MOON

Ø 3/20-12/20

D0194247

PACIFIC CREST TRAIL

SCENIC TRAIL

Drive & Hike

PACIFIC
CREST TRAIL

CAROLINE HINCHLIFF

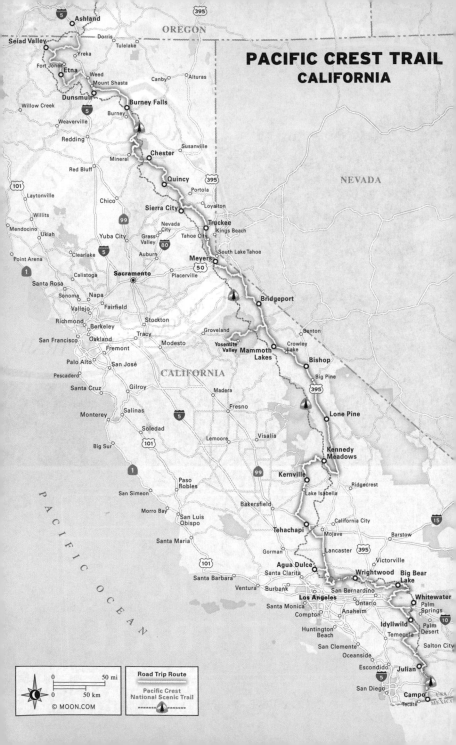

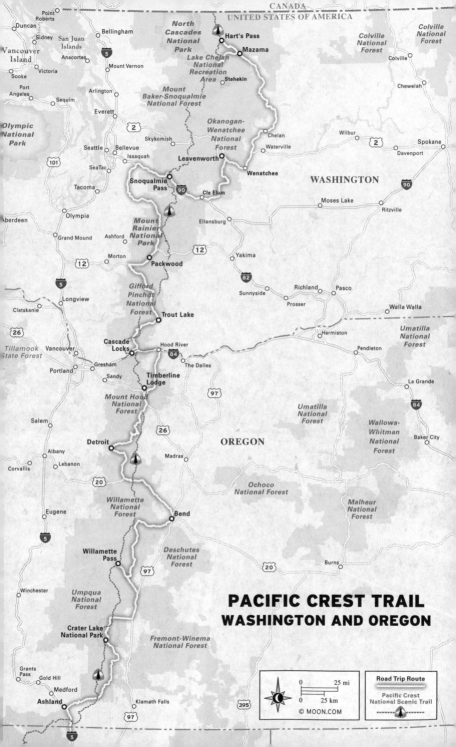

PACIFIC CREST TRAIL
WASHINGTON AND OREGON

CONTENTS

DISCOVER
the Pacific Crest Trail

"I wish I could do that."

When I tell people I hiked the Pacific Crest Trail, this is the response I get. I understand the sentiment—I still reminisce about the summer of 2014 that I spent trekking through the wilderness of California, Oregon, and Washington with a 30-pound backpack strapped to my hips and near-destroyed sneakers laced around my aching feet. My thru-hike was an epic journey that forever changed my perspective on happiness and success.

Cheryl Strayed's bestselling book *Wild* (and the subsequent film) turned the PCT into a household name. The trail is now known as one of the best ways to experience the rugged, scenic West, but for many reasons—family, career, health, finances—most people are unable to venture into the wilderness for five months. Almost everyone, though, gets a few days of vacation every year and can squeeze a road trip into the plan.

This is your accessible, approachable route to the most beautiful places on the 2,650-mile trail. From Campo to Canada, this road trip parallels the PCT, offering many of the same spectacular opportunities (without the giant backpack or the gruesome blisters). Gaze out over the vast expanse of the desert ranges. Marvel at the rugged, towering High Sierra and the formidable Cascade volcanoes. Wander the misty, mossy rainforests of the Pacific Northwest. There's much more to see than hiking trails: visit steaming natural hot springs, paddle wild and scenic rivers on a whitewater raft, cruise down rocky slopes on a mountain bike, or amble through thick woods on horseback. Historic and charming trail towns peppered along the route welcome weary hikers and cater to the adventurous spirit.

You don't have to quit your job or leave your life behind to have an authentic PCT experience. After exploring the trail as both a thru-hiker and a road-tripper, I can assure you that this version is just as spectacular (and considerably more comfortable).

This road trip is the answer to your wish—a guide for hikers and road-trippers alike to experience the stunning beauty and wild splendor of the Pacific Crest Trail.

10 TOP EXPERIENCES

1 **Hike an Alpine Landscape:** Wade across glacier-fed streams and wander through wildflower-speckled meadows on the flanks of remote **Mount Jefferson** (page 316).

^ ^
^ ^

2 **Soak in Hot Springs**: Follow the PCT along the banks of the Mojave River and over a rainbow-painted bridge to reach **Deep Creek Hot Springs,** a desert oasis on the north side of the San Bernardino Mountains (page 85).

3 **Drive a Scenic Byway:** Zoom along a legendary stretch of the **Angeles Crest Scenic Byway** through the rugged San Gabriel Mountains, stopping for views of Los Angeles and the Mojave Desert more than a mile below (page 87).

4 **Gaze at Mountain Peaks:** Enjoy the views from Whitney Portal, the gateway to the highest peak in the lower 48 states, sky-piercing **Mount Whitney** (page 124).

^^^
^^

5 **Explore Yosemite's High Country:** Experience the national park's high Sierra via Tioga Pass, with stops to admire alpine **Tuolumne Meadows** (page 170).

6 **Wander Amid Waterfalls:** Dip your toes into an ice-cold plunge pool below **Burney Falls,** where thousands of natural springs cascade over a basalt cliff (page 244).

>>>

7 **Climb a Volcano:** Journey through a volcanic wonderland to summit **Lassen Peak,** the southernmost volcano in the Cascade Mountain range (page 239).

8 **Cruise Around a Sunken Caldera**: Descend into **Crater Lake**'s ancient caldera and motor across the surface of the deepest, clearest lake in America (page 290).

9 **Swim in Mountain Lakes**: Splash into warm **Deep Lake** and fill your belly with fresh huckleberries in this unheralded wilderness area between three volcanoes (page 354).

>>>

10 **Leave Civilization Behind:** Escape to remote, secluded **Stehekin** village in the North Cascades, accessible only by boat or hiking trail (page 385).

PLANNING YOUR TRIP

Where to Go

Southern California

East of San Diego, the Pacific Crest Trail begins its northbound journey from the border near Campo. The trail passes through mountains to visit the old mining town of **Julian** before grazing past austere **Anza-Borrego Desert State Park** to climb into the artsy town of **Idyllwild.**

Big Bear Lake is a hub for year-round sports and recreation. Near the **Angeles Crest Scenic Byway,** hikers can summit **Mount Baden-Powell,** the second-highest peak in the San Gorgonio Mountains. As the PCT traces the western edge of the **Mojave Desert,** it showcases the fascinating geology at **Vasquez Rocks.**

Central California

The Sierra Nevada, with its sky-scraping spires and granite towers, couldn't be more different from the desert. **Mount Whitney,** the tallest point in the Lower 48, looms on the western horizon above **Lone Pine,** a Wild West town on U.S. 395. **Bishop** is a fantastic base camp from which to access **Sequoia and Kings Canyon National Parks** from the east (as long as you're willing to hike in). The PCT travels north through **Mammoth Lakes,** a luxurious resort town, before entering lush meadows and granite domes of Tuolumne Meadows in **Yosemite National Park.**

Northern California

From **Sonora Pass,** the PCT traverses ragged ridgelines above sparkling **Lake Tahoe** before heading through the rocky Sierra Buttes massif and into **Lassen Volcanic National Park,** where geothermal activity abounds. Ice-cold **Burney Falls** is a scenic stopover and the trail town of **Mount Shasta** offers great views of its namesake volcano. At **Castle Crags State Park,** granite monoliths loom over the I-5 freeway below.

Oregon

Elegant **Ashland** is home to tasty restaurants, beautiful shops, and world-class theater. Nearby **Crater Lake National Park** is the best place to learn about Oregon's volcanic legacy. Outdoor enthusiasts bond over craft beers in **Bend,** home to more than 20 microbreweries. An hour's drive from Portland, **Mount Hood** is a year-round destination for hiking, skiing, sightseeing, and dining at the historic **Timberline Lodge.**

Washington

The PCT enters Washington in the dramatic **Columbia River Gorge** before tracing the western base of **Mount Adams** and entering the wild, roadless **Goat Rocks Wilderness.** Views of the state's biggest volcano (known locally as "The Mountain") are incredible in **Mount Rainier National Park.** Isolated **Stehekin** is a quaint, remote town at the southern tip of **North Cascades National Park,** where the PCT exits civilization before entering Canada.

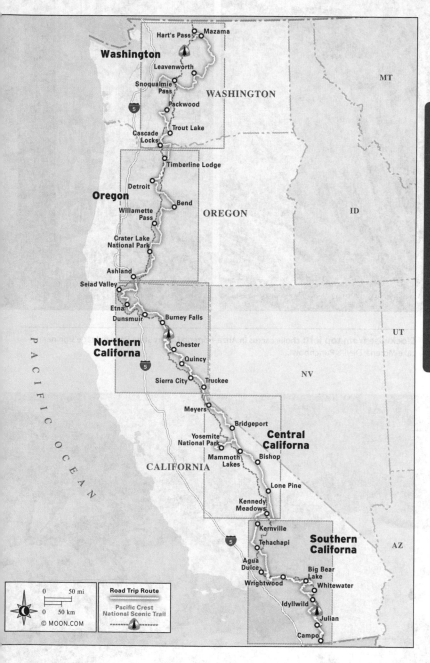

Washington
Hart's Pass
Mazama
Leavenworth
Snoqualmie Pass
WASHINGTON
Packwood
Trout Lake
Cascade Locks
Timberline Lodge
Oregon
Detroit
Bend
Willamette Pass
OREGON
Crater Lake National Park
Ashland
Seiad Valley
Etna
Dunsmuir
Burney Falls
Northern Californa
Chester
Quincy
Sierra City
Truckee
Meyers
Bridgeport
Central Californa
Yosemite National Park
Mammoth Lakes
Bishop
CALIFORNIA
Lone Pine
Kennedy Meadows
Kernville
Tehachapi
Southern Californa
Agua Dulce
Big Bear Lake
Wrightwood
Whitewater
Idyllwild
Julian
Campo

MT
ID
UT
NV
AZ

PACIFIC OCEAN

0   50 mi
0   50 km
© MOON.COM

Road Trip Route
Pacific Crest National Scenic Trail

Clockwise from top left: cholla cactus in Anza-Borrego Desert State Park; mileage sign near Lake Morena; Devil's Punchbowl.

When to Go

Spring

Most PCT thru-hikers begin at the Mexican border in **April**, when desert temperatures are still mild and wildflowers are blooming. This is the best time of year to explore the **Southern California** region of the PCT, which means the trail and nearby towns can be extremely busy.

If planning to explore this area March-May, **reserve accommodations and campgrounds in advance.** Snow still covers the regions farther north until May or June, and many seasonal roads will still be closed.

Summer

Summer is your best bet for a contiguous trip along the Pacific Crest Trail—the snow has melted in the mountains, mountain passes are open, and the weather is generally quite pleasant (with two exceptions: Anza-Borrego Desert State Park and the Mojave Desert, where temperatures are only hospitable during fall, winter, and spring). **National parks** are busy during the summer, as are resort towns like **Mammoth Lakes** and **Lake Tahoe**, so expect to share the trails with others, and be sure to **reserve accommodations in advance**, especially if you're traveling on a weekend.

Autumn

Autumn can be quite beautiful on the PCT, despite earlier sunsets and potentially chilly temperatures. Thru-hikers finish their journey in the North Cascades in **September and October**, racing to beat the season's first snows. The **Eastern Sierra** in particular is known for spectacular fall colors each autumn, when needles on larch trees turn yellow and huckleberry bushes light up the granite hillsides in red hues.

Winter

Most of the Pacific Crest Trail is at elevations of 5,000 feet or more, so accessing the trail during the winter months is difficult at best. To make the most of the winter months, visit the resort towns of **Big Bear, Mammoth Lakes, Lake Tahoe,** or **Mount Shasta** in California; **Bend** in Oregon; or **Leavenworth** in Washington. If you're determined to do some winter hiking, trails in **Anza-Borrego** and **Agua Dulce** are good bets.

Hikers without avalanche expertise and the appropriate winter gear are advised to visit the PCT between April and October. Regions including the High Sierra, Oregon, and Washington may not be accessible until late June or early July.

Know Before You Go

Weather

Most of the Pacific Crest Trail experiences heavy winter snow **November-April** and is inaccessible by car or on foot. Southern California sections are best explored in **spring,** when water flows in the seasonal streams, wildflowers explode in color, and daytime temperatures are hospitable.

Plan to visit the High Sierra, Northern California, Oregon, and Washington during **summer** and **fall,** when snows have melted and all the roads are open.

Wildfires close sections of the trail every year, and are most common **July-September.** Be prepared with an alternative route should your planned destination be closed due to fire.

Reservations, Permits, and Passes

With the exception of some parts of Southern California, most destinations on your road trip are only accessible half the year, which means they can get crowded when they're open. Make **reservations** for campgrounds and accommodations as far in advance as

Clockwise from top left: John Muir Wilderness; Maple Pass Loop; wildflowers on the Naches Peak Loop.

possible, especially if you'll be traveling on holiday weekends.

Some national parks require **entrance fees** ($15-35), as do some state parks, and **backcountry permits** may be required for overnight stays in addition to the entrance fee. The Mount Whitney Zone, Sequoia and Kings Canyon, John Muir Wilderness, Yosemite, Lassen, Obsidian Trail, Mount Rainier, and North Cascades require advance permit registrations and enforce quotas. While some permits may be available on short notice, permits in extremely popular areas (Mount Whitney, Sequoia and Kings Canyon, and Yosemite) are awarded by application or lottery up to eight months in advance. Other wilderness areas may require free permits available at regional ranger stations or self-issued at the trailhead. Sometimes permitting is completed online through www.recreation.gov or www.nps.gov.

If you plan to camp in California, you'll need a **California campfire permit** (www.preventwildfireca.org) for campfires, barbecues, and portable stoves. Visits to national forests in Southern California require a **California Adventure Pass** ($5/day or $30/year).

In Oregon and Washington, a **Northwest Forest Pass** ($5/day or $30/year) is required to visit national forests; a **Discover Pass** ($10/day or $30/year) is required at Washington state parks. December through April, winter recreation areas require a **Sno-Park Permit** ($5-42) to park in snow-cleared lots.

If you plan to cross the Canadian border to visit the northern terminus of the Pacific Crest Trail in Manning Park, British Columbia, you'll need a valid **passport.**

What to Bring

In addition to the **Ten Essentials** (see page 417), bring your backpack and at least two water bottles. Trekking poles can assist with long hikes and stream crossings. If camping, pack a tent, a sleeping pad, sleeping bag, and a pillow, a camp chair, and an outdoor kitchen set with cookware and dishes. A tarp or awning is a wonderful luxury in sunny California, where many campsites are exposed to the sun.

Driving Guide

You'll need a reliable car to get from place to place. Most local towns are accessible by car—any car will do, although you'll suffer in summer in a vehicle without air-conditioning.

While some parts of the Pacific Crest Trail are accessible by road, reaching the trailheads in more remote areas may require long drives on unpaved forest roads. A high-clearance, all-wheel-drive vehicle is recommended.

Getting There and Back

This trip starts in San Diego, where you can fly into **San Diego International Airport** (SAN, 619/400-2400, www.san. org) and rent a car. There are plenty of grocery stores and outdoor retailers if you need to stock up on food and travel necessities. The southern terminus of the Pacific Crest Trail is east of downtown San Diego on Highway 94.

Southern California can also be accessed via airports in the greater Los Angeles area, including busy **Los Angeles International Airport** (LAX, 855/463-5252, www.flylax.com), smaller **Ontario International Airport** (ONT, 909/544-5300, www.flyontario.com), and relatively calm **Palm Springs International Airport** (PSP, 760/318-3800, www.palmspringsca.gov).

Sections of the PCT in the Sierra Nevada and Northern California are quite remote—that distance is part of their appeal. For travel in this area, fly into **Sacramento International Airport** (SMF, 916/929-5411, www.sacramento. aero/smf) or **Reno-Tahoe International Airport** (RNO, 775/328-6400, www.

Best Festivals

♦ **PCT Days** (Cascade Locks, OR, Aug.): With an outdoor retailer expo, raffle prizes, food and beer vendors, film screenings, and camping, this event is a celebration of all things trail related.

♦ **Oregon Shakespeare Festival** (Ashland, OR, Feb.-Oct.): Eleven plays and 300 shows are performed near downtown's Lithia Park.

♦ **High Sierra Music Festival** (Quincy, CA, July): This is the home of a party with music, art, costumes, and playshops.

♦ **Bend Brewfest** (Bend, OR, Aug.): Breweries from all over the state gather in Bend for a weekend of food, beer, music, and art.

♦ **Oktoberfest** (Leavenworth, WA, Oct.): This Bavarian-themed event draws big crowds over three weekends in October.

♦ **Buckner Orchard Harvest Fest** (Stehekin, WA, Oct.): Celebrate a bounty of orchard-grown produce at this annual festival near North Cascades National Park.

renoairport.com) and plan to spend a few hours driving from the airport

Portland International Airport (PDX, 877/739-4636 or 503/460-4234, www.flypdx.com) is the best hub for visits to Oregon and the southern part of Washington State.

Your road trip ends in the North Cascades, three hours northeast of **Seattle-Tacoma International Airport** (SEA, 800/544-1965 or 206/787-5388, www.portseattle.org/sea-tac). Or you may choose to end your trip in Canada, as many thru-hikers do. **Vancouver International Airport** (YVR, 604/207-7077, www.yvr.ca) is three hours northwest of North Cascades National Park.

No one road parallels the Pacific Crest Trail in its entirety, but some major routes provide consistent access to the mountain passes and twisty roads that reach the trail. In Southern California, most trail towns can be accessed near **I-15** or **Highway 14.** Scenic **U.S. 395** is your primary route through Central California and the High Sierra. Destinations in Northern California are sprinkled along **Highway 89** and **I-5.** In Oregon and Washington, **I-5** parallels the trail on the west side of the mountain range, while **U.S. 97** provides a similar route to the east.

Rental Cars

Rent a car at the **airport,** keeping in mind what you'll need to stay comfortable during your travels. Consider extra space for camping gear, fold-down seats that allow for sleeping in the car, or a high-clearance vehicle to travel on bumpy dirt roads in the mountains. Ask about any related fees for taking the car on unpaved roads. If you're planning a one-way trip, confirm that you can return the rental car in a different location than where you rented it (this may incur a fee).

Camper vans and **RVs** are fantastic options for this road trip, if you're comfortable driving a larger vehicle. Some single-lane, twisty mountain roads may prohibit trailers, but you can still have a delightful trip even if you skip those options.

Driving Tips

This road trip spends time on both high-speed highways and curvy mountain byways. Speed limits vary from 30-80 mph.

Drivers in California move fast—don't be alarmed when they want to pass (and don't feel pressured to exceed speed limits just because others are). Observe laws and common courtesy and keep right except to pass. Watch for **wildlife** on the roads, especially during **dawn and dusk,** when many animals emerge from the woods to graze. Deer, raccoons, rabbits, squirrels, and birds are all common sights on roadways across the Pacific Crest Trail.

Most rental cars are equipped with **GPS,** but this trip enters remote areas where satellite and cell phone coverage may be spotty or nonexistent. Bring a road atlas so you can plan routes and orient yourself when GPS becomes unreliable.

Road Conditions

While some parts of Southern California are accessible year-round, most of the PCT is buried in snow between December and April. In winter, many **mountain roads into high-elevation areas may close,** including sections of the Angeles Crest Scenic Byway, all the roads leading into the remote high country of the Sierra Nevada, and Highway 89 through Lassen in California; Crater Lake Rim Drive and McKenzie Pass in Oregon; and Forest Road 23 and the North Cascades Highway in Washington. Other winter routes are plowed but require traction

tires and/or tire chains—expect these conditions near Big Bear, Mammoth Lakes, Lake Tahoe, Mount Shasta, and across all the mountain passes in Oregon and Washington.

Fueling Up

Be sure you have plenty of gas in the tank before heading into remote areas. Gas is plentiful in **Southern California,** where the PCT skirts major urban areas; however, gas stations along U.S. 395 are few and far between where fuel is at a premium (in Mammoth Lakes and Lee Vining, for example, the price can exceed $5 per gallon). Plan to fill your tank in Tehachapi, Bishop, or even the state of Nevada, where prices are more reasonable.

Expect elevated gas prices to continue through the small towns between Truckee and Burney; once you hit the I-5 corridor near Mount Shasta, the prices start to drop.

Gas stations are peppered sporadically along U.S. 97 through **Oregon,** but it's wise to fill the tank for adventures into the mountains.

There are two remote sections—no gas, services, or cell phone reception—in **Washington:** Forest Road 23, between Trout Lake and Packwood, and the North Cascades Highway, between Mazama and Marblemount.

HIT THE ROAD

This road trip follows the traditional thru-hiker's journey, which starts in spring near the California-Mexico border and runs north to the border with Canada.

21 Days on the Pacific Crest Trail

California in 12 Days
DAY 1: SAN DIEGO TO JULIAN
95 mi/153 km, 2.5 hr
Take Highway 94 east for one hour to the rural community of **Campo** and visit the **Pacific Crest Trail Southern Terminus Monument** on the U.S.-Mexico border. Head north on the **Sunrise Highway** to Mount Laguna, where the **Garnet Peak Trail** leads to a spectacular viewpoint overlooking **Anza-Borrego Desert State Park.**

Stop at the **Pine House Café** for a draft beer and a bowl of chili before spending the night in **Julian,** 30 minutes north on Highway 79.

DAY 2: JULIAN TO IDYLLWILD
90 mi/145 km, 1.5 hr
Wake up and grab breakfast at **Granny's Kitchen** before heading north to **Idyllwild** via Highways 79, 371, 74, and 243. A hike on the **Deer Springs Trail** showcases the towering granite massifs of the **San Jacinto Mountains.**

Catch some live music at **Café Aroma** during dinner before retreating to your cozy cottage or hotel room.

DAY 3: IDYLLWILD TO WRIGHTWOOD
160 mi/260 km, 4 hr
Get ready for a long day of driving on twisty scenic byways that traverse three unique mountain ranges and offer incredible views in every direction. Fuel up with coffee at **Higher Grounds** before making the two-hour trek via Highways 243 and 38 to **Big Bear Lake.** Hike the **Cougar Crest Trail** to enjoy panoramic views of Big Bear Lake and the **San Bernardino Mountains,** then drive 90 minutes west to **Wrightwood** on Highways 18 and 138.

Enjoy a frosty pint and a handcrafted sandwich at **Wrightwood Brew Co.** before bedding down for the night at **Blue Ridge Primitive Campground.**

DAY 4: WRIGHTWOOD TO TEHACHAPI
170 mi/275 km, 3 hr
Take a morning stroll on the Pacific Crest Trail along **Blue Ridge** to see the sun light up the **San Gabriel Mountains,** then head west on the **Angeles Crest Scenic Byway** to trace the path of the PCT through the remarkably rugged range. After stopping at **Newcomb's Ranch** for lunch, follow the Angeles Forest Highway north and Highway 14 south to the tiny town of **Agua Dulce,** where you can walk through **Vasquez Rocks,** a group of otherworldly sandstone formations that have been the filming site of countless movies and TV shows.

Head north on Highway 14 and Tehachapi Willow Springs Road to **Tehachapi,** where you can grab dinner at **Red House BBQ** and get a comfy hotel room.

DAY 5: TEHACHAPI TO KENNEDY MEADOWS
126 mi/203 km, 4.5 hr
Take a 90-minute scenic route through the Piute Mountains on **Caliente Bodfish Road** to the town of **Kernville,** where you can hop on a **whitewater rafting** trip on the Kern River and sip on a craft beer at **Kern River Brewing Company.** Afterward, stock up on water, food, and camping supplies in Kernville before making the twisty, three-hour drive on Mountain Highway 99 and **Sherman Pass Road** to **Kennedy Meadows,** a remote community high on the Kern Plateau.

Clockwise from top left: Anza-Borrego from Garnet Peak; Cougar Crest trail; California poppies in Tehachapi.

On the way, stop at 9,200-foot **Sherman Pass** to gaze out over the Sequoia National Forest and South Sierra Wilderness. Pitch your tent in **Kennedy Meadows Campground** alongside PCT hikers preparing to enter the High Sierra.

DAY 6: KENNEDY MEADOWS TO MOUNT WHITNEY
100 mi/161 km, 2.5 hr

Let yourself get nice and hungry before visiting **Grumpy Bear's Retreat,** where breakfasts are served with unlimited 10-inch pancakes. Take Nine Mile Canyon Road east to U.S. 395 and head north to **Lone Pine,** stopping at the **Eastern Sierra Interagency Visitor Center** to learn fascinating details about the region's natural wonders.

The **Whitney Portal Road** delivers you to the eastern base of the highest peak in the lower 48 states—14,505-foot **Mount Whitney.** Hike to **Lone Pine Lake** to soak up the views, then drive back to town to visit the **Museum of Western Film History.** Find unlikely (and delicious) Chinese food at **Merry Go Round** for dinner and grab a motel room at the **Dow Villa,** a historic motel where many Western film stars have stayed over the years.

DAY 7: MOUNT WHITNEY TO BISHOP
95 mi/153 km, 2.5 hr

Get up early to beat the heat and eat breakfast at **Alabama Hills Café** before exploring the **Alabama Hills** via **Movie Road** stopping for the brief hike to **Mobius Arch.** On your way north via U.S. 395, stop at **Manzanar National Historic Site** for a glimpse into a chilling era in U.S. history during World War II.

Next, continue north to **Onion Valley Road,** and follow this twisty westbound road to Onion Valley Campground. Make the trek to 11,700-foot **Kearsarge Pass** for a stunning, panoramic view into **Kings Canyon National Park** and the path of the PCT through what John Muir called the "Range of Light."

Continue north on U.S. 395 to **Bishop,** where you can satisfy your hiker hunger (and thirst) at **Mountain Rambler Brewery** with artisan pizza and craft beer before retreating to your hotel room in town.

DAY 8: BISHOP TO TUOLUMNE MEADOWS
120 mi/193 km, 3.5 hr

Stock up on pastries and lunch sundries at **Erick Schat's Bakkery** before heading north on U.S. 395 and Highway 203 to **Mammoth Lakes.** Take the shuttle to **Devils Postpile National Monument,** where the Pacific Crest Trail passes beneath a dramatic formation of columnar basalt. For a longer hike, walk south along the San Joaquin River to **Rainbow Falls.** Or, to save time, opt to skip the shuttle trip to the monument altogether and have a picnic lunch at scenic **Horseshoe Lake** instead, just south of town on Lake Mary Road.

Return to Mammoth Lakes and head north on U.S. 395 to **June Lake,** where Highway 158 makes a scenic loop past four sparkling lakes below craggy Sierra peaks. Stop at **June Lake Brewing** for a creative craft brew and some Hawaiian soul food from **Ohanas395.**

End the day with a scenic evening drive on **Tioga Pass Road** (13 miles north of June Lake), which travels over 9,900-foot **Tioga Pass** into **Yosemite National Park.** Make sure you've got a reservation for a campsite at **Tuolumne Meadows Campground.**

DAY 9: TUOLUMNE MEADOWS TO LAKE TAHOE
180 mi/290 km, 4 hr

Grab a breakfast burrito to go at **Tuolumne Meadows Lodge** and hike to the top of **Lembert Dome,** where you'll find a lovely vantage of the area's namesake meadows and surrounding granite massifs.

Travel east back over Tioga Pass and north on U.S. 395 through Lee Vining

Clockwise from top left: Alabama Hills; Kearsarge Pass trail; Tuolumne Meadows.

to **Bridgeport,** stopping for lunch at **High Sierra Bakery.** It's a two-hour drive on Highway 89 over Monitor Pass and through the town of Meyers to the western shore of sparkling **Lake Tahoe,** the second-deepest lake in the country.

Stretch your legs during a scenic walk through **Emerald Bay State Park** before driving 45 minutes north to **Truckee** to enjoy happy hour at one of the city's many urbane restaurants. Relax into a waterfront hotel room at **Loch Leven Lodge** on **Donner Lake.**

DAY 10: LAKE TAHOE TO LASSEN
160 mi/260 km, 3.5 hr

Fuel up for the day at famous breakfast joint **Squeeze In,** then follow Highways 89 and 49 for an hour to **Sierra City,** where you can take a short walk on the PCT to **Loves Falls** or do a longer hike to the top of the **Sierra Buttes Lookout Tower.**

Next, take Highway 89 past the western shore of Lake Almanor to the town of **Chester** to enjoy a treat at **Pine Shack Frosty** and pick up camping supplies at the supermarket. It's a 30-minute drive into **Lassen Volcanic National Park,** where you can see bubbling mud pots, smell steaming fumaroles, and, if you're up for it, hike to the top of **Lassen Peak.** Set up camp at **Summit Lake Campground** in the national park.

DAY 11: LASSEN TO DUNSMUIR
120 mi/193 km, 2.5 hr

Keep your headlight handy and head north out of the park on Highway 89 to **Subway Cave,** a huge underground lava tube, before continuing north for a day of majestic waterfalls.

An hour north, near the town of Burney, check out **Burney Falls,** where dozens of springs surge out of a 130-foot cliff next to the rushing cascade of Burney Creek and splash into a misty plunge pool.

Heading northwest toward Mount Shasta, take I-5 south to the town of

Dunsmuir, where craft brews and tasty burgers await you at **Dunsmuir Brewery Works.** Enjoy the short, easy trail to **Hedge Creek Falls** before retiring to your perfectly appointed overnight caboose at **Railroad Park Resort.**

DAY 12: DUNSMUIR TO
ASHLAND, OREGON
100 mi/161 km, 3 hr

After breakfast at **The Wheelhouse** in historic downtown Dunsmuir, drive a few minutes south on I-5 to **Castle Crags State Park** for a hike to **Castle Dome** and stunning views of snowcapped **Mount Shasta.** After your hike, head north on I-5 past the mighty volcano and into the state of Oregon. A scenic drive on **Mount Ashland Ski Road** takes you to the top of Mount Ashland (30 minutes one-way from I-5), paralleling the PCT most of the way.

Before you retreat to your hotel room, treat yourself to a nice dinner at one of Ashland's world-class restaurants and shop for hiking snacks at **Ashland Food Co-Op.**

Oregon in 4 Days
DAYS 13: ASHLAND TO CRATER LAKE
90 mi/145 km, 2 hr

Enjoy a decadent breakfast at **Morning Glory** before heading east out of town on **Dead Indian Memorial Road.** Take Highways 140 and 62 to **Crater Lake National Park** and hike down to the crystal clear lake's lapping shore on the **Cleetwood Cove Trail.**

After a **volcano boat cruise** around the lake, catch the sunset at the **Watchman Overlook** before retreating to historic **Crater Lake Lodge** for an elegant Pacific Northwest-themed dinner in the dining room and a soft bed in a cozy guest room.

DAY 14: CRATER LAKE TO BEND
120 mi/193 km, 2.5 hr

Hike from Crater Lake Lodge to the top of **Garfield Peak** to get a bird's-eye view of Crater Lake, Mount McLoughlin,

Best Trail Towns

Famous for their warm hospitality, natural beauty, and small-town charm, these are the towns that make lasting impressions on Pacific Crest Trail hikers.

Travertine Hot Springs in Bridgeport

♦ **Mount Laguna, CA:** Nestled in a sparse pine forest atop a dramatic mountain ridge, the tiny community of Mount Laguna defies Southern California stereotypes. Visit during the spring to walk through mountain meadows and marvel at the many different bird species that make Mount Laguna an annual stop during their migration.

♦ **Idyllwild, CA:** Catch live music every night of the week in this artsy mountain town, which is also home to fantastic restaurants and great shops. Trails into Mount San Jacinto State Park depart from the edges of town, leading to the PCT and the top of Mount San Jacinto.

♦ **Lone Pine, CA:** Find yourself transported to the Wild West in Lone Pine, where you can explore the filming locations of hundreds of movies and TV shows. Mount Whitney, the tallest peak in the Lower 48, dominates the western skyline.

♦ **Bridgeport, CA:** Without the crowds of the more popular areas farther south, Bridgeport is a no-frills town in the Eastern Sierra with craft beer, nice views, and two beautiful natural hot springs. Hike on the PCT at nearby Sonora Pass.

♦ **Truckee, CA:** Not far from Lake Tahoe, this sophisticated mountain town has fantastic restaurants, great shops, and plenty of opportunities for year-round outdoor recreation at nearby Donner Lake and Donner Summit.

♦ **Mount Shasta, CA:** In 2018, Mount Shasta became the first official Pacific Crest Trail Town. Castle Crags State Park is nearby, and the town is surrounded by some of the most rugged terrain in Northern California. Mount Shasta itself, a 14,180-foot volcano, is visible from about 500 miles of the PCT.

♦ **Ashland, OR:** Quaint, elegant, and friendly, Ashland is a city that perfectly balances natural beauty with modern luxury. It's known for its great restaurants, shopping, and theater.

♦ **Cascade Locks, OR:** Framed by the steep canyon walls of the Columbia River Gorge, Cascade Locks showcases thick forests and huge waterfalls, two of Oregon's trademarks. The PCT travels right through town.

♦ **Trout Lake, WA:** Mount Adams looms larger-than-life above this peaceful community, where hikers and outdoor enthusiasts come for food, rest, and relaxation.

♦ **Stehekin, WA:** With no roads to the outside world, Stehekin is a town at the northern tip of Lake Chelan that can only be reached by foot or by boat. Craggy peaks surround the town and are reflected in the lake's surface.

Mount Thielsen, and the surrounding terrain. Drive north on U.S. 97 and the **Cascade Lakes Scenic Byway** to the city of **Bend.**

Stop for lunch at woodsy **Brown Owl,** then rent a tube to **float the Deschutes River** through the center of town. Visit a few craft breweries with your **Bend Ale Trail** passport in hand and spend the night at a hotel in town.

DAY 15: BEND TO MOUNT HOOD
110-220 mi/177-355 km, 2.5-5 hr

Start your day with a scenic loop on the **McKenzie Pass-Santiam Pass Scenic Byway,** popping into **Sisters Coffee** for breakfast beforehand. Allow plenty of time to stop for photos during the wow-worthy drive through bizarre lava fields, incredibly pointy peaks, and thundering waterfalls. Stop at the **Dee Wright Observatory** or hike to **Matthieu Lakes** on the PCT.

Take U.S. 97 and 26 north to **Mount Hood,** Oregon's tallest volcano, grab a campsite at **Frog Lake Campground,** and head to **Mt. Hood Brewing** for dinner and beers.

DAY 16: MOUNT HOOD TO CASCADE LOCKS
70 mi/113 km, 1.5 hr

After stuffing your belly to your heart's content at the famous **Timberline Lodge buffet,** hike on the Timberline Trail to **Paradise Park.**

Take Highway 35 and I-84 through Hood River and the **Columbia River Gorge** to the town of **Cascade Locks.** Gaze at the **Bridge of the Gods** from your picnic table at **Thunder Island Brewing,** then relax in a comfy river-view room at the **Columbia River Inn.**

Washington in 5 Days
DAY 17: CASCADE LOCKS TO MOUNT RAINIER NATIONAL PARK
140 mi/225 km, 4 hr

Start with breakfast at **Bridgeside,** then cross the Bridge of the Gods and drive for an hour on Highways 14 and 141 to **Trout Lake,** where **Mount Adams** looms larger-than-life. Hike to the top of **Sleeping Beauty** to get a lay of the land, including five massive Cascade volcanoes.

Take a twisty, three-hour drive on Forest Road 23 and U.S. 12 to **Packwood,** where you can stock up on camping supplies and groceries. Enter **Mount Rainier National Park** on Highway 123 and drive to the top of **Chinook Pass,** where the PCT crosses Highway 410. The **Naches Peak Loop** is an easy hike with incredible views of the mountain and surrounding terrain. Pitch a tent at **Lodgepole Campground,** just east of the pass.

DAY 18: MOUNT RAINIER NATIONAL PARK TO LEAVENWORTH
190 mi/305 km, 4 hr

The steep terrain of the Northern Cascades doesn't allow for northbound travel by road, so from here you'll make a two-hour drive to **North Bend** on Highways 410, 169, 18, and I-90. Get lunch at **North Bend Bar & Grill** before climbing back over the mountains at **Snoqualmie Pass.**

It's another two hours on I-90 and U.S. 97 to **Leavenworth,** an adorable Bavarian village on the eastern edge of the craggy Cascade Range. If you have time, head west on U.S. 2 for an evening hike on the PCT to **Lake Valhalla,** or explore the bustling streets of Leavenworth. Sip a craft brew and sink your teeth into a locally made wurst at **Munchen Haus** before settling into your hotel room.

DAY 19: LEAVENWORTH TO STEHEKIN
55 mi/89 km, 1 hr

You've got a boat to catch, so pack an overnight bag and scoot out of your hotel early to drive one hour to the **Lady of the Lake,** where you'll be shuttled across **Lake Chelan** to **Stehekin,** a remote town at the northern tip of the lake with no roads to the outside world.

Ride the **red bus** to **Stehekin Pastry Company** for mouthwatering cinnamon

Clockwise from top left: Crater Lake Lodge; Mount Hood near Paradise Park; Naches Peak Loop trail.

rolls, marvel at 300-foot Rainbow Falls, and hike on the **Agnes Gorge Trail.** Dine and spend the night at the **North Cascades Lodge at Stehekin.**

DAY 20: STEHEKIN TO NORTH CASCADES NATIONAL PARK
115 mi/185 km, 2.5 hr

Ride the boat back down the lake and hop into your car for a 1.5-hour drive on U.S. 97 and Highways 153 and 20 to **Mazama.** Deli sandwiches at the **Mazama Store** are surprisingly gourmet considering the remote location. On your way to **North Cascades National Park,** stop at **Washington Pass Overlook** for a jaw-dropping vantage of the highway's route through the formidable mountain range. Hike into the national park on the **Maple Pass Loop** hike and enjoy incredible views of glacier-fed lakes beneath craggy peaks.

Retreat to a luxurious, modern **Rolling Huts** for the night, or stake out your tent at **Early Winters Campground.**

DAY 21: NORTH CASCADES NATIONAL PARK TO CANADA
250 mi/405 km, 5.5 hr

To get one last glimpse of the Pacific Crest Trail before the end of your trip, make the precarious drive to beautiful **Hart's Pass,** where the national scenic trail meets the highest point in Washington State accessible by road. North of this point, no more roads cross the PCT.

Descend from the pass and drive west on **Highway 20** through the national park, pausing for views at **Ross Lake** and **Diablo Lake Overlooks.** Stop in **Newhalem** and walk along the **Trail of Cedars,** where a suspension bridge crosses the **Skagit River.**

From here, head back to Seattle on I-5 to complete your trip, or continue north to Canada. The PCT ends in a quiet patch of forest in **Manning Park,** British Columbia, about eight miles south of **Manning Park Resort.** To visit, cross the border at Sumas and head east on BC Highways 1 and 3.

Weekend Getaways

You may not have 21 days to drive the entirety of the Pacific Crest Trail. But, if you find yourself in a nearby city, you can spend a weekend exploring some of the best the trail has to offer.

From San Diego

Head east for one hour on I-8 to the **Sunrise Highway,** which twists into piney **Mount Laguna** (page 53). Hike on the PCT along Laguna Mountain Ridge to gaze out over the stark beauty of Anza-Borrego Desert State Park, then reward yourself with comfort cuisine and craft brews at **Pine House Café.** Spend the night at **Laguna Mountain Lodge.**

Wake up and head to breakfast at **Mom's Pies** in the old mining town of **Julian** (page 57), north on Highway 79. Tour the historic **Eagle Mine** then hike to the top of **Volcan Mountain,** where you can see the path of the PCT running through the desert far below. Stop at **Volcan Mountain Winery** for a tasting, then catch some live music with dinner at **Wynola Pizza.**

From Los Angeles

Follow the **Angeles Crest Scenic Byway** (accessible via I-210 in La Cañada Flintridge or Highway 138 at Cajon Junction) to **Wrightwood** (page 86), an adorable mountain town nestled among towering pine trees. After grabbing a beer at **Wrightwood Brew Co.,** enjoy an easy hike on the PCT at **Blue Ridge,** where you can watch the sun set over the big city below. Bed down for the night in a cozy **Grand Pine Cabin.**

Walk to **Cinnamon's Bakery** in the morning for breakfast. A hike to the top of **Throop Peak** showcases the rugged terrain of the San Gabriel Mountains,

Go Wild

Bridge of the Gods

Fans of Cheryl Strayed's book *Wild* and the movie starring Reese Witherspoon won't want to miss the chance to visit these filming locations.

♦ **Tehachapi, CA:** While most of the movie was filmed in Oregon, producers knew Cheryl's first few steps on the Pacific Crest Trail in the **Mojave Desert** had to be filmed in its actual geographic location to convey what Cheryl saw at the start of her journey. To visit this iconic spot, take Highway 58 east from Tehachapi for 10 miles and exit toward Cameron Canyon Road. Here at **Tehachapi Pass** (page 97), the PCT departs from the north side of the highway among dry, dusty hills peppered with desert shrubs and Joshua trees.

♦ **Ashland, OR:** By the time Cheryl reached Ashland, she had hit her stride and was gaining confidence as a long-distance hiker. Scenes were filmed at shops and restaurants along **Main Street** (page 273) and at **The Breadboard** (page 282), where Cheryl sinks her teeth into a juicy burger.

♦ **Crater Lake, OR:** It's easy to see why Cheryl felt such a baffling sense of disbelief upon her first glimpse of Crater Lake. The lake's deep blue color (the result of ultra-clear water that absorbs every shade of light except blue) is remarkable. Walk in her footsteps on the **Crater Lake Rim Trail** (page 290).

♦ **Cascade Locks, OR:** The finale of Cheryl's captivating story occurs at the northern end of the Oregon section of the Pacific Crest Trail. In Cascade Locks, the historic **Bridge of the Gods** (page 332) stretches over a narrow section of the mighty Columbia River, offering passage from Oregon into Washington. You can cross the bridge by car or foot; you can also admire it from town while enjoying a meal or walking through the **Cascade Locks Marine Park** (page 333).

and views from the top stretch from the Pacific Ocean across the Mojave Desert.

From Sacramento

Follow U.S. 50 and Highway 88 east to **Carson Pass** (page 192), where the PCT runs through wildflower-strewn **Meiss Meadow.** Continue southeast on Highways 88, 89, and U.S. 395 for two hours to **Bridgeport** (page 176), where you can grab some pub food at **Rhino's Bar and Grill** and soothe your tired hiking muscles in **Travertine Hot Springs.** Spend the night in the historic **Bodie Hotel.**

In the morning, visit **High Sierra Bakery** for heavenly pastries, then drive northeast on U.S. 395 and Highway 108 to the top of **Sonora Pass** (page 176), where a hike to the top of windy **Sonora Peak** rewards with expansive views across the high country of Yosemite and the Emigrant Wilderness. Return via Highway 108, stopping at **Kennedy Meadows Resort & Packstation** for dinner.

From Reno

Head west on I-80 to **Truckee** (page 212), exiting the freeway to take Donner Pass Road along the north shore of **Donner Lake** and all the way up to **Donner Pass.** Just before the top, stop at **McGlashan Point** to see ancient petroglyphs in the rocks and the old Central Pacific Railroad tunnel cut into the hillside. Step onto the PCT on Old Donner Summit Road to hike through the Sugar Bowl ski area to **Donner Peak.**

On your way back to Truckee, get an artisan ice cream cone at **Little Truckee Ice Creamery** or go straight to **Old Town Tap** for swanky cocktails and gourmet pizza. A charming hotel room awaits you at the historic **Truckee Hotel.**

The next morning, grab a cup of coffee for the road at **Dark Horse Coffee Roasters** and drive south on Highway 89 to the **Fire Sign Café** for a home-style breakfast and freshly squeezed juice. Once you're fueled up, make the 30-minute drive on Barker Pass Road to the Barker Pass trailhead, where the PCT shares a path with the **Tahoe Rim Trail.** Hike north to **Twin Peaks** for epic views of Lake Tahoe and the surrounding Granite Chief Wilderness.

After your hike, take Highways 28 and 431 to soak up as many Lake Tahoe views as possible.

From Portland

Drive east on U.S. 26 to the historic **Timberline Lodge** (page 320), where you can gaze up at the 11,250-foot summit of volcanic **Mount Hood** while sipping a decadent hot chocolate. Walk along the PCT to the **Zigzag Canyon** overlook, or all the way to **Paradise Park** if you're in the mood for a longer hike. Spend the night at Timberline Lodge, taking advantage of the year-round outdoor hot tub.

The next morning, take Highway 35 to scenic **Hood River** (page 325), stopping on the way to hike to **Tamanawas Falls.** Reward yourself with waterfront dining at **Riverside.** The trail town of **Cascade Locks** (page 331) is a 30-minute drive west on I-84, where you can check out the **Bridge of the Gods** and the PCT's passage over the Columbia River into Washington State.

From Seattle

The PCT crosses I-90 at **Snoqualmie Pass** (page 372), east of Seattle. Stop at **Red Mountain Coffee** for espresso and a breakfast burrito before making the trek to the **Kendall Katwalk,** where the trail is cut into a steep granite slope in the Alpine Lakes Wilderness. Satisfy your hiker hunger at **North Bend Bar & Grill** and spend the night in town.

Make reservations to visit **Goldmyer Hot Springs** the next day—the natural hot spring is nestled deep in the mossy, fern-filled Middle Fork Snoqualmie River Valley. Pack a picnic lunch, as you'll be hiking five miles (each way) to reach the springs.

Hiker Hunger

Multiday treks through the wilderness do wonders for the appetites of thru-hikers. The following best restaurants are the best for hungry hikers, with big portions, great deals, or impressive buffet spreads.

Idyllwild, CA: If you find yourself in town on a Tuesday, stop at **Los Gorditos** for Taco Tuesday specials. With authentic street-style tacos for just $0.99 apiece, you can fill your belly for just a few bucks.

Big Bear, CA: After climbing 7,000 feet from the desert floor into the San Bernardino Mountains, PCT hikers flock to **Himalayan Restaurant** for lunch specials that include an entrée, *aaloo mattar*, lentils, rice, naan, and salad—all for $12 or less.

Kennedy Meadows, CA: The hiker breakfast at **Grumpy Bear's Retreat** in-

Grumpy Bear's Retreat in Kennedy Meadows

cludes eggs, bacon, potatoes, and all-you-can-eat pancakes. Each pancake is 10 inches in diameter—good luck eating more than one! For lunch, try The General: a double bacon cheeseburger, stacked high with lettuce, tomato, and pickles between two toasted buns, served with fries.

Bishop, CA: The dining room may be casual at **Back Alley Bowling**—it's a bowling alley after all—but it's the best spot in the Owens Valley for fresh and tasty surf-and-turf! Try the steak and shrimp entrée for $20, or visit Thursday-Sunday for prime rib.

Etna, CA: The beef for the $8 burgers and dogs at **Dotty's** is raised just two miles away at the owners' family farm. Served with red onion marmalade between two buns from Grain Street Bakery, a burger this good—not to mention this stylish—would easily sell for twice as much in one of the West Coast's trendy food cities.

Seiad Valley, CA: Find out if you have what it takes to win the pancake challenge at **Seiad Café** by digging into a stack of five 13-inch pancakes. If you can finish them all in less than two hours, your meal is on the house. According to the café owners, only four people have ever succeeded!

Timberline Lodge, OR: Watch in awe as ravenous backpackers fill their plates with mountains of food at the famous **Cascade Dining Room** breakfast and lunch buffets. With an elegant setting and a divine array of fresh, flavorful foods, this buffet attracts everyone from mud-crusted thru-hikers to polished luxury travelers.

Cascade Locks, OR: If you're craving some fresh veggies, the all-you-can-eat salad bar at **Bridgeside** is just $8. Pile your plate as many times as you'd like with all the typical salad bar fixings—leafy greens, raw vegetables, cheeses, olives, dressings, nuts, and seeds—plus broccoli slaw, potato salad, and pasta salad.

Stehekin, WA: The giant cinnamon rolls at **Stehekin Pastry Company** are legend and PCT hikers for days before their arrival in town. As this is the last stop in civilization for Canada-bound hikers, many take cinnamon rolls to go when they hit the trail. Ride the red bus or walk to the bakery to see (and taste) what makes these pastries famous.

Best Hikes

Ready to hit the dirt? Here are some of the best hikes along the Pacific Crest Trail.

Southern California
LAGUNA MOUNTAIN RIDGE (PAGE 55)
4.5 mi/7.2 km one-way, 2-3 hr
The rocky Laguna Mountains loom 4,000 feet above Anza-Borrego Desert State Park. Hike along the top of the range's dramatic eastern escarpment to admire the geology and stark beauty of this arid region.

MOUNT BADEN-POWELL (PAGE 88)
9 mi/14.5 km, 4.5-5 hr
The Pacific Crest Trail is gently graded as it ascends to the top of the second-highest peak in the San Gorgonio Mountains, making this peak a quite reasonable endeavor compared to its nearby counterparts. Views from the top stretch out over downtown Los Angeles, the Pacific Ocean, the San Bernardino and San Jacinto Mountains, and the Mojave Desert.

Central California
KEARSARGE PASS (PAGE 131)
9 mi/14.5 km, 6 hr
While most of the John Muir Trail (JMT) remains out of reach for day hikers, this challenging hike to the top of 11,700-foot Kearsarge Pass provides a sneak peek into the route of the JMT and PCT through Sequoia and Kings Canyon National Park.

LONG LAKE AND BISHOP PASS (PAGE 137)
11.2 mi/18 km, 7-8 hr
Every moment feels magical on the path to Bishop Pass, where you're surrounded by sparkling lakes, sky-piercing peaks, vibrant wildflowers, colorful terrain, and tumbling waterfalls. Options for shorter hikes along this gorgeous trail are plentiful.

Crater Lake and Wizard Island from Garfield Peak

LEMBERT DOME (PAGE 171)
2.8 mi/4.5 km, 2-3 hr

Inside Yosemite National Park, the trail to the top of Lembert Dome showcases the unique geology of the park and provides a gorgeous vantage point over lush Tuolumne Meadows.

SONORA PEAK (PAGE 178)
7.7 mi/12.4 km, 4 hr

Hikers find solitude on the PCT near Sonora Pass, which is far less crowded than the national parks farther south and arguably just as beautiful.

Northern California
TWIN PEAKS (PAGE 205)
11.2 mi/18 km, 6 hr

The Pacific Crest Trail overlaps with the Tahoe Rim Trail for 50 miles on the southwest side of Lake Tahoe. Explore this scenic section of the Granite Chief Wilderness with stunning views of the oh-so-blue lake below.

SIERRA BUTTES LOOKOUT TOWER (PAGE 221)
5.5 mi/8.9 km, 3 hr

This hike along the PCT leads to the top of a craggy massif with a defunct lookout tower. Unless you're afraid of heights, you'll want to climb the historic tower's steep stairs to soak up the 360-degree views of the northern Sierra Nevada.

DEADFALL LAKES AND MOUNT EDDY (PAGE 254)
8.6 mi/13.8 km, 5 hr

Mount Shasta looks magnificent from your vantage on top of 9,025-foot Mount Eddy, the tallest peak in the Trinity Alps range. The trail to the top visits multiple alpine lakes along the way.

Oregon
CRATER LAKE RIM (PAGE 290)
6 mi/9.7 km one-way, 3 hr

While the official PCT is plotted through a different area of the national park, this popular alternate follows the western rim of Crater Lake, a volcanic caldera filled with pristine, crystal clear water. This hike offers the best views of Wizard Island, the cone-shaped island in the lake.

OBSIDIAN TRAIL (PAGE 306)
11.8 mi/19 km, 6-7 hr

Explore the evidence of Oregon's volcanic past on the Obsidian Trail, framed by the glaciated mountainsides of North Sister and Middle Sister. The trail twists through forest and lava fields before arriving at Obsidian Falls, where glassy black rocks shimmer in the creek bed.

JEFFERSON PARK (PAGE 316)
12.5 mi/20.1 km, 6-7 hr

The hike to Jefferson Park isn't easy, but the wildflower-speckled meadows and warm, swimmable lakes make the effort well worth it. Start early so you can relax for a few hours midday in the meadows.

Trail Magic

Sometimes hikers need a little help and encouragement during their travels on the Pacific Crest Trail. Trail Magic is the act of doing something nice for hikers without asking for anything in return. Residents in communities near the PCT play a huge part in making this trail so welcoming—buying hikers a beer, giving them a ride to the post office, or offering a place to sleep for the night. You can get involved, too, by visiting trail towns during hiking season, or giving to an organization.

Volunteer Opportunities

♦ The Pacific Crest Trail is one of the most popular hiking trails in the country, and it needs routine maintenance to remain safe and navigable. The **Pacific Crest Trail Association** (www.pcta.org/volunteers) organizes local trail crews for projects in California, Oregon, and Washington. If you prefer to lend your skills in administration or events, volunteer at the PCTA's office in Sacramento or during various annual events across all three PCT states.

♦ The **Washington Trails Association** (www.wta.org/get-involved) maintains trails within Washington, including the PCT.

♦ Volunteers staff the **Mountaineers Lodge at Stevens Pass** (www.mountaineers. org/volunteer) each August-September, welcoming PCT hikers and overseeing the property.

Trail Communities

♦ **Wrightwood, CA:** This town has three fantastic breakfast joints and a brewery with a multilevel outdoor patio.

♦ **Kennedy Meadows, CA:** The sense of excitement is in the air at Kennedy Meadows as hikers prepare to leave the desert behind and enter the High Sierra. Both restaurants in town serve hearty fare and have outdoor seating areas.

♦ **Independence, CA:** This community in the Eastern Sierra has a hiker-themed hotel, a post office, and a couple of tasty food options. It's the closest town to Kearsarge Pass, a popular entry-exit point onto the PCT.

♦ **Sierra City, CA:** Hikers come first in Sierra City, where all three eateries cater to hungry backpackers during the summer.

♦ **Etna, CA:** The city park turns into a campground during late summer when thru-hikers stop in town to rest and resupply.

♦ **Cascade Locks, OR:** Participate in the thru-hiker beer program at the local brewery: Buy a beer in advance for a random hiker and design a coaster with your own personal message.

♦ **Trout Lake, WA:** The town's general store has benches on the front porch where hikers can relax. The huckleberry milkshakes down the street are popular in hot weather.

♦ **Packwood, WA:** Hikers stay here to eat, resupply, or wait out bad weather.

Washington
KILLEN CREEK MEADOWS (PAGE 355)
10 mi/16.1 km, 5 hr

Thanks to its remote location, Mount Adams sees a fraction of the visitors that Mount Hood and Mount Rainier experience each year. This hike along the PCT offers larger-than-life views of Mount Adams, as well as panoramic mountain vistas including Mount St. Helens, Goat Rocks, and Mount Rainier.

NACHES PEAK LOOP (PAGE 365)
3.6 mi/5.8 km, 1.5-2 hr

Mount Rainier can be seen from miles in every direction, but it's hard to appreciate its magnitude without seeing it up close. Admire its icy splendor on this loop hike near Chinook Pass, where the PCT traces the eastern edge of Mount Rainier National Park.

HART'S PASS (PAGE 396)
5.4 mi/8.7 km, 2 hr

Surrounded by formidable, craggy peaks in all directions, hiking at Hart's Pass is humbling, to say the least. If you're willing to brave chilly temps, visit in early October when yellow larch trees and fiery red huckleberry bushes light up the mountainsides.

Southern California

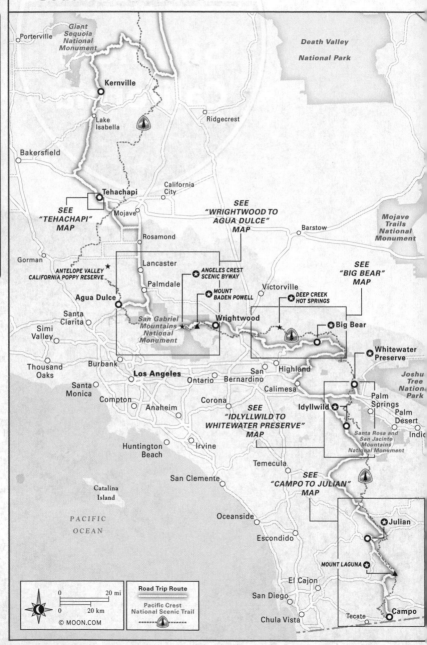

Southern California

Porterville

Giant Sequoia National Monument

Death Valley National Park

Kernville

Lake Isabella

Ridgecrest

Bakersfield

California City

Tehachapi

SEE "TEHACHAPI" MAP

Mojave

Rosamond

SEE "WRIGHTWOOD TO AGUA DULCE" MAP

Barstow

Mojave Trails National Monument

Gorman

ANTELOPE VALLEY CALIFORNIA POPPY RESERVE

Lancaster

SEE "BIG BEAR" MAP

Palmdale

ANGELES CREST SCENIC BYWAY

Agua Dulce

Santa Clarita

Simi Valley

San Gabriel Mountains National Monument

MOUNT BADEN POWELL

Wrightwood

Victorville

DEEP CREEK HOT SPRINGS

Big Bear

Whitewater Preserve

Thousand Oaks

Burbank

Los Angeles

Ontario

San Bernardino

Highland

Joshua Tree National Park

Santa Monica

Compton

Anaheim

Corona

Calimesa

Idyllwild

Palm Springs

Palm Desert

Indio

SEE "IDYLLWILD TO WHITEWATER PRESERVE" MAP

Santa Rosa and San Jacinto Mountains National Monument

Huntington Beach

Irvine

Temecula

SEE "CAMPO TO JULIAN" MAP

San Clemente

Catalina Island

PACIFIC OCEAN

Oceanside

Escondido

Julian

MOUNT LAGUNA

El Cajon

San Diego

Chula Vista

Tecate

Campo

0   20 mi
0   20 km

© MOON.COM

Road Trip Route

Pacific Crest National Scenic Trail

Highlights

★ **Mount Laguna:** Gaze across Anza-Borrego Desert State Park from the top of Laguna Mountain Ridge, a forested, subalpine habitat east of San Diego (page 53).

★ **Julian:** Taste local wines and indulge in fresh-baked apple pie in Julian, a popular historic mining town (page 57).

★ **Eagle Rock:** Stroll along the PCT through lush oak forest and rolling hills to one of the most iconic destinations on the southern PCT (page 65).

★ **Idyllwild:** Granite rock faces tower above Idyllwild, an adorable mountain town tucked into a pristine canyon below Mount San Jacinto (page 66).

★ **Whitewater Preserve:** This river valley between the San Jacinto and San Bernardino Mountains is where white sands, springtime wildflowers, and blue skies abound (page 75).

★ **Big Bear:** Big Bear Lake is a popular four-season resort town where you can find something fun to do every month of the year (page 77).

★ **Deep Creek Hot Springs:** Relax at Deep Creek Hot Springs, a heavenly trailside oasis of hot pools with a cool running creek under cottonwood trees (page 85).

★ **Angeles Crest Scenic Byway:** Follow this twisty scenic route through the San Gabriel Mountains, stopping for spectacular views of Los Angeles to the south and the Mojave Desert to the north (page 86).

★ **Mount Baden-Powell:** Summit the second-highest peak in the San Gabriel Mountains while hiking along the Pacific Crest Trail (page 88).

★ **Vasquez Rocks:** Explore an otherworldly formation of sandstone that was a popular spot for intergalactic TV and film scenes (page 95).

Between the palm-lined beaches of the coast and the vast expanse of the Mojave Desert, the 2,650-mile Pacific Crest Trail traverses towering mountain ranges up to 10,000 feet (3,048 m).

This well-worn path starts inauspiciously along the United States border with Mexico before winding its way north through the desert, showcasing a diverse collection of wildflowers, desert shrubs, cacti, rock formations, Joshua trees, pines, and cedars. The rocky and forested alpine landscape defies the stereotypic Southern California scenery—you won't find palm trees, skyscrapers, or traffic jams here. What you'll encounter instead is solitude and an authentic wilderness experience, just a few miles from one of the most populated regions of the country.

A robust and well-maintained highway system provides many opportunities to access the Pacific Crest Trail, experience the wilderness, and discover the appeal of this surprisingly scenic desert region. Your driving route closely parallels the PCT, crossing the trail multiple times and even overlapping at a few points. North of the trail's southern terminus, the scenic Sunrise Highway climbs into Mount Laguna, a subalpine ridge overlooking Anza-Borrego Desert State Park. The Pines to Palms Highway and the Banning-Idyllwild Panorama Highway offer exploration into the San Jacinto Mountains between greater Los Angeles and Palm Springs.

Continuing north, drive the Rim of the World Scenic Byway to Big Bear, a year-round recreation hub in the San Bernardino Mountains. North of L.A., the Angeles Crest Scenic Byway stretches east out of Wrightwood into the steep, dramatic San Gabriel Mountains. Descend toward the desert floor on the Angeles Forest Highway before passing through the quaint town of Agua Dulce and crossing the westernmost corner of the Mojave Desert on Highway 14.

Highway 58 leads into Tehachapi, nestled in a high-elevation valley between Bakersfield and the Mojave Desert. Heading north, the Caliente Bodfish Road climbs out of Tehachapi to Lake Isabella at the southern base of the Sierra Nevada. Along the entire route through Southern California, charming towns provide an oasis of hospitality for hikers, outdoor adventurers, and travelers.

Planning Your Time

The Pacific Crest Trail begins on the Mexico-U.S. border in a tiny town called Campo, about an hour east of San Diego, and traverses five unique mountain ranges before entering the Sierra Nevada 700 miles later. Though the trail itself is miles away from big cities, sections of the PCT are reachable in less than two hours from either San Diego or Los Angeles. Both cities offer a convenient base for exploration.

Plan **one week** to hike the best sections of the trail, explore nearby trail towns, and cruise along the scenic highways for breathtaking views of the valleys below.

When to Go

Though Southern California weather is mild, visits to these PCT sections are most rewarding in **spring** and **fall,** when the temperatures are moderate and all roads are open. High-elevation mountain roads including the Sunrise Highway in Mount Laguna and the Angeles Crest Scenic Byway near Wrightwood may be affected by winter closures; when open, these roads parallel the PCT and offer the same panoramic vistas as the national scenic trail itself. Depending on the weather, you may find snow in these high-elevation regions even during the summer months.

Day Trips on the PCT

With just a 2-3 hour drive, it's possible to leave the urban sprawl of the big cities behind for day trips to trail towns and scenic stretches of the PCT.

From San Diego
Close to the PCT's southern terminus, **Lake Morena** has several day hikes on the PCT, including the trail to **Kitchen Creek Falls.** Near Julian, the small community of **Warner Springs** offers an opportunity to hop on the PCT for the hike to **Eagle Rock.**

From Los Angeles
The mountains east of L.A. beckon hikers, with multiple access point along the PCT. In the San Gabriel Mountains, the town of **Wrightwood** offers a chance to climb the PCT up **Mount Baden-Powell.** In the San Jacinto Mountains, the town of **Idyllwild** is home to the **Devils Slide Trail** below Tahquitz Peak. North of L.A., the tiny town of **Agua Dulce** offers a chance to walk the PCT through the otherworldly **Vasquez Rocks.**

In the low-elevation desert regions—Lake Morena, Eagle Rock, Whitewater Preserve, and Vasquez Rocks—sections of the PCT are accessible year-round, but are most enjoyable in the cooler **winter** months.

Getting There

Car
Most of the roads near the Pacific Crest Trail can be driven year-round. Rush hour traffic in the cities can be bad on weekdays, but less so in small, remote mountain communities where the trail is located. In winter, many roads close due to ice, rain, or snow. If driving to Mount Laguna, Idyllwild, Big Bear, or Wrightwood in the winter, check road conditions online with **CalTrans** (www. dot.ca.gov).

From San Diego
San Diego is the most convenient travel hub from which to start this drive. From downtown San Diego, **Highway 94** heads 50 miles (81 km) east, becoming a rural, two-lane highway midway to **Campo.** This is the best way to reach the southern terminus of the PCT. From Campo, it's a 30-mile (48-km) drive north to reach Mount Laguna.

For travelers wishing to skip the start in Campo, **I-8** offers easier and more direct access from San Diego to **Mount Laguna,** where the scenic Sunrise Highway climbs north into the 6,000-foot mountains. This route is affected by snow and may experience seasonal closures in the winter months. It takes about an hour to make the 55-mile (89-km) drive from downtown San Diego to Mount Laguna.

From Mount Laguna, **Highway 79** leads 20 miles (32 km) north into **Julian.** This is a popular day-trip destination for San Diegans, who use east-west Highway 78 instead to reach the quaint mountain town in about two hours. The route involves taking I-15 north out of San Diego for about 20 miles (32 km) to Poway, then heading 35 miles (56 km) east on Highway 78. Note that this stretch of road can become clogged with traffic during rush hour.

From Julian, Highway 79 continues 23 miles (37 km) north to **Warner Springs,** then another 22 miles (35 km) north to Aguanga, where you turn east onto **Highway 371** and begin the ascent into the San Bernardino National Forest. Highway 371 continues 20 miles (32 km) northeast until it meets the junction with Highway 74. Turn north here to follow the **Pines to Palms Highway** (Hwy. 74) for about 12 miles (19.3 km), to where it

Best Restaurants

★ **Pine House Café, Mount Laguna:** On the Sunset Highway, stop at this 1942 roadhouse for rustic comfort food and live music (page 56).

★ **Mom's Pies, Julian:** This mountain town is known for its apple pies and this is the best place for a delicious slice (page 60).

★ **Café Aroma, Idyllwild:** This gorgeous cafe serves unforgettable breakfasts and dinners both inside and outdoors on a scenic patio (page 73).

★ **Silverwood Sushi and Grill, Silverwood Lake:** Enjoy colorful sushi in the middle of nowhere on this rural section of road between the San Bernardino and the San Gabriel Mountains (page 86).

★ **Cinnamon's Bakery, Wrightwood:** Satisfy your hiker hunger with their decadent "thru-hiker" sandwich (page 92).

★ **Home Made, Agua Dulce:** Hang with locals and PCT thru-hikers alike over breakfast on this small café's outdoor patio (page 97).

★ **Red House BBQ, Tehachapi:** Enjoy delicious brisket and pulled pork at "Tehachapi's only real barbecue joint" (page 99).

meets the **Idyllwild-Banning Panoramic Highway** (Hwy. 243) at Mountain Center. Highway 243 continues north into Idyllwild. (Highway 243 receives snow in the winter; seasonal accessibility varies.)

From Los Angeles

Los Angeles is a more convenient base from which to explore the sections of the PCT from Idyllwild into Big Bear, the Angeles National Forest, Agua Dulce, and Tehachapi. From L.A., Idyllwild is 130 miles (209 km) east along I-10, a drive that can take anywhere from 3-5 hours in traffic. Accessible from I-10, **Highways 38** and **18** lead 50 miles (81 km) north into **Big Bear,** where the elevation rises above 6,000 feet (1,829 m) (vehicles are required to carry chains in winter).

From Big Bear, **Highway 138** connects west from the San Bernardino Mountains to the San Gabriel Mountains via Cajon Pass between Big Bear and **Wrightwood.** (Wrightwood receives winter snow, but the roads remain open year-round.)

West of Wrightwood, **Highway 2**

navigates the spine of the San Gabriel Mountains; sections of the road are affected by seasonal winter closures.

Highway 2 meets the **Angeles Forest Highway** (County Rd. N3) 50 miles (81 km) west of Wrightwood, then travels north for 25 miles (40 km) before intersecting with **Highway 14. Agua Dulce**, a tiny community on the PCT near Vasquez Rocks, is located near Highway 14 just 10 miles (16.1 km) west of its intersection with the Angeles Forest Highway. Alternatively, you can reach Agua Dulce from Los Angeles by taking I-5 north to exit 162, then heading east on Highway 14 for 14 miles (22.5 km). Allow 45 minutes for this drive.

North of Agua Dulce, Highway 14 connects to Highway 58, which leads into the town of **Tehachapi. Highway 58** to Tehachapi closes occasionally during the winter in icy or snowy conditions. Tehachapi is 106 miles (171 km) north of Los Angeles, about a 2.5-hour drive on I-5 north, Highway 14 north, and Highway 58 west.

Best Accommodations

★ **Alter Experiences, Mount Laguna:** Pamper yourself with a luxurious glampsite, built for you by Alter Experiences (page 57).

★ **Julian Lodge, Julian:** Historic, yet modern, this affordable B&B offers easy access to downtown Julian (page 61).

★ **Idyllwild Inn, Idyllwild:** With rental cabins that date to 1910, 1924, and 1953, this is the most historic place to stay in Idyllwild (page 75).

★ **Robin Hood Resort, Big Bear:** Stay just steps away from Big Bear's lakeshore and downtown shops and restaurants (page 83).

★ **Blue Ridge Primitive Campground, Wrightwood:** The PCT travels right through this primitive campground, which sports views of the San Gabriel River Basin (page 93).

Air

To start your trip near the beginning of the Pacific Crest Trail at the California-Mexico border, fly into **San Diego International Airport** (SAN, 619/400-2404, 3225 N. Harbor Dr., www.san.org). San Diego is the most convenient metropolis to the southernmost towns along the trail: Campo, Mount Laguna, and Julian.

Destinations farther north on the PCT, including the communities of Idyllwild, Big Bear, Wrightwood, and Tehachapi, are closer to the greater Los Angeles area and can be reached more quickly from airports in this region. **Los Angeles International Airport** (LAX, 1 World Way, 855/463-5252, www.flylax.com) is the biggest and busiest airport. Depending on when your flight arrives, you may find yourself fighting some of the nation's worst traffic just to get out of town and into the mountains.

Ontario International Airport (ONT, 2500-2900 E. Airport Dr., 909/544-5300, www.flyontario.com) is far less busy than LAX, and it's closer to the PCT. It's about a 90-minute drive from the airport to Idyllwild or Big Bear, and under an hour's drive to Wrightwood (depending on traffic, of course).

If the thought of sitting in freeway gridlock doesn't sound like the way to kick off your road trip into the wilderness, you can avoid the metro area altogether by flying into **Palm Springs International Airport** (PSP, 3400 E. Tahquitz Canyon Way, 760/318-3800, www.palmspringsca.gov). The airport is serviced by most international airlines and is about an hour's drive from the town of Idyllwild.

Train

Amtrak (800/872-7245, www.amtrak.com) offers rail service to a number of stations within 50 miles of the Pacific Crest Trail: San Diego (Santa Fe Station, 1050 Kettner Blvd.), Los Angeles (Union Station, 800 N. Alameda St.), San Bernardino (1170 W. 3rd St.), Victorville (16858 D St.), and Palm Springs (Palm Springs Station Rd.). You'll need to rent a car or hop on a bus to access the PCT from any of these urban hubs.

Bus

Greyhound (800/231-2222, www.greyhound.com) offers bus service to San Diego (1313 National Ave., 619/515-1100) and Los Angeles (1716 E. 7th St., 213/629-8401).

BoltBus (877/265-8287, www.boltbus.com) also serves Los Angeles from select locations in California (Barstow, Fresno, Oakland, San Francisco, San Jose) and Nevada (Las Vegas).

You can take a **FlixBus** (855/626-8585, www.flixbus.com) to San Diego, San Bernardino, Anaheim, Los Angeles, or Bakersfield. Once arriving in one of these urban hubs, you'll need to rent a car to access the wilderness areas near the Pacific Crest Trail.

Campo and Lake Morena

The rural community of Campo lies 1.5 miles (2.4 km) north of the Pacific Crest Trail's Southern Terminus on the U.S. border with Mexico. Campo (Spanish for "countryside") and the surrounding valley is settled with horse ranches, old-fashioned windmills, and easy, winding roads. The area is quiet—a far cry from the eight-lane freeways of nearby San Diego—with bright blue skies and rolling green hills.

Lake Morena is a famous fishing and hiking destination with a lovely campground. Lake Morena is also a stopping point along the Pacific Flyway, the bird migration route between South America and Alaska. Visits to the area during the spring reward campers with a musical array of birdsong from diverse species: orioles, flycatchers, finches, sparrows, thrushes, and jays. It's 5 miles (8 km) north of Campo.

Getting There

Campo is 53 miles (85 km) east of San Diego. From San Diego, take Highway 94 east for 50 miles (81 km). The multi-lane freeway transitions into a rural two-lane highway at Rancho San Diego, about halfway between downtown San Diego and Campo. If you need gas or snacks, make any necessary stops in the first 25 miles (40 km).

The second half of the drive is quite scenic, as it follows a meticulously maintained byway through rolling hills of chaparral and granite boulders. The Mexico border wall is also within view, and U.S. Border Patrol agents are very active in this area. If you're an international traveler, keep your passport handy.

You can also get to Campo from the **El Cajon Transit Center** (S. Marshall Ave. and Palm Ave., El Cajon, 619/233-3004, www.sdmts.com, $5-7.50) on the 891 bus.

Sights

The 2,650-mile **Pacific Crest National Scenic Trail** begins 50 miles east of San Diego on the U.S. border with Mexico. Originally built in 1988, the **Southern Terminus Monument** (along with a matching structure at the Northern Terminus) was designed to commemorate the 20th anniversary of the National Trails System Act. The Act designated both the PCT and its eastern counterpart, the Appalachian Trail, as national scenic trails. A new monument was installed in 2016.

The monument is made of five hand-painted fir pillars, stained and lettered with the Pacific Crest Trail logo. The monument sits on a hill next to the Mexican border with a sweeping view of the Campo Valley's ranches and granite-speckled mountains on the horizon. For northbound thru-hikers, this vista is the first of many panoramic views to come. For those on a southbound journey, the monument marks the end of their epic adventure.

You can drive right up to the monument in Campo. From the Campo Green Store at the intersection of Forest Gate Road and Highway 94, follow Forest Gate Road south for 1.5 miles (2.4 km).

Hiking
Morena Butte

Distance: 8.2 mi/10.5 km round-trip

Duration: 4.5 hours

Elevation change: 1,280 ft/390 m

Effort: Moderate/Strenuous

Trailhead: Morena Reservoir Road

Campo to Julian

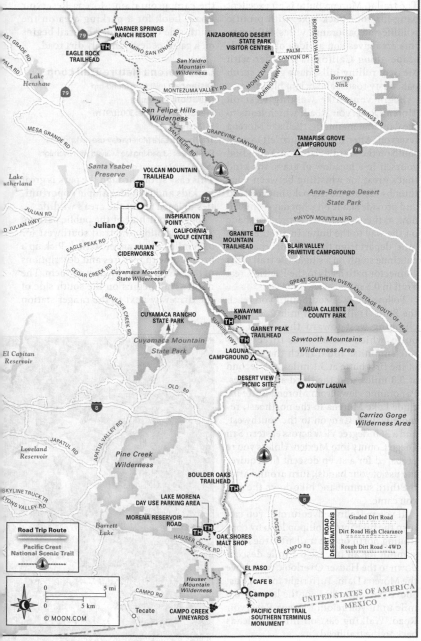

Road Trip Route

Pacific Crest National Scenic Trail

DIRT ROAD DESIGNATIONS	
	Graded Dirt Road
	Dirt Road High Clearance
	Rough Dirt Road - 4WD

0 — 5 mi
0 — 5 km

© MOON.COM

Pass/Fee: $3 parking fee (waived with overnight stay in Lake Morena County Park)

The trail to Morena Butte is an excellent bang-for-your-buck hike, with prolific wildlife and panoramic vistas. Hiking in this area gives you an idea of the landscape along California's border with Mexico: rolling hills, dark green scrub oak, dusty roads, and bright blue skies.

Begin your hike walking west on Morena Reservoir Road, which leads to the dam that maintains the Lake Morena reservoir. After 1.3 miles, turn left to walk south on the Ward's Flat Loop. You'll find yourself in a meadow of grass, the kind that's great for whistling between your thumbs. California live oaks line the road and provide shade on a hot day—enjoy it now, as these are the last sources of shade on the way to the butte. In another 0.25 mile, depart from the wide dirt road and continue south on a single-file trail. This connector path leads to the Pacific Crest Trail in 0.5 mile.

Follow the PCT south until you reach the Butte Trail cutoff at mile 2.5. Begin climbing west toward the top of the butte, which actually has three separate summits. You'll reach the summit of the first butte at 3.1 miles, the second at 3.8 miles, and the third at 4.1 miles. Panoramic views from Morena Butte include Lake Morena to the northeast, remote Hauser Canyon to the southwest, and a 360-degree view across eastern San Diego County into Mexico. Unless you're prepared for a steep descent (it requires the use of your hands), turn around after the third summit and hike down the way you came.

If you're feeling adventurous, you can turn the hike into a lollipop loop by continuing north on the trail after the third summit for an intense 0.5 mile descent down to the Hauser Overlook, just above the Morena Dam. Turn right to head east above the south shore of the lake for 0.5 mile until you rejoin Morena Reservoir Road. Walking east on this road leads back to the trailhead.

Getting There

The trailhead is located 0.5 mile west of the campground on Morena Reservoir Road. Look for a parking area on the south side of the road. The trail begins on a gated pedestrian-only dirt road.

Lake Morena Nature Trail Loop ᴾᶜᵀ

Distance: 1 mi/1.6 km round-trip
Duration: 30 minutes
Elevation change: 300 ft/91 m
Effort: Easy
Trailhead: Lake Morena day-use parking area
Pass/Fee: $3 parking fee (waived with overnight stay in Lake Morena County Park)

This easy stroll through the park is great for kids and provides ample opportunities to learn about the area's wildlife.

Begin your hike at the public parking area and follow the trail southwest for 0.25 mile to the ranger station. Pick up a brochure with pictures and descriptions of the park's plants to identify them. The nature trail begins on the south side of the driveway next to the ranger station

and leads through a chaparral environment of scrub oak, live oak, manzanita, whitethorn, and buckwheat. Turn left at the intersection with the Pacific Crest Trail to head north. The PCT will lead you back to the park's entrance. Complete the loop by walking along the eastern edge of the campground and turning left to walk toward the restrooms and return to the parking area.

Guided hikes on the Lake Morena Nature Trail are offered on some Saturdays. Call the park (619/579-4101) for dates and times.

Kitchen Creek Falls 🅿️

Distance: 5.1 mi/8.2 km round-trip
Duration: 2.5 hours
Elevation change: 880 ft/268 m
Effort: Moderate
Trailhead: Pacific Crest Trail at Old Highway 80

During the winter and spring, Kitchen Creek pours south out of the Laguna Mountains and creates waterfalls on the way. This hike along the PCT leads to some of these seasonal waterfalls.

From the parking area, walk northeast on the Pacific Crest Trail, crossing under I-8 at 0.3 mile. The trail curves to the south, then bends northeast again at 1 mile as it ascends a rocky hill. There are nice west-facing views between 1.5-2.3 miles where the trail is cut into the western slopes of rocky foothills. Reach a trail junction at 2.3 miles and veer left, departing from the PCT and descending toward Kitchen Creek to see the falls. Arrive at the creek at 2.5 miles. The creek bed is made up of huge, smooth boulders. Return the way you came, or to make this a longer hike, return to the PCT and continue north toward Mount Laguna.

Getting There

The PCT trailhead at Old Highway 80 is 13 miles (20.9 km) north of Campo, about a 20-minute drive. Take Highway 94/Campo Road north for 1.5 miles (2.4 km) and turn left to continue north on

wildflower bloom at Lake Morena

Buckman Springs Road. In 10 miles (16.1 km), turn right to head south on Old Highway 80 for 2 miles (3.2 km). The trailhead parking area is on the west side of the road.

Recreation

Fishing is one of the most popular activities in **Lake Morena County Park** (2550 Lake Morena Dr., 858/565-3600, www.sdparks.org, 6am-sunset Oct.-Mar., 5:30am-sunset Apr.-Sept., parking $3), where trophy largemouth bass are caught regularly. Anglers can pay the fishing fee ($5-7), then rent a motorboat ($30-50) or a rowboat ($15-25) to fish for bass, bluegill, crappie, or catfish.

Lake Morena is 7.5 miles (12.1 km) north of Campo. From Campo, head north on Highway 94 for 1.5 miles (2.4 km), then turn left onto Buckman Springs Road. In 3.5 miles (5.6 km) turn left onto Lake Morena Drive and continue 4.3 miles (6.9 km).

Entertainment and Events
Wine-Tasting
Campo Creek Vineyards (29556 Hwy. 94, 619/402-8733, www.campocreekvineyards.com, noon-4pm Sat., 1pm-4pm Sun., by appt. Mon.-Fri., $10) features mild, easy-drinking wines, including an award-winning viognier that's perfect for a warm outdoor afternoon. This small, family-run winery feels nothing like the fancy, luxurious tasting rooms in Napa. You'll taste wine in view of the Mexican border wall, a fleet of tractors, and at least three shaggy (and quite friendly) family dogs.

Food

Café B (1247 Sheridan Rd., 619/478-5415, www.cafebcampo.com, 7am-8:30pm Mon.-Thurs., 7am-9pm Fri.-Sat., $7-9) has an extensive café menu, featuring hot

From top to bottom: welcome to Campo sign; wines in the Campo Creek Vineyards tasting room; Mexican cuisine at El Paso.

breakfast sandwiches, salads, and custom wraps for lunch, plus from-scratch pizza and a full espresso bar.

El Paso (31464 Hwy. 94, 619/478-9045, 7am-8pm Mon.-Sat., 8am-8pm Sun., $6-9) is a Mexican food stand on the road between Campo and Lake Morena. The tacos are larger than average and served with house-made red or green salsa. One taco with a side of beans is a satisfying lunch. Take food to go, or enjoy it at one of the stand's shaded tables.

If you're planning to cook at camp, or need some snacks for the drive, the **Campo Green Store** (31080 Hwy. 94, 619/478-5494, 8am-8pm daily) has an impressive selection of goods, including local wines and fresh produce. You'll also find high-quality Pacific Crest Trail merchandise and gifts like hats, maps, and patches.

Don't be alarmed by the bars on the windows and the appearance of a possibly sketchy mini-mart. Inside **Oak Shores Malt Shop** (2425 Lake Morena Dr., 619/478-5845, www.oak-shores-malt-shop.business.site, 7am-9pm daily, $8-14), a delicious menu of sandwiches, burgers, and pizzas awaits. This convenience store/restaurant combo is a staple for long-distance hikers on their way through Lake Morena, after they've completed the first 20 miles of the Pacific Crest Trail.

Accommodations and Camping

Lake Morena County Park (2550 Lake Morena Dr., 619/478-5473, www.sdparks.org, $28-50) has 86 campsites and 10 cabins on a beautifully groomed property. Take advantage of the large, clean bathrooms, with plenty of hot water in the coin-operated showers.

★ Mount Laguna

Mount Laguna is the smallest town in Southern California, with only 54 residents. At an elevation of more than 6,000 feet, this ridgeline habitat blends alpine and desert environments; the landscape is peppered with Jeffrey pine trees, prickly pear cactus, mistletoe, and manzanita. The area features gorgeous scenery and abundant wildlife, including a number of bird species that flourish in post-burn environments.

Getting There

Mount Laguna is a one-hour drive east of downtown San Diego. From San Diego, follow I-8 east to exit 47. Turn left from the off-ramp and continue north on S1 to Mount Laguna.

From Campo, it's a 30-minute drive north. Head east on Highway 94 to Buckman Springs Road and turn left. Drive north on Old Buckman Springs Road for 9.5 miles (15.3 km). Take the left fork to meet up with Old Highway 80 in less than a mile. Turn left to travel east; the road leads to a freeway overpass, crosses I-8, and heads onto San Diego County Route 1, the Sunrise Highway.

The **Sunrise Highway** (San Diego County Route 1 or S1) is the only paved thoroughfare in Mount Laguna, with access to campgrounds, businesses, and the Pacific Crest Trail. The Sunrise Highway meets I-8 at exit 47, 1 mile (1.6 km) west of a tiny town called Pine Valley, which has a grocery store, two motels, a gas station, and a couple of casual restaurants.

Scenic Drive

The scenic drive along the **Sunset Highway** (S1) closely parallels the Pacific Crest Trail, offering drivers many of the same panoramic views as hikers on the trail: rolling green chaparral hills to the west and the dramatic, rocky eastern descent into the Colorado Desert.

This scenic 24-mile (39-km) stretch of Sunrise Highway begins east of the town of Pine Valley where it intersects with I-8. Head northeast, following signs for Mount Laguna. Around mile marker 17, the highway reaches 5,000 feet (1,524 m) in elevation and winds through Mount

Laguna's version of the Sierras—a subalpine environment of pine trees, granite peaks, and epic views. Stop at the **Pine House Café** (mile marker 23) for a meal, snack, beer, or coffee.

The **Desert View Picnic Site** (mile marker 24) is another worthy stop for a picnic snack or lunch. Views from this perch extend over the Colorado Desert, Anza-Borrego Desert State Park, and the San Felipe Valley. Even the Salton Sea, California's largest lake, can be seen on clear days. Continue north on the highway to Kwaaymii Point (mile marker 30) for more spectacular east-facing views before meeting up with Highway 79 at mile marker 37, just north of Cuyamaca Rancho State Park.

Allow about 35 minutes for this drive, more if you plan to stop for photos or hikes.

Hiking
Desert View Trail Loop

Distance: 1 mi/1.6 km round-trip
Duration: 30 minutes
Elevation change: 120 ft/37 m
Effort: Easy
Trailhead: Desert View Picnic Site
Pass/Fee: Adventure Pass ($30 annually/$5 daily) (waived with overnight stay at Burnt Rancheria Campground)

There's no easier way to say you've hiked part of the Pacific Crest Trail than to amble along the Desert View Trail. The path connects the Desert View Picnic Area to Burnt Rancheria Campground and provides a sneak peek at the views PCT hikers enjoy during their trek along the eastern edge of the Laguna Mountains. Pick up a printed guide at the **Mount Laguna Visitor Center** (Sunrise Hwy. and Los Huecos Rd., 619/473-8547, 1pm-5pm Fri., 9am-5pm Sat., 9am-3pm Sun.) before you go to learn about local flora and fauna, designated with numbered signposts along the trail.

The Desert View Trail is accessible at the northeast edge of the Desert View Picnic Site loop. Look for the trail marker near the southeast edge of the parking area. Walk south and bear right at the trail junction at 0.2 mile. The chaparral landscape is dotted with pines and California black oaks (the state's only native oak), offering shade in the spring and summer and a delight of colorful foliage in the fall. You'll find yourself on the northern edge of Burnt Rancheria Campground at 0.5 mile (and if you're camping there, this trail can be accessed near campsite 77). Bear left to continue east for another 0.1 mile before meeting up with the Pacific Crest Trail. Walk north, back toward the parking area, and gaze out across the expanse of the desert. You may notice a white orb on nearby Monument Peak: the Laguna Observatory.

Getting There
Desert View Picnic Site is located on the east side of the Sunrise Highway near mile marker 24.

Garnet Peak

Distance: 2.2 mi/3.5 km round-trip
Duration: 1.5 hours
Elevation change: 500 ft/152 m
Effort: Easy/Moderate
Trailhead: Garnet Peak
Pass/Fee: Adventure Pass ($30 annually/$5 daily)

Garnet Peak's jagged and dramatic eastern cliff juts out over Anza-Borrego Desert State Park. The views from the top are spectacular, especially if you're up early enough to catch the sunrise over the desert horizon. No cliff-scaling is necessary to get to the viewpoint at the top—the hike actually climbs up the gently sloping western side of the peak.

The Garnet Peak Trail begins in an open, mostly flat area with a few blackened tree snags, evidence of the 2013 Chariot Fire. You won't do much climbing until you cross the Pacific Crest Trail at 0.6 mile; this is where the Garnet Peak Trail gets steeper as it ascends (15-20 percent grade), and the trail is rocky in places. Endure for another 0.5 mile before

the trail bends to the right; in another 0.1 mile, it reaches the rocky summit.

Hold onto your hat (the peak is known for high winds) and enjoy an impressive view including the Laguna Mountains, the Cuyamaca Mountains, and the expanse of the desert 4,000 feet (1,219 m) below. Even the Salton Sea, more than 35 miles away, is visible on clear days.

Getting There

From the Desert View Picnic Site, drive 4.2 miles (6.8 km) north on the Sunrise Highway and look for the dirt parking area on the right side of the road (the eastern side) just north of mile marker 27. There is room for one or two cars in this parking area. If you see Pine Creek Road on the left, you've gone too far.

Laguna Mountain Ridge

Distance: 4.5 mi/7.2 km one-way
Duration: 2-3 hours
Elevation change: 500 ft/152 m
Effort: Easy/Moderate

view from Garnet Peak

Trailhead: Kwaaymii Point

Pass/Fee: Adventure Pass ($30 annually/$5 daily)

This hike along Laguna Mountain Ridge showcases the dramatic eastern slope of the Laguna Mountains with Anza-Borrego Desert State Park 4,000 feet (1,219 m) below.

Start your hike at Kwaaymii Point, a popular jump-off spot for hang gliders, walking north on the Pacific Crest Trail. Right away, you're rewarded with expansive desert views, and it will stay this way throughout the entire hike. Keep right at the first trail junction to stay on the PCT, and continue along the ridgeline, looking down on Cottonwood Canyon and the Sawtooth Mountains to the east. The trail continues north past Oriflamme Mountain and meets up with the Sunrise Highway at 4.5 miles. Arrange a shuttle to end your hike here or turn around to head south on the PCT back to Kwaaymii Point.

Getting There

Kwaaymii Point is located on the east side of the Sunrise Highway near mile marker 30, about a 10-minute drive north from Burnt Rancheria Campground.

Food

The ★ **Pine House Café** (9849 Sunrise Hwy., 619/473-8857, www.pinehousecafe.com, 5pm-7pm Thurs., noon-8pm Fri., 8am-8pm Sat., 8am-6pm Sun., $9-18) is a roadhouse-style restaurant serving rustic and elegant comfort food from its original timber frame structure, built in 1942 when Mount Laguna was a busy U.S. Air Force base. Pine House is must-stop for weary and ravenous hikers. The seasonal rotating menu features chili (both meat and vegetarian) and soup, entrée specials, local craft beer, and juicy burgers. The berry cobbler is a delight if you've got a hankering for a sweet treat. Live musicians play country, folk, and rock 'n' roll Friday and Saturday nights. The scene is always family-friendly.

There's also a full **espresso bar** (9am-2:30pm Fri., 8am-2:30pm Sat.-Sun.) with mochas, chai lattes, and non-dairy milks.

Accommodations

Chilly weather and sub-freezing temps are common November-March, when there's nothing better than warming up next to a fireplace after a long day outside in the cold. The 17 cabins and 12 motel rooms at **Laguna Mountain Lodge** (10678 Sunrise Hwy., 619/473-8533, www.lagunamountain.com, rooms $70-100, cabins $90-215) all have a cozy cabin vibe, wood-burning stoves, and full baths. Rooms have microwaves and refrigerators, while cabins have kitchenettes with sinks. Pets are allowed in some of the cabins. The on-site **general store** (9am-5pm daily) carries groceries, beer and wine, gifts, books, and camping supplies, including firewood.

Camping

In the Cleveland National Forest, **Burnt Rancheria Campground** (mile marker 23, Sunrise Hwy., 858/673-6180), www.fs.usda.gov, Apr.-Oct.) has 109 large, well-maintained campsites within walking distance of Pine House Café and the general store. Some of the sites have pergolas, which can provide valuable shade in the hot summer months (bring your own tarp to affix across). From the campground, you can walk right onto the Desert View Trail and connect to the PCT. Coin-operated showers are also available.

The **Laguna Campground** (mile marker 26, Sunrise Hwy., 619/473-2082, www.fs.usda.gov, year-round) is located 3.5 miles (5.6 km) north of Burnt Rancheria in the Laguna Mountain Recreation Area. It has 104 sites and offers most of the same amenities, minus the direct PCT access or pergolas. Located next to Laguna Meadow, this is a peaceful and picturesque place to spend the night.

Reservations (877/444-6777, www.

recreation.gov, $25) for both campgrounds are available.

★ **Alter Experiences** (619/642-7015, www.alterexperiences.com, $99-350) will build a "glampsite" for you: a glamorous campsite with an oversized canvas ground tent or a suspended tree tent. It sets the scene at an existing campsite at Burnt Rancheria or Laguna Campground with hotel-like amenities including a therapeutic mattress, fluffy pillows, blankets or sleeping bags, toiletries, an outdoor kitchen, campfire seating, and even a carpet with lounge chairs. The result is an ultra-luxurious and uber-comfortable campsite under the stars, perfect if you're new to camping, don't have your own camping gear, or simply feel like being pampered for the weekend.

Information and Services

The **Laguna Mountain Visitor Center** (Los Huecos Rd. and Sunrise Hwy., 800/832-1355, 1pm-5pm Fri., 9am-5pm Sat., 9am-3pm Sun.) sells printed maps of Laguna Mountain Recreation Area ($3). Pick one up here or at the Laguna Mountain Lodge to get a sense of the highway route, biking and hiking trails (including the PCT), campgrounds, picnic areas, and parking lots.

★ Julian

Julian is a historic mining town known mostly for apple pie and antiques, but it's quickly becoming a culinary destination and a popular hub for outdoor recreation. Although the desert isn't far, Julian's lush hillsides are covered in live oaks, manzanita, and cottonwood trees. This charming area has managed to maintain its historical appeal while adapting to the desires of modern foodies, tech-savvy travelers, and outdoor adventurers. The food and wine scene is burgeoning, and the local business owners love to feed hungry hikers.

The Pacific Crest Trail crosses Highway 78 at Scissors Crossing, 12 miles (19.3 km) east of Julian, so this town makes a convenient base from which to explore.

Getting There

Julian is 20 miles (32 km) northeast of Mount Laguna and 65 miles (105 km) northeast of San Diego.

From Mount Laguna, take the Sunrise Highway north for 14 miles (22.5 km) to the junction with Highway 79. Turn right and continue north for 6 miles (9.7 km). Turn left onto Main Street to arrive in downtown Julian. Allow about 30 minutes for the drive.

From San Diego, the drive takes about 1.5 hours. Follow I-8 east for 37 miles (60 km) to exit 40. Turn left onto Japatul Valley Road/Highway 79, which travels north through Cuyamaca Rancho State Park. You'll arrive in Julian in 23 miles (37 km).

Street parking in downtown Julian is limited and can be tough to find on weekends. Park in the lot on the corner of 4th and B Streets ($5) to avoid the frustration of looking for a spot.

Sights

Julian's Main Street is lined with shops, bakeries, and restaurants. Buskers play music on summer weekends. Expect to share the sidewalks and streets with many other visitors.

The historic **Eagle Mining Co.** (2320 C St., 760/765-0036, www.theeaglemining. com, 10am-4pm daily, $10 cash or check only) offers an exciting glimpse into Julian's beginnings as a mountain gold mining town in the 1870s. Take the tour to try your hand at panning for gold, and walk through the mine, ducking through pitch-black tunnels (with lanterns, of course). Along the way stop to see the old mining equipment and learn about what life was like for the gold miners.

Inspiration Point Scenic Overlook (423 Inspiration Point Rd.) is 2.5 miles (4 km) south of Julian on Highway 79. The point looks out over the town of Banner, Anza-Borrego Desert State Park, and Scissors Crossing, where the Pacific Crest Trail crosses the San Felipe Valley floor.

Canine enthusiasts won't want to miss **California Wolf Center** (470 K Q Ranch Rd., 760/765-0030, www.californiawolfcenter.org, 8am-4pm daily, $20-30 adults, children under 5 free), a conservation, research, and education facility dedicated to the recovery of wild wolves. Your two-hour tour begins with a slideshow and educational presentation about the history of wolves and current recovery efforts. Next, follow your tour guide to outdoor enclosures where you can view both Mexican and North American gray wolves. Tour days and times vary throughout the year; **reservations** are required.

Hiking
Volcan Mountain Preserve

Distance: 5 mi/8 km round-trip
Duration: 2.5 hours
Elevation change: 1,200 ft/366 m
Effort: Moderate
Trailhead: Volcan Mountain

Views from Volcan Mountain look out over the route of the Pacific Crest Trail as it traverses Scissors Crossing and the San Felipe Valley. Near the summit, interpretive panels map the course of the national scenic trail through the desert, pointing out prominent peaks on the horizon to the south and west. From your vista point, you'll get sweeping views from the crest, including the lush, green hills to the west, and the expanse of the desert to the east.

Begin your hike at the preserve entrance by walking through the exquisite fin-like wood gates into the garden. In 0.3 mile, the trail meanders through an oak grove that local acorn woodpeckers are quite fond of. Stay left at the junction of the Five Oaks Trail; you'll take that route on the way back. There's a small plateau with a westward lookout point at 1.1

miles, where the Five Oaks Trail rejoins the main trail. This is a great turnaround point if you've had enough elevation gain for the day.

Otherwise, continue up the hillside on the wide dirt road, which makes a big bend to the right at 1.7 miles. At 1.9 miles, stop to study the interpretive panels and look through telescopes to identify the peaks in your line of sight. Your view to the east over the San Felipe Valley is just 0.2 mile farther, and there's another diagram, this time with the PCT plotted through the center. To round out the views, walk 0.1 mile to the Charles Powell Memorial Bench and gaze over the town of Julian to the south. The road loops at the top of the peak and you're on your way back down.

Getting There
Take Farmer Road northwest out of downtown Julian for 2 miles (3.2 km). Turn right on Wynola Road, then take your first left to continue onto Farmer Road. The trailhead parking area is on the east side of the road. Park off-pavement and walk east on the dirt road for 0.2 mile to the park entrance.

Entertainment and Events
Autumn (Sept.-Nov.) is Julian's busiest time of year, when the town and surrounding orchards celebrate the harvest season with pumpkin patches and gourd picking, hay rides, apple picking, pie-baking contests, and beer and wine tastings. Check online (www.visitjulian.com/to-see-do/calendar) for a full list of activities and events.

The **Taste of Julian** (www.atasteofjulian.com, May, $25-30) is an annual "rural dining adventure." This self-guided culinary tour offers a chance to experience many of Julian's restaurants and eateries, including wine, beer, cider, and pie, of course. A shuttle service ($10) from stop to stop is also available.

Wine- and Cider-Tastings and Craft Breweries

Two boutique wineries are conveniently located at the base of Volcan Mountain Preserve. Their tasting rooms are a perfect stop after your hike.

Volcan Mountain Winery (1255 Julian Orchards Dr., 760/765-3267, www.volcanmountainwinery.com, 11am-5pm Thurs.-Mon.) produces wine from traditional grapes like pinot gris, pinot noir, and malbec, as well as some lesser known, but highly noteworthy European varietals like carignan and mourvedre. Try the apple wine: a dry, sparkling wine that tastes like a sauvignon blanc but bubbles like a champagne.

Menghini Winery (1150 Julian Orchards Dr., 760/765-2072, www.menghiniwinery.com, 11am-4pm Mon.-Fri., 10am-5pm Sat.-Sun.) is a family-owned winery up the road from Volcan. Sunny apple orchards and vineyards surround the rustic tasting room.

Julian Hard Cider (4470 Julian Rd., Wynola, 760/765-2500, www.julianhardcider.biz, 11am-6pm Sun.-Mon., 11am-8pm Fri.-Sat.) makes cider from apples, cherries, pears, raspberries, and more. Its Miner's Saloon tasting room is located in Julian Station, an original 1943 apple packing facility, and has 10 cider flavors on tap. Sip some cider, then wander through Julian Station to nibble on chocolate, eat tacos, view local art, or catch live music on the weekend.

If you're curious about what makes Julian apples the best, learn about the cider-making process at **Julian Cider Works** (17552 Harrison Park Rd., 760/331-7453, www.julianciderworks.com, 2:30pm-6pm Thurs.-Fri., noon-6pm Sat.-Sun., $8). The tasting room is located in a barn on the 200-acre Kenner Ranch outside Julian. The owners are dedicated

From top to bottom: Eagle Mine entrance; Volcan Mountain Preserve; Volcan Mountain Winery.

to the craft of cider-making as well as the education around it.

Tom Nickel worked in San Diego breweries for years before striking out on his own in the mountains east of the city. The result is **Nickel Brewing Company** (1485 Hollow Glen Rd., 760/765-2337, www.nickelbeerco.com, 2pm-8pm Mon.-Thurs., 11:30am-9pm Fri., 11am-9pm Sat., 11am-8pm Sun.), a brewery with 16 creative and expertly crafted beers on tap. Order a tasting flight (served in muffin tins), then grab a seat on the dog-friendly outdoor patio, nestled among pine and apple trees with a great view of Volcan Mountain to the north. Fill up a growler to share at your campsite.

Shopping

Julian is a great stop for artisan and handmade goods, picnic supplies, and everyday clothing. **Julian Market & Deli** (2022 Main St., 760/765-2606, 8am-7pm daily) has it all: groceries, camping gear, clothing, and household goods. If you're visiting during the spring, look for the *Welcome PCT! Hikers* sign above the front door.

Crow and Lilac (2608 B St., 760/842-3331, www.crowandlilac.com, 1pm-5pm Mon. and Thurs., 11am-5pm Fri.-Sun.) is a gallery and boutique with a carefully curated collection of art, handmade skin care, jewelry, and gifts. The wood-paneled interior gives the shop a distinct mountain feel, but the merchandise is modern and elegant.

Food

If you like apple pie, candied apples, or apple turnovers, you'll love eating in Julian. The exceptional quality of the apples in Julian is the result of a unique combination of elevation, air quality, soil composition, and botanical diversity. ★ **Mom's Pies** (2119 Main St., 760/765-2472, www.momspiesjulian.com, 7am-5pm Mon.-Thurs., 7am-5:30pm Fri. and Sun., 7am-6pm Sat., $5-18) bakes variations on the theme, like apple-boysenberry

and apple-cherry pies with buttery, flaky crusts. Not in the mood for apples? The chocolate-pecan pie is nothing short of decadent, while the rhubarb-strawberry is tangy and tart.

The locals take advantage of the great lunch special at **Apple Alley Bakery** (2122 Main St., 760/765-2532, 8:30am-5pm daily, $4-16) where you can order a sandwich, a soup or salad, and a slice of warm pie for just $11. Spinach wraps are on the menu, too, with a choice of chicken, roast beef, veggies, and sauces, plus a few gluten-free items. The bakery also serves a variety of pie flavors (caramel-apple is its specialty).

If you've got plans for an early morning adventure, **Granny's Kitchen** (1921 Main St., 760/765-2900, www.grannyskitchenjulian.com, 5am-3pm Mon.-Wed. and Fri., 7am-5pm Sat.-Sun., $8-14) can serve you breakfast before you embark. Egg sandwiches, breakfast burritos, and omelets are on the menu until 11:30am. Lunch sandwiches, like the salmon BLT, hot pastrami, and chicken pesto salad, are crafted to order and served with home-style coleslaw.

Romano's Restaurant (2718 B St., 760/765-1003, www.romanosrestaurantjulian.com, 11am-8:30pm Sun.-Tues. and Thurs., 4pm-8:30pm Wed., 11am-9pm Fri.-Sat., $11-24) has been dishing up rustic Italian fare in Julian since 1982. The menu is extensive, with pastas, salads, sandwiches, and traditional entrées like eggplant parmesan and chicken marsala.

Julian Grille (2224 Main St., 760/765-0173, www.juliangrille.com, 11am-4pm Mon., 11am-8pm Tues.-Thurs. and Sun., 11am-9pm Fri.-Sat., $11-27) looks like a house from the outside, but the inside has been transformed into a beautiful dining space with hardwood floors, ornate windows, and beautifully restored 1920s touches. Pasta, seafood, and steaks are on the menu; the Reuben sandwich is a favorite.

Jeremy's on the Hill (4354 Hwy.

78, Wynola, 760/765-1587, www.
bestrestaurantinjulian.com, 11am-8pm
Sun.-Thurs., 11am-9pm Fri.-Sat., $15-
32) is a leader in Julian's culinary development. The upscale menu highlights
ingredients from local farms and producers with wild-caught fish, grass-fed
beef, quinoa salad bowls, and fresh vegetables. Insider tip: Before it was a fine-
dining destination, the building was the
home of Tom's Chicken Shack. Jeremy's
still sells fried chicken on Friday nights.
Call ahead to make a reservation or order
chicken to go; it often sells out.

Wynola Pizza (4355 Hwy. 78, Wynola,
760/765-1004, www.wynolapizza.com,
11am-8pm Sun.-Wed., 11am-9pm Thurs.-
Sat., $10-20) has live music on Friday and
Saturday nights (6pm-9pm), plus a hearty
American-Italian menu of pizzas, salads,
and meat or seafood entrées. Look for the
big red barn on the south side of the highway in Wynola, 3.6 miles (5.8 km) north
of Julian.

Accommodations

Located downtown, ★ Julian Lodge
(2720 C St., 760/765-1420, www.
julianlodge.com, $149-179) is the most
affordable hotel of its caliber: upscale,
comfortable, and with more privacy than
the popular B&Bs in the area. The modern hotel was designed to feel historic.
It's within steps of the town's bakeries,
restaurants, museums, shops, post office,
and library. Rooms are painted in pas-
tels and elegantly furnished. Coffee and
tea are available in-room, and a deluxe
continental breakfast is served downstairs daily.

Dog lovers will want to stay at the
Eagle's Nest (2609 D St., 760/765-
1252, www.eaglesnestbnb.com, $175-
195), where they'll be greeted by four
friendly and loving golden retrievers.
Inside, all rooms have fireplaces and

From top to bottom: tasting flight at Nickel
Brewing Company; Apple Alley Bakery & Coffee;
Jeremy's on the Hill.

air-conditioning; some rooms have king beds, mountain views, or private entrances with access to an outdoor patio. The sunny courtyard and seasonal swimming pool are available for all guests to enjoy.

The **Apple Tree Inn** (4360 Hwy. 79, Wynola, 760/765-0222, www. julianappletreeinn.com, $129-149) has remodeled rooms with private entrances, soft and fluffy beds, hardwood floors, and bright, clean bathrooms. Plus you're just across the street from Wynola Pizza for live music and next door to Jeremy's for gourmet cuisine. The outdoor swimming pool is open during warm summer months. It's 4 miles (6.4 km) northwest of Julian.

Tuck yourself away in the woods for a private getaway at the **Artist's Loft Cabins** (Pine Hills, 760/765-0765, www. artistsloft.com, $175-185, 2-night minimum weekends). The luxurious mountain cabins offer accouterments like French doors, screened-in porches, California king beds, wood-burning stoves, territorial views, and do-it-yourself gourmet breakfast (without someone else's schedule to adhere to).

Camping

Cuyamaca Rancho State Park (14592 Hwy. 79, 760/765-3023, www.parks. ca.gov) has four campgrounds, plus cabins rentals that sleep up to eight people. Campground **reservations** (800/444-7275, www.reservecalifornia.com, $30-75) are required weekends April-October and are accepted year-round. The park is 10 miles (16.1 km) south of Julian. Nearby Lake Cuyamaca offers boat rentals, fishing, hiking, and wildlife.

Information and Services

The **Julian Chamber of Commerce** (2129 Main St., 760/765-1857, www.visitjulian. com, 10am-4pm daily) has an office in the town hall that is brimming with brochures and handouts about hiking trails, shopping, restaurants, accommodations, and camping. The staff is friendly and helpful.

Anza-Borrego Desert State Park

Anza-Borrego is located within the Colorado Desert, a small section of the Sonoran Desert, northeast of San Diego and east of Julian. The park gets its name from two separate entities: explorer San Juan de Anza, and the Spanish word for sheep. As California's largest state park, Anza-Borrego is home to 16 native cactus species, and visitors flock to see its stunning wildflower bloom each spring. The flowers aren't the park's only draw: the night skies in Anza-Borrego are breathtaking, with no light pollution to dim the sparkle of the stars. The area is a favorite location for astronomers and photographers.

The Pacific Crest Trail grazes the western edge of the park in two places: along

the northern base of Granite Mountain, and through the San Felipe Hills between Julian and Warner Springs.

Getting There

Anza-Borrego Desert State Park is 75 miles (121 km) northeast of San Diego and 15 miles (24 km) east of Julian.

From Julian, follow Highway 78 east for 11 miles (17.7 km) down winding Banner Grade to Scissors Crossing. Turn right on S2 to head south toward Agua Caliente, or to reach Borrego, drive 7 miles (11.3 km) north on Highway 78. Turn left (north) on S3 and drive 7 miles (11.3 km) to the junction with Borrego Springs Road. Turn left (west) and follow Borrego Springs Road 5.3 miles (8.5 km) to Borrego Springs.

The visitors center is located at the west end of Palm Canyon Drive, about 2 miles (3.2 km) from Christmas Circle.

Scenic Drive

At Scissors Crossing, the Pacific Crest Trail crosses Highway 78 and Highway S2, also known as the **Great Southern Overland Stage Route.** This route has been in use since the 1700s, when it was a dusty path traveled by Spaniards. It eventually became one of the routes in the westward expansion of the United States. Highway S2 travels north-south between Warner Springs and Ocotillo. Driving along this 65-mile (105-km) stretch of highway is a great way to see the stark, wondrous beauty of **Anza-Borrego Desert State Park,** which borders both sides of the highway at certain points along this drive.

For an abbreviated trip, drive 22 miles (35 km) from Scissors Crossing to Agua Caliente County Park. As you drive south you'll see Granite Peak to the west framed by 6,000-foot Laguna Mountain Ridge. Near mile marker 39, drive through Box Canyon; upon emerging into the flat-lands, look northeast to see Whale Peak

Anza-Borrego Desert State Park

on the horizon. Arrive at Agua Caliente near mile marker 26, a seasonal campground and hot springs resort open during the winter months.

Scissors Crossing is 11 miles (17.7 km) east of Julian via Highway 78 and 20 miles (32 km) south of Warner Springs via S2. Allow an hour to travel from Scissors Crossing to Agua Caliente and back, more if you plan to stop for photographs.

Hiking

Granite Mountain Loop

Distance: 7.4 mi/11.9 km round-trip
Duration: 4-5 hours
Elevation change: 3,100 ft/945 m
Effort: Strenuous
Trailhead: Granite Mountain

Climb to the top of 5,550-foot Granite Mountain from the desert floor to gaze out over the Pacific Crest Trail's route through Scissors Crossing and the San Felipe Hills. Make it a shorter, more moderate excursion by hiking to the lower-elevation **eastern summit** (5.2 mi/8.4 km rt, 1,900 ft/579 m, moderate), which provides territorial views of Anza-Borrego Desert State Park.

Begin your hike by walking west on the Granite Mountain Trail for 1 mile as it meanders up the eastern side of the peak. At the trail junction at 1 mile, stay right and climb northwest on the north fork (you will return on the other trail). The steepness increases over the next 1.5 miles before the trail rejoins the south fork at 2.4 miles. This is the eastern summit, and views from this vantage point include Box Canyon to the south, Blair Valley to the southeast, the Pinyon Mountains on the eastern horizon, Earthquake Valley to the northeast, and the San Felipe Hills to the north. Laguna Mountain Ridge towers high on the western horizon. Return to the parking area by taking the south fork trail back down the hill.

To continue to the western summit of Granite Mountain (7.4 mi/11.9 km rt, 3,100 ft/945 m, strenuous), follow the west-bound trail as it ascends through the chaparral. Between 3-3.4 miles, the trail traces a narrow ridgeline and the climb from here to the top is quite steep. Your reward from the western summit at 3.5 miles is an expansive view of the surrounding terrain, including the path of the PCT as it skirts the northern edge of Granite Mountain. Return the way you came, opting for the south fork on the way back, where the trail splits at 4.8 miles.

Getting There

The Granite Mountain trailhead is 5.5 miles (8.9 km) south of Scissors Crossing, about a 10-minute drive. Take S2 south for 4.5 miles (7.2 km). Just after the stagecoach Trails RV resort, turn right onto an unnamed dirt road. Follow it west for 1 mile to the parking area.

Camping

The 140 campsites at **Agua Caliente County Park** (39555 S-2, 760/765-1188, www.sdparks.org, Labor Day-Memorial Day) are framed by Anza-Borrego's dusty desert hills, dotted with cactus, cholla, and ocotillo. Reservations include access to the hot springs resort, with man-made pools fed by natural mineral springs. The park is very popular in the winter, when daytime desert temperatures are mild and the hot springs are a treat. The resort closes in the summer due to inhospitable weather. **Reservations** (877/565-3600, http://reservations.sdparks.org, $29-34) are recommended.

Tamarisk Grove Campground (5960 Yaqui Pass Rd., 760/767-4205, www.parks.ca.gov) has 27 sites with amenities and plenty of shade. **Reservations** (800/444-7275, www.reservecalifornia.com, $25) are available. It's 7 miles (11.3 km) east of Scissors Crossing,

Prefer to rough it, away from other campers? You won't find any amenities or services at **Blair Valley Primitive Campground** (aside from pit toilets), but you will find solitude and serenity.

To camp here, bring plenty of water for cooking, drinking, and washing and be prepared for extreme temperatures (hot days and cold nights are typical).

Blair Valley is 6 miles (9.7 km) south of Scissors Crossing on San Diego County Route 2 (S2). The Ghost Mountain and the Pictograph Trails are both nearby.

Information and Services

For maps, wildlife brochures, and hiking information, visit the **Anza-Borrego Desert State Park Visitor Center** (300 Palm Canyon Dr., Borrego Springs, 760/767-4205, www.parks.ca.gov, 9am-5pm daily Oct. 1-May 31, 9am-5pm Sat.-Sun. and holidays June 1-Sept. 30).

Warner Springs

In Warner Springs, the Pacific Crest Trail departs from the cactus-speckled desert and enters groves of oak trees in rolling, wildflower-strewn hills. The PCT crosses Highway 79, the main route through town, making this small community an easy place for road-trippers to step onto the national scenic trail.

Hiking

★ Eagle Rock 🅿🄲🅃

Distance: 6.4 mi/10.3 km round-trip
Duration: 2.5-3 hours
Elevation change: 850 ft/259 m
Effort: Easy
Trailhead: Pacific Crest Trail/Barrel Springs/Eagle Rock

Eagle Rock is one of the most iconic locations on the southern portion of the Pacific Crest Trail. The natural boulder formation bears a striking resemblance to its namesake raptor.

Start your hike at the PCT trailhead on the south side of Highway 79, just west of the fire station. Walk south on the PCT through a grove of live oaks and scrub oaks along a seasonal creek, which flows in winter and spring. You'll pass through two cattle gates at 0.2 mile and 0.3 mile

before entering an open range where you may encounter a few cows. The trail is lush, shady, and lovely for the next mile as it follows the creek. Around 1.6 miles, the trail enters open meadows. At 1.9 miles, stop and look at the ridgeline on the eastern horizon—Palomar Mountain Observatory is the shiny metal ball on the mountaintop. Continue hiking through meadows peppered with California poppies and purple lupine in the spring. Your destination is unmistakable at 3.2 miles: a massive pile of boulders in the shape of an eagle about to take flight.

Insider tip: Daytime temperatures during the summer can be punishing in this region. Do this hike during the spring, or plan to hike in the morning or evening.

Getting There

Park off-pavement on Highway 79 west of the fire station. The trail begins on the south side of the cement highway bridge. Look for a sign with the Pacific Crest Trail logo.

Shopping

At **2-Foot Adventures** (760/614-1151, www.2footadventures.com), you can pick up all kinds of backcountry gear—backpacks, clothing, cooking equipment, snacks, footwear (including expert shoe fitting), and more—vended out of a completely restored 1968 Airstream trailer. The owners abide by thru-hiker seasonality, and spend mid-March-mid-May in the parking lot at the **Warner Springs Community Resource Center** (30950 Hwy. 79, 760/782-0670, www.wscrcenter.org).

Accommodations and Food

The only place to stay is the **Warner Springs Ranch Resort** (31652 Hwy. 79, 760/782-4200, www. warnerspringsranchresort.com, $109), which also happens to have the only restaurant, the only gas station, and a beautiful golf course. Rooms are in quaint ranch-style cottages designed to feel like the "Old West"; all have free Wi-Fi and private bathrooms. Choose from rooms with one queen bed or two double beds.

The **Golf Grill** (760/782-4271, 7:30am-5pm Wed.-Thurs., 7:30am-7:30pm Fri.-Sun., $10-20) has a big patio overlooking rose gardens and the golf course. All the standard breakfast items are served in the morning. Burgers, sandwiches, salads, and Mexican fare make up the lunch and dinner menus. Local wines are highlighted on the menu.

Information and Services

Warner Springs is a small town with few services and amenities. The nearest large town is Ramona, 30 miles (48 km) south on Highways 78/79.

Getting There

Warner Springs is 70 miles (113 km) northeast of San Diego and 22 miles (35 km) north of Julian. From Julian, take Highway 79 north for 22 miles (35 km) to Warner Springs, a 30-minute drive.

To more closely follow the path of the PCT through Anza-Borrego Desert State Park, take Highway 78 east from Julian for 11 miles (17.7 km), down the twisty Banner Grade to Scissors Crossing, then turn left to head north on San Felipe Road/San Diego County Route 2. The road parallels the Pacific Crest Trail for 16 miles (26 km)—look east into the San Felipe Hills to get an idea of the PCT's path through this area. At the T intersection, turn right onto Highway 79 and drive east for 3.5 miles (5.6 km) to Warner Springs. Allow about 45 minutes for this drive.

★ Idyllwild and Mount San Jacinto State Park

The alpine community of Idyllwild sits high in the San Jacinto Mountains west of Palm Springs. The town is surrounded by Mount San Jacinto State Park, where Mount San Jacinto towers above the desert at almost 11,000 feet.

The state park is laced with wilderness trails. The Pacific Crest Trail traverses the spine of this mountain range, showcasing panoramic views of Palm Springs and the surrounding desert cities, as well as the hills descending into the town of Hemet and the southeastern suburbs of San Bernardino.

Getting There

Idyllwild is 110 miles (177 km) southeast of Los Angeles, 110 miles (177 km) northeast of San Diego, and 60 miles (97 km) north of Warner Springs.

From Warner Springs, follow Highway 79 north for 20 miles (32 km), then turn right to head west on Highway 371. In 12 miles (19.3 km), turn left at the intersection with Highway 74 (the Pines to Palms Highway) and travel north for 12 miles (19.3 km) to Mountain Center. Turn right onto the Banning-Idyllwild Panoramic Highway (Highway 243) and climb for 4 miles (6.4 km) to reach downtown Idyllwild.

Sights

Harmony Tree Monument (Ridgeview Dr. and Village Center Dr.) is an exquisite wood carving of wild animals—a bear, a cougar, an eagle, and more—designed by artist David Roy to honor the town of Idyllwild. However, there's something very interesting about the sculpture you can't see: no nails, screws, or bolts are responsible for its structure. In fact, nothing but Gorilla Glue holds the statue's four primary log segments together.

Scenic Drive

The **Banning-Idyllwild Panoramic Highway** (Highway 243) showcases the incredible biodiversity of Southern California, from the hot, sandy desert through boulder-speckled chaparral and into subalpine forests and the massive granite slabs of the San Jacinto Mountains. The 29-mile (47-km) stretch

Idyllwild to Whitewater Preserve

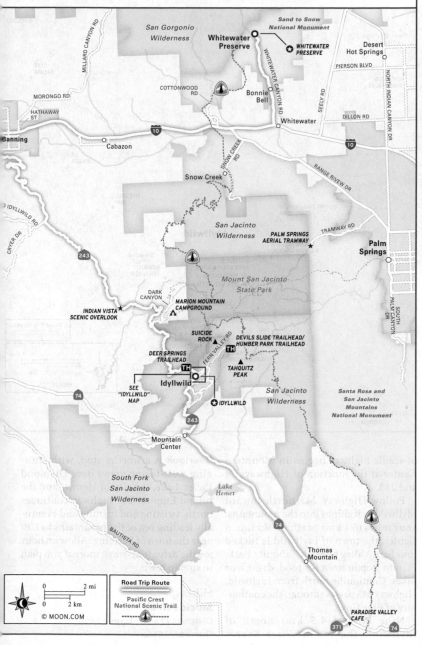

Idyllwild

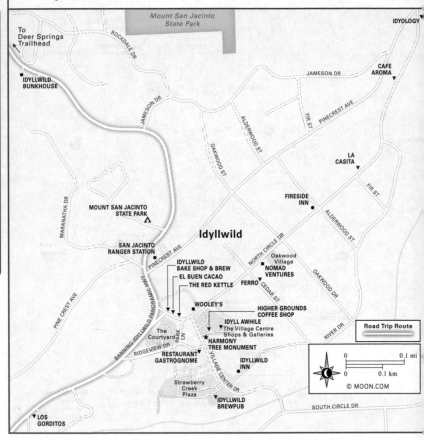

of scenic highway begins in Mountain Center at the junction of Highways 74 and 243.

Follow Highway 243 north toward Idyllwild as it climbs into the mountains. Four miles (6.4 km) north of Mountain Center, the town of Idyllwild is tucked into Fern Valley beneath Tahquitz Peak. Plan to stop in town for food, drinks, or hikes. Continuing north from Idyllwild, Highway 243 passes through the community of Pine Cove.

Nine miles (14.5 km) north of Idyllwild, the **Indian Vista Scenic**

Overlook is a worthy stop, with stunning west-facing views over Diamond Valley Lake, the city of Hemet, and the Inland Empire. The highway continues north, twisting and turning and eventually leading out of the mountains to I-10 near the town of Banning. Allow an hour for the drive (one-way), more if you plan to stop in town.

Hiking
Suicide Rock
Distance: 7.2 mi/11.6 km round-trip
Duration: 3.5 hours

Elevation change: 1,850 ft/564 m
Effort: Moderate
Trailhead: Deer Springs
Pass/Fee: Adventure Pass ($30 annually/$5 daily)

Suicide Rock is a massive granite formation that juts out of the northwestern canyon wall above Fern Valley, Strawberry Creek, and the town of Idyllwild. Start your hike on the Deer Springs Trail, which climbs from Highway 243 toward the crest of the San Jacinto Mountains, then continue onto the Suicide Rock spur trail, where you can look out over Idyllwild to Tahquitz Rock and the other side of the valley.

Begin your hike by following the Deer Springs Trail north out of the parking area through manzanita, cedar, oak, and pine trees. You'll enter San Jacinto State Park at 0.7 mile. Big granite boulders abound (look for an interesting mushroom-shaped boulder at the 0.9-mile mark). The trail makes a small horseshoe bend at 1.5 miles, and the clearing there is a great spot to stop for a water break on a hot day. Continue for another 0.8 mile to the Suicide Rock spur trail at 2.3 miles, and turn right to head south on the spur. (The sign says 1 mile, but the viewpoint is actually 1.3 miles from this point.) In the springtime, keep your eyes peeled for snow plants: vibrant red fungal formations that grow low to the ground. The trees and plants begin to thin as you approach the viewpoint, and Tahquitz Rock appears across the valley. At the trail's end, you stand 2,000 feet (610 m) above Idyllwild, gazing west toward the foothills of Mountain Center, Hemet, and the Inland Empire.

Getting There

The Deer Springs trailhead is 0.9 mile north of downtown Idyllwild on Highway 243. Look for a gravel parking area on the east side of the highway.

Devils Slide

Distance: 4.8 mi/7.7 km round-trip
Duration: 2.5 hours

Elevation change: 1,650 ft/503 m
Effort: Moderate
Trailhead: Devils Slide
Pass/Fee: Adventure Pass ($30 annually/$5 daily) and free Devils Slide permit at Idyllwild Ranger Station

There's a reason Devils Slide is the most popular trail in Idyllwild. Views along this path include Suicide Rock to the north, Tahquitz Peak towering just above, and a stunning perspective of Fern Valley.

The trail starts in Humber Park (in the northeast corner of town) and climbs to a five-trail intersection called Saddle Junction, where it meets the Pacific Crest Trail.

Start your hike at the south end of the Humber Park parking lot. The trail switchbacks through the trees twice in the first 0.3 mile, then follows the mountainside's contour for 0.3 mile before another set of switchbacks. Stop here and turn around to behold 8,800-foot Tahquitz Peak, also known as Lily Rock, towering above. Large ponderosa pine trees in this area are a sight to see, some stripped of their outer bark and exposing the candy-cane striping of the trunk. At 1 mile, views across Fern Valley offer a vantage of Marion Mountain, one of the tallest peaks in the San Jacinto Mountains. (San Jacinto itself is the tallest, but from here, it's hidden behind Marion.) For the next mile, manzanita trees create intermittent green tunnels that block valley views but offer precious shade on warm days. Your best view of Suicide Rock is at 2.3 miles, and your turnaround point is the intersection with the Pacific Crest Trail at 2.4 miles. On your way down, check out the trail itself, expertly hewn into the mountainside.

The Devils Slide Trail is the most heavily used trail in Idyllwild. Daily quotas are in place to protect the ecosystem. Stop by the **San Jacinto Ranger Station** (54270 Pine Crest Ave., 909/382-2921, 8am-4pm Fri.-Mon., 8am-noon Tues.) early to get your permit, or call ahead to confirm availability.

Getting There

The Devils Slide trailhead is located in Humber Park, 2.5 miles northeast of downtown Idyllwild. It takes about 10 minutes to drive there from the intersection of Highway 243 and North Circle Drive.

Drive northeast on North Circle Drive for 0.7 mile then turn right onto South Circle Drive. Take the first left, heading north on Fern Valley Road. In 0.5 mile, turn left to stay on Fern Valley Road. Arrive at Humber Park in 1.3 miles. The trailhead is located in the southeast corner of the parking area.

Deer Springs-PCT-Devils Slide

Distance: 10.6 mi/17.1 km one-way
Duration: 6 hours
Elevation change: 3,400 ft/1,036 m
Effort: Strenuous
Trailhead: Deer Springs
Pass/Fee: Adventure Pass ($30 annually/$5 daily)

A popular and beautifully constructed section of trail showcases some of the best views of Suicide Rock to the northwest, Tahquitz Peak to the south, and the steep canyon walls of Fern Valley. This horseshoe hike traces the upper walls of Fern Valley, giving hikers a chance to experience part of the Pacific Crest Trail's route through the San Jacinto Wilderness.

Your journey into the San Jacinto Mountains begins at 5,600 feet (1,707 m) where the Deer Springs Trail departs from Highway 243. The trail climbs through sparse oak, pine, and cedar forest for the first 2.3 miles, gaining 1,300 feet (396 m) of elevation before reaching the Suicide Rock spur. Continue straight to head north on the Deer Springs Trail toward Strawberry Junction. A series of 11 tight switchbacks over the next 0.5 mile bring you to a clearing with a sweeping territorial view to the southwest. You'll reach another viewpoint at 3.2 miles, this time facing the mountain community of Pine Cove and, far below, the Inland Empire. Between here and your intersection with the PCT are some

outstanding trees: massive ponderosa and Jeffrey pines, along with towering cedars.

Your trail meets the Pacific Crest Trail at 4 miles at Strawberry Junction. Turn right at the junction to head east along the southbound PCT, stopping at the boulder field at 4.6 miles to soak up the west-facing views over Diamond Valley. Here the PCT makes a sharp left and travels northeast along the base of Marion Mountain. At 5.3 miles, cross Strawberry Creek, which flows all the way down to Idyllwild and right through the center of town. Views of Fern Valley and the massive rock faces that tower above Idyllwild are awesome on this stretch. At 6.2 miles, the Pacific Crest Trail makes a sharp right and begins to descend south toward Saddle Junction. Your hike will be downhill from here.

Meet the Devils Slide Trail at 8.1 miles and turn right to head west, back toward town. Your ending point, Humber Park, is 2.4 miles down the Devils Slide Trail, through clusters of manzanita bushes, lofty pine trees, and remarkable granite boulders.

The Devils Slide Trail terminates at Humber Park, which is three miles northeast of the Deer Springs trailhead. Be sure to arrange for a shuttle at Humber Park or leave a vehicle in the parking lot to avoid a road walk back to your car at Deer Springs.

Recreation

Rock climbers from all over Southern California flock to Idyllwild to scale 8,840-foot **Tahquitz Peak,** which resembles the shape and size of rocks in Yosemite. Despite its ominous name, **Suicide Rock** is another popular monolith among climbers. **Vertical Adventures** (800/514-8785, www.vertical-adventures. com, $95-395) offers half-day or full-day lessons as well as guided climbs.

Winter

During the winter months, the San

Jacinto Mountains are covered in snow. Daytime temps average in the 40s, making Idyllwild an ideal place to grab your sled (or your snowshoes) and enjoy the winter weather. Due to limited parking near town, you'll want to visit one of the designated snow play areas. **Mount San Jacinto State Park** (25905 Hwy. 243, 951/659-2607, www.parks.ca.gov, 8am-4pm daily, $10/day) is within blocks of the city's shops and restaurants. **Humber Park** (24559 Fern Valley Rd., 909/382-2921, www.fs.usda.gov) provides access to Devils Slide Trail and Ernie Maxwell Trail, which can be fun on snowshoes. Limited entry permits are not required during the winter months, but an Adventure Pass ($30 annually/$5 daily) is required to park at Humber Park.

Entertainment and Events
Wine-Tasting and Craft Breweries
The sheer magnitude of **Idyllwild Brewpub** (54423 Village Center Dr., 951/659-0163, www.idyllwildbrewpub.com, noon-10pm Fri., 11am-10pm Sat., 11am-8pm Sun., $8-20) is extraordinary. Its sleek, urban design—a blend of hardwoods, bright lights, metallics, and marble—sets it apart from other restaurants in Idyllwild. There are more than 20 house beers on tap and a creative cocktail list. The pub fare menu is elevated: truffle fries, charred Brussels sprouts, steak salad, mussels, and gourmet hot dogs with kraut, plus burgers, fish-and-chips, and buffalo wings. A large deck overlooks Strawberry Creek.

Idyll Awhile (54245 N. Circle Dr., 951/659-9463, www.idyll-awhile.com, 1pm-8pm Mon.-Thurs., 1pm-9pm Fri., noon-9pm Sat., noon-7pm Sun., $11-14) is a cozy wine shop and bistro with a long list of by-the-glass pours. Wine tastings change weekly and include red and white wines from around the world.

From top to bottom: downtown Idyllwild; Devils Slide trail; giant trees on the Deer Springs trail.

Six rotating beers are also on tap. The bistro menu offers meats, cheeses, small plates, sandwiches, and flatbreads. More than just a place to sip wine, the shop is a prime spot to relax and socialize: Monday is game night and local musicians play Friday-Sunday evenings.

Shopping

You can't miss **Wooley's** (54274 N. Circle Dr., 951/659-0017, www.wooleys.com, 10:30am-5pm daily) with its giant hat-shaped sign. Step inside to see the astonishing selection of hats, visors, boots, sweaters, belts, sunglasses, foxtails, sheepskins, and local art. Every ounce of space in the shop is stocked with something you might need for your travels, or a sweet memento to bring back home.

Nomad Ventures (54415 N. Circle Dr., 951/659-4853, www.nomadventures. com, 9am-5pm daily) is the local outfitter, staffed with extremely friendly and helpful outdoor experts specializing in hiking and rock climbing. The small shop is well furnished with shoes, clothing, hats, backpacks, sleeping bags, cooking equipment, and more. If it's something you need to explore the San Jacinto Mountains, you'll find it here.

Food

Many Idyllwild restaurants are open six days per week (often closed on Monday, Tuesday, or Wednesday), and their hours vary seasonally. Some restaurants suggest calling ahead of time if you're making the drive exclusively to visit their spot. Idyllwild prides itself on promoting local musicians and artists—almost every night of the week, you can catch live music acts in Idyllwild's restaurants.

If you've driving to Idyllwild from Warner Springs, you'll drive right past the **Paradise Valley Café** (61721 Hwy. 74, Mountain Center, 951/659-3663, www.

From top to bottom: Idyllwild Brewpub sign; Wooley's; outdoor dining on Strawberry Creek at Idyology.

theparadisevalleycafe.com, 8am-3pm Mon.-Tues., 8am-8pm Wed.-Sat., 8am-6pm Sun., $9-15), where hikers, bikers, and horseback riders are well-fed on burgers and diner fare. The Pacific Crest Trail is only 1 mile (1.6 km) east of the restaurant, so it's extremely popular with hikers who have been trekking through the desert heat. Traditional breakfast fare includes omelets and French toast. For lunch and dinner, choose from 15 different burgers along with sandwiches, salads, and a handful of entrées like chicken burritos, fish tacos, and spaghetti marinara. Beer and wine are served, too. The café is 17 miles (27 km) south of Idyllwild, at the intersection of Highways 371 and 74.

Stepping into **Restaurant Gastrognome** (54381 Ridgeview Dr., 951/659-5055, www.gastrognome.com, 10am-9pm Sun.-Mon. and Thurs., 10am-9:30pm Fri.-Sat., $15-38) is like stepping back in time. Rich red carpeting, exposed wooden beams, and a large stone hearth give the interior a cozy, cabin-like feel. The restaurant opened in 1973, and the menu still features vintage classics like steamed artichokes, roast duck, and shrimp scampi, as well as a wide array of New American items including salads, soups, fresh seafood, steaks, and chops. The dog-friendly patio, surrounded by stonemasonry and towering pines trees, gives diners a view of Marion Mountain and the northern canyon walls of Fern Valley.

Post-modern and polished, **Ferro** (25840 Cedar St., 951/659-0700, www.ferrorestaurant.com, 5pm-9pm Mon.-Tues. and Thurs., 5pm-10pm Fri., 11:30am-4pm and 5pm-10pm Sat., 11:30am-4pm and 5pm-9pm Sun., $12-38) serves fine Italian fare in a sleek, elegant setting. The menu features a delightful array of imported cheeses, cured meats, fresh seafood, and bright, colorful vegetables. Choose from traditional Italian appetizers, salads, pizzas, and pastas. If you aren't fluent in Italian, prepare

to learn a few words—the knowledgeable servers are happy to explain the menu items. On the elegant outdoor patio in back, live music acts play 2-3 nights per week during the spring and summer.

The gorgeous marble bar, exquisite wooden interior, and multilevel indoor/outdoor patio make ★ **Café Aroma** (54750 N. Circle Dr., 951/659-5212, www.cafearomaidyllwild.com, 11am-9pm Fri.-Tues., $12-29) an unforgettable place to eat, drink, or watch live music. Breakfast favorites like omelets, pancakes, steak and eggs, and eggs Benedicts are served until 4pm. Soups, salads, and pastas are available all day, while dinner specials like osso buco and scallops start at 5pm. The live music acts are varied—everything from a Sunday morning harp to Saturday night blues. Art installations change seasonally.

With a double-level outdoor deck along Strawberry Creek, **Idyology** (54905 N. Circle Dr., 951/659-5962, www.idyologyidyllwild.com, 4pm-midnight Mon.-Fri., noon-2am Sat., 8am-midnight Sun., $14-28) is a local favorite for specialty cocktails and creative burgers. The menu's "hillbilly favorites" include armadillo eggs, fried chicken, and nachos made with your choice of tortilla or potato chips. Remarkable interior decor (leather couches set around a stone hearth with animal-print blankets), a full bar, and a pool table all make indoor dining or drinking equally alluring.

The Red Kettle (54220 N. Circle Dr., 951/659-4063, www.perrysredkettle.com, 7am-2pm daily, $8-13) is Idyllwild's go-to breakfast joint, with omelets, scrambles, breakfast burritos, griddlecakes, and oats. Originally a candy and soda shop, the building has been here since the 1920s, and it retains its old-fashioned charm with red-plaid curtains and a diner-style breakfast counter. Red umbrellas and pine trees shade the outdoor patio.

Higher Grounds Coffee Shop (54245 N. Circle Dr., 951/659-1379, www.

⚑ Side Trip: Palm Springs Aerial Tramway

If you aren't in the mood for a strenuous hike, the **Palm Springs Aerial Tramway** (1 Tram Way, Palm Springs, 888/515-8726, www.pstramway.com, 10am-8pm Mon.-Thurs., 8am-9pm Fri.-Sat., 8am-8pm Sun. late May-late Aug. and holidays, 10am-8pm Mon.-Fri., 8am-8pm Sat.-Sun. Sept.-June, $26 adults, $24 seniors, $17 children ages 3-10) is a fantastic way to visit the high-elevation areas of the San Jacinto Mountains. Departing from Chino Canyon in Palm Springs, the tram travels 2.5 miles up to 8,500 feet (2,591 m) in about 10 minutes. Views from the rotating tramcar (the world's largest) are stunning and include dramatic Chino Canyon, the surrounding granite peaks, and the desert cities of Coachella Valley to the east. A museum with natural history exhibits awaits in the three-story visitors building at the top, along with two restaurants and a bar.

Peaks Restaurant (11am-8:30pm, $15-42) is a fine-dining restaurant with huge floor-to-ceiling windows that face east over the dramatic edge of the mountains and the desert cities sprawling below. The menu features upscale New American cuisine; **reservations** (760/325-4537) are recommended. Casual **Pines Café** (11am-8:30pm, $8-18) is a cafeteria-style deli with soups, sandwiches, salads, hot entrées, and pizza. If you're just in the mood for a drink, the **Lookout Lounge** is a full liquor bar on the same level as the restaurant. A network of hiking trails departs from the building, including the trail to the summit of Mount San Jacinto.

Getting There

The Palm Springs Aerial Tramway isn't far from Idyllwild as the crow flies, but the 48-mile (77-km) drive around the north side of the mountain range takes about an hour. From Idyllwild, head north on Highway 243 for 24 miles (39 km). Following signs for I-10, turn right (east) onto Lincoln Street and left (north) onto Hargrave Street, then turn right and merge onto I-10 east. Continue for 11 miles (17.7 km) to exit 111, then follow Highway 111 southeast for 8 miles (12.9 km). Turn right to head west on Tram Way to arrive at the parking area.

---

highergroundscoffee.com, 6am-7pm Sun.-Thurs., 6am-9pm Fri.-Sat.) serves 100 percent organic, fair-trade coffee and espresso from Idyllwild Coffee Roasters. High ceilings, exposed wooden beams, and big windows give the café a lofty feel. The outdoor patio is a sunny spot to enjoy the mountain views. Signature drinks are named after nearby trails and mountains: the PCT Sunrise smoothie is a refreshing treat on a warm summer day. Pastries and light café fare are in the cold case if you need a snack.

Idyllwild Bake Shop & Brew (54200 N. Circle Dr., 951/659-4145, www.idyllwildbakeshopandbrew.tumblr.com, 6:30am-4pm Mon.-Thurs., 6:30am-5pm Fri., 7am-5pm Sat., 7am-4pm Sun.) is a cute coffee shop in the center of town. Fill up with tasty coffee, baked goods, grilled sandwiches served on house-made bread,

and tater tots with gourmet toppings like bacon, avocado, and white truffle oil. Window seats are perfectly positioned to watch what's going on outside.

Tucked away at the end of a charming alleyway, **El Buen Cacao** (54200 N. Circle Dr., 760/333-7690, www.elbuencacao.com, 10am-5pm Mon.-Fri., 10am-6pm Sat.-Sun., $5-6) is a tiny chocolate shop with an outdoor patio. The owners handle the entire chocolate-making process—from roasting to winnowing to grinding the cocoa beans. Their wholesome, tasty treats feature only three ingredients: chocolate, sugar, and a special flavor like orange, hazelnut, or espresso. Sipping chocolates and specialty beverages are served as well.

Idyllwild may be nestled way up in the mountains, but it's still in Southern California, the home of fantastic Mexican cuisine. **La Casita** (54650 N. Circle Dr., 951/659-6038, www.idyllwildlacasita. com, 11am-8pm daily, $10-20) does $1.50 taco nights on Mondays and Thursdays. Tacos are just $0.99 on Tuesdays at **Los Gorditos** (26290 Hwy. 243, 951/659-2842, www.gorditosidyllwild.com, 11am-8pm Tues. and Fri.-Sun., $8-20).

Accommodations
The cottages at **The Fireside Inn** (54540 N. Circle Dr., 951/659-2966, www. thefiresideinn.com, $80-130) are located within walking distance of downtown shops and restaurants. Stone hearths and knotty pine paneling give each cabin a quaint mountain feel. Each cottage features a fireplace; most have kitchens. You'll also get a 10 percent discount at Wooley's, the nearby hat and accessory shop.

A fourth-generation family business, the ★ **Idyllwild Inn** (54300 Village Center Dr., 888/659-2552, www.idyllwildinn. com, $110-160) is the oldest hotel in town with rental cabins dating back to 1910, 1924, or 1953. The pet-friendly cabins have fireplaces, private decks, free Wi-Fi, and full kitchens. Hotel rooms feature quilted beds, stone fireplaces, and artisan bed frames carved by the same artist who made the Harmony Tree Monument outside the hotel.

Knotty pine paneling and red-flannel sheets at the **Idyllwild Bunkhouse** (25525 Hwy. 243, 951/659-2201, www. idyllwildbunkhouse.com, $139-209) give this mountain lodge a lumberjack feel. Most rooms have kitchenettes and private entrances, and some are pet-friendly. Panoramic west-facing views from rooms, suites, and cabins look over the forested edge of the San Jacinto Mountains.

Camping
The 33 sites at **San Jacinto State Park Campground** (25905 Hwy. 243, 951/659-2607, www.parks.ca.gov) are within walking distance of downtown. Some sites have RV hookups while others are designed for tents only. Coin-op showers are clean and spacious. The campground is surrounded on three sides by a nature trail perfect for walking pets or boisterous kiddos. **Reservations** (800/444-7275, www.reservecalifornia.com, $25) are strongly recommended, especially on weekends.

At 6,400 feet, **Marion Mountain Campground** (52745 Forest Rd. 4S02, 909/382-2922, www.fs.usda.gov, late May-early Oct.) is 7 miles (11.3 km) north of Idyllwild, nestled on a west-facing slope. The campground has nine first-come, first-served sites and 16 sites available by **reservation** (877/444-6777, www.recreation.gov, $10). The Marion Mountain Trail departs from the west edge of the campground, leading to the Pacific Crest Trail and San Jacinto Peak.

Information and Services
The **San Jacinto Ranger Station** (54270 Pine Crest Ave., 909/382-2921, www. fs.usda.com, 8am-noon and 12:30pm-4pm Fri.-Tues.) has a great 3D relief map of the nearby mountains and trail systems. Knowledgeable rangers can recommend hiking and biking trails, advise on campsites, and provide information about wildlife. You can also pick up detailed hike listings, wildlife and tree descriptions, and recommendations for things to do in Idyllwild. More services are available in the towns of Hemet (Highway 74) to the west or Palm Springs to the east via I-10.

★ Whitewater Preserve

Whitewater Preserve (9160 Whitewater Canyon Rd., Whitewater, 760/325-7222, www.wildlandsconservancy.org, hours and access varies) is a pristine stretch of arid river valley between the San Jacinto and the San Bernardino Mountains, surrounded by the San Gorgonio Wilderness. Formerly a trout farm, the

2,800-acre preserve has been converted into a lush little oasis, shaded by cottonwoods and sycamores with picnic areas, wading pools, camping, trails, and access to the Pacific Crest Trail as it travels through the Sand to Snow National Monument.

Getting There

Whitewater Preserve is near San Gorgonio Pass between Idyllwild and Big Bear, 5 miles (8 km) north of I-10. From Idyllwild, take Highway 243 north for 25 miles (40 km), then merge onto I-10 eastbound. After 13 miles (20.9 km), take exit 114 toward Whitewater. Turn left to head north onto the freeway overpass, then make another left onto Whitewater Canyon Road. Follow for 5 miles (8 km) to arrive at the preserve.

From Los Angeles, follow I-10 east for 95 miles (153 km), then take exit 114 toward Whitewater. Turn left to head north onto the freeway overpass, then make another left onto Whitewater Canyon Road.

Follow for 5 miles (8 km) to arrive at the preserve.

Hiking
Red Dome 🅟🅒🅣

Distance: 4.3 mi/6.9 km round-trip
Duration: 2 hours
Elevation change: 400 ft/122 m
Effort: Easy
Trailhead: Whitewater Trail

This easy hike along the Whitewater River is a great way to experience the stark and varied beauty of the Sand to Snow National Monument, including diverse wildlife and fascinating geological features.

Start your hike at the north end of the parking lot next to the ranger station. Stay to the right of the wading pool (unless you want to splash in) and continue north along the rock-lined path toward the palm trees. Turn left at 0.2 mile to head west toward the PCT and Red Dome. Cross the Whitewater River, which is only a creek for about half the

Whitewater Preserve

year. You'll enter the San Gorgonio Wilderness at 0.6 mile and meet up with the Pacific Crest Trail at 0.7 mile. During the spring, this stretch of trail is rife with cactus blooms: bright pink beavertail and vibrant yellow cholla blossoms. Keep your eyes peeled for bighorn sheep—they're often spotted on the steep cliffs on either side of the river valley.

Follow the PCT along the edge of the riverbed for another 1.4 miles to reach the Red Dome, an outcropping of brick-red boulders next to the river. This river crossing is your turnaround point, as well as a great spot to picnic or splash in and cool off.

Camping

Camping at Whitewater Preserve is free, and on hot, windy days, the grassy, shaded preserve is a luxurious delight. There aren't any designated sites or parking spaces, just a large field and shared parking area. Picnic tables, water spigots, and bathrooms are all on-site.

Arrive before 4:30pm to make camping arrangements with the ranger, or call ahead of time to make a **reservation** (760/325-7222).

Information and Services

The historic, beautifully restored **ranger station** (9160 Whitewater Canyon Rd., 760/325-7222, www. wildlandsconservancy.org, 8am-5pm daily except Thanksgiving, Christmas, and New Year's Day) has a large, 3D relief map of the surrounding mountains and plenty of information about the area's wilderness. Check in here for overnight camping.

★ Big Bear

Big Bear is a mountain town with hiking trails, ski resorts, restaurants, cabin rentals, and a big reservoir that's popular for boating and fishing. Located 95 miles (153 km) east of Los Angeles in the San Bernardino Mountains, it's a popular escape for both winter and summer recreation.

The Pacific Crest Trail enters Big Bear from the east, climbing out of the desert into the pine-spotted hills around Big Bear Lake. The trail then turns west and traverses 8,000-foot Bertha Ridge above the sunny north shore, offering gorgeous views of the lake and snow-dusted peaks, including Mount San Gorgonio.

Getting There and Around

From Whitewater Preserve, the Pacific Crest Trail climbs due north to the eastern edge of the Big Bear Basin. No roads parallel this route; instead, you'll need to make a big horseshoe bend to the east or the west.

Once you've arrived in Big Bear, **Mountain Transit** (909/878-5200, www. mountaintransit.org, $1.50-5) offers bus service along Big Bear Boulevard near the Village, around the eastern edge of the lake to the Discovery Center and Serrano

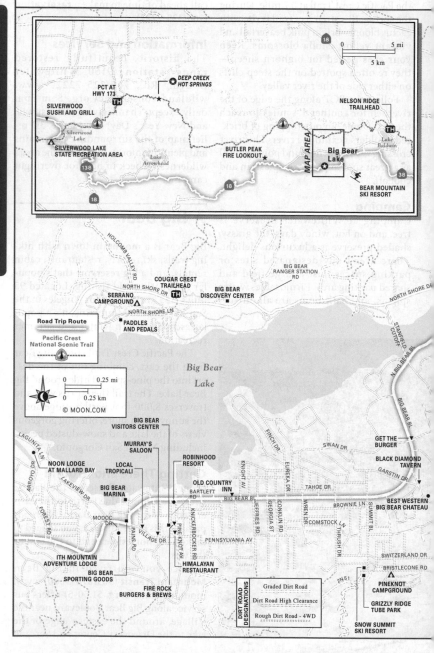

Big Bear Lake

DEEP CREEK HOT SPRINGS

PCT AT HWY 173
TH

SILVERWOOD SUSHI AND GRILL

Silverwood Lake

SILVERWOOD LAKE STATE RECREATION AREA

Lake Arrowhead

BUTLER PEAK FIRE LOOKOUT

NELSON RIDGE TRAILHEAD
TH

Lake Baldwin

MAP AREA

Big Bear Lake

BEAR MOUNTAIN SKI RESORT

0   5 mi
0   5 km

HOLCOMB VALLEY RD

BIG BEAR RANGER STATION RD

COUGAR CREST TRAILHEAD
TH

BIG BEAR DISCOVERY CENTER

NORTH SHORE DR

SERRANO CAMPGROUND

NORTH SHORE LN

NORTH SHORE DR

STANFIELD CUTOFF

N. BIG BEAR BL

Road Trip Route
Pacific Crest National Scenic Trail

PADDLES AND PEDALS

0   0.25 mi
0   0.25 km
© MOON.COM

Big Bear Lake

BIG BEAR BL

BIG BEAR VISITORS CENTER

MURRAY'S SALOON

ROBINHOOD RESORT

LAGUNITA LN

NOON LODGE AT MALLARD BAY

ARROYO DR

LAKEVIEW DR

LOCAL TROPICALI

BIG BEAR MARINA

FOREST RD

MODOC DR

PAINE RD

VILLAGE DR

PINE KNOT AV

OLD COUNTRY INN

BARTLETT RD

BIG BEAR BL

KNICKERBOCKER RD

JEFFRIES RD

GEORGIA ST

CONKLIN RD

PENNSYLVANIA AV

KNIGHT AV

FINCH DR

EUREKA DR

SWAN DR

TAHOE DR

WREN DR

COMSTOCK LN

BROWNIE LN

SUMMIT BL

THRUSH DR

GET THE BURGER

BLACK DIAMOND TAVERN

GARSTIN DR

BEST WESTERN BIG BEAR CHATEAU

SWITZERLAND DR

ITH MOUNTAIN ADVENTURE LODGE

BIG BEAR SPORTING GOODS

FIRE ROCK BURGERS & BREWS

HIMALAYAN RESTAURANT

2N 51

BRISTLECONE RD

PINEKNOT CAMPGROUND

GRIZZLY RIDGE TUBE PARK

SNOW SUMMIT SKI RESORT

DIRT ROAD DESIGNATIONS
Graded Dirt Road
Dirt Road High Clearance
Rough Dirt Road - 4WD

Campground, and over Nelson Ridge where the PCT crosses Highway 18.

Western Option

The western option brings you through the eastern edge of the Inland Empire and into Big Bear via the **Rim of the World Scenic Byway.** This route is quite scenic in the high-elevation areas, but is likely to be more heavily traveled and may involve rush hour traffic through Beaumont, Calimesa, and Redlands before entering the national forest near Mountain Home Village.

To take this 86-mile (138-km) route (about an hour and 45 minutes with no traffic) from Whitewater, follow Whitewater Preserve Road south for 5 miles (8 km) and merge onto I-10 west. After 29 miles (47 km), take exit 85 to Oak Glen Road and turn right to head northeast. After 4.2 miles (6.8 km), turn left onto Bryant Street, follow for 2.5 miles (4 km), then turn right onto Highway 38 east, the Rim of the World Scenic Byway. After 39 miles (63 km), make a left turn onto East Bear Boulevard and follow for 5.5 miles (8.9 km) into town.

Eastern Option

The eastern option takes you through the town of **Yucca Valley,** across Johnson Valley, and into the northeast corner of Big Bear Basin. Long-distance territorial views of the desert are breathtaking, and this is the best way to see the San Gorgonio's dramatic eastern escarpment in the Sand to Snow Monument.

To take this 90-mile (145-km) route (about an hour and 45 minutes with no traffic) from Whitewater, follow Whitewater Preserve Road south for 5 miles (8 km) and merge onto I-10 east. Take exit 117 for Highway 62 toward Yucca Valley and follow for 21 miles (34 km). Make a left onto Highway 247 north (Old Woman Springs Road) and continue for 40 miles (64 km). Turn left on Camp Rock Road (an easy turn to miss—pay close attention around

the 39-mile mark), follow for 5 miles (8 km), and continue onto Highway 18. This road will deliver you to Big Bear Lake in 17 miles (27 km).

Sights

Views from the top of 8,500-foot **Butler Peak Fire Lookout** are spectacular: the entire Big Bear Valley spread out before you, nestled between the dramatic ridgelines of the San Bernardino Mountains. Nearby Lake Arrowhead is visible, too, along with the high desert and the suburban cities of the Inland Empire. You can drive to the lookout, but you'll have to hike 0.15 mile up a steep and rocky slope to climb the tower's ladders and soak up the best views.

Getting There

From the Big Bear Discovery Center, follow Highway 38 west for 2.5 miles (4 km) to Fawnskin. As Highway 38 bends to the left, stay right onto Rim of the World Drive and continue for 1.3 miles (2.1 km). Make a left to head southwest on Forest Road 2M13 and follow for 2.1 miles (3.4 km). The turnoff for Butler Peak is a sharp left onto Forest Road 2N13C. Continue for 2.5 miles (4 km) to the end of the road.

Scenic Drive

The 110-mile (177 km) **Rim of the World Scenic Byway** traverses the spine of the San Bernardino Mountains between Gorgonio Pass and Cajon Pass. Views along the way are absolutely spectacular as the road twists and turns along steep edges that provide vantages into valleys thousands of feet below. This route begins in Redlands at the intersection of Mill Creek Road and Garnet Street, climbs east to Onyx Peak (where it meets the Pacific Crest Trail), turns west to trace the southern shore of Big Bear Lake, winds past Lake Arrowhead and Silverwood Lake, and ends in Cajon Junction at the intersection of I-15 and Highway 138.

The byway is open year-round, but chains may be required during the winter when Big Bear receives snow. Allow three hours to drive the entire route, more if you plan to stop in Big Bear.

Hiking

Hiking is ideal during the spring due to weather conditions, and it also happens to be shoulder season for tourism, so you'll get more solitude on the trails (and better deals in town) during the months of March, April, and May.

Cougar Crest

Distance: 5.6 mi/9 km round-trip
Duration: 2.5 hours
Elevation change: 960 ft/293 m
Effort: Moderate
Trailhead: Cougar Crest

The Cougar Crest Trail is the easiest, most scenic way to access the Pacific Crest Trail as it traverses the ridge on the north side of Big Bear Lake.

The trail begins on a wide dirt path departing from the northeast corner of the parking lot. Walk north for 0.6 mile to reach a wooden bench (the first of many along this trail) where the trail bends right and then makes a sharp left to continue north. The path narrows as it ascends through the sparse cedar and pine forest. Catch your first views of Big Bear Lake at 1.3 miles, where you'll find another bench, as well as a sneak peek at 11,500-foot San Gorgonio Peak on the southern horizon. Continue northwest along the trail, over expertly crafted granite steps. Look for bright orange Indian paintbrush flowers cropping out from the rock formations along the trail. San Gorgonio comes into clear view at 2 miles, where there are three benches to sit and gaze.

You'll reach the Pacific Crest Trail junction at 2.4 miles; walk east on the PCT along Bertha Ridge for an additional 0.4 mile and soak up the views of Big Bear Lake framed by the tallest mountains in the San Bernardino Range.

Big Bear Lake from Cougar Crest

Nelson Ridge PCT

Distance: 2.2 mi/3.5 km round-trip
Duration: 1-1.5 hours
Elevation change: 500 ft/152 m
Effort: Easy
Trailhead: Pacific Crest Trail

This Pacific Crest Trail hike along Nelson Ridge offers sweeping views of the high desert and a high-elevation vantage of the eastern Big Bear Lake basin.

Start your hike walking south, away from Highway 18 and into a sparse, arid forest. The trail climbs for the first 0.4 mile, then turns east and begins to descend. Look to the west at 0.5 mile for a view of the Baldwin Lake community and Big Bear City. Continue for another 0.7 mile to get a great east-facing vantage of Lone Valley (in the foreground), Granite Peaks, and Johnson Valley (beyond the ridgelines). Over the next 0.4 mile, the trail gently descends, then climbs again. You'll reach another vista point at 1.1 miles, overlooking the vast expanse of the Mojave Desert, including the Johnson Valley and the Fry Mountains from your perch at 6,800 feet. Turn around here.

Make it a longer hike by continuing south on the Pacific Crest Trail. You'll get more scenic desert vistas, cross seasonal Arrastre Creek at 8 miles, reach Deer Spring at 10 miles, and eventually reach Onyx Summit—the trail's intersection with Highway 38—at 13 miles.

Getting There

Nelson Ridge is 9.5 miles (15.3 km) northeast of Big Bear Lake. From Big Bear Lake Village, follow Big Bear Boulevard (Highway 18) eastbound for 3.5 miles (5.6 km) to Division Drive. Turn left to head north for 0.3 mile, then turn right onto West North Shore Drive (Highway 18 east). Follow for 5.7 miles (9.2 km). The Pacific Crest Trail parking area is on the south side of Highway 18 at the crest of a hill.

Recreation
Summer

During the summer months, Big Bear Lake is the main draw for tourists and visitors to the area, offering a cool, refreshing escape from the Southern California heat.

Rent a kayak or stand-up paddleboard at **Paddles and Pedals** (40545 N. Shore Dr., 909/936-2907, www.paddlesandpedals.com, hours vary daily May-Oct., $20-25/hour, $55-70 half day, $85 full day) on the north shore near Serrano Campground. Bicycles are also available to rent ($10/hour, $30 half day, $40 full day) and ride along the paved lakefront path. Hours vary depending on weather conditions; call ahead to confirm availability.

Big Bear Lake is full of trout, bass, catfish, crappie, and carp. Pick up your fishing license at **Big Bear Marina** (500 Paine Ct., 909/866-3218, www.bigbearmarina.com, 8am-5pm daily), just seven blocks west of the Village. The marina rents pontoon boats ($80-130/hour) and

fishing boats ($55/2 hours), as well as pedal boats, kayaks, and stand-up paddleboards ($25-40/hour). Call ahead to reserve your rental watercraft. You can also charter a 21-foot boat for wakeboarding, waterskiing, and tubing ($175/hour), and your package includes top-of-the-line watersports equipment.

Winter

Big Bear has two ski resorts within a few miles of each other. Views from the slopes show off the beautiful San Bernardino Mountains all covered in snow and Big Bear Lake in the basin below. At 8,800 feet, **Bear Mountain** (43101 Goldmine Dr., 844/462-2327, www.bigbearmountainresort.com, 9am-4pm Mon.-Fri., 8:30am-4pm Sat.-Sun. Dec.-Mar., $70-110) is higher in elevation and has an extensive terrain park. It's southeast of downtown, about a 10-minute drive. Lift tickets are valid for same-day use at both Bear Mountain and **Snow Summit** (880 Summit Blvd.), located on the slopes that rise south out of Big Bear Village.

In addition to downhill slopes, Snow Summit is home to **Grizzly Ridge Tube Park** (880 Summit Blvd., 909/866-5766, 10am-5pm daily Dec.-Mar., $25-35). Ski, snowboard, and equipment **rentals** ($31-55) are available at both locations.

Shopping

Big Bear Sporting Goods (40544 Big Bear Blvd., 909/866-3222, www.bigbearlakesportinggoods.com, 8am-5pm Mon.-Thurs., 8am-7pm Fri., 7am-6pm Sat., 7am-5pm Sun.) is a one-stop shop for shoes, clothing, accessories, camp cooking equipment, water bottles, snacks, guidebooks, and maps. Plenty of gear for fishing, boating, and climbing is in stock, too. Staff is friendly and

From top to bottom: Highway 38 on Big Bear Lake's north shore; Nelson Ridge on the PCT; burger and onion rings at Murray's Saloon.

knowledgeable about all the opportunities for outdoor recreation in the area.

Food

Dubbed the "Five Star Dive Bar" by locals, **Murray's Saloon** (672 Cottage Ln., 909/866-1444, 10am-2am Mon.-Fri., 8am-2am Sat.-Sun., $10-14) is a popular spot for beers, cocktails, and nightly karaoke. The food is surprisingly fresh and tasty, especially considering the price point. In addition to traditional pub fare like burgers and fries, you'll find items like seared ahi with sautéed vegetables.

For the best Bloody Mary, visit **Old Country Inn** (41126 Big Bear Blvd., 909/866-5600, www. oldcountryinnrestaurant.com, 8am-3pm Mon.-Wed., 8am-8pm Thurs. and Sun., 8am-9pm Fri.-Sat., $12-17). Hungry for brunch, too? There's something for everyone on the varied food menu. German sausages like bratwurst, knockwurst, and bockwurst are served with eggs. American breakfast favorites including omelets, skillets, French toast, waffles, and eggs Benedicts are available, too, along with a few Mexican dishes.

Fire Rock Café Burgers & Brews (618 Pine Knot Ave., 909/878-0696, www. firerockburgersandbrews.com, 11am-9pm daily, $12-14) is a rock and roll-themed burger joint with creative ingredients and preparations—think bourbon-whiskey glaze, bacon-infused beef, and fig marmalade. Most diners opt for tater tots over fries. Burgers with just the traditional fixings are available, too. Despite the AC/DC blasting through the speakers, it's kid-friendly, and like almost everywhere in this mountain town, welcomes dogs on the outdoor patio.

Local Tropicali (40616 Village Dr., 909/878-0499, www.osotropicali.com, 11am-5pm Mon. and Thurs., 11am-8pm Fri.-Sat., 11am-6pm Sun., $10-14) is a fusion restaurant serving Pacific island-style cuisine. Teriyaki bowls and poke bowls are served with sweet and spicy meat, wild-caught fish, tofu, tropical fruit, rice, and your choice of housemade sauces. There are some sweet options, too (Belgian waffles with tropical fruit), plus cold-brew coffee and smoothies.

You might have to wait a few minutes for your food at **Get the Burger** (42151 Big Bear Blvd., 909/866-8800, www.gettheburger.com, 11:30am-5pm Wed.-Sun., $7-10), a Hollywood-themed burger joint famous for its special sauce, but the decadent, juicy burgers are worth the wait. Pair yours with sweet potato fries, onion rings, or a milkshake at this 1950s-style burger shack.

Himalayan Restaurant (672 Pine Knot Ave., 909/878-3068, www. himalayanbigbear.com, 11am-9pm Sun.-Thurs., 11am-10pm Fri.-Sat. $10-19) brings the high-elevation cuisine of Nepal, Tibet, and northern India to Big Bear Village. The curries, masalas, tandoori dishes, soups, and salads on the menu are spicy, flavorful, and fresh. Lunch specials (including your choice of a chicken, lamb, fish, shrimp, or vegetarian entrée with *aaloo mattar,* lentils, rice, naan, and salad) are a great way to experience the diversity of this restaurant's cuisine, as are the thali specialty plates during dinner.

Accommodations

Big Bear is a popular mountain escape for residents of Los Angeles and it's one of the largest towns the Pacific Crest Trail passes through. In addition to the dozens of hotels, hostels, and campgrounds in the area, entire homes and cabins are available for rent. Rates for Big Bear accommodations are seasonal and tend to be lowest in spring and highest in winter.

The ★ **Robin Hood Resort** (40797 Big Bear Blvd., 800/990-9956, www. robinhoodresorts.com, $110-175), perched right on the corner of the highway and Big Bear's iconic downtown village, is friendly and welcoming to PCT hikers and outdoor enthusiasts. Some rooms have two or three beds. Jacuzzi spa rooms are available as well. Here, you're steps away from the lakeshore and its recreation opportunities—fishing, kayak rental, pontoon boat cruises—as well as the dozens of restaurants and shops on Pine Knot Avenue.

If you have a penchant for smart, sleek design and modern amenities, **Noon Lodge at Mallard Bay** (214 S. Lagunita Ln., 909/866-2526, www.noonlodge. com, $180-260) will impress you with its textiles and revamped vintage design. Cabins, studios, and lofts are available with various features and sleeping arrangements. A seasonal pool, lawn games, and bicycles for guest use round out that luxury vacation feeling.

ITH Mountain Adventure Lodge (657 Modoc Dr., 909/866-2532, www. ithhostels.com) has fun, colorful decor with dorm-style beds ($19-39) as well as private rooms ($49-59 shared bath, $79-109 private bath). The beautiful living area is well appointed with huge leather couches, a fireplace, and musical instruments to play. Additional perks include daily breakfast, wine and appetizers each evening, and shuttles to/from San Diego if you're traveling without a car.

If you've stayed at a Best Western or two, you may have a "seen one, seen 'em all" attitude toward the franchise establishments, but the **Big Bear Chateau** (42200 Moonridge Rd., 909/866-6666, www.bestwestern.com, $130-160) is quite memorable. Affectionately dubbed "Chateau Le Bear" by some of the locals who frequent the hotel bar, this elegant castle features an ornate, marble-clad lobby, a luxurious outdoor pool and hot tub, and fireplaces in every room.

Camping

Pine Knot Campground (Forest Service Rd., 909/866-8550, www.fs.usda.gov, late Apr.-late Oct.) is a perfectly manicured campground in the heart of Big Bear Lake. Friendly hosts are happy to provide local information about the town. **Reservations** (877/444-6777, www. recreation.gov, $29-31) are available. It's located at the bottom of Snow Summit Ski Resort, 2 miles (3.2 km) from the shops and restaurants in Big Bear Village.

Serrano Campground (40800 North Shore Dr., Fawnskin, 909/866-8021, www.fs.usda.gov, mid-Mar.-late Nov.) has 93 sites and 16 double sites on the north shore of the lake. It's the closest developed campground to the Cougar Crest Trail, the best way to access the PCT in the Big Bear region. It's also just 0.5 mile from the Big Bear Discovery Center, the area's nature-focused visitors center. Showers are available. **Reservations** (877/444-6777, www.recreation.gov, $35) are recommended.

Lavish Cabins (909/771-6550, www. lavishcabins.com, from $75) has a number of cozy, comfortable, and luxurious homes for rent in the area. During the spring (Big Bear's shoulder season), the family-operated management company is happy to accommodate requests for early check-in or late checkout.

Most of the cabins and condos for rent through **Big Bear Vacations** (877/417-6504, www.bigbearvacations.com, from $150) are on the south side of the lake, within a few miles of the waterfront and the village's restaurants. The rental interiors include outdoorsy features like stone fireplaces, exposed wooden beams, and cozy blankets. Some are pet-friendly.

Information and Services

Upon arriving in Big Bear, visit the **Discovery Center** (40971 North Shore Dr., Fawnskin, 909/382-2790, www. fs.usda.gov, 9am-4pm Thurs.-Mon.) to talk with rangers about trail conditions, learn about the local wildlife, grab some printed maps, and pick up a Forest Adventure Pass (the pass you'll need to park at trailheads within the San Bernardino, Angeles, Los Padres, or Cleveland National Forests).

The chamber of commerce staffs a **visitors center** (630 Bartlett Rd., 909/866-7000, www.bigbear.com, 9am-5pm daily) in the village, with local hiking maps and information about recreation, activities, food, camping, and lodging.

Silverwood Lake

Between the towns of Big Bear and Wrightwood, the Pacific Crest Trail crosses a valley between the San Bernardino and the San Gabriel Mountain Ranges. Within this valley is Silverwood Lake, a reservoir fed by the Mojave River and surrounded by mountains 3,000 feet (914 m) above. Silverwood Lake is a popular spot for outdoor recreation on sunny days. The PCT traces the path of the Mojave River as it cuts through Luna Canyon on its way to Silverwood Lake.

Getting There

Silverwood Lake is 40 miles (64 km) west of Big Bear Lake, about an 80-minute drive. Take Highway 18 west out of Big Bear for 31 miles (50 km) to Highway 138. Exit onto Highway 138, heading north toward Crestline. The road twists and turns for the next 5 miles (8 km), descending through woodsy hills, then straightens out and heads west for another 5 miles (8 km) to Silverwood Lake.

Alternatively, from the Los Angeles area, take I-15 north to exit 131 at Cajon Junction. Exit the freeway and head east on Highway 138 for 10.5 miles (16.9 km) to Silverwood Lake.

Hiking

TOP EXPERIENCE

★ Deep Creek Hot Springs PCT

Distance: 12 mi/19.3 km round-trip
Duration: 6 hours, plus more for soaking
Elevation change: 1,500 ft/457 m
Effort: Moderate
Trailhead: Pacific Crest Trail at Highway 173
Pass/Fee: Adventure Pass ($30 annually/$5 daily)

A remote and gorgeous desert oasis, Deep Creek Hot Springs is nestled between the steep walls of Luna Canyon on the north side of the San Bernardino Mountains. The cool, refreshing Mojave River runs westbound through the canyon, and at the springs, hot pools of varying temperatures line the southern bank. There are no roads leading to the hot springs, but you can hike in on the Pacific Crest Trail as it follows the path of the river.

Starting from the parking area, walk northeast on the Pacific Crest Trail for 0.8 mile to the bank of the Mojave River, then walk across the southern edge of a large earthen dam. The PCT climbs a hill on the northeast side of the dam before making a sharp right turn to head southeast. Follow the path of the Mojave River as the PCT traces its twists and turns. The trail is relatively flat until mile 4, when you'll cross the river on a painted rainbow bridge. The trail begins to gain elevation; reach the high point of your hike at 5.4 miles.

You'll arrive at the hot springs at 6 miles, where a sandy beach shaded by cottonwood trees is nestled into a river bend. Steep canyon walls make the entire hot springs area feel secluded (and it is, with the nearest roads being miles away). Four different hot pools are built into the southern edge of the river; their edges are made from smooth river rocks so they blend in beautifully with the surroundings. There are plenty of boulders and beach areas to relax and enjoy this sunny, scenic area. Note that clothing is optional. No facilities exist here—pack out everything you brought with you, and follow Leave No Trace guidelines.

Insider tip: This area is subject to very hot weather during the spring, summer, and fall. Start your hike early in the morning to allow plenty of time for hiking before the sun gets too hot.

Getting There

The PCT trailhead at Highway 173 is 11 miles (17.7 km) north of Silverwood Lake. Take Highway 138 north for 2.5 miles (4 km), then turn right to head east on Highway 173. The trailhead parking

Deep Creek Hot Springs

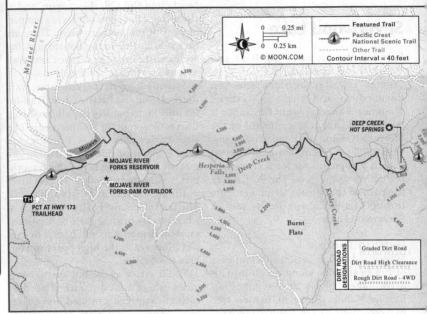

area is on the north side of the road in 8 miles (12.9 km).

Food

★ **Silverwood Sushi and Grill** (13910 Hwy. 138, Hesperia, 760/389-2200, 11:30am-9pm Thurs.-Tues., $9-28) is a diamond in the rough—a sushi restaurant in the middle of nowhere, on a rural section of Highway 138 between Silverwood Lake and Cajon Pass. While cows graze in pastures outside, satisfy your hiker hunger with fresh, colorful sushi, bento boxes, soups, stir-fries, and Korean barbecue, plus beer and wine. Bamboo plants and high ceilings in the restaurant give the space an airy, natural feel.

Camping

The Pacific Crest Trail traces the northwest shore of **Silverwood Lake State Recreation Area** (13988 Sawpit Canyon Rd., Hesperia, 760/389-2281, www.parks. ca.gov, 7am-7pm daily), a popular spot for boating, fishing, and summer recreation. If it's cold in Big Bear or Wrightwood, chances are good that camping here will be much warmer! Campsites at Mesa Campground, on the west edge of the lake, are available for **reservations** (800/444-7275, www.reservecalifornia. com, $45-50).

★ Wrightwood and the Angeles Crest Scenic Byway

Scenic drives and year-round outdoor recreation are the hallmarks of the quaint mountain town of Wrightwood, nestled onto the northeastern slope of the San Gabriel Mountains. The Pacific Crest Trail traverses the 8,000-foot ridge above the town. Although Wrightwood is less than two hours from downtown Los Angeles, the quiet, pine-lined streets feel like a different world. Friendly Wrightwood businesses welcome hikers, skiers, bikers, and outdoor enthusiasts with downtown gathering places, craft beer, and tasty food.

Getting There

Wrightwood is 65 miles (105 km) west of Big Bear and 30 miles (48 km) northwest of San Bernardino.

From Big Bear, follow Highway 18 (Rim of the World Scenic Byway) for 30 miles (48 km). Take the exit for Highway 138 west, traveling north and west for 43 miles (69 km) as the highway passes through the community of Crestline, traces the southwest edge of Silverwood Lake, and crosses I-15 at Cajon Junction. Nine miles (14.5 km) west of Cajon Junction, turn left onto Highway 2, and you'll arrive in Wrightwood after 5 miles (8 km).

From San Bernardino, follow I-215 north to I-15. Take exit 131 at Cajon Junction and turn left onto Highway 138 west. Nine miles (14.5 km) west of Cajon Junction, turn left onto Highway 2, and you'll arrive in Wrightwood after 5 miles (8 km).

TOP EXPERIENCE

Scenic Drive

The **Angeles Crest Scenic Byway** (Hwy. 2) is a 66-mile, two-lane highway that traverses the spine of the San Gabriel Mountains, crossing the Pacific Crest Trail six times. Views on this route are breathtaking as the road winds along dramatic, steep mountainsides up to 8,000 feet (2,438 m) above Los Angeles and San Bernardino. The rugged granite mountains are peppered with pines, cedars, and oaks, and the arid expanse of the Mojave Desert sprawls below the northern edge of the range. Views traveling west on the highway out of Wrightwood alternate between north-facing desert vistas, the urban sprawl of L.A. to the south, up-close-and-personal views of the granite San Gabriel Mountains, and wildlife (including bighorn sheep). The PCT crosses the highway at **Inspiration Point** (5.5 mi/8.9 km west of Wrightwood), which looks out over (from west to east) Mount Baden-Powell, Vincent Gulch, the San Gabriel River, Pine Mountain Ridge, Mount Baldy, and Blue Ridge. The **Grassy Hollow Visitor Center** (Hwy 2, 626/821-6737, www.grassyhollow.net, 10am-4pm Sat.-Sun.) is 0.5 mile west of Inspiration Point.

Vincent Gap is the trailhead for Mount Baden-Powell; the PCT crosses the highway here. **Dawson Saddle** (13.5 mi/22.5 km west of Wrightwood) is the highest point on the highway at 7,900 feet. Highway 2 meets the PCT again at **Islip Saddle,** where a network of trails sprawls out in different directions. Stop at the **Jarvi Memorial Vista** and Picnic Area (20 mi/32 km west of Wrightwood) to enjoy views of Kratka Ridge, the San Gabriel Wilderness, and Mount Islip, then travel through three tunnels bored into the southern edge of Mount Williamson. Between Cloudburst Summit (26 mi/42 km west of Wrightwood) and Three Points, the PCT and the highway route are almost identical. The highway turns south, continuing to the **Chilao Visitor Center** (626/796-5541, www.fs.usda.gov, 9am-4pm Sat.-Sun.), while the PCT turns north toward Pacifico Mountain. If you're hungry, stop at **Newcomb's Ranch** (626/440-1001, www.newcombsranch.com, 9am-4pm Thurs.-Fri., 7am-4pm Sat.-Sun., closed Mon.-Wed. and during severe weather conditions), a restaurant just west of the Chilao Visitor Center. This roadhouse is popular with motorcyclists and racecar enthusiasts.

Allow at least an hour to travel between Wrightwood and Chilao Visitor Center, more if you plan to stop for photographs or hikes.

Highway 2 is closed between Islip Saddle and Vincent Gap during the winter. It may also close west of Islip Saddle during ice, snow, avalanches, or rock

Wrightwood and the Angeles Crest Scenic Byway

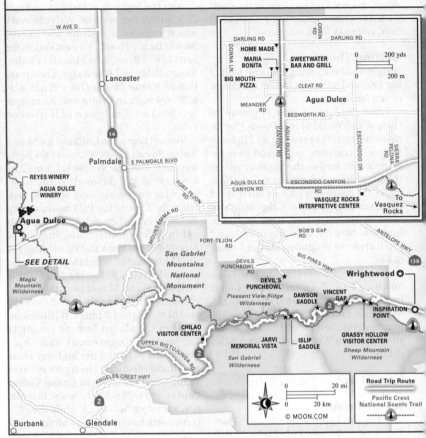

slides. Check the CalTrans website (www.dot.ca.gov) before your trip to ensure the road is open.

Hiking
★ Mount Baden-Powell

Distance: 9 mi/14.5 km round-trip
Duration: 4.5-5 hours
Elevation change: 2,800 ft/853 m
Effort: Strenuous
Trailhead: Vincent Gap

This popular hike along the Pacific Crest Trail climbs from Highway 2 to the top of the 9,400-foot peak, the second-highest in the San Gabriel Range. What looks like a steep climb is actually graded moderately over more than 35 switchbacks.

Begin your ascent at Vincent Gap, walking west from the parking area onto the northbound PCT. The shady trail is forested with oaks, pines, cedars, and firs. Reach a bench at 1 mile and enjoy east-facing views. A short spur trail to Lamel Spring is located at 1.8 miles. The trees begin to thin around the 3-mile mark, and limber pines (which only grow at high elevation) begin to appear, their trunks gnarled and branches

Mount Baden-Powell, Wrightwood

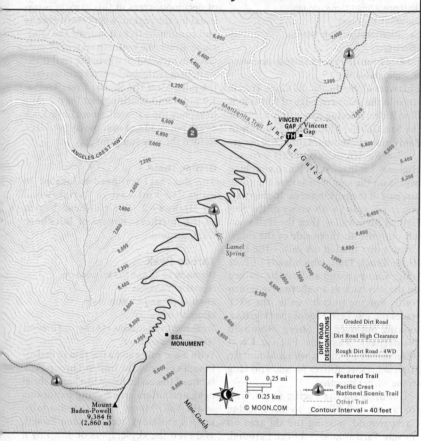

windswept. Views get more dramatic as you continue to climb. The southeast-facing lookout point at 4.3 miles is on the edge of a near-sheer drop into Mine Gulch. Look east for fantastic views of Mount Baldy (the tallest San Gabriel peak) and Pine Mountain Ridge. At 4.4 miles, veer left to the summit where the Pacific Crest Trail bends right and continues westbound. It's just 0.1 mile to the rounded mountaintop.

A plaque at the mostly bare summit introduces Lord Baden Powell as the founder of the Boy Scouts, but you'll be busy gazing out over the Mojave Desert, the entire San Gabriel Range, the San Bernardino Mountains, and the sprawling metropolis of Los Angeles far below.

Getting There

Vincent Gap is 9.5 miles (15.3 km) west of Wrightwood on Highway 2. The parking lot at Vincent Gap fills up quickly, especially on weekends. Plan to arrive early, though you'll still share the trailhead with other mountain enthusiasts.

Blue Ridge PCT

Distance: 4.5 mi/7.2 km round-trip
Duration: 2-2.5 hours
Elevation change: 650 ft/198 m
Effort: Easy
Trailhead: Inspiration Point, 5.5 miles (8.9 km) west of Wrightwood on Hwy. 2

This walk along the Pacific Crest Trail is cut into the southern edge of 8,000-foot Blue Ridge, offering panoramic views of the San Gabriel Mountains and Mount Baldy, the tallest mountain in the range.

The Pacific Crest Trail crosses Highway 2 at Inspiration Point; your hike begins on the southern side of the road, just east of the parking area. Right away, you're rewarded with views of the San Gabriel River valley, then the trail veers left onto the northern side of the ridge. Cross a dirt road at 0.8 mile—the Blue Ridge Truck Trail, which leads to Blue Ridge Campground and can be walked on the way back as an alternative return route. For the next 0.7 mile, the PCT traces the southern edge of the ridgeline, looking out over the Sheep Mountain Wilderness. Pass the Pacific Crest Reservoir at 1.5 miles, which Mountain High ski resort utilizes for snowmaking in the winter months.

Continue on the Pacific Crest Trail for another 0.5 mile to Blue Ridge Campground, passing the ski area on the way. Turn around at the campground, or make it a longer hike by continuing southbound on the PCT on the ridgeline above the town of Wrightwood.

Cooper Canyon Falls PCT

Distance: 4.2 mi/6.8 km round-trip
Duration: 2.5 hours
Elevation change: 860 ft/262 m
Effort: Moderate
Trailhead: Buckhart

This hike to serene, lush Cooper Canyon Falls is all downhill on the way there, and the trail is well shaded for the climb back up to your car.

Start by walking northeast on the Buckhart Trail, following the western bank of a seasonal creek. The abundance of deciduous trees in this canyon is unusual for the region, where stark granite and coniferous trees dominate the landscape. Reach the southern edge of Cooper Canyon at mile 1.3, where the trail turns west, then switchbacks east again to reach the falls. Meet the Pacific Crest Trail at 1.9 miles and continue east for 0.2 mile to explore the waterfall, where Little Rock Creek pours 30 feet over mossy boulders. Return the way you came.

Getting There

The Buckhart trailhead is located 26 miles (42 km) east of Wrightwood on Highway 2. The trailhead begins in the northeast corner of Buckhorn Campground.

Throop Peak

Distance: 3.9-4.4 mi/6.3-7.1 km round-trip
Duration: 2-2.5 hours
Elevation change: 1,200 ft/366 m
Effort: Moderate
Trailhead: Dawson Saddle, 13.5 miles (21.7 km) west of Wrightwood on Hwy. 2

With fewer miles and a fraction of Baden-Powell's crowds, the trail to Throop Peak is one of the easier hikes to a San Gabriel peak and offers an amazing panorama at the top: Mount San Antonio (also known as Baldy), Mount Baden-Powell, and even the skyscrapers of downtown Los Angeles are visible from the summit. You'll see the ocean on a clear day, along with expansive views of the high desert to the north.

Start your hike at 7,900-foot Dawson Saddle, the highest point on Highway 2. The Throop Peak Trail is on the south side of the highway, just east of the parking area. Make three wide switchbacks as you climb away from the road, then begin a steady ascent up the peak's northern arm. The forest of sugar pines, incense cedars, and lodgepole pines thins at 0.4 mile, allowing expansive views of the surrounding peaks and the Antelope

Valley. The trail bends slightly southeast at 1 mile around an 8,550-foot knob, then continues south again for another 0.5 mile. Views at 1.5 miles showcase the Mojave Desert and the northern foothills of the San Gabriel Range.

Follow the trail as it turns west and intersects with the Pacific Crest Trail at 1.9 miles. Turn right to head northbound on the PCT and look for a trail junction on the right leading up the mountainside. (The PCT veers to the left, continuing southwest below the base of the summit.) The remaining 0.2 mile to the top of the peak is steep, but the 360-degree views are well worth the effort: Iron Fork Basin, Mount Burnham, and Mount Baden-Powell to the east; Mount Hawkins and Copter Ridge to the south; Angeles Crest Scenic Byway 1,500 feet (457 m) below, and greater Los Angeles spread out before you. A plaque built into a rock pile introduces Amos Throop for whom the peak was named.

Turn around here for a 4.4-mile hike, or shave off 0.5 mile and make it a lollipop loop by following the trail north past the plaque. This 0.3-mile alternative route rejoins the original trail at 2.5 miles.

Recreation

Mountain High Resort (24510 Hwy. 2, 888/754-7878, www.mthigh.com, 9am-4pm Mon.-Thurs., 9am-10pm Fri., 8:30am-10pm Sat.-Sun., Nov.-Mar., $45-79) is just minutes west of Wrightwood. Skis, snowboards, and equipment are available for rent. In addition to skiing and snowboarding, the resort has a tubing park ($25-30). If you don't want to drive in winter conditions, **Rally Bus** (855/725-5928, www.rallybus.co, from $40) offers shuttle service from San Diego or Los Angeles to Mountain High.

The ski resorts around Wrightwood are covered in snow during winter months, but there are ample opportunities to enjoy the terrain throughout all four seasons.

Sky High Disc Golf Course (Table Mountain Rd., 760/316-7828, www.mtnhigh.com, noon-9pm Fri., 8am-9pm Sat., 8am-6pm Sun., $9), at Mountain High's north resort, opens each spring and with 27 holes is Southern California's only disc golf course above 6,000 feet. Located on the north side of the mountain range, the course looks out over the high desert and the cities below.

If you've ever looked up at a hawk zipping through the air and wondered what it feels like to fly above the forest floor, you're in luck. The guides at **Ziplines at Pacific Crest** (6014 Park Dr., 760/705-1003, www.ziplinespc.com, 9am-5pm daily, $109-209) strap you into a harness, clip you onto a zipline, and (after a thoroughly informative and educational training session) send you soaring through the trees, hundreds of feet above the canyon floor at speeds up to 60 miles per hour. The result is a ride that's thrilling, exciting, and only a little bit scary. The knowledgeable guides share information about geology and ecology throughout the tour.

Entertainment and Events

The **Wrightwood Inn** (1350 Hwy. 2, 760/249-5039, 3pm-2am Sun.-Tues. and Thurs.-Fri., 11am-2am Wed. and Sat.) is a local watering hole serving beer and cocktails in a two-story alpine-style hut. Karaoke on Tuesday and Thursday-Saturday draws town residents and visitors alike.

There are five core brews on tap at **Wrightwood Brew Co.** (1257 Apple Ave., 760/488-3163, www.wwbrewco.com, noon-8pm Mon.-Thurs., 11am-10pm Fri.-Sat., 11am-8pm Sun.) plus seasonal beers on rotation. Not a beer drinker? Classic mimosas, hibiscus mimosas, and select local wines are poured, too. The brewpub serves fresh, handmade sandwiches, salads, wraps, and garlic bread. The multilevel deck, a popular hangout spot, overlooks downtown Wrightwood.

Shopping

Mountain Hardware (1390 Hwy. 2, 760/249-3653, www.mtnhardware.com, 8:30am-5:30pm Mon.-Sat., 8:30am-4:30pm Sun.) is a one-stop shop for all things PCT-related: gifts and souvenirs, camping supplies, backpacking food, and outdoor clothing. The hardware store is staffed with friendly, knowledgeable locals who are happy to provide information about the town and the trails.

Vendors at the year-round **Friday Farmers Market** (1275 Hwy. 2, 760/316-4119, www.wrightwoodcfm.org, 4pm-7pm Fri.) sell fresh produce, eggs, and meats, of course, but you'll also find locally made jewelry, soaps, gifts, clothing, and wood carvings. Food trucks are also on-site serving creative artisan fare.

Food

Village Grind (6020 Park Dr., 760/249-5501, www.wrightwoodrestaurants.com, 6am-6pm daily, $3-10) is a cozy, cabin-like coffee shop serving espresso, coffee, tea, wine, beer, and café cuisine like breakfast burritos, oatmeal, baked goods, sandwiches, and soups. Most of the tables are outside on the large deck. The shop extends their hours into the evening for live music and special events.

For a super tasty breakfast under $10 (including coffee), visit ★ **Cinnamon's Bakery** (1350 Hwy. 2, 760/249-5588, www.cinnamonsbakerywrightwood.com, 5am-2pm daily, $5-9). In addition to baked goods, the shop serves breakfast sandwiches, bowls, and burritos, plus biscuits and gravy, croissants, and bagels. Hearty sandwiches and wraps are on the lunch menu, including the decadent "thru-hiker" sandwich with turkey, bacon, avocado, cheese, garlic-scallion cream cheese, jalapeño, caramelized onion, and tomato.

Portions at **Grizzly Café** (1455 Hwy. 2, 760/249-6733, www.grizzlycafe.com,

From top to bottom: PCT near Blue Ridge; Cinnamon's Bakery; Racoon Saloon.

7am-9pm daily, $9-11) are big, and breakfast is popular: corned beef hash and eggs, country-fried steak and eggs, omelets, pancakes, waffles, and cinnamon rolls. The lunch and dinner menus feature classic American dishes including soups, salads, sandwiches, burgers, pastas, and entrées. The outside patio is a pleasant place to dine.

Mile High Pizza (5996 Cedar St., 760/249-4848, www.milehighpizza.com, 3:30pm-8pm Mon.-Thurs., 2pm-9pm Fri., 11:30am-9pm Sat., 11:30am-8pm Sun., $6-20) is a casual, colorful counter-service pizza joint with beautiful potted plants and gardens out front.

Evergreen Café (1269 Evergreen Rd., 760/249-6393, 7am-8pm Sun.-Thurs., 7am-9pm Fri.-Sat., $7-12) is a busy breakfast spot with all the breakfast classics. The café is small but has a porch for outdoor dining, and the owners decorate the restaurant seasonally. In the back, the **Racoon Saloon** is a popular dive bar with pool tables and a jukebox. Order food from Evergreen Café to eat in the bar.

Accommodations

Seasonal rates apply to the hotels and cabins in town, with the winter months being more expensive.

Grand Pine Cabins (6045 Pine St., 760/249-9974, www.grandpinecabins. com, $85-140 summer, $155-275 winter) are right downtown, steps from Wrightwood's restaurants. Cabins feature wood-paneled walls, custom pine branch headboards, red quilts on the beds, and remodeled bathrooms. Some cabins have fireplaces and kitchenettes. There's a cute outdoor seating area under Jeffrey and ponderosa pines.

Also within walking distance to everything downtown, **Cedar Lodge Motel** (5995 Cedar St., 760/249-5062, www. cedarlodgewrightwoodca.com, $129-219) has six different comfy rooms with elegant decor, some with sleeper sofas, dining tables, and cozy armchairs. All rooms include a mini-fridge, coffeemaker, and free Wi-Fi.

Camping

Camping in the Wrightwood area is limited to spring, summer, and fall when the mountains aren't covered in snow.

Table Mountain Campground (Table Mountain Rd., 760/249-3526, www. fs.usda.gov, May-Oct.) is on the north side of the San Gabriel slopes, only a few minutes' drive from Wrightwood, and overlooks the high desert. It shares space with the Sky High Disc Golf Course. **Reservations** (877/444-6777, www.recreation.gov, $23-46) are recommended. To get there, take Highway 2 west from Wrightwood for 2.4 miles (3.9 km) to the turn for Table Mountain.

Camp like a backpacker at ★ **Blue Ridge Primitive Campground** (661/269-2808, www.fs.usda.gov, free with Adventure Pass). Blue Ridge, at 8,000 feet (2,438 m) above sea level, forms part of the continental Pacific Crest. It towers above the town of Wrightwood and is home to Mountain High, the seasonal ski resort. This is a primitive campground: vault toilets, no electricity, and no running water, so make sure you bring enough water for cooking, washing, and drinking. All eight sites are first-come, first-served. Campsites on the south side of the campground have marvelous territorial views of the San Gabriel River Basin and greater Los Angeles. The PCT travels right through the campground, and both north- and south-bound day hikes are incredibly scenic.

To get there, head west on Highway 2 from Wrightwood for 5.5 miles (8.9 km) to Inspiration Point and turn left to head east on Blue Ridge Road. Continue 3 miles (4.8 km). The road is open May-October and is accessible for most passenger vehicles.

Information and Services

Big Pines Information Station (3 mi/4.8 km west of Wrightwood on Hwy 2,

760/249-3504, www.fs.usda.gov, 8:30am-3:30pm Fri.-Tues.) has free guides for easy, moderate, and strenuous hikes in the area surrounding Wrightwood, and detailed information about nearby campgrounds.

Grassy Hollow Visitor Center (6 mi/9.7 km west of Wrightwood on Hwy 2, 626/821-6737, www.grassyhollow. net, 10am-4pm Sat.-Sun.) is located directly on the Pacific Crest Trail, near Inspiration Point. Pick up a Forest Adventure Pass or a campfire permit (seasonal restrictions may apply). Shaded picnic tables on the south side of the parking lot have stunning views of Alder Gulch and the San Gabriel River.

If you're entering the San Gabriel Mountains from the west (via La Cañada Flintridge), you'll pass the **Chilao Visitor Center** (626/796-5541, www.fs.usda. gov, 9am-4pm Sat.-Sun.) on your way to Wrightwood. Geometric architecture, informative exhibits, and a detailed 3D relief map of Los Angeles make this a worthy stop.

The visitors center is 26 miles (42 km) east of La Cañada Flintridge and 33 miles (53 km) west of Wrightwood on Highway 2.

Agua Dulce

Agua Dulce is a blink-and-you'll-miss-it town in the dusty hills between Los Angeles and the high desert cities east of the mountains. Hikers on the Pacific Crest Trail enter the area through Vasquez Rocks, a world-famous geological site, and then walk right through the center of town as the trail follows Agua Dulce Canyon Road past horse ranches, homes, and a sprinkling of restaurants and family businesses. This community is so small, lodging and camping options here are slim-to-none; plan to explore Agua Dulce and Vasquez Rocks during the day but spend the night elsewhere. Newhall and Lancaster are just a

30-minute drive away. Nearby PCT towns Wrightwood and Tehachapi have services and accommodations as well.

Getting There

Agua Dulce is northwest of Wrightwood, a 1-2-hour drive depending on the route you choose.

If driving here directly from Los Angeles, take I-5 north toward Santa Clarita for 24 miles (39 km), then take exit 162 onto Highway 14. Follow for 14 miles (22.5 km) to exit 15 onto Agua Dulce Canyon Road.

Angeles Crest Scenic Byway

To follow the path of the Pacific Crest Trail and explore the San Gabriel Mountains, take this twisty 80-mile (129-km) route. Allow about two hours for the drive, more if you stop for photos or hikes.

From Wrightwood, take Highway 2 west for 41 miles (66 km). You'll cross the PCT six times between Inspiration Point and the Chilao Visitor Center. Make a hard right onto Upper Big Tijunga Canyon Road and follow it north for 9 miles (14.5 km) to meet the Angeles Forest Highway. Turn right to head north out of the mountains. Drive north for 16 miles (26 km), then merge onto Highway 14 south. Take exit 19 toward Agua Dulce.

This route is subject to road closures and winter conditions December-March.

Highway 138

This 55-mile (89-km) route through the high desert is faster (about an hour), and is advisable during the winter when Highway 2 may be closed.

Take Highway 2 east out of Wrightwood for 5 miles (8 km), then turn left to head west on Highway 138. Continue for 30 miles (48 km), then turn left to continue west on Pearblossom Highway for 4.5 miles (7.2 km). Merge onto Highway 14 south and take exit 19 toward Agua Dulce.

🏳 Side Trip: Devil's Punchbowl

The dramatic **Devil's Punchbowl** is worth a side trip. Situated along the Punchbowl Fault (part of the greater San Andreas Fault system), this slanted sandstone surges out of the northern side of the San Gabriel Mountains, creating a narrow, dramatic canyon where the mountains meet the high desert. A one-mile hiking loop to the canyon floor showcases the geology, unique to this region.

The **visitors center** (28000 Devils Punchbowl Rd., Pearblossom, 661/944-2743, www.parks.lacounty.gov, 9am-5pm Tues.-Sun.) has diagrams that explain the geologic formation, as well as a number of live snakes and taxidermy.

Devil's Punchbowl

Getting There

Devil's Punchbowl is 24 miles (39 km) east of Wrightwood and 25 miles (40 km) west of Agua Dulce, in the northern foothills of the San Gabriel Mountains.

From Wrightwood, take Highway 2 west to the Big Pines Information Station. Veer right at the intersection of Big Pines Highway (County Rte. 4) to head northwest and follow for 15 miles (24 km). Stay straight onto Valyermo Road, follow for 2.5 miles (4 km), and turn left to head west on Fort Tejon Road. Continue straight onto Pallet Creek Road for 2 miles (3.2 km), make a left on Longview Road, follow for 1 mile (1.6 km), take a left on Tumbleweed Road, and continue for 3 miles (4.8 km) to the Devils Punchbowl parking area.

From Agua Dulce, take Escondido Canyon Road to Highway 14 north and follow for 11 miles (17.7 km). Take exit 30 toward Pearblossom Highway and continue for 2 miles (3.2 km). Make a right on Barrel Springs Road, follow for 3.5 miles (5.6 km), make a right on Cheseboro Road, and then a left on Mount Emma Road. In 3.5 miles (5.6 km), turn right to head southeast on Fort Tejon Road. Follow for 4.8 miles (7.7 km) to Longview Road and make a right. Take a left on Tumbleweed Road and continue for 3 miles (4.8 km) to the Devils Punchbowl parking area.

Hiking

★ Vasquez Rocks 🅟

Distance: 3.5 mi/5.6 km round-trip

Duration: 1.5-2 hours

Elevation change: 350 ft/107 m

Effort: Easy/Moderate

Trailhead: Pacific Crest Trail

This hike through world-famous Vasquez Rocks showcases incredible, otherworldly rock formations where dozens of movies and TV shows have been filmed. Hike here in the springtime to see the desertlike terrain blanketed in green grass and colorful wildflowers.

Begin your hike by taking a 0.1 mile spur trail north out of the parking area to the Pacific Crest Trail. Make a right to walk south on the PCT through sagebrush. In 0.2 mile, you'll get up close and personal with some of the park's smaller, more subtle rock formations. Continue as the terrain flattens out, then follow the PCT as it makes a sharp right turn to head southeast along the upper rim of Escondido Canyon. You'll reach a trail junction at 1.2 miles—stay straight, departing from the PCT, to continue exploring Vasquez Rocks and climb to

⚑ Side Trip: Antelope Valley California Poppy Reserve

Walk through endless fields of orange California poppies, the state flower, at the **Antelope Valley California Poppy Reserve** (15101 Lancaster Rd., Lancaster, 661/724-1180, www.parks.ca.gov, sunrise-sunset daily, $10). Wildflower blooms vary each year, often peaking **late March-early April**. Eight miles of easy trails cross the park, where meadowlarks, snakes, lizards, bobcats, and coyotes roam. The park is open year-round, but visit between March 1st and Mother's Day (mid-May) when the poppies are in bloom and the interpretive center is open. Inside, see educational wild-flower and wildlife exhibits, as well as photographs, watercolors, and stained-glass art. The Pacific Crest Trail traverses the mountains just south of the reserve in the Angeles National Forest.

Getting There

The reserve is located in the Antelope Valley, about 45 minutes north of Agua Dulce and an hour south of Tehachapi.

From Agua Dulce, take Escondido Canyon Road to Highway 14 north. Follow for 25 miles (40 km) through Palmdale and Lancaster, then take exit 44 to Avenue I. Turn left to head west for 10 miles (16.1 km), then continue straight onto Lancaster Road. The entrance is on the right after 4 miles (6.4 km).

From Tehachapi, take Tehachapi Willow Springs Road south for 25 miles (40 km). Turn right to head west on Highway 138, then make a left to go south on 110th Street for 5 miles (8 km). Take a right onto Avenue I for 1 mile (1.6 km) and make a right onto Lancaster Road. The entrance is on the right after 4 miles (6.4 km).

---

higher-elevation parts of the park. Your trail makes a big horseshoe bend at 1.6 miles and begins ascending the western edge of the sandstone formations as you travel north. Territorial views from this east-facing ridge include Escondido Canyon, Pelona Valley to the north, and the Magic Mountain Wilderness to the south. The highest point is 2,200 feet (671 m) at 2.2 miles.

Descend in a northwest direction. At 2.7 miles, veer right to follow the main trail, or take a tiny 0.1-mile detour straight ahead to get a closer look at the sandstone massifs before you return to your primary route.

Continue west through sandy sagebrush flats, then along the northern edge of the largest rock formations. At 3 miles, there is a well-marked trail junction. Continue straight to head back toward the parking area, or take a little detour along the ridgeline to soak up some good views.

Getting There

Vasquez Rocks Natural Area Park is located on the southeast side of Agua Dulce. Stop at the **interpretive center** (10700 W. Escondido Canyon Rd., 661/268-0840, parks.lacounty.gov, 8am-5pm daily) to pick up a park map. There are many trails in the park, only some of which are labeled, so you'll want to carry a map or GPS with you while you explore.

The parking area for the trailhead is 0.2 mile past the interpretive center, in a large dirt lot on the east side of the road.

Entertainment and Events
Wine-Tasting

Agua Dulce Winery (9640 Sierra Hwy., 661/268-7402, www.aguadulcewinery.com, 10am-5:30pm daily, $10) has a tasting room on a beautiful, expansive vineyard with gazebos and walking paths. The property also has an animal sanctuary including a mini horse, an alpaca, and some interesting birds. The luxurious vibe in the tasting room and throughout the vineyard feels more like Napa than rural desert mountains. The $10 tasting fee is waived with any bottle purchase. Wine Wednesdays feature special pricing: $5 glasses and tastings.

Reyes Winery (10262 Sierra Hwy., 661/268-1865, www.reyeswinery.com, 11am-5pm Sat.-Sun., $10) is an award-winning family winery with cabernet sauvignon, merlot, syrah, chardonnay, and muscat grapes on the estate. The beautiful vineyard and tasting room are framed by the Sierra Pelona Mountains, where the Pacific Crest Trail climbs out of Agua Dulce toward the Antelope Valley.

Food

Locals hang out on the outdoor patio at ★ **Home Made** (33359 Agua Dulce Canyon Rd., 661/268-5005, 6:30am-3pm daily, $11-17) to enjoy fresh American breakfast and lunch fare and catch up on the town happenings. The menu includes egg dishes, waffles, and pancakes for breakfast, satisfying savory sandwiches for lunch, and homemade desserts.

Visit **Maria Bonita** (33311 Agua Dulce Canyon Rd., 661/268-8004, 11am-9:30pm daily, $12-20) on Tuesdays for $1 taco night. Relax into one of the restaurant's comfy green booths and reward yourself after a day of hiking in the desert sun with enchiladas, burritos, fajitas, and blended margaritas.

Other food options in town include **Sweetwater Bar and Grill** (33310 Agua Dulce Canyon Rd., 661/268-0688, www.sweetwaterbargrill.com, 7:30am-9pm Mon., 7am-9pm Tues.-Thurs. and Sun., 7am-close Fri.-Sat., $11-16) and **Big Mouth Pizza** (33323 Agua Dulce Canyon Rd., 661/268-7500, www.bigmouthpizza.com, 11am-9pm Sun.-Thurs., 11am-10pm Fri.-Sat., $10-20), a casual Italian American eatery with pizzas, pastas, salads, and sandwiches.

Tehachapi

Tehachapi is a small city in a mountain valley between Bakersfield and Mojave. Pacific Crest Trail hikers receive a warm welcome in this friendly town after hiking across the western edge of the hot, dry Antelope Valley into the Tehachapi Mountains. At almost 4,000 feet, Tehachapi differs from its low-elevation neighbors in that it experiences four distinct seasons, and the town motto encourages everyone to "come up, eat up, stay up, and play up."

The original vision for the Pacific Crest Trail plotted the entire route along the crest, but during the trail's initial creation, the mountains southwest of Tehachapi Valley proved to be impassable due to unyielding private landowners. The national scenic trail was instead routed through the Mojave Desert, along dirt roads and the California Aqueduct, and through fields of wind turbines on the east side of Tehachapi. Happily, a conservation easement was approved in 2014, and plans are in the works to route the PCT where it belongs: in the mountains.

Scenic Drive

The **Caliente Bodfish Road** travels 51 miles (82 km) through the Piute Mountains between Tehachapi and Lake Isabella. This winding mountain road parallels the Pacific Crest Trail, which is just 20 miles (32 km) to the east, as it climbs toward the southern base of the Sierra Nevada. A scenic drive on this road takes you through grassy, wildflower-speckled hillsides, quaint cattle ranches, and the tiny settlement of Havilah, which was the Kern County seat many years ago.

Starting from Tehachapi, head west on Highway 58 for 14 miles (22.5 km), then turn right to head north on Bealville Road, following signs for Caliente. (The scenic portion begins here.) After 2 miles (3.2 km), the road becomes Caliente

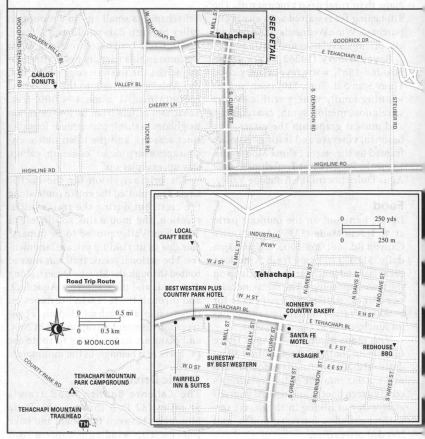

Bodfish Road. The byway climbs into the hills, twisting and turning through meadows and oak groves. During the spring, these hillsides are covered in purple, pink, yellow, and white wildflowers. About 15 miles (24 km) north of Highway 58, enter **Walker Basin,** a gorgeous, grassy valley where cows graze and wildflowers blanket the meadows in the spring. Stop at the historical plaque at Rankin Ranch to read a brief history of settlement in the valley.

Continue another 10.5 miles (16.9 km) north to the historic town of Havilah.

History buffs will want to stop at the Kern County Courthouse Museum, a building constructed in 1968 as a replica of an 1868 original. It's another 9.5 miles (15.3 km) from Havilah into the city of Lake Isabella.

Hiking
Tehachapi Mountain

Distance: 5 mi/8 km round-trip
Duration: 2.5-3 hours
Elevation change: 1,950 ft/594 m
Effort: Moderate
Trailhead: Tehachapi Mountain

Your hike begins at the southern end of Tehachapi Mountain Park Campground. Walk south from the trailhead and follow the Tehachapi Mountain Trail as it switchbacks twice in the first 0.1 mile before intersecting a wide dirt road. Turn right to walk south and follow the road up the hill. At 0.6 mile, the road takes a sharp turn to the left and the trees open up to allow expansive views of Tehachapi and the Cummings Valley. If you're hiking in the spring, look for bright orange patches of California poppies on the mountains across the valley. The road switchbacks twice more in the next mile before narrowing to a smaller, single-file trail at 1.7 miles. A sign appears indicating that you're only 0.88 mile from the summit, known as both Woody's Peak and Tehachapi Mountain. Get ready—this is where the trail gets steep.

The pine trees thin out at a false summit halfway up; from here you can enjoy southwestern views of the Tehachapi Mountains. Continue walking south along a saddle and through a grove of giant ponderosas and Jeffrey pines, then up a steep slope to reach the summit at almost 8,000 feet.

Getting There
Tehachapi Mountain Park is 8 miles (12.9 km) southwest of the town of Tehachapi. The trailhead is located at the southern end of County Park Road (in the Tehachapi Mountain Park Campground). There is a turnaround and parking area near the restrooms.

Entertainment and Events
The sheer number of beers on tap at **Local Craft Beer** (365 Enterprise Way, 661/822-2337 www.localcraftbeer.net, 4pm-10pm Mon.-Thurs., 2pm-midnight Fri., noon-midnight Sat., noon-10pm Sun., $5-7) is baffling. At least 25 delicious, high-quality brews are poured on any given day, all of which are brewed in-house and include New England-style IPAs, sours, stouts, porters, and pale ales. Select a flight of four or eight beers to satisfy your curiosity.

No food is served, but **Tehachapi Restaurants Xpress** (661/379-4105, 10am-9pm Mon.-Sat., 10am-8pm Sun., $5 fee), a local restaurant delivery service, will deliver food from any eatery in town.

Food
★ **Red House BBQ** (426 E. Tehachapi Blvd., 661/822-0772, 11am-8pm Wed.-Mon., $9-16) touts itself as "Tehachapi's only real barbecue joint." The extensive menu is impressive and features everything from pit beef, brisket, and pulled pork to popcorn shrimp and catfish, and even pastrami and hot links. The mouthwatering side dishes include hush puppies, sweet potato fries, cornbread, and fried okra. This is a one-of-a-kind local lair, and the eccentric (like an indoor waterfall) interior decor gives you plenty to look at while you wait. The big portions attract hungry thru-hikers, and you're likely to see them milling around in the backyard eating area. The owners even invite long-distance PCT hikers to camp in the grass.

The first sushi restaurant in town, **Kasagiri** (128 E. F St., 661/822-7533, 11:30am-1:30pm and 5pm-8pm Mon.-Fri., 5pm-8:30pm Sat., $10-25), opened in 1990 with the intention of feeding relocated Japanese employees at the nearby Honda plant. Over the years, the fresh and creative cuisine attracted Tehachapi locals and visitors. In addition to sushi (sashimi, nigiri, and rolls), popular menu items include a chicken and asparagus sauté, king salmon steak, and beef teriyaki.

Kohnen's Country Bakery (125 W. Tehachapi Blvd., 661/822-3350, www.kohnenscountrybakery.com, 6am-6pm daily, $8-10) is a German-style bakery and a bustling lunch spot on the main drag. Try the popular grilled Cubano panini or a custom sandwich with your choice of deli meats, veggies, and cheese on slices of traditional European breads:

graubrot, sourdough, *sechskorn*, or sheep-herders. Bakery rolls, croissants, cookies, and sweet treats like eclairs and cream puffs are in the cold case.

If you're in the mood for a treat, **Carlos' Donuts** (20011 W. Valley Blvd., 661/809-8936, 6am-noon, $1-6) has delectable donuts—if you can make it there before they're sold out. Mexican pastries like cream-filled *pañuelos*, sweet and savory empanadas, and *polvorones* (Mexican wedding cookies) are popular. Craving a hearty, savory breakfast instead? Carlos makes breakfast burritos, too.

Accommodations

You can't miss the **Santa Fe Motel**'s (120 W. Tehachapi Blvd., 661/822/3184, www.santafemotelca.com, $60) charming, bright vintage sign. The rooms are nothing fancy, but they're clean and feature microwaves and mini-fridges. The fixtures and paint still retain some of the art-deco vibes of the 1960s.

Downtown Tehachapi is quite walkable.

Three chain hotels on the same downtown block provide easy pedestrian access to the town's best restaurants and shops: **SureStay by Best Western** (418 W. Tehachapi Blvd., 661/822-5591, www.bestwestern.com, $109-114), **Fairfield Inn & Suites** (422 W. Tehachapi Blvd., 661/822-4800, www.marriott.com, $129-179), and **Best Western Plus Country Park Hotel** (420 W. Tehachapi Blvd., 661/823-1800, www.bestwestern.com, $129-139). All have rooms with Wi-Fi, desks, mini-fridges, and microwaves. Guest laundry and free breakfasts are available. They're right across the street from the train tracks, and the train traffic is constant—every 15 minutes during peak times. If you're a light sleeper, pick up some earplugs from the front desk.

Camping

If you're eager to escape the lights and sounds of the locomotive parade, **Tehachapi Mountain Park Campground** (17350 Water Canyon Rd., 661/822-4632,

California poppies in Walker Basin

www.kerncounty.com, $18) has 61 first-come, first-served sites located 15 minutes southwest of town. The campground's peaceful, forested quietude includes access to hiking trails such as the Tehachapi Mountain Trail to Woody's Peak, as well as complimentary showers for campers.

The park is open year-round, but winter snows cause road closures. The park advises all winter travelers to carry tire chains.

Getting There and Around

Tehachapi is located about 70 miles (113 km) north of Agua Dulce and 120 miles (193 km) north of Los Angeles.

From Agua Dulce, drive north on Agua Dulce Canyon Road for 1.8 miles (2.9 km). Turn right and travel east on Sierra Highway for 6.5 miles (10.5 km) to merge onto Highway 14 north. In 39 miles (63 km), take exit 61 and make a sharp left onto Backus Road. You'll come to a T-junction at Tehachapi Willow Springs Road in 7.5 miles (12.1 km). Turn right to head north. As the road climbs into the hills, you'll travel through wind farms and cross the Pacific Crest Trail at the intersection of Oak Creek Road and Cameron Canyon Road. To reach downtown Tehachapi, continue 5.5 miles (8.9 km) and make a left on Highline Road, then turn right on Curry Street.

Alternatively, from Los Angeles, take I-5 north to Highway 14 north. Continue north on Highway 14 for 60 miles (97 km) to Backus Road. Take a left on Backus Road then follow route above.

Central
California

Central California

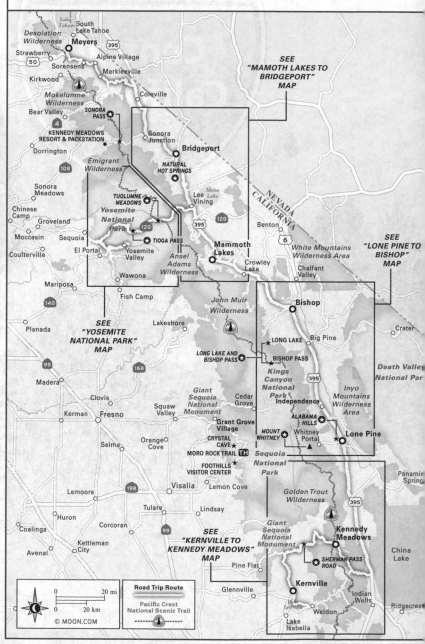

Lake Tahoe

Desolation Wilderness

South Lake Tahoe

Meyers

395

Strawberry

50

Sorensens

Alpine Village

Kirkwood

Markleeville

Mokelumne Wilderness

Coleville

Bear Valley

4

SONORA PASS

KENNEDY MEADOWS RESORT & PACKSTATION

Dorrington

Sonora Junction

Bridgeport

108

Emigrant Wilderness

NATURAL HOT SPRINGS

Sonora Meadows

TUOLUMNE MEADOWS

Lee Vining

Mono Lake

Chinese Camp

Groveland

Yosemite National Park

120

NEVADA

CALIFORNIA

SEE "MAMOTH LAKES TO BRIDGEPORT" MAP

Moccasin

Sequoia

El Portal

120

TIOGA PASS

Yosemite Valley

395

Benton

6

Coulterville

Ansel Adams Wilderness

Mammoth Lakes

White Mountains Wilderness Area

SEE "LONE PINE TO BISHOP" MAP

Mariposa

140

Wawona

Fish Camp

Crowley Lake

Chalfant Valley

SEE "YOSEMITE NATIONAL PARK" MAP

Planada

Lakeshore

John Muir Wilderness

Bishop

Crater

99

Madera

168

LONG LAKE

Big Pine

Death Valley National Par

Clovis

Squaw Valley

Giant Sequoia National Monument

Cedar Grove

LONG LAKE AND BISHOP PASS

BISHOP PASS

Kings Canyon National Park

395

Inyo Mountains Wilderness Area

Kerman

Fresno

Grant Grove Village

Independence

Panamint Spring

Selma

Orange Cove

CRYSTAL CAVE

MORO ROCK TRAIL TH

MOUNT WHITNEY

ALABAMA HILLS

Whitney Portal

Lone Pine

Lemoore

198

FOOTHILLS VISITOR CENTER

Sequoia National Park

Huron

Visalia

Lemon Cove

Golden Trout Wilderness

Coalinga

Tulare

Lindsay

395

China Lake

Kettleman City

Corcoran

Giant Sequoia National Monument

Kennedy Meadows

Avenal

99

SEE "KERNVILLE TO KENNEDY MEADOWS" MAP

Pine Flat

SHERMAN PASS ROAD

Indian Wells

Glennville

Kernville

Ridgecrest

Lake Isabella

Weldon

Road Trip Route

Pacific Crest National Scenic Trail

0 — 20 mi
0 — 20 km

© MOON.COM

Highlights

★ **Sherman Pass Road:**
Leave the desert behind on
this twisty mountain road
to Kennedy Meadows (page
116).

★ **Mount Whitney:** The
serrated edge of Mount
Whitney pierces the sky as it
towers over the Owens Valley
(page 124).

★ **Alabama Hills:** Explore
the natural rock arches and
towering boulders of the
Alabama Hills with the dramatic Sierra Nevada in the
background (page 124).

★ **Kearsarge Pass:** Hike
to this 11,700-foot mountain
pass for a sneak peek of
Kings Canyon National Park
(page 131).

★ **Long Lake and Bishop
Pass:** Walk past alpine lakes
and lush wildflower mead-
ows as waterfalls tumble
down around you (page
137).

★ **Natural Hot Springs:**
Soothe your tired muscles in
steaming mineral pools with
stunning views of the Eastern
Sierra (page 154).

★ **Tioga Pass:** The highest
highway pass in the High
Sierra offers high country
views of Yosemite (page
168).

★ **Tuolumne Meadows:**
Gaze at alpine meadows
blanketed in wildflowers and
surrounded by granite peaks
and domes (page 170).

★ **Sonora Pass:** This
high mountain pass travels
through dramatic, wind-
swept volcanic terrain next
to crusty hoodoo towers of
lava rock (page 178).

Your journey into the Sierra Nevada begins about 40 miles (64 km) west of the Pacific Crest Trail at the southern base of the mountain range.

These mountains represent the end of Southern California's arid, dry desert and the beginning of an alpine wonderland. The southern half of this magnificent mountain range is mostly impenetrable by road, with the exception of a few winding mountain passes, while the remote interior remains the province of backpackers.

For road-trippers, U.S. 395 parallels the spine of the Sierras, albeit 8,000 feet (2,438 m) below the route of the Pacific Crest Trail. From the floor of the Owens Valley, the pointed peaks and steep spires of the Sierra Nevada are breathtaking, especially set against the bright blue skies of late spring and early summer.

Crowning these peaks is 14,505-foot Mount Whitney, the highest point in the lower 48 states, a draw for backpackers and day hikers alike. Beyond Mount Whitney, the Pacific Crest Trail routes into Sequoia and Kings Canyon National Parks and through the John Muir Wilderness, sharing a path with the 211-mile John Muir Trail for much of its length.

As you cruise north along U.S. 395, the towns of Lone Pine, Bishop, and Mammoth Lakes provide convenient bases from which to explore the eastern edge of the mountain range. The rich history of the Eastern Sierras is best experienced with a stop in these trail communities, where you can learn more about the region's remarkable past. Each town has its own appeal, with quirky museums, down-home restaurants, cozy lodgings, and a host of outdoor activities.

The Pacific Crest Trail enters Yosemite National Park in the high country on the east side of the park. A scenic drive on Tioga Pass Road delivers you from U.S. 395 to Tuolumne Meadows, where you can step onto the PCT to marvel at the national park's granite glacier-sculpted domes. At 9,900 feet (3,018 m), Tioga Pass is the tallest highway pass in the Sierra Nevada, and the road closes every winter.

North of Yosemite, Highway 108 departs from U.S. 395 and climbs to Sonora Pass (also closed in the snowy winter months), where the PCT crosses the highway. The nearby town of Bridgeport provides a handful of dining and overnight options for travelers.

Planning Your Time

The Pacific Crest Trail stretches 250 miles (405 km) through the wild, rugged Sierra Nevada. Reaching this remote, mountainous area requires at least a half-day's drive from major cities. Plan at least **one week** to visit the most beautiful parts of the PCT, some of which are only accessible via out-and-back trips on roads that depart from U.S. 395. Start at the southern base of the Sierras in Kennedy Meadows, then travel north along U.S. 395 through the towns of Lone Pine, Bishop, and Mammoth Lakes, all convenient hubs for accessing Sequoia Kings Canyon National Park and the John Muir Wilderness. Finish your visit to this area in Yosemite National Park and Sonora Pass.

Don't miss the opportunity to see the jagged summit of Mount Whitney, the tallest peak in the lower 48, looming over Lone Pine and the Owens Valley. **If your time is limited,** spend it in Mammoth Lakes, where you can step directly onto the PCT, surrounded by the rugged beauty of the High Sierra—sparkling lakes, roaring waterfalls, and sky-piercing peaks.

When to Go

Plan to visit this area during the **summer** and **early fall** when roads are open and snow has melted from the trails. Hikes

Day Trips on the PCT

The remote Eastern Sierra offers long drives, few towns, and epic multiday backpacking trips along the PCT and John Muir Trail (JMT). For the best day hikes near the PCT in this region, pair the following:

Lone Pine

This Wild West town is the gateway to Mount Whitney. Though some folks try to tackle Whitney in a day, a more sensible option is to use Lone Pine as a base for day hikes from the **Cottonwood Pass** trailhead. The trail to **Chicken Spring Lake** accesses the southernmost alpine lake on the Pacific Crest Trail.

Independence

This blink-and-you'll-miss-it town on U.S. 395 is the entry point for the scenic hike to **Kearsarge Pass,** the eastern gateway to **Kings Canyon National Park**.

Bishop

Home to multiple outfitters, delicious pastries, and varied restaurants, Bishop is one of the best bases in the Eastern Sierra. Fuel up here for the challenging day hike through the John Muir Wilderness to **Bishop Pass.**

Mammoth Lakes

This resort town caters to outdoors lovers in winter and summer. Take the shuttle into **Devils Postpile National Monument** to hike the trail to **Minaret Falls,** a short but lovely jaunt on the PCT.

Yosemite

The PCT shares trails near **Tuolumne Meadows** with the JMT—you'll meet lots of thru-hikers here in summer. The popular trail to **Glen Aulin** follows the PCT north along the Tuolumne River.

during the months of June and July can be quite pleasant, but be prepared for mosquito attacks early in the summer when snow is still melting. Afternoon thunderstorms are common in July, although the weather generally remains quite sunny. During August and September, wildfires are common and some trails may be closed due to fire activity. Check www.inciweb.nwcg.gov for live updates about fire conditions.

While U.S. 395 is open year-round, other mountain roads are subject to heavy snowfall and many **roads close in winter.** Horseshoe Meadow Road and Whitney Portal Road near Lone Pine are closed between November and May, along with Onion Valley Road to Kearsarge Pass. Westbound roads near Big Pine and Bishop, including Glacier

Lodge Road and Highway 168, close each winter.

Mammoth Lakes is a popular ski resort during the winter; roads are open year-round, but traction tires or chains may be advised or required. Tioga Pass Road and Highway 108 over Sonora Pass are the two highest-elevation highway passes in the Sierra Nevada. They close each year between November and May.

Getting There

From the southern California town of Tehachapi, the PCT road trip travels north to Kernville before curving east to follow U.S. 395 north for much of the route.

Car

From Tehachapi, enjoy this scenic

Best Restaurants

★ **Grumpy Bear's Retreat, Kennedy Meadows:** Home of the famous hiker breakfast, this tavern offers a scenic place to eat in Kenney Meadows (page 119).

★ **Alabama Hills Café & Bakery, Lone Pine:** Dine beneath a hand-painted mural of the Alabama Hills at Lone Pine's best breakfast place (page 127).

★ **Still Life Café, Independence:** Dine on traditional French cuisine in the tiny town of Independence (page 132).

★ **Erick Schat's Bakkery, Bishop:** The best bakery hands-down on any road trip (page 141).

★ **Black Sheep Coffee Roasters, Bishop:** This narrow café serves excellent espresso drinks and tasty breakfast treats (page 142).

★ **Mammoth Brewing Company, Mammoth Lakes:** Enjoy classic brews or rotating seasonals plus pub food while gazing at the Mammoth Crest (page 157).

★ **Warming Hut Scratch Kitchen, Mammoth Lakes:** Creative breakfasts include a choice of three types of pancakes with tons of add-ons (page 158).

★ **Whoa Nellie Deli, Lee Vining:** Expect a line for the best food you'll ever order at a gas station (page 166).

★ **High Sierra Bakery, Bridgeport:** Handmade doughnuts, croissants, and baked goods complement this bakery's hearty sandwiches and espresso drinks (page 180).

60-mile route north to Kernville, about a 90-minute drive on a twisting byway. Take **Highway 58** west for 14 miles (22.5 km) to Bealville Road, then head north and continue as the road becomes Caliente Bodfish Road, arriving in **Lake Isabella** in 34 miles (55 km). Merge onto Highway 178 east and take exit 43 toward Wofford Heights. Continue north onto Wofford Heights Road/Highway 155 for 11 miles (17.7 km) into Kernville.

Alternatively, take busy, well-traveled roads. Follow Highway 58 west for 27 miles (43 km) to exit 121 for Comache Drive. Head north on Comanche Drive to Highway 178 east toward Lake Isabella. Take exit 43 toward Wofford Heights and continue north onto Wofford Heights Road/Highway 155 for 11 miles (17.7 km) into Kernville.

Kernville connects to U.S. 395, your primary path through the Sierra Nevada region, via two potential routes. North of Kernville, **Mountain Highway 99** and **Sherman Pass Road** climb northeast to Kennedy Meadows. Sherman Pass Road (open June-October) continues east out of Kennedy Meadows, becoming Kennedy Meadows Road and then Nine Mile Canyon Road, arriving at U.S. 395 near Pearsonville. South of Kernville, Sierra Way heads southeast out of town and meets Highway 178, which heads east and meets Highway 14 near Indian Wells. U.S. 395 is just 6.5 miles (10.5 km) north.

To skip Kernville and start your Sierra Nevada journey in **Lone Pine** instead, head directly to Lone Pine from Tehachapi by following **Highway 58** east for 18 miles (29 km) to Highway 14. Follow **Highway 14** north for 45 miles (72 km), continuing north as the highway

Best Accommodations

★ **Frandy Park Campground, Kernville:** Sleep in a covered wagon on the bank of the Kern River (page 114).

★ **Dow Villa Hotel & Motel, Lone Pine:** Built in 1957, this historic hotel is an homage to the area's Wild West film history (page 128).

★ **Mount Williamson Motel and Base Camp, Independence:** These hiker-friendly cabins are a beacon to weary PCTers (page 133).

★ **Onion Valley Campground, Independence:** This campground provides the easiest access to Kearsarge Pass, a popular entry/exit point for most PCT and JMT hikers (page 133).

★ **Hostel California, Bishop:** This colorful hostel is popular with thru-hikers, backpackers, and climbers (page 143).

★ **Mammoth Mountain Inn, Mammoth Lakes:** A stay here offers a central location for all recreation in Mammoth Lakes (page 160).

★ **Reds Meadow Resort and Pack Station, Mammoth Lakes:** These motel rooms and cabins offer easy access to Devils Postpile and the PCT (page 160).

★ **June Lake Campground, June Lakes:** Relax on the shore of June Lake, where campsites are shaded by aspen and pines with views of the surrounding 12,000-foot peaks (page 164).

★ **Tuolumne Meadows Campground, Yosemite National Park:** The largest campground in the park is a crossroads for thru-hikers and road-trippers (page 174).

★ **Kennedy Meadows Resort & Packstation, Sonora Pass:** This historic lodge rents cabins with kitchenettes and bathrooms within a few miles of Sonora Pass (page 180).

merges with U.S. 395 north. Arrive in Lone Pine 65 miles (105 km) later.

As **U.S. 395** stretches north for almost 200 miles (320 km) toward Tahoe, stops along the way offer out-and-back trips to Whitney Portal, Kings Canyon, Yosemite, and Sonora Pass.

Air

Meadows Field Airport (BFL, 3701 Wings Way, Bakersfield, 661/391-1800, www. meadowsfield.com) is the most convenient airport to Tehachapi and Kernville, both within an hour's drive. American Airlines and United Airlines serve this airport.

Major airlines serve the **Fresno**

Yosemite International Airport (FAT, 5175 E. Clinton Way, 800/244-2359, www. flyfresno.com), the major Central Valley air hub. Fresno is 160 miles (260 km) from Kernville, about a 2.5-hour drive.

Los Angeles is one of the most airport-dense metropolitan areas in the country. **Los Angeles International Airport** (LAX, 1 World Way, 855/463-5252, www.flylax. com) has the most flights. From L.A., it's a 2.5-hour drive to Kernville or Tehachapi and the starting point of your PCT road trip.

Reno is more convenient to the northern destinations in this region (including Sonora Pass and Yosemite) than airports farther south. The **Reno-Tahoe**

International Airport (RNO, 2001 E. Plumb Ln., Reno, NV, 775/328-6400, www.renoairport.com) is 110 miles (177 km) from Bridgeport, about a two-hour drive.

The **Sacramento International Airport** (SMF, 6900 Airport Blvd., 916/929-5411, www.sacairports.org) is 180 miles (290 km) from Bridgeport, about a 3.5-hour drive.

More than 900 planes arrive or depart **McCarran International Airport** (LAS, 5757 Wayne Newton Blvd., Las Vegas, NV, 702/261-5211, www.mccarran.com) every day. Terminal 1 hosts domestic flights, while Terminal 3 has domestic and international flights. Las Vegas is 300 miles (485 km) from Tehachapi and the southern starting point on U.S. 395, about a four-hour drive.

Train

Amtrak's (www.amtrak.com) *San Joaquin* line stops in Fresno (2650 Tulare St.) between Sacramento and Bakersfield with seven trains daily.

Bus

The **Eastern Sierra Transit Authority** (www.estransit.com) offers public transportation along U.S. 395 with stops in Lone Pine, Bishop, Mammoth, Bridgeport, and Reno.

Kernville

Located at the southern base of the majestic Sierras, Kernville marks your entry into these wild mountains. The town is about 40 miles (64 km) west of the Pacific Crest Trail. While nearby Lake Isabella is a common PCT resupply point, Kernville is a more scenic stop for road-trippers. The Kern River, which flows right through town, is the first major river to meet the PCT since the trail's southern terminus at the Mexico border. The recreation opportunities along this river draw visitors from all over the

region. After all that desert driving, stop in Kernville to cool off: Splash into the river, hop onto a whitewater rafting trip, or sit down for a frosty beer.

Sights

Stretch your legs in the shade of cottonwoods, sycamores, and pine trees at **Riverside Park** (10 Kern River Dr., 6am-10pm daily), a waterfront haven with a riverwalk, picnic tables, and a playground. The park is in downtown Kernville, steps from restaurants and shops. Be prepared to meet the park's friendly ducks, who aren't shy about asking to share your lunch.

Hiking
Skinner Peak ⓟ

Distance: 8.5 mi/13.7 km round-trip
Duration: 5 hours
Elevation change: 1,800 ft/549 m
Effort: Moderate
Trailhead: Pacific Crest Trail at Bird Spring Pass

Hike along the PCT to the top of Skinner Peak for territorial views of the boulder-laden, chaparral-blanketed Scodie Mountains.

From the trailhead at Bird Spring Canyon Road, follow the Pacific Crest Trail northeast as it begins a steady, moderate climb up the mountainside. The trail switchbacks six times between miles 1.5 and 2.7, ascending into the Scodie Mountains. South-facing vistas stretch out across Bird Spring Canyon, with Wyley's Knob as the most prominent peak across the canyon. When the trail straightens out and heads northwest around 2.8 miles, gaze down into Horse Canyon to the east. At 3.3 miles, the trail traces the ledge of 7,100-foot Skinner Peak's southeastern arm. To climb to the top of the peak (the highest in the Scodie range), look for a small, unmarked cutoff trail at 3.8 miles heading southwest, away from the PCT. Follow this path west, keeping the summit of the peak in sight when the trail becomes hard to follow. From the top at 4.2 miles,

Kernville to Kennedy Meadows

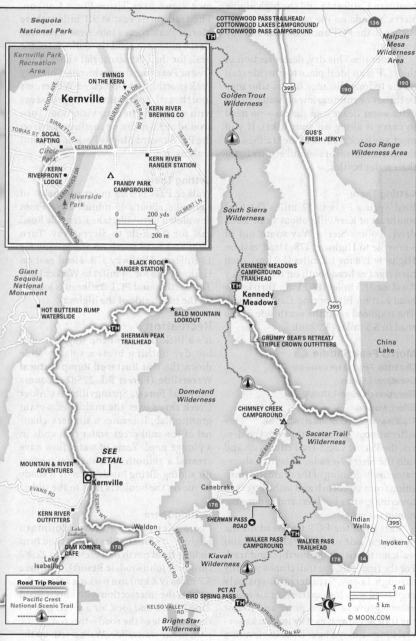

Sequoia National Park

COTTONWOOD PASS TRAILHEAD/
COTTONWOOD LAKES CAMPGROUND/
COTTONWOOD PASS CAMPGROUND

Malpais Mesa Wilderness Area

Kernville Park Recreation Area

Kernville

EWINGS ON THE KERN

KERN RIVER BREWING CO

SCODIE AVE
SIRRETTA ST
BUENA VISTA DR
SIERRA DR
SIERRA WY

TOBIAS ST
SOCAL RAFTING

KERNVILLE RD.

Circle Park

KERN RIVERFRONT LODGE

KERN RIVER DR
BURLANDO RD

KERN RIVER RANGER STATION

FRANDY PARK CAMPGROUND

GILBERT LN

Riverside Park

0   200 yds

0   200 m

Golden Trout Wilderness

South Sierra Wilderness

Giant Sequoia National Monument

BLACK ROCK RANGER STATION

KENNEDY MEADOWS CAMPGROUND TRAILHEAD

Kennedy Meadows

HOT BUTTERED RUMP WATERSLIDE

BALD MOUNTAIN LOOKOUT

SHERMAN PEAK TRAILHEAD

GRUMPY BEAR'S RETREAT/
TRIPLE CROWN OUTFITTERS

China Lake

Domeland Wilderness

CHIMNEY CREEK CAMPGROUND

Sacatar Trail Wilderness

CANEBRAKE RD

SEE DETAIL

MOUNTAIN & RIVER ADVENTURES

Kernville

EVANS RD

KERN RIVER OUTFITTERS

SIERRA WY

Lake Isabella

Weldon

Canebrake

SHERMAN PASS ROAD

Indian Wells

Inyokern

DAM KORNER CAFE

Lake Isabella

KELSO VALLEY RD

KELSO CREEK RD

WALKER PASS CAMPGROUND

WALKER PASS TRAILHEAD

Kiavah Wilderness

PCT AT BIRD SPRING PASS

KELSO VALLEY RD

Bright Star Wilderness

BIRD SPRING CANYON RD

Road Trip Route

Pacific Crest National Scenic Trail

0   5 mi

0   5 km

© MOON.COM

Coso Range Wilderness Area

GUS'S FRESH JERKY

look out over this ecological transition zone between the desert mountains of Southern California and the high alpine Sierra Nevada on the northern horizon. Return to the PCT and head back the way you came.

Insider tip: This dry, desert section of the PCT is an ideal place to provide trail magic to long-distance hikers who may be thirsty or running low on water. Bring extra water (leave it in the car—no need to carry it along on your hike). If you meet any backpackers at the trailhead at the start or finish of your hike, offer to fill their water bottles.

Getting There
Bird Spring Pass is 32 miles (52 km) southeast of Kernville, about a one-hour drive. Follow Sierra Way south out of Kernville to Highway 178. Head east on Highway 178 for 1.2 miles (1.9 km), then turn right to head south on Kelso Valley Road for 11.5 miles (18.5 km). Turn left to head east on Bird Spring Canyon Road. The trailhead is on the north side of the road in 5.5 miles (8.9 km).

Morris Peak Saddle 🚶
Distance: 7 mi/11.3 km round-trip
Duration: 3.5 hours
Elevation change: 1,370 ft/418 m
Effort: Moderate
Trailhead: Pacific Crest Trail at Walker Pass

After almost 700 miles through the desert, the Pacific Crest Trail climbs up and into the Sierra Nevada. This hike showcases the beginning of the dramatic transition from sagebrush and Joshua trees to towering granite boulders and panoramic mountain vistas.

Start from the PCT trailhead on the northwest side of the parking area and walk northeast on the northbound trail. For the first mile, the trail climbs steadily through tawny, arid terrain, sparsely populated with Joshua trees. At 1.1 miles, enter a grove of piñon pines and follow the trail northwest as it switchbacks several times. Enjoy a brief lapse in elevation

gain between 1.8 and 2.5 miles, where the trail is relatively flat and provides nice views over Three Pines Canyon. The trail turns east at 3.1 miles where Morris Peak comes into view. Continue for 0.4 mile onto a saddle southwest of the peak for the best territorial views of the Owens Peak (north/northwest), Chimney Peak (north), and Domeland Wilderness (northeast) areas, three rugged areas with very little human visitation. Turn around at 3.5 miles, or continue north on the PCT toward Morris Peak and Mount Jenkins.

Getting There
Walker Pass is 37.5 miles southeast of Kernville, about a 45-minute drive. From downtown Kernville, take Kernville Road east for 0.5 mile to Sierra Way. Turn right and head south on Sierra Way for 13 miles to Highway 178. Head east on Highway 178 for 24 miles to Walker Pass. The northbound PCT trailhead is located on the north side of the highway.

Recreation
It's a little bit out of the way, but on a hot day nothing beats a splashy slide down the **Hot Buttered Rump Natural Waterslide** (Forest Rd. 22S82, Sequoia National Forest, Springville). As Alder Creek flows over the middle of a giant granite slab, it creates a slippery channel of ice-cold creek water that ends in a plunge pool. Years of water flow have created a smooth rock surface, perfect for sliding. Bring lunch to enjoy a shady picnic on the boulders next to the slide.

Getting There
From Kernville, follow Mountain Highway 99 for 21 miles (34 km) and turn right to head north on Forest Road 22S82 (just past Johnsondale Resort). Continue 5.7 miles (9.2 km) to a parking area on the right at the intersection with Forest Road 22S83. Park and look for a green gate on the west side of the road—this road is the path to the waterslide. Walk north up the

road for 0.7 mile to an obvious (but un-marked) footpath on the right. This path leads down to the waterslide at the confluence of Alder Creek and Dry Meadow Creek.

Whitewater Rafting

Whitewater rafting is Kernville's biggest draw, and this exciting activity attracts visitors from all over Southern California. Trips explore various sections of the Kern River, from Class II and III to Class IV rapids. Book a trip on the Kern River with an expert guide; after being snugly secured in a life jacket and a helmet, you'll splash your way past boulders and through waves with lots of help from your fellow paddlers. Be prepared to get completely soaked!

Guides

River trips are popular and can fill quickly. Most outfitters accept reservations up to three months in advance. Book your rafting trip and a riverfront campsite at the same time with **Mountain & River Adventures** (15775 Sierra Way, 800/861-6553, www.mtnriver.com, Mar.-Oct., $42-230). Mountain & River offers one-day and multiday whitewater rafting trips on the Kern River as well as guided kayaking on Lake Isabella (Mar.-Oct. $68), rock climbing ($68), stand-up paddleboarding (year-round, $68), and mountain biking (Feb.-Oct., $68-140). Their 34 campsites ($54, 2-night minimum) include picnic tables, fire rings, and access to restrooms with hot showers.

SoCal Rafting (11101 Kernville Rd., 888/537-6748, www.socalrafting.com, Mar.-July, $33-90) offers three-hour and six-hour rafting trips on the Kern. Try a guided paddle-tubing trip (July-Aug., $44-120) if you'd rather be in command of your own single-size watercraft.

Kern River Outfitters (6602 Wofford Blvd., 760/376-3370, www.kernrafting.com, Apr.-Aug., $79-415) has been running trips on the Kern River since 1980. Family-friendly trips offer options for more or less excitement, depending on how adventurous you are about whitewater.

Entertainment and Events

Owned by a former Olympic whitewater kayaker, **Kern River Brewing Company** (13415 Sierra Way, 760/376-2337, www.kernriverbrewing.com, 11am-9pm Sun.-Thurs., 11am-9:30pm Fri.-Sat., $10-13) brews beers that reflect the adventurous spirit of the town. Every day, the brewery fills with smiling, sun-kissed faces of those fresh off the river or out of the mountains. Choose from a refreshing array of beers including pale ales, IPAs, red ales, brown ales, and stouts. Order craft beer in flights, pints, or bottles to go. Burgers, sandwiches, and hearty salads can fuel you up before or after your outdoor adventure.

Food

Ewings on the Kern (125 Buena Vista Dr., 760/376-2411, www.ewingsonthekern.com, 11am-9pm Mon.-Fri., 7am-9pm Sat.-Sun., $16-36) is perched on a cliff overlooking the Kern River. The restaurant's outside sign promises "Dining, Drinks & Views," and it doesn't disappoint on any of these three accounts. Inside, the place is reminiscent of a rustic log cabin, with exposed wooden beams and dining tables set next to picture windows overlooking the river. Local beers and fancy cocktails are available at the exquisite copper-top bar. A covered outdoor deck looks directly down onto the river, where you might see whitewater rafts or kayaks paddling past. The meat-and-potato menu sticks to ribs, burgers, sliders, barbecue, and steaks, with the addition of tasty side dishes and salads. Entrée alternatives include seared ahi tuna and shrimp linguini alfredo.

Fuel up for your outdoor adventure with breakfast at the **Dam Korner Café** (6303 Lake Isabella Rd., Lake Isabella, 760/379-8770, 6am-9pm daily, $10-13). This casual, charming American diner

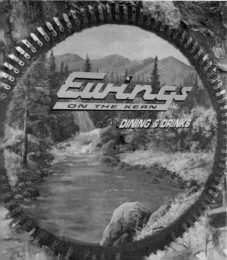

pairs hearty, satisfying breakfasts—omelets, French toast, pigs in a blanket, steak and eggs, scrambles—with hot, strong coffee. Service is prompt and friendly. Lunch and dinner are served, too.

Accommodations

Suites and cottages at **Kern Riverfront Lodge** (113 Kern River Dr., 760/376-1396, www.kernriverfrontlodge.com, $89-179) look out on Riverside Park and the Kern River. The decor is casual and charming, with wood-paneled walls and exposed brick. All rooms include full kitchens, fireplaces, and free Wi-Fi. The outdoor patio has a barbecue and plenty of seating.

Camping

★ **Frandy Park Campground** (11252 Kernville Rd., 760/531-4151, www.frandy.net, $41-100 Feb.-Oct., $35-88 Nov.-Jan.) is in downtown Kernville on the south side of the riverbank. All 90 campsites have access to bathrooms with full plumbing and coin-op showers. Some sites have electric hook-ups, picnic tables, or fire rings. In addition to tent sites and RV sites, the campground offers accommodations in **covered wagons** (from $125, plus cost of campsite) that sleep six guests among a king-size bed and two twin bunks. This is glamping at its finest, with LED lighting and an air-conditioning and heater unit in the wagon.

There are more than a dozen riverside campgrounds along a 20-mile stretch of road between Kernville and Sherman Pass Road. This road, known as Sierra Way (close to town) and Mountain Highway 99 (north of town), follows the path of the Kern River. Seasonal availability varies. Stop by the **Kern River Ranger Station** (11380 Kernville Rd., 760/376-3781, www.fs.usda.gov,

From top to bottom: Riverside Park in Kernville; Kern River Brewing Company; Ewings on the Kern.

8am-4:30pm Mon.-Fri.) to find out which campgrounds are open.

Rub elbows with fellow PCT hikers and backpackers at **Walker Pass Campground** (Hwy. 178, Onyx, 661/391-6000, www.blm.gov, free). Piñon pines, desert shrubs, and even a few Joshua trees surround the campground. There are 2 sites with parking spaces and 11 walk-in sites. Each site has a picnic table and fire ring, and pit toilets are nearby. No water is available; be sure to bring plenty for drinking, washing, and cooking (and, if you want to, some to share with backpackers who may be thirsty or running low on water).

The campground is open year-round, but it's not uncommon to see snow here during the winter months. The Walker Pass Campground is 35 miles (56 km) east of Lake Isabella on Highway 178/Isabella Walker Pass Road.

Information and Services

Stop by the **Kern River Ranger Station** (11380 Kernville Rd., 760/376-3781, www.fs.usda.gov, 8am-4:30pm Mon.-Fri.) for up-to-date information about campgrounds, trail conditions, and weather. Dozens of free brochures and printouts are available with information about hikes and recreation in the surrounding Sequoia National Forest. Detailed maps, guidebooks, and gifts are available for purchase.

Kennedy Meadows

Kennedy Meadows is a small mountain community with homes, campgrounds, two eateries, and a seasonal general store, all set high on the Kern Plateau at the southern edge of the Sierra Nevada. This is a special place for the Pacific Crest Trail, as it marks the southern gateway to a 200-mile stretch of pristine, high-elevation wilderness with no road crossings. Kennedy Meadows itself is quite remote—the drive to get there is long,

there aren't any services along the way, cell phone reception is spotty at best, and winter snows make access challenging (or impossible). If you're looking for the offerings of a bona fide town, head north on U.S. 395 to Lone Pine or Bishop.

During the summer, Kennedy Meadows may feel like the hot, dry desert, but the granite peaks on the horizon promise an exciting setting for northbound travelers. The South Fork of the Kern River flows south through the meadows, surrounded by arid piñon and juniper forests on its journey from its headwaters in the High Sierra.

Getting There

From Kernville, take the scenic route on **Sherman Pass Road** (late May/early June-Oct./early Nov.). Head north out of Kernville on Sierra Way/Mountain Highway 99 for 19 miles (31 km), then turn right to drive east on Sherman Pass Road. Follow for 44 miles (71 km) to Kennedy Meadows. This 65-mile (105-km) drive takes about three hours.

To save time or reach Kennedy Meadows during the winter from Kernville, take Sierra Way southeast out of town for 13.5 miles (21.7 km) to Highway 178. Turn east and continue on Highway 178 for 32 miles (52 km) to Highway 14, then head north on Highway 14 and continue straight as it merges with U.S. 395. Two miles (3.2 km) north of Pearsonville, turn left on **Nine Mile Canyon Road** to head west for 10 miles (16.1 km), continuing straight when the road name changes to Kennedy Meadow Road (also known as Sherman Pass Road) for an additional 14 miles (22.5 km). Allow two hours for this 87-mile (140-km) drive.

Bald Mountain Lookout

It's an easy 0.3-mile stroll to 9,400-foot **Bald Mountain Lookout** (Bald Mtn. Lookout Rd., Sequoia National Forest, 760/376-3781, www.fs.usda.gov, 9:30am-6pm Thurs.-Mon. May-Nov.)

for 360-degree views of the South Sierra's Kern Plateau. You can see plenty from the bald summit itself, but climb the two sets of stairs to the top of the brace metal lookout tower for an even better vantage point. Views to the south stretch over the Domeland Wilderness and Trout Creek. Pine Mountain and Kennedy Meadows rise to the east, with neighboring Beach Ridge to the northwest. Kern Peak, Mount Whitney, and Sequoia National Park's Kern River Canyon are visible on the northern horizon. You can drive to the lookout anytime the road is open (approx. late May-early Nov.), but the tower itself is closed Tuesday-Wednesday and during high winds.

Getting There

Bald Mountain is 20 miles (32 km) west of Kennedy Meadows in the Sequoia National Forest.

From Kernville, follow Sierra Way north out of town for 3 miles (4.8 km), continuing straight when it becomes Mountain Highway 99 at Riverkern. Continue north for 16 miles (26 km), then turn right to head east on Sherman Pass Road for 25 miles (40 km). Turn right onto Forest Road 21S97, then make an immediate right to head south on Forest Road 22S77. This bumpy dirt road climbs 1.8 miles (2.9 km) to the base of the lookout.

From Kennedy Meadows, head west on Sherman Pass Road for 18.5 miles (29.8 km). Make a sharp left to head east on Forest Road 21S97, then an immediate sharp right onto 22S77. This bumpy dirt road climbs 1.8 miles (2.9 km) to the base of the lookout.

Scenic Drive
★ Sherman Pass Road

The steep, twisty road out of the Kern River Valley to 9,200-foot Sherman Pass is exciting for a few reasons. For one, the drive itself is exhilarating as the road twists up through the colossal, dramatic slopes of the southwestern Sierra on a narrow road, offering scenic vistas into canyons far below and endless mountains on all horizons. Also, the climb into this region represents the end of Southern California's arid, dry desert regions and the beginning of exhilarating new habitat on the Pacific Crest Trail: the pristine alpine wonderland known as the Sierra Nevada. The southern half of this magnificent range is mostly impenetrable by road, and only two mountain pass highways actually traverse it: Sherman Pass Road out of Kernville, and Tioga Pass Road from Lee Vining. Although the Sherman Pass Road is narrow at times, the entire route is paved and friendly to all passenger vehicles.

Sherman Pass Road (late May/early June-Oct./early Nov.) begins at about 4,000 feet (1,219 m) above sea level, 16 miles (26 km) north of the town of Kernville on Mountain Highway 99. From there it makes a 5,000-foot ascent over the course of 15.5 miles (25 km) to a scenic vista point and parking area at Sherman Pass, 35 miles (56 km) northeast of Kernville. Sneak peeks of some of the continent's tallest mountains, including Mount Whitney, can be seen on the northern horizon. There is no better place to get a sense of the southern Sierra Nevada and the Sequoia National Forest than Sherman Pass. Allow about an hour to get from Kernville to the top of Sherman Pass, more if you plan to stop for photos. From Sherman Pass, it's another 45-minutes drive (30 mi/48 km) to Kennedy Meadows.

Hiking
Sherman Peak

Distance: 5 mi/8 km round-trip
Duration: 2.5-3 hours
Elevation change: 1,110 ft/338 m
Effort: Moderate
Trailhead: Sherman Peak

You can see Mount Whitney and the southern Sierra on the horizon from the vista point at Sherman Pass without even getting out of your car, but the 2.5-mile hike to the top of Sherman Peak takes the views to the next level. The trail delivers you to the top of a 9,900-foot butte with a 360-degree vantage point, endless mountains in all directions.

Start your hike at the vista point parking lot and cross Sherman Pass Road (late May/early June-Oct./early Nov.) to reach the trailhead on the west side of the road. The trail climbs for just 0.2 mile, then descends for the next 0.3 mile before beginning the steady climb toward the peak through a forest of red fir and western white pine. The scenery begins to change at 1.3 miles as you hike alongside a field of granite scree and rocks striped with shades of red, and at 1.5 miles, the radio towers atop your destination come into view. Pay close attention to the trail at 1.6 miles—after a right-hand turn, it's tempting to keep hiking straight up the steep hillside, but the trail bends to the left and continues northwest through a patch of buckthorn. At 1.9 miles, you'll begin the ascent up the west side of the peak where the views start to get really good. Don't be alarmed if you feel more out of breath than usual! Remember, high-elevation hiking makes your lungs work harder. The trail intersects with a dirt road—the Sherman Peak 4x4 trail—at 2.3 miles; turn left and follow the road to the top of the peak. Soak up the panoramic views of Kern Canyon, Mount Whitney, Mount Langley, and Olancha Peak to the north; the path of the PCT through the Domeland and Owens Peak Wildernesses to the southeast; and the impressive, twisting route of the Sherman Pass Road out of the southern Kern River Valley.

Getting There
This is a great hike to stop for if you're driving the Sherman Pass Road between Kernville and Kennedy Meadows. The Sherman Peak trailhead is located

From top to bottom: Kennedy Meadows; Nine Mile Canyon Road; Bald Mountain Lookout.

at Sherman Pass, on the west side of Sherman Pass Road (across the road from the vista point parking lot).

From Kernville, follow Sierra Way/Mountain Highway 99 for 19 miles (31 km) to Sherman Pass Road. Turn right to head northeast for 15 miles (24 km) to Sherman Pass. Allow about an hour for this drive.

From Kennedy Meadows, head west on Forest Road 22S05/Sherman Pass Road for 29 miles (47 km). Allow an hour and 45 minutes for this drive.

Pacific Crest Trail to Kern River Bridge PCT

Distance: 4.1 mi/6.6 km round-trip
Duration: 2 hours
Elevation change: 465 ft/142 m
Effort: Easy
Trailhead: Kennedy Meadows Campground

This Pacific Crest Trail hike is an easy amble along the South Fork of the Kern River into the South Sierra Wilderness.

Start your hike at the north end of the Kennedy Meadows Campground loop and walk north on the PCT. Granite boulders, junipers, piñon pines, and sagebrush are your company. Listen for the rushing sounds of whitewater at 0.4 mile as the trail nears the river. You'll get closest to the water between 0.6 and 0.8 mile—on a hot day, you may be tempted to tread through the brush to cool off in the river, but wait until the bridge if you can, where access is easier. See a scraggly, lightning-struck tree at 1.5 miles, and the bridge comes into view at 1.9 miles. Continue for another 0.1 mile to reach the bridge and a towering piñon pine on the west side of the river.

Make it a longer hike or a backpacking trip by continuing north on the PCT toward Clover Meadow, Beck Meadow, and Olancha Peak.

Shopping

If you're in need of new shoes, clothing, a backpack, water filtration, cookware, or pretty much anything

view from the summit of Sherman Peak

backpacking-related, you're in luck. **Triple Crown Outfitters** (98837 Kennedy Meadows Rd., Inyokern, 559/850-4453, www.triplecrownoutfitters.com, 9am-3pm daily year-round) is a backpacking and outdoor gear shop located next to Grumpy Bear's Retreat on the southeast end of the Kennedy Meadows community. The shop is owned and operated by two long-distance backpackers who are knowledgeable and passionate about backpacking gear.

Food

If you've read *Wild* or seen the movie, you may remember the **Kennedy Meadows General Store** (967440 Beach Meadow Rd., 559/850-5647, www.kennedymeadowsgeneralstore.com, 9am-5pm daily May-Oct., 9am-5pm Sat.-Sun. Nov.-Apr.) as one of the first places Cheryl Strayed stopped to rest and resupply on her journey. (The scene in the movie was actually filmed elsewhere at a lookalike locale.) The store

sells bagged ice, ice cream, camping supplies, backpacking food, and snacks, and the burger shack out back (11am-4pm daily May-Oct.) serves burgers and fries. The food is nothing fancy, but it hits the spot if you're hungry and not in the mood to cook for yourself or make the drive down out of the mountains. While there isn't any seating inside the store, an outdoor deck on the south side of the store's Old West-style building is shady during some parts of the day, and picnic tables look south over the meadows. Visiting Kennedy Meadows on a Saturday? Stick around after dinner for an outdoor movie night under the stars.

★ **Grumpy Bear's Retreat** (98887 Kennedy Meadow Rd., 559/850-2327, www.grumpybearsretreat.com, 8am-10pm daily Apr.-July, 8am-10pm Wed.-Sun. Aug.-Sept., 8am-10pm Fri.-Sun. Oct.-Mar., $7-12) is the only other restaurant on the Kern Plateau, and it's set up more like a tavern, serving beer and wine at an indoor bar with cushy barstools. There are tables inside as well, and a shady outdoor dining area with north-facing views of the river valley. The famous hiker breakfast is a plate of eggs, bacon, and potatoes next to a 10-inch monster pancake (offered as "all you can eat," in case a pancake the size of a medium pizza isn't big enough). Fresh-smoked beef jerky is available to go, and during the summer, the retreat hosts chili cook-offs and barbecues. During the off-season, check the event calendar on the website to find out about prime rib dinners, holiday brunches, and catfish fry dinners.

Camping

The Pacific Crest Trail runs right through **Kennedy Meadows Campground** (County Rd. J41, www.fs.usda.gov, $10) in the Inyo National Forest. The 37 campsites are just steps from the trail, and the Kern River flows along the western edge of the campground. Bring plenty of water for drinking, cooking, and washing—pit toilets and fire rings are the only amenities. The Kennedy Meadows store is accessible via a short drive or a three-mile walk. This campground is open year-round, but expect snow and chilly temps during the winter.

Getting There: The campground is 26.8 miles (43.1 km) northwest of U.S. 395. From U.S. 395, exit north of Pearsonville and follow paved Nine Mile Canyon Road west to Country Road J41, just east of the Kennedy Meadows General Store. Follow J41 north for 3 miles (4.8 km) to the campground. Plan at least one hour for the long drive.

Chimney Creek Campground (Chimney Peak Rd., Inyokern, www.blm. gov, free) is 17 miles (27 km) southeast of Kennedy Meadows. The 36 sites are usually less populated than the Kennedy Meadows Campground. In summer, there is potable water from a spigot at the end of a one-mile road. The PCT passes along the southern edge of the campground. Though the dirt access road to the campground is bumpy, it is suitable for passenger vehicles. All campsites have picnic tables, and pit toilets are nearby. The campground is open year-round.

Getting There: From Kennedy Meadows, follow Kennedy Meadows Road south for 13 miles (20.9 km). Turn right and continue south on Chimney Basin Road. The well-signed campground will be on your left in 4 miles (6.4 km). From U.S. 395, take Nine Mile Canyon Road west for 10.5 miles (16.9 km), then head south on Chimney Basin Road for 4 miles (6.4 km).

Information and Services

Kennedy Meadows is a remote area with no cell phone reception. Prepare for a safe trip to this area by bringing plenty of water and maps of the area. The **Black Rock Ranger Station** (Sherman Pass Rd., 760/376-3781, www.fs.usda.gov, 8:30am-4:30pm Thurs.-Mon. May-Nov.) is 13 miles (20.9 km) west of Kennedy Meadows and is an excellent resource for

hiking maps, wilderness permits, local area information, and burn permits (required for campfires, barbecue grills, and propane camp stoves).

The Kennedy Meadows General Store sells gasoline for upward of $5 per gallon. Fill your tank in Kernville or Pearsonville instead before you drive into the mountains.

Lone Pine

The small, Western-themed town of Lone Pine is located on U.S. 395 and serves as the gateway to some of the highest peaks in the Sierra Nevada.

About 12 miles (19.3 km) west of Lone Pine lies Whitney Portal and the trail to Mount Whitney, the tallest peak in the continental United States. Although Mount Whitney isn't on the PCT, many hikers choose to spend a day summiting the peak, while some descend from the mountain to rest and recharge in Lone Pine. Located at 4,000 feet (1,219 m) in elevation, the Owens Valley is up to 10,000 feet (3,048 m) below the Sierra Nevada and White Mountains. Daytime temperatures in the valley during the summer can be punishing, even when high-elevation weather is pleasant. Visits to Lone Pine during the early summer or late fall offer mild weather when the trails aren't covered in snow.

Getting There

Lone Pine is on U.S. 395, 80 miles (129 km) north of Kennedy Meadows and 57.5 miles (93 km) south of Bishop. From Kennedy Meadows, follow Kennedy Meadows Road east for 14 miles (22.5 km), continuing east when it becomes Nine Mile Canyon Road. Continue down the grade for 9 miles (14.5 km) to U.S. 395, then turn left and drive north for 55 miles (89 km). Allow 90 minutes for this drive.

It takes about two hours to drive from Kernville or Tehachapi to Lone Pine.

Lone Pine to Bishop

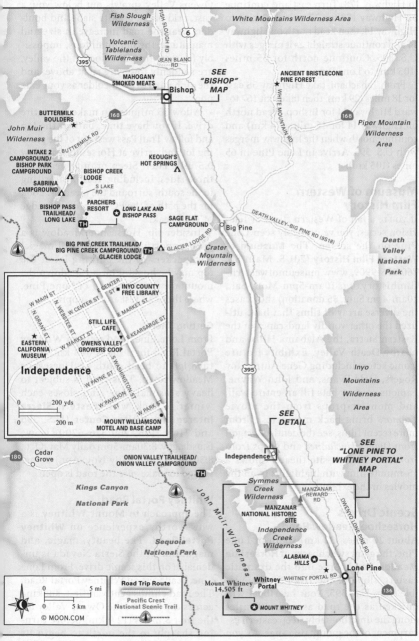

From Kernville, take Sierra Way southeast out of town for 13.5 miles (21.7 km) to Highway 178. Turn east and continue on Highway 178 for 32 miles (52 km) to Highway 14, then head north on Highway 14 and continue straight as it merges with U.S. 395. Continue north for 65 miles (105 km) to Lone Pine.

From Tehachapi, take Highway 58 east for 18 miles (29 km), then take exit 167 toward Highway 14 for Bishop. Head north on Highway 14 for 46 miles (74 km) and continue north when the highway merges with U.S. 395. Arrive in Lone Pine in 65 miles (105 km).

Museum of Western Film History

If you're a fan of Western films or television series, you've probably seen Lone Pine on the screen. The **Museum of Western Film History** (701 S. Main St., 760/876-9909, www.museumofwesternfilmhistory.org, 10am-5pm Mon.-Sat., 10am-4pm Sun., $5 donation) showcases the diverse array of films that have utilized the otherworldly landscapes of the Eastern Sierra, the Alabama Hills, and nearby Death Valley. Exhibits feature iconic actors including Gene Autry, Roy Rogers, Dale Evans, and John Wayne. Famous cowboy hats fill an entire wall, and monster props from the movie *Tremors* bring back memories. From more recent films, see the dentist's wagon from *Django Unchained* and props from *Ironman*. The on-site theater shows a 15-minute film with highlights from the movies in the exhibits.

Scenic Drives
Horseshoe Meadow Road

About 20 miles (32 km) south of Lone Pine, the giant switchbacks of **Horseshoe Meadow Road** carve into the dramatic eastern slope of the High Sierra, visible from U.S. 395. Your heartbeat will quicken as the road ascends 19 miles along the unfathomably steep eastern escarpment of the mountain range. As you climb more than a vertical mile in elevation (4,000-10,000 ft/1,219-3,048 m), the Owens Valley sprawls out below you: a vast, arid plain; granite slabs and boulders near the road increase in size and magnitude; the mountaintops, impossibly far away from the floor of the valley, are suddenly towering right above; and the air begins to grow colder as your ears pop.

Allow 35 minutes to make the entire drive. If you have time, park at the top and follow Trail Pass west out of the parking lot and arrive at Horseshoe Meadow 0.5 mile later. Steep granite peaks on three sides, including Trail Peak rising to the south, surround the meadow. Look for the path of the PCT cut into the edge of Trail Peak.

Insider tip: Horseshoe Meadow is a great opportunity to offer trail magic! Backpackers in the parking lot at the top may be hopeful for a ride down the mountain into the town of Lone Pine, where they can rest and resupply.

Getting There

From Lone Pine, head west on Whitney Portal Road for 3 miles (4.8 km), then turn left to head south on Horseshoe Meadow Road. This road is subject to heavy seasonal snow and closes each winter. Check with **Eastern Sierra Interagency Visitor Center** (U.S. 395 and Hwy. 136, 760/876-6200, www.fs.usda.gov, 8:30am-5pm daily May-Oct., 8:30am-4:30pm daily Nov.-Apr.) before you go to make sure the road is open.

Whitney Portal Road

The approach to Mount Whitney is a wow-worthy experience on **Whitney Portal Road.** The beauty, magic, and magnitude of the Sierra Nevada is undeniable on this scenic drive. From Lone pine, head west on Whitney Portal Road. The road climbs gently at first, snaking across the floor of the Owens Valley for the first 8 miles (12.9 km) before turning sharply to the north to begin its ascent into the mountains. The next dramatic turn takes the road 180 degrees to face Lone Pine Peak (which many travelers on U.S. 395 mistake for Mount Whitney). At the 10-mile mark, the road turns west again and enters a narrow granite canyon where Lone Pine Creek flows off Mount Whitney's eastern flanks and down into the Owens Valley. By the time you arrive at the portal, you've climbed 4,300 feet (1,311 m) in just 12 miles (19.3 km). (Don't be surprised if the temperature drops by 10-20 degrees during the course of your drive.) You'll recognize Mount Whitney by the "needles" on its south side; this craggy group of granite pinnacles leads to the massive summit.

Whitney Portal is just that: A passage from the dry, dusty Owens Valley into another world where waterfalls tumble over towering cliffs and granite spires reach astonishing heights.

Whitney Portal Road and the parking area at its terminus can be extremely busy in the summer months, in part because the visitation season is short—the road is only open **May-November.** If possible, plan to visit during shoulder season (May or Sept.-Oct.) or on a weekday so that you can savor the experience with fewer crowds.

Explore the area by parking and walking to the western edge of the parking lot to see Lone Pine Creek Falls cascading hundreds of feet down steep granite canyon walls. Day hike destinations from the Portal include Meysan Lakes, Lone Pine Lake, and Lower Boy Scout Lake.

Destinations beyond these lakes require entering the Mount Whitney Zone, where **wilderness permits** are required May-October. For more information about the lottery, and to download an application, visit www.fs.fed.us/r5/inyo or call the wilderness permit information and reservation line for Inyo

From top to bottom: Museum of Western Film History; Alabama Hills; PCT near Trail Pass.

★ Mount Whitney

One of the most famous climbing or backpacking trips in California is **Mount Whitney** (www.nps.gov/seki). At 14,505 feet (4,421 m), Whitney is the highest peak in the continental United States, and this must-do trek draws intrepid hikers and climbers from around the world. Whitney also marks the southern end of the 211-mile (340 km) John Muir Trail and makes for a dramatic end or beginning for thru-hikers doing the whole trail. While the Pacific Crest Trail shares much of its path through the High Sierra with the John Muir Trail, the two routes diverge near Mount Whitney. Although the peak isn't technically part of the PCT, many PCT hikers choose to detour from the PCT for one day to summit.

Mount Whitney is located at the far eastern edge of Sequoia National Park, but there are no roads leading there from the west. The only vehicle access is via Whitney Portal Road from Lone Pine.

The climb to the top of Mount Whitney is a very challenging hike, even for very fit hikers. The trek is 22 miles round-trip with 6,700 feet (2,042 m) of elevation gain. While some hikers do attempt the feat in one day, starting as early as 3am to finish before dark, an overnight backpacking trip makes better sense for most people.

Permits

Permits are required for anyone entering the Mount Whitney Zone—even day hikers. May-October, there's a quota for hikers; those who want to hike must enter the February lottery in order to have a good chance of getting a permit for the following summer.

For more information about the lottery, and to download an application, contact the National Forest (760/873-2483, recreation.gov). November-April, hikers still need a permit, but there are no quotas in place. Pick up a permit in person at the **Interagency Visitor Center** (U.S. 395 and Hwy. 136, south of Lone Pine, 760/876-6200, www.fs.fed.us/r5/inyo, 8am-5pm daily May-Oct., 8:30am-4:30pm daily Nov.-Apr.). During the off-season, you can self-register for a permit if the visitors center is closed.

If all that sightseeing stirs up your appetite, stop at the **Whitney Portal Store** (238 S. Main St., Lone Pine, 760/876-0030, www.mountwhitneyportal.com, 9am-6pm daily May and Oct., 8am-8pm daily June and Sept., 7am-9pm daily July-Aug., $11-14) for a cheeseburger, bacon cheeseburger, veggie burger, or patty melt. Lunch service starts at 11am. Beers and sodas are available, too.

★ Alabama Hills

At the foot of the Eastern Sierras, a few miles west of Lone Pine, sits a jumbled collection of otherworldly rock formations. If the enormous boulders and rounded arches look eerily familiar, that's because you probably have seen them before—on screen. Hundreds of movies and television shows (particularly Westerns) have been filmed in these hills, including *Django Unchained* (2012), *Gladiator* (2000), *Tremors* (1990), *Star Trek* (1980s-1990s), *Around the World in 80 Days* (1956), and the *Lone Ranger* (1938). The landscape has served as a substitute for everywhere from India to Afghanistan.

Take the 3-mile **Movie Road** driving tour through the weathered terrain, stopping often to take pictures—the natural arches and rock formations in the wilderness permit information and reservation line for **Inyo National Forest** (760/873-2483, www.fs.fed.us/r5/inyo and www.recreation.gov). November-April, hikers still need a permit, but there are no quotas in place. Pick up a permit in person at the **Mount Whitney Ranger Station** within the **Interagency Visitor Center** (U.S. 395 and Hwy. 136, 2 mi/3.2 km south of Lone Pine, 760/876-6200, www.fs.fed.us/r5/inyo, 8am-5pm daily May-Oct., 8:30am-4:30pm daily Nov.-Apr.). During the off-season, you can self-register for a permit if the visitors center is closed.

There are a few hike destinations from Whitney Portal that do not enter the Mount Whitney Zone and can be done without wilderness permits: Meysan Lakes, Lone Pine Lake, and Lower Boy Scout Lake.

Hikers rest after a strenuous climb to the summit of Mount Whitney

Camping

The nearest campground is **Whitney Portal Campground** (end of Whitney Portal Rd., 6 mi/9.7 km west of Lone Pine, 877/444-6777, www.recreation.gov, 44 sites, mid-May-Oct., $21) in the Inyo National Forest; it's 7 miles (11.3 km) from the trailhead. Twenty-five walk-in sites are located near the **Mount Whitney trailhead** (first-come, first-served, one-night limit, $12).

foreground add scale, contrast, and perspective to the Sierras' jagged peaks on the western horizon. Stop to see Mobius Arch, the most famous formation, by hiking a 0.6-mile loop trail accessible from Movie Road. Pick up a self-guided tour map at the **Lone Pine Chamber of Commerce** (120 S. Main St., 760/876-4444, 8:30am-4:30pm Mon.-Fri.) or online at www.lonepinechamber.org.

Insider tip: Summer temperatures in the Alabama Hills can climb into the triple digits during the middle of the day. Visits during the morning or evening, or during the spring or fall, provide the most comfortable weather for sightseeing and hiking.

The Alabama Hills are located on BLM land, and **overnight camping** is permitted. A California campfire permit (www.preventwildfireca.org) is required for campfires and stoves. There

are no amenities or services; bring plenty of water for drinking, washing, and cooking.

Getting There

From Lone Pine, drive west on Whitney Portal Road for 3 miles (4.8 km) and turn right to head north on Movie Road. The trailhead for Mobius Arch is located on the north side of Movie Road in 1.5 miles (2.4 km), where the road makes a big bend to the east.

Hiking

Chicken Spring Lake 🅟🅒🅣

Distance: 8.8 mi/14.2 km round-trip
Duration: 5 hours
Elevation change: 1,440 ft/439 m
Effort: Moderate
Trailhead: Cottonwood Pass

Hike to the southernmost snow-fed, alpine lake on the Pacific Crest Trail, soaking up views of lush meadows, granite spires, and limber pines along the way.

The trail begins at Horseshoe Meadow and heads west from the parking area. Stay straight at the junction at 0.3 mile and follow a sign for Cottonwood Pass, continuing west. The first 1.5 miles are flat as the trail follows the northern edge of the expansive meadow, crossing Cottonwood Creek twice. The sandy trail will give your ankles a workout—boots and trekking poles are helpful. The trail switchbacks at 1.8 miles, zigging and zagging over the next 1,000 feet (305 m) of elevation to deliver you to Cottonwood Pass. The marvelous landscape is themed in the High Sierra's trademark color palette: blue sky, tree bark, grassy meadows, and white granite. The trail meets the PCT at 3.7 miles before turning right to head north, leveling out with only another 100 feet of elevation before reaching **Chicken Spring Lake** at 4.4 miles.

Return the way you came, or follow the longer **Cottonwood-Trail Pass Loop** (12.2 mi/19.6 km rt, 1,720 ft/524 m, moderate) to see more of the PCT's path through this area. Continue south on the Pacific Crest Trail at Cottonwood Pass for 4.8 miles, returning to Horseshoe Meadow via the 1.8-mile **Trail Pass Trail.** This additional hike showcases peaceful, pristine Big Whitney Meadow and a number of 14,000-foot peaks west inside Sequoia National Park.

Getting There

Cottonwood Pass trailhead is located 23 miles (37 km) southwest of Lone Pine, about a 40-minute drive. Head west on Whitney Portal Road for 3 miles (4.8 km), then turn left to head south on Horseshoe Meadow Road. This 19-mile (31-km) road zigzags up the steep edge of the mountain range and delivers you to Horseshoe Meadow. The trailhead is located at the end of the road.

Lone Pine Lake

Distance: 5.3 mi/8.5 km round-trip
Duration: 3 hours
Elevation change: 1,780 ft/543 m
Effort: Moderate
Trailhead: Whitney Portal

Although some people actually accomplish it in a day, the 22-mile round-trip hike to the summit of the highest mountain in the lower 48 states, Mount Whitney, is best approached as an overnight backpacking trip. This shorter hike gives you a chance to explore part of the route, soaking up the incredible landscape of the high-elevation Eastern Sierra on your way to Lone Pine Lake.

Starting from Whitney Portal, head north out of the parking area on the Mount Whitney Trail. The trail turns west and crosses the North Fork of Lone Pine Creek at 0.7 mile. Stay left at the junction here to head south toward Lone Pine Lake. Climb south up the eastern edge of Thor Peak, following the path of Lone Pine Creek. At 2.5 miles, take the left fork onto the Lone Pine Lake Trail. Arrive at the lake in 0.2 mile. The glassy, serene wonder is framed by towering granite spires. Return the way you came.

A **wilderness permit** is required to continue climbing south on the Mount Whitney Trail past Lone Pine Lake. Contact the **Interagency Visitor Center** (U.S. 395 and Hwy. 136, 2 mi/3.2 km south of Lone Pine, 760/876-6200, www. fs.fed.us/r5/inyo, 8am-5pm daily May-Oct., 8:30am-4:30pm daily Nov.-Apr.) for details.

Recreation
Rock Climbing

Rock climbers love Lone Pine's Alabama Hills for the diversity of routes and the delightful High Sierra backdrop. With hundreds of rock formations, there is something for climbers of every level to explore. **California Rock Guides** (120 S. Main St., 888/797-6867, www. californiarockguides.com, Apr.-Nov., $87-175) offers full- and half-day guided climbs with instruction. Helmets, rock shoes, harnesses, and all technical equipment is provided for you. Custom and private climbs are also available.

Whitney Base Camp & Climbing School (701/391-5432, www.whitneybasecamp. com, $140-350) offers climbing classes, backpacking trips, and women's climbing retreats. Rock climbing instruction includes introductory skills, multi-pitch climbing, scouting, and rigging. Some classes are geared toward couples and families.

Fishing
The Owens River tributaries are famous for year-round fishing. Golden, rainbow, and brook trout, bass, catfish, and crappie are among the most popular catches. Fishing is good at the Whitney Portal Pond, located along Lone Pine Creek in the Whitney Portal Campground, 13 miles (20.9 km) west of Lone Pine on Whitney Portal Road. Review the California fishing regulations at www. wildlife.ca.gov/regulations.

Shopping
Big Willi Mountaineering Co. (120 S. Main St., 760/878-8325, www.bigwillimc. com, 9am-5pm Thurs.-Mon.) is a tiny shop, filled to the brim with everything you need for an adventure: clothing, equipment, accessories, and snacks (including the best deal in town on Clif Bars). The knowledgeable staff is happy to provide up-to-date information about trail conditions and local weather.

Elevation (150 S. Main St., 760/876-4560, www.sierraelevation.com, 9am-6:30pm Sun.-Thurs., 9am-7pm Fri.-Sat.) is a well-stocked source for climbing, hiking, and camping gear. Crampons, snowshoes, and bear canisters are available for rent.

Packed to the gills with essential goods for fishing, hiking, camping, and traveling, **Gardner's True Value** (104 S. Main St., 760/876-4208, www.truevalue. com, 8am-6pm Mon.-Sat.) is a one-stop shop with camp stoves, cookware, fishing equipment, blankets, tents, air mattresses, bug repellent, automotive products, and more.

Entertainment and Events
Lone Pine celebrates the heritage of the film industry during the **Lone Pine Film Festival** (www.lonepinefilmfestival.org, early Oct.). The first movie was filmed in Owens Valley in 1920, and more than 400 films, 100 television episodes, and countless commercials have been filmed near Lone Pine since then. Weekend festival events include film screenings, tours through the Alabama Hills to notable film locations, guest speakers, and rodeo shows. Special guests to the festival in the past include singer-actor Roy Rogers, actress Peggy Stewart, and stunt performer Diamond Farnsworth.

Food
Bustling ★ **Alabama Hills Café & Bakery** (111 W. Post St., 760/876-4675, www. alabamahillscafe.com, 6am-2pm Mon.-Thurs., 6am-3pm Fri.-Sun., $9-13) is the town's best breakfast joint, with eggs Benedicts, omelets, scrambles, breakfast burritos, pancakes, French toast, warm pastries, and vegetarian options on the menu. Lunch is also popular, with fresh sandwiches packed with colorful veggies and served with a side of fruit. Hand-painted murals inside depict the Alabama Hills in a series of comical cartoon sketches.

Lone Pine is a Wild West-themed town, and most of the restaurants and businesses have adopted the motif, decking out their interiors with wood paneling and wagon wheels. Then there's **Merry Go Round** (212 S. Main St., 760/876-4115, www.merrygornd.com, 11am-2pm Wed.-Fri., 4:30pm-8:30pm daily, $13-23), a one-of-a-kind Szechuan restaurant housed in a circular building with booths arranged within the curved front windows. The restaurant serves tasty, alluring food—barbecued duck, kung pao shrimp, beef,

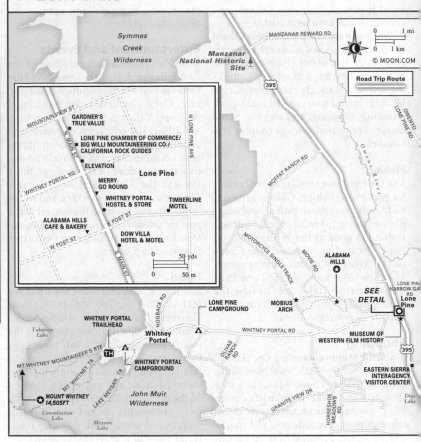

Lone Pine

and chicken, sweet and sour dishes, noodles of all kinds, and a variety of Chinese American appetizers. In a tourist town where many things seem overpriced, Merry Go Round provides the best value. Locals love the lunch special.

Forgot to pick up hiking snacks? **Gus's Fresh Jerky** (580 Hwy. 395, Olancha, 760/764-2822, www.freshjerky.com, 9am-6:30pm daily, $5-20) has you covered. The tender brisket jerky is so good you'll be tempted to gobble it up before you hit the trail. Beef, buffalo, elk, turkey, and venison jerky are available in small and large sizes. The shop also vends stuffed olives, spiced pistachios, local honey, and dried fruit (figs, cantaloupe, spicy mango, banana chips). Though the building's exterior may appear junky and covered in stickers, you don't want to miss tasting the high-quality snacks inside. Gus's is 25 miles (40 km) south of Lone Pine on U.S. 395, about a 25-minute drive.

Accommodations

History buffs and movie enthusiasts will love staying at ★ **Dow Villa Hotel & Motel** (310 S. Main St., 760/876-5521, www.dowvillamotel.com, $70-170). The main building was constructed in 1957 to accommodate movie and TV stars filming nearby, and the hallways of the two-story historic hotel section are lined with film memorabilia from decades past. Historic hotel rooms feature vintage furnishings and beds covered with Pendleton blankets. Some rooms have private baths, while budget rooms utilize shared hallway baths for a lower rate. A more modern wing of motel rooms with ground-level entrances is next door. After a long day of exploring, the outdoor swimming pool is a fantastic place to cool off in the evening, with views of Lone Pine Peak and Mount Whitney.

Timberline Motel (215 E. Post St., 760/876-4555, www.lonepine-motel. com, $110-140) is located off the main drag of noisy U.S. 395. Eight clean and cozy rooms feature comfy beds, fleece blankets, coffeemakers, microwaves, and mini-fridges. Restaurants and businesses are all within walking distance. Rooms are pet-friendly, and Wi-Fi is free.

Whitney Portal Hostel and Hotel (238 S. Main St., 760/876-0030, www. mountwhitneyportal.com, $31-203) has shared rooms with bunk beds, as well as private rooms with double or queen beds. All rooms have attached bathrooms, and in-room amenities include microwaves, coffeemakers, and mini-fridges. Whitney Portal Store (7am-9pm July and Aug., 8am-8pm June and Sept., 9am-6pm May and Oct.) on the 1st floor has souvenirs and clothing. Showers ($7) are available à la carte at the store if you're camping or staying elsewhere.

Camping

Lone Pine Campground (7 mi/11.3 km west of Lone Pine, Whitney Portal Rd., 760/937-6070, www.fs.usda.gov, late Apr.-Dec.) is a beautiful place to spend the night with spectacular views in all directions. From your campsite at 6,000 feet (1,829 m), you'll wake up to watch the sun illuminate the needles of Mount Whitney and the spires of the High Sierra. Campsites are distributed along a loop next to Lone Pine Creek. Some sites have shade, but most are completely exposed—if you're visiting in the summer, bring a tarp or shade device. **Reservations** (877/444-6777, www. recreation.gov, $22) are recommended April-October.

Camping at the **Whitney Portal Campground** (13 mi/20.9 km west of Lone Pine, Whitney Portal Rd., 760/937-6070, www.fs.usda.gov, mid-May.-Oct.) offers an escape from the hot, arid Owens Valley. The campground is located at 8,000 feet (2,438 m) in a narrow granite canyon near the eastern base of Mount Whitney. Nearby hiking trails lead to Meysan Lakes, Lone Pine Lake, and the summit of Mount Whitney. Some of the 44 campsites are available on a walk-in basis, but **reservations** (877/444-6777, www. recreation.gov, $24) are recommended at this beautiful and popular destination.

Located near Horseshoe Meadow, 24 miles (39 km) southwest of Lone Pine, **Cottonwood Lakes** and **Cottonwood Pass Campgrounds** (Horseshoe Meadow Rd., 760/876-6200, www.fs.usda.gov, June-Oct., $6) are great places to spend the night if you plan to do some high-elevation hiking. Set at an elevation of almost 10,000 feet (3,048 m), camping here can help hikers acclimate before hiking the PCT, JMT, or to Mount Whitney. Situated in sandy meadows surrounded by limber pines, Cottonwood Lakes has 13 sites while Cottonwood Pass holds 18 sites. Each site has a fire pit and picnic table; piped water and pit toilets are located throughout the campground. All sites are first-come, first-served with a one-night stay limit.

Getting There
From Lone Pine, drive west on Whitney Portal Road for 3 miles (4.8 km), then turn left to head south on Horseshoe Meadow Road for 19 miles (31 km) to Cottonwood Pass Campgrounds.

Information and Services

Eastern Sierra Interagency Visitor Center (U.S. 395 and Hwy. 136, 760/876-6200, www.fs.usda.gov, 8am-5pm daily May-Oct., 8:30am-4:30pm daily Nov.-Apr.) is a gorgeous facility with information about national forest and wilderness areas in the region. Rangers are on site to issue wilderness permits and answer questions about the parks. A huge, three-dimensional relief map of the Owens Valley, the High Sierra, and Death Valley provides a fascinating perspective of the area, including the Pacific Crest Trail's route along the eastern edge of the Sierra Nevada. An on-site gift shop stocks guidebooks and maps, along with souvenirs. Even the landscaped gardens outside are gorgeous, with views of the surrounding ridgelines.

Stop by the **Lone Pine Chamber of Commerce** (120 S. Main St., 760/876-4444, www.lonepinechamber.org, 8:30am-4:30pm Mon.-Fri.) to pick up driving maps and local activity guides.

Showers are available at **Whitney Portal Hostel and Hotel** (238 S. Main St., 760/876-0030, www.mountwhitneyportal.com, $7), even if you're staying elsewhere, and there's free Wi-Fi at **Lone Star Bistro** (107 N. Main St., 760/876-1111, 7am-5pm Mon.-Thurs., 7am-6pm Fri.-Sun.).

Getting Around

Eastern Sierra Transit (www.estransit.com, $3-59) provides weekday service along U.S. 395, stopping in Lone Pine outside of McDonald's (601 S. Main St.). The *Lone Pine Express* travels between Bishop and Lone Pine. Northbound bus service from Lone Pine travels all the way to Reno on the *Reno-Lone Pine* route, and southbound buses go as far south as Lancaster on the *Lancaster* route. Buses depart 3-4 times per day.

Manzanar

The Manzanar War Relocation Center was one of 10 internment camps in the western United States where Japanese Americans were interred between 1942 and 1945. The **Manzanar National Historic Site** (5001 Hwy. 395, Independence, 760/878-2194, www.nps.gov, 9am-4:30pm daily, free) offers visitors a chance to consider this dark time in American history and learn more about it by exploring the grounds and walking through informative, heartrending exhibits about the internment. While most of the camp's buildings have been demolished, the visitors center is located in what was once the high school auditorium. Just inside the entrance, photos and multimedia displayed in this space tell the stories of the men, women, and children ordered to leave their homes and spend three years in Manzanar, as well as the other military-style camps across the American West. Also portrayed in these articles and photos are popular opinions of some white Americans during World War II, which can be shocking. Further into the museum, walk through life-size models of the camp's barracks and look around to imagine what daily life was like for the American citizens held prisoner here inside a square mile of barbed wire. Eerie and haunting, the property sprawls out under the heat of the sun in the stark, stunning Owens Valley. Explore the site on a 3.2-mile driving tour that visits reconstructed barracks, rock gardens and ponds, and the camp cemetery. Pick up a tour map in the visitors center.

Getting There

Manzanar is 9.5 miles (15.3 km) north of Lone Pine and 48 miles (77 km) south of Bishop on U.S. 395.

Independence

Independence is a blink-and-you'll-miss-it town 15 miles (24 km) north of Lone Pine with two gas stations, a library, a museum, and a couple of restaurants. Smaller and less touristy than Lone Pine, this historic settlement is worthy of a stop. Learn about the history of the Owens Valley, splash in Independence Creek, spend the night at a cozy motel, or get a scrumptious bite to eat. Kearsarge Pass, 13 miles (20.9 km) west of Independence, is a popular entrance and exit point for PCT and John Muir Trail hikers. The trail to the top of the pass offers day hikers a glimpse into the spectacular interior of Kings Canyon National Park.

Getting There

Independence is 16 miles (26 km) north of Lone Pine and 42 miles (68 km) south of Bishop on U.S. 395.

Eastern California Museum

The **Eastern California Museum** (155 N. Grant St., 760/878-0258, www.inyocounty.us/ecmsite, 10am-5pm daily, free) portrays Inyo County and the Eastern Sierra in its entirety, with exhibits about every aspect of the region's history. While the museum may be modest in size and design, it's brimming with artifacts. Popular exhibits include woolly mammoths and fossils; a set of pioneer dentures made from coyote teeth; an extensive collection of beautifully woven Paiute baskets; an in-depth biography of Norman Clyde, famous mountaineer; and a riveting exposition about how the Los Angeles Aqueduct forever changed the landscape and culture of the Owens Valley.

Hiking
★ Kearsarge Pass

Distance: 9 mi/14.5 km round-trip
Duration: 6 hours
Elevation change: 2,600 ft/792 m
Effort: Strenuous
Trailhead: Onion Valley

This spectacular hike to Kearsarge Pass is gratifying from the very first step on the trail, with multiple waterfalls, vibrant wildflowers, and sweeping vistas, all visible from the parking lot. It only gets better as you climb to pristine lakes and craggy peaks. The view from the 11,900-foot pass offers a sneak peek into the John Muir Wilderness and the PCT's route through Kings Canyon National Park.

Your hike begins at 9,200 feet at the end of Onion Valley Road. Depart from the western edge of the parking area on the Kearsarge Pass Trail. The trail climbs 550 feet (168 m) in the first mile, with three different waterfalls in view, tumbling down from the alpine lakes above. At 0.4 mile, stay left at the trail junction to continue west on the Kearsarge Pass Trail. The snow-crusted granite spires above are part of 13,000-foot University Peak.

At 1.3 miles, step to the edge of your first waterfall. Little Pothole Lake, the first of five lakes, comes into view at 1.4 miles, along with more whitewater tumbling in from the lakes above. In June and July, look for columbine, Indian paintbrush, and pink penstemon nestled into the rocks. Past Little Pothole, continue through a boulder field at 2.2 miles and pass sparkling **Gilbert Lake** (4.4 mi/7.1 km rt, 1,300 ft/396 m, moderate) at 10,400 feet (3,170 m). This is a great spot for a picnic; it's also a popular backpacking destination. You can stop here for a 4.4-mile round-trip hike and be completely satisfied with its beauty.

To get a peek into the incredible interior of the Sierra Nevada, continue following the trail west through a whitebark pine forest and past Flower Lake at 2.6 miles. A viewpoint above Heart Lake appears at 3.4 miles. As you approach tree line, at around 11,400 feet (3,475 m), shade becomes sparse. The last mile follows a series of 12 switchbacks up a sunny, rocky slope where you suddenly

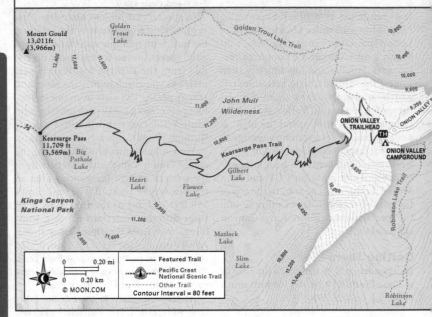

Kearsarge Pass Trail, Independence

find yourself eye level with the massive peaks you gazed up at from the parking lot. Sunscreen is critical on every hike, but you'll especially want to protect yourself from the sun during this exposed stretch.

At 4.5 miles, you reach **Kearsarge Pass** (9 mi/14.5 km rt, 2,600 ft/792 m, strenuous) This is the eastern boundary of Kings Canyon National Park, and the views are stunning. Spy Kearsarge Pinnacles, Kearsarge Lakes, and Bullfrog Lake to the southwest; Mount Bago's red volcanic crater to the west; Mount Rixford to the northwest; and Mount Gould to the north.

While not technically part of the Pacific Crest Trail, Kearsarge Pass is a critical entry and exit point for thruhikers. The trail connects to the PCT a few miles beyond the pass. Backpackers can overnight at Kearsarge Lakes, one mile from the pass. A **wilderness permit** and a **bear canister** are required.

Insider's Tip: The Onion Valley trailhead is a great place to provide **trail magic!** Offer backpackers a ride to or from the town of Independence, where they can rest and resupply.

Getting There

From Independence, follow Onion Valley Road west for 13 miles (20.9 km) to the campground. The trailhead is located at the western edge of the parking area. Allow about 25 minutes for the drive. Onion Valley Road **closes in winter** (November-April). Snow may remain on the road and trails well into June.

Food

★ **Still Life Café** (135 S. Edwards St., 760/878-2555, noon-3:30pm and 5:30pm-9pm Mon.-Sat., noon-9pm Sun., $13-19) is a surprising find in a tiny town, a restaurant serving traditional French cuisine like escargot in buttery herb sauce, tuna niçoise salad with haricot verts, pomme frites, and *croque monsieur* with béchamel sauce. Cheeseburgers are on the menu, too, if you're in the mood for something less French. Nightly specials feature seasonal cuisine influenced by both French and American styles. Ask about the French wines (not listed on the menu), and be prepared for a leisurely evening—this romantic, charming place is no fast-food restaurant.

Owens Valley Growers Coop (149 S. Edwards St., 760/915-0091, www. owensvalleygrowerscooperative.com, 10am-2pm and 5pm-10pm Fri., 10am-2pm and 5pm-9pm Sat.-Sun.) sells locally grown produce, as well as local art from throughout eastern California.

Accommodations and Camping

Named for the second-tallest mountain in the Sierras, ★ **Mount Williamson Motel and Base Camp** (515 S. Edwards St., 760/878-2121, www.mtwilliamsonmotel. com, $85-135) has hiker-friendly cabins in downtown Independence. Beautifully furnished and decorated with art featuring bighorn sheep, the eight cabins are modern and clean, and three of them are pet-friendly. A complimentary breakfast is served during hiking season (June-Sept.).

If you're eager for some great views, but not so keen on a strenuous hike, you're in luck. ★ **Onion Valley Campground** (13 mi/20.9 km west of Independence, Onion Valley Rd., 760/937-6070, www.fs.usda. gov, May-Nov.) is nestled into a pristine, 9,200-foot valley amid tumbling waterfalls and snow-crusted granite peaks. The 29 campsites are small and closely packed—plan to befriend your neighbors—and include picnic tables and fire pits. Vault toilets are available, but there is no drinking water; bring plenty for drinking, washing, and cooking. The Kearsarge Pass Trail, a critical entry/exit

From top to bottom: Kearsarge Pass trail; Gilbert Lake on the way to Kearsarge Pass; Still Life Café.

point for most PCT and JMT hikers, is mere steps from the campground, and there's a large parking lot for day hikers. Shorter trails, including Robinson Lake and Copper Lake, also depart from Onion Valley. Campsites here fill quickly; **reservations** (877/444-6777, www.recreation.gov, $23) are recommended.

Information and Services

Get free internet access at **Inyo County Free Library** (168 N. Edwards St., 760/878-0260, www.inyocounty.us/library, noon-5pm Tues. and Thurs.-Fri., noon-8pm Wed., 10am-1pm Sat.), located on the ground floor of the historic courthouse.

Showers ($5/person) are available at the **Chevron Station** (130 S. Edwards St., 661/824-4250, 6am-10pm Mon.-Fri., 7am-10pm Sat.-Sun.).

Getting Around

Eastern Sierra Transit (www.estransit.com, $3-59) stops in front of the Inyo County Courthouse (168 N. Edwards St.). Independence is served by the *Lone Pine Express, Lancaster Route,* and *Reno-Lone Pine* routes. Northbound bus service from Independence travels all the way to Reno, and southbound buses go as far south as Lancaster. Buses depart six times per day (three times each direction).

Big Pine

Big Pine is another small town along U.S. 395 in the Owens Valley surrounded by majestic 14,000-foot peaks. East-west roads departing from Big Pine provide access into the Sierra Nevada to the west, as well as the White Mountains on the east side of the valley.

Getting There

Big Pine is 26 miles (42 km) north of Independence and 15 miles (24 km) south of Bishop on U.S. 395.

To get to the Glacier Lodge and Big Pine

Creek hiking trails, take Crocker Avenue/Glacier Lodge Road west out of Big Pine for 10.5 miles (16.9 km). Glacier Lodge Road is subject to winter closures between December and March.

Ancient Bristlecone Pine Forest

East of Big Pine near the Nevada border is yet another amazing California wilderness area. Little visited but worth a trip on its own, **Ancient Bristlecone Pine Forest** is a section of the Inyo National Forest in the White Mountains where the world's oldest trees reside. The bristlecone pines can be even older than the coastal redwoods and sequoias. With gnarled and twisted trunks, ancient bristlecone pines are believed to be up to 1,000 years older than any other trees in the world. For many years, a tree named **Methuselah** was thought to be the oldest at the ripe age of about 4,750, but an even older specimen was discovered in 2013. To protect these trees, the Forest Service won't reveal their exact locations, but

don't worry—almost all the trees around here are beautiful to behold.

There are two main groves of trees that you won't want to miss. The **Schulman Grove** is where you'll find the **Ancient Bristlecone Pine Forest Visitor Center** (Hwy. 168, 23 mi/37 km east of Big Pine, 760/872-1220, www.fs.usda.gov/inyo, 10am-5pm Fri.-Sun. mid-May-late June and mid-Oct., 10am-5pm daily late June-mid-Oct., $3 pp or $6/car).

Getting There

In Big Pine at the junction of U.S. 395 and Highway 168, take Highway 168 east for 13 miles (20.9 km) to White Mountain Road. Turn left (north) on White Mountain Road and drive 10 miles (16.1 km) to the visitors center in Schulman Grove. Plan one hour for the long and winding drive.

Hiking
North Fork Trail

Distance: 11.5 mi/18.5 km round-trip

Duration: 7 hours
Elevation change: 2,600 ft/792 m
Effort: Strenuous
Trailhead: Big Pine Creek

Hike along Big Pine Creek into a magnificent lake basin framed by sky-piercing granite Sierra peaks. While the Pacific Crest Trail traverses the valley south of these same peaks, explore the northern lake basin to get a taste of what this section of trail has to offer.

The North Fork Big Pine Creek Trail departs from the northwest corner of the parking area. Stay straight at the trail junction at 0.25 mile, continuing west. At 0.8 mile, get a gorgeous view of the South Fork Valley, framed by Kid Mountain and Mount Alice. The trail bends right at 1 mile, following the north shore of the creek. Switchback up a steep slope around the 2.8-mile mark and enjoy some waterfalls tumbling over boulders through the forest of Jeffrey pines. Arrive at Big Pine Creek Wilderness Ranger Camp at 3.6 miles, set within **Cienaga Mirth** (7.2

Ancient Bristlecone Pine Forest

mi/11.6 km rt, 1,600 ft/488 m, moderate). This lush creekside location offers a wonderful place to picnic, rest, or turn around. Be sure to check out the stone cabin built by Lon Chaney in 1929.

To continue to the lake basin, follow the trail west as it traces the contour of Sky Haven (the peak rising to the north) and Big Pine Creek. Stay left at the trail junction at 5.2 miles as the North Fork Trail bends south. (The trail climbing up the hillside to the north leads to Black Lake.) **First Lake** awaits you at 5.5 miles, then **Second Lake** at 5.7 miles (11.5 mi/18.5 km rt, 2,600 ft/792 m, strenuous). These sparkling lakes are bright turquoise, framed by 13,000-foot Temple Crag. Bring a map and compass to identify all the majestic peaks on the horizon.

Make it a longer hike or a backpacking trip by continuing on the North Fork Big Pine Creek Trail to Third, Fourth, Fifth, Sixth, and Seventh Lakes, or Black Lakes. Spending the night in the John Muir Wilderness requires a **wilderness permit**—the closest place to get one is the **White Mountain Public Lands Information Center** (798 N. Main St., Bishop, 760/873-2500, 8am-5pm daily May-Oct., 8am-4pm daily Nov.-Apr.).

Getting There

The Big Pine Creek trailhead is 10.5 miles east of Big Pine. From U.S. 395, head east on West Crocker Avenue (Glacier Lodge Rd.) and drive 10.5 miles to the end of the road. The parking area is located on the south side of the road next to the restrooms.

Accommodations

Established in 1917, **Glacier Lodge** (100 Glacier Lodge Rd., 760/938-2837, www. glacierlodge395.com, Apr.-Nov.) is an old-fashioned mountain resort with a tiny general store that serves delicious home-style breakfast, lunch, and dinner. Wondering where the lodge is? The namesake lodge burned to the ground in 1988, but plans are in the works for a beautiful new building sometime in the 2020s. In the meantime, enjoy the property, situated at 8,000 feet (2,438 m) in elevation by staying in one of seven unique cabins ($159-299) that have showers and kitchens; towels and linens are provided, and pets ($20/day) are welcome. Campsites ($28-50) in a pine grove near the creek have picnic tables, fire rings, and access to potable water and pit toilets. Reservations are recommended during July and August. Wi-Fi is available ($5/day) near the general store.

Camping

Two campgrounds are located in the Inyo National Forest along Glacier Lodge Road, convenient to hiking trails in Big Pine Creek. **Sage Flat Campground** (Glacier Lodge Rd., 8 mi/12.9 km west of Big Pine, www.fs.usda.gov, May-Oct., $25) has 28 sites shaded by Jeffrey pines and cottonwoods. Peaceful campsites are nestled along Big Pine Creek, just 1.5 miles (2.4 km) east of the Big Pine Creek trailhead. Campsites have picnic tables, fire rings, and bear-proof food storage containers. Pit toilets and potable water are on-site. **Big Pine Creek Campground** (Glacier Lodge Rd., 9.5 mi/15.3 km west of Big Pine, www.fs.usda.gov, May-Oct.) is at the end of the road, just steps from the trailhead. While some walk-up sites are available, **reservations** (877/444-6777, www.recreation.gov, $21) are recommended at this popular campground.

Getting Around

Eastern Sierra Transit (www.estransit. com, $3-59) has three stops in Big Pine: Bartell Road and Newman Street, U.S. 395, and Dewey, Reynolds, and Juniper Roads. Big Pine is serviced by the *Lone Pine Express, Lancaster,* and *Reno-Lone Pine* routes. Northbound bus service from Big Pine travels to Reno, and southbound buses to Lancaster, both routes with stops along U.S. 395. Buses depart six times per day (three times each direction).

Bishop

Bishop is an outdoor enthusiast's paradise in the Owens Valley. Situated between two 14,000-foot mountain ranges, the opportunities to explore the wilderness are endless—from rock climbing and hiking to horseback riding and fishing. To the west, the glorious Sierra Nevada's snowcapped peaks beckon from the highway. To the east lie the equally impressive White Mountains. With a variety of restaurants and comfy accommodations, Bishop offers a convenient base that lures thru-hikers from the high-elevation wilderness into the valley to recharge.

Getting There
Bishop sits at the north end of the Owens Valley. From Lone Pine, it's 58 miles (93 km) north along U.S. 395 and 42 miles (68 km) southeast of Mammoth Lakes.

Scenic Drive
West of Bishop, **Highway 168** climbs 22 miles (35 km) from the valley floor, through the Inyo National Forest, and into the John Muir Wilderness, showcasing what the famous naturalist and conservationist referred to as the "Range of Light."

From downtown Bishop, drive west on Highway 168. Meet the edge of Bishop Creek after about 9 miles (14.5 km) and follow its path into the mountains through a valley, cruising through Dutch Johns Meadow after 12 miles (19.3 km). During the drive, spy the 12,000-foot peaks of Mount Emerson and Table Mountain on the horizon, which are snowcapped most of the year. At 15 miles (24 km), turn south onto South Lake Drive and continue for 7 miles (11.3 km) to the end of the road.

The scenic drive ends with a bang at a roaring waterfall pouring out of South Lake. Head to the Bishop Pass trailhead parking lot and hop out to soak up the views, which are spectacular (the kind of sights you would normally need to lace up your hiking boots and sweat for): South Lake stretches out among towering granite walls with waterfalls plummeting down their sides into the lake below, and quaking aspen sparkle in the wind. This place is so beautiful, you may feel like staying awhile.

One mile north of the lake, **Parcher's Resort** (5000 South Lake Rd., 760/873-4177, www.parchersresort.net, Memorial Day weekend-mid-Oct.) offers boat rentals (starting at $15/hour) at the resort's boat launch near the Bishop Pass trailhead.

Alternatively, rather than taking the South Lake cutoff, continue on Highway 168 through Aspendell, a small resort community in Jawbone Canyon, to Lake Sabrina, where you'll find more jaw-dropping views of the High Sierra: granite peaks, spires, and ridges surrounding a glistening, glacier-fed lake. At Lake Sabrina Boat Landing, find boat rentals, a fishing shop with tackle and bait, and a café with wine, beer, snacks, and homemade pie. The Lake Sabrina Trail departs from the northeast side of the lake, and **Sabrina Campground** (760/873-2400, www.fs.usda.gov, 18 sites, May-Oct., $26) is less than a mile from the lakeshore.

Hiking
★ Long Lake and Bishop Pass
Distance: 11.2 mi/18 km round-trip
Duration: 7-8 hours
Elevation change: 1,000-2,600 ft/305-762 m
Effort: Strenuous
Trailhead: Bishop Pass
If you can only do one hike in the entire High Sierra, make it this one—the Bishop Pass Trail's route through the John Muir Wilderness shows hikers what makes the High Sierra such a magical place. In addition to its astonishing beauty, this trail provides options for hikes and backpacking trips of various levels and lengths. On its way to the pass, the path traces the edges of sparkling alpine lakes with views

Bishop

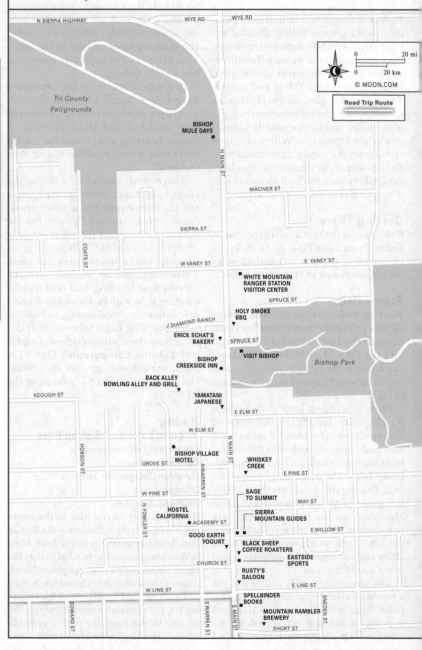

N SIERRA HIGHWAY — WYE RD — WYE RD

Tri County Fairgrounds

BISHOP MULE DAYS

MACIVER ST

SIERRA ST

W YANEY ST — E YANEY ST

WHITE MOUNTAIN RANGER STATION VISITOR CENTER

SPRUCE ST

HOLY SMOKE BBQ

J DIAMOND RANCH

ERICK SCHAT'S BAKERY

SPRUCE ST

VISIT BISHOP

BISHOP CREEKSIDE INN

Bishop Park

BACK ALLEY BOWLING ALLEY AND GRILL

KEOUGH ST

YAMATANI JAPANESE

E ELM ST

W ELM ST

BISHOP VILLAGE MOTEL

GROVE ST

WHISKEY CREEK

W PINE ST

E PINE ST

SAGE TO SUMMIT

MAY ST

HOSTEL CALIFORNIA

ACADEMY ST

SIERRA MOUNTAIN GUIDES

E WILLOW ST

GOOD EARTH YOGURT

BLACK SHEEP COFFEE ROASTERS

CHURCH ST

EASTSIDE SPORTS

RUSTY'S SALOON

E LINE ST

W LINE ST

SPELLBINDER BOOKS

MOUNTAIN RAMBLER BREWERY

SHORT ST

0   20 mi
0   20 km

© MOON.COM

Road Trip Route

HOBSON ST

COATS ST

N MAIN ST

N WARREN ST

N FOWLER ST

S WARREN ST

S MAIN ST

SNEDEN ST

EDWARD ST

of raging waterfalls, sky-piercing peaks, and wildflowers in every color.

Start your hike at 9,800 feet (2,987 m) in elevation and walk south on the **Bishop Pass Trail** out of the parking area. The first 0.5 mile follows the east shore of South Lake through a grove of quaking aspen before ducking into the shade of lodgepole and white pines. The trail switchbacks through a boulder field around mile 1.5, and aptly named Chocolate Peak comes into view within 0.3 mile. Just before reaching Long Lake, the sharp spires of 13,000-foot Cloudripper become visible behind Chocolate Peak. Around the 2-mile mark, the trail arrives at lovely **Long Lake** (4 mi/6.4 km rt, 1,000 ft/305 m, moderate); this is a fantastic place for a picnic. Turn around here for a 4-mile round-trip hike, or continue hiking to see more waterfalls, wildflowers, and colorful, mineral-rich rock formations.

Waterfalls tumble over rocks between Spearhead Lake (at 3.5 miles), Saddle Rock Lake (at 3.7 miles), and **Bishop Lake** (at 4.4 miles; 8.8 mi/14.2 km rt, 2,100 ft/640 m, strenuous). Look for Indian paintbrush and rock cress sprouting from the boulders, and lupine and columbine blooms near the marshy areas. Picture Puzzle Peak and Mount Agassiz, part of the Inconsolable Range, can be seen in their full glory at the 4-mile mark, where you'll cross the tree line. Shade is sparse from this point forward.

Begin the steep ascent to the summit of Bishop Pass on a set of stone stairs expertly constructed into the boulders. The last mile of switchbacks is challenging, even for very fit hikers, as the trail suddenly increases in elevation to almost 12,000 feet (3,658 m). Take your time and reach the high point of the hike at 5.6 miles, where 11,972-foot Bishop Pass is announced on a sign. From the top of **Bishop Pass** (11.2 mi/18 km rt, 2,600 ft/792 m, strenuous), you can gaze south over the Pacific Crest Trail's route through Dusy Basin as you stand atop the divide that separates the John Muir Wilderness from the Owens Valley.

Make it a longer hike or a backpacking trip by continuing on the Bishop Pass Trail for another 6 miles to where it meets the Pacific Crest Trail. Backpacking trips in the John Muir Wilderness require a **wilderness permit**—get one in advance at the **White Mountain Public Lands Information Center** (798 N. Main St., Bishop, 760/873-2500, 8am-5pm daily May-Oct., 8am-4pm daily Nov.-Apr.).

Getting There

From Bishop, take Highway 168 west for 14.7 miles (23.7 km) to South Lake Road. Turn left onto South Lake Road and drive 7.1 miles (11.4 km) south to the Bishop Pass trailhead.

Rock Climbing

Bishop is home to the **Buttermilk Boulders,** an area famous among rock climbers. With thousands of boulders and hundreds of established routes, there's something for climbers of all levels. To learn more about routes and activities in this area, stop by **Sage to Summit** (312 N. Main St., 760/872-1756, www.sagetosummit.com, 9am-9pm daily), where you can rent a climbing guidebook (or buy one, if you're so inclined) and talk to knowledgeable staff.

The Buttermilks are 10 miles (16.1 km) west of Bishop. Head west on Highway 168 for 7 miles (11.3 km), then turn right onto Buttermilk Road. After about 3.5 miles (5.6 km), you'll begin to see numerous roads and trails leading from the main road toward popular rock climbing sites.

Sierra Mountain Guides (213 N. Main St., 760/648-1122, www.sierramtnguides.com, 9am-5pm Mon.-Fri., $150) lead day and multiday trips into the Sierras, focusing on snow, ice, rock, and trails. These expertly led trips are fantastic ways to explore new territory while expanding your skill set in mountaineering, climbing, or back-packing. Gear rental is available—all you need to bring is a sense of adventure.

Entertainment and Events

A proud Bishop establishment since 1947, **Rusty's Saloon** (112 N. Main St., 760/873-9066, 9am-2am daily) is a popular local dive bar with pool tables, dartboards, and a shuffleboard table. Games of pool are free during happy hour (4pm-6pm), and local and domestic beers are on tap. If your visit falls anywhere near a national holiday, expect to see the entire bar decorated accordingly. Live music on Saturday nights varies from local rock bands to karaoke.

Every Memorial Day weekend, thousands of people caravan to Bishop for **Mule Days** (760/872-4263, www.muledays.org, late May), an equestrian festival with riding classes, workshops, and mule shows ($15, with packages available). There's also a fair with vendor booths selling authentic Western gear, as well as tasty food, and live music acts play each evening. On Saturday morning, a parade with mules, wagons, and riders proceeds north through town from South and Main Streets/U.S. 395 to the fairgrounds (be aware that this parade re-routes vehicle traffic along the side streets). RV spaces (from $150) are available for camping at the fairgrounds. Hotels in the Bishop area fill up quickly around Memorial Day weekend—book a few months in advance to guarantee space.

Shopping

Eastside Sports (224 N. Main St., 760/873-7520, www.eastsidesports.com, 9am-6pm Sun.-Thurs., 9am-8pm Fri.-Sat.) is a spacious and well-stocked gear shop with clothing, shoes, hats, accessories, maps, guidebooks, and gear for hikers, climbers, mountaineers, and boaters. The shop rents gear as well, and the staff's expertise in pack- and shoe-fitting

Bishop Pass Trail

ensures you'll be guided toward the right size and fit for your adventure.

Geared toward runners, hikers, and climbers, **Sage to Summit** (312 N. Main St., 760/872-1756, www.sagetosummit. com, 9am-9pm daily) is an outdoor retailer with a comprehensive selection of clothing, equipment, and accessories. Bear canisters, climbing equipment, and ski equipment are available for rent. The store's **indoor climbing gym** ($15/day) is a great place to practice and learn new skills before heading out into the Owens Valley boulders.

Need something to read aloud around the campfire? **Spellbinder Books** (124 S. Main St., 760/873-4511, www. spellbinderbookstore.com, 9am-5:30pm Mon.-Fri., 10am-5pm Sat., 10am-2pm Sun.) has old-fashioned bookstore charm with handmade signs and a carefully curated collection of books to satisfy your literary cravings. Local area guidebooks are plentiful, as are works of fiction, poetry, non-fiction, and photo essays. The staff is passionate and knowledgeable about the store's inventory as well as the Bishop area.

Food

★ **Erick Schat's Bakkery** (763 N. Main St., 760/873-7156, www.schatsbakery. com, 6am-6pm Sat.-Thurs., 6am-7pm Fri., $4-12) is a haven for hungry hikers and travelers in need of a treat. The bakeshop is a famous Bishop destination. The enormous, European-style space features a lovely outdoor patio and two rooms brimming with baked goods: one dedicated to hundreds of bread loaves, with creative combinations of nuts, cheeses, grains, fruits, and spices, and another stacked with cookies, cakes, pastries, doughnuts, and more. Deli sandwiches are crafted to order with the bakery's own fresh bread and your choice of meats, veggies, and condiments. Daily seasonal soups are popular, too.

At **Holy Smoke BBQ** (772 N. Main St., 760/872-4227, www. holysmoketexasstylebbq.com, 11am-9pm Wed.-Mon., $11-18), tender, juicy meat is served with thick and sweet Texas-style barbecue sauce and accompanied with "sidekicks" like smokehouse beans, outlaw coleslaw, and cornbread, of course. This casual, counter-service joint serves food on red cafeteria trays. Choose from pulled pork, tri-tip beef, ribs, hickory-smoked chicken, brisket, and sausages. If you're hankerin' for something sweet, try the banana pudding—it's heavenly.

Modern and refined **Yamatani Japanese** (635 N. Main St., 760/872-4801, www.yamatanibishop.com, 5pm-9:30pm Sun.-Thurs. 4:30pm-10pm Fri.-Sat., $9-20) serves fresh, colorful sushi and teriyaki. Sushi rolls are divided into four categories to help undecided diners navigate their choices: standard, cooked, signature, and "outside the box." Creative appetizers and vegetarian options round out the menu. Dine inside at a peaceful table or in the lovely bamboo garden out front.

Back Alley Bowl and Grill (649 N. Main St., 760/873-5777, www.thebackalleybowlandgrill.com, 4pm-10pm Mon., 11am-10pm Tues.-Sat., 11am-9:30pm Sun., $8-20) serves what you'd expect at a bowling alley—nachos, chicken wings, hot dogs—but the cuisine is surprisingly upscale and includes gourmet burgers, steaks, and seafood. (This is probably the only place in the Owens Valley where you can order lobster!) There's no public bowling on league night (Wed.), but the restaurant is worth a visit.

The gourmet sandwiches at **Mahogany Smoked Meats** (2345 N. Sierra Hwy., 760/873-5311, www.smokedmeats.com, 7am-6pm daily, $8-10) are house-made with meat, cheese, and fresh veggies on toasted bread. The shop also sells smoked meats, fish, cheese, bacon, sausages, and jerky, plus pickles, mustards, and jams. Hearty breakfast burritos are served before 10am. This is a great place to stock up on gourmet picnic supplies and gifts.

★ **Black Sheep Coffee Roasters** (232 N. Main St., 760/872-4142, www.blacksheepcoffeeroasters.com, 6:30am-6pm Mon.-Thurs., 6:30am-7pm Fri.-Sat., 7am-6pm Sun., $3-10) is a charming little coffee shop squeezed into a narrow storefront along Bishop's downtown strip. The seating is plentiful for such a small space, but there's also a lovely garden out back. Espresso drinks, tea lattes, and smoothies are popular. Breakfast options include quiches, bagels, and granola.

One part wine bar, one part frozen yogurt parlor, and one part organic café, **Good Earth Yogurt** (251 N. Main St., 760/872-2020, www.goodearthyogurt.com, 11am-9pm Sun.-Thurs., 11am-10pm Fri.-Sat., $5-24) can supply whatever you want. The elegant white interior is inviting and refreshing. Choose from front tables or a cozy seating area in the back, or sit at the bar to enjoy a glass of wine,

From top to bottom: Long Lake on Bishop Pass; Back Alley Bowl and Grill; Bishop Creekside Inn.

a grilled panini, a charcuterie plate, or a cup of organic frozen yogurt.

Mountain Rambler Brewery (186 S. Main St., 760/258-1348, www.mountainramblerbrewery.com, 11:30am-10:30pm Sun.-Thurs., 11:30am-11:30pm Fri.-Sat., $9-16) is one of only two microbreweries in the Owens Valley (the other is in Indian Wells, an hour south of Lone Pine). The diverse house brews include pale ales, porters, stouts, hefeweizen, IPAs, and lagers. The kitchen serves burgers, salads, pizzas, fries, nachos, and a handful of gourmet items like wild Alaskan king salmon, lamb empanadas, and Thai meatballs.

Whiskey Creek (524 N. Main St., 760/873-7777, www.whiskeycrk.com, 11am-9pm Sun.-Thurs., 11am-10pm Fri.-Sat., $12-31) has been in business in Bishop since 1924, and although it's been remodeled, its historical charm is its primary appeal. While the quiet, genteel dining room is an option, the full menu is available in the bar, where you can get a better sense of the restaurant's heritage. A large, wooden wraparound bar is finished with brass details and lined with leather stools. Something about this place makes you want to order a cognac to sip on while you await your meal. The food menu includes hearty American classics like steaks, pastas, burgers, and grilled seafood.

Accommodations
Bishop
Bishop Creekside Inn (725 N. Main St., 760/872-3044, www.bishopcreeksideinn.com, $140-190) is a lovely hotel built along the edge of Bishop Creek. The log cabin-style lobby is a luxurious place to relax, as are the waterfront patios. Rooms are lavish and elegant, with dark woods, leather detailing, and plush furnishings; many overlook the creek. The hotel is centrally located, within steps of Bishop's best restaurants, the city park, and the historic downtown area.

Rooms and suites at **Bishop Village Motel** (286 W. Elm St., 888/688-5546, www.bishopvillagemotel.com, $80-120) are nothing fancy, but they're quiet and peaceful, set on a residential street away from busy U.S. 395. The outdoor pool is a fantastic place to relax and beat the summer heat.

★ **Hostel California** (213 Academy Ave., 760/399-6316, www.thehostelcalifornia.com, $60-100) is a quirky, colorful hostel popular with hikers, backpackers, and climbers. Dorm beds and private rooms are available, and there are communal hangout areas. Relax on the huge couch in the living room, or take advantage of the piano, extensive movie collection, and board games. Outside areas have shaded picnic tables. A large, well-stocked kitchen is available for use. Wi-Fi is free throughout the property. Borrow one of the hostel's bikes to zip around town.

Bishop Pass
There are two resorts on South Lake Road, near the Bishop Pass trailhead, South Lake, and Lake Sabrina. **Bishop Creek Lodge** (2100 South Lake Rd., 760/873-4484, www.bishopcreekresort.com Apr.-Oct.) is a resort with cabins, a café, and a small general store. Pet-friendly cabins sleep 2-8 guests and include bathrooms, kitchens, and linens. Outside each cabin, enjoy the mountain scenery at your picnic table, barbecue, and campfire ring. **Parchers Resort** (5001 South Lake Rd., 760/873-4177, www.parchersresort.net, mid-May-late Oct., $130-295) offers accommodations in cozy cabins with kitchens, linens, and housekeeping services.

Camping
Several campgrounds are in the Inyo National Forest near Bishop. Popular **Bishop Park** (Hwy. 168, 12 mi/19.3 km west of Bishop, 760/873-2400, www.fs.usda.gov, 21 sites, first-come, first-served, Apr.-Oct., $26) is right on the banks of Bishop Creek, with flush toilets

and space for RVs. Another nice option is **Intake 2** (Hwy. 168, 16 mi/26 km west of Bishop, 8 sites, first-come, first-served, Apr.-Oct., $26), located near Intake Two Lake. Though it's cold, the lake does offer anglers the chance to catch trout. **Sabrina Campground** (Hwy. 168, 18 mi/29 km west of Bishop, 18 sites, first-come, first-served, late May-Sept., $26) is at 9,300 feet (2,835 m) elevation, making it low on oxygen but high on views. Lake Sabrina is nearby, and it's a good trout-fishing destination.

Note that showers are not available at any of the national forest campgrounds, but you can buy a shower at **Bishop Creek Lodge** (2100 South Lake Rd., 760/873-4484, www.bishopcreekresort.com, Apr.-Oct., $6 for a 10-minute token, $1 for soap and towel) and **Parchers Resort** (5001 South Lake Rd., 760/873-4177, www.parchersresort.net, mid-May-late Oct., $6 for a 10-minute shower, $1 each for soap and towel).

A nice place to stay near Bishop is **Keough's Hot Springs** (800 Keough Hot Springs Rd., 760/872-4670, www.keoughshotsprings.com, swim pass $10-75 adults, $7-55 children). The swimming pool is heated by natural hot springs, so it's open year-round, as is the campground and other facilities. Lodging options include "dry" tent or RV sites ($28), campsites with water and electricity ($33), four tent cabins ($110-125), and a mobile home ($140).

To get to Keough's, travel 6 miles (9.7 km) south of Bishop on U.S. 395. When you see the big blue sign on your left, turn right. You'll be there in less than 10 minutes.

Information and Services

Bishop Visitor Center (690 N. Main St., 760/873-8405, www.bishopvisitor.com, 10am-5pm Mon.-Fri., 10am-4pm Sat.) is your source for information about Bishop's businesses: restaurants, accommodations, shops, and outfitters/guides.

Rangers at the **White Mountain Ranger Station Visitor Center** (798 N. Main St., 760/873-2500, www.fs.usda.gov, 8am-5pm daily) are knowledgeable about current road, trail, and weather conditions. Get your wilderness permit here, along with a bear canister rental if you need one. Maps and guidebooks are available in the bookstore.

Showers are available at **Wash Tub Coin-Op Laundry** (326 N. Warren St., 760/873-6627, 7am-6pm, $5 including soap and towel, no time limit).

Getting Around

Eastern Sierra Transit Authority (760/872-1901, www.estransit.com) offers bus service to and from Bishop. Routes travel U.S. 395, providing service to/from Bishop on the *Reno-Lone Pine, Lancaster, Mammoth Express,* and *Lone Pine Express* routes. The *Bishop Creek Shuttle* ($5, two departures daily mid-June-Labor Day) runs east-west along Highway 168 between Bishop, South Lake, and Lake Sabrina.

⬥ Detour: Sequoia and Kings Canyon National Parks

Sequoia and Kings Canyon National Parks offer some of the tallest and oldest trees on earth, myriad hiking trails, thriving wildlife, and smaller crowds than their more famous neighbor to the north.

Sequoia and Kings Canyon National Parks lie on the western side of the Sierras, parallel to U.S. 395. Roads only enter these parks from the west side, and no road connects to the parks from the east. To loop a visit to these parks into your road trip, you have two options: backpack into the parks via several remote wilderness trails accessible from U.S. 395 or add 5-6 hours to your drive, detouring from the east to the west.

Getting There and Around

Reaching the entrances to Sequoia and Kings Canyon will require either backtracking on U.S. 395 to Tehachapi or continuing north on U.S. 395 and crossing Yosemite National Park. Either route will add at least another day of driving and bypasses much of the glorious Eastern Sierra scenery.

From the West

For road-trippers who wish to access these parks from the west, the most direct route is to head north from Tehachapi and save the route up U.S. 395 for another trip. To do this, take Highway 58 west from Tehachapi; you'll reach Bakersfield in about 40 miles (64 km). From Bakersfield, follow Highway 99 north for 70 miles (113 km) to Visalia and Highway 198. Head east on Highway 198 for 30 miles (48 km) to reach the **Ash Mountain** entrance to **Sequoia National Park.**

From the East

Those who want it all—the Eastern Sierras and the western national parks—can backtrack 188 miles (305 km) south to Tehachapi and continue 140 miles (225 km) northwest from there to the **Ash Mountain** entrance of **Sequoia National Park.**

From Bishop, the Tioga Pass entrance to Yosemite National Park is 76 miles (122 km) north on U.S. 395. When open, Tioga Pass Road (Highway 120) leads 45 miles (72 km) west across the High Sierra to connect with Big Oak Flat Road north of Yosemite Valley. From there, travelers must navigate through Yosemite Valley then south through the park along Highway 41. Highway 41 exits the park near Wawona and continues 67 miles (108 km) south to Fresno. From Fresno, follow Highway 180 east to reach the **Big Stump** entrance of **Kings Canyon National Park.**

From top to bottom: giant sequoias; view from Moro Rock; Kings Canyon National Park.

The drive from Yosemite to this entrance is 150 miles (242 km) and can take 3.5-5 hours in good weather. Note that roads along this route may close in winter. If following this route, two park entrance fees will apply.

Entering the Park

Two entrances are most convenient for entering **Sequoia and Kings Canyon National Park** (559/565-3341, www.nps. gov/seki, 7-day vehicle pass $30, foot or bicycle $15) from the north or south.

The **Ash Mountain entrance** (Highway 198) enters Sequoia National Park from the south. Inside the park, Highway 198 becomes Generals Highway. Driving north, you'll pass the Foothills Visitor Center, Giant Forest Museum, the General Sherman Tree, and the Lodgepole Visitor Center and Village.

The main portal to the north is the **Big Stump entrance** (Highway 180), which enters Kings Canyon National Park. Past the entrance station, turn left to follow Highway 180 into the park. For Kings Canyon National Park, continue straight; you'll be at Grant Grove Village in about 3.5 miles (5.6 km). To reach Sequoia National Park, turn right onto Generals Highway and head south toward Lodgepole Visitor Center and Village.

Visitors Centers

The **Foothills Visitor Center** (47050 Generals Hwy., Three Rivers, 559/565-4212, 8am-4:30pm daily) is 1 mile (1.6 km) north of the Ash Mountain entrance and also serves as the park headquarters. It includes a bookstore and exhibits about the nearby area, and ranger talks and walks begin here. You can also buy Crystal Cave tickets (ticket sales 8am daily May-late Oct.) or get a wilderness permit (late May-late Sept., $15 for up to 15 people). Check the office behind the visitors center in summer, or self-register for a permit outside the office the rest of the year for free.

The **Kings Canyon Visitor Center** (83918 Hwy. 180 E., 559/565-4307, 8am-5pm daily May-Oct., 9am-4pm daily Nov.-May) is near Grant Grove, 3 miles (4.8 km) from Highway 180. This is the place to get maps and information about camping and hiking, ranger talks, and other park activities; check weather conditions and road closures for the whole park; explore the well-designed exhibits about park ecology and history; and chat with park rangers.

When to Go

Summer is high season in the parks. From May to September, a quota for backpacking permits is in effect, and campgrounds fill most summer weekends. Several of the park's roads close in **winter** (Nov.-May). Generals Highway usually remains open; however, heavy snows can rapidly change conditions and make it difficult to predict when major roads will be plowed. Check www.nps. gov/seki or call 559/565-3341 for current road conditions.

Permits and Regulations

Permits ($15) are required for overnight stays in the backcountry. There's a quota for permits during high season (May-Sept.). You can reserve a permit up to two weeks in advance by downloading the application form online (www.nps. gov/seki) and sending it in with payment, or you can stand in line at 1pm the day before your hike for a first-come, first-served permit. When the quota season ends in late September, permits are free and you can self-register at the permit station. Bear canisters are required; rent one from the ranger station if you don't have your own.

Scenic Drives
Generals Highway

Generals Highway is the main road running north-south through the two parks; it connects Highway 180 (Kings Canyon National Park) in the north to Highway

Backpacking the Rae Lakes Loop

For moderate backpackers, the premier trip is the **Rae Lakes Loop** in Kings Canyon. This 46-mile (74-km) loop trail gains more than 5,000 feet (1,524 m) of elevation and takes about 10 days to complete. The shady trail is beautiful, with terrain that varies from flat and pleasant to rolling to some mettle-testing rock scrambling and stream crossing.

Most hikers start the loop from either the Bubbs Creek or Woods Creek trailheads in Kings Canyon, but it's also possible to enter the trail from the east via Kearsarge Pass (Inyo National Forest permit required). The PCT joins the Rae Lakes Loop for about 12 miles, from the Bubbs Creek junction to the Woods Creek suspension bridge. Several campsites dot the well-marked and popular trail along this scenic stretch.

A backcountry **permit** ($15) is required and is available at the permit station at Roads End. A permit quota is in effect May-September. Download an application online (www.nps.gov/seki) and submit it with payment. When the quota season ends in late September, permits are first-come, first-served. Self-register at the permit station. A bear canister is required.

198 (Sequoia National Park) in the south. Cruise its winding curves for a lovely trip through Sequoia National Park, with numerous stops to stretch your legs and visit unique sights.

From the Ash Mountain entrance, stop at the Foothills Visitor Center to inquire about tickets to **Crystal Cave.** The immense underground cave is only accessible via a guided tour. Continue north, stopping at the **Giant Forest** to see the 275-foot-tall **General Sherman Tree.** Nearby **Moro Rock** offers a view of the national park from an impressive granite dome. It's accessible by a short but steep 0.3-mile hike that ascends 300 vertical feet. At the **Lodgepole** area, you'll find supplies and a campground.

Generals Highway winds its way north to the Grant Grove area and the entryway into Kings Canyon.

Kings Canyon Scenic Byway

In **Grant Grove,** a short walk leads to the **General Grant Tree,** an enormous giant sequoia. Northeast of Grant Grove, Highway 180 becomes the **Kings Canyon Scenic Byway,** and it offers tremendous views of this vast canyon. The drive starts at 6,600 feet (2,012 m) at Grant Grove, weaving down as far as 3,000 feet (914 m) around Convict Flat before climbing back

up to 5,000 feet (1,524 m) before its terminus at **Road's End.** Cedar Grove Village is located within Kings Canyon and offers camping, lodging, and the only services in this area.

In mid- to late October, the eastern part of Highway 180 closes past the junction of Highway 180 with Generals Highway.

Food

The Lodgepole area has a **market** (9am-6pm daily late Mar.-early May, 8am-9pm daily early May-late Oct.) and **deli** (9am-6pm daily early Mar.-early May, 8am-8pm daily early May-late Oct.). The closest thing to a restaurant is the **Peaks Restaurant** (64740 Wuksachi Way, 559/625-7700, www.visitsequoia.com, 7:30am-10am, 11am-2:30pm, and 5pm-9pm daily, $13-34) in Wuksachi Lodge. Reservations are advised.

Grant Grove Restaurant (Hwy. 180 at Generals Hwy., 559/335-5500, 7am-10am, 11:30am-3:30pm, and 5pm-8pm daily, $13-25) serves three meals daily, while the **Grant Grove Market** (86728 Hwy. 180, 7am-9pm daily early May-late Oct., 9am-6pm late Oct.-early May) sells a few staples.

Accommodations and Camping

Most lodging and campgrounds in Sequoia National Park are centered in the Lodgepole area or along Generals Highway. Lodgepole is located on Generals Highway 22 miles (35 km) north of the Ash Mountain entrance. Stay overnight at the **Wuksachi Lodge** (64740 Wuksachi Way, Sequoia National Park, 866/807-3598, www.visitsequoia.com, $114-279) or plan to camp at **Lodgepole** (214 sites, year-round, reservations summer only 877/444-6777, www.recreation.gov, May-Sept., $22) or **Dorst Creek** (222 sites, reservations 877/444-6777, www.recreation.gov, late June-Labor Day, $22-70) campgrounds.

The Grant Grove area of Kings Canyon National Park is located near the Big Stump entrance, accessed via Highway 180. It is home to three campgrounds, lodging, and a visitors center. Your overnight options include a range of choices at **Grant Grove Cabins** (877/436-9615 or 866/807-3598, www.visitsequoia.com, $61-140) and the **John Muir Lodge** (86728 Hwy. 180, 866/807-3598, www.visitsequoia.com, $95-212). Campgrounds in the area include **Azalea** (110 sites, year-round, summer $18), **Sunset** (159 sites, summer only, $22-40), and **Crystal Springs** (49 sites, summer only, $18-40).

For those planning to backpack the Rae Lakes Loop, there are campsites in the Cedar Grove area of Kings Canyon.

Mammoth Lakes

The town of Mammoth Lakes is located east of Yosemite, about 28 miles (45 km) south of Tioga Pass. The gorgeous mountain scenery, along with multiple alpine lakes, natural hot springs, and dependable snowfall, has established Mammoth Lakes as a prime tourist destination. Outdoor recreation—especially skiing—is the town's main reason for existence. In summer, the area's convenient access to the John Muir Wilderness lures hikers and backpackers from all over the world. Indeed, for hikers, Mammoth Lakes is one of the best places to experience the Sierra Nevada. Multiple trailheads offer access to the PCT, and the town is a popular destination for resupplies.

In winter, the roads are subject to the whims of weather, though they rarely close. It's best to carry chains and to check weather reports before starting out.

Getting There

Car

U.S. 395 is the main access road to the Mammoth Lakes area. To get to the town of Mammoth Lakes from U.S. 395, turn onto Highway 203, which will take you right into town. Allow about 45 minutes to drive there from Bishop.

Expect a seven-hour drive from San Francisco if the traffic and weather cooperate. If you fly into Reno, the drive out to Mammoth takes about 3.5 hours.

In the winter, be aware that it snows at Mammoth Lakes more than it does in almost any other place in California. Carry chains! Even if the weather is predicted to be clear for your visit, having chains can prevent a world of hurt and the need to turn back in a sudden storm. The longer you plan to stay, the more you should stock your car with items such as ice scrapers, blankets, water, food, and a full tank of gas whenever possible. For the latest traffic information, including chain control areas and weather conditions, call Caltrans (800/427-7623).

Air

The nearest airport is the **Mammoth Yosemite Airport** (MMH, 1200 Airport Rd., 760/934-3813, www.ci.mammoth-lakes.ca.us). Alaska Airlines serves the airport year-round; United Express also flies December 15-April 30. In winter, nonstop flights run to Mammoth from Los Angeles, San Francisco, Denver, Las Vegas, and San Diego.

For a major transportation hub, fly to

Mammoth Lakes

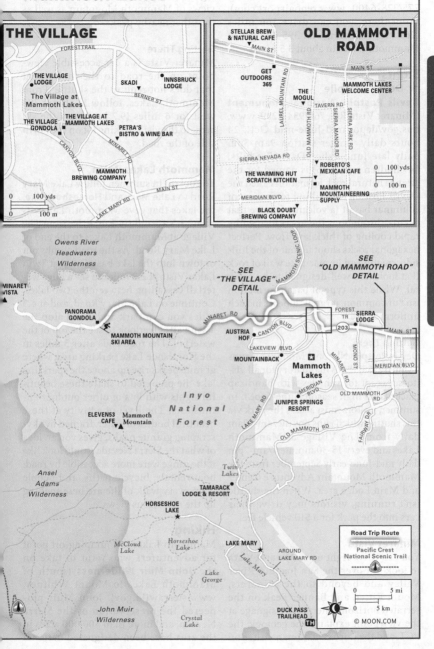

THE VILLAGE

FOREST TRAIL

THE VILLAGE LODGE
INNSBRUCK LODGE
SKADI
The Village at Mammoth Lakes
BERNER ST
THE VILLAGE GONDOLA
THE VILLAGE AT MAMMOTH LAKES
PETRA'S BISTRO & WINE BAR
CANYON BLVD
MINARET RD
MAMMOTH BREWING COMPANY
LAKE MARY RD
MAIN ST

0   100 yds
0   100 m

OLD MAMMOTH ROAD

STELLAR BREW & NATURAL CAFE
MAIN ST
MAIN ST
GET OUTDOORS 365
THE MOGUL
MAMMOTH LAKES WELCOME CENTER
TAVERN RD
LAUREL MOUNTAIN RD
SIERRA MANOR RD
SIERRA PARK RD
OLD MAMMOTH RD
SIERRA NEVADA RD
ROBERTO'S MEXICAN CAFE
THE WARMING HUT SCRATCH KITCHEN
MAMMOTH MOUNTAINEERING SUPPLY
MERIDIAN BLVD
BLACK DOUBT BREWING COMPANY

0   100 yds
0   100 m

Owens River Headwaters Wilderness

MINARET VISTA

SEE "THE VILLAGE" DETAIL

MAMMOTH SCENIC LOOP

SEE "OLD MAMMOTH ROAD" DETAIL

PANORAMA GONDOLA
MAMMOTH MOUNTAIN SKI AREA

MINARET RD
FOREST TR
SIERRA LODGE
203
AUSTRIA HOF
CANYON BLVD
LAKEVIEW BLVD
MOUNTAINBACK
MONO ST
MAIN ST
MERIDIAN BLVD

★ Mammoth Lakes

MINARET RD

Inyo National Forest

ELEVEN53 CAFE Mammoth Mountain

JUNIPER SPRINGS RESORT
MERIDIAN BLVD
OLD MAMMOTH RD
LAKE MARY RD
OLD MAMMOTH RD
FAIRWAY DR

Ansel Adams Wilderness

Twin Lakes

TAMARACK LODGE & RESORT
HORSESHOE LAKE ★

McCloud Lake
Horseshoe Lake
LAKE MARY
AROUND LAKE MARY RD
Lake Mary

Lake George

John Muir Wilderness

Crystal Lake

DUCK PASS TRAILHEAD

Road Trip Route

Pacific Crest National Scenic Trail

0   5 mi
0   5 km

© MOON.COM

the **Reno-Tahoe International Airport** (RNO, 2001 E. Plumb Ln., Reno, NV, 775/328-6400, www.renoairport.com). From there, you can drive 166 miles (265 km) south on U.S. 395 and get to Mammoth Lakes in about 3.5 hours.

Sights
★ Devils Postpile

Devils Postpile National Monument (Minaret Vista Rd., 760/934-2289, www.nps.gov/depo, mid-June-mid-Oct., 24 hours daily, ranger station 9am-5pm daily late June-Labor Day, $7 adults, $4 children ages 3-15) is named for the strange natural rock formation called the Devils Postpile, a striking formation of columnar basalt (a volcanic feature that occurs throughout the area) formed by rapid cooling of thick lava flow. Perfect hexagonal rocks shoot up out of the hillside, creating an immaculate wall of rock that looks too well-designed to be natural. While this type of basalt formation isn't uncommon, it rarely appears in such uniform shape.

Getting There

Devils Postpile National Monument runs a **shuttle** ($8) that's mandatory for all visitors, except for vehicles with handicap placards, in high season (June-Sept.). In summer, visitors must access the park via this shuttle, which runs hourly 7am-10am daily from The Village at Mammoth Lakes and every 15-30 minutes 7am-7pm daily mid-June-early September from the Mammoth Mountain Adventure Center and Main Lodge area. When the shuttle isn't running, visitors may drive their cars into the park for a $10 vehicle fee.

Minaret Vista

You can drive right up to **Minaret Vista** to look out over the San Joaquin River Valley and beyond to the Minarets, Mount Ritter, and Banner Peak on the serrated horizon. Interpretive signage at the viewpoint explains the geology, the PCT, and the impact of human visitation on the delicate Sierra Nevada habitat. It's a great place to have a picnic and enjoy views of Mammoth Mountain as well as the other nearby peaks.

Getting There

Minaret Vista is a car-accessible viewpoint on the road to the monument that does not require the shuttle. From Mammoth Lakes, follow Highway 203 west for 6 miles (9.7 km), past the ski area, to the vista parking lot on the north side of the road.

Mammoth Lakes Basin

To cool off in summer, follow Lake Mary Road to **Lake Mary** and **Horseshoe Lake**, the lakes that gave Mammoth Lakes its name. It's a 5-mile (8-km) drive from The Village at Mammoth Lakes to the end of Lake Mary Road. As the road climbs out of town into the lake basin, stop at Twin Lakes Vista at 2.2 miles to see a huge waterfall cascading between the two lakes. Continue on Lake Mary Road, and at 4.3 miles you can park and stand atop the Twin Falls Overlook to see the top of the waterfall. The road ends after 5 miles in the Horseshoe Lake parking area, where granite peaks rise up above the sparkling lake. Be prepared to share these beautiful sights with lots of other outdoor enthusiasts. The level of activity at these beautiful bodies of water, framed by skyscraping granite peaks, gives you an idea of what the Sierra Nevada would look like if the range were more accessible by road: boat rentals, bicycle paths, and people from every walk of life are here soaking up the marvelous views.

Hiking

Mammoth Lakes is a jumping-off point for adventurers who want to take on the **John Muir Wilderness** (south of Mammoth Lakes to Mount Whitney, www.sierrawild.gov). John Muir pioneered the preservation of the Sierra Nevada, and more than 500,000 acres in the area have been designated national wilderness areas in his honor. Day hikers are welcome, and there's plenty to see. Check with the Inyo and Sierra National Forests (www.fs.usda.gov) for trail maps of the area.

The main attractions in the John Muir Wilderness are the **John Muir Trail** (JMT, 211 miles Yosemite-Mount Whitney, www.johnmuirtrail.org) and the **Pacific Crest National Scenic Trail** (PCT, 2,650 miles, www.pcta.org), both among the holiest of grails for backpacking enthusiasts from around the world.

If you're planning an overnight camping trip in the John Muir or Ansel Adams Wilderness areas of the Sierra National Forest, you must first obtain a **wilderness permit.** You can apply for these up to one year in advance by downloading an application (www.fs.usda.gov/sierra) or by calling 559/297-0706. If you reserve in advance, there is a charge of $5 per person for the permit. On the other hand, if you're willing to be flexible, you can just show up at a ranger station no more than 24 hours before your trip begins and apply in person. There is no charge for these "walk-up" permits, though their availability is not guaranteed.

If you're planning an overnight in the Inyo National Forest, you can apply for your permit in person at the **Mammoth Lakes Welcome Center** (Hwy. 203, 3 mi/4.8 km west of U.S. 395, 760/924-5500, www.visitmammoth.com, 8am-5pm daily), at the entrance to Mammoth Lakes, or online (www.fs.usda.gov/inyo).

Minaret Falls 🅿️

Distance: 2.6 mi/4.2 km round-trip
Duration: 1.5-2 hours
Elevation change: 200 ft/61 m
Effort: Easy
Trailhead: Devils Postpile

Minaret Creek tumbles thousands of feet from its headwaters at Minaret Lake to the San Joaquin River, cascading over

From top to bottom: Devils Postpile; Minaret Vista; Rainbow Falls.

smooth granite near the Pacific Crest Trail. Get up close and personal with the falls on this easy hike along the PCT.

Starting at the Devils Postpile trailhead, walk south for 0.2 mile, then turn right to walk west and cross the pedestrian bridge over the Middle Fork of the San Joaquin. On the other side of the bridge, follow the northbound PCT as it makes a sharp right and heads north along the riverbank. Stay right at the trail junction at 0.7 mile to continue on the PCT. Arrive at the waterfall at 1.3 miles. The best viewpoints aren't on the main trail itself, and many long-distance hikers walk right by without even stopping to check them out; step off the trail toward the towering rock wall, following the sound of the falls, to get the best views of the creek as it spills over the granite boulders. Turn around to head back to your starting point, or make it a longer hike by continuing north on the PCT for another 1.3 miles to Soda Springs Campground or 4.2 more miles to Agnew Meadows. The shuttle stops at both of these places, so you can get a ride back to your car.

Getting There

Reaching this trailhead requires taking the **Reds Meadow shuttle** (7:15am-7pm daily June-Sept., $8 adults, $4 children ages 3-15) into the Devils Postpile National Monument. Catch the bus at **Mammoth Mountain Adventure Center** (10001 Minaret Rd., 800/626-6684).

Rainbow Falls

Distance: 3.6-5 mi/5.8-8 km round-trip
Duration: 2-3 hours
Elevation change: 500 ft/152 m
Effort: Easy
Trailhead: Devils Postpile

The Middle Fork of the San Joaquin River tumbles more than 100 feet at Rainbow Falls. You can see this massive sight by walking an easy 2 miles downhill (keeping in mind that you'll have to walk back uphill afterward). The trail

follows the bank of the San Joaquin River through sparse forests and into the exposed remains of the 1992 Rainbow Fire. Although some scrub and small trees have flourished since the fire, the lack of tall trees enables a great sightline to the spiky Minarets and the hulking mound of Mammoth Mountain.

From the shuttle drop-off in the parking lot, walk south along the Devils Postpile Trail, stopping in 0.5 mile to check out Devils Postpile, a fascinating formation of columnar basalt. Continuing south, you'll encounter trail crossings at 0.6, 0.8, and 1.4 miles. These junctions are well signed; at all points, continue south toward Rainbow Falls. Turn right at 2.5 miles to head west down the hill to the viewpoint. After 0.1 mile you'll see and hear the majestic waterfall tumbling down into a pool between granite cliffs. Continue down the hill to the viewing platform on the north side of the trail. The single-drop cascade is as wide as the river itself, forming a thick veil as

it falls. Afternoon light creates a rainbow in the mist above the plunge pool.

Return the way you came for a 5-mile round-trip hike, or shorten the hike to 3.6 miles by catching the shuttle at Reds Meadow instead. To take advantage of this shortcut, veer right at 2.9 miles and follow the trail signs toward Reds Meadow and the shuttle stop. This climb is a bit steeper, but it shaves off 1.4 miles.

Getting There

Reaching this trailhead requires taking the **Reds Meadow shuttle** (7:15am-7pm daily June-Sept., $8 adults, $4 children ages 3-15) into the Devils Postpile National Monument. Catch the bus at **Mammoth Mountain Adventure Center** (10001 Minaret Rd., 800/626-6684).

Duck Pass

Distance: 7.5 mi/12.1 km round-trip
Duration: 4 hours
Elevation change: 1,750 ft/533 m

Effort: Moderate/Strenuous
Trailhead: Duck Pass

You don't have to be a backpacker to see the best of the Sierra Nevada, and this hike proves it. Glistening, turquoise lakes and craggy granite spires are the hallmarks of this beautiful trek through the valley between Cold Water Creek and Mammoth Creek.

Begin your hike by climbing southeast out of the parking area on the Duck Pass Trail. The first mile is steep and gains 650 feet. Stop to peek through the trees at 0.5 mile and see Lake Mary with Mammoth Mountain looming behind. You can hear the roar of Mammoth Creek at 0.8 mile; take the cutoff trail to the east to get a look at the waterfall. Visit **Arrowhead Lake** by forking left (southeast) at 0.9 mile, or continue on the main trail. Walk through a boulder field at 1.1 miles, past a perfect little swimming hole in Mammoth Creek at 1.4 miles, and arrive at beautiful **Skelton Lake** at 1.6 miles (3.2 mi/5.1 km rt, 900 ft/274 m, moderate).

Duck Lake

This is a fantastic picnic spot, place to swim, or potential turnaround point.

The views get better as the trail ascends along the south shore of the lake, past the creek and through meadows, to **Barney Lake** at 2.6 miles (5.2 mi/8.7 km rt, 1,170 ft/357 moderate). Framed by talus and scree fields below the 11,500-foot mountains that make up the Mammoth Crest, Barney Lake is another splendid place to relax, make a splash, and enjoy the views.

The trail gets steeper on its way to Duck Pass, leaving the vegetation of the valley behind and entering the sheer, rocky slopes above tree line. Climb 500 feet, stopping along the way for territorial views of Mammoth Mountain and the lakes you just hiked past. At 3.7 miles, reach the top of **Duck Pass** (7.5 mi/12.1 km rt, 1,750 ft/533 m, moderate), where sparkling sapphire Duck Lake spreads out below you. Look for Pika Lake, the smaller lake to the east, and the creek that cascades over the isthmus between the two bodies of water.

Make it a longer hike or a backpacking trip by continuing south on the Duck Pass Trail for 1.8 miles to where the trail meets the **Pacific Crest Trail.** Head south on the PCT (also the John Muir Trail) for 2.2 miles to Purple Lake, or hike 11 miles north toward Reds Meadow. Note that a backpacking **permit** and a **bear canister** are required for any overnight stays.

Getting There

Duck Pass trailhead is 5 miles (8 km) south of the town of Mammoth Lakes. From the Village, take Lake Mary Road south for 3.6 miles (5.8 km). Turn left to continue south on Around Lake Mary Road for 0.6 mile, then turn left to head southeast on Coldwater Creek Campground Road. The parking area for the trailhead is at the end of the road.

★ Natural Hot Springs

Long Valley, a giant caldera about 10 miles (16.1 km) east of Mammoth Lakes, was formed by a volcanic eruption 7,500 years ago, and the ground is still rife with volcanic activity. Hot springs abound in this shallow crater, and there are plentiful opportunities to soak. With Mammoth Mountain and the Minarets on the western horizon, Mount Morgan and Mount Baldwin to the south, the White Mountains to the east, and the Benton Range to the north, the views from the steamy tubs in this basin are marvelous. Visit at sunset to see the western sky light up above the craggy mountain peaks.

If you're interested in seeing some volcanic activity but don't want to soak, you can look down on bubbling, bright turquoise springs at **Hot Creek Geological Site** (Hot Creek Hatchery Rd., www.fs.usda.gov, sunrise-sunset daily, free) from a hiking trail above the creek. No swimming is allowed in this dangerously hot water.

Wild Willy's Hot Spring

Follow a short boardwalk to three soaking pools of varying temps at **Wild Willy's Hot Spring.** The pools are about two feet deep at most, perfect for wading or sitting, and the hot water bubbles right up out of the ground in front of your eyes. There is room for about two dozen people among all the pools.

Getting There

From Mammoth Lakes, follow Highway 203 east for 3 miles (4.8 km) and merge onto U.S. 395 South. Take the exit for Benton Crossing Road eastbound toward Whitmore Hot Springs. Follow for 2.6 miles (4.2 km) and make a hard right on an unnamed dirt road. The parking area is located 1.7 miles (2.7 km) later, where the road ends and the boardwalk begins. Follow the path east for 0.25 mile to the tubs.

Crab Cooker Hot Springs

Crab Cooker Hot Springs has a handcrafted stone tub with water piped in from a spring about 30 feet away. There is only room for four or five people.

Getting There

From Mammoth Lakes, follow Highway 203 east for 3 miles (4.8 km) and merge onto U.S. 395 South. Take the exit for Benton Crossing Road eastbound toward Whitmore Hot Springs. Follow for 2.5 miles (4 km) and turn left on an unnamed dirt road. After 1.1 miles (1.8 km), make the first right onto another dirt road and follow for 0.7 mile to the dead end where you can park. Walk south on the footpath for 0.25 mile to the tub.

Hilltop Hot Springs

Hilltop Hot Springs is another small, concrete tub with natural spring water piped in and incredible views of the surrounding terrain.

Getting There

From Mammoth Lakes, follow Highway 203 east for 3 miles (4.8 km) and merge onto U.S. 395 South. Take the exit for Benton Crossing Road eastbound toward Whitmore Hot Springs. Follow for 2.7 miles (4.3 km), then look for a parking area and a tub on the west side of the road.

Recreation
Mountain Biking

Come summertime and melting snow, Mammoth Mountain transforms from a ski resort to a mountain bike mecca. The **Mammoth Mountain Bike Park** (1 Minaret Rd., 800/626-6684, www. mammothmountain.com, 8am-6pm daily June-Sept., $16 for trail access, $49 for trail, gondola, and shuttle access) spans much of the same terrain as the ski areas, with almost 90 miles of trails that suit all levels of biking ability. The park headquarters is at the **Mammoth Mountain Adventure Center** (Main Lodge, 1 Minaret Rd., 760/934-0706 or 800/626-6684, 8am-6pm daily June-Sept.), at the Main Lodge at Mammoth Mountain. You can also buy bike park tickets at the Mountain Center at the Village (760/924-7057).

Skiing and Snowboarding

The premier downhill ski and snowboard mountain is **Mammoth Mountain** (1 Minaret Rd., 760/934-2571, lodging and lift tickets 800/626-6684, snow report 888/766-9778, www. mammothmountain.com, lifts 8:30am-4pm daily Nov.-May, $169 adults, $139 seniors, $139 children ages 13-18, $68 children ages 5-12). More than two dozen lifts, including three gondolas and 10 express quads, take you up 3,100 vertical feet (945 m) to the 3,500 acres of skiable and boardable terrain; there are also three pipes. Guests at Eagle Lodge, Canyon Lodge, Mammoth Mountain Inn, the Main Lodge, or The Village at Mammoth Lakes enjoy the convenience of a lift or gondola right outside their door. All these, plus the Mill Café and McCoy Station halfway up the mountain, offer hot drinks, tasty snacks, and a welcome spot to rest during a long day of skiing.

The easiest runs on the mountain cluster around the ski school and the lower area near the Mammoth Mountain Inn; **beginner tickets** ($69 adults, $57 seniors, $57 children ages 13-18, $28 children ages 5-12) are available and provide access to chairs 7, 11, 15, and 17. If you're an intermediate skier, take the Panorama Gondola up to Panorama Lookout at the top of the mountain and then ski all the way down the east side of the mountain along the intermediate-to-harder ridge runs. Advanced skiers favor the bowls and chutes at the front of the mountain, and hard-core experts go west from Panorama Lookout to chase the dragon.

Gondola Rides

Mammoth Mountain (1 Minaret Rd., 760/934-2571) has two gondolas to whisk you up the mountain while relaxing and enjoying the view; only one is open year-round.

The **Panorama Gondola** (7:30am-midnight daily May-Oct., last ride at 11:15pm; 8:30am-4pm daily Nov.-Apr.,

Mammoth Lakes to Bridgeport

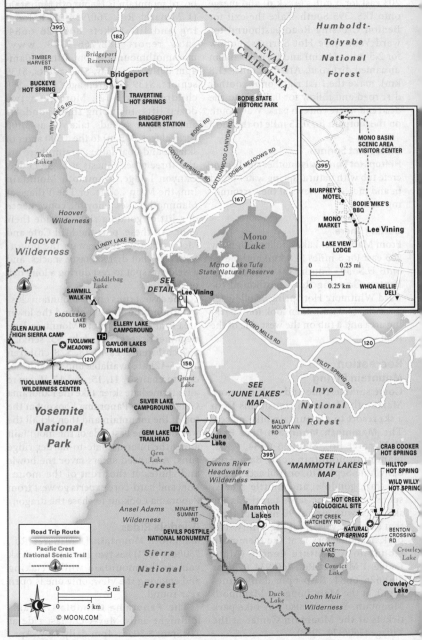

Bridgeport

TIMBER HARVEST RD

BUCKEYE HOT SPRING

TWIN LAKES RD

Bridgeport Reservoir

TRAVERTINE HOT SPRINGS

BRIDGEPORT RANGER STATION

BODIE STATE HISTORIC PARK

NEVADA
CALIFORNIA

Humboldt-Toiyabe National Forest

Twin Lakes

Hoover Wilderness

Hoover Wilderness

BODIE RD

COYOTE SPRINGS RD

COTTONWOOD CANYON RD

DOBIE MEADOWS RD

LUNDY LAKE RD

Mono Lake

Mono Lake Tufa State Natural Reserve

MONO BASIN SCENIC AREA VISITOR CENTER

MURPHEY'S MOTEL

BODIE MIKE'S BBQ

MONO MARKET

LAKE VIEW LODGE

Lee Vining

0   0.25 mi
0   0.25 km

WHOA NELLIE DELI

Saddlebag Lake

SAWMILL WALK-IN

SADDLEBAG LAKE RD

GLEN AULIN HIGH SIERRA CAMP

TUOLUMNE MEADOWS

ELLERY LAKE CAMPGROUND

GAYLOR LAKES TRAILHEAD

SEE DETAIL

Lee Vining

MONO MILLS RD

PILOT SPRING RD

120

TUOLUMNE MEADOWS WILDERNESS CENTER

Yosemite National Park

120

158

Grant Lake

SEE "JUNE LAKES" MAP

Inyo National Forest

SILVER LAKE CAMPGROUND

GEM LAKE TRAILHEAD

June Lake

BALD MOUNTAIN RD

Gem Lake

Owens River Headwaters Wilderness

395

SEE "MAMMOTH LAKES" MAP

CRAB COOKER HOT SPRINGS

HILLTOP HOT SPRING

WILD WILLY HOT SPRING

Ansel Adams Wilderness

MINARET SUMMIT RD

Mammoth Lakes

HOT CREEK GEOLOGICAL SITE

HOT CREEK HATCHERY RD

NATURAL HOT SPRINGS

BENTON CROSSING RD

MINARET SUMMIT RD

DEVILS POSTPILE NATIONAL MONUMENT

CONVICT LAKE RD

Convict Lake

Crowley Lake

Road Trip Route

Pacific Crest National Scenic Trail

Sierra National Forest

Duck Lake

John Muir Wilderness

Crowley Lake

0   5 mi
0   5 km

© MOON.COM

last ride at 3:15pm; $34-39 adults, $29 youth age 13-18, children under age 12 free with adult) runs from the Main Lodge at Mammoth to McCoy Station. After stopping there, the gondola goes to the top of the 11,053-foot mountain. From the top, views extend as far as 400 miles on a clear day. In winter, the gondola is extremely popular with skiers: Intermediate-level skiers get off at McCoy to access the trails there; the top of the mountain is for experts only. The Panorama Gondola closes for maintenance mid-May through mid-June.

In winter, the **Village Gondola** (8:30am-4pm Nov.-Apr., free) transports passengers from The Village at Mammoth Lakes to Canyon Lodge.

The ride to the top takes about 20 minutes. Stop for a meal or a snack at the **Eleven53 Café** (760/934-0745, 10:30am-3:30pm daily May-Oct., 11am-2pm daily Nov.-Apr., $8-20).

One of the most popular reasons to ride up is to ride down—on a mountain bike. In summer, 70 miles of trails are open for biking, and 25 miles of hiking trails are available. A **day pass** ($43 over age 12, $22 children under age 13) includes all-day access to both the Panorama Gondola and the shuttle. Hikers only pay to ride the gondola up; walking down is free. If you're not a skier, you can still ride the Panorama Gondola to the top and back in winter ($24 adults, $20 seniors over age 64, $19 children ages 13-17, $8 children ages 7-12).

The Panorama Gondola is sometimes closed in October for maintenance between the two big seasons. The Village Gondola sometimes operates in summer for special events.

Entertainment and Events
Breweries
You can't miss ★ **Mammoth Brewing Company** (18 Lake Mary Rd., 760/934-7141, www.mammothbrewingco.com, 10am-9:30pm Sun.-Thurs., 10am-10:30pm Fri.-Sat., $5-8), a big beautiful

building at the base of Lake Mary Road. There are two large indoor seating areas, and picnic tables at the outdoor beer garden look south toward the Mammoth Crest. Explore the variety of beers by ordering a flight, featuring either classic brews or rotating seasonals. The brewery's own imperial root beer is a special treat, a chance for non-drinkers (or those underage) to taste something brewed on-site. Inside the brewery on the main level, **The Eatery** (3:30pm-9pm Mon.-Thurs., 11:30am-9pm Fri.-Sun.) puts a worldly spin on brewpub eats, dishing up sumptuous, creative items like naan tacos, Korean short ribs, banh mi sandwiches, carne asada French fries, and goat cheese flatbread pizzas.

Tucked into a tiny space in a strip mall, **Black Doubt Brewing** (452 Old Mammoth Rd., 760/525-0462, www.blackdoubtbrewing.com, 2:30pm-9pm Mon.-Fri., 11:30am-9pm Sat.-Sun., $5-8) couldn't be more different from the town's other brewery. It's a nano-brewing operation, meaning brewers make no more than 100 gallons at a time, and beers are only sold on-site. The owners aim to create unusual and hard-to-find beers like hazy IPAs and sour beers. Although there isn't much room inside the bar for a band, musicians do play some nights of the week. No food is served—feel free to bring your own.

Shopping
Get Outdoors 365 (3183 Main St., 760/923-0191, www.getoutdoors365.com, 8am-8pm daily summer, 9am-7pm daily winter) is a gear shop in an alpine-style A-frame hut, packed with clothing, gear, footwear, and accessories for kids and adults. They also rent mountain bikes, town bikes, skis, and snowboards.

If you need it for an adventure in the Sierras, you'll find it at **Mammoth Mountaineering Supply** (361 Old Mammoth Rd., 760/934-4191, www.mammothgear.com, 8am-8pm daily). The shop has a huge collection of gear for skiing, mountaineering, climbing, hiking, and backpacking. In addition to brand-new gear, a selection of used equipment is for sale at huge discounts from the retail price. Ski equipment, sleeping bags, tents, and bear canisters are available for rent.

The Village at Mammoth Lakes (www. villageatmammoth.com) offers lodging, dining (the standard chains plus a few local places), and shopping—all organized around a central pedestrian plaza. In summer, the plaza is sprinkled with outdoor benches, tables with umbrellas, and recently planted greenery as it tries to impersonate an actual village square. Concerts and outdoor movies are presented here in the warmer months.

Food

Stellar Brew and Natural Café (3280 Main St., 760/924-3559, www. stellarbrewnaturalcafe.com, 5:30am-6pm daily, $8-12) is a coffee shop and café with local art on the walls, a spacious front porch, and great views of the Mammoth Crest from outdoor and window tables. Sink your teeth into a breakfast burrito, Buddha bowl, or lunch wrap with organic veggies, tempeh, natural meats, cheeses, nuts, seeds, and sauces. Espresso, coffee, tea, and smoothies are available, too.

Almost always busy, **Roberto's Mexican Café** (271 Old Mammoth Rd., 760/934-3667, www.robertoscafe.com, 11am-10pm daily, $12-18) is popular among locals. The large menu includes everything you expect (like burritos, tacos, carne asada), plus noteworthy house specialties like menudo, Mexican pizza, lobster taquitos, and duck quesadillas. Eat in the main dining room downstairs, the exquisite garden patio, or the upstairs loft bar, where wood-carved palm trees decorate the liquor shelves.

Petra's Bistro and Wine Bar (6080 Minaret Rd., 760/934-3500, www. petrasbistro.com, 5:30pm-9:30pm Tues.-Sun. year-round, $23-36) offers a seasonal menu that's designed to please the palate and a wine list that's worth a visit

itself. The by-the-glass offerings change nightly, and your server will happily cork your unfinished bottle to take home. Two dining rooms and a wine bar divide the seating, and the atmosphere feels romantic without being too dark. Reservations are a good idea during ski season.

The popular gourmet establishment **Skadi** (94 Berner St., 760/914-0962, www. skadirestaurant.com, 5:30pm-9:30pm Wed.-Sun., $24-32) describes its menu as "alpine cuisine." The restaurant, co-owned by a chef and a rancher, offers a creative menu of fresh local meat and plants to their best advantage. Consider ordering a couple of items from the ample selection of appetizers for a "small plates" experience. Don't skip dessert!

When hiker hunger sets in, head to **The Mogul Restaurant** (1528 Tavern Rd., 760/934-3039, www.themogul.com, 5:30pm-close daily, $20-40) for steaks, prime rib, lamb, fresh fish, and pastas. The American classics on the menu are rich and satisfying, and the portions are generous. Stop by for happy hour (5:30pm-6:30pm), when bottled beer starts at only $2.50—a steal in this town during the ski season.

Fuel up before your outdoor adventure at the ★ **Warming Hut Scratch Kitchen** (343 Old Mammoth Rd., 760/965-0549, 7am-3pm Mon.-Thurs., 7am-6pm Fri.-Sun., $6-14), where creative breakfasts are crafted in hashes, pancakes, smoothies, and chia parfaits. The pancakes are especially fun: Choose from three batters, then select your mix-ins from a delightful array of fruits, meats, veggies, nut butters, and sweets. Pair your meal with an espresso drink or a fresh-squeezed OJ, lemonade, or even a house-made cranberry juice. The après-ski menu, available 3pm-6pm, features hearty sandwiches and a selection of savory sharable appetizers.

Accommodations

The **Innsbruck Lodge** (913 Forest Trail between Hwy. 203 and Sierra Blvd.,

760/934-3035, www.innsbrucklodge.com, $85-295) offers economy rooms with twin beds, plus a table and chairs. Other rooms have queen or king beds, and some include kitchenettes. All have access to the motel whirlpool tub and the lobby with its stone fireplace. The quiet North Village location is on the ski area shuttle route for easy access to the local slopes. It's also an easy walk to most restaurants and other Village attractions. The inn requires a two-night stay on weekends during ski season.

The **Sierra Lodge** (3540 Main St., 760/934-8881 or 800/356-5711, www.sierralodge.com, $99-199) offers reasonably priced nonsmoking rooms right on the ski shuttle line. Rooms have either a king or two double beds, a kitchenette, and plenty of space for gear. The decor is simple in cool, relaxing blues. Breakfast, cable TV, and internet access are included. This small motel's rates are rock-bottom in the off-season and on weekdays in winter.

One of the best things about the **Tamarack Lodge & Resort** (163 Twin Lakes Rd., 760/934-2442, www.tamaracklodge.com) is that you can cross-country ski right to your door. The 11 lodge rooms ($100-269) and 35 cabins ($179-749) range from studios to three-bedroom units that sleep up to nine. Tamarack prides itself on its rustic atmosphere, so accommodations have fireplaces or woodstoves, but no televisions.

From the outside, the ornate, carved-wood, fringed **Austria Hof** (924 Canyon Blvd., 760/934-2764 or 866/662-6668, www.austriahof.com, $150-188) might be a ski hotel tucked into a crevice of the Alps. Inside, you'll find the most stylish of American appointments. Some of the peaceful motel rooms come with king beds and spa tubs. Austria Hof's location adjacent to the Canyon Lodge and

From top to bottom: Hot Creek Geological Site; Stellar Brew and Natural Cafe; Reds Meadow Resort and Pack Station.

the free gondola to the Village make it a great base camp. In the evening, head down to the **Austria Hof Restaurant** ($27-49) for hearty German fare. The Hof also boasts several lavish condos ($245-395) with 1-3 bedrooms during winter.

Across the street from Mammoth Mountain's Main Lodge and right beside the Panorama Gondola is the ★ **Mammoth Mountain Inn** (10400 Minaret Rd., 760/934-2581 or 800/626-6684, www.themammothmountaininn. com). The main building at the inn features standard hotel rooms ($111-467). The nearby East-West Building features condos that range from studios ($249) to one-bedrooms ($329) to deluxe two-bedrooms with lofts that can sleep up to 11 people ($769/night in ski season). All rooms and condos have flat-screen TVs in addition to all the amenities you'd expect in an upscale ski lodge.

Juniper Springs Resort (4000 Meridian Blvd., 760/924-1102 or 800/626-6684, www.juniperspringsmammoth.com, $249-1,100) has absolutely every luxury amenity to make your vacation complete. Condos come in studios, 1-3 bedrooms, and townhouses. The interiors have stunning appointments, from granite-topped kitchen counters to 60-inch flat-screen TVs. Baths include deep soaking tubs. The resort also features heated pools year-round and six outdoor heated spas. The on-site **Talons Diner** (760/934-0797 or 760/934-2571, hours vary) serves breakfast and lunch, and the **Daily Grind** (3pm-7pm Fri., 7am-11am and 3pm-7pm Sat., and 7am-11am Sun.) provides coffee, snacks, breakfast, and lunch year-round. Juniper Springs is located next door to the Eagle Lodge, which serves as one of the Mammoth Mountain base lodges, complete with a six-seat express chairlift up to the main ski area.

The company that owns Juniper Springs also owns the luxury condo complex at **The Village Lodge** (1111 Forest Trail, 760/934-1982 or 800/626-6684, www.mammothmountain.com,

$239-1,200), which is even closer to the ski mountain. Check them out if you can't get the condo of your dreams at Juniper.

For a fine condo rental, try **Mountainback** (435 Lakeview Blvd., 800/468-6225, www.mountainbackres. com, $200-500, 2-night minimum, $60-85 booking fee). This complex has an array of all-two-bedroom units, some that sleep up to 10. Every individual building has its own outdoor spa, and the complex has a heated pool and a sauna. Every condo is decorated differently. Check the website for photos.

★ **Reds Meadow Resort and Pack Station** (1 Reds Circle, 760/934-2345, www.redsmeadow.com, mid-June-Oct. $60-230) is located within Devils Postpile. Spend the night in a backpackers' cabin ($60 pp, $100 for 2 people) with bunk beds, which includes one shower per person at communal showers. A-frame mountain cabins sleep up to six people and include a full kitchen and an upstairs sleeping loft. Motel rooms with private bathrooms and heaters are located in cabin-style duplexes with wood-paneled walls. Don't expect televisions or phones in the resort's rustic accommodations, just comfy beds in a peaceful, forested setting.

Camping

There are three campgrounds (www. fs.usda.gov, first-come, first-served, late June-early Oct., $23) near the Pacific Crest Trail north of Devils Postpile: **Pumice Flat** (27 sites), **Minaret Falls** (27 sites), and **Soda Springs** (28 sites). Campgrounds are on the Middle Fork of the San Joaquin River along Minaret Summit Road, which parallels the PCT between Reds Meadow and Agnew Meadows. Campsites include picnic tables, fire rings, and bear-proof food storage containers. All sites are first-come, first-served and tend to fill up, especially on busy summer weekends. Arrive by noon to see if any sites are available.

Getting There

These campgrounds are 12 miles (19.3 km) west of Mammoth Lakes, about a 35-minute drive. From Mammoth Lakes, take Minaret Road northwest out of town and past the ski area. Check in at the Minaret Vista entrance station (6 mi/9.7 km west of town) to inquire about campsite availability. From there, continue on Minaret Summit Road for 6 miles (9.7 km). Campgrounds are located on the west side of the road.

Information and Services

The town of Mammoth Lakes has an awesome visitors center. **Mammoth Lakes Welcome Center** (2510 Main St., 760/924-5500 or 888/466-2666, www.visitmammoth.com, 8am-5pm daily) is jointly run by the U.S. Forest Service, the town of Mammoth Lakes tourism bureau, the Eastern Sierra Interpretive Association, and the National Park Service. Staff can help you with everything from condo rentals and restaurant reservations to the best recreation options. They're also your best resource for camping information, weather travel advisories, updates on snowmobile trails, and backpacking permits.

Getting Around

Parking in Mammoth Lakes in the off-season is a breeze. In the winter, it can get a bit more complicated, as constant snow removal means that parking on the street is illegal throughout town. Most of the major resorts and hotels offer heated parking structures, and many of the restaurants, bars, and ski resorts have plenty of parking in their outdoor lots.

Shuttles and Buses

The **Eastern Sierra Transit Authority** (ESTA, 760/920-3359 or 760/914-1315, www.estransit.com) runs a number of bus lines, including the CREST line, which takes passengers from Lone Pine through Bishop, Mammoth, Lee Vining, and other stops on the way to the Reno Greyhound station and the Reno-Tahoe International Airport. The trip from the Reno Airport to Mammoth Lakes takes 3.5 hours ($46 adults, $42 children and seniors). The ESTA also operates local bus routes around Mammoth Lakes, including the **June Mountain Shuttle** ($14.50 round-trip), which takes skiers from Mammoth Lakes to the June Lake ski area. Some routes only run on certain days of the week, so check the schedule ahead of time for updated info.

The **Mammoth Transit System** (www.visitmammoth.com, Nov.-May, free) offers complimentary rides all over town in the winter, freeing visitors from their own cars most of the time. You can download a copy of the transit map from the website.

Devils Postpile National Monument (760/934-2289, www.nps.gov/depo, adults $8, children ages 3-15 $4) runs a shuttle that's mandatory for all visitors (except for vehicles with handicap placards) in high season (June-Sept.). In summer, visitors must access the park via this shuttle, which runs hourly 7am-10am daily from The Village at Mammoth Lakes and every 15-30 minutes 7am-7pm daily mid-June-early September from the Mammoth Mountain Adventure Center and Main Lodge area.

◆ Side Trip: June Lake

June Lake is 20 miles (32 km) north of Mammoth Lakes and 13.5 miles (19.3 km) south of Lee Vining, tucked into a lake basin on the eastern edge of the Ansel Adams Wilderness. This quaint resort town is arranged along Highway 158, which departs from U.S. 395 and makes a scenic loop around June Lake, Gull Lake, Silver Lake, and Grant Lake before rejoining the busy thoroughfare. In the summer, June Lake attracts hikers, anglers, and outdoor enthusiasts eager to cool off in the refreshing lakes. A small ski hill—at least compared to

Mammoth—rises above the lake's southern shore. The Pacific Crest Trail passes through the Ansel Adams Wilderness on its way between Mammoth and Yosemite. Westbound trails from June Lake provide access into this stunning, serene section of the High Sierra.

Getting There

June Lake is just west of U.S. 395, about halfway between Mammoth Lakes and Lee Vining. From Mammoth, take Highway 203 east for 3.5 miles (5.6 km), then merge onto U.S. 395 north. Follow for 14.5 miles (23.3 km), then turn left to drive west on Highway 158. Arrive in June Lake in 2.5 miles (4 km). Allow about 25 minutes for the drive.

Scenic Drive

Take a 16-mile (26-km) drive along the **June Lake Loop** to see three gorgeous alpine lakes framed by towering granite Sierra peaks. From U.S. 395, take Highway 158 south for 2.5 miles (4 km), passing the namesake lake and arriving in the small resort town. There are a handful of places to stop for a bite or just hop out of the car for some views. Continue south for another mile past June Mountain Ski Area and follow the road as it bends northwest underneath the steep face of Carson Peak. If you're in the mood for a hike, stop just north of Silver Lake Resort (4.5 mi/7.2 km from June Lake) to explore the Rush Creek Trail as it ascends into the Ansel Adams Wilderness. The PCT is just over the western mountain crest you can see from the road. Highway 158 continues north past 9,500-foot Reversed Peak and Grant Lake. Grant Lake's surroundings feel stark compared to the other lakes along the loop—rather than a wooded, forested setting, the lake is surrounded mainly by sand and volcanic soil. Rejoin U.S. 395 after 16 miles (26 km).

June Lake

Hiking
Gem Lake

Distance: 6.6 mi/10.6 km round-trip
Duration: 3-4 hours
Elevation change: 2,080 ft/634 m
Effort: Strenuous
Trailhead: Rush Creek

Climb onto the mountainside above the June Lake Loop for a spectacular hike that includes a waterfall and two sparkling alpine lakes, all framed by the stunning granite Sierra backdrop.

The Rush Creek Trail heads south out of the parking area, crossing Alder Creek at 0.1 mile and following the path of the highway. At 1.5 miles, catch a glimpse of Rush Creek (south of the trail) as it plunges and crashes hundreds of feet down the eastern side slope. Reach **Agnew Lake** at 2.1 miles (4.2 mi/6.8 km rt, 1,330 ft/405 m, moderate) and walk past the outlet of Rush Creek, where the waterfall begins.

The Rush Creek Trail continues along the north shore of Agnew Lake, then climbs a ridgeline to arrive at **Gem Lake** at 2.9 miles (6.6 mi/10.6 km rt, 2,080 ft/634 m, strenuous). Continue to 3.3 miles where there is a small campsite and a place to access the lakeshore.

Make this a longer hike by continuing for 3 more miles on the Rush Creek Trail to meet the Pacific Crest Trail west of Waugh Lake. Note that overnight stays in the Ansel Adams Wilderness require a **permit,** which can be obtained in advance at **Mammoth Lakes Welcome Center** (2510 Main St., 760/924-5500 or 888/466-2666, www.visitmammoth.com, 8am-5pm daily).

Getting There
Rush Creek trailhead is 4.5 miles (7.2 km) west of the town of June Lake. Follow Highway 158 south past Silver Lake Resort. Park in the trailhead parking area on the west side of the road near Silver Lake Campground. The trail departs from the southwest corner of the parking area.

Reversed Peak
Distance: 6.9 mi/11.1 km round-trip
Duration: 4 hours
Elevation change: 1,970 ft/600 m
Effort: Moderate/Strenuous
Trailhead: Reversed Peak

Reversed Peak rises high above the lakes in the June Lake Loop. Climb to the top to get a birds-eye view of the lake basin and the snowy peaks surrounding it.

From the trailhead, the Reversed Peak Trail climbs steeply west onto the southern edge of a steep butte, switchbacking twice before reaching a relatively flat section at 0.9 mile. Enjoy the pleasant, level walk until 2 miles where you're faced with a choice: stay right at this trail junction to gently loop back to the parking area and enjoy views of June Lake along the way, or stay left to begin the steep 1,100-foot ascent to the top of the peak. To make the climb, follow the trail northwest up the southern base of Reversed Peak.

Views from the top are spectacular: all three lakes in the June Lake Loop, Mono Lake stretching out into the high desert to the east, and towering Sierra spires all around. Head back down the way you came, or stay left at the trail junction

at 4.9 miles to make a scenic loop back down to the parking area.

Getting There
Reversed Peak trailhead is 1.6 miles (2.6 km) southwest of the town of June Lake. Head south on Highway 158 for 1.2 miles (1.9 km), then turn right onto Northshore Drive, heading north. Continue for 0.4 mile and look for the trailhead on the west side of the road.

Skiing and Snowboarding
Built onto a north-facing slope above June Lake, **June Mountain Ski Area** (3819 Hwy. 158, 760/934-2571, lodging and lift tickets 888/586-3686, snow report 760/934-2224, www.junemountain.com, lifts 8am-4pm daily Dec.-Mar., $119-139 adults, $98-114 seniors and children ages 13-18) is small compared to Mammoth Mountain, but it's still a very popular ski destination. Chairlifts lead to June Mountain Summit and Rainbow Summit, both above 10,000 feet (3,048 m) in elevation. Most runs are intermediate or advanced, although there are three easy runs.

Food
Quirky and bubbling with personality, **June Lake Brewing** (131 S. Crawford Ave., 858/668-6340, www.junelakebrewing. com, noon-8pm Sun.-Thurs., noon-9pm Fri.-Sat., $5-10) is a casual counter-service brewery with just a few bar stools and two long tables for seating. Brewery operations are on display right behind the counter. Beers are listed on the menu in order from mildest (saisons, brown ales, pales) to wildest (double IPAs, porters, strong ales). Get a pint, or order a flight to sample a few of the house brews.

You can order food outside in the parking lot from **Ohanas395** (www. ohanas395.com, noon-5pm daily, $6-14). The food truck serves "Hawaiian soul food," including tacos, fries, burritos, and Hawaiian favorite loco moco: a burger patty on a bed of rice, topped with a fried egg and smothered in gravy.

Accommodations

The inexpensive **Boulder Lodge** (2282 Hwy. 158, 760/648-7533 or 800/458-6355, www.boulderlodgejunelake.com, $88-375) provides an array of options, from simple motel rooms to multiple-bedroom apartments and even a five-bedroom lake house. The Boulder Lodge goes back a few decades with its decor—the browns, wood paneling, and faux leather furniture recall the 1950s. But the views of June Lake and the recreation area surrounding the lodge are timeless.

Adorable chalet-style cabins at **June Lake Pines** (2733 Hwy. 158, 760/648-7522, www.junelakepines.com, $165-275) have everything you want in a vacation cabin: cozy living spaces with woodstoves, full kitchens, soft linens, and wood-paneled walls to remind you that you're in the mountains. The location is ideal, right downtown near June Lake's restaurants. Cabins range from one to three bedrooms, and some are pet-friendly.

Camping

Near the south shore of the lake, campsites at ★ **June Lake Campground** (2470 Boulder Dr., www.fs.usda.gov, late Apr.-mid-Oct.) are shaded by aspen and pine trees, with views of the area's 12,000-foot peaks all around. Each site has a picnic table and a fire ring. Bathrooms with flush toilets and bear-proof food storage containers are nearby. June Lake Marina is just south of the campground.

Silver Lake Campground (Hwy. 158, 4.5 mi/7.2 km west of June Lake, www.fs.usda.gov, late Apr.-mid-Oct.) is on the west side of the June Lake Loop, just a few minutes' drive from town. The Rush Creek Trail leading into Ansel Adams Wilderness is nearby.

Both of these campgrounds fill quickly—**reserve** (877/444-6777, www.recreation.gov, $21-23) in advance to guarantee a spot.

June Lake

Information and Services

The nearest visitors centers are the **Mammoth Lakes Welcome Center** (2510 Main St., 760/924-5500 or 888/466-2666, www.visitmammoth.com, 8am-5pm daily) and **Mono Basin National Forest Scenic Area Visitor Center** (U.S. 395, 760/647-3044, www.fs.usda.gov, 9am-4:30pm Thurs.-Mon. mid-Apr.-mid-May and Oct., 8am-5pm daily mid-May-Sept., closed in winter).

Lee Vining

At the junction of U.S. 395 and Highway 120, Lee Vining is the eastern gateway to Yosemite National Park. The small town is a welcoming place for travelers and has a variety of restaurants and lodging. Set between Mono Lake and towering Sierra peaks, Lee Vining showcases a unique eastern California landscape. The Pacific Crest Trail crosses Highway 120 near Tuolumne Meadows, 21 miles

(34 km) west of Lee Vining. Some services in Lee Vining **close in winter,** when Highway 120 closes.

Getting There

Lee Vining is on U.S. 395, about 30 miles (48 km) north of Mammoth Lakes.

From June Lake, head north on Highway 158 for 2.5 miles (4 km), then drive north on U.S. 395 for 11 miles (17.7 km).

From Mammoth, take Highway 203 east for 3.5 miles (5.6 km), then drive north on U.S. 395 for 26 miles (42 km).

Mono Lake

Mono Lake is an eerie attraction in the Eastern Sierra. The beautiful yet unusual lake is nestled within a dry desert valley, its glassy surface reflecting a craggy skyline of ragged tufa towers. Fed by an average of 7 inches of rain and snowfall every year, Mono Lake loses approximately 45 inches of water annually to evaporation. As the water evaporates, the remaining salt levels turn the water alkaline and minerals collect into huge stores of calcium carbonate, which solidify into strange-looking tufa towers. Within the lake sit two large islands.

Negit Island is a volcanic cinder cone that serves as a nesting area for California gulls. **Paoha Island** was created when volcanic activity pushed sediment from the bottom of the lake up above the surface. Visitors can walk the interpretive trail along the **South Tufa Area** ($3 adults, children under 16 free, open June-Sept.) to learn more about the fascinating geology of the area. Free guided one-hour tours are offered daily in summer at 1pm. Reserve your spot in advance online (www.monolake.org).

Mono Lake is located in the Mono Basin, which is part of the Inyo National Forest. One of the best viewpoints of the lake is on the grounds of the **Mono Basin National Forest Scenic Area Visitor Center** (U.S. 395, 760/647-3044, www.fs.usda.gov, 9am-4:30pm Thurs.-Mon.

mid-Apr.-mid-May and Oct., 8am-5pm daily mid-May-Sept., closed in winter). In summer, you can enjoy an oddly buoyant swim in its heavily salted waters or take a boat trip around the silent, uninhabited islands.

Getting There

From Lee Vining, take U.S. 395 south for 1.5 miles (2.4 km) and turn left (east) on Forest Road 1N44. Drive 0.5 mile then turn right onto Test Station Road. Stay on Test Station Road for about 4 miles (6.4 km), turning left to enter the South Tufa Area.

To reach the visitors center from Lee Vining, head north on U.S. 395 instead and drive 0.5 mile to Visitor Center Drive on the left. Follow Visitor Center Drive to the visitors center.

Food

For a unique dining experience, stop in at the Tioga Gas Mart for a meal at the ★ **Whoa Nellie Deli** (22 Vista Point Dr., Hwy. 120 and U.S. 395, 760/647-1088, www.whoanelliedeli.com, 6:30am-9pm daily Apr.-Nov., $8-23). The dinner menu includes tasty sashimi, lobster taquitos, or fish tacos with mango salsa and ginger coleslaw, with options for lighter fare. The hearty morning breakfast includes a grilled rib eye steak and eggs. Expect to wait in line to order at the counter, then wait again to pick up your food. Seating, both indoor and out, is at a premium during high-traffic mealtimes. Heaven help you if you arrive at the same time as a tour bus.

For Wild West atmosphere and spicy barbecue sauce, dine at **Bodie Mike's Bar B-Q** (51357 U.S. 395, 760/647-6432, 11am-10pm daily summer, $7-26), where you can dig into barbecued ribs, chicken, beef, brisket, and more. The rustic atmosphere—rough-looking wood, red-checked tablecloths—and local patrons in cowboy boots complete the dining experience. At the back of the dining room is a small, dark bar that attracts local characters.

Mono Lake at sunset

The **Mono Market** (51303 U.S. 395, 760/647-1010, www.leeviningmarket. com, 7am-10pm daily summer, 7:30am-8pm daily winter) is a great place to pick up freshly made breakfast sandwiches, pastries, and wraps on the go.

Accommodations

Lee Vining offers no-frills motels and lodges on the shores of eerily still Mono Lake. Rent clean, comfortable, affordable lodgings at **Murphey's Motel** (51493 U.S. 395, 760/647-6316 or 800/334-6316, www. murpheysyosemite.com, year-round, $80-175). Rooms include one or two queen beds with cozy comforters, TVs, and tables and chairs. Its central location in downtown Lee Vining makes dining, shopping, and trips to the visitors center convenient.

At the intersection of Highway 120 and U.S. 395, stay at the comfortable and affordable **Lake View Lodge** (51285 U.S. 395, 800/990-6614, www. lakeviewlodgeyosemite.com, rooms $149-179, cottages $164-299). The aptly named lodge offers both motel rooms and cottages (summer only). From basic rooms to larger accommodations with a kitchen, you'll enjoy the simple country-style decor, the outdoor porches, and the views of Mono Lake. All rooms have TVs with cable, and internet access is available.

Camping

Several campgrounds cluster along the entrance road to Tioga Pass in the Inyo National Forest. **Ellery Lake** (Hwy. 120, Upper Lee Vining Canyon, 760/873-2400, www.fs.fed.us, $21) boasts 14 first-come, first-served campsites perched at 9,500 feet elevation, with running water, pit toilets, and garbage cans. Located 1.6 miles from Highway 120 is **Sawmill Walk-In** (Saddlebag Rd., 760/873-2400, www. fs.fed.us, June-Oct., $16). This primitive, hike-in campground has an astonishing 9,800-foot elevation that will, after a day or two, prepare you for any high-altitude activity you want to engage in. Sites are first-come, first-served; there is no water.

Information and Services

The **Mono Basin National Forest Scenic Area Visitor Center** (U.S. 395, 760/647-3044, www.fs.usda.gov, 9am-4:30pm Thurs.-Mon. mid-Apr.-mid-May and Oct., 8am-5pm daily mid-May-Sept., closed in winter) is located off U.S. 395 at the edge of Mono Lake. Inside, you can pick up backpacking permits, maps, and other information on the area. The visitors center fronts the lake, offering picturesque views.

Yosemite National Park

The Pacific Crest Trail enters Yosemite National Park near Tuolumne Meadows, a lush valley in the park's high country, and only one highway traverses this high-elevation terrain. **Tioga Pass Road** (Highway 120) is Yosemite's own "road less traveled." The pass crosses Yosemite east to west, leading from Lee Vining and Mono Lake in the east to the populous west edge of the park. Along the pass, you'll find a number of developed campgrounds, plus a few natural wonders that many visitors to Yosemite never see. At 9,940 feet in elevation, Tioga Pass is the highest highway pass in California, and snowy conditions close the road November-May.

Getting There

Travelers can enter Yosemite National Park from the east near the town of Lee Vining where U.S. 395 connects with **Highway 120/Tioga Pass Road.** Tioga Pass Road travels 45 miles (72 km) across Yosemite's high country, eventually connecting to Big Oak Flat Road at Crane Flat on the west side of the park. The Pacific Crest Trail crosses the highway at Tuolumne Meadows, 20 miles (32 km) west of Lee Vining, where a vast network of hiking trails spread out into some of the park's most beautiful terrain.

Tioga Pass closes in winter (November or December) and reopens in the spring, usually in May or June.

Entering the Park

Yosemite National Park (209/372-0200, www.nps.gov/yose, $35/vehicle, $20 pedestrians and bicycles, $30 motorcycles) is open daily year-round. There are five park entrances, two of which close in winter, and entrance fees are valid for seven days. The best source of comprehensive, well-organized, and seasonal information is available in the *Yosemite Guide.*

The national park **annual pass** (https://store.usgs.gov/pass, $80) allows access to all national parks for one year. Passes are available online, at the entrance stations, and at visitors centers in the park.

Visitors Centers

The **Tuolumne Meadows Visitor Center** (Tioga Pass Rd., west of Tuolumne Meadows Campground, 209/372-0200, hours vary, late May-mid-Sept.) is housed in a small building where you can get info along with a great map and guide to Tuolumne Meadows.

You can secure wilderness permits at the **Tuolumne Meadows Wilderness Center** (off Tioga Pass Rd., 8 mi/12.9 km west of Tioga Pass and 2 mi/3.2 km east of Tuolumne Meadows Visitor Center, 209/372-0309, 8am-5pm daily late May-mid-Oct.).

When to Go

Tioga Pass Road (Highway 120) is closed in winter, and "winter" can come at almost any time at this elevation. To check weather conditions and road closures, call 209/372-0200.

Permits and Regulations

A wilderness permit is required for all overnight stays in the backcountry. You can apply for a permit online (www.nps.gov/yose) or stand in line to grab a first-come, first-served permit when the wilderness office opens. In summer, you can get a free wilderness permit in any of the wilderness offices. Bear-proof canisters are required in the backcountry and can be rented from the **Tuolumne Meadows Wilderness Center** (209/372-0309, 8am-5pm daily late May-mid-Oct., $5 for up to 2 weeks, $95 security deposit required).

★ Tioga Pass Road

The **Tioga Pass Road** (Highway 120) is the eastern gateway to Yosemite from U.S. 395. This section of highway stretches from Lee Vining all way across the crest of the Sierra Nevada, eventually

Yosemite National Park

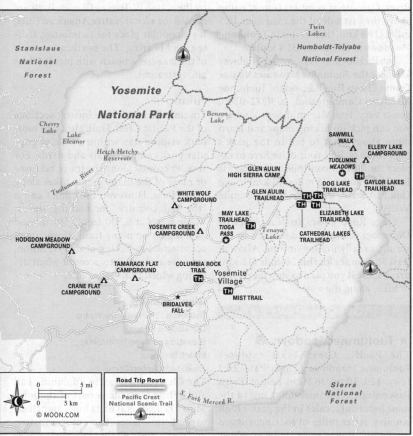

Stanislaus National Forest

Yosemite National Park

Twin Lakes

Humboldt-Toiyabe National Forest

Cherry Lake

Lake Eleanor

Benson Lake

Hetch Hetchy Reservoir

Tuolumne River

GLEN AULIN HIGH SIERRA CAMP

WHITE WOLF CAMPGROUND

GLEN AULIN TRAILHEAD

SAWMILL WALK

ELLERY LAKE CAMPGROUND

TUOLUMNE MEADOWS

DOG LAKE TRAILHEAD

GAYLOR LAKES TRAILHEAD

MAY LAKE TRAILHEAD

YOSEMITE CREEK CAMPGROUND

TIOGA PASS

Tenaya Lake

ELIZABETH LAKE TRAILHEAD

HODGDON MEADOW CAMPGROUND

TAMARACK FLAT CAMPGROUND

COLUMBIA ROCK TRAIL

Yosemite Village

CATHEDRAL LAKES TRAILHEAD

CRANE FLAT CAMPGROUND

MIST TRAIL

BRIDALVEIL FALL

0   5 mi
0   5 km
© MOON.COM

Road Trip Route

Pacific Crest National Scenic Trail

S. Fork Merced R.

Sierra National Forest

continuing into California's Central Valley. Reaching heights upward of 9,940 feet (3,030 m) in elevation, this twisty mountain road offers road-trip travelers an exclusive inside look at the majestic interior of the High Sierra, much of which is too treacherous to be reached by car. Enjoy a scenic 20-mile (32-km) drive on this road between U.S. 395 and Tuolumne Meadows, where the PCT crosses the highway on its way through Yosemite National Park.

Starting from Lee Vining, head west and begin your ascent as the road follows the path of Lee Vining Creek. Giant peaks and granite domes loom on the western horizon, and the vegetation begins to thin as you approach tree line. The road twists south, arriving at **Ellery Lake** at 9 miles (14.5 km) and **Tioga Lake** at 11 miles (17.7 km). These turquoise, glacier-fed lakes make fantastic picnic spots and offer opportunities to marvel at the granite peaks towering above the road. Reach **Tioga Pass** in 12 miles (19.3 km), the high point of the drive, where you'll enter the national park. There's a meadow at around 14.5 miles (23.3

km), where the road begins to follow the path of the Dana Fork of the Tuolumne River. Gaze up at **Lembert Dome,** rising above the east side of the road near 18.5 miles (29.8 km), then arrive in **Tuolumne Meadows** at 19.5 miles (31.4 km).

The Pacific Crest Trail crosses Highway 120 near the **Tuolumne Meadows Visitor Center** (Tioga Pass Rd., west of Tuolumne Meadows Campground, 209/372-0200, hours vary, late May-mid-Sept.), where you can pick up hiking maps and learn more about what to see in the park's high country. End your drive here to explore the PCT, or continue on Tioga Pass Road for another 38 miles (61 km) to Big Oak Flat Road, which leads to Yosemite Valley.

Tioga Road closes in November or December each year and reopens in the spring, usually in May or June. Allow at least 30 minutes for this 20-mile (32-km) drive, more if you plan to stop for photos or hikes along the way.

TOP EXPERIENCE

★ Tuolumne Meadows 🅟🅒🅣

The Pacific Crest Trail explores **Tuolumne Meadows** (Tioga Pass Rd./ Hwy. 120, 10 mi/16.1 km east of Tioga Pass entrance, summer only), one of the most beautiful locales in the park's high country. After miles of soaring, rugged mountains, these serene alpine meadows almost come as a surprise. They are brilliant green and dotted with wildflowers in spring, gradually turning to golden orange as fall approaches. The waving grasses support a variety of wildlife, including yellow-bellied marmots. You may see moraines and boulders left behind by long-gone glaciers. Stop the car and get out for a quiet, contemplative walk along the PCT through the meadows.

Tenaya Lake

Right off Tioga Pass Road is **Tenaya Lake** (Tioga Pass Rd., 10 mi/16.1 km west of Tuolumne Meadows), a natural gem

nearly a mile long and framed by granite peaks. The body of water was formed by the action of Tenaya Glacier. Both are named for a local Native American chief. It's a popular place for swimming, fishing, and boating. The northeastern side of the lake has a beach with picnic tables and restrooms.

Hiking

Yosemite is one of the busiest sections of the Pacific Crest Trail, although most park visitors stay within a mile of popular park campgrounds and roads. For smaller crowds along the trails, take one or more of the many scenic hikes along Tioga Pass. However, they don't call it "the high country" for nothing; the altitude starts at 8,500 feet (2,591 m) and goes higher on many trails. If you aren't accustomed to hiking at this elevation, take the altitude into account when deciding which trails to explore.

Glen Aulin 🅟🅒🅣

Distance: 12 mi/19.3 km round-trip
Duration: 6-8 hours
Elevation change: 800 ft/244 m
Effort: Strenuous
Trailhead: Lembert Dome

The Glen Aulin Trail to Tuolumne Fall and White Cascade is part of the John Muir Trail. Several of its forks branch off to pretty little lakes. There are some steep and rocky areas on the trail, but if you've got the lungs for it, you'll be rewarded by fabulous views of the Tuolumne River alternately pooling and cascading right beside the trail. This hike gets crowded in the high season—expect to meet plenty of thru-hikers. In the hot summertime, many hikers trade dusty jeans for swimsuits and cool off in the pools at the base of both White Cascade and Tuolumne Fall. If you want to spend the night, enter the High Sierra Camp lottery; if you win, you can arrange to stay at the Glen Aulin camp. If you do this, you can take your hike a few miles farther, downstream to

Tuolumne Meadows Hikes

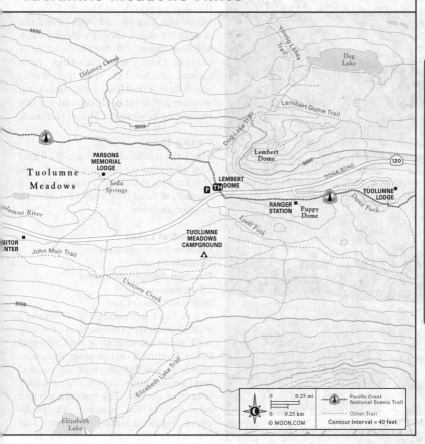

California Fall, Le Conte Fall, and finally Waterwheel Fall.

Lembert Dome

Distance: 2.8 mi/4.5 km round-trip
Duration: 2-3 hours
Elevation change: 850 ft/259 m
Effort: Moderate
Trailhead: Dog Lake

Lembert Dome rises like a giant shark's fin from Tuolumne Meadows. Seeing this granite dome, you may be inspired to climb it for views of the Pacific Crest Trail's path through the meadow.

From the trailhead, follow the signs to Dog Lake before taking a left at a trail junction toward the dome. Follow the marked path to avoid exposed sections that are dangerous due to steep drops. The last section of the hike involves a steep ascent. This is a fine vantage point to take in the rising or setting sun.

May Lake

Distance: 2.5 mi/4 km round-trip
Duration: 1.5-2.5 hours
Elevation change: 400 ft/122 m
Effort: Moderate

Trailhead: May Lake parking lot

May Lake sits peacefully at the base of the sloping granite of Mount Hoffman. While the hike to and from May Lake is only 2.5 miles, there's a steady, steep 400-foot climb from the trailhead up to the lake. One of Yosemite's High Sierra Camps perches here. For truly hard-core hikers, a trail leads from the lake up another 2,000 vertical feet and 6 miles round-trip to the top of Mount Hoffman.

Getting There

May Lake trailhead is 13 miles (20.9 km) west of Tuolumne Meadows and 1 mile (1.6 km) southwest of Tenaya Lake on Tioga Pass Road (Highway 120), about a 25-minute drive.

Cathedral Lakes

Distance: 8 mi/12.9 km round-trip
Duration: 4-6 hours
Elevation change: 1,000 ft/305 m
Effort: Moderate
Trailhead: Cathedral Lakes

If you can't get enough of Yosemite's granite-framed alpine lakes, take the long walk out to one or both of the Cathedral Lakes. Starting at ever-popular Tuolumne Meadows, you'll climb about 800 vertical feet over 3-4 miles, depending on which lake you choose. The picture-perfect lakes show off the dramatic rocky peaks above, the surrounding evergreens, and the crystalline waters of Yosemite at their best. Bring water, munchies, and a camera!

Getting There

Cathedral Lakes trailhead, part of the John Muir Trail, is 0.5 mile west of Tuolumne Meadows Visitor Center on Highway 120.

Elizabeth Lake

Distance: 4.6 mi/7.4 km round-trip

From top to bottom: Tuolumne River in Yosemite's high country; the PCT through Tuolumne Meadows; Tuolumne Falls

Duration: 4-5 hours
Elevation change: 1,000 ft/305 m
Effort: Moderate
Trailhead: Back side of Tuolumne Meadows Campground

Originating at the Tuolumne Meadows Campground's horse camp, the trail to Elizabeth Lake starts with a real climb through a boulder-strewn forest. Don't give up: The path levels out after 1,000 vertical feet, meandering along a little creek and through a meadow. The destination is a picturesque subalpine lake with an impressive mountain wall as a backdrop. The 10,823-foot horn of Unicorn Peak tops the northernmost edge of the rocky ridge. Hop into the chilly water to cool off before returning down the same trail.

Gaylor Lakes and Granite Lakes

Distance: 3-6 mi/4.8-9.7 km round-trip
Duration: 3-6 hours
Elevation change: 700-1,000 ft/213-305 m
Effort: Moderate
Trailhead: Parking lot just west of the Tioga Pass entrance station, on the north side of the road

If you're willing to tackle longer, steeper treks, you will find an amazing array of small scenic lakes within reach of Tioga Pass. The Gaylor Lakes trail starts high (almost 10,000 feet elevation) and climbs a steep 600 vertical feet up the pass to the Gaylor Lakes valley. Once you're in the valley, you can wander at will around the lovely Granite Lakes, stopping to admire the views out to the mountains surrounding Tuolumne Meadows. You can also visit the abandoned 1870s mine site above Upper Gaylor Lake. It's one of Yosemite's less crowded hikes.

Getting There

Gaylor Lakes trailhead is 8 miles (12.9 km) east of Tuolumne Meadows.

Rock Climbing

Many of Yosemite's spectacular ascents are not beginners' climbs. The best place to start is the **Yosemite**

Mountaineering School (209/372-8344, www.yosemitepark.com, $175-215). Here you'll find "Go Climb a Rock" classes for beginners, perfect for older kids or adult team-building groups. You'll also find guided climbs out of Yosemite Valley and Tuolumne Meadows. If you're looking for a one-on-one guided climb experience, you can get it through the school. Also available are guided hikes and backpacking trips as well as cross-country skiing lessons and treks in winter.

Food

The **Tuolumne Meadows Grill** is located in the tent-like store and serves basic fare, including burgers, hot dogs, and breakfast items.

The **Tuolumne Meadows Lodge Dining Room** (Tuolumne Meadows Lodge, 209/372-8413, www.travelyosemite.com, 7am-9am and 5:30pm-8pm daily mid-June-mid-Sept., $10-29), located along the Tuolumne River, is open for breakfast and dinner. While breakfast options are limited, dinner is more varied and can include steak, trout, a burger, or beef stew. Reservations are required for dinner.

The **White Wolf Lodge Dining Room** (White Wolf Lodge, www.travelyosemite. com, 7:30am-9:30am and 6pm-8pm daily mid-June-early Sept., $29 adults, $26 seniors, $10 children) serves up one main item each night with a few sides in a wooden building on the grounds. Dinner reservations are required.

Accommodations

All the lodges, hotels, and cabin-tent clusters in Yosemite are run by the same booking agency. For **reservations**, contact the Yosemite Park concessionaire (888/413-8869, outside U.S. 602/278-8888, www.travelyosemite.com). Coming to Yosemite in the summer? Make reservations 6-9 months in advance, especially if you have a specific lodging preference. If you wait until the week before your trip, you may find the park sold out.

Tuolumne Meadows Lodge

(mid-June-mid-Sept., $135) offers rustic lodgings and good food in a gorgeous subalpine meadow setting. Expect no electricity, no private baths, and no other plush amenities. What you will find are small, charming wood-frame tent cabins that sleep up to four, central bath and hot shower facilities, and a dining room. The tent cabins have beds and wood-burning stoves. The location is perfect for starting or finishing a backcountry trip through the high country.

The rustic **White Wolf Lodge** (mid-June-early Sept., $135-155) sits back in the trees off Tioga Pass. Amenities are few, but breathtaking scenery is everywhere. With only 28 cabins, it's a good place to get away from the crowds. You can rent either the standard wood-platform tent cabin with use of central bath and shower facilities, or a solid-wall cabin with a private bath, limited electricity, and daily maid service. All cabins and tent cabins include linens and towels.

Camping

Yosemite visitors who favor the high country tend to prefer to camp. Accordingly, most of Yosemite's campgrounds are along Tioga Pass Road, away from the Valley's tourist crowds. All campgrounds fill spring-fall, and reservations can be hard to come by. Make **reservations** (877/444-6777, www.recreation.gov) at least five months in advance. Campgrounds outside the park boundaries are often less expensive and require less advance planning.

★ **Tuolumne Meadows Campground** (Tioga Pass Rd. at Tuolumne Meadows, 877/444-6777, www.recreation.gov, reservations advised, July-mid-Sept., $26) hosts the largest campground in the park, with more than 300 individual campsites. The campground sprawls among trees and boulders. All the sites include fire rings and picnic tables along with food lockers to keep the bears at bay. Expect Tuolumne to be crowded for the whole of its season. Tuolumne is RV-friendly

and has most necessary services, including food and showers available at the Tuolumne Meadows Lodge. Half the campsites can be reserved via the reservation system, while the other half are first-come, first-served.

Other good-size campgrounds off Tioga Pass Road include **Crane Flat** (877/444-6777, www.recreation.gov, 166 campsites, reservations required, July-Sept., $26) and **White Wolf** (74 campsites, no reservations, July-early Sept., $18), and **Hodgdon Meadow** (877/444-6777, www.recreation.gov, 105 campsites, reservations required mid-Apr.-mid Oct., open year-round, $26) at the west edge of the park.

If you're looking to ditch the RV traffic and crowded visitor areas, head for tent-only **Yosemite Creek** (75 sites, first-come, first-served, July-Sept., $12). There are few amenities and no on-site potable water, which makes it a good fit for campers willing to rough it. The creek flows right through the campground, perfect for cooling off on a hot day. (Treat water before drinking.) Another no-frills option is **Tamarack Flat** (Tioga Pass Rd., 52 sites, first-come, first-served, late June-Sept., $12), located on Tamarack Creek, which is closer to Yosemite Valley.

The backcountry **High Sierra Camps** (888/413-8869, www.travelyosemite.com, open seasonally, unguided trips $152-159 adults, $81-85 children, guided trips from $700 adults, $375 children, includes meals and lodging) offer far more than your average backcountry campground. These hike-in camps provide tent cabins with amenities, breakfast and dinner in camp, and a box lunch to take along during the day. Choose from among the Merced Lake, Vogelsang, Glen Aulin, May Lake, and Sunrise Camp—or hike from one to the next. Unfortunately, you can't just make a reservation to stay in a High Sierra Camp. In the fall, a lottery takes place for spots at High Sierra Camps through the following summer. You'll need to submit an application if you want to join the lottery, and even if you get a spot, there's no guarantee you'll get your preferred dates. If you want to experience the Yosemite backcountry, plan for a summer when you can be flexible in your dates, and start making your arrangements a year in advance.

Getting Around
Bus
The **Yosemite Area Regional Transportation System** (YARTS, 877/989-2787, www.yarts.com, daily July-Aug., Sat.-Sun. only June and Sept., $4-32) operates buses along Highway 120 that connect the park with Mammoth Lakes, June Lake, and Lee Vining. Online reservations are recommended to guarantee a spot.

Shuttle
The seasonal **Yosemite Valley to Tuolumne Meadows Hikers Bus** (209/372-1240, www.travelyosemite.com, daily early mid-June-mid-Sept., $5-14.50 one-way) ferries hikers between Tuolumne Meadows and the Valley. The eastbound bus departs Yosemite Village daily at 8am, arriving at Tuolumne Meadows Store at 10am. Stops along the way include Crane Flat, White Wolf, May Lake, Olmstead Point, and Tenaya Lake. The westbound bus departs Tuolumne at 2pm and arrives in Yosemite Valley at 4pm. Make a reservation to guarantee space on the bus.

◆ Detour: Yosemite Valley

In summer, it's possible to squeeze in a trip to Yosemite Valley from Tuolumne Meadows. The drive from the Tioga Pass entrance is 65 miles (105 km) south and can take 2-3 hours. The Valley's sights, waterfalls, and day hikes can fill a lifetime, but here's what you can pack into one day.

Getting There
From Tioga Pass, drive 46 miles (74 km) west along Tioga Pass Road (Highway 120) to the junction with Big Oak Flat Road. Turn left and follow Big Oak Flat Road for 17 miles (27 km) into Yosemite Valley.

Sights
Stop at **Bridalveil Fall** for a photo op, then continue on to the **Yosemite Valley Visitor Center** (shuttle stop 1), where you'll leave your car for the day. At the visitors center, check for any open campsites or tent cabins at Half Dome Village, and confirm your reservations for dinner later at the **Majestic Yosemite Hotel** (shuttle stop 3). Explore **Yosemite Village,** stopping for picnic supplies and water, then board the Valley Shuttle Bus. The shuttle provides a great tour of the park for free, with multiple points to hop on and off.

Hiking
Choose one of the valley's stellar day hikes (tip: not Half Dome). Take the Valley Shuttle Bus to Happy Isles (shuttle stop 16) and the trailhead for the challenging **Mist Trail** (5.4 mi/8.7 km round-trip, 5-6 hours, strenuous). This hike is best done in spring when the waterfalls are at their peak, but it's still gorgeous at any time of year. Hike to the Vernal Fall Footbridge (1.6 mi/2.6 km round-trip) and gaze at the Merced River as it spills over Vernal Fall.

Hardier souls can continue on the strenuous trail to the top of Vernal Fall (2.4 mi/3.9 km round-trip) and enjoy a picnic lunch soaking in the stellar views of the valley below. Return via the John Muir Trail back to the Happy Isles trailhead and the Valley Shuttle.

Food
With all that hiking, you probably built up an appetite. Fortunately, you've made reservations at the **Majestic Yosemite Hotel Dining Room** (209/372-1489,

◆ Side Trip: Bodie State Historic Park

The town of Bodie sprang up around a gold mine in 1877. It was never a nice place to live. The weather, the work, the scenery, and, some say, the people all tended toward the bleak or the foul. By the 1940s mining had dried up, and the remote location and lack of other viable industry in the area led to Bodie's desertion.

Today **Bodie State Historic Park** (end of Hwy. 270, 13 mi/20.9 km east of U.S. 395, 760/647-6445, www.parks.ca.gov, 9am-6pm daily Apr.-Oct., 9am-4pm daily Nov.-Mar., $8 adults, $5 children ages 1-17) is the largest ghost town in California. Its structures are preserved in a state of "arrested decay," which means you get to see each house and public building just as it was when it was abandoned: dust and broken furniture and trash and all. It would take all day to explore the town on foot, and even then you might not see it all.

A visit to Bodie takes you back in time to a harsh lifestyle in an extreme climate, miles from the middle of nowhere. As you stroll down the dusty streets, imagine the whole town blanketed in 20 feet of snow in winter and scorched by 100°F temperatures in summer, with precious few trees around to provide shade. In a town filled with rough men working the mines, you'd hear the funeral bells tolling at the church every day. Few families came to Bodie (though a few hardy souls did raise children in the hellish town), and most of Bodie's women earned their keep the old-fashioned way: The prostitution business boomed while mining did.

Take a 50-minute **Stamp Mill Tour** (11am, 1pm, and 3pm daily Memorial Day-Labor Day, $6) to learn how gold was extracted from rocks in this town's heyday. Like many other relics in this town, the Stamp Mill is in miraculously decent shape considering its age, and you'll get to walk right through it.

Free history talks are offered daily during the summer. Inquire at the kiosk at the western edge of the park.

Getting There

To reach Bodie, take U.S. 395 north of Lee Vining to Highway 270 and turn east. Drive 10 miles (16.1 km) to the end of the paved road, and then continue another 3 miles (4.8 km) on a rough dirt-and-gravel road to the ghost town. Note that Highway 270, Cottonwood Canyon Road, and other access roads are subject to winter closures. Check the park website or call 760/616-5040 to find out about current road conditions.

7am-3pm, 5:30pm-9pm daily). Change out of your shorts and hiking shoes (and maybe take a shower at Half Dome Village), and then catch the Valley Shuttle to the Majestic Yosemite Hotel (shuttle stop 3). Grab a drink in the bar and spend some time enjoying the verdant grounds and stellar views of this historic building. After dinner, take the shuttle back to Yosemite Village, where your car awaits, and immediately start planning your return trip.

Bridgeport and Sonora Pass

Set in a broad river valley between the Sierra Nevada and the Bodie Hills, Bridgeport is a small town on U.S. 395 with a sprinkling of necessities and comforts for weary travelers (including two delightful natural hot springs). It makes a convenient base camp for hikers who want to explore 9,600-foot Sonora Pass, where the Pacific Crest Trail traverses the Emigrant and Carson-Iceberg Wilderness areas. Volcanic ridges, sparse vegetation, and rocky outcroppings dominate the terrain in this region.

Sonora Peak Trail

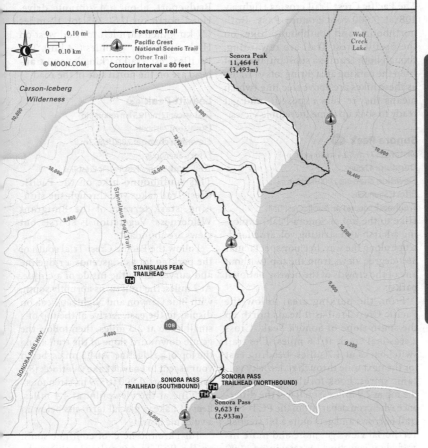

Getting There

Bridgeport is 25 miles (40 km) north of Lee Vining on U.S. 395. Sonora Pass is located 31 miles (50 km) west of Bridgeport, high in the Sierra Nevada. It takes about 45 minutes to drive there. Follow U.S. 395 north for 17 miles (27 km), then turn left to head west on Highway 108. Arrive at Sonora Pass in 15 miles (24 km). Note that while U.S. 395 is open year-round, Sonora Pass is only accessible approximately May-October—Highway 108 closes each winter due to heavy snows.

Sights

Mono County Museum (129 Emigrant St., 760/932-5281, www.monocomuseum.org, 9am-4pm Tues.-Sat., $2 adults, $1.50 seniors, $1 children ages 6-17) features photographic exhibits about nearby ghost towns Bodie and Aurora. Hundreds of historic artifacts from early settlers line the walls—see everything from snowshoes to shotguns, plus an old phonograph (i.e., record player). Precious rocks and gems are also on display, along with Paiute baskets.

Hiking

★ Sonora Pass

The Pacific Crest Trail crosses Highway 108 at 9,600-foot Sonora Pass. Both northbound and southbound hikes on the Pacific Crest Trail are rewarding, though both require a substantial ascent from the parking area. Bring lots of water, as these hikes are above tree line (which means they're very exposed), and get ready to soak up some incredible views.

Sonora Peak

Distance: 7.7 mi/12.4 km round-trip
Duration: 4 hours
Elevation change: 2,000 ft/610 m
Effort: Strenuous
Trailhead: Sonora Pass/Pacific Crest Trail

Hike to the top of Sonora Peak, exploring a harsh and striking volcanic landscape along the way, to enjoy spectacular 360-degree views from the top (without any of the crowds of the nearby national parks).

From the parking area, follow the Pacific Crest Trail as it heads north up the south slope of Sonora Peak. Cross a seasonal creek at 1.6 miles. The trail switchbacks at 1.7 miles, heading east for the next mile through red, rocky volcanic spires. Look for the spur trail to the top at 2.9 miles. You'll feel the difference when you depart from the PCT—the trail narrows and gets quite a bit steeper. Territorial views get sets more and more incredible as you climb the remaining 1,000 feet to the summit over the next mile. If you feel out of breath, keep in mind that you're hiking above 10,000 feet in elevation! Take your time and keep your eyes on the summit; the trail can be easy to lose here if you don't pay close attention. Views from the top stretch out over Bridgeport Valley to the east, Hoover Wilderness and Yosemite National Park to the south, Carson-Iceberg Wilderness to the north, and the stunning beauty of the High Sierra all around. Return the way you came.

Getting There

Sonora Pass is 32 miles (50 km) west of Bridgeport, about a 45-minute drive. Head north on U.S. 395 for 17 miles (27 km), then turn left to head west on Highway 108 for 15 miles (24 km). The Pacific Crest Trail parking lot and trailhead are on the north side of the road.

Leavitt Peak

Distance: 12 mi/19.3 km round-trip
Duration: 7-8 hours
Elevation change: 2,800 ft/853 m
Effort: Strenuous
Trailhead: Sonora Pass/Pacific Crest Trail

This southbound hike on the Pacific Crest Trail takes you through the stunning, stark terrain of the Emigrant Wilderness. Vegetation is sparse, but views are abundant.

Follow the Pacific Crest Trial south of the parking lot as it ascends a ridgeline and curves along the inside of a cirque. At 2 miles, the trail turns abruptly south, with Blue Canyon and Nightcap Peak on display to the east. Arrive at the top of a small knob at 2.3 miles, then follow the gentle downward slope of the trail along the top of a ridgeline. At 4.3 miles, begin your ascent to **Leavitt Lake Overlook** (8.8 mi/14.2 km rt, 1,900 ft/579 m, strenuous), arriving at the viewpoint at 4.4 miles. Leavitt Lake, a glacial tarn, sits below in a volcanic bowl.

Turn around here, or continue south on the PCT to 4.9 miles. Look for the Leavitt Peak Trail on the right, heading west up **Leavitt Peak** (12 mi/19.3 km rt, 2,800 ft/853 m, strenuous). The ascent is grueling, from 10,860 feet at the PCT to 11,540 at the top of the peak, but the views at the top stretch for miles in every direction. Gaze south into Kennedy Creek Valley, more than 3,000 feet below. Once you've had enough, return the way you came.

Getting There

Sonora Pass is 31 miles (50 km) west of Bridgeport, about a 45-minute drive.

Head north on U.S. 395 for 17 miles (27 km), then turn left to head west on Highway 108 for 15 miles (24 km). The Pacific Crest Trail parking lot and trailhead are on the south side of the road.

Hot Springs

Bridgeport is home to two hot springs in gorgeous natural settings.

Travertine Hot Springs

At **Travertine Hot Springs,** two hot pools steam next to a large boulder striped with mineral deposits. Views across Bridgeport Valley to the Sierra Nevada on the horizon are stunning, especially in spring or early summer when the peaks are still covered in snow. Because these springs are so easy to access, they can become crowded. Note that clothing is optional.

Getting There

Take U.S. 395 south out of Bridgeport for 0.5 mile. Turn left to head east on Jack Sawyer Road (just before the ranger station) and continue for 1 mile (1.6 km) to the springs.

Buckeye Hot Springs

Buckeye Hot Springs doesn't have the views, but its location along Buckeye Creek provides the opportunity to splash between hot and cold water. Like Travertine, the hot water here cascades over a neighboring boulder and creates colorful mineral deposits.

Getting There

Buckeye is 10 minutes west of Bridgeport, about a 20-minute drive. From Bridgeport, head south on Twin Lakes Road for 7.2 miles (11.6 km), following the road as it twists and turns. Make a right onto Buckeye Road (just past Doc & Al's Resort), heading north for 2.8

From top to bottom: main street in Bridgeport; Travertine Hot Springs in winter; High Sierra Bakery.

miles (4.5 km). Stay right at the turnoff for the campground, following the road as it bends east. Park in the parking lot 0.4 mile later and walk down the short trail to the hot spring.

Entertainment and Events

Bridgeport's **Big Meadow Brewing** (241 Main St., 951/265-4553, 2pm-6pm Mon.-Thurs., 2pm-7pm Fri.-Sat., noon-5pm Sun.) isn't that big, but it's a fantastic spot to enjoy a beer after a hike. Be prepared to share the bar with locals, visitors, and maybe a friendly dog or two. The tasty and diverse beers range from light pilsners and blondes to medium-dark red ales and porters. The brewery is located just behind the tasting room bar and you can watch the operations through the window.

Food

Don't miss the handmade doughnuts, croissants, and breads at ★ **High Sierra Bakery** (172 Main St., 760/914-4002, www.highsierrabakery.com, 6am-3pm daily, $3-10). Cinnamon rolls, cookies, and Danishes beckon from the case, too. Craving something more savory? Hearty salads and sandwiches with house-made bread are sure to satisfy. Coffee and espresso drinks are made with locally roasted beans.

The **Bridgeport Inn** (205 Main St., 760/932-7380, www.thebridgeportinn. com, 7am-9pm Thurs.-Tues. mid-Mar.-mid-Nov., $10-30) offers the most genteel dining experience around. Steaks, fish, and salads are served in the dining room of a historic inn.

For something more budget friendly, cross the street to **Rhino's Bar & Grill** (226 Main St., 760/932-7345, 11am-8pm Mon.-Tue. and Thurs., 8am-8pm Fri.-Sun., $10-23), a dive bar that serves surprisingly good food. Don't let the tin tackers on the wood-paneled walls and the neon beer signs in the windows dissuade you. The burgers, steaks, pizzas, and sandwiches are delicious and the breakfast isn't bad either.

Accommodations

Rooms at **Bodie Hotel** (281 Main St., 760/616-1977, www.bodievictorianhotel. com, $60-125) are decked out in traditional Victorian decor like damask-print wallpaper, ornate bedside lamps, and intricately carved wooden bedframes. The historic building is reminiscent of boardinghouses that were popular during the California gold rush, except that each room now has its own private bathroom. Some rooms are quite small, but all are big in personality, and each one is different. Step through the front doors into the red-carpeted parlor to get a sense of the place before booking your room here.

★ **Kennedy Meadows Resort & Packstation** (Hwy. 108, 41 mi/66 km west of Bridgeport, 209/965-3911 or 209/965-3900, www.kennedymeadows.com, late Apr.-early Oct.) is a great place to stay if you plan to explore Sonora Pass, which is just 10 miles (16.1 km) to the east. The resort offers sleeper cabins with kitchenettes and bathrooms ($110) and furnished cabins with bedrooms, bathrooms, full kitchens, and linens ($110-215). The historic lodge, built in 1941, is home to a general store with groceries and camping supplies. On the south side of the lodge, a restaurant serves breakfast, lunch, and dinner daily and a saloon pours beer, wine, and liquor every day starting at 11am.

Camping

Located on Highway 108 between Bridgeport and Sonora Pass, **Sonora Bridge Campground** (www.fs.usda.gov, late Apr.-early Oct., $20) has 23 first-come first-served campsites with picnic tables, fire rings, and access to pit toilets. Sites are shaded by Jeffrey pines, and the West Walker River flows right through the campground.

Getting There

Head north on U.S. 395 out of Bridgeport for 17 miles (27 km), then make a left to head west on Highway 108. The campground is on the north side of the highway in 2 miles (3.2 km).

Information and Services

Stop by the **Bridgeport Ranger Station** (75694 U.S. 395, 760/932-7070, www.fs.usda.gov, 8am-4:30pm Mon.-Fri.) to get hiking maps and find out current conditions in the Hoover, Emigrant, and Carson-Iceberg Wilderness areas, as well as the Humboldt-Toiyabe National Forest.

Getting Around

Eastern Sierra Transit Authority (760/872-1901, www.estransit.com, $5-13) serves Bridgeport on the *Reno-Lone Pine* and *Bridgeport Gardnerville* routes. Buses depart from 121 Emigrant Street.

Northern
California

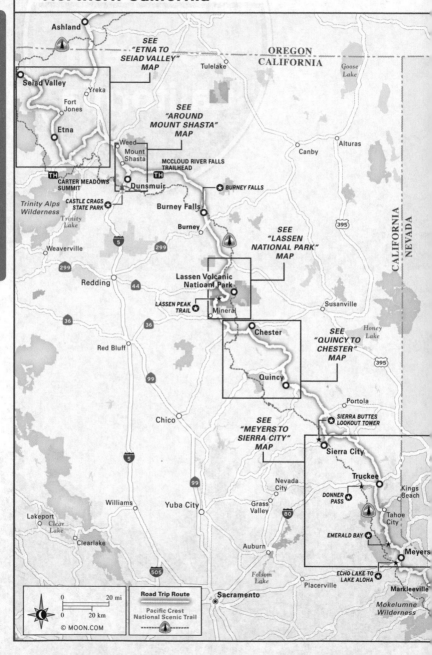

Northern California

Ashland

SEE "ETNA TO SEIAD VALLEY" MAP

OREGON
CALIFORNIA

Tulelake

Goose Lake

Seiad Valley

Yreka

Fort Jones

Etna

SEE "AROUND MOUNT SHASTA" MAP

Canby

Alturas

Weed

Mount Shasta

MCCLOUD RIVER FALLS TRAILHEAD

TH CARTER MEADOWS SUMMIT

Dunsmuir

CASTLE CRAGS STATE PARK

BURNEY FALLS

Trinity Alps Wilderness

Trinity Lake

Burney Falls

Burney

SEE "LASSEN NATIONAL PARK" MAP

395

Weaverville

299

Redding

44

Lassen Volcanic National Park

LASSEN PEAK TRAIL

Mineral

Susanville

36

Red Bluff

36

Chester

SEE "QUINCY TO CHESTER" MAP

Honey Lake

99

Quincy

395

5

Chico

Portola

SIERRA BUTTES LOOKOUT TOWER

SEE "MEYERS TO SIERRA CITY" MAP

Sierra City

99

Williams

Yuba City

Nevada City

Grass Valley

80

Truckee

Kings Beach

DONNER PASS

Tahoe City

Lakeport

Clear Lake

Clearlake

505

Auburn

EMERALD BAY

Meyers

ECHO LAKE TO LAKE ALOHA

Markleeville

Folsom Lake

Placerville

Sacramento

Mokelumne Wilderness

CALIFORNIA NEVADA

0   20 mi
0   20 km

Road Trip Route

Pacific Crest National Scenic Trail

© MOON.COM

Highlights

★ **Echo Lake to Lake Aloha:** Explore the lake-studded Desolation Wilderness during this lollipop-loop hike on the Pacific Crest Trail to picturesque Lake Aloha (page 195).

★ **Emerald Bay:** See sparkling Lake Tahoe at its best from this picturesque perch overlooking the bay (page 198).

★ **Donner Pass:** Check out ancient petroglyphs, historic railroad tracks, and the present-day route of the Pacific Crest Trail while enjoying fantastic views over Donner Lake (page 212).

★ **Sierra Buttes Lookout Tower:** Climb a formidable set of historic stairs to a lookout tower with panoramic views of the Northern Sierra Nevada (page 221).

★ **Lassen Peak Trail:** Set foot on an active volcano as you hike to the top of the 10,462-foot summit (page 239).

★ **Burney Falls:** Feel the spray of California's most beautiful waterfall, where Burney Creek tumbles 130 feet into a vibrant plunge pool and hundreds of natural springs pour out of the surrounding cliffs (page 244).

★ **Castle Crags State Park:** For breathtaking views of Mount Shasta, explore the steep terrain in this forested park, a hotspot for hikers and rock climbers (page 252).

Northern California offers a greater sense of solitude than the famously popular areas farther south, yet the Pacific Crest Trail is much easier to reach by car.

From Bridgeport, U.S. 395 heads north toward Lake Tahoe, veering left to follow Highway 89, your primary route through this chapter. As the scenic drive curves north along the west shore of the deep blue lake, multiple viewpoints compete for your attention while trailheads lure hikers west into the Desolation Wilderness and sections of the PCT. North of Lake Tahoe, the historic town of Truckee offers travelers access to Donner Pass.

Highway 89 leads through Sierra City, Quincy, and Chester—quaint, historic towns en route to Lassen Volcanic National Park. Here you'll meet Lassen Peak, the first of a dozen volcanoes on the northern section of the Pacific Crest Trail. These massive, snowcapped peaks dominate the skyline and can be seen from 50 miles away. Explorers in this region are rewarded with views of golden, rolling hills speckled with wildflowers; craggy, granite-crusted mountains ringed by dense alpine forests; and crystal clear lakes.

At I-5 near Dunsmuir, the PCT passes through Castle Crags State Park, where 14,180-foot (4,322-m) Mount Shasta sparkles on the horizon. Follow Highway 3 to Etna, the gateway to the Trinity Alps and the Marble Mountain Wilderness, before winding along the Scott River Road to Seiad Valley, where the PCT prepares to enter the state of Oregon.

Planning Your Time

The Northern California stretch of the PCT offers more than a dozen convenient base camps from which to explore the trail, the biggest of which include South Lake Tahoe, Truckee, Lassen Volcanic National Park, and the city of Mount Shasta. Tahoe and Lassen are quite busy during the summer months, when travelers **book reservations months in advance** (do your part to reserve your accommodations). However, if you want to experience more solitude during your hikes and explorations, plan to **stay in smaller, lesser-known towns** like Sierra City and Etna.

When to Go

Hiking season in this region can be short, thanks to snow that sticks around well into June and wildfires that spark every summer. As a general rule, lower-elevation destinations receive less snow and are accessible earlier in the year than lofty mountaintops. Schedule your travels between **July and September** to experience the best wilderness conditions; October can be beautiful as well, but tends to be a bit chillier.

Getting There

Your PCT road trip departs from U.S. 395 in Bridgeport and travels into the heart of the Sierra Nevada, where Lake Tahoe beckons.

Car

The most scenic and most direct route from **U.S. 395** to **Lake Tahoe** is via Highway 89 over Monitor Pass, which is open approximately June-October, depending on weather patterns that year. If Monitor Pass is closed during your travels, stay north on U.S. 395 to Gardnerville, then take Highways 756 and 207 to U.S. 50, which delivers you into South Lake Tahoe.

Highway 89 is your primary route through Lake Tahoe, the Northern Sierra, Lassen Volanic National Park, and Burney Falls. While most of Highway 89 is open year-round, sections near Lake Tahoe are subject to closures, and the

Day Trips on the PCT

The gateway cities of San Francisco, Sacramento, and Reno, Nevada, offer convenient access to the Pacific Crest Trail in the Lake Tahoe region and beyond.

Markleeville
South of this historic town is **Ebbetts Pass,** where the PCT ascends into the Mokelumne Wilderness at **Kinney Lakes.**

South Lake Tahoe
Near **Meyers,** south of the lake, the PCT traverses the Desolation Wilderness on the hike from **Echo Lake** to Lake Aloha.

Truckee
Near this charming little city, easily accessible off I-80, the PCT climbs to **Donner Peak** for scenic views of Donner Lake.

Sierra City
This rustic small town is the gateway to the **Sierra Buttes,** where the PCT traverses craggy terrain over a scenic lake basin.

---

other sections may be affected by winter snows. Chains or traction tires may be advised or required.

As most mountain passes are subject to closure during the winter months, when Northern California destinations receive hundreds of inches of snow, summer is the only time to see the PCT through this region.

Air
The nearest commercial airport is in Nevada at the **Reno-Tahoe International Airport** (RNO, 2001 E. Plumb Ln., Reno, NV, 775/328-6400, www.renoairport. com). It's also possible to fly into the **Sacramento International Airport** (SMF, 6900 Airport Blvd., 916/929-5411, www. sacramento.aero). Car rentals are available at both airports.

Train
Amtrak's (800/872-7245, www.amtrak. com) *Coast Starlight* stops in Dunsmuir (5750 Sacramento Ave.) en route between Sacramento and Klamath Falls.

The *Capital Corridor* route departs Sacramento for travel to South Lake Tahoe at one of two unstaffed locations: the South Y Transit Center (1000 Emerald Bay Rd.) and the South Lake Tahoe Transit Center (4114 Lake Tahoe Blvd.). The *California Zephyr* departs the San Francisco Bay Area (5885 Horton St., Emeryville) with a stop in Sacramento (401 I St.) before arriving in Truckee (10065 Donner Pass Rd.).

Bus
Eastern Sierra Transit (800/922-1930, www.estransit.com) provides bus transportation between Reno, Carson City, and Gardnerville in Nevada and Bridgeport, California, all of which can be convenient hubs from which to start your trip through this region, although a car will be required to reach most trailheads and destinations.

Tahoe Area Regional Transit (800/736-3635, www.tahoetruckeetransit.com) offers service between Carson City, Nevada, and South Lake Tahoe on the 19X line.

Best Restaurants

★ **Stonefly, Markleeville:** This upscale American restaurant is a pleasant surprise off Highway 89 (page 189).

★ **Meyers Downtown Café, Meyers:** South of Lake Tahoe, this tasty breakfast joint serves plenty of carbs for a day on the lake (page 196).

★ **Bridgetender Tavern, Tahoe City:** A diverse menu and a shady outdoor patio make this the perfect place to relax for a bite or drink (page 210).

★ **Old Town Tap, Truckee:** Owned by PCT hikers, this popular restaurant serves rustic Italian cuisine and craft cocktails (page 219).

★ **Buckhorn Bar and Mountain Creek Restaurant, Sierra City:** Dine on American classics while surrounded by a lush garden with a babbling waterfall (page 223).

★ **Quintopia Brewing, Quincy:** This bright and spacious brewery is a great place to get a cold beer or a satisfying bite after a hike (page 228).

★ **Cravings Café, Chester:** The best breakfast in Chester is at this friendly café with a community vibe (page 234).

★ **Yaks on the Five, Dunsmuir:** This one-of-a-kind café is known for grass-fed beef burgers with decadent toppings and delectable bourbon-caramel sticky buns (page 250).

★ **Tree House Restaurant, Mount Shasta:** Located inside a Best Western Plus, this is one of the best restaurants in town (page 258).

★ **Denny Bar Co., Etna:** This polished restaurant-bar-distillery operation sources local grains and products for their sophisticated menu items (page 261).

★ **Seiad Café, Seiad Valley:** Home of the thru-hiker pancake challenge, the only restaurant in Seid Café is, fortunately, a good one (page 264).

Markleeville

Markleeville is a quaint, historic community nestled in the mountains southeast of Lake Tahoe, about 45 minutes from the lakeshore. Despite its proximity to the lake, this town sees far fewer visitors than any of the waterfront destinations, and it's a great base camp from which to explore the 10,000-foot peaks, dramatic river canyons, and wildflower-speckled meadows of the Carson-Iceberg and Mokelumne Wilderness areas. The Pacific Crest Trail crosses the Alpine State Highway (Highway 4) at Ebbetts Pass, 18 miles (29 km) south of Markleeville.

Getting There

Markleeville is 63 miles (101 km) northwest of Bridgeport, about a 75-minute drive. Head north on U.S. 395 for 40 miles (64 km), then take Highway 89 northwest for 17.5 miles (28.2 km) over Monitor Pass. At the T intersection with Highway 4, turn right to continue north on Highway 89 for 5 miles (8 km) to Markleeville.

During the winter, **Highway 89 is**

Best Accommodations

★ **Carson River Resort, Markleeville:** If you're planning to explore the PCT near Ebbetts Pass, you'll want to stay here (page 191).

★ **Basecamp Tahoe South, South Lake Tahoe:** This stylish boutique hotel is designed to appeal to outdoor enthusiasts (page 203).

★ **General Creek Campground, Tahoma:** This campground in Sugar Pine Point State Park is a great place for a family vacation or an overnight trip (page 211).

★ **Redlight Hostel, Truckee:** The amenities at this part hostel, part speakeasy, make any stay here memorable (page 219).

★ **Sardine Lakes Campground, Sierra City:** This popular campground is near the Sardine Lakes, the Sierra Buttes, and the PCT (page 225).

★ **Silver Lake Campground, Quincy:** Camp at this gorgeous and remote place in the mountains west of town (page 231).

★ **Summit Lake Campgrounds, Lassen Volcanic National Park:** Located on the main road in the heart of the national park, these two campgrounds are extremely popular (page 241).

★ **Mossbrae Hotel, Dunsmuir:** The nicest place to stay in Dunsmuir is at this boutique hotel located close to the main drag (page 251).

★ **Panther Meadows, Mount Shasta:** This is the most popular campground in the area, perched on the slopes of Mount Shasta (page 258).

★ **Alderbrook Manor, Etna:** Popular with PCT hikers, this manor has traditional bed-and-breakfast rooms as well as rooms in a bunkhouse (page 263).

★ **Indian Scotty Campground, Seiad Valley:** This gorgeous riverside campground offers access to hiking trails into the Marble Mountain Wilderness and connecting with the PCT (page 265).

closed between U.S. 395 and Markleeville (approx. Nov.-June). From Bridgeport, follow U.S. 395 for 62 miles (100 km) to Gardnerville, then head west on Riverview Drive/Dresslerville Road. After 4 miles (6.4 km), turn left to head south on Highway 88 for 10.5 miles (16.9 km), then turn left to continue south on Highway 89 for 6.5 miles (10.5 km) to arrive in Markleeville. Allow about 90 minutes for this drive in normal road conditions, more in bad weather.

Five miles (8 km) south of Markleeville, both Highway 89 and Highway 4 (Alpine State Highway) are closed during the winter, which means the way you came in is the only way out of town.

Hiking
Noble Lake

Distance: 8.5 mi/13.7 km round-trip
Duration: 4 hours
Elevation change: 1,670 ft/509 m
Effort: Moderate
Trailhead: Pacific Crest Trail at Ebbetts Pass

Venture into Noble Canyon, a deep river valley in the Carson-Iceberg Wilderness, and relax at a sparkling lake below 10,000-foot Tryon Peak.

Begin your hike in the parking area on

the east side of Highway 4 at Ebbetts Pass and follow the PCT south out of the lot. For the first mile, the trail heads southeast as it traces the bottom of a steep, crumbly ridgeline. The trail makes an abrupt turn north at 1.3 miles, then south at 1.5 miles as it begins to descend down into Noble Canyon. Highland Peak looms on the eastern horizon, the tallest peak on the canyon's eastern edge. Cross Noble Creek at 2.8 miles and continue south on the PCT when you meet the Noble Canyon Trail at 3.2 miles. Ascend the southern wall of Noble Canyon over the next mile before reaching Noble Lake at 4.2 miles, a sunny spot with grassy slopes and lots of wildflowers in the early summer. Return on the northbound PCT after enjoying the views.

Upper Kinney Lake

Distance: 4.2 mi/6.8 km round-trip
Duration: 2 hours
Elevation change: 620 ft/189 m
Effort: Easy
Trailhead: Pacific Crest Trail at Ebbetts Pass

Enjoy an easy stroll along the PCT between 9,000-foot peaks to a sparkling alpine lake, perfect for swimming or sunbathing on a warm summer day.

Starting from Highway 4, walk north on the PCT, gazing at round, crumbly Ebbetts Peak rising above the trail to the west. Pass Sherrold and Dorothy Lakes at 0.5 mile as the trail traverses a ridgeline above Kinney Reservoir. After 1 mile, begin to descend toward the lake. The trail navigates giant boulders and sparse, high-elevation vegetation for the next 0.7 mile before reaching the shore of Upper Kinney Lake. Where the trail forks, take either route around the lake, stopping for photos or a picnic. Should you choose to explore it, there is also an old dirt road leading down the hill to Lower Kinney Lake that departs from the southwest corner of the upper lake. After exploring, return on the PCT to Ebbetts Pass.

Recreation

West of downtown Markleeville, **Grover Hot Springs State Park** (3415 Hot Springs Rd., 530/694-2248, www.parks.ca.gov, 10am-7pm daily Apr.-Oct., 10am-7pm Thurs.-Tues. Nov.-Mar., $10 adults, $5 children) is home to forested hiking trails, a large meadow, a campground, and hot springs, of course. Fresh hot spring water is piped into a large manmade pool daily. An adjacent cold pool offers a refreshing reprieve from the hot water, especially in the summer when daytime temps creep into the 80s. The pools are located at the southern edge of the meadow, nestled in a valley below towering Sierra Nevada peaks and ridges.

Entertainment and Events

Despite its ominous name, the **Death Ride** (530/694-2475, www.deathride.com) attracts hundreds of bicyclists every July who ride 129 miles and climb more than 15,000 feet (4,572 m) in elevation during the event. The course includes both sides of Monitor Pass, both sides of Ebbetts Pass, and the east side of Carson Pass. Hikers on the Pacific Crest Trail at Ebbetts Pass and Carson Pass share the road with these hard-core cyclists during mid-July while they scout the route and complete the race. Note that all three passes are subject to closure for vehicles on the day of the ride, which is usually the second Saturday in July.

Food

Alps Haus (14841 Hwy. 89, 530/694-9494, www.alpshauscafe.com, 7am-3pm daily, $6-11) is the place for breakfast, lunch, and sweet treats. The space seems at first like a coffee shop, but the staff makes delicious bowls, burritos, sandwiches, and salads from scratch. Gluten-free bread is available, and substitutions/special menu requests are welcome. In addition to espresso drinks made with locally roasted coffee, the café has a large selection of bottled beer and cider. Wi-Fi is free, too.

You may forget you're in a tiny mountain town when you step inside ★ **Stonefly** (14821 Hwy. 89, 530/694-9999, www.stoneflyrestaurant.com, hours vary seasonally $12-36), an upscale American restaurant with an open kitchen, a wood-fired pizza oven, and a colorful assortment of fresh, seasonal items on the menu. Appetizers like chicken liver mousse and mushroom marsala are paired with creative pizzas and entrées featuring steak, pork, and seafood. Artisanal desserts are delicate and delightful.

Accommodations

The only hotel in Markleeville, **Creekside Lodge** (14820 Hwy. 89, 530/694-2511, www.creekside-lodge.com, $88-187) is right downtown, just steps from the town's restaurants. While the architecture and amenities are modern, the colorful quilts and wooden furnishings remind you that you're at a mountain lodge. Most of the 12 rooms have king beds; there are some options for full or twin beds, as well as one unit with a kitchenette. As a nudge from the property owners to get outside and enjoy the surrounding mountains, you won't find a TV in your room, but free Wi-Fi is available. Some rooms are pet-friendly. Coffee, tea, and hot chocolate are complimentary for guests and available in the common area near the ice machine.

★ **Carson River Resort** (12399 Hwy. 89, 530/694-2229, www.carsonriverresort. com, campsites $20-30, cabins $90-170) is a relaxed, old-fashioned resort on the bank of the Carson River with cabins and an RV-friendly campground. Each of the heated log cabins has a unique layout; all have private baths, some have a kitchenette with microwave and coffeemaker, some have a full kitchen, and some have an outdoor deck with a barbecue grill.

From top to bottom: waterfall in Grover Hot Springs State Park; Alps Haus; Sorensen's Resort cabin in winter.

Wi-Fi is free throughout the property. The friendly, welcoming owners and staff are passionate and knowledgeable about the area's opportunities for fishing, hiking, and outdoor recreation. Pets are welcome. The resort is just a short drive from downtown Markleeville on Highway 89.

Halfway between Markleeville and Meyers, **Sorensen's Resort** (14255 Hwy. 88, 530/694-2203, www.sorensensresort. com) is an adorable, Scandinavian-style resort with perfectly appointed log cabins ($215-270), a bed-and-breakfast ($145-175), **café** (7:30am-4pm and 5pm-8:30pm daily, dinner reservations recommended), and gift shop with an impressive selection of guidebooks. The resort feels far away from it all, but it's remarkably convenient to the offerings of the nearby areas, including hikes at Carson Pass and explorations in South Lake Tahoe. Coffee, tea, and hot chocolate are complimentary for guests all day.

Camping

You can camp all year at **Grover Hot Springs State Park Campground** (3415 Hot Springs Rd., 530/694-2248, www. parks.ca.gov). Campsites are within a few minutes' walk of the large hot and cold spring-fed pools, and a network of hiking trails within the state park is accessible from the campground as well. The main campground is open between Memorial Day and Labor Day and has 75 sites with picnic tables, bear-proof storage lockers, fire pits, and access to bathrooms with showers. Reservations are recommended (800/444-7275, www. reservecalifornia.com, $25), especially on busy summer weekends. During the winter, the park turns the day-use picnic area into 20 first-come, first-served campsites with availability for tents and RVs under 18 feet. (Be warned: This area is subject to 3-5 feet of snow in the winter.)

Markleeville Campground (Hwy. 89, 1 mi/1.6 km east of Markleeville, late Apr.-early Sept., $18) is the closest campground to the historic downtown area. Campsites are shaded by pines and cottonwoods along Markleeville Creek. Each campsite has a fire ring, picnic table, bear-proof storage locker, and access to potable water and vault toilets.

There are two campgrounds close to the PCT at Ebbetts Pass. **Silver Creek** (Hwy. 4, 5.5 mi/8.9 km east of Ebbetts Pass, early June-early Sept., $18) is the more developed of the two, with picnic tables, bear-proof storage lockers, fire rings with grills, vault toilets, potable water, and campground hosts who sell firewood. Make advance reservations (877/444-6777, www.recreation.gov) to guarantee a spot.

Farther west is **Bloomfield** (Highland Lakes Rd., 2 mi/3.2 km west of Ebbetts Pass, early June-early Sept., $12), a quiet campground along the North Fork Mokelumne River. Twenty first-come, first-served campsites include picnic tables, fire rings, and access to vault toilets and potable water. At 7,780 feet (2,371 m), this campground can experience cold weather year-round, especially at night, so be prepared.

Information and Services

Alpine County Chamber of Commerce Visitor Center (3 Webster St., 530/694-2475, www.alpinecounty.com, 8am-4pm daily May-Aug., 8am-4pm Mon.-Fri., 10am-4pm Sat. Sept.-Nov., 8am-2pm Mon.-Fri. Dec.-Apr.) has a large selection of maps, guidebooks, and brochures with information about hikes, camping, recreation, food, and lodging in the area. History buffs will want to pick up a free *Alpine County Visitors Guide* here to see the list and map of over 30 historical points of interest in Markleeville.

⚑ Detour: Carson Pass

Midway between Markleeville and Meyers, Highway 88 splits south off Highway 89 toward 8,564-foot (2,613-m) Carson Pass.

Getting There

Carson Pass is 20 miles (32 km) south of Meyers, about a 25-minute drive. Take Highway 89 south for 11 miles (17.7 km), then head west on Highway 88 for 9 miles (14.5 km).

Hiking

Winnemucca Lake Loop

Distance: 6 mi/9.7 km round-trip
Duration: 3 hours
Elevation change: 900 ft/274 m
Effort: Moderate
Trailhead: Winnemucca/Pacific Crest Trail at Carson Pass
Pass/Fee: $5/day or $20/year

Stroll through grassy wildflower meadows beneath snowcapped Sierra peaks and visit two (or three) pristine lakes along the way.

Walk southwest out of the parking area along the PCT as it meanders through a conifer grove. After 1 mile, enter the meadow near Frog Lake and enjoy views of the water to the east. At 1.2 miles, depart from the PCT and walk south on the Winnemuca Wildflower Trail as it traces the western base of 9,500-foot Elephant's Back. Reach the high point of the hike (9,000 ft/2,743 m) around 2.2 miles, where the trail begins to flatten out and then descend to the shores of Winnemucca Lake. Round Top and the Sisters loom on the southern horizon above the lake. Take a hard right at 2.6 miles onto a northbound pack trail that departs from the Winnemucca Wildflower Trail and heads toward Woods Lake Campground. You can detour west at 4 miles to check out the campground and the lake, or continue north to reach Woods Lake Road at 4.6 miles. Turn right to walk east along the dirt road as it parallels Highway 88 and leads back to the PCT parking area.

Getting There

Carson Pass is 20 miles (32 km) south of Meyers, about a 25-minute drive. Take

Highway 89 south for 11 miles (17.7 km), then head west on Highway 88 for 9 miles (14.5 km). The parking area is on the south side of the highway.

Round Lake

Distance: 10 mi/16.1 km round-trip
Duration: 5 hours
Elevation change: 1,380 ft/421 m
Effort: Moderate
Trailhead: Meiss/Pacific Crest Trail at Carson Pass
Pass/Fee: $5/day or $20/year

Lofty lava rocks, weather-beaten trees, and colorful wildflowers are the hallmarks of this hike along the Pacific Crest and Tahoe Rim Trails to a picture-perfect alpine lake.

Follow the northbound PCT as it heads west out of the parking area and twists around the southwestern side of Red Lake Peak. After climbing and descending down the northern side of a ridgeline, cross the Upper Truckee River on large boulders at 2.5 miles. Depart from the PCT at 2.7 miles, veering north on the Tahoe Rim Trail toward Round Lake. An expansive meadow is lush in the early summer and bright golden in the fall. Walk through patches of conifer forests and small meadows as the trail continues to descend, reaching Round Lake at 5 miles. The towering lava rocks framing the eastern shore of the lake look like giant sand castles and make for fantastic photo ops. Return the way you came, or make it a longer hike by continuing on the Tahoe Rim Trail toward Highway 89 (you can arrange a shuttle to meet you there, or park a car that will be waiting for you).

Getting There

Carson Pass is 20 miles (32 km) south of Meyers, about a 25-minute drive. Take Highway 89 south for 11 miles (17.7 km), then head west on Highway 88 for 9 miles (14.5 km). The parking area is on the north side of the highway.

Camping

Just west of Carson Pass, **Woods Lake Campground** (Woods Lake Rd., 2 mi/3.2 km south of Hwy. 88, www.fs.usda.gov, late June-mid-Oct., $24) is a first-come, first-served campground with 25 sites at 8,200 feet (2,499 m) in elevation. In addition to Woods Lake itself, there are other lakes within hiking distance, including Round Top Lake, Winnemucca Lake, and Frog Lake. The PCT is a short hike away via the Winnemucca Lake Trail or Woods Lake Road. The campground is surrounded by huge Sierra peaks, including Elephant's Back, Round Top, Black Butte, and Red Lake Peak. Sites have picnic tables, fire rings, bear-proof storage lockers, and access to pit toilets and potable water. No motors are allowed on Woods Lake, so many campers bring kayaks and canoes to enjoy the peaceful scenery of the Mokelumne Wilderness. Sites here are popular; arrive between 1pm-2pm to secure a site when other campers are checking out.

Information and Services

The **Carson Pass Information Station** (Hwy. 88, 8.5 mi/13.7 km west of Hwy. 88/89 junction, 209/295-4251, www. fs.usda.gov, 9am-4pm Mon.-Thurs., 8am-5pm Fri.-Sun.) is most convenient for hikes and adventures near Carson Pass.

Round Lake

Meyers

South of Lake Tahoe, Highway 89 and U.S. 50 bring travelers to the awe-inspiring lake basin through a residential community called Meyers, south of South Lake Tahoe. South of Meyers, the Pacific Crest Trail joins paths with the Tahoe Rim Trail near Carson Pass before crossing U.S. 50 at Echo Summit. The PCT traces the ridgelines above Lake Tahoe while Highway 89 traces the western shore of the lake.

Getting Around

Meyers is located near the junction of Highway 89/U.S. 50. From Markleeville, follow Highway 89 north for 24 miles (39 km), about a 30-minute drive. Continue northeast on U.S. 50 for 5-7 miles (8-11.3 km) to reach the heart of South Lake Tahoe.

Hiking

★ Echo Lake to Lake Aloha PCT

Distance: 12.5 mi/20.1 km round-trip
Duration: 6-7 hours
Elevation change: 1,870 ft/570 m
Effort: Moderate
Trailhead: Echo Lake Chalet
Pass/Fee: Desolation Wilderness permit required (free, self-issue permits available at trailhead or at Lake Tahoe Basin Management Unit ranger station at U.S. 50/ Highway 89 junction in Meyers)

This picturesque hike to Lake Aloha is in one of the busiest wilderness areas in the entire country, but the region's incredible beauty makes it easy to see why the trail to Lake Aloha is so popular.

Start with a relatively flat walk along the northern shore of Lower Echo Lake to **Upper Echo Lake** (5 mi/8 km rt, 610 ft/186 m, easy). Stop at 2.7 miles to look behind you for a scenic view of both lakes. Now your elevation gain begins.

At 3.6 miles, reach the spur trail for little **Tamarack Lake** (7.4 mi/11.9 km, 890 ft/271 m, moderate), which sits in a basin below Ralston Peak. Take the spur to visit the lake, or continue on the PCT as it climbs up a steep hillside beneath Keith's Dome. Look down to see Tamarack Lake below.

At 4.6 miles, meet the Lake of the Woods Trail and stay left to head west toward the lake. Climb for 0.2 mile to 8,400 feet (2,560 m), the high point of the hike, and reach **Lake of the Woods** at 5.3 miles (11 mi/17.7 km rt, 1,790 ft/546 m, moderate). There's a great chunk of granite in the water that makes an awesome spot to take pictures of the giant boulders, domes, and crags surrounding the lake.

Continue west/northwest on the Lake of the Woods Trail to **Lake Aloha**, which you'll reach right around the 6-mile mark (12.5 mi/20.1 km rt, 1,870 ft/570 m, moderate). This unique lake is full of granite islands that are fun to swim between on warm summer days. Walk along the shoreline until you meet the PCT at 6.6 miles, then turn right to head southeast back toward Echo Lake.

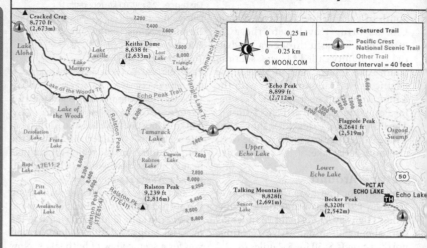

Echo Lake Trail to Lake Aloha, Meyers

If you're tired on the way back, stop at the **water taxi** dock (530/659-7207, www.echochalet.net, 8:30am-5pm daily late May-early Sept., $15/person, 3-person min.) at Upper Echo Lake and catch a boat back. The ride across the lake shaves off the remaining 2.5 miles, and it's a lovely way to enjoy the area. You can also catch the boat on the way there, shortening the hike to 7.5 miles (instead of 12.5 miles).

Tip: Lake Aloha, Upper Echo Lake, and Lower Echo Lake are drained each fall. To see this area in its splendor, visit before the snow in winter.

Getting There

The trailhead is a 20-minute drive from Meyers. From Meyers, take U.S. 50 west for 5.5 miles. Turn right on Echo Summit Road and drive east for 0.6 mile. Stay left to head north on Echo Lakes Road/Forest Route 11N05 for one mile to Echo Lake Chalet. The trailhead is near the shore of the lake, between the buildings and the pier.

Winter Sports

West of Echo Summit, **Sierra-at-Tahoe** (1111 Sierra-at-Tahoe Rd., Twin Bridges, 530/659-7453, www.sierraattahoe.com, 9am-4pm Mon.-Fri., 8:30am-4pm Sat.-Sun. Dec.-Apr., $110 adults, $100 youth ages 13-22, $76 seniors 65-69, $45 children ages 5-12 and seniors 70 and over) has 2,000 skiable acres, 14 lifts, and six terrain parks. Every Tahoe resort has its own personality, and the vibe at Sierra-at-Tahoe is young and playful. The PCT traverses the ridgelines east of the ski area, and backcountry skiers are fond of the area.

Food and Accommodations

Known for delicious food and warm hospitality, ★ **Meyers Downtown Café** (3200 U.S. 50, 530/573-0228, 6am-2pm Tues.-Sun., $8-11) is everything you could want in a breakfast joint: a hearty, satisfying selection of both sweet and savory breakfast classics, all served with hot coffee and a smile. Eat outside on the shady patio or inside where it's warm. Upstairs, **The Divided Sky** (530/577-0775, www.thedividedsky.com, 2pm-2am daily, $8-12) is a local watering hole with daily

Meyers to Sierra City

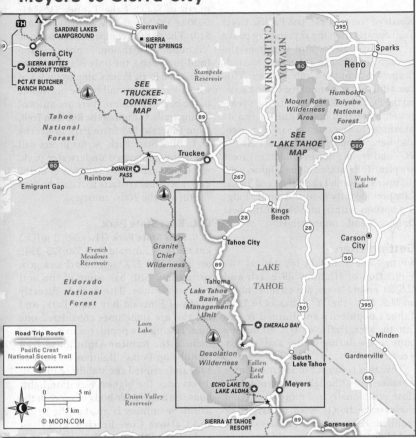

SARDINE LAKES CAMPGROUND
Sierraville
SIERRA HOT SPRINGS

CALIFORNIA
NEVADA

395
Sparks

Sierra City
SIERRA BUTTES LOOKOUT TOWER
PCT AT BUTCHER RANCH ROAD

80
Reno

Stampede Reservoir

SEE "TRUCKEE-DONNER" MAP

Mount Rose Wilderness Area
Humboldt-Toiyabe National Forest

89

Tahoe National Forest

431
580

Truckee

SEE "LAKE TAHOE" MAP

80
DONNER PASS
Rainbow

267

Washoe Lake

Emigrant Gap

28

Kings Beach

Carson City

French Meadows Reservoir

Granite Chief Wilderness

Tahoe City

89

28

50

Eldorado National Forest

LAKE TAHOE

395

Tahoma
Lake Tahoe Basin Management Unit

Loon Lake

50

Minden

EMERALD BAY

Road Trip Route

Pacific Crest National Scenic Trail

Desolation Wilderness
Fallen Leaf Lake

South Lake Tahoe

Gardnerville

0   5 mi
0   5 km
© MOON.COM

Union Valley Reservoir

ECHO LAKE TO LAKE ALOHA
Meyers

88

SIERRA AT TAHOE RESORT

89
Sorensens

soups, huge salads, toasted sandwiches, shareable appetizers, and a sunny outdoor deck. More than just a restaurant-bar, "The Sky" is also a popular spot for live music most nights of the week: open mic, reggae, bluegrass, and rock.

The Pacific Crest Trail passes right through **Echo Chalet** (9900 Echo Lakes Rd., 530/659-7207, www.echochalet.net, open Memorial Day-Labor Day, $137-297), a rustic resort on the shores of Lower Echo Lake with historic cabin rentals. The cabins, called "chaletlees," were built in 1947 and retain their authentic charm with

knotty pine interiors and the complete absence of phones, TVs, radios, or microwaves. Cabin kitchenettes include small refrigerators, two-burner cooktops, coffeemakers, toasters, and counters with stools. Electricity and hot running water allow for a sense of luxury while still experiencing the refreshing sense of being removed from modern society. A boat ramp is nearby, along with the water taxi, which provides boat access to the western edge of Upper Echo Lake. The on-site general store has a limited selection of grocery items, camping supplies, and souvenirs.

South Lake Tahoe

North of Sonora Pass, the Pacific Crest Trail departs from the skyscraping peaks of the High Sierra and traverses the western rim of Lake Tahoe, the second-deepest lake in the United States. This beautiful region is one of the busiest areas on the PCT, thanks to Lake Tahoe's year-round recreation opportunities and its proximity to Sacramento, San Francisco, and Reno. Opportunities to access the PCT and explore nearby wilderness areas are plentiful. Located along Highway 89, the towns of South Lake Tahoe and Tahoe City provide tasty food and comfy lodging options within minutes of the best trailheads and campgrounds.

Getting There

South Lake Tahoe is located at the Y-junction of Highway 89 north and U.S. 50. From Meyers, drive 5 miles north on U.S. 50 to the "Y". Thanks to Lake Tahoe's popularity and limited routes into the area, traffic on U.S. 50 may be quite severe during winter and/or busy weekends.

This area is subject to intense **winter weather** and although major routes do close occasionally, it's more likely that **chains** or traction tires will be advised or required. Highway 88 near Carson Pass and Highway 89 near Emerald Bay close frequently during winter storms. Be prepared to take an alternate route.

Alternatively, from Reno, follow I-580 South for 36 miles (58 km) to Carson City, then take U.S. 50 west for 25 miles (40 km) to reach South Lake Tahoe.

Sights
★ Emerald Bay

Driving north from South Lake Tahoe, Highway 89 passes through **Emerald Bay State Park**. Pull over at **Inspiration Point** (Hwy. 89, 8 mi/12.9 km north of South Lake Tahoe) for stunning views of Lake Tahoe's pristine waters and forested shorelines.

Continue north to reach **Emerald Bay State Park** (Hwy. 89, 10 mi/16.1 km north of South Lake Tahoe, 530/541-3030 or 530/525-3345, www.parks.ca.gov, $10). The park encompasses the historic Vikingsholm mansion; Fannette Island (mid-June-Feb.), the only island in Lake Tahoe; the Eagle Point Campground; and a boat-in campground on the north side of the bay. In addition, there are miles of hiking trails, including the **Rubicon Trail,** from Emerald Bay State Park to nearby D. L. Bliss State Park. Scuba divers will enjoy the designated underwater park, where you can see the remains of boats, cars, and some artifacts that date back to the turn of the 20th century.

D. L. Bliss State Park

D. L. Bliss State Park (Hwy. 89, 2 mi/3.2 km north of Emerald Bay, 530/525-3345 or 530/525-7277, www.parks.ca.gov, spring-fall, $10) has some of the best views in Tahoe. The park is directly north of Emerald Bay State Park, and the two are sometimes considered one unit. Hiking is a popular activity; trails include the **Rubicon-Lighthouse Trail** to Rubicon Point's lighthouse, built in 1919 and restored and stabilized in 2001; it was once the highest-elevation lighthouse on a navigable body of water in the world. Swimming is great at the Lester and Calawee Cove Beaches, and trout and salmon fishing are also popular from D. L. Bliss's shores. There are three campgrounds within the park, too.

Recreation
Backpacking

If you decide to backpack into the Carson-Iceberg, Mokelumne, or Desolation Wilderness areas, an **overnight wilderness permit** is required. During the summer, you can obtain a permit at the **Carson Pass Information Station** (Hwy. 88, 8.5 mi/13.7 km west of Hwy. 88/89 junction, 209/295-4251, www.fs.usda.gov, 9am-4pm Mon.-Thurs., 8am-5pm Fri.-Sun.) or the **Taylor Creek Visitor**

Lake Tahoe

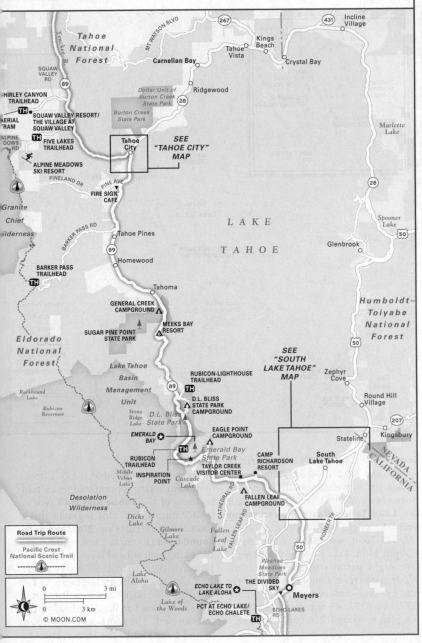

Tahoe National Forest

Truckee R.

SQUAW VALLEY RD

89

SHIRLEY CANYON TRAILHEAD
TH

AERIAL TRAM
TH
SQUAW VALLEY RESORT/ THE VILLAGE AT SQUAW VALLEY

ALPINE MEADOWS RD
TH
FIVE LAKES TRAILHEAD

ALPINE MEADOWS SKI RESORT

PINELAND DR

Granite Chief Wilderness

BARKER PASS RD

MT WATSON BLVD

267

Carnelian Bay

Dollar Unit of Burton Creek State Park

Burton Creek State Park

Ridgewood

28

Tahoe City

Tahoe Vista

Kings Beach

Crystal Bay

Incline Village
431

SEE "TAHOE CITY" MAP

PINE AVE
FIRE SIGN CAFE

Marlette Lake

28

Spooner Lake

50

Tahoe Pines
89

Homewood

Tahoma

GENERAL CREEK CAMPGROUND

SUGAR PINE POINT STATE PARK

MEEKS BAY RESORT

LAKE TAHOE

Glenbrook

Humboldt–Toiyabe National Forest

50

Eldorado National Forest

Lake Tahoe Basin Management Unit

Rockbound Lake

Rubicon Reservoir

89

RUBICON-LIGHTHOUSE TRAILHEAD
TH

D.L. BLISS STATE PARK CAMPGROUND

Stony Ridge Lake

D.L. Bliss State Park

EAGLE POINT CAMPGROUND

EMERALD BAY

RUBICON TRAILHEAD
TH

INSPIRATION POINT

Middle Velma Lake

Emerald Bay State Park

Cascade Lake

TAYLOR CREEK VISITOR CENTER

CAMP RICHARDSON RESORT

SEE "SOUTH LAKE TAHOE" MAP

Zephyr Cove

Round Hill Village

207

Stateline

South Lake Tahoe

Kingsbury

NEVADA
CALIFORNIA

Desolation Wilderness

Dicks Lake

Gilmore Lake

Fallen Leaf Lake

CATHEDRAL RD

FALLEN LEAF RD

FALLEN LEAF CAMPGROUND

50

PIONEER TR

Washoe Meadows State Park

Lake Aloha

ECHO LAKE TO LAKE ALOHA

THE DIVIDED SKY

Meyers

Lake of the Woods

PCT AT ECHO LAKE/ ECHO CHALETE
TH

ECHO LAKES RD

ECHO LAKES

Road Trip Route

Pacific Crest National Scenic Trail

0   3 mi
0   3 km

© MOON.COM

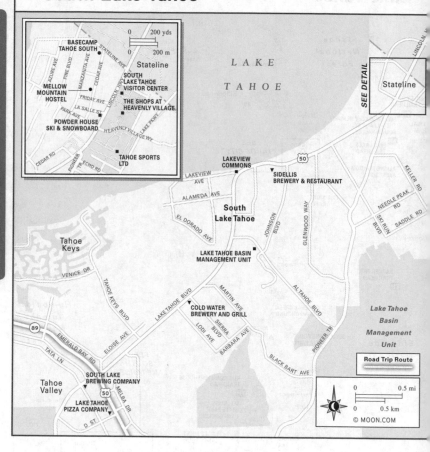

South Lake Tahoe

Center (Hwy. 89, 3 mi/4.8 km north of South Lake Tahoe, 530/543-2600, www.fs.usda.gov, 8am-4:30pm daily). Between November and April, you'll need to visit the **Lake Tahoe Basin Management Unit** (35 College Dr., South Lake Tahoe, 530/543-2600, www.fs.usda.gov, 8am-4:30pm Mon.-Fri.) to obtain a permit. Overnight permits in the Desolation Wilderness are on a quota system to prevent overuse—**reserve** yours in advance (877/444-6777, www.recreation.gov) if you plan to backpack out of Echo Lake.

Mountain Biking

While it's never allowed on the PCT itself, mountain biking is permitted on certain sections of the **Tahoe Rim Trail** (www.tahoerimtrail.org). One segment that's accessible is the ride from **Big Meadow to Round Lake** (10 mi/16.1 km round-trip). To reach the trailhead from South Lake Tahoe, drive south on U.S. 50 to Highway 89. Continue south on Highway 89 for about 5 miles, until the Tahoe Rim Trail crosses the road at Big Meadow, where you can park. The trail heads south, past Round Lake and to the Upper Truckee

River. When you near the river, you'll see a sign warning that the trail is about to join the Pacific Crest Trail and cyclists must turn around.

Entertainment and Events

One of the best ways to experience Lake Tahoe's gorgeous shoreline is with live music every Thursday during the **Live at Lakeview** (Lakeview Commons, U.S. 50 at Lakeview Ave., www.liveatlakeview.com, free) summer concert series. Bands play on an outdoor stage with Lake Tahoe and the Sierra Nevada as their stunning backdrop. Food and craft vendors are on-site with tasty vittles and local goods for sale. Summer temperatures are typically warm and pleasant, but bring layers in case evening temps drop. Free parking is available at **South Lake Tahoe Recreation Center** (1180 Rufus Allen Blvd.).

Breweries

Cold Water Brewery and Grill (2544 Lake Tahoe Blvd., 530/544-4677, www.tahoecoldwaterbrewery.com, 11am-9pm Mon.-Thurs., 11am-10pm Fri.-Sat., 10am-9pm Sun., $16-29) has a somewhat fancy menu for a brewery—salmon with coconut quinoa, pork chops with apricot chutney, farro with butternut squash and pomegranate—and the dining room is sleek and elegant. The brews are diverse as well, from stout to wheat beer, and the brewers promise there's something for everyone.

As many as 15 beers are on tap at **South Lake Brewing** (1920 Lake Tahoe Blvd., 530/578-0087, www.southlakebeer.com, 2pm-9pm Mon.-Thurs., noon-11pm Fri.-Sat., noon-9pm Sun., $5-7). If you can't choose just one, try a tasting flight, served on a miniature ski. There's no food, but you can bring your own. The modern, industrial-style taproom is spacious, with a big bar and plenty of table seating. The brewery's large selection of board games and lawn games are fun ways to pass the time while you sip. Children (and dogs!) are welcome.

The wood-paneled interior at **Sidellis** (3350 Sandy Way, 530/600-3999, www.sidellis.com, $6-13) is cozy on a winter day, and the outdoor patio, set back a block or two from the busy main drag, is relaxing in the summer. This is a smaller operation than the other breweries in the area, and you can feel the family-owned vibe. The food menu includes salads, sandwiches, and shareable appetizers, many featuring house-fermented sauerkraut or house-pickled veggies. The brewery's most well-known beer is the Clockwork White, a white ale with orange and coriander notes, but the IPA and porter are popular as well. Ask about the selection of barrel-aged beers while you're there.

Shopping

For athletic equipment and apparel, check out **Tahoe Sports Limited** (4000 Lake Tahoe Blvd., 530/542-4000, www.tahoesportsltd.com, 9am-7pm daily summer, 9am-7pm Mon.-Thurs., 8am-8pm Fri.-Sun. winter).

You can rent or buy a wide array of winter equipment at **Powder House Ski & Snowboard** (4045 Lake Tahoe Blvd., 530/542-6222, www.tahoepowderhouse.com, 7am-8pm Mon.-Fri., 7am-9pm Sat.-Sun.), with eight locations in South Lake Tahoe, including one at Heavenly Village (1001 Heavenly Village Way, Heavenly Village, 530/541-6422, 7am-8pm Mon.-Fri., 7am-9pm Sat.-Sun.) right next to the gondola.

At the upscale **Shops at Heavenly Village** (1001 Heavenly Village Way, www.theshopsatheavenly.com), you'll find a **Patagonia** (530/542-3385, www.patagonia.com, 8:30am-7pm Mon.-Thurs., 8:30am-8pm Mon.-Thurs., 8:30am-9pm Fri., 8am-9pm Sat., 8am-8pm Sun. summer, 8:30am-8pm Fri., 8am-8pm Sat., 8am-7pm Sun. winter) and a **Quiksilver** (530/542-4857, www.quiksilver.com, 10am-6pm Mon.-Fri., 9:30am-7pm Sat.-Sun.). You'll pay a premium for clothing here, but if you're in

the mood to go shopping, malls don't get much nicer than this. At the good-size **North Face** (4118 Lake Tahoe Blvd., 530/544-9062, www.skiheavenly.com, 8am-8pm daily), you can rent recreational gear as well as buy it. If you catch yourself in the sun without shades, visit **Heavenly Eyes** (4080 Lake Tahoe Blvd., 775/586-6116, www.skiheavenly.com, 9am-7pm Mon.-Fri., 9am-8pm Sat.-Sun. summer, 8am-7pm Mon.-Fri., 8am-8pm Sat.-Sun. winter) to pick up some sunglasses or goggles.

Food

If you're famished after a long day of hiking or driving, pizza at **Lake Tahoe Pizza Company** (1168 Emerald Bay Rd., 530/544-1919, www.laketahoepizzaco. com, 4pm-9:30pm Mon.-Thurs., 4pm-10pm Fri.-Sat., 3pm-9pm Sun., $8-23) doesn't disappoint. The cabin-like space is welcoming and cozy, with a big chimney and rustic wooden booths. In addition to pizzas with any toppings you desire and a specialty crust of your choice (including corn crust and gluten-free for those with dietary restrictions), hearty calzones, an all-you-can-eat salad bar, spaghetti, and house-made pizza dough chips are on the menu. Local beers are on tap; wine and soft drinks are available, too.

Accommodations

Accommodations can be pricey in South Lake Tahoe, but the rates are more reasonable at **Mellow Mountain Hostel** (4081 Cedar Ave., 530/600-3272, www. mellowmountainhostel.com), the only hostel in town. Choose from beds in 4-person and 8-person female-only or coed dorm rooms (from $29); private rooms for 1-2 people are available as well (from $79). A shared kitchen facility is available for guests, along with laundry, outdoor picnic tables, and a communal

From top to bottom: Emerald Bay; lakeshore in South Lake Tahoe; tasting flight at Sidellis.

living room with couches and a foosball table.

With a wide variety of options, ★ **Basecamp Tahoe South** (4143 Cedar Ave., 530/208-0180, South Lake Tahoe, www.basecamptahoesouth.com, $119-332) has the perfect room for every group. Accommodations at this stylish boutique hotel include rooms with one king bed, two queens, two full beds, a family room for 4-6 guests, or the Explorer's Club (sleeps up to 8). There's even a room option with a huge tent set up inside called The Great Indoors, where you can camp without actually, well, being outside. Rooms are decorated in modern mountain style with nods to Lake Tahoe's natural beauty and native wildlife. Enjoy the seasonal pool and rooftop hot tub, or roast marshmallows over one of the outdoor fire pits. All 73 rooms include complimentary Wi-Fi and a continental breakfast.

Camp Richardson (1900 Jameson Beach Rd., South Lake Tahoe, 530/541-1801 or 800/544-1801, www.camprichardson.com, $95-262) is a full-spectrum resort with 33 rooms and suites featuring rustic furnishings and luxurious fabrics. Rooms in the hotel are comfortable and quaint, with private baths and upscale amenities. The 38 individual cabins offer full kitchens and linens but no TVs or phones. The resort also offers sites for tents, campers, and RVs ($35-45). Guests enjoy use of the beach, the lounge, and the marina. Facilities include the excellent **Beacon Bar and Grill,** the **Mountain Sports Center,** and a coffee shop.

Camping

The two great state parks have gorgeous campgrounds. **Emerald Bay State Park** (Hwy. 89, 10 mi/16.1 km north of South Lake Tahoe, 22 miles (35 km) south of Tahoe City, 800/444-7275, www.reserveamerica.com, $35) has the 100-site Eagle Point Campground and a boat-in campground (July-Sept.) on the north side of the bay. Campsites include fire rings, and restrooms and showers are available in the park. Of the 150 sites at **D. L. Bliss State Park** (Hwy. 89, 2 mi/3.2 km north of Emerald Bay, 800/444-7275, www.parks.ca.gov, May-Sept., $35-45), the beachfront campsites are worth the premium price. All sites have picnic tables, bear-proof food lockers, and grills. Hot showers, flush toilets, and potable water are available in the park.

The U.S. Forest Service runs 206 sites at **Fallen Leaf Lake Campground** (Fallen Leaf Lake Rd., off Hwy. 89, 3 mi/4.8 km north of U.S. 50, 530/543-2600 or 877/444-6777, www.recreation.gov, mid-May-mid-Oct., $32-34). RVs up to 40 feet are welcome, though there are no hookups or dump stations. Each campsite has a barbecue grill, a picnic table, and a fire ring. There are modern baths with flush toilets, and some restrooms even have free showers. The campground is 0.25 mile north of Fallen Leaf Lake.

Information and Services

For information about hiking, camping, and exploring the wilderness areas surrounding Lake Tahoe, visit one of three Forest Service visitors centers or offices. The **Lake Tahoe Basin Management Unit** (35 College Dr., South Lake Tahoe, 530/543-2600, www.fs.usda.gov, 8am-4:30pm Mon.-Fri.) is in central South Lake Tahoe near restaurants and accommodations. If you're heading north on Highway 89 toward Emerald Bay or Tahoe City, stop at the **Taylor Creek Visitor Center** (Hwy. 89, 3 mi/4.8 km north of South Lake Tahoe, 530/543-2600, www.fs.usda.gov, 8am-4:30pm daily May-Oct.).

Brochures and pamphlets at the **South Lake Tahoe Visitor Center** (4114 Lake Tahoe Blvd., 530/542-4637, www.tahoesouth.com, 9am-5pm daily) provide more info about the city's hotels, restaurants, and opportunities for recreation. Staffers are friendly and knowledgeable about the area.

Getting Around

In the South Lake Tahoe area, local public transportation is provided by **BlueGO** (530/541-7149, www.bluego.org, $2-5 adults), which runs buses, trolleys, and ski shuttles. The cheerful-looking trolley can help you get around the South Shore without driving. Routes and schedules vary, so consult the website for details.

Tahoe City

Tahoe City is located on scenic Highway 89 between South Lake Tahoe and Truckee. With plenty of food and lodging options offering views of the sparkling lake, Tahoe City is a convenient base camp from which to explore destinations on Tahoe's western rim, including Barker Pass, Alpine Meadows, and Squaw Valley—all located on or near the Pacific Crest Trail.

Getting There

From South Lake Tahoe, follow Highway 89 north for 27 miles (43 km) to Tahoe City. Allow 45 minutes for this scenic drive, more if you plan to spend time at Emerald Bay or D. L. Bliss State Parks along the way, both worthy stops with incredible views.

Highway 89 near Emerald Bay often **closes in winter.** You'll need to drive around the east shore of the lake to get to Tahoe City from South Lake Tahoe. Chains or traction tires may also be required during certain parts of this drive.

Sights

Z'berg Sugar Pine Point State Park

Z'berg Sugar Pine Point State Park (Hwy. 89, Tahoma, 530/525-7982, www.parks.ca.gov, $10) is located on the West Shore, north of Emerald Bay and a few miles south of the town of Homewood. The park is split into two sections. Sugar Pine Point includes the General Creek Campground, the Ehrman Mansion (a beautifully preserved 12,000-square-foot

house built in 1903), the visitors center, and a gift shop. The smaller Edwin L. Z'berg Natural Preserve features the Sugar Pine Point Lighthouse.

The park features tours of the historic Ehrman Mansion, ski trails from the 1960 Winter Olympics, and great camping, among other attractions.

Tahoe Maritime Museum

The **Tahoe Maritime Museum** (5205 W. Lake Blvd., Homewood, 530/525-9253, www.tahoemaritimemuseum.org, 10am-4:30pm Thurs.-Tues. late May-Oct., 10am-4:30pm Fri.-Sun. Oct.-late May, $5 adults, children under 13 free) explores the marine history of Lake Tahoe. Located on the West Shore, the museum resembles an old boathouse and has a great collection of historic boats that share the history of the lake. It also houses photos and artifacts related to the lake's history. You'll learn about "gentlemen's racing"; steam ferries, like the 1896 *Tahoe,* which used to take people around the lake in the days before roads circumnavigated it; and fishing, which has been part of the lake's culture for more than a century. Young visitors will enjoy a children's learning area with exhibits about small and midsize boats and activities designed just for them.

Gatekeeper's Museum and Marion Steinbach Indian Basket Museum

Together, the **Gatekeeper's Museum and Marion Steinbach Indian Basket Museum** (130 W. Lake Blvd., Tahoe City, 530/583-1762, www.northtahoemuseums.org, 10am-5pm daily early June-Sept., noon-4pm Wed.-Sun. Oct.-late May, $5 adults, $4 seniors, under age 13 free accompanied by an adult) offer an in-depth history of society around the lake. You'll find transcribed oral histories, photographs, dolls, costumes, and many other artifacts displayed in attractive and unusual pine-and-glass cases that match the wooden floors of the galleries. The authentic Native American artifacts include

Tahoe City

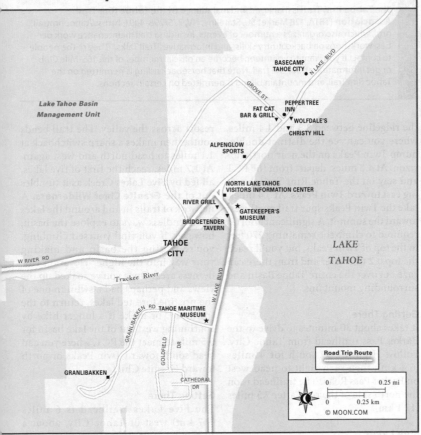

a large collection of baskets and caps made of willow, tule, and pine needles, among other things.

Hiking
Twin Peaks via Tahoe Rim Trail 🅿

Distance: 11.2 mi/18 km round-trip
Duration: 6 hours
Elevation change: 2,060 ft/628 m
Effort: Strenuous
Trailhead: Barker Pass

The Tahoe Rim Trail and the Pacific Crest Trail overlap for 50 miles on the southwest side of the mighty lake. This

hike shows off the region's best features: fields of wildflowers, craggy mountainsides, and of course, the oh-so-blue surface of Lake Tahoe.

Start by walking west out of the parking area on the northbound PCT/TRT. The trail traces the south base of Barker Peak, alternating through lush meadows and sparse pine forests, before turning north around 1.9 miles and cutting along the inside of a steep cirque where the views of the lake and the unique geology of the Granite Chief Wilderness are spectacular. Switchbacks lead to the top of

The Tahoe Rim Trail

The **Tahoe Rim Trail** is managed and maintained by the **Tahoe Rim Trail Association** (TRTA, 128 Market St., Stateline, NV, 775/298-4491, https://tahoerimtrail.org), which also organizes a number of events, including trail maintenance work parties, workshops on backcountry skills, and informative "Trail Talks." They're the people to contact if you want to volunteer, become an official member of the 165-Mile Club, or get information about the trail. Note that horseback riding is permitted on the Tahoe Rim Trail, and mountain biking is permitted on certain sections.

the ridgeline between 3.3 and 4.4 miles, where you can see the distinct double-hump Twin Peaks on the near north horizon. At 4.8 miles, depart from the PCT and stay on the Tahoe Rim Trail, heading east toward Twin Peaks. At 5.4 miles, take the Twin Peaks spur trail northwest toward the summit. A significant effort is required to climb the remaining 270 feet to the top of Twin Peaks, but you'll reach the top 0.2 mile later and from there can gaze out over the entire Tahoe Basin and surrounding mountains.

Getting There

It takes about 30 minutes to drive to the Barker Pass trailhead from Tahoe City. Follow Highway 89 south for 4 miles (6.4 km), then turn right to head west on Barker Pass Road. The trailhead is on the north side of the road after 7.5 miles (12.1 km).

Five Lakes

Distance: 4-5 mi/6.4-8 km round-trip
Duration: 2-3 hours
Elevation change: 1,120 ft/341 m
Effort: Moderate
Trailhead: Five Lakes

Follow a gently graded trail out of Alpine Meadows to a lake basin on Lake Tahoe's western rim. The Five Lakes Trail begins by ascending west up the southern base of a craggy peak called KT-22. The north side of the peak, inside the Squaw Valley ski resort, is home to one of Tahoe's steepest ski runs. There isn't much shade between 0.8 and 1.6 miles, but you do get great views of the Alpine Meadows ski resort across the valley. The trail bends south, then makes a sharp switchback at 1.1 miles to head north and west again. At 1.7 miles, reach the first of five lakes, all fed by Five Lakes Creek as it tumbles out of the **Granite Chief Wilderness.** A network of trails in and around the lakes offers endless ways to explore the basin; however, if you find yourself climbing, you're exiting the basin and making your way into the higher-elevation wilderness area. Once you've soaked up the views and perhaps had a swim in one of the pristine forested lakes, return to the trailhead, or make it a longer hike by continuing west out of the lake basin for 0.5 mile to meet the PCT, where you can head south toward Twin Peaks or north toward Granite Chief.

Getting There

The Five Lakes trailhead is 6 miles (9.7 km) west of Tahoe City, about a 10-minute drive. Take Highway 89 north for 3.8 miles (6.1 km), then turn left to head west toward Alpine Meadows on Alpine Meadows Road. The trailhead is on the north side of the road in 2.1 miles (3.4 km).

Shirley Canyon to High Camp

Distance: 3 mi/4.8 km one-way
Duration: 2 hours
Elevation change: 1,920 ft/585 m
Effort: Moderate
Trailhead: Shirley Canyon

Hike along Shirley Creek to the 8,200-foot High Camp in Squaw Valley, then coast your way back down as you enjoy the views from the windows of the **Aerial Tram** (800/403-0206, www.squawalpine. com, $46 adults, $25 children ages 5-17, children ages 4 and under and Ikon pass holders free). While this hike is short, it can be steep at times, and the high-elevation terrain makes it a lung buster. Of course, if you aren't in the mood for a climb, take the tram up to High Camp and hike back down on the trail.

Starting at the Shirley Canyon trailhead on Squaw Peak Way, hike northwest on the Shirley Canyon Trail, following the path of Squaw Creek. Pass your first waterfall at 0.5 mile and reach Shirley Lake at 2 miles. To continue to the Aerial Tram, stay left at the trail junction at 2.2 miles and hike southeast. As you climb away from the lake, views of the surrounding high country are spectacular: granite peaks covered with lush meadows and colorful wildflowers (in early summer) or bathed in gold (in the fall). The brilliant blue surface of Lake Tahoe comes into view as you approach 8,200-foot High Camp, where you'll meet the tram.

Note: For interactive maps of the trails in and around Squaw Valley, download the Squaw Alpine Summer App (https:// squawalpine.com/other/mobile-app).

Getting There
Squaw Valley is 8 miles (12.9 km) northwest of Tahoe City, about a 15-minute drive. Take Highway 89 north for 5 miles (8 km), then turn left to head west on Squaw Valley Road. Once you reach the resort, continue onto Squaw Peak Road. The trailhead is at the northwest corner of the Squaw Peak Road/Squaw Peak Way loop.

Guided Rim Hikes
In summer, nonprofit **Tahoe Rim Trail Association** (TRTA, 128 Market St., Stateline, NV, 775/298-4491, https:// tahoerimtrail.org) runs several 14-day thru-hikes ($1,725), during which participants cover all 165 miles and bag

elevation gains and losses totaling 27,500 feet. The cost includes food, trip leaders, transportation to and from the trail, and delivery of meals and supplies to key locations along the way by a group of "Trail Angels"—which greatly reduces the weight of your backpack on a trek of this length. These trips fill up fast, so call early to get on the list.

If you're not up for hiking the whole trail in one bite, you might love the TRTA's Segment Hiking Program (membership fee $550), where you can join the expert guides as they hike the whole trail over the course of 10-13 weeks through the summer. The program fills quickly; register through the website or contact the trail-use director (775/298-4491, lindseys@tahoerimtrail.org).

Recreation
Aerial Tram
Entertainment options include skiing and ice-skating in the winter, hiking in summer, and the **Aerial Tram** (800/403-0206, hours vary, daily winter and summer, Sat.-Sun. spring and fall, $46 adults, $25 children ages 5-17, children ages 4 and under and Ikon pass holders free) up to **High Camp** (1960 Squaw Valley Rd., Olympic Valley, 530/584-1000, www. squawalpine.com) at 8,200 feet (2,499 m) elevation. At High Camp, you can play tennis or paintball, roller-skate, soak in a hot tub, browse the **Olympic Museum** (www.squawalpine.com/olympic-museum, free with Aerial Tram ride), or just stand outside and enjoy the incredible views of Lake Tahoe and the Granite Chief Wilderness. In summer there's often live music at the base of the mountain; various other special events offer year-round fun for adults and kids.

Winter Sports
Granlibakken (725 Granlibakken Rd., Tahoe City, 530/583-4242 or 800/543-3221, www.granlibakken.com, lift tickets $16-30, lodging $165-665) is a lovely, historic resort that dates to the turn of the

20th century, when the original Tahoe Tavern was built on this site. The Tahoe Tavern was the site of the 1932 and 1936 U.S. Olympic trials, and over the years it has hosted various national championships, Junior Olympics, and other competitions. Granlibakken still offers some downhill skiing, but those who crave the excitement of bigger mountains should sleep here and take advantage of the package deals with other resorts, which include discount lift tickets and shuttle transportation to one of seven other ski areas.

Alpine Meadows (2600 Alpine Meadows Rd., Tahoe City, 530/583-4232 or 800/441-4423, www.squawalpine. com, mid-Nov.-mid-May, $89-159 adults, $72-114 youth ages 13-17 and seniors 70 and over, $63-87 children ages 5-12) is a sprawling resort that encompasses both sides of two Sierra peaks, Scott and Ward. With a full range of trails, an all-day every-day ski school, and state-of-the-art rental equipment, Alpine is ideal for all levels of skiers. Beginners will particularly enjoy their new "rocker" skis, which make steering easier than ever, and the scenic network of green trails. An intermediate skier can have a great time at Alpine, especially coming off the Summit Six or the Roundhouse Express chairlifts. On the south side, from Scott Peak off the Lakeview Chair, all ski runs are blue. Alpine devotes considerable space to what it refers to as "Adventure Ski Zones." These are large clusters of black-diamond and double-black-diamond bowls and runs intended for expert skiers only. Thirteen lifts serve the mountains, including three high-speed chairs. If you're an expert, take just about any chair up the mountain, and you'll find exhilarating ways down. The Scott Chair leads to a bunch of single-black-diamond runs on the front of the mountain, as does the Summit Express six-passenger chair at the back of Ward Peak. You can get to Art's Knob from the Sherwood Express. Alpine has two terrain parks:

Tiegel, with a few small snow features for beginners and young adventurers, and Howard's Hollow, which usually has more features for medium-level skiers and snowboarders.

Squaw Valley (1960 Squaw Valley Rd., Olympic Valley, 530/583-6985, www. squawalpine.com, mid-Nov.-mid-May, $89-159 adults, $72-114 youth ages 13-17 and seniors 70 and over, $63-87 children ages 5-12) was the headquarters for alpine sports during the 1960 Winter Olympics. Today it is perhaps the most popular ski resort in California, with practically every amenity and plenty of activities, from geocaching to ziplining, but skiing and snowboarding remain the most important pursuits. Squaw Valley has a great ski school with plenty of fun for new skiers and boarders of all ages along with a wide selection of intermediate slopes. Some slopes are long, such as those served by the Squaw Creek, Red Dog, and Squaw One Express lifts—perfect for skiers who want to spend more time on the snow than on the lifts. But the jewels of Squaw are the many black-diamond and double-black-diamond slopes and the two terrain parks. Whether you prefer trees, moguls, narrow ridges, or wide-open vertical bowls, you'll find your favorite at Squaw. The slopes off KT-22 are legendary with skiers around the world. If you want to try freestyle for the first time, head for Belmont Park. During the day, especially weekends and holidays, expect long lines at the lifts, crowds in the nice big locker rooms, and still more crowds at the numerous restaurants and cafés.

Entertainment and Events

The annual **WinterWonderGrass** (Squaw Valley, www.winterwondergrass.com, late Mar. or early Apr., prices vary) is a huge outdoor celebration of music, food, art, and entertainment held at the base of the Squaw Valley ski hills. Past headliners have included Greensky Bluegrass, Trampled by Turtles, Leftover Salmon,

The Devil Makes Three, The Infamous Stringdusters, and Yonder Mountain String Band. There are craft brew tasting booths and local food trucks onsite to keep everyone well fed. Lodging is available within Squaw Valley ski resort. Free shuttle buses run from the Squaw Valley clock tower to Tahoe City and Truckee.

If you think yoga and partying don't belong together, you haven't been to **Wanderlust** (Squaw Valley, www.wanderlust.com, mid-July, $120-400), an annual festival of yoga, meditation, mindfulness, and entertainment. Take your yoga practice to the next level during daytime classes with world-famous instructors, then dance the night away as DJs and music producers take over stage. The gathering offers opportunities for both quiet contemplation and adventurous play in the surrounding Granite Chief Wilderness.

Shopping

Packed to the brim with high-quality outdoor goods and supplies, **Alpenglow Sports** (415 N. Lake Tahoe Blvd., 530/583-6917, www.alpenglowsports.com, 10am-6pm Mon.-Fri., 9am-6pm Sat.-Sun.) is Tahoe City's oldest outdoor shop. Find clothes and gear for hiking, camping, and all backcountry adventures. Winter merchandise focuses mostly on skiing while summer items are geared toward hiking and water play. True to the upscale vibe of the Lake Tahoe region, some stylish casual clothes, accessories, and souvenirs are also for sale.

You might think of **The Village at Squaw Valley** (1750 Village East Rd., Olympic Valley, 530/584-1000, www.squawalpine.com) as a ski area, but it's more like a small town where you could easily spend hours rambling around eating and shopping. Souvenir seekers can go straight to **Squaw One Logo Company**

From top to bottom: Barker Pass trailhead; views from the PCT near Twin Peaks; rugged red terrain in Granite Chief Wilderness.

(530/584-6250, www.squawalpine.com, 9am-6pm daily). If you're in need of outdoor gear and clothing, check out **North Face** (530/452-4365, www.northface.com, 9am-5pm Mon.-Fri., 8am-6pm Sat.-Sun.).

Food

Start your day with a fresh, down-home breakfast at **Fire Sign Café** (1785 W. Lake Blvd., 530/583-0871, 7:30am-2:30pm daily, $8-12), a busy family-owned breakfast-and-lunch joint popular with Tahoe locals. Delicious eggs Benedicts, French toast, and three-egg omelets are favorites; plenty of gluten-free and vegetarian options are available, too. Expect a wait for a table on weekend mornings.

Fat Cat Bar & Grill (599 N. Lake Blvd., 530/583-3355, www.fatcattahoe.com, noon-9pm Mon.-Thurs., noon-10pm Fri., 11am-10pm Sat., 11am-9pm Sun., $9-14) is great for casual, inexpensive dining, especially if you like entertainment with your food. Thursday is karaoke night, and Friday and Saturday nights have live music (from 9pm). The menu includes sandwiches, salads, and delicious grass-fed beef burgers. The café also has free wireless internet access.

For a casual, delicious meal, enjoy the shady outdoor patio at ★ **Bridgetender Tavern** (65 W. Lake Blvd., 530/583-3342, www.tahoebridgetender.com, 11am-11pm Mon.-Thurs., 11am-midnight Fri., 9am-midnight Sat., 9am-11pm Sun.), or sit inside at a table or at the beautifully hewn wooden bar. The menu is diverse, featuring classic American favorites like sandwiches, salads, burgers, and fry baskets as well as "Fresh Mex" items like ahi poke tacos, street-style tacos, and hearty veggie burritos. Globally inspired daily specials range from jambalaya to hangar steak with chimichurri to udon noodle bowls. Stop by for happy hour (4:15pm-6:15pm Mon.-Thurs.), when drinks and selected appetizers are discounted.

The **River Grill** (River Rd. at Hwy. 89 and Hwy. 28, 530/581-2644, www.rivergrilltahoe.com, 5pm-close daily, $19-45) overlooks the Truckee River as it pours out of Lake Tahoe. Eat outside on the rustic heated wooden porch, enjoying the river view while listening to live music, or sit indoors in the casually elegant dining room, complete with a fireplace. Happy hour (5pm-6:30pm daily) features discounted drinks and food in the bar and at the outdoor fire pit.

Long before fusion cuisine was popular, you could find it at **Wolfdale's** (640 N. Lake Blvd., 530/583-5700, www.wolfdales.com, 5:30pm-10pm Wed.-Mon., $15-35), an upscale waterfront restaurant serving a delightful selection of both Asian and New American plates since 1978. Everything about the restaurant is elegant, from the modern dishware to the airy outdoor patio. The small seasonal menu is heavy on seafood, but also includes tasty beef and game meats in season. Save room for the delicious desserts.

Christy Hill Lakeside Bistro (115 Grove St., 530/583-8551, www.christyhill.com, 5pm-9:30pm daily summer, 5pm-9pm daily winter, $21-33) is an ideal spot for a delicious, seasonally inspired dinner with a view. Entrées range from fresh cannelloni with homemade lemon ricotta to Moroccan spiced lamb loin. Be sure to ask your server about wine pairings from the incredible wine list. If you're just in the mood for a drink and a snack, the outdoor **Sand Bar** (beer and wine only) offers casual seating on the back deck.

More than half a dozen restaurants, snack bars, and coffee shops at **The Village at Squaw Valley** (1750 Village East Rd., Olympic Valley, 530/584-1000, www.squawalpine.com) offer sushi, pizza, high-end wine, and more. Two of the most popular restaurants are **Mamasake Sushi** (1850 Village South Rd., 530/584-0110, www.mamasake.com, 11:30am-9pm Mon.-Thurs., 11:30am-10pm Fri.-Sun., $6-76) and **Fireside Pizza Co.** (1985 Squaw Valley Rd., 530/584-6150, www.firesidepizza.com, noon-9pm Mon.-Thurs., noon-10pm Fri., 11:30am-10pm

Sat., 11:30am-9pm Sun., $13-26), plus several other eateries.

Accommodations

Just like its counterpart in South Lake Tahoe, **Basecamp Tahoe City** (955 N. Lake Tahoe Blvd., 530/580-8430, www. basecamptahoecity.com, $120-332) is stylish and modern, with a distinct mountain-chic design. Exposed wood, natural textiles, and regional artwork are on display in every room. Guests choose from king or queen beds and enjoy complimentary breakfast, free Wi-Fi, and access to the property's outdoor fire pits.

Within walking distance to most of Tahoe City's best restaurants, the **Pepper Tree Inn** (645 N. Lake Blvd., 530/583-3711 or 800/624-8590, www.peppertreetahoe. com, summer $96-213, winter $105-175) is also located right across the street from the waterfront Lakeside Trail. Rooms include fridges, microwaves, and coffeemakers, and all guests are invited to take advantage of an outdoor swimming pool, free wireless internet access, and on-site laundry facilities. North-facing rooms on the upper levels have views of the lake, and some rooms have oversized whirlpool tubs.

To stay as close to the mountains and the PCT as possible, get a condo at **The Village at Squaw Valley** (1750 Village East Rd., Olympic Valley, 866/818-6963, www.squawalpine.com, 1-bedroom condo $99-700, 3-bedroom $299-1,300) and hike right out your front door. Elegant, modern condos range from compact studios perfect for singles or couples to three-bedroom homes that sleep up to eight. Condos have full kitchens—some even have granite countertops—as well as a living room with a TV and maybe a fireplace, and a dining table. Included in the price is use of the Village's eight outdoor hot tubs, five saunas, five fitness rooms, and heated underground parking garage.

Camping

Every campsite at ★ **General Creek Campground** (Sugar Pine Point State Park, Hwy. 89, Tahoma, 800/444-7275, www.reserveamerica.com, mid-May-mid-Sept., $25-35) has a picnic table, a charcoal grill, and ample space for a tent or camper. Some sites are ADA-compliant. Amenities include clean showers (you can get a hot five-minute shower for $0.50). The campground in this wooded, wildlife-filled park can get crowded in midsummer, so make reservations in advance. In the off-season, there are 16 sites available on a first-come, first-served basis.

Not far from Sugar Pine Point State Park, the Washoe Tribe runs the **Meeks Bay Resort** (7941 Hwy. 89, Tahoma, 530/525-6946 or 877/326-3357, www. meeksbayresort.com, May-Oct., tent sites $20-30, RV sites $30-50). The 14 tent sites and 23 RV sites all have a two-night minimum; pets are not allowed. The resort features a sandy beach and a marina (530/525-5588) where you can rent single kayaks and pedal boats ($20/hour) and double kayaks, canoes, and paddleboards ($30/hour). You can also launch your own boat ($15 one-way, $25 round-trip) or rent a slip ($60/night, $360 weekly).

Information and Services

The Lake Tahoe Visitor Bureau maintains the **North Lake Tahoe Visitor Information Center and Chamber of Commerce** (100 N. Lake Blvd., Tahoe City, 530/581-6900, www.gotahoenorth.com, 9am-5pm daily). This spacious, beautiful facility has hundreds of pamphlets and publications to help you take advantage of the Tahoe region during your stay.

For medical attention, the **Tahoe Forest Hospital** (10121 Pine Ave., Truckee, 530/587-6011, www.tfhd.com) has the closest emergency room.

Getting Around

Tahoe Truckee Area Regional Transit (TART, 530/550-1212 or 800/736-6365, www.laketahoetransit.com) is the North Shore's public bus system. Buses ($1.75 adults one-way, $0.85 youth/senior/disabled, 24-hour pass $3.50 adults, $1.75 youth/senior/disabled) run between Tahoma, Tahoe City, Truckee, Kings Beach, and Incline Village, Nevada, with many stops along the way. During the summer and winter seasons, TART also offers service between Squaw Valley, Tahoe City, and Truckee on the Highway 89 route.

Truckee-Donner

Northwest of Lake Tahoe, Truckee is a sophisticated little mountain town with a historic downtown strip. Dining and shopping in Truckee feels like being in a big city, and it's no coincidence as the town is a popular relocation destination for reformed urbanites.

Following I-80 west of Truckee, Donner Lake sprawls south toward Donner Pass, offering plentiful recreation opportunities in summer and skiing at nearby resorts in winter.

On the ridgelines west of the lake, the Pacific Crest Trail traverses Donner Pass near the Sugar Bowl ski area and Donner Summit on I-80.

Getting There

From Tahoe City, follow Highway 89 north for 15 miles (24 km); allow about 20 minutes. Truckee is located along I-80, 100 miles (161 km) northeast of Sacramento and 30 miles (48 km) southwest of Reno, Nevada.

While it doesn't happen often, both Highway 89 and I-80 are subject to closure in severe winter weather. Traction tires or chains may be advised or required during more typical winter conditions.

Sights
Donner Memorial State Park

Donner Memorial State Park (12593 Donner Pass Rd., off I-80, 530/582-7894, www.parks.ca.gov, sunrise-sunset daily year-round, $5-10 parking) is a great place to experience the lush beauty that the ill-fated Donner Party was heading to California to find. Near the entrance to the park is the **Pioneer Monument,** a massive structure celebrating the courage and spirit of the Donners and others who made their way west in harder times.

The **visitors center** (530/582-7892, 10am-5pm daily year-round) offers uplifting information about the human and natural history of the area. The 0.5-mile **nature trail** at the visitors center is an easy self-guided trek through a forest of Jeffrey and lodgepole pines past the site of the cabin built by the Murphy family during the Donner Party's layover here in the winter of 1846-1847. A moving plaque at the cabin site lists those who perished and those who survived. The trail continues over a creek and through the campground. Guided nature hikes are offered from the museum daily starting at 10am during summer.

★ Donner Pass

Donner Pass (Donner Pass Rd., 8.5 mi/14 km west of Truckee, 80, 530/587-3558, www.exploredonnersummit.com or www.donnersummithistoricalsociety. org) is one of the legendary natural landmarks of the North Tahoe region. Take a scenic drive on Donner Pass Road (the former U.S. 40) to McGlashan Point and the Donner Lake Overlook, where you can enjoy sweeping views of Donner Lake and the surrounding mountains. To see Native American petroglyphs, climb the varied rock faces south of the highway at McGlashan Point. While you're there, check out the 1,659-foot railroad tunnel carved into the mountainside. It was completed in 1868, but is now defunct.

Truckee and Donner Pass

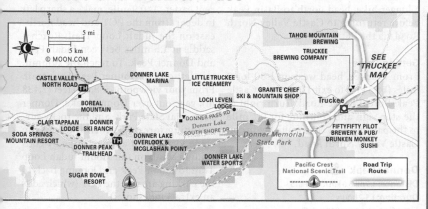

TAHOE MOUNTAIN BREWING
TRUCKEE BREWING COMPANY
SEE "TRUCKEE" MAP
GRANITE CHIEF SKI & MOUNTAIN SHOP
LITTLE TRUCKEE ICE CREAMERY
DONNER LAKE MARINA
LOCH LEVEN LODGE
Truckee
CASTLE VALLEY NORTH ROAD TH
BOREAL MOUNTAIN
DONNER PASS RD
Donner Lake
SOUTH SHORE DR
FIFTYFIFTY PILOT BREWERY & PUB/ DRUNKEN MONKEY SUSHI
CLAIR TAPPAAN LODGE
DONNER SKI RANCH
Donner Memorial State Park
SODA SPRINGS MOUNTAIN RESORT
DONNER LAKE OVERLOOK & MCGLASHAN POINT
DONNER PEAK TRAILHEAD TH
SUGAR BOWL RESORT
DONNER LAKE WATER SPORTS

Pacific Crest National Scenic Trail   Road Trip Route

0   5 mi
0   5 km
© MOON.COM

The Pacific Crest Trail crosses Donner Pass Road 0.5-mile west of McGlashan Point.

Donner Camp Picnic Ground Historical Site

If you want to learn more about what really happened to the Donner Party, visit the **Donner Camp Picnic Ground Historical Site** (Hwy. 89, 2.5 mi/4 km north of Truckee, www.fs.usda.gov/tahoe, May-Oct., free). The site is in the Tahoe National Forest, and it's a good place to stop for a picnic, a hike, or a mountain-bike ride. This is also where 25 members of the Donner Party, who had left Springfield, Illinois, in April 1846 on their way to new lives in California, stopped to repair their wagons in the fall after being slowed down by an ill-fated shortcut through Hastings Cutoff. It was only October when they got here, but a blizzard hit hard. Some of the party ended up staying the whole winter, and some, as you may know, never left.

The interpretive loop trail that begins and ends here is short and fairly flat, with signs along the way that illuminate the Donner Party's history.

Hiking
Castle Peak

Distance: 7 mi/11.3 km round-trip
Duration: 4 hours
Elevation change: 1,900 ft/579 m
Effort: Moderate
Trailhead: Castle Valley North Road

Hike to the top of Castle Peak, a giant rocky outcrop that towers over Donner Lake and the I-80 corridor, and get territorial views of the Truckee region.

Begin your hike by walking north out of the parking area on the road. The Pacific Crest Trail follows a similar path just east of your route. Ascend gradually through the forest, crossing a jeep trail at 0.7 mile and continuing northwest to stay on the Castle Valley North Road. Meet the PCT at a junction at 1.8 miles and continue north (up the hill) for 0.1 mile before the Castle Peak Trail splits off to the east. Follow the Castle Peak Trail northeast as it ascends an arm of the mighty butte. Enjoy the views during a short flat section at 2.5 miles before the elevation gain picks up again. At 3 miles, reach the western edge of the rocky top and turn right to head south on the Castle Peak Trail toward the summit. Reach your high point at 3.5 miles, the top of Castle Peak, where you can marvel at the rugged beauty of the Northern Sierra. Return the way you came, or to make it a longer hike, head north to Basin Peak before returning to Castle Valley North Road via the PCT.

Getting There

From Truckee, head west on I-80 for 9 miles (14.5 km) to exit 176 toward Castle Peak/Boreal Ridge Road. Turn right at the stop sign and continue for 0.1 mile to the parking area. The route begins on Castle Valley North Road.

Donner Peak

Distance: 3.5 mi/5.6 km round-trip
Duration: 1.5-2 hours
Elevation change: 940 ft/287 m
Effort: Moderate
Trailhead: Pacific Crest Trail at Donner Pass Road

Views from the top of Donner Peak show off Donner Lake and Truckee, as well as Donner Pass Pass as the scenic byway twists through a steep mountain pass.

Begin by walking south on the PCT.

The switchbacks in the first 0.25 mile keep the trail graded well to make the ascent easier. At 0.9 mile, make a sharp left to depart from the PCT and head northeast on the Judah Loop Trail. Reach a saddle at 1.5 miles between Judah Peak and Donner Peak. To reach the summit, stay left on the Donner Peak Spur trail. From your viewpoint at 8,000 feet (2,438 m), gaze out over Donner Lake, Donner Memorial State Park, and the rocky surrounding forests. Return the way you came, or make it a longer hike by continuing south on the Mount Judah Loop Trail to Judah Peak and looping back to the parking area on the PCT (which adds an extra 3 miles total).

Recreation

During the warm, dry summer months, locals and visitors alike love to splash into Donner Lake. Rent kayaks, stand-up paddleboards, canoes, and pedal boats at **Donner Lake Watersports** (Donner Memorial State Park, 12593 Donner

Donner Lake

Pass Rd.; Donner Lake Marina, 15695 Donner Pass Rd., 530/582-1999, www.donnerlakemarina.com, 9am-5pm Mon.-Fri., 8am-6pm Sat.-Sun., $20-30/hour). Surrounded by rocky, snowcapped peaks, Donner Lake offers some of the best views of Truckee's mountains. Look to the hills southwest of the lake to see the old railroad grade cut into the mountainside.

Winter Sports

Truckee is less than an hour's drive from half a dozen popular ski areas, each with their own appeal. Rentals are available at all resorts.

The biggest resort at Donner Pass is **Sugar Bowl** (629 Sugar Bowl Rd., Norden, 530/426-1111, www.sugarbowl.com, 9am-4pm daily Dec.-Apr., $118-125 adults, $97-103 youth ages 13-22 and seniors 65-74, $69-72 children ages 6-12 and seniors 75 and over), with 12 lifts and 1,540 skiable acres. The terrain is mostly intermediate and advanced, but there are a few hills appropriate for beginners.

Food is available at numerous outlets in the Village Lodge, Judah Lodge, and mid-mountain near the Mt. Lincoln chairlift, with options ranging from outdoor barbecue to fine dining with white tablecloths.

Donner Ski Ranch (19320 Donner Pass Rd., Norden, 530/426-3635, www.donnerskiranch.com, 9am-4pm daily Dec.-Apr., $75 adults, $65 youth ages 13-17 and seniors 70 and over, $35 children ages 7-12, $18 children age 6 and under) is a low-key, family-friendly ski area that prides itself on being more affordable than other Tahoe-area resorts. For those who aren't interested in skiing or boarding, the tubing hill (10am-4pm daily, $28) offers an alternative for winter fun. The humble, no-frills lodge has a café, a bar, and a wraparound deck for sunny outdoor seating.

The only resort with night skiing is **Boreal** (19749 Boreal Ridge Rd., Soda Springs, 530/426-3666, www.rideboreal.com, 9am-9pm daily Dec.-Apr., $79 adults, $69 youth ages 13-17 and seniors 60-69, $49 children ages 6-12, $34 seniors 70 and over, $5 children age 5 and under, $39 children ages 6-12 after 3pm). The mountain has eight lifts, including two magic carpets for kids and beginners. Boreal is known for its park terrain, with multiple rails, half-pipes, and jumps. Playland Tubing offers all-day ($54) or 90-minute ($39) sessions on the tubing hill. Food and beverage options include three cafés, a "waffle cabin," and a full bar.

Soda Springs (10244 Soda Springs Rd., Soda Springs, 530/426-1010, www.skisodasprings.com, 10am-4pm Mon. and Thurs.-Fri., 9:30am-4pm Sat.-Sun. Dec.-Apr., $50 adults, $45 youth ages 13-17, $40 children ages 6-12, $5 children age 5 and under) is Boreal's smaller sister resort. With just three lifts and two magic carpets, it's an approachable resort for kids or those new to snow sports. It also has Planet Kids ($40 per kid-adult combo), a snow play park with tubing

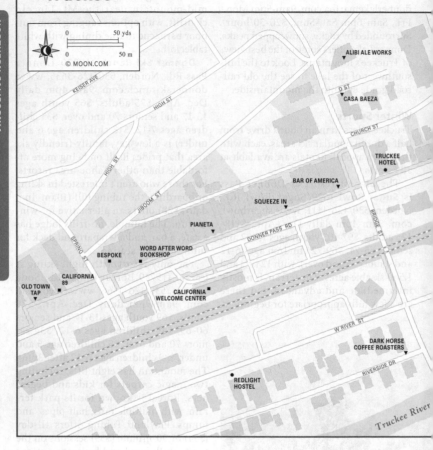

Truckee

0   50 yds

0   50 m

© MOON.COM

carousels and lanes, learn-to-ski areas, and play structures for kids seven and under to frolic in.

Entertainment and Events

Every Thursday evening during the summer, Truckee's downtown is transformed into a bustling street fair with dozens of booths featuring local art and artisan goods, plus food trucks, a beer garden, and a stage with live music for **Truckee Thursdays** (www. truckeethursdays.com, 5pm-8:30pm Thurs. June-Aug., free). This event is not

only fun, it's also the best way to meet locals and get a sense of this mountain town's friendly vibe.

If you're in the mood for some nightlife, the **Bar of America** (10040 Donner Pass Rd., 530/587-2626, www. barofamerica.com, 11am-11:30pm Mon.-Thurs., 11am-12:30am Fri., 10am-12:30am Sat.-Sun., $9-17) serves cocktails, food, and local beers. Bands tend to play here Thursday-Saturday and usually don't charge a cover. The outdoor patio is a nice place to hang out on summer evenings.

Breweries

Microbrews at **Alibi Ale Works** (10069 Bridge St., 530/536-5029, www.alibialeworks.com, noon-10pm Sun.-Wed., noon-midnight Thurs.-Sat.) are creative, diverse, and numerous. In addition to classic styles like IPAs, pale ales, porters, and stouts, Alibi takes pride in crafting unique sours, saisons, and traditional German styles, among others. The space is bright and modern, with lots of seating at the bar and the large dining area. Pub grub includes sourdough pretzels, gourmet nachos, and 2-3 upscale entrées with ingredients from local farms and food purveyors.

Beers at **Fiftyfifty Pilot Brewery & Pub** (11197 Brockway Rd., 530/587-2337, www.fiftyfiftybrewing.com, 11am-9pm daily) are hop-heavy IPAs and pale ales, plus some hazy IPAs and other seasonal rotators. If you're hungry, the food menu features all the classic beer-and-food pairings: burgers, pizza, fish-and-chips, and sandwiches, plus shareable appetizers, soups, and salads.

There are two industrial-chic taprooms on the west end of Truckee. Stop at **Truckee Brewing Company** (10736 Pioneer Trail, 530/562-9569, www.truckeebrewco.com, 3pm-9:30pm Mon.-Thurs., 2pm-9:30pm Fri.-Sun., $5-7) to taste a few IPAs, a pale ale, and perhaps a porter, sour, kolsch, or red ale. Just around the corner, you'll find **Tahoe Mountain Brewing** (10990 Industrial Way, 530/587-3409, www.tahoebrewing.com, 3pm-8pm Thurs.-Fri., noon-8pm Sat., noon-5pm Sun., $5-8), where creative brews and barrel-aged beers are the specialties.

Shopping

Truckee has a cute downtown strip with a number of specialty shops, mainly vending local art, gifts, and luxury clothing. You can visit most of these shops during a stroll along Donner Pass Road between Spring Street and Bridge Street.

One particularly lovely shop is **Bespoke** (10130 Donner Pass Rd., 530/582-5500, www.bespoketruckee.com, 10am-6pm Sun.-Thurs., 10am-8pm Fri.-Sat.), which has a beautifully curated collection of local and regional handmade goods: home decor, stationery, clothing, accessories, books, jewelry, and art.

Find regional guidebooks and natural history guides along with novels, poetry, and kids' books at **Word After Word Bookshop** (10118 Donner Pass Rd., 530/536-5099, www.wordafterwordbooks.com, 10am-6pm Sun.-Thurs., 10am-8pm Fri.-Sat.), a locally owned bookstore set back from the street in Truckee's shopping district. The cozy shop is packed to the brim with quality titles, the staff is friendly, and dogs are welcome.

You may recognize some familiar signage at **California 89** (10156 Donner Pass Rd., 530/214-8989, www.california89.com, 10am-6pm daily), a retail shop named for the scenic byway that traces the western edge of Lake Tahoe. Highway 89 also parallels the Pacific Crest Trail for much of its journey through Northern California, passing through Markleeville, Meyers, Truckee, Quincy, Lassen Volcanic National Park, Burney Falls, and Mount Shasta. The store has a nicely curated selection of high-quality Tahoe- and California-themed apparel and accessories that make great gifts or keepsakes from your road trip.

If you're in need of hiking clothing or outdoor gear, your best bet is **Granite Chief Ski & Mountain Shop** (11368 Donner Pass Rd., 530/587-2809, www.granitechief.com, 8am-6pm daily), which rotates inventory seasonally to reflect the sports of the moment. During the summer, hiking and backpacking gear is plentiful, along with boating, biking, climbing, and camping equipment, while the winter store selection focuses mostly on skiing and snowboarding. The staff is friendly and knowledgeable about the outdoor recreation opportunities in the greater Truckee area.

Food

Dark Horse Coffee Roasters (10009 W. River St., 530/550-9239, www. darkhorsetruckee.com, 7am-5pm daily, $3-6) is a unique place to enjoy a cup of joe before heading out for a day of exploring. The quirky basement café, with its mix of vintage and modern decor, is also the place where the single-origin beans are roasted. If you need breakfast too, pastries and tasty breakfast burritos are available.

The gigantic menu at the **Squeeze In** (10060 Donner Pass Rd., 530/587-9814, www.squeezein.com, 7am-3pm daily, $15-30) is a bit overwhelming, but it's impossible to choose poorly from the delicious breakfast and lunch classics. Although there are now 10-plus franchised Squeeze In restaurants, this location in Truckee is where it all began, and the long, narrow space in a historic building with exposed brick and over-the-top decor retains its authentic charm.

Reservations are coveted at **Pianeta** (10096 Donner Pass Rd., 530/587-4694, www.pianetarestauranttruckee.com, 5pm-9pm daily, $20-49), an elegant Northern Italian restaurant with delectable house-made pastas, fresh and colorful salads, and a curated selection of perfectly executed meat dishes. Romantic lighting and exposed brick walls add to the old-world feel. Many locals opt to visit for happy hour (5pm-6pm Sun.-Thurs.), when you can grab a spot at the bar without reservations and preview some of the antipasti, salads, and bruschetta items from the full menu.

While burgers are ubiquitous, there aren't many restaurants near the PCT where you can satisfy a sushi craving, so you may want to take advantage of the opportunity to dine at **Drunken Monkey** (11253 Brockway Rd., 530/582-9755, www.drunkenmonkeysushi. com, 11:30am-9pm Sun.-Thurs.,

From top to bottom: main street in Truckee; Squeeze In; cocktails at Old Town Tap.

11:30am-9:30pm Fri.-Sat., $12-19). Fresh, colorful fish is delivered daily and turned into satisfying rice bowls, sashimi, and maki and temaki rolls. Delicious noodles, tempura, teriyaki, and salads are also on the menu. The space is bright, clean, and casual, and there's a nice outdoor patio for summertime dining.

Both family-friendly and urbane, ★ **Old Town Tap** (10164 Donner Pass Rd., 530/563-5233, www.oldtowntaptruckee. com, noon-10pm Mon.-Thurs., noon-midnight Fri.-Sat., 11am-10pm Sun., $12-17) has broad appeal: rustic Italian cuisine, creative pizzas from the imported specialty oven, craft beer, local wines on tap, and exquisite cocktails to impress even the most discerning alcohol aficionados. The restaurant is popular with all types of Truckee locals and visitors, from families with small children to ravenous skiers at the end of a day of shredding. The owners are PCT hikers and supporters—look for trail-themed art on the walls.

Tequila enthusiasts won't want to miss **Casa Baeza** (10010 Bridge St., 530/587-2161, www.casabaezatruckee. com, 11:30am-9pm Mon.-Thurs., 11:30am-10pm Fri.-Sat., 9am-9pm Sun., $10-16) famous among locals for fantastic margaritas and a tequila selection that is downright impressive. Belly up to the wooden bar for a cocktail or beer, or grab a seat in the colorful dining room. The menu features all the classic Mexican American dishes, plus all-day breakfast, daily soups, and shareable appetizers.

In need of a treat after a sweaty hike? At the west edge of Donner Lake, **Little Truckee Ice Creamery** (15628 Donner Pass Rd., 530/587-2884, www. truckeeicecream.com, 12:30pm-6:30pm Sun.-Thurs., 12:30pm-8pm Fri.-Sat., $3-7) vends freshly made ice cream, sorbet, and dairy-free coconut ice cream at an adorable "scoop shop" with an outdoor patio. Salted caramel, strawberry, cookies and cream, and chocolate brownie are a few favorites. Rotating pop-up food trucks park in the lot next to the shop some days. Check the website or call the creamery to find out what food items may be available.

Accommodations

The **Truckee Hotel** (10007 Bridge St. at Donner Pass Rd., 530/587-4444, www. truckeehotel.com, $79-229) is a beautifully restored historic building from the early days of Truckee. In operation since 1873, rooms are designed in a Victorian fashion, with high ceilings and clawfoot tubs. Most of the 36 rooms have shared baths in the hall that are clean and comfortable, with either a shower or a bathtub and a privacy lock. The 3rd- and 4th-floor rooms are accessible only via stairs. Breakfast is included, and the hotel is also home to one of Truckee's most popular restaurants, **Moody's** (530/587-8688, www.moodysbistro.net, 11:30am-9pm Mon.-Fri., 11am-10pm Sat.-Sun., $20-46) with pizzas, pastas, and upscale American cuisine.

One part hostel, one part speakeasy-style bar, ★ **Redlight Hostel** (10101 W. River St., 530/536-0005, www. redlighttruckee.com) has both female-only and mixed-gender dorm rooms ($59-69), private rooms with shared bathrooms ($99-119), private rooms with en suite bathrooms ($139), and studio suites with a full kitchen ($159-199). Brilliant additions to the shared sleeping spaces include white-noise machines to drown out potential night noises from cohabitants. Between 4pm and 10pm, a sauna is available for hostel guests, and Wi-Fi is complimentary throughout the building. Stepping into the **bar** (5pm-9pm Sun.-Wed., 4pm-11pm Thurs.-Sat.), with its red damask-print wallpaper and gold-trimmed mirrors, is like stepping into a scene from a film. Creative cocktails are on the bar menu, of course, along with beer, wine, and a few appetizers and treats.

Outside of downtown Truckee,

Donner Pass Road follows the northern shore of Donner Lake, where a number of beautiful homes overlook the water. Quietly nestled among these houses and with a prime waterfront location is **Loch Leven Lodge** (13855 Donner Pass Rd., Donner Lake, 530/587-3773, www.lochlevenlodge.com, $130-200). The vintage neon sign out front hints that the property has been there for quite some time; indeed, it's been housing visitors to Donner Lake since 1952. Rooms have been updated and feature modern amenities. All rooms have views of the lake, coffeemakers, fridges, microwaves, and flat-screen TVs; some rooms have full kitchens. The lodge has a private dock from which to launch boats and rafts, and the outdoor hot tub is a lovely place to catch the sunset after a day of hiking.

If you're planning to hike on the PCT or any trails at Donner Summit, you may want to spend the night at the top of Donner Pass to get an early start. Since 1934, the Sierra Club has run the **Clair Tappaan Lodge** (19940 Donner Pass Rd., Norden, 530/426-3632 or 800/679-6775, www.ctl.sierraclub.org, $65-75). Accommodations are pretty basic, mostly men's or women's dormitories with shared bathrooms, but there are a few small rooms available for couples and larger rooms for families. You'll need to provide your own bedding or sleeping bag. Overnight lodging (Sierra Club members $65, nonmembers $70, children ages 4-13 $50, children under age 4 free) includes three home-cooked meals. Rates in winter and on weekends and holidays are usually $5 more. Communal spaces include a toasty library with a wood-burning stove, a hot tub, a recreation room, and extensive grounds.

Camping

Donner Memorial State Park (12593 Donner Pass Rd., off I-80 west of downtown Truckee, 800/444-7275, www.reserveamerica.com, reservations late May-mid-Sept., first-come, first-served mid-Sept.-late May, $35) offers a spacious, tree-filled campground with easy access to the lake, a nice visitors center, and trails in the park. It has 152 sites spread across three campgrounds: Ridge Campground (May-Oct.), Creek Campground (June-Sept.), and Splitrock (June-Sept.). Sites include fire rings and picnic tables, and there are restrooms with coin-op showers.

Information and Services

Truckee has a comprehensive **California Welcome Center** (10065 Donner Pass Rd., 530/587-8808, www.visitcalifornia.com, 8:45am-6pm Mon., 9am-6pm Tues.-Sun.) with free internet access on your computer or theirs, public baths, huge brochure racks, and friendly advice. The center is attached to the town's Amtrak station, perfect if you're coming from Reno or San Francisco.

If you need medical attention, the **Tahoe Forest Hospital** (10121 Pine Ave., 530/587-6011, www.tfhd.com) has a full-service emergency room, among other services.

Getting Around
Bus

Tahoe Truckee Area Regional Transit (TART, 530/550-7451, www.tahoetruckeetransit.com, $1.75 adults one-way, $0.85 youth/senior/disabled; 24-hour pass $3.50 adults, $1.75 youth/senior/disabled) provides service between Truckee, Tahoe City, Squaw Valley, and Incline Village, Nevada, as well as in-town routes between the Truckee Tahoe Airport, downtown Truckee, Donner Memorial State Park, and Donner Lake.

Train

You can reach Truckee by train on **Amtrak's** (10065 Donner Pass Rd., 800/872-7245, www.amtrak.com) *California Zephyr* route, which provides train service between Chicago and San Francisco, with many stops in between.

Sierra City

Sierra City is a historic mountain town nestled in a forested valley next to the Yuba River, which is famous for its summertime swimming holes. To get there, depart from Highway 89 for a twisty drive along Highway 49, the Yuba River Scenic Byway. The unassuming community is also the gateway to the Sierra Buttes, a distinct, striking massif with steep, craggy slopes. The Pacific Crest Trail crosses Highway 49 three miles east of Sierra City before zigzagging its way into the Sierra Buttes.

Getting There

Sierra City is 46 miles (74 km) northwest of Truckee, about an hour's drive. Take Highway 89 north for 28 miles (45 km), past Sierraville, then turn left to head west on Highway 49. This winding route climbs up and over Yuba Pass before arriving in Sierra City in 18 miles (29 km). While this route is open all year, it is subject to winter weather. Chains or traction tires may be advised or required. Also note that Highway 49 closes every time I-80 closes (as a preventative measure for truck and trailer traffic that twisty Highway 49 cannot accommodate).

Sights

In California, almost every town near the path of today's Pacific Crest Trail began as a gold mining town in the 1800s, and the **Kentucky Mine Museum** (100 Kentucky Mine Rd., 530/862-1310, www. sierracountyhistory.org, 10am-4pm daily Memorial Day-Labor Day, $2 adults, $0.50 children) is the best place to see (and hear) a historic stamp mill in action. Explore the museum's historic artifacts on your own, or take a one-hour guided tour (11am and 2pm daily, $7 adults, $3.50 children). The historic stamp mill, built into a hillside on the east side of town, consists of a three-story wooden building with heavy metal machinery inside and a tall bridge where the ore cars were wheeled out of the mountain and into the mill.

Hiking
Loves Falls
Distance: 1 mi/1.6 km round-trip
Duration: 30 minutes
Elevation change: 200 ft/61 m
Effort: Easy
Trailhead: Pacific Crest Trail at Highway 49

Cross the North Yuba River at Loves Falls, where the PCT spans the river on a bridge high above the cascades.

Start on the Pacific Crest Trail on the south side of the highway, and walk northeast on the southbound PCT. At the 0.3 mile mark, you can look southeast across the river canyon to see Milton Creek pouring down a steep hillside and joining the Yuba. Arrive at the bridge over Loves Falls at 0.4 mile, a multi-tier cascade with mini-falls and deep pools. While none of the falls are particularly impressive on their own, the beauty of this stretch of river is found in the magnificent gorge that the water has carved over thousands of years, and the bizarre shapes it has eroded into the boulders.

Make it a longer hike by continuing south on the PCT and/or making a loop through Wild Plum Campground.

★ Sierra Buttes Lookout Tower
Distance: 5.5 mi/8.9 km round-trip
Duration: 3 hours
Elevation change: 1,550 ft/472 m
Effort: Moderate
Trailhead: Pacific Crest Trail at Butcher Ranch Road

Hike to the top of 8,850-foot Sierra Buttes, then climb a formidable set of historic stairs to a lookout tower with panoramic territorial views of the Northern Sierra Nevada and the nearby Lakes Basin.

From the trailhead, walk south on the Pacific Crest Trail. After the first 0.7 mile, the trail flattens a bit as it traverses a ridge with fantastic early summer wildflowers. Meet the Sierra Buttes Trail at

Sierra Buttes Lookout Tower, Sierra City

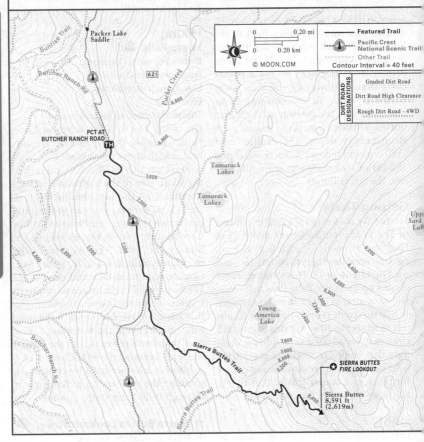

1.1 miles. The PCT veers right, but stay straight to remain on the Sierra Buttes Trail and begin your steady ascent up the massif. At 1.5 miles, take the left fork to a scenic viewpoint where you can look down on crystal clear Young America Lake. Return to the main trail and meet your first switchback at 2.2 miles. The last 0.2 mile of the hike is on a defunct dirt road that lookout tower employees used when the tower was in service. At 2.7 miles, the lookout tower and the set of 180 stairs leading up to it come into view. Closer to a ladder than a typical set of stairs, this staircase is incredibly steep. Views from the top are the absolute best in the entire region. Upper and Lower Sardine Lakes sparkle to the northeast, and on a clear day, you can see all the way to Mount Lassen (100 miles away). Note: If you're afraid of heights, the see-through grated platform on the fire lookout could make you queasy.

Getting There

From Sierra City, head east on Highway 49 for 4.9 miles (7.9 km), then turn left to head north on Gold Lake Highway.

Follow for 1.3 miles (2.1 km), turn left (west) on Packer Lake Road, and turn right after 0.3 mile to stay on Packer Lake Road. Arrive at the trailhead in 4.6 more miles (7.4 km).

Recreation

If you're eager to warm up on a chilly day or soothe tired hiking muscles, head back over Yuba Pass to **Sierra Hot Springs** (521 Campbell Hot Springs Rd., Sierraville, 530/994-3773, www.sierrahotsprings. org, 3-hour soak $20 pp Mon.-Thurs., $25 pp Fri.-Sun., plus $5 membership fee). This quirky resort houses its hottest spring-fed pool in a geodesic dome with stained glass and skylights. There are adjacent cold-plunge pools, as well as two outdoor warm pools ranging 98-100°F. Note that clothing is optional in all the pools. Overnight accommodations in the lodge ($66-132) and camping ($33-39 pp) are available should you want to spend the night—use of the springs is included in nightly rates. The pools are open 24 hours, but arrive between 9:30am-5pm to check in.

There's no better way to pass the time on a hot summer afternoon than by splashing into one of the nationally acclaimed **Yuba River swimming holes.** The entire river is thronged with deep pools, and you need not wander far from town to discover one. If you're staying at Buttes Resort, where some cabins have decks overlooking the river, there is a path leading from the southern edge of the property down to a great swimming hole. There are also premium spots at Wild Plum Campground on the east edge of town.

Entertainment and Events

Despite being such a small community, Sierra County holds community events at least monthly, from holiday dinners and chili cook-offs to film festivals and poetry and music shows. Some events are held in nearby towns Downieville or Sierra Valley. Check the events board at the **Sierra City Visitor Center** (Main St./ Hwy. 49 and Butte St.) to find out what's happening in the near future.

Food

Don't leave town without eating at the **Red Moose Café** (224 Main St., 530/862-1024, www.redmoosecafe.com, 8am-2pm Wed.-Sun. Apr.-Sept., closed Oct., 8am-2pm Thurs.-Sun. Nov.-Mar., $8-12), a cute breakfast-and-lunch joint with tasty scrambles, breakfast burritos, French toast, biscuits and gravy, and mimosas. Fish-and-chips are the lunchtime specialty, but burgers, soups, and sandwiches are popular, too. Two beers are on tap, with more available in bottles. You may find yourself ordering another just to continue a friendly chat with the owners while you sit at the historic wooden bar.

Drinking and dining at the ★ **Buckhorn Bar and Mountain Creek Restaurant** (225 Main St., 530/862-1171, www.buttesresort.com, 4pm-8pm Tues., 4:30pm-8:30pm Wed.-Sun., bar open 1pm-close Wed.-Sun., late Apr.-mid-Oct., $12-28) is a unique Sierra City experience. The building's river-stone and knotty pine interior gives it a distinct historical feel; you can almost imagine yourself as an early resident of this old mining town while sipping on your cold beer or cocktail. The outdoor dining area is built into a lush, terraced garden with a waterfall babbling through the center. Tuesday is taco night, but the regular menu features classic American favorites with an upscale twist, including some vegetarian and vegan options (encouraged by visiting PCT hikers, some of whom have very different tastes than the residents of this rural area).

Hikers like to relax on the porch outside **Sierra Country Store & Deli** (213 Main St., 530/862-1560, www. sierracountrystore.com, 10am-5pm daily Apr.-Oct., 10am-5pm Tues.-Sun. Nov.-Mar., $6-10) eating ice cream and taking advantage of the store's free Wi-Fi. This old-fashioned store harks back to the days

when shop owners worked downstairs and slept upstairs in an attached apartment (and in fact, this owner still does). The store has groceries, beer and wine, liquor, camping supplies, souvenirs, and a deli with fresh coffee, breakfast burritos, sandwiches, burgers, and pizzas.

Accommodations

Cabins at **Buttes Resort** (230 Main St., 530/862-1170, www.buttesresort.com, $95-160) are charming and perfectly appointed with cozy plaid linens, kitchens or kitchenettes, and porches or patios, some of which have views of the Yuba River in the canyon just south of the resort. Units vary in size, sleeping between 2-6 guests, and some units have fireplaces. Sierra City's restaurants are just steps away.

Upstairs from the Red Moose Café, the **Red Moose Inn** (224 Main St., 530/862-1024) has a few renovated rooms for rent with cozy cabin-like decor and antique touches. Call ahead for availability, which is limited during the summer when PCT hikers are in town.

Yuba River Inn (510 Main St., 530/862-1122, www.yubariverinn.com, $99-190) has ten cabins of varying size to accommodate singles, couples, or families. Most cabins have full kitchens, backyards with barbecues, and satellite TV. The location on the east edge of town is quiet and peaceful, and the resort has private riverfront property on the Yuba River.

Campgrounds

Located on Haypress Creek south of the PCT, **Wild Plum Campground** (Wild Plum Rd., 2 mi/3.2 km west of Sierra City, www.fs.usda.gov) has 47 sites with picnic tables, fire rings, bear-proof food boxes, and access to vault toilets. The Yuba River, Loves Falls, and the PCT are a short walk away via the Wild Plum

From top to bottom: Loves Falls in winter; Sierra Buttes Lookout Tower; Sierra Country Store.

Access Trail. **Reservations** (877/444-6777, www.recreation.gov, $24) are recommended on summer weekends when many Californians flock to the Yuba River to swim and cool off.

★ **Sardine Lakes Campground** (Sardine Lake Rd., 7 mi/11.3 km north of Sierra City, www.fs.usda.gov) is a popular campground near Sardine Lakes, the pristine lakes just north of the Sierra Buttes, where the rugged massif towers above the lake basin. All 29 sites include picnic tables, bear-proof storage lockers, fire rings, and access to potable water and vault toilets. Explore the lakes on the Sardine Lake Trail, part of which is a boardwalk over the water, or hike west on the Tamarack Connection Trail to reach the PCT from the campground. Make **reservations** (877/444-6777, www.recreation.gov) to guarantee a spot at this scenic and popular spot.

Information and Services

Sierra County staffs a **visitors booth** (Main St./Hwy. 49 and Butte St.) in summer. Public restrooms are available year-round.

Sierra Country Store (213 Main St., 530/862-1850, www.sierracountrystore. com) has a laundromat available to the public. During the summer, expect to share the space with PCT hikers, some of whom definitely smell like they've been living outside for months.

The nearest medical care is in Truckee at **Tahoe Forest Hospital** (10121 Pine Ave., 530/587-6011, www.tfhd.com).

Quincy

North of Sierra City on Highway 89, Quincy is the humble heart of a region known as the "Lost Sierra," so named for its tendency to be overlooked in favor of more popular regions near Tahoe. Located between the Middle Fork and the North Fork of the iconic Feather River, one of 12 nationally designated rivers in

the original 1968 Wild and Scenic Rivers Act, Quincy spreads out in a valley surrounded by forested mountains. West of town, the Pacific Crest Trail traverses ridgelines near Bucks Lake, a popular outdoor recreation area during northeastern California's hot summers.

Getting There

Quincy is 46 miles (74 km) northwest of Sierra City. Take Highway 49 east for 5 miles (8 km), then turn left to head north on Gold Lake Highway for 15 miles (24 km). Turn left onto Highway 89, traveling north for 26 miles (42 km) to Quincy.

Gold Lake Highway is closed between December and April due to heavy snowfall. From Sierra City, head east on Highway 49 for 18 miles (29 km), then travel north on Highway 89 for 41 miles (66 km). Allow about 75 minutes for this drive.

Roads in and around Quincy are subject to winter weather, and while they rarely close, chains or traction tires may be advised or required during the winter.

Sights

Driving around Quincy, you can't help but notice the colorful geometric patterns on historic barns and downtown buildings. These are Barn Quilts, each unique pattern created by community volunteers and local 4-H clubs. You can see many of the quilts during a self-guided driving or biking tour of the valley. Pick up a map of the tour route at the Plumas County Museum or in the brochure rack at Feather River Outdoors.

Plumas County Museum (500 Jackson St., 530/283-6320, www.countyofplumas. com, 10am-4pm Tues.-Sat., free) is the best place to learn about the varied past of Quincy and Plumas County. From gold mining, railroad construction, and timber to today's recreation, Quincy has been a hub of outdoor activity since the 1850s. Some of the museum's most fascinating exhibits highlight the lives and times of the Maidu people, who inhabited the

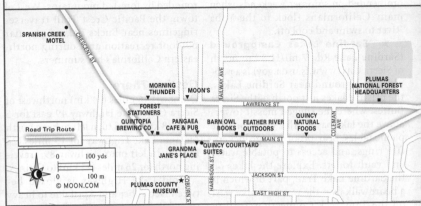

Quincy

valley for hundreds of years before white settlers arrived. In addition to exhibits with art, artifacts, clothing, dolls, baskets, skis, and musical instruments inside the building, the exhibit yard is full of historic equipment and tools used by gold miners and loggers.

Hiking
Spanish Peak (PCT)

Distance: 7.4 mi/11.9 km round-trip

Duration: 3-4 hours

Elevation change: 1,520 ft/463 m

Effort: Moderate

Trailhead: Gold Lake Trail at Silver Lake Campground

Hike to the top of Spanish Peak, a lofty mountaintop above Quincy and the American Valley, and enjoy sweeping territorial views of the Lost Sierra.

Begin your hike in Silver Lake Campground, where the Gold Lake Trail departs from the end of the road and heads east for 0.1 mile before turning south and ascending the ridgeline south of Silver Lake. Get a great view of Spanish Peak's rocky dome summit at 1 mile, and stay right to continue southwest up the hill on the Granite Gap Trail. Pass small Mud Lake at 1.2 miles, surrounded by the Sierra's trademark smooth, weather-aged granite. Get ready—the trail climbs significantly over the next mile. Meet the Pacific Crest Trail at 2 miles and veer left to head south on the PCT. From here forward, the trail stays pretty level as it heads southeast, traversing a ridge-line above sparkling Gold Lake in the basin below. At 3.3 miles, depart from the PCT and turn left to head east on a dirt road toward the summit of Spanish Peak. Arrive at the top at 3.7 miles, enjoying 360-degree views of the Bucks Lake Wilderness, Bucks Lake itself to the southwest, and the town of Quincy to the east.

Return the way you came, or make it a longer hike by continuing south on the PCT to Bucks Summit. You may choose to arrange a shuttle to pick you up or leave a car at the Bucks Summit trailhead for a one-way hike.

Getting There

Silver Lake Campground is 15 miles (24 km) west of Quincy, about a 35-minute drive. Take Bucks Lake Road west out of Quincy for 9 miles (14.5 km), then turn right onto Silver Lake Road and continue for 6 miles (9.7 km) to the campground.

Recreation
Bucks Lake (16469 Bucks Lake Rd., 530/283-4243, www.buckslakemarina. com) is an outdoor recreation hub 17

miles (27 km) southwest of Quincy, especially popular between Memorial Day and Labor Day for swimming, boating, waterskiing, and fishing. There are a few restaurants and casual resorts on the south shore of the lake, as well as a marina with boat rentals and a general store. The Pacific Crest Trail crosses Bucks Lake Road at Bucks Summit, 4 miles east of the lake and 13 miles (20.9 km) west of Quincy.

Getting There: From Quincy, follow Bucks Lake Road for 17 miles (27 km). During the winter, the road is only open as far as Bucks Summit, and chains may be required.

One of the most popular outdoor activities near Quincy is mountain biking. Forested mountains surround the entire town, and while the PCT itself isn't bike-friendly, many other trails are. **Feather River Outdoors** (530/283-0455, www.featherriveroutdoors.com, Apr.-Nov., $25-55) operates a bike shuttle to Mount Hough and Mills Peak, so you can cruise up to the top in an SUV and ride your bike back down the trails. Bike rentals are available for one-day ($50-85) or three-day ($125-195) increments.

Entertainment and Events

Every 4th of July weekend, Quincy is flooded with visitors for the annual **High Sierra Music Festival** (Plumas County Fairgrounds, 204 Fairground Rd., 530/283-6272, www.highsierramusic.com, $300 for 4-day pass, plus parking), a joyful gathering of music, art, and community. Dozens of live bands play throughout the weekend on multiple stages, and headliners in the last few years include Dispatch, Umphrey's McGee, String Cheese Incident, Ween, Ben Harper and the Innocent Criminals, Thievery Corporation, Dr. Dog, Lord Huron, and more. Attendees get silly, dressing up in costumes, painting faces,

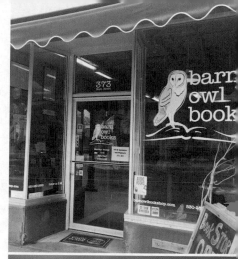

From top to bottom: Barn Owl Books; Quintopia Brewing; Ranchito Motel.

and just generally being playful during the event. Daily "body and spirit playshops" are offered, featuring yoga, Pilates, and dancing. Food vendors are on-site with a variety of cuisines. There are multiple camping options, both on-site and in nearby designated areas, some locations sunnier than others (consider bringing a shade tarp) and some friendly for RVs and trailers.

Shopping

Your go-to spot for anything and everything outdoor related is **Feather River Outdoors** (375 Main St., 530/283-0455, www.featherriveroutdoors.com, 10am-6pm Mon.-Fri., 9:30am-4:30pm Sat.), where you can find new and used gear for hiking, biking, boating, skiing, and fishing. There are plenty of camping and backpacking supplies, and the shop has a decent selection of clothing and accessories. Store owners and staff are friendly, passionate, and knowledgeable about the Quincy area. Summer rental options include mountain bikes ($50-85 daily), kayaks, and stand-up paddleboards ($40-50 daily); snowshoes, skis, and snowboards are available to rent during the winter ($25-45 daily). Note that bike shuttles still run on Sundays during the summer even though the store is closed.

The outdoor store shares a space with **Barn Owl Books** (373 Main St., 530/283-2665, www.barnowlbookshop.indielite.org, 10am-6pm Mon.-Fri., 9:30am-4:30pm Sat.), a family-owned bookshop with a great selection of local area guides, fiction, kids' books, and gifts.

Find locally made goods and unique gifts at **Forest Stationers** (531 Main St., 530/283-2266, 9:30am-5:30pm Mon.-Fri.), an office supply store with a curated collection of socks, stationery, jewelry, candles, leather goods, clothing, and toys.

Food

Restaurants in Quincy cater to locals, many of whom work downtown during the week but spend the weekends at home or in the mountains. Numerous downtown businesses are closed on Saturday, Sunday, Monday, or Tuesday. Check the hours ahead of time before setting your sights on a specific spot.

Stop at ★ **Quintopia Brewing** (541 Main St., 530/289-6530, www.quintopiabrewing.com, 3pm-9pm Wed.-Fri., noon-9pm Sat., noon-7pm Sun., $7-10), a bright and spacious new downtown brewery with big windows and a modern vibe. Choose between crispy battered, shoestring, or sweet potato fries, then select from a list of themed "loaded fries" toppings (among them Thai sweet chili, chicken masala, beef chili cheese, and Reuben), or keep it simple with a pretzel, arugula salad, grilled cheese sandwich, or a bowl of chili instead. Beers run the gamut from light to dark with medium-bodied options in between. The taproom is open five days a week, and the brewing facility just down the street is open on select Mondays seasonally—call ahead to get the schedule.

Owned and operated by a mother-daughter team who each specialize in different bakery items, **Grandma Jane's Place** (445 Main St., 530/616-5656, 6am-4pm Tues.-Sat., $4-8) vends a wide array of both sweet and savory fare. During Quincy's summer wedding season, bakers are busy with special-order cakes but still make time to stock the storefront with items for regular customers. If you go, try the flaky ham and cheese pastry, a breakfast burrito, or a piece of coffee cake.

Pangaea Café & Pub (461 Main St., 530/283-0426, www.pangaeapub.com, 11:30am-8:30pm Mon.-Fri., $10-13) is a bustling, family-friendly pub with juicy burgers, filling salads, wraps, and sandwiches with globally inspired flavors. There are plenty of options for vegetarians, vegans, and omnivores alike, including wheat-free and dairy-free choices. Local beers on tap are in constant rotation, varying with the seasons. The café also serves fresh, sustainable sushi and

⚐ Side Trip: Belden

Belden on the Feather River

Thirty miles (48 km) northwest of Quincy on Highway 70, the Pacific Crest Trail travels right through **Belden Town Resort and Lodge** (14785 Belden Town Rd., Belden, 530/283-9662, www.beldentown.com, $98-150), a rustic riverfront resort with hotel rooms, cabin rentals, and a large **restaurant-bar** (8am-10pm daily May-Oct., 11am-7pm daily Nov.-Apr.) overlooking the Feather River. Many long-distance hikers stop here for a cold beer or a satisfying meal on their way through. Although it's a bit out of the way, the pretty drive along the Feather River Scenic Byway and the unique location of this eccentric resort make Belden Town a worthy detour. Cabins include full kitchens, while hotel rooms have microwaves, mini-fridges, and TVs. Campsites, some with RV hookups, are also available.

Note: Tickets are required to enter Belden during annual festivals (www.beldentown.com/events.cfm). Third-party agencies handle bookings for the events and all the resort's overnight accommodations. These weekend parties feature live music and/or DJs, and a large stage is set up in the middle of the resort.

makes a mean stir-fry with seasonal veggies over rice. Take advantage of the free Wi-Fi.

You'll recognize **Moon's** (497 Lawrence St., 530/283-9900, www. moons-restaurant.com, 5pm-8:30pm daily May-Oct., 5pm-8:30pm Thurs.-Mon. Nov.-Apr., $15-20) by its beautiful river-stone exterior. Despite being one of the fancier restaurants in this casual town, its cozy and warm wooden interior still retains the quirky, rustic charm Quincy is known for. The house-baked garlic bread is a must, as are the hearty baked potatoes with decadent toppings. The menu primarily features pizza, pasta, and sumptuous salads, along with some upscale steak, chicken, and seafood entrées. Patio dining is nice in the summer.

You may forget you're far from the coast when you step inside **Mill Creek Fish 'N Chips** (1760 E. Main St., 530/283-0312, 11am-8pm Tues.-Sat., $9-15), a cute little seafood restaurant with tasty fry baskets, beef and wild game burgers, sandwiches, and, surprisingly, tacos. The place is decked out floor-to-ceiling with nautical decor. Fair prices, delicious food, and friendly service make this a worthy stop after a day in the car or in the mountains.

Patti's Morning Thunder (557 Lawrence St., 530/283-3300, www.

morningthundercafe.com, 6:30am-2pm Mon.-Fri., 7am-2pm Sat.-Sun., $7-12) is a cozy breakfast and lunch spot with lots of hometown charm. Enjoy generous portions of omelets and scrambles with fresh veggies, decadent French toast, and waffles, plus hearty salads and sandwiches. Outdoor dining on the shady front patio is a delight during the warm summer months.

Stop for hiking snacks and high-quality groceries at **Quincy Natural Foods** (269 Main St., 530/283-2528, www.qnf. coop, 7am-8pm Mon.-Sat., 8am-8pm Sun.), where you can get fresh-ground peanut and almond butter, crisp seasonal produce, and locally baked breads. This is the best place in town for local, organic, and specialty items. If you need a meal or snack on the go, check out the selection of healthy and delicious options in the case by the bakery items.

Accommodations

Located on the 2nd floor of a beautifully restored 1908 building, **Quincy Courtyard Suites** (436 Main St., 530/283-1401, www.quincycourtyardsuites.com, $149-189) has four apartment-style suites. Studio suites accommodate two guests and have a kitchenette with a microwave, coffeemaker, and mini-fridge. The larger suites accommodate up to four guests and feature a full kitchen. Private baths are modern and luxurious with clawfoot tubs. Coffee, tea, and Wi-Fi are complimentary during your stay, and there's an on-site laundry room for guests. Note: Suites can only be accessed via staircase.

Spanish Creek Motel (233 Crescent St., 530/283-1200, www.spanish-creek-motel-us, $79-92) is an affordable downtown option within walking distance of Quincy's brewery, restaurants, and shops. The furnishings are a bit outdated, but the wood-paneled walls are charming. Rooms have heat, air-conditioning units, microwaves, and mini-fridges. Wi-Fi is free throughout the property,

and continental breakfast is included with every stay.

A few miles east of downtown, the **Ranchito Motel** (2020 E. Main St., 530/283-2265, www.ranchitomotel. com, $76-95) is another no-frills option. Rooms are spread out among multiple buildings in a forested setting with various outdoor picnic and barbecue areas. All rooms have a mini-fridge, microwave, and coffeemaker; three rooms have kitchenettes with a stove, oven, and kitchen sink. Unless you want a room with a kitchenette, ask for a room in the original front building, which has a more charming early California mission style (the newer buildings are fairly plain). Some rooms are pet-friendly, and Wi-Fi is free throughout the property. If you want to watch a movie, you can check out a DVD from the extensive collection in the lobby.

PCT hikers will love the theme at cozy and quaint **Pacific Crest Cabins** (8298 Bucks Lake Rd., Meadow Valley, 530/616-0710, www.pacificcrestcabins.com, $175), where knotty pine cabins have full kitchens, private baths, fireplaces, and free Wi-Fi in a peaceful setting in Meadow Valley, 8 miles (12.9 km) west of downtown Quincy. Cabins here are convenient to Bucks Summit, Silver Lake, and Spanish Peak.

An overnight stay at **Feather River Hot Springs** (21986 Hwy. 70, Twain, 925/783-2913, www.featherriverhotsprings.com, Apr.-Nov., $20 tents, $45 RVs, $154-163 cabins) includes a soak in a mineral-rich riverside pool. Campsites and cabins are located on a shady patch of land between the Feather River and the scenic highway through the canyon. Woodsy, renovated cabins sleep 2 adults and include a queen bed, dresser, mini-fridge, microwave, coffeemaker, and dishes. All overnight guests have access to a large outdoor kitchen. If you're in the mood for a soak, but prefer to spend the night elsewhere, make reservations for a two-hour dip in the springs ($25). Feather River Hot

Quincy to Chester

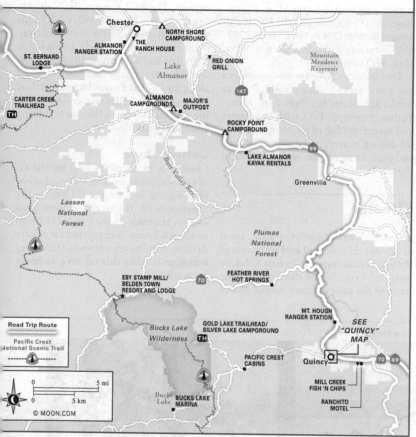

Springs are located 14 miles northwest of Quincy on Highway 70.

Camping

Ideal for tent camping, ★ **Silver Lake Campground** (Silver Lake Rd., www. fs.usda.gov, May-Oct., free) has nine first-come, first-served sites on the east edge of the lake with picnic tables, fire rings, and access to vault toilets. Bring plenty of water for drinking, washing, and cooking. Swimming isn't allowed in the lake, but nonmotorized paddle boating is permitted. The campground is

the access point for the Gold Lake Trail, which connects with trails leading to the PCT and the top of Spanish Peak. Silver Lake Campground is 15 miles (24 km) west of Quincy, about a 35-minute drive. Take Bucks Lake Road west out of Quincy for 9 miles (14.5 km), then turn right onto Silver Lake Road and continue for 6 miles (9.7 km) to the campground.

Information and Services

For info, free handouts, and pamphlets about the wilderness areas and national forests surrounding Quincy, stop at the

Plumas National Forest Headquarters (159 Lawrence St., 530/283-2050, www.fs.usda.gov, 8am-4:30pm Mon.-Fri.) in downtown Quincy, or visit the **Mt. Hough Ranger District** (39696 Hwy. 70, 530/283-0555, www.fs.usda.gov, 8am-4:30pm Mon.-Fri.) north of town.

The **Quincy Chamber of Commerce** has a self-serve visitor booth (Plumas Bank, 336 Main St., 9am-5pm Mon.-Thurs., 9am-6pm Fri.) with brochures and magazines full of recommendations for dining, overnight accommodations, and outdoor recreation opportunities in Plumas County.

Chester

Follow Highway 89 north to the tiny town of Chester, 25 miles (40 km) southeast of the southern entrance to Lassen Volcanic National Park. While the town's proximity to the national park is what draws most visitors, its prime waterfront location on beautiful Lake Almanor is a close second. The PCT crosses the Volcanic Legacy Scenic Byway 8 miles (12.9 km) west of Chester, and the trail's halfway point between Mexico and Canada is just 10 trail miles (16.1 km) south of the highway. Chester is one of the snowiest places along the PCT, and many businesses close up shop for the entire winter—visit during the summer when the sun is shining and the town is alive.

Getting There

Chester is 46 miles (74 km) northwest of Quincy, about an hour's drive. Follow Highway 89 for 44 miles (71 km) to the junction with Highway 36, then head east on Highway 36 for 2 miles (3.2 km) to reach Chester. Be prepared for winter driving conditions between December and March, when this region gets heavy snowfall.

Lake Almanor

Hiking
Butt Mountain  (PCT)

Distance: 10.3 mi/16.6 km round-trip
Duration: 5 hours
Elevation change: 1,950 ft/594 m
Effort: Moderate
Trailhead: Carter Creek

Spectacular views from the top of Butt Mountain include Lassen Peak, Lake Almanor, and the surrounding volcanic terrain.

From the trailhead, walk south on the Carter Creek Trail and meet the PCT at 1.3 miles. Turn left to walk east on the northbound PCT and begin to climb a hillside of manzanita bushes as the trail ascends toward Butt Mountain on switchbacks. You'll reach 7,000 feet in elevation at 1.9 miles, and over the next few miles, the PCT alternates between sparse forests, little meadows, and rocky volcanic terrain. Arrive at the Butt Mountain Trail cutoff at 4.6 miles and turn left to hike north and ascend the peak. It's only another 0.6 mile to the summit, but

there's little to no shade. Views from the top make it all worth it: the entire surface of Lake Almanor to the east, Lassen Peak on the northern horizon (the southernmost volcano in the Cascade Range), and 360-degree views of the wild and forested lands of northeastern California. Return the way you came for a 10.3-mile hike, or make it a longer hike by continuing in either direction on the PCT.

Getting There

Carter Creek trailhead is 18 miles (29 km) southwest of Chester. Before you go, stop by the **Almanor Ranger Station** (900 Hwy. 36, 530/258-2141, www.fs.usda.gov, 8am-4:30pm Mon.-Fri.) for maps and directions. Thanks to an unsigned network of dirt roads, it can be tricky to get here; use your car's odometer to follow these directions.

Head west on Highway 36 for 8 miles (12.9 km), then turn left to head south on Lost Creek Road for 0.4 mile. At the T intersection, make a hard right to drive west on an unsigned dirt road for 0.7 mile, then veer left and continue west on this road. After 2.3 miles (3.7 km), veer left to continue west for another 1 mile (1.6 km), then make a left at the T intersection to travel south for 4.8 miles (7.7 km). The trailhead is located on the south side of the road where the road crosses Carter Creek.

Recreation

Boating is one of the most popular summertime activities on Lake Almanor, where the summers are hot and dry. For a fun and splashy workout, rent a kayak or stand-up paddleboard at **Lake Almanor Kayak Rentals** (29529 Hwy. 89, Canyon Dam, 530/284-7372, www.lakealmanorkayaks.com, 9am-6pm daily May-Sept., $60-80/day), or if you're in the mood for an outing on a motorized craft, you can rent a ski boat ($194 for 2 hours, $469 all day), pontoon boat ($140 for 2 hours, $334 all day), fishing boat ($55 for 2 hours, $115 all day), or Jet Ski ($69/hour or $483 all day) at **Major's Outpost** (3000 Almanor Dr., 8am-8pm daily May-Sept.)

Shopping

B&B Booksellers (278 Main St., 530/258-2150, www.stoverlanding.com/b, 9am-5pm Mon.-Sat., 9am-3pm Sun.) is an adorable, three-level bookstore attached to Cravings Café. Thanks to the unique multilevel layout, the store is able to stock a huge selection of books, toys, accessories, journals, yarn, and gifts. Some books are even on display in the café, which is a beloved gathering place for locals.

Focused on biking and kayaking, **Bodfish Bicycles & Quiet Mountain Sports** (149 Main St., 530/258-2338, www.bodfishbicycles.com, 10am-5pm Tues.-Sat., noon-4pm Sun., closed Sun. and Thurs. in winter) is owned and operated by a passionate bicyclist nicknamed Bodfish who draws his own adventure maps, which you can see in the store and on the website. Inventory varies seasonally, but year-round you can find clothing, accessories, and gear for nonmotorized, human-powered outdoor sports.

Food

As is the case in many small towns, many of Chester's family-run restaurants are closed midweek when tourism is slow. Check the hours in advance to make sure your planned destination will be open to serve you.

The most iconic restaurant in Chester is **Pine Shack Frosty** (321 Main St., 530/258-2593, 11am-7pm Sun.-Tues., 11am-8pm Fri.-Sat. May-Sept., $5-10), an old-school fast-food joint with tasty burgers, sandwiches, and fry baskets. Broasted chicken and ribs are on the menu, too. As for cold treats, it's a tough choice between soft-serve ice cream or an ice cream shake—there are more than three dozen flavors available for the shakes. Nothing beats this spot for a post-hike meal. As an added bonus, according to a wooden sign out front, your

entire purchase is free if Lassen Peak erupts while you're ordering.

The **Ranch House** (669 Main St., 530/258-4226, 11am-8pm Wed.-Fri., 7am-8pm Sat.-Sun., $9-13) is a family-friendly restaurant-bar with local beers on tap and a full liquor selection. The restaurant serves soups, salads, sandwiches, and, during dinner hours, nice steak, chicken, and seafood entrées. Eat out back on the shady patio in the summer, or slide into a cozy wooden booth if you prefer the comfort of air-conditioning. Weekend brunch is popular with locals and visitors alike.

The best breakfast in town is at ★ **Cravings Café** (278 Main St., 530/258-2229, 7am-2pm Thurs.-Mon., $8-12). Choose from breakfast burritos, croissants, hashes, omelets, biscuits and gravy, French toast, and waffles. The long list of sides and à la carte items allows you to customize your meal to personal perfection. Big east-facing windows allow for lots of morning sun to shine on the dining tables. It's located in the same building as B&B Booksellers.

The sign outside says "fine homemade cookin," and it's true at the **Kopper Kettle** (243 Main St., 530/258-2698, 6am-9pm daily, $10-18) a vintage diner—think wood paneling and brick-red leather booths—with all-day breakfast and American comfort food classics. In addition to all the standard breakfast offerings, choose from hearty salads and wraps, grilled sandwiches, and dinner entrées like pot roast and steak and prawns. Service is prompt and very friendly at this popular locals' hangout.

Although it's a little bit out of the way, the **Red Onion Grill** (303 Peninsula Dr., 530/596-1800, www.redoniongrill.com, 5pm-8:30pm daily, closed Mon.-Tues. Dec.-Mar., $14-39) is well worth the trip. The upscale menu features steaks grilled to order, expertly seasoned seafood, delectable flatbreads, and some tasty appetizers. For the ultimate dining experience, order the Steakhouse Mixed Grill for two: juicy cuts of both filet mignon and rib eye, plus a fire-grilled shrimp skewer, parmesan baked potato, and sautéed seasonal veggies.

Accommodations

Built in 2008, **Antlers Motel** (268 Main St., 530/258-2722, www.antlersmotel. com, $90) is a nice place to stay in downtown Chester. Rooms are decorated in a "modern lodge theme" with moose-and-forest-print linens, all including mini-fridges, coffeemakers, TVs, and decorative fireplaces. The front desk has a large selection of board games if you want to relax in your room without screen time.

St. Bernard Lodge (44801 Hwy. 36, Mill Creek, 530/258-3382, www. stbernardlodge.com, $102-115) is a charming bed-and-breakfast with seven rooms, all appointed with knotty pine interiors, cozy quilts, robes, and slippers. While all rooms have a sink and mirror, full bathrooms are down the hall. For breakfast (8am-10am), overnight guests order from a menu of scrambles, omelets, and pancakes. The lodge's location is convenient to Lassen Volcanic National Park, about 10 minutes closer to the park's entrance than the town of Chester.

Camping

If you're planning to camp in or near Chester, you may as well choose a waterfront location on Lake Almanor, where the views are grand and the water is inviting.

North Shore Campground (Hwy. 36/89, 530/258-3376, www. northshorecampground.com, Apr.-Oct., tents $26-36, RVs $40-56) is 2 miles (3.2 km) east of Chester with 130 sites for tents and RVs. Facilities include picnic tables, fire rings, drinking water, restrooms with flush toilets and showers, and a small store.

Almanor North and South Campgrounds (877/444-6777, www. recreation.gov, May-Sept., $15-100) are operated by the **Almanor Ranger District** (530/258-2141, www.fs.fed.us). Situated directly on the lake, the 104 campsites offer great views of Lassen as well as biking, hiking, and fishing. Facilities include picnic tables, fire rings, drinking water, vault toilets, and a boat ramp. To reach the campgrounds, turn right on Highway 89 2 miles (3.2 km) west of Chester and drive 6 miles (9.7 km) to County Road 310; turn left for the campground.

Rocky Point Campground (916/386-5164 or 530/284-1785, www.pge.com, May-Oct., $23-46) is at the southwest end of Lake Almanor, with 131 sites for tents and RVs. Facilities include picnic tables, fire rings, drinking water, and vault toilets. You can reserve most of those sites online starting in early March; 24 sites are first-come, first-served only.

Information and Services

Find dozens of free brochures, pamphlets, and visitor publications just inside the front door at **Cravings Café** (278 Main St.), or for information about hikes and nearby national forests, visit the **Almanor Ranger Station** (900 Hwy. 36, 530/258-2141, www.fs.usda.gov, 8am-4:30pm Mon.-Fri.). For a comprehensive overview of the economic region surrounding Chester, visit the **Lake Almanor Area Chamber of Commerce** (www. lakealmanorarea.com).

Lassen Volcanic National Park

Lassen Volcanic National Park (www.nps. gov/lavo, 530/595-4480, 9am-5pm daily, visitors center 530/595-4480, 9am-5pm daily Apr.-Oct., 9am-5pm Wed.-Sun. Nov.-Mar.) is one of the oldest national parks in the United States, filled with ample hiking trails, lovely ponds, and several campgrounds with amazing views of the surrounding volcanic terrain. The centerpiece of the park, Lassen Peak is an active volcano with a long recorded history of eruptions, the last of which occurred in 1914-1917.

Highway 89 runs south-north through the park, making it easy for summer road-trippers to take in the park's best features, including numerous areas of active volcanic activity. The scenic drive takes you from the stark slopes and jagged rocks of the most recent eruption around the back to an enormous ancient crater, the remains of a long-gone volcano. Beyond the bounds of the national park, national forest lands allow for additional exploration. Half the park is only accessible via dirt roads and backcountry trails, which include the PCT.

Getting There

From Chester, follow Highway 36 west for 25 miles (40 km), then continue north on Highway 89 as it enters the park.

From I-5 at Red Bluff, take exit 649 toward Highway 36 east. Continue east for 46 miles (74 km) to the junction with Highway 89, then turn north and enter the park.

During the winter, the road is only plowed as far as the Kohm Yah-mah-nee Visitor Center. Explorations farther into the park require snowshoes or skis.

Entering the Park

Most road-trippers will access the park via the south entrance along **Highway 89,** also known as the Volcanic Legacy Scenic Byway. This entrance leads to the Kohm Yah-mah-nee Visitor Center, which is open year-round. From here, the 30-mile (48-km) park road circles eastward around Lassen Peak to reach Manzanita Lake and the north entrance of the park. Visitors entering the park from the north via Highway 44 should stop at the Loomis Museum near Manzanita Lake. Note that the north entrance is open in summer only.

The **park entrance fee** is $25 for vehicles, $20 for motorcycles, and $12 for travelers on foot. The entrance fee decreases to $10 in winter. All entrance fees are valid for seven days.

Visitors Centers

The **Kohm Yah-mah-nee Visitor Center** (21820 Lassen National Park Hwy., 530/595-4480, www.nps.gov/lavo, 9am-5pm daily Apr.-Oct., 9am-5pm Wed.-Sun. Nov.-Mar.) is a modern, state-of-the-art facility located at the south entrance to the park. An auditorium shows films, interactive exhibits illuminate local geology and ecology, and a well-stocked snack bar and souvenir shop keeps visitors busy. There's also an attractive amphitheater, a first-aid center, and large modern restrooms. Outside, strategically placed benches offer great spots to enjoy lunch or a snack with gorgeous views of the mountains. A short interpretive trail follows paved walkways with informative signage. The visitors center is accessible even when the park road closes due to snow.

Entering the park from the north, you'll find visitors services at the **Loomis Museum** (530/595-6140, 9am-5pm Fri.-Sun. mid-May-mid-June, 9am-5pm daily mid-June-Oct., free), which offers a wonderful opportunity to learn about the history of Mount Lassen and the 1914-1915 eruptions photographed by Mr. B. F. Loomis. This interpretive museum offers a rare chance to see, through photos, the devastation and stages of regrowth on the volcanic slopes. The museum was named

Lassen Volcanic National Park

*Thousand Lakes
Wilderness*

HAT CREEK RIM
OVERLOOK

CAVE
CAMPGROUND   SUBWAY CAVE

89

44

HAT CREEK
RESORT & RV PARK

*Lassen
National
Forest*

44

89

BUTTE LAKE RD

LOOMIS
MUSEUM

*Chaos Crags
Trail*

*Butte
Lake*

MANZANITA LAKE
CAMPGROUND

CHAOS
CRAGS

89

Noble Trail

*Lassen
Volcanic
National
Park*

SUMMIT LAKE NORTH
TRAILHEAD/
SUMMIT LAKE NORTH
CAMPGROUND

Lassen Peak
10,460 ft

TH

LASSEN PEAK
TRAILHEAD

TH

SUMMIT LAKE SOUTH
CAMPGROUND

SULPHUR
WORKS

BUMPASS
HELL

*Juniper
Lake*

WARNER VALLEY
CAMPGROUND

*Brokeoff
Mountain*

DRAKESBAD
GUEST RANCH

KOHM YAHMAHNEE
VISITOR CENTER

CHESTER WARNER VALLEY RD

89

THE VILLAGE
AT CHILDS MEADOW

36

Mineral

HIGHLANDS RANCH
RESORT

89

Road Trip Route

Pacific Crest
National Scenic Trail

0   2.5 mi

0   2.5 km

© MOON.COM

for the photographer, who later became a major player in the push to make Mount Lassen a national park.

When to Go

The park's rugged weather and isolated location means that a visit here offers an opportunity to explore a largely unspoiled wilderness—but only in **summer.** Although it is officially open year-round, snow completely buries the area between October and June, closing the main road through the park and making even the lower-altitude campground snowy and cold. Unless you're an avid winter recreation fan, the only time to visit Lassen is the height of summer; most visitors pick August and early September.

Permits and Regulations

Backcountry camping is permitted at Lassen; several hike-in campgrounds offer some minimal facilities and a way to lessen your impact on the landscape. A free wilderness permit is required; there are no quotas. To apply for a permit, download an application online (www.nps.gov/lavo) and submit it prior to your trip. Permits are also available in the park at the Loomis Museum (530/595-6140, 9am-5pm Fri.-Sun. mid-May-mid-June, daily 9am-5pm mid-June-Oct.) and the Kohm Yah-mah-nee Visitor Center (530/595-4480, www.nps.gov/lavo, 9am-5pm daily Apr.-Oct., 9am-5pm Wed.-Sun. Nov.-Mar.).

Scenic Drive

From the south entrance, the park road becomes the **Lassen Volcanic National Park Highway** (also known as Highway 89 and the Volcanic Legacy Scenic Byway) as it winds north 30 miles (48 km) to Manzanita Lake. Stop at **Sulphur Works** (1 mi/1.6 km from entrance) for a peek at some bubbling, steaming mud pots. A boardwalk runs along the road, and a parking area is nearby, making it easy for visitors to examine these fascinating geothermal features.

Continue 5.5 miles (8.9 km) north to **Bumpass Hell,** where you'll find a colorful and varied area of volcanic geothermal activity. From the parking lot, a trail leads to clusters of boiling mud pots, fumaroles, steaming springs, and pools of steaming water. The unmistakable smell of sulfur offers more evidence that this volcano is anything but extinct. Boardwalks are strategically placed through the area, creating safe walking paths for visitors.

In 0.5 mile, catch a glimpse of the trail to the top of **Lassen Peak** where it looms at 10,457 feet (3,187 m) in elevation. Even if you're not up to the hike, it's worth stopping at the trailhead parking lot to gaze up at the peak and enjoy beautiful Lake Helen just below.

Summit Lake (9 mi/14.5 km north of Lassen Peak) attracts campers to its two scenic campgrounds. An easy walk circumnavigates the lake for those who want to stretch their legs.

The Hot Rock turnout offers great views of the **Devastated Area.** When Mount Lassen blew its top in 1915, a tremendous part of the mountain (including all life on its slopes) was destroyed. Boiling mud and exploding gases tore the side off Lassen's peak, killing all vegetation in the area. Today this "devastated area" includes an interpretive walk through a small part of the disrupted mountainside, now filled with some of the world's youngest rocks, as well as grasses, shrubs and tall pine trees. The Devastated Area has ample parking, and the interpretive walk is flat and wheelchair accessible.

The broken and decimated area known as **Chaos Crags** (11.8 mi/19 km north of Summit Lake) was caused by a massive avalanche about 300 years ago. Today visitors can see a wealth of new life, including a broader-than-average variety of coniferous trees.

In one mile, turn left for sparkling **Manzanita Lake,** which has plentiful camping, cabins, and water sports in summer. The Loomis Museum and the park's north entrance are just ahead. Stop at the museum to get an in-depth look at the park's history and the people who fought for its preservation.

Continue your scenic drive beyond the park's northern boundary by exiting the park and heading northeast on Highway 44/89 to Old Station. After 13 miles (20.9 km), stay straight to head north on Highway 89, then make your first right to see the **Subway Cave,** a long, underground lava tube formed by volcanic activity less than 20,000 years ago. Aptly named, the cave is as large as an underground train tunnel. You can walk all the way through the cave, which is completely dark—a flashlight or headlamp is absolutely necessary!

Cap your adventure and cross paths with the Pacific Crest Trail at the **Hat Creek Rim Overlook** (3.7 mi/6 km north of Old Station on Highway 44). This vista point showcases the unique geological fissures, crevices, and fractures of the Hat Creek Valley, and interpretive signage provides a nice overview of the area's ancient and recent history. Lassen Peak is on display to the south, and Mount Shasta, the next-nearest Cascade volcano, shimmers on the northern horizon. Despite its stark beauty, this 30-mile stretch of the PCT (known as Hat Creek Rim) is dreaded among long-distance hikers due to a complete absence of water sources. While most hikers choose to bear the extra weight and carry enough water for the entire stretch, some are lucky enough to get resupply support, making arrangements with a friend to meet them halfway with water.

Hiking

Thanks to the extreme weather conditions in this part of California, which range from blistering heat to blustering snowstorms, there's a fairly short window in which you can hike comfortably in Lassen Volcanic National Park. Most hikers choose to explore this area between July and September; be prepared for various types of weather when you visit. The **Pacific Crest Trail** traverses 17 miles of high-elevation terrain through the national park, a few miles east of the highway and park entrances, offering lots of challenge and solitude.

TOP EXPERIENCE

★ Lassen Peak Trail

Distance: 5 mi/8 km round-trip
Duration: 3-4 hours
Elevation change: 2,000 ft/610 m
Effort: Strenuous
Trailhead: Lassen Peak

The must-do hike for any serious hiker is Lassen Peak Trail. This path not only takes you to the highest point in the national park, it also offers a unique perspective of the stark volcanic terrain in the rest of the park and beyond. The climb to the top is dramatic, challenging, and worth it. It's not actually a long hike—only 5 miles round-trip—but the trail gains more than 2,000 vertical feet in only 2.5 miles on the way up. The trail is well graded and has many switchbacks, which help manage the steepness. Exhibits along the way explain some of the fascinating views of volcanic remains, lakes, wildlife, and rock formations. The recent (by geologic standards) eruption and prevailing weather conditions leave this peak without much plant life, which means nothing blocks your views downward and outward; it also means there's little to no shade, so dress accordingly. Only the last 0.25 mile or so actually involves any scrambling over large rocks; most of the trail is just a steady upward walk. From the summit, marvel at the 360-degree views of the volcanic landscape below and Mount Shasta shimmering in the distance.

Summit Lake to Echo Lakes

Distance: 4.4 mi/7 km round-trip
Duration: 2.5 hours
Elevation change: 810 ft/246 m

Effort: Moderate

Trailhead: Summit Lake

This pleasant hike through a lake-studded forest gives you a taste of the national park backcountry, plus a delightful opportunity to cool off in a pristine alpine lake when the weather is hot.

Start your hike at the Summit Lake trailhead and walk south toward the Summit Lake campgrounds. After 0.4 mile, you'll reach the shore of Summit Lake. When the trail forks at 0.5 mile, stay left to head east on the Echo Lakes/ Twin Lakes Trail. The path rises 6,700 feet to 7,100 feet over the next 0.7 mile before delivering you to the top of the plateau around the 1.2-mile mark. The views of Lassen Peak are stunning.

At a trail junction at 1.4 miles, stay straight to continue east toward **Echo Lake** (4.4 miles/7 km round-trip) and descend to reach the lakeshore. This is a fantastic swim spot on hot days, which are common during the summer.

Turn around here or extend the hike by continuing 1.4 miles to **Upper Twin Lake** (7.2 miles/11.5 km round-trip). **Lower Twin Lake** (8.4 miles/13.5km round-trip) is 0.5 mile beyond Upper Twin; the Pacific Crest Trail traces the eastern edge of Lower Twin Lake.

Make this a lollipop-loop by circling Lower Twin Lake, returning to the Echo Lake Trail, and walking west back to the Summit Lake trailhead (8.4 miles round-trip).

Getting There

The Summit Lake trailhead and parking area are located on the east side of Highway 89, 0.3 mile north of the Summit Lake North Campground.

From top to bottom: Lassen Peak from Highway 89; sunset at Manzanita Lake; backcountry lake in Lassen Volcanic National Park.

Recreation

There's no better way to enjoy a hot, sunny day in the park than paddling around Manzanita Lake, where Lassen Peak looms large above the water. Rent kayaks, canoes, and stand-up paddleboards at the **Manzanita Lake Camper Store** (in the Manzanita Lake Campground, 530/335-7557, www.lassenlodging.com, 10am-4pm daily late May-late Sept., $15-30/hour).

Food

Dining options are limited inside the park. If you're camping, shop in Chester and bring lots of food with you. There's decent food available at **Kohm Yah-mah-nee Visitor Center** (Hwy. 89, 530/595-4480, www.nps.gov/lavo, 9am-5pm daily Apr.-Oct., 9am-5pm Wed.-Sun. Nov.-Mar.), where the snack bar sells burgers, slices of pizza, hot coffee, and ice cream. Hours can vary during the winter.

Part of the year, the small **Manzanita Lake Camper Store** (8am-8pm daily summer, 9am-5pm daily late spring and early fall) sells gifts, camping supplies, hot food, snacks (including s'mores for campfires), and ice cream. The park's only gas station is located right behind the camp store and is available 24 hours per day.

If you're in the mood for a nice restaurant meal and you're willing to drive 10 miles (16.1 km) out of the park, **Highlands Ranch Resort** (41515 Hwy. 36, Mill Creek, 530/595-3388, www.highlandsranchresort.com, 7:30am-9pm daily mid-May-Oct., 4:30pm-9pm Thurs., 8am-9pm Fri.-Sun. Nov.-mid-May) has a huge, magnificent dining room and deck overlooking Childs Meadow. Open for breakfast, lunch, and dinner, the restaurant and bar serve upscale American cuisine that doesn't disappoint. The dinner menu ($17-39) features steaks, pastas, and chicken entrées, while breakfast and lunch ($8-17) keeps things more casual with egg dishes, sandwiches, burgers, and salads.

Accommodations and Camping
Inside the Park

The ★ **Summit Lake North** (46 sites, 877/444-6777, www.recreation.gov, late June-Sept., $24) and ★ **Summit Lake South** (48 sites, 877/444-6777, www.recreation.gov, late June-late Sept., $22) campgrounds are some of the most popular in the park. Reservations are recommended, but some sites are designated walk-up only. While you're here, swim in Summit Lake, easily accessing its banks from trails and campsites. These two developed campgrounds have fire rings, picnic tables, access to potable water, and toilets (flush in North Summit, pit toilets only in South). At 7,000 feet (2,134 m) elevation, the Summit Lake campgrounds are among the highest in the park. If you've been living or traveling at lower elevations, it may take some time to get used to the thin air. Bring layers for potentially chilly nights.

Located close to the north entrance, pleasant and serene **Manzanita Lake Campground** (179 sites, 877/444-6777, www.recreation.gov, May-Oct. or first snowfall, $26) is the largest campground in Lassen. Manzanita Lake has a full slate of amenities, including flush toilets, potable running water, fire rings or pits, picnic tables in all campsites, and an RV dump station, and it's the only place in the park where showers are available, in the nearby camp store (quarters required). Trailers and campers up to 35 feet are allowed. Advance reservations are recommended.

Remote **Warner Valley Campground** (18 sites, June-Sept., $16) is set along the south edge of the park near the PCT. A small gem of a semi-developed campground, Warner Valley has pit toilets and drinking water as well as tables and fire pits at each site. Trailers are not allowed at this first-come, first-served campground—although the dirt road is only one mile long, it's too rough for large campers and RVs to navigate.

◈ Side Trip: Drakesbad

Drakesbad Guest Ranch, Warner Valley

The Pacific Crest Trail runs right through **Drakesbad Guest Ranch** (end of Warner Valley Rd., Chester, 866/999-0914, www.lassenlodging.com/drakesbad, June-mid-Oct., $220-243/day single adult, $394-464/day double adult, $162-185/day each additional adult, $75/day children ages 7-14, 2-night minimum), a rustic 1880s ranch that's been beautifully maintained and transformed into a serene backcountry retreat. Choose from rooms in the lodge, cabins, and bungalows for overnight accommodations, all including three gourmet meals each day (reservations are required). Most overnight accommodations are without electricity, but kerosene lanterns and gas heat keep them comfortable. Spend your time at the ranch taking guided trail rides through the national park ($75-190) on one of the ranch's horses. You're within steps of hiking trails, including the PCT, which crosses Warner Valley Road 0.5 mile east of the main lodge building. The ranch even has a wonderful warm swimming pool that's fed by the water from a local hot spring. Bring your tackle along on a walk or a ride to take advantage of the fishing available in the local lakes and streams; the ranch can also connect you with local guides from the Lake Almanor Fly-Fishing Company (530/258-3944, http://almanorflyfishing.com).

Getting There

Drakesbad is only 17 miles (27 km) from Chester, but it's a long drive on a winding road to get there—allow about 50 minutes. From Chester, head west on Feather River Drive for 0.7 mile, then turn left to continue west on Warner Valley Road and continue for 16 miles (26 km) to the guest ranch.

Outside the Park

Everything about **Highlands Ranch Resort** (41515 Hwy. 36, Mill Creek, 530/595-3388, www.highlandsranchresort.com, $279-489) is luxurious. Seven newly constructed cottages are arranged along the edge of serene Childs Meadow and feature private entrances, elegant furnishings, luxury linens, gas fireplaces, and lovely views of the meadow through floor-to-ceilings windows. Two cottages even have private outdoor hot tubs. The on-site restaurant leaves nothing to be desired, serving three meals a day with a full bar, dining room, and outdoor deck. The property is only a 15-minute drive from the southwest entrance to the national park, and the cottages book out months in advance during the park's busy summer season.

Across the highway and far more casual than the ranch, **The Village at Childs Meadow** (41500 Hwy. 36, Mill Creek, 530/595-3388, www. thevillageatchildsmeadow.com, open daily mid-May-Oct., Thurs.-Sun. only Nov-mid-May, $169-179) has 19 renovated motel rooms with TVs, mini-fridges, and coffeepots. There are also seven tent camping sites and an RV park with 22 spaces (May-Oct., $25-35) with picnic tables and fire rings. Campers have access to showers, laundry facilities, horseshoe pits, an outdoor community center for cooking, and a dump station.

Lassen Mineral Lodge (Hwy. 36, Mineral, 530/595-4422, www. minerallodge.com, May-early Nov., $85-115) is on Highway 36 near the southwest entrance to the park. The lodge offers 20 small motel-style rooms with private baths and few frills; pets are not allowed. The lack of TVs and telephones encourages visitors to get out and enjoy the park and its surrounding landscape. Hiking and fishing are favorite pastimes of lodge guests. The on-site **Mineral Lodge Restaurant** (8am-8pm daily summer, 8am-7pm Sat., 8am-6pm Sun. winter, $12-21) has a bar and is open to non-guests.

Near the northern junction of Highways 44 and 89, the tiny community of Old Station offers some convenient options. **Hat Creek Resort & RV Park** (12533 Hwy. 44, Old Station, 530/335-7121, www.hatcreekresortrv.com, mid-Apr.-Oct.) is a laid-back fishing resort with waterfront cottages ($129-219), luxury cabins ($89-204), yurts ($69-149), motel rooms ($69-154), and campsites ($25-57). Amenities vary among the different types of accommodations, but most include coffeemakers, microwaves, and fire rings with grates. Property amenities include free hot showers, laundry, a phone, an RV dump station, sports courts, and a convenience store with a deli, camping supplies, and firewood.

Just across the highway from Subway Cave, **Cave Campground** (Hwy. 89, 13 mi/20.9 km north of Lassen Volcanic National Park north entrance, www. fs.usda.gov, Apr.-Oct., $16) has 46 first-come, first-served campsites with fire rings, picnic tables, and barbecues. Flush toilets and potable water are available on-site. Hat Creek, a popular fishing stream, borders the campground, and it's an easy walk to explore the Subway Cave.

Information and Services

Chester (25 mi/40 km southeast of the park on Highway 36) is the closest real town to the national park, and has a comprehensive range of stores and restaurants to outfit you for your travels.

If you're approaching the park from the west, stop for supplies, food, and services in **Red Bluff,** 50 miles (81 km) west of the south entrance along Highway 36.

McArthur-Burney Falls Memorial State Park

One of the most beautiful waterfalls in California is at **McArthur-Burney Falls Memorial State Park** (24898 Hwy. 89, Burney, 530/335-2777, www.parks.ca.gov, $10). No less a naturalist than Theodore Roosevelt declared these falls one of the wonders of the world. The state park is located halfway between Mount Lassen and Mount Shasta. The Pacific Crest Trail travels right through the park, entering near Highway 89 and leaving via a dam over the western edge of Lake Britton. Opportunities for sightseeing and nature walks are plentiful within the park, where five miles of hiking trails branch out into the forest.

Getting There

McArthur-Burney Falls Memorial State Park is located on Highway 89 near the town of Burney. From the north entrance to Lassen Volcanic National Park, follow Highway 89 north for 41 miles (66 km) to the state park entrance. Allow about 45 minutes for the drive.

From I-5 near Redding, take exit 680 and head east on Highway 299 for 54 miles (87 km) to the town of Burney, 10.5 miles (16.9 km) south of the state park on Highway 299.

While Highways 89 and 299 don't often close during the winter, they are subject to snow and icy conditions. Chains or traction tires may be advised or required during intense weather conditions.

Sights

TOP EXPERIENCE

★ Burney Falls

Burney Falls is one of nature's greatest masterpieces, a 130-foot cliff where Burney Creek flows over the edge in two distinct cascades as dozens of underwater springs come surging out of the rock on both sides of the stream. While stronger in the spring, the creek flows true year-round and is just as beautiful in September as in April. You don't even have to hike to reach the falls; they're right by the parking lot. Still, it's more than worth your time to get out of your car and take a walk around the grounds of the woodsy state park. Be sure to walk all the way down the paved path to the pool at the base of the falls, where the powerful spray will douse you in a cool, refreshing mist. For views from every angle, take the one-mile hike around the waterfall, crossing both the Rainbow Bridge and Fishermen's Bridge over Burney Creek.

Pro tip: Most locals choose to enter the state park from the west side of the creek to avoid the congestion of the main parking lot and the summertime crowds in the fee area. To take advantage of this "back way," find the intersection of Highway 89 and Clark Creek Road (1.5 mi/2.4 km south of the park's main entrance station) and head northwest on Clark Creek Road for 1.7 miles (2.7 km). Look for a dirt parking area on the east side of the road. Walk east on the trail out of the parking area for 0.25 mile, crossing the PCT on the way, to get to Burney Creek and the trail around the falls.

Pit 3 Dam

Most of the Pacific Crest Trail's water crossings are via wooden pedestrian bridges, logs, or river rocks, but the national scenic trail crosses Lake Britton in a very unusual way. Here, hikers simply walk across the **Pit 3 Dam,** built in 1925. Located on the western edge of the lake, just west of McArthur-Burney Falls State Park, this is where the Pit River escapes from the Lake Britton reservoir to resume its natural form as a whitewater river. Most of the year, the dam completely contains the lake, but if you happen to visit in the late spring, you may see the torrential cascade of water as Lake Britton overflows across the 130-foot dam, which is about as tall as Burney Falls.

The Pit River is an unusual river in itself, one of only three rivers with headwaters on the eastern side of the Cascade Crest that manage to cross the divide to empty into the Pacific Ocean. (The other two are the Klamath, which the PCT crosses in Seiad Valley, near the California-Oregon border, and the Columbia, where the Bridge of the Gods acts as the PCT's official crossing between Oregon and Washington.)

Getting There

From the intersection of Highway 89 and Clark Creek Road, head northwest on Clark Creek Road for 6.5 miles (10.5 km). You can walk or drive across the dam (be mindful of hikers and pedestrians if you're driving across). You may choose to turn the trip into a scenic drive around Lake Britton by staying right on Forest Road 37N05 after crossing the dam and heading east back to Highway 89.

Recreation

The **Falls Loop Trail** is the busiest path in the park, as it shows off the centerpiece waterfall, but there are other options to explore. The Pacific Crest Trail is plotted through the southwest corner of the park, between Burney Creek and Clark Creek Road. Walk north on the Burney Creek Trail to a peninsula in Lake Britton with a fishing pier and a swimming beach, or walk east out of the Pioneer Campground on the Pioneer Cemetery Trail to visit a historic cemetery site.

When a railroad line between the towns of Burney and McCloud ceased operation in 2005, the tracks were repurposed to create the **Great Shasta Rail Trail** (www.greatshastarailtrail.org), an 80-mile (129-km) path for nonmotorized recreation and travel. The red cinder trail cuts through the serene forests and rivers of northeastern California, offering a convenient way to get some exercise

From top to bottom: Burney Creek; Lake Britton Bridge; Art's Outpost.

and enjoy some fresh air. Currently, 40 miles is open to the public for walking, biking, snowshoeing, cross-country skiing, and horseback riding; the remaining 40 miles are under construction and/or awaiting critical bridge repair. Among these defunct bridges is the **Lake Britton Bridge,** made famous in the 1986 movie *Stand by Me.* While it isn't safe or legal to walk across, you can stand at the end of the bridge and gaze across the decaying tracks, picturing the scene from the film. The bridge can be accessed via Eagle Mountain Lane, a dirt road on the east side of Highway 89, 3 miles (4.8 km) north of the entrance to the state park.

Food

No food is available in the park, but it's only a 15-minute drive to the town of Burney, where you'll find a handful of restaurants and stores.

To fill up for a big day of adventuring, head to the **Blackberry Patch** (37453 Hwy. 299, 530/335-3902, 6am-8pm daily June-Sept.; 6am-8pm Fri.-Sun. and 6am-2pm Mon.-Thurs. Apr.-May and Oct.; 6am-3pm daily Mar.-Nov., $8-12) for a homestyle diner meal and a hot cup of a coffee. During July and August, you're likely to share the place with lots of hungry PCT hikers. Service is friendly and prompt, and the homemade pies aren't bad either.

Art's Outpost (37392 Main St., 530/335-2835, 4:30pm-9pm Tues.-Sat., $17-26) is like a combination of a swanky steak house and your favorite dive bar. Sip on a cocktail or a beer in the red-light lounge, then enjoy a deep-fried appetizer before sinking your teeth into a juicy piece of prime rib, rib eye, or sirloin. Big salads, chicken entrées, spaghetti, and ravioli are the other house specialties. Art's is a great spot for a date, special occasion, or just a satisfying stop at the end of a long day.

Burney's oldest bar and restaurant, **The Rex Club** (37143 Main St., 530/335-4184, www.burneyrexclub.com, 11am-8pm Tues.-Sat., $14-24), is exactly the type of restaurant you expect to find in a rural mountain town: cedar shingles on the outside, dark wood interior, taxidermy animals on the wall, a big fireplace, and a hearty menu of meat and potatoes. White tablecloths give the place an extra bit of elegance, and the menu does feature a nice variety of veggies, poultry, seafood, and pasta, along with soups, salads, and sandwiches.

Taqueria La Fogata (37063 Hwy. 299, 530/335-3338, 11am-7:30pm Mon.-Fri., noon-7:30pm Sat., $6-16) is a colorful café with fresh, tasty Mexican cuisine. The authentic street tacos are a great deal, as are the lunch specials, which come with rice and beans. Food arrives quickly after ordering, and the self-serve salsa bar is another perk.

Accommodations

Burney Motel (37448 Main St., 530/335-4500, www.theburneymotel.com, $89-99) is an affordable option in town. The rooms are nothing special, but they do offer air-conditioning, free Wi-Fi, mini-fridges, microwaves, and coffeemakers. Walk across the street to the Blackberry Patch for breakfast, then down the block to Art's Outpost for dinner.

If you prefer a little more space than a motel room, **The Rex Club** (37143 Main St., Burney, 530/335-4184, www.burneyrexclub.com, $95-105) has four cabins behind the restaurant with en suite bathrooms and full kitchens. Beds are cozy, all cabins offer satellite TV, and one unit is pet-friendly.

Camping

The state park **campground** (Hwy. 89, 530/335-2777, reservations May-Sept. 800/444-7275, www.reserveamerica.com, year-round, $35) has 102 reservable campsites and three primitive hike-in/bike-in sites. It also has 24 cabins ($105) with heaters and platform beds. Facilities include restrooms with flush toilets, showers, picnic tables, and fire rings.

Outside the park on the north shore of

Lake Britton, **Dusty Campground** (Eagle Mountain Ln., 2 mi/3.2 km north of the state park entrance on Hwy. 89, 530/335-2777, Mar.-Nov., $8) is a first-come, first-served campground in Lassen National Forest with seven waterfront sites. The bridge from the movie *Stand by Me* is in sight from the campground. Vault toilets and potable water spigots are in the center of the campground. Each site has a picnic table, a fire ring, and immediate access to the lake for swimming and boating.

North Shore Campground (Forest Rd. 37N05, 4 mi/6.4 km north of the state park entrance on Hwy. 89, www.recreation.pge.com, Apr.-Sept., $16) is across Lake Britton from the state park's swimming beach and fishing pier. Waterfront sites have beautiful views of the forested lakeshore and prime access for water activities. All 29 sites have fire rings, picnic tables, and access to vault toilets and potable water.

Information and Services

Stop by the state park **visitor center and gift shop** (24898 Hwy. 89, 530/335-2777, www.burneyfallspark.org, 11am-3pm daily) for informative displays about the formation of the falls, hands-on learning activities for kids, and a well-stocked gift shop with souvenirs and guidebooks.

◆ Detour: McCloud

When driving Highway 89 between Burney Falls and Mount Shasta, you'll pass right through the town of McCloud. It's perfectly restored historic buildings are backdropped by magnificent snow-covered Mount Shasta.

Getting There

McCloud is on Highway 89, 42 miles northwest of McArthur-Burney Falls Memorial State Park and 9.5 miles east of the Highway 89/I-5 junction.

McCloud Falls

Stop at **McCloud Falls** (Fowler Camp Rd. off Hwy. 89, 5.5 mi/9km east of McCloud) to admire three gorgeous waterfalls along the McCloud River. You can drive up to each of the viewpoints or park and walk through the woods on the McCloud River Trail (5 mi/8km, 2 hours) to see them all. Lower Falls (near Fowlers Camp) is the easiest waterfall to see. From here, walk 1.3 miles (2 km) to Middle Falls, the largest and most dramatic of the three. The cascade pours over a wide part of the McCloud River. In 0.5 mile, you'll reach Upper Falls, which shoots out of a narrow basalt channel, spraying into a vibrant plunge pool below.

Food and Accommodations

Stop at **Floyd's Frosty** (125 Broadway Ave., 530/964-2394, 11am-7pm daily May-Sept., 11am-6pm Sat.-Sun. Oct.-Apr., $6-12), where the signature "Logger Burger" includes two beef patties, two pieces of cheese, and bacon, served with fries.

For upscale dining in the McCloud Mercantile building, the **McCloud Meat Market & Tavern** (231 Main St., 530/524-3639, www.mccloudmeatmarket.com, 1pm-10pm Fri.-Sun., 4pm-10pm Mon. and Thurs., $7-16) serves salads, sandwiches, tacos, and entrées with nice appetizers and fancy cocktails. A few doors down, the **White Mountain Café** (241 Main St., 530/964-2005, 8am-2pm Wed.-Mon., $7-12) is a fantastic breakfast and lunch joint with high ceilings and old-fashioned stools at the counter.

The **McCloud Hotel** (408 Main St., 530/964-2822, www.mccloudhotel.com, $169-279) is an impressive inn surrounded by lush gardens. In addition to the 12 rooms and four suites, the hotel is home to the elegant **Sage Restaurant** (530/964-2822, 5:30pm-8pm daily late May-early Sept. 5:30pm-8pm Wed.-Sun. mid-Sept.-mid-May, $18-32) and the more casual yet still gorgeous **Axe &**

Rose Pub (530/408-8322, 11:30am-9pm daily, $7-14).

Before leaving town, cross the highway for a beer at **Siskiyou Brew Works** (110 Squaw Valley Rd., 530/925-5894, www.siskiyoubrewworks.com, 4pm-7pm Wed.-Thurs. and Sun., 4pm-8pm Fri., 12:30pm-8pm Sat., $10-23), a family-run brewery and pizzeria housed in a big red barn. The unique German- and English-style beers are brewed with both European and local hops. (Some of the hops are grown right outside the barn.) Pizzas come in three sizes—sapling, second growth, and old growth—and feature a housemade beer-pizza sauce.

Dunsmuir

Cut into a cleft in the mountains just south of Mount Shasta, Dunsmuir is a historic railroad town along the Sacramento River and I-5. Known for its waterfalls, the town's motto is, "Home of the best water on earth." Outdoor recreation and dining are the primary draws to Dunsmuir, and the Pacific Crest Trail is plotted through the mountains a few miles south of town near Castle Crags State Park.

Getting There

Dunsmuir is located on I-5 between the town of Mount Shasta and Castle Crags State Park, about 48 miles (77 km) north of Redding.

From McArthur-Burney Falls Memorial State Park, follow Highway 89 north for 50 miles (81 km), then take I-5 south for another 5.5 miles (8.9 km) to exit 730. This drive takes about an hour.

From I-5 near Redding, take I-5 north for 48 miles (77 km) to exit 729. Allow 55 minutes.

Sights

Don't miss **Hedge Creek Falls,** where Hedge Creek shoots through a gap in a chunky basalt cliff and pours down the hillside toward the Sacramento River. Although you wouldn't know it while you're there, this waterfall is right next to the interstate, and walking along the trail to reach the falls only takes a few minutes. Once you're there, the roar of the waterfall completely drowns any freeway noise, and the dense woods surrounding the creek create a feeling of being deep in the wild, rather than right next to a giant roadway. You can even walk behind the falls through an amphitheater-like cave.

Getting There: The parking area for Hedge Creek Falls is at the intersection of Mott Road and Siskiyou Avenue, on the west side of I-5 exit 732. The short trail to the falls begins on the west side of Mott Road.

If you want another opportunity to stretch your legs, a walk through **Dunsmuir Botanical Gardens** (4841 Dunsmuir Ave., 530/235-4740, www.dunsmuirbotanicalgardens.org, sunrise-sunset daily, free) is a lovely option, featuring both native plants and introduced perennial flowers. Paths through the gardens (located inside Dunsmuir City Park) eventually lead to the Sacramento River, where a trail provides a serene escape from the nearby freeway.

Entertainment and Events

Dunsmuir is the home of the annual **State of Jefferson Brewfest** (Dunsmuir City Park, 4841 Dunsmuir Ave., 530/235-2177, www.jeffersonbrewfest.com, first Sat. in Aug., $5 general admission ages 13 and over, $35 beer garden ticket, children 12 and under free), where more than 80 commercial craft breweries and home brewers gather to taste beer and enjoy the sunshine. Live bands play in the evening, and food vendors are on-site to keep everyone well fed.

Shopping

Dunsmuir Hardware (5836 Dunsmuir Ave., 530/235-4538, www.dunsmuirhardware.com, 8:30am-5:30pm Mon.-Sat., 10am-4pm Sun.) was founded

Around Mount Shasta

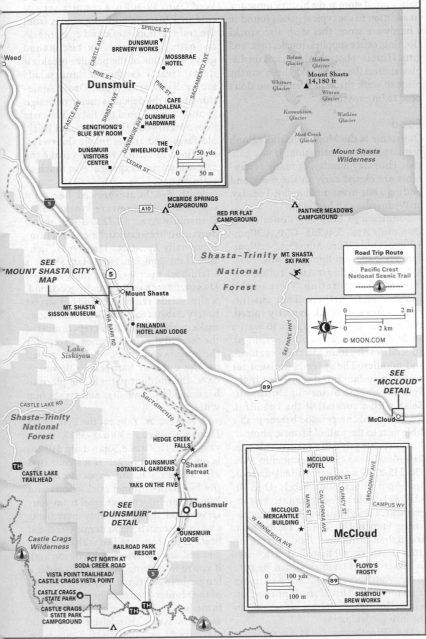

Dunsmuir

- SPRUCE ST.
- CASTLE AVE
- PINE ST.
- DUNSMUIR BREWERY WORKS
- MOSSBRAE HOTEL
- SHASTA AVE
- PINE ST.
- SACRAMENTO AVE
- CAFE MADDALENA
- DUNSMUIR HARDWARE
- SENGTHONG'S BLUE SKY ROOM
- DUNSMUIR AVE
- THE WHEELHOUSE
- DUNSMUIR VISITORS CENTER
- CEDAR ST.
- 0   50 yds
- 0   50 m

Mount Shasta Wilderness

- Bolam Glacier
- Hotlum Glacier
- Mount Shasta 14,180 ft
- Whitney Glacier
- Wintun Glacier
- Konwakiton Glacier
- Watkins Glacier
- Mud Creek Glacier

- Weed
- 5

- MCBRIDE SPRINGS CAMPGROUND
- A10
- RED FIR FLAT CAMPGROUND
- PANTHER MEADOWS CAMPGROUND

- *Shasta–Trinity National Forest*
- MT. SHASTA SKI PARK
- SKI PARK HWY

Road Trip Route

Pacific Crest National Scenic Trail

- 0   2 mi
- 0   2 km
- © MOON.COM

- SEE "MOUNT SHASTA CITY" MAP
- 5
- Mount Shasta
- WA BARR RD
- MT. SHASTA SISSON MUSEUM
- FINLANDIA HOTEL AND LODGE

- Lake Siskiyou
- CASTLE LAKE RD
- *Shasta–Trinity National Forest*
- CASTLE LAKE TRAILHEAD

- Sacramento R.
- 89
- SEE "MCCLOUD" DETAIL
- McCloud

- HEDGE CREEK FALLS
- DUNSMUIR BOTANICAL GARDENS
- Shasta Retreat
- YAKS ON THE FIVE
- SEE "DUNSMUIR" DETAIL
- Dunsmuir
- DUNSMUIR LODGE

- Castle Crags Wilderness
- RAILROAD PARK RESORT
- PCT NORTH AT SODA CREEK ROAD
- VISTA POINT TRAILHEAD/ CASTLE CRAGS VISTA POINT
- CASTLE CRAGS STATE PARK
- CASTLE CRAGS STATE PARK CAMPGROUND
- 5

McCloud

- MCCLOUD HOTEL
- DIVISION ST
- QUINCY ST
- BROADWAY AVE
- CAMPUS WY
- MCCLOUD MERCANTILE BUILDING
- MAIN ST
- CALIFORNIA ST
- W MINNESOTA AVE
- FLOYD'S FROSTY
- 89
- SISKIYOU BREW WORKS
- 0   100 yds
- 0   100 m

in 1894 by Dunsmuir's first mayor, Alexander Levy, and today's shop acts as both a retail store and a history museum. In addition to the typical goods found in a hardware store, this shop also stocks clothing, office supplies, music, toys, and gifts. Historic photos and artifacts on display around the store make this a worthy place to walk through even if you don't need to buy anything.

Food

Dunsmuir is the Mount Shasta region's primary dining destination. If you can, visit Thursday-Sunday, as many restaurants are closed early in the week and finding a bite to eat on Monday, Tuesday, or Wednesday can be tough.

Sengthong's Blue Sky Room (5841 Dunsmuir Ave., 530/235-4770, 4:30pm-8:30pm Thurs.-Sun. Apr.-Oct., 4:30pm-8pm Fri.-Sat., 5pm-8pm Sun. Nov.-Mar., $18-25) is a Southeast Asian fusion restaurant incorporating Vietnamese, Laotian, and Northern Thai cuisine. Food is fresh, colorful, expertly spiced, and cooked to order (expect to wait a while for your meal on busy evenings). Specialties include curries, seafood, and noodles. The space is unusual for an Asian restaurant, designed to highlight the unique history of Dunsmuir: Relax with a cocktail at the beautiful, old-fashioned cherrywood bar, or grab a table next to the wall of historic photos.

A surprising find in a town of this size, **Café Maddalena** (5801 Sacramento Ave., 530/235-2725, www.cafemaddalena.com, 5pm-9pm Thurs.-Sun., Feb.14-Dec. 31, $21-28) is a chic Mediterranean restaurant with a delightful seasonal menu featuring French, North African, Spanish, and Italian influences. Find everything from ricotta ravioli to grilled artichokes to zataar-spiced lamb shoulder. Be sure to ask your server about wine pairings from the curated list of small-production wines. During the summer, sit outside on the lush garden patio.

The Wheelhouse (5841 Sacramento Ave., 530/678-3502, www.thewheelhousedunsmuir.com, 7am-3pm Wed.-Sun. $9-20) is a counter-service café in a historic building across from the train station. Steak and eggs, breakfast hash, French toast, and biscuits and gravy are some of the popular breakfast items. Hearty sandwiches and salads are available after 11am. Order something from the delicious menu, or design your own meal from the list of à la carte items. Hardwood floors, exposed brick, old-fashioned arches in the doorways, and floor-to-ceiling windows make the café a historical experience as much as a dining one.

With 6-8 house-brewed beers on tap, **Dunsmuir Brewery Works** (5701 Dunsmuir Ave., 530/235-1900, www.dunsmuirbreweryworks.com, 11am-10pm daily Apr.-Oct., 11am-9pm Tues.-Sat., 11am-8pm Sun. Nov.-Mar., $8-16) is a laid-back microbrewery in downtown Dunsmuir with unexpectedly good food. Soups, salads, sandwiches and burgers on hearty ciabatta rolls, ribs, and bratwursts make up the menu. Chefs prepare most of the food in the open kitchen, except for the burgers and meats, which are grilled on the outdoor barbecue. On sunny days, the outdoor patio is the place to be, shaded by umbrellas and twisty hop vines.

A meal at ★ **Yaks on the Five** (4917 Dunsmuir Ave., 530/678-3517, www.yaks.com, 11:30am-8:30pm daily, $10-16) is one you won't forget. If it's your first visit to the restaurant, expect to sample the bourbon-caramel sticky buns and listen to an informative spiel from your server about the high-quality ingredients and from-scratch menu items. Grass-fed beef burgers come stacked with fresh veggies and sauces bursting with flavor; and, if you're wondering, yes you can order a burger between two sticky buns instead of the regular brioche. The array of costume jewelry covering the inside windows, the flashy chandeliers hanging in every room, and the colorful murals on the walls make this place anything but an ordinary burger joint.

Accommodations and Camping

Spend the night in a refurbished train car at **Railroad Park Resort** (100 Railroad Park Rd., 530/235-4440, www.rrpark.com, $155-210), complete with modern amenities. Each caboose is adorned with a knotty pine interior and a theme from one of the historic U.S. railroad lines. Railroad cars feature a full private bathroom, a kitchenette with a mini-fridge and a microwave, and air-conditioning. Other on-site overnight options include vintage cabins ($145-155) with the same amenities as the train cars, as well as tent and RV sites ($29-42) with picnic tables, fire rings, and access to bathrooms with showers. Guest laundry facilities and a game room with a pool table are extra bonuses that may interest some travelers.

Dunsmuir Lodge (6604 Dunsmuir Ave., 530/235-2884, www.dunsnmuirlodge.com, $63-158) is a comfy, clean downtown motel in a park-like setting. Each room has a small refrigerator, a coffeemaker, and a flat-screen TV. Some rooms are pet-friendly, Wi-Fi is included in your stay, and the shady outdoor area has barbecues for guest use. Downtown shops and restaurants are one mile north of the lodge.

★ **Mossbrae Hotel** (5734 Dunsmuir Ave., 530/235-7019, www.mossbraehotel.com, $119-209) is a downtown boutique hotel with seven guest rooms. Silky linens, heat-controlled bathroom tiles, and modern design give the rooms a luxurious feel. All rooms include a kitchenette with a mini-fridge, microwave, coffeemaker, and sink. Some rooms have windows overlooking Dunsmuir's main drag, where restaurants and shops are located.

From top to bottom: Hedge Creek Falls; Dunsmuir's historic downtown; burger at Yaks on the Five.

Information and Services

Stop by the Dunsmuir Chamber of Commerce & Visitors Center (5915 Dunsmuir Ave., 530/235-2177, www.dunsmuir.com) for maps and brochures with info about the town's restaurants, accommodations, and outdoor recreation opportunities.

Getting Around

For many years, Dunsmuir's economy and culture revolved around the train, and you can still travel to and from the area this way. The **Amtrak** *Coast Starlight* route makes a stop at Dunsmuir Station (5750 Sacramento Ave., 800/872-7245, www.amtrak.com) on its journey between Seattle and Los Angeles.

★ Castle Crags State Park

Just a few miles south of Dunsmuir on I-5, **Castle Crags State Park** (20022 Castle Creek Rd., Castella, 530/235-2684, www.parks.ca.gov, $10/vehicle) is home to some unique Northern California terrain. The park has 4,350 acres of land, including very dramatic granite peaks and cliffs, with 28 miles of hiking trails snaking through the forests and peaks. The Pacific Crest Trail traverses the park, offering views of the rocky towers above. You can hike or rock-climb to the very top of the spectacular 6,000-foot crags to take in the stunning views. The park's campground is a convenient place to spend the night if you plan to explore the Pacific Crest Trail or other trails in the park.

Getting There

Castle Crags is one of the easiest PCT access points in California to find. The park is just 6 miles (9.7 km) south of Dunsmuir and about 13 miles (20.9 km) south of the city of Mount Shasta. Take I-5 exit 724 at Castella. Turn west onto Castle Creek Road, and the park is less than 0.5 mile.

Castle Crags State Park

Hiking

If you don't have much time to explore or aren't in the mood for a hike, you can still get a fantastic view of Castle Crags. After entering the gate, drive through the park following the signs for "Vista Point." A paved walk of no more than 0.25 mile from the **Vista Point** parking lot leads to a spectacular overlook with views of 14,180-foot (4,322-m) Mount Shasta to the north, Castle Crags to the west, and the dramatic, forested Sacramento River canyon below.

Crags Trail to Castle Dome

Distance: 5.7 mi/9.2 km round-trip
Duration: 3-3.5 hours
Elevation change: 2,180 ft/664 m
Effort: Strenuous
Trailhead: Vista Point parking lot
Pass/Fee: Castle Crags State Park entrance fee ($10)

While there are plenty of hiking trails throughout the park, the Crags Trail is the most scenic as it makes a beeline for 4,800-foot Castle Dome. From there, you

can admire the park's dramatic cliffs with Mount Shasta as a backdrop. On a sunny day, Mount Lassen and mountains in Oregon including Mount McLoughlin are also in sight.

Starting from the Vista Point parking lot, walk west through the woods on the wide, flat Root Creek Trail for 0.4 mile, then stay left onto the signed Crags Trail. Cross the PCT at 0.5 mile and begin your ascent into the park's high country. Arrive at a junction with the Bob's Hat Trail at 0.8 mile, but continue straight, heading west on the Crags Trail. Cross a few seasonal, snow-fed creeks between 1.3 and 1.7 miles as the trail heads north. Right around 2 miles, the scenery starts to change as the trail departs from the woods and enters the rocky, exposed faces of the crags. Views from here to the top are fantastic, including Root Creek's giant waterfall in the canyon below the trail, and Mount Shasta shimmering in the distance. Reach the summit at 2.9 miles, where the smooth granite rocks resemble the terrain in Yosemite and the High Sierra. Castle Dome itself is just east of the trail's end.

Take the same route back to your car, or to mix it up, take Bob's Hat Trail to the PCT, which connects back to the Root Creek Trail.

Root Creek Falls 🅿🅲🆃

Distance: 5 mi/8 km round-trip
Duration: 2-3 hours
Elevation change: 810 ft/247 m
Effort: Easy
Trailhead: Pacific Crest Trail at Soda Creek Road

If you aren't in the mood for a strenuous hike to the top of Castle Dome, opt for this gently graded hike along the PCT to a stunning waterfall beneath the park's trademark granite towers.

Begin your hike on the northbound PCT, which actually heads south for the first 0.4 mile as it climbs out of the Sacramento River Valley and the I-5 corridor. The trail turns west and stays pretty flat between 0.4 and 1.3 miles, meandering through the forest. Depart from the PCT at 1.6 miles, making a hard right to walk north on the Root Creek Trail. Continue as the trail bends northwest and meets Root Creek at 2 miles. It's only another 0.5 mile to the waterfall viewpoint, but the trail can be hard to follow. Stay on the south side of the creek, and climb west up the embankment as the canyon begins to narrow. Your final destination is a vista point where the multi-tier waterfall and Castle Dome are both visible.

Getting There
This trailhead is outside the boundaries of Castle Crags State Park. Take I-5 to exit 726, then look for the signed PCT parking area on the west side of the interstate.

Camping
The state park **campground** (www. reserveamerica.com, reservations May-Sept., first-come, first-served Oct.-Apr., $25) has 64 sites as well as 12 environmental sites ($15) available year-round on a first-come, first-served basis. Some sites are close to the freeway and can be loud, but others are tucked deep enough in the pines to feel miles away from civilization. Sites have picnic tables, fire rings, and bear-proof storage lockers; bathrooms with flush toilets and showers are nearby.

Mount Shasta

The city of Mount Shasta sits on the western base of an enormous dormant volcano of the same name, the second-tallest in the Cascade Range behind Washington's Mount Rainier. In 2018, Mount Shasta was named as the first official Pacific Crest Trail Town, and its proximity to multiple PCT access points makes it a convenient base camp for exploring some of Northern California's most famous peaks and ridgelines.

Getting There
The town of Mount Shasta is located directly on I-5 about 60 miles (97 km) north of Redding and 60 miles (97 km) south of the Oregon-California border. From McArthur-Burney Falls Memorial State Park, follow Highway 89 north for 48 miles (77 km), then turn right on South Mount Shasta Boulevard and continue north into town.

Sights
Mt. Shasta Sisson Museum
If you find yourself gazing up at 14,180-foot Mount Shasta and wondering how on earth it was created, visit the **Mt. Shasta Sisson Museum** (1 N. Old Stage Rd., 530/926-5508, www.mtshastamuseum. com, 10am-4pm daily Memorial Day-Labor Day, 1pm-4pm Mon.-Thurs., 10am-4pm Fri.-Sun. Labor Day-Sept. 30, 10am-4pm Fri.-Sun. Oct.-mid-Dec. and Apr.-Memorial Day, $1 donation suggested) where short films and exhibits explain how Shasta and all the other Cascade volcanoes were formed. History exhibits showcase the more recent past, including Native American arts and artifacts. Kids will love the interactive exhibits where they can walk though a volcano, climb onto a fire truck, play dress-up with old-fashioned clothes, and more. But it's not just for kids: Adults say they were surprised at how much they learned and enjoyed the place.

Hiking
Deadfall Lakes and Mount Eddy 🄿🄲🅃
Distance: 8.6 mi/13.8 km round-trip
Duration: 5 hours
Elevation change: 2,590 ft/789 m
Effort: Strenuous
Trailhead: Deadfall Meadow
Hike to the top of Mount Eddy, the tallest peak in the Trinity Alps, for fantastic views of the surrounding ranges and larger-than-life Mount Shasta.

Begin your hike by walking southeast on the Deadfall Lakes Trail, admiring the wildflowers if you're there in early

Mount Shasta City

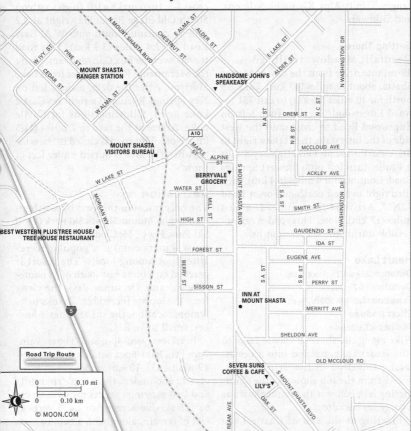

MOUNT SHASTA RANGER STATION

HANDSOME JOHN'S SPEAKEASY ▼

A10

MOUNT SHASTA VISITORS BUREAU ■

BERRYVALE GROCERY ▼

BEST WESTERN PLUS TREE HOUSE/ TREE HOUSE RESTAURANT

INN AT MOUNT SHASTA ●

SEVEN SUNS COFFEE & CAFE ▼

LILY'S ▼

Road Trip Route

0   0.10 mi
0   0.10 km

© MOON.COM

summer. At the junction with the Pacific Crest Trail at 1.6 miles, take a right onto the southbound PCT and follow for 0.2 mile to the shore of **Lower Deadfall Lake** (3.6 mi/5.5 km rt, 870 ft/265 m, moderate), the largest of the Deadfall Lakes. Mount Eddy and the Trinity Divide tower above the eastern edge of the water's surface.

Return 0.2 mile back to the PCT-Deadfall Lakes Trail junction, turn right, and ascend east up the ridgeline on the Deadfall Lakes Trail, arriving at the next lake at 2.4 miles. Vegetation begins to

thin as you climb, reaching yet another lake at 2.6 miles. Meet the **Mount Eddy Trail** at 3.1 miles (6.2 mi/10 km rt, 1,540 ft/469 m, moderate). Rocky and exposed, this destination feels like a summit itself, and views of the lakes below are incredible.

To reach the actual **Mount Eddy Summit** (8.6 mi/13.8 km rt, 2,590 ft/789 m, strenuous), depart from the Deadfall Lakes Trail and take the Mount Eddy Trail northeast up to the 9,025-foot peak, arriving at the top at 4.3 miles. Take in the incredible views of Mount Shasta, the

I-5 corridor far below, and the convergence of Northern California's mountain ranges: Trinity Alps, Klamaths, Salmons, and Siskiyous.

Getting There
Deadfall Meadow trailhead is a 45-minute drive from the city of Mount Shasta, about 27 miles (43 km). Take I-5 north for 10 miles (16 km) to exit 751 toward Edgewood/Gazelle. Turn left on Edgewood Road to cross onto the west side of the interstate, then take a right to drive northwest on Old Highway 99. In 0.4 mile, turn left onto Stewart Springs Road. Continue for 4 miles (6.4 km), then turn right to head north on Forest Road 42N17. Arrive at the trailhead in 10.4 miles (17 km). Note: This road is not accessible during the winter months.

Heart Lake
Distance: 2.6 mi/4.2 km round-trip
Duration: 1.5-2 hours
Elevation change: 800 ft/244 m
Effort: Moderate
Trailhead: Castle Lake

Hike along the shore of Castle Lake to tiny Heart Lake, nestled into a north-facing ridgeline in the Trinity Alps. Views from the top showcase the shimmering lake below with Mount Shasta as a gorgeous backdrop.

Starting at the end of Castle Lake Road, walk southwest on the Little Castle Lake Trail as it follows the water's shore and ascends up a ridgeline on the lake's west side. At the trail junction at 0.5 mile, stay right onto the Heart Lake Trail. Arrive at Heart Lake at 0.9 mile, a tiny lake with incredible views of Black Butte and Mount Shasta. Picnic, swim, or relax here, or continue west past Heart Lake on the Castle Overlook Trail to a viewpoint at 6,200 feet (1,890 m) that offers even better views of the surrounding scenery.

Getting There
Castle Lake is 10 miles (16.1 km) southwest of the city of Mount Shasta, about a 20-minute drive. To get there from the downtown area, head west on Lake Street, cross I-5, then make a left to go south on South Old Stage Road. Stay right at 0.2 mile to continue south onto W.A. Barr Road for 2.4 miles (3.9 km). This road travels over the Box Canyon Dam, where the Sacramento River escapes from Lake Siskiyou. After the dam, make a left on Ney Springs Road and a right on Castle Lake Road, following signs for Castle Lake. Arrive at the lake in 7 miles (11.3 km). Note: This road is closed in the winter when the area is buried under feet of snow.

Recreation
The only resort in this part of Northern California, **Mount Shasta Ski Park** (4500 Ski Park Hwy., McCloud, 530/926-8610, www.skipark.com) is a popular recreation spot among locals. The resort is perched on a butte just south of its namesake volcano. On sunny days, the views from the top are incredible. Thanks to its remote location, the ski area has a low-key, small-town feel.

In **winter** (9am-4pm Sun.-Thurs., 9am-7pm Fri., 9am-6pm Sat., Dec.-Apr., $39-49 adults, $33-40 seniors, $16-40 children ages 12 and under), three triple chair lifts and two moving carpets provide access to 425 skiable acres with 1,435 vertical feet of terrain, along with a **tubing park** (9am-4pm Fri.-Sun., $15-20 for 3 hours).

In **summer** (www.mtshastasummer. com, June-Oct.), activities include scenic chairlift rides ($20), an alpine disc golf course (free with purchase of chairlift), and a mountain biking park ($35).

Entertainment and Events
Local watering hole and hangout **Handsome John's Speakeasy** (316 Chestnut St., 530/261-0456, 2pm-11pm Mon.-Thurs., 11am-midnight Fri.-Sat., $4-12) is a great place to grab a pint after a hike. While the space isn't exactly a secret underground bar, it is set back from the street and has a best-kept-secret vibe

about it. This is the cheapest place to get a beer in town, and the rotating taps feature a good variety of microbrews from regional breweries. Play Ping-Pong, relax on the outdoor patio, or enjoy some live music on select weekend evenings. The food menu changes seasonally, but usually includes tacos, grilled meats, barbecue, and pizza.

Food

Seven Suns Coffee and Café (1011 S. Mt. Shasta Blvd., 530/926-9701 or 530/926-9700, 6am-4pm daily, $7-12) is a great little coffee shop with tasty breakfast and lunch options in the form of local baked goods, burritos, wraps, and salads. It makes all sorts of coffee and espresso drinks and sells beans by the pound. There's a spacious porch on the south side with umbrella-shaded tables, but the prime spot on a beautiful, sunny morning is the front sidewalk, where the mighty volcano is in view.

Both a high-end food market and a town gathering place, **Berryvale Grocery** (305 S. Mt. Shasta Blvd., 530/926-1576, www.berryvale.com, store 8am-8pm daily, café 8am-7pm daily) is popular with locals and PCT hikers. (The laundromat across the street leaves them with time to kill.) The café serves tasty soups, sandwiches, and burritos with plenty of meat and vegetarian options, as well as gluten-free and dairy-free offerings.

One of the nicest restaurants in Mount Shasta is **Lily's** (1013 S. Mt. Shasta Blvd., 530/962-3372, www.lilysrestaurant.com, 8am-2pm and 5pm-9pm daily, $12-24), a casual yet elegant eatery with a bright, spacious interior and a lovely outdoor patio. Breakfast is a full selection of omelets, pancakes, and other American favorites, plus a few specialties including huevos rancheros and biscuits and gravy. Lunch is burgers, salads, and choices like the eggplant hoagie and the walnut dal

From top to bottom: Heart Lake; Seven Suns Coffee and Cafe; Inn at Mount Shasta.

burger. Dinner entrées feature hearty steaks, fresh seafood, and a colorful array of seasonal vegetable sides. Vegetarian and vegan options are available for all three meals.

One of the best places in town to eat is at the ★ Tree House Restaurant (530/926-3101, www.treehouserestaurantmtshasta. com, 6:30am-10:30am and 5pm-9pm daily, $13-24), located inside the Best Western Plus. The eggs Benedicts and griddle cakes are popular during breakfast, and a few other options are available as well. During dinner, menu highlights include steaks, pastas, burgers, and seafood, along with soups and salads. Cooper's Bar and Grill (10:30am-10pm Mon.-Thurs., 10:30am-11pm Fri.-Sun., $6-10) has its own comprehensive bar menu with tasty burgers, tacos, wings, fry baskets, and flatbreads.

Accommodations

There are a number of inexpensive lodging options on the south side of town, most of them with similar amenities. The nicest is the Inn at Mount Shasta (710 S. Mt. Shasta Blvd., 530/918-9292, www.innatmountshasta. com, $79-179), a remodeled motel with clean and modern décor. Rooms feature wildlife artwork (foxes, birds, elk, and more) and include mini-fridges, microwaves, and coffeemakers. Many of Mount Shasta's restaurants are within walking distance, including Seven Suns Coffee and Lily's.

The Finlandia Hotel and Lodge (1621 S. Mt. Shasta Blvd., 530/926-5596, www. finlandiamotelandlodge.com, $65-125) offers comfortable rooms, from a single room with a queen bed at the low end to a suite with a king bed and a kitchen at the top. Some rooms are pet-friendly. The lodge ($200-250) can sleep up to eight people; amenities include three bedrooms, a fully equipped kitchen, a sauna, an outdoor spa, and a wood-burning fireplace crafted out of lava rock.

One of the most popular places to stay (and eat!) in Mount Shasta is the Best Western Plus Tree House (111 Morgan Way, 530/926-3101, www.bestwestern. com, $162-230), near the main drag and I-5. Rooms come with microwaves, fridges, and blow-dryers as well as wireless internet access. This large, full-service hotel has an indoor pool, a hot tub, and a fitness center. A full hot breakfast is included. There's a computer station in the lobby. The on-site Tree House Restaurant (530/926-3101, www.treehouserestaurantmtshasta.com, 6:30am-10:30am and 5pm-9pm daily, $13-24) serves breakfast and dinner. Popular with the locals, especially during happy hour (3pm-6pm), Cooper's Bar and Grill (10:30am-10pm Mon.-Thurs., 10:30am-11pm Fri.-Sun., $6-10) serves tacos, burgers, pasta, cocktails, wine, and beer.

Camping

The Shasta-Trinity National Forest (Shasta Ranger District, 530/926-4511, www.fs.usda.gov, 8am-4:30pm Mon.-Fri.) manages three campgrounds on Mount Shasta. All are popular and fill quickly on summer weekends. Reservations are not accepted; visit on weekdays when it's easier to find space. McBride Springs (12 sites, first-come, first-served, late May-Oct., $10) is conveniently located on the mountain at 5,000 feet (1,524 m), just 4 miles (6.4 km) from Mount Shasta city. Facilities include drinking water, vault toilets, and picnic tables.

★ Panther Meadows (Everitt Memorial Hwy., 1.7 mi/2.7 km past Bunny Flat, 15 sites, first-come, first-served, mid-July-Nov., free) is 14 miles (22.5 km) northeast of Mount Shasta city at an elevation of 7,500 feet (2,286 m) on the slopes of Mount Shasta. Due to the high elevation, it can be cold at night and snowed-in well into summer. Although this is a walk-in campground, it is only 100-500 feet from the parking lot to the campsites. Facilities include picnic tables, fire rings, and vault toilets; bring your own water. The maximum stay is three nights.

The third campground is **Red Fir Flat** (530/926-4511, $12), a group site (8-75 people) available by reservation. Facilities include picnic tables, fire rings, and vault toilets, but not drinking water.

Dispersed camping is allowed throughout the Shasta-Trinity National Forest. A wilderness permit is required on Mount Shasta itself. Otherwise, anywhere you want to sleep is fair game, though you do need a campfire permit, available for free at any ranger station. For permits and information, contact the **Mount Shasta Ranger Station** (204 W. Alma St., 530/926-4511, www.fs.usda.gov, 8am-4:30pm Mon.-Sat. summer, 8am-4:30pm Mon.-Fri. fall-spring).

Information and Services

At the **Mount Shasta Visitors Bureau** (300 Pine St., 530/926-4865, ext. 203, http://visitmtshasta.com) you'll find information about hotels, restaurants, and local recreation; the staff is also helpful with driving directions to nearby sites.

For wilderness permits and trail advice, head for one of the local ranger stations. The **Mount Shasta Ranger Station** (204 W. Alma St., 530/926-4511, www.fs.usda.gov, 8am-4:30pm Mon.-Sat. summer, 8am-4:30pm Mon.-Fri. fall-spring) can supply wilderness passes, plus park maps and information about current mountain conditions.

The town of Mount Shasta has a full-service hospital, **Mercy Medical Center Mount Shasta** (914 Pine St., 530/926-6111, www.mercymtshasta.org), with a 24-hour emergency room.

Etna

In a picturesque valley surrounded by mountains, the town of Etna is the gateway to Northern California's most remote mountain ranges. A handful of surprisingly sophisticated food and beverage options in this quaint community make Etna a more appealing culinary destination than a typical rural town.

South of town, the Pacific Crest Trail traverses stunning alpine ridgelines through the Trinity Alps, the Russian Wilderness, and the Marble Mountain Wilderness. Day hikes along the PCT in these often-overlooked areas are plentiful.

Getting There

Etna is located in the Scott Valley, 60 miles (97 km) northwest of the city of Mount Shasta. The fastest way there is through Yreka (allow 65 minutes for the drive). Take I-5 north for 33 miles (53 km) to exit 773, then follow Highway 3 south to Etna.

For a slightly longer, but more scenic option, take I-5 north for 10 miles (16 km) to exit 751, exiting onto Old Highway 99 north toward Gazelle. Head north on Old Highway 99 for 10 miles (16 km), then make a left to head southwest on Gazelle-Callahan Road. After 25 miles (40 km), meet Highway 3 and continue west and north for 14 miles (22.5 km) to Etna.

Hiking
South Fork Lakes 🅿ᴄᴛ
Distance: 4.4 mi/7.1 km round-trip
Duration: 2 hours
Elevation change: 1,390 ft/424 m
Effort: Moderate
Trailhead: Carter Meadows Summit

Hike along the Pacific Crest Trail to the South Fork Lakes Trail, which leads to two pristine lakes in a steep alpine cirque.

Beginning at Carter Meadows Summit, walk south on the southbound PCT, crossing a seasonal stream at 0.4 mile. Views are already incredible as the Trinity Alps spread out before you. Blue Jay Ridge looms on the eastern horizon above Noland Gulch. The trail descends to cross the South Fork Scott River at 0.9 mile. Meet the South Fork Lakes cutoff at 1.1 miles. Make a right to depart

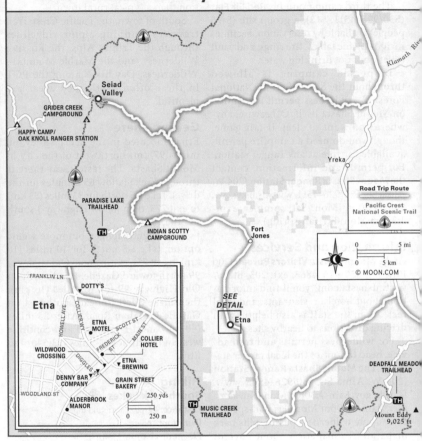

Etna to Seiad Valley

from the PCT, climbing toward the lake basin. You'll climb 900 feet over the next 0.9 mile as you ascend toward the lakes, arriving at the eastern lake at 2.2 miles. Continue to the western lake if you wish. These lakes are cold in the early summer when snowmelt is still strong, but perfect for swimming in August when daytime temps soar.

Note: Free overnight wilderness permits are required in the Trinity Alps. Pick one up at the Callahan Guard Station or the Forest Service district office in Fort Jones.

Getting There

Carter Meadows Summit is 24 miles (39 km) south of Etna, about a 35-minute drive. Take Highway 3 south for 12 miles (19.3 km) to Callahan, then make a right to continue south onto Callahan-Cecilville Road. The trailhead and parking area is on the south side of the road after 12 miles (19.3 km).

Statue Lake

Distance: 5.5 mi/8.9 km round-trip
Duration: 3-4 hours
Elevation change: 1,620 ft/494 m

Effort: Strenuous

Trailhead: Music Creek

If you're up for an adventure, the hike to Statue Lake is a worthy challenge. Follow the Pacific Crest Trail for most of the hike, then venture off-trail to a picturesque destination in the Russian Wilderness.

From the Music Creek trailhead, hike eastward up the switchbacks for 0.9 mile to meet the PCT. Make a right to walk south and enjoy the mostly flat section of the national scenic trail as it gently follows the contours of a ridgeline. Right around the 2.1-mile mark, as the PCT curves west-northwest, look for an overland route up the ridgeline to the south. Your destination sits in the curve of the ridgeline above you. Once you get to the top, you'll be so glad you did. Bizarre granite boulders emerge around the surface of a crystal clear snow-fed lake. It's easy to spend hours here, marveling at the scenery and enjoying the solitude.

Return the way you came. For a longer hike, opt to stay on the northbound PCT past the Music Creek trailhead and head toward Paynes Lake.

Note: Free wilderness permits are required for overnight stays in the Russian Wilderness. If you plan to camp, pick one up in advance at the Callahan Guard Station or the Forest Service district office in Fort Jones.

Getting There

Music Creek trailhead is only 28 miles (45 km) south of Etna, but the twisting mountain roads to get there result in a 70-minute drive. Don't worry: The roads are scenic, and the hike is worth the drive. From Etna, head south on Main Street/Sawyers Bar Road for 19 miles (31 km), crossing the PCT at Etna Summit. Make a hard left to travel south on Forest Road 40N54 (just before Idlewild Campground). Continue for 9.1 miles (14.6 km) to the trailhead.

Food

A pioneer in the "ranch-to-restaurant" concept, **Dotty's** (404 Hwy. 3, 530/476-3303, www.dottysburger.com, 11am-8pm daily, $7-9) is a surprisingly gourmet burger joint with beef from the owner's ranch just two miles down the road. In fact, many of the burger fixings and other ingredients are locally sourced as well (including tasty beers from Etna Brewing). Etna is known for dry, hot summers, and nothing beats a soft-serve ice cream from Dotty's on a summer afternoon.

After selling his breads and pastries on the street corner for years, Etna mayor Erik Ryberg opened a brick-and-mortar location in downtown Etna by popular demand. Stop by **Grain Street Bakery** (445 Main St., www.grainstreetbakery.com, 8am-2pm Wed. and Fri., 8am-6pm Thurs., 8am-noon Sat., $4-8) for heavenly croissants, hearty sourdough loaves, and mouthwatering tarts, cheesecakes, and cookies. Grain Street items proudly use grains from the surrounding Scott Valley. Selection varies based on the day of the week. Fresh coffee is always available in the sunny storefront.

Stepping into ★ **Denny Bar Company** (511 Main St., 530/467-5155, www.dennybarcompany.com, 11am-10pm Wed.-Sat., 11am-7pm Sun., $13-26) feels like being transported to a big city somewhere far away from the rural, 700-person town of Etna. The sophisticated menu features wood-fired pizzas with delicate, gourmet toppings; sumptuous salads, and a delightful array of seafood, poultry, steak, and pork dishes with delectable sauces and hearty sides—duck confit, coffee-crusted rib eye, and house-smoked Columbia River steelhead salmon, to name a few. On weekends and select quiet weekdays, distillery tours are offered. Call ahead to inquire.

Popular with visiting PCT hikers, **Wildwood Crossing** (405 Main St., 530/467-5544, 7am-4pm Mon.-Fri., 8am-1pm Sat., $5-8) is a coffee shop café with a full food menu, free Wi-Fi, and a cute

downtown location. In addition to any coffee or espresso beverage you could want, choose from home-style sandwiches, burritos, salads, and wraps.

Up the road in Fort Jones, **Five Marys Burgerhouse** (11825 Main St., Fort Jones, 530/468-4555, www.fivemarysburgerhouse.com, 11am-9pm Mon.-Wed., 11am-10pm Thurs., 11am-11pm Fri.-Sat., $10-18) is yet another farm-to-table restaurant with meats and ingredients sourced from the nearby Five Marys Farm. The restaurant space was converted in 2017 from an old tavern, and despite the delightfully contemporary menu, the place retains its historical charm. Make the 15-minute drive north out of Etna (or stop here on your way to Seiad Valley) for juicy burgers, chicken-fried steak, carne asada tacos, or chili mac and cheese. If you're in the mood for something green, the salads don't disappoint.

Etna Brewing (131 Callahan St., 530/467-5277, www.etnabrew.com, noon-8pm Wed.-Sat., $9-11) is a laid-back local hangout with a killer outdoor patio. Beers are diverse, running the spectrum from light to dark with lots of medium-bodied brews in between. Named after local influencers in both the brewery and the town of Etna itself, the beers impart the brewer's obvious sense of local pride. The food menu is decent as well: burgers, soups, sandwiches, salads, and wraps.

Accommodations

Etna Motel (317 Collier Way, 530/467-5338, www.theetnamotel.com, $74) is an affordable option downtown within walking distance to Main Street. The rooms are nothing special, but they're clean, quiet, and air-conditioned. Each of the 10 rooms has a mini-fridge, microwave, flat-screen TV, and access to complimentary Wi-Fi.

From top to bottom: Denny Bar Company; appetizer at Five Marys Burgerhouse in Fort Jones; Collier Hotel.

Right downtown, **Collier Hotel** (143 Collier Way, 530/598-9642, www. collierhotel.com, $90-169) is a hotel and vacation rental in a beautiful rooming house built in 1897. Room options include 700-square-foot suites as well as the more standard 250-square-foot hotel rooms. The place has a nice blend of modern furnishings and antique accents to remind you of the historical significance.

At ★ **Alderbrook Manor** (836 Sawyers Bar Rd., 530/467-3917, www. alderbrookmanor.com), rooms in the main B&B ($120-145) have a Victorian design, with pastels and ornamental furnishings. Full breakfast, complimentary Wi-Fi, and a glass of wine in the afternoon are included. More casual is the Hiker Hut ($35), where four bunk beds and a sleeper couch are set up in a miniature barn. There is a bathroom inside with a shower and a flush toilet. Wi-Fi is included and laundry facilities are on-site for guests.

Information and Services

The nearest ranger station is **Callahan Guard Station** (12534 Hwy. 3, 530/467-3365, www.fs.usda.gov, hours vary seasonally), where you can pick up wilderness permits and learn about current conditions in the backcountry. Overnight stays in all the wilderness areas near Etna require free wilderness permits. California campfire permits are also required.

Seiad Valley

There isn't much to see in Seiad Valley besides rugged mountain scenery, and that's precisely the appeal of this quiet, remote community along the Klamath River just south of the California-Oregon border. You may be surprised to see roadside pay phones on the Klamath River Highway east of Seiad Valley, where cellular coverage is slim-to-none. The Pacific Crest Trail travels right through town, and hikers stop to rest, resupply, and eat at a charming little restaurant next to the post office.

Getting There

Seiad Valley is 52 miles (84 km) northwest of Etna, about an 80-minute drive. Take Highway 3 north for 11 miles (17.7 km) to Fort Jones, then head west on Scott River Road for 30 miles (48 km) to Highway 96 (also known as the Klamath River Highway). Seiad Valley is another 11 miles (17.7 km) west on Highway 96.

Note: Scott River Road is maintained for winter travel, but traction tires or chains may be advised or required during winter snows. If you are not comfortable or experienced driving in winter conditions, opt to reach Seiad Valley via Yreka and Highway 96 (described below).

You can also reach Seiad Valley from I-5. Starting in Yreka, head north on Highway 263 for 8 miles (12.9 km), then head west on Highway 96 for 43 miles (69 km). Allow about 70 minutes for this drive.

From Ashland, Oregon, drive south on I-5 into California and take exit 786 toward the Klamath River Highway. Follow Highway 96 west for 45 miles (72 km) to Seiad Valley. Allow about 90 minutes for the drive.

Hiking

The Pacific Crest Trail is plotted right through town, but due to the trail's low elevation near Seiad Valley, this section of trail doesn't offer any panoramic vistas or rewarding views. Instead, follow Scott River Road south of town to access nearby trails at higher elevations that connect to the PCT, climb to the top of dramatic ridgelines, and visit sparkling, swimmable lakes.

Paradise Lake

Distance: 4.2 mi/6.8 km round-trip
Duration: 2 hours
Elevation change: 1,430 ft/436 m
Effort: Moderate
Trailhead: Paradise Lake

The Paradise Lake Trail is one of the shortest, easiest ways into this remote section of the Pacific Crest Trail's route through the Marble Mountain Wilderness. See beautiful wildflowers in the early summer or visit in the late summer or early fall to see the hillsides lit in colorful hues. This 2.1-mile hike to the lake alternates between mixed conifer forest (some of the most diverse in the entire continent!) and grassy meadows. It can be hot during the summer, especially when the trees thin, so be prepared. Paradise Lake itself is small, right on the PCT, and makes a great spot for a picnic.

Getting There

Paradise Lake trailhead is 39 miles (63 km) from Seiad Valley, about an hour and 20 minutes. Head east on Highway 96 for 10.5 miles (16.9 km), then turn right to travel south on Scott River Road for 16.5 miles (26.6 km). At Indian Scotty Campground, turn right onto Forest Road 44N45 and continue for 11.5 miles (18.5 km), following signs for Paradise Lake.

Food

The only restaurant in town, charming ★ **Seiad Café** (44721 Hwy. 96, 530/496-3360, 7am-2pm daily, $8-12) serves up hearty, satisfying breakfasts and lunches in a cozy diner-style space next to the post office and the store. Breakfast fare includes all the standards: bacon, eggs, sausage, potatoes. Lunch is sandwiches, soups, salads, and fries. The coffee is great, too. Famous among hikers is the pancake challenge: Eat all five 13-inch pancakes and your plate is free! Good luck—while hundreds of hungry PCT hikers have attempted, only four people have ever won the challenge. Those who've tried say you're better off just ordering a regular menu item.

You can restock next door at **Seiad Valley Store** (44719 Hwy. 96, 530/496-3399, 6am-8pm Mon.-Sat., 9am-5pm Sun.), a convenience store with packaged food items as well as some fresh groceries, clothing, and camping supplies.

Klamath River Valley

Camping

Camp like the backpackers do at **Grider Creek Campground** (Grider Creek Rd., www.fs.usda.gov, open year-round but subject to winter snows, free), a quiet, forested campground just south of town. The small campground has only 10 sites, each with a picnic table, fire ring, and access to vault toilets. No potable water is available, so bring plenty of your own for drinking, cooking, and washing. The PCT is plotted right through the campground; during July and August, you'll meet northbound thru-hikers emerging from the Marble Mountain Wilderness. If you're so inclined, this is a great place to offer trail magic to weary hikers—cold drinks and satisfying snacks are always appreciated!

Getting There: Grider Creek Campground is 6 miles (9.7 km) south of Seiad Valley, about a 15-minute drive. From Seiad Café, follow Highway 96 east for 1.2 miles (1.9 km) to Walker Creek Road. Turn right to head south, then stay right to continue onto westbound Grider Creek Road as it follows the shore of the Klamath River and then turns south. The

campground is at the end of the road in 4.8 miles (7.7 km).

South of Seiad Valley on Scott River Road, ★ **Indian Scotty Campground** (Forest Rd. 44N45, www.fs.usda.gov, May 15-Oct. 15, $10) is a gorgeous riverside campground with convenient access to hiking trails that lead into the Marble Mountain Wilderness and connect with the PCT, including the Paradise Lake Trail and the Canyon Creek Trail. Campsites are bordered by the Scott River and surrounded by the rugged peaks in the Klamath range. Drinking water is available, and each site has a picnic table, fire ring, and access to pit toilets.

Getting There: Indian Scotty is 28 miles (45 km) south of Seiad Valley, about a 45-minute drive. Take Highway 96 east for 11 miles (17.7 km), then turn right and head south on Scott River Road for 17 miles (27 km). Look for the campground on the south side of the road.

Information and Services

The most convenient ranger station to your road trip is the **Salmon/Scott River Ranger Station** (11263 N. Hwy. 3, Fort Jones, 530/842-6131, www.fs.usda.gov, 8am-4:30pm Mon.-Fri.), about 15 minutes north of Etna and an hour southeast of Seiad Valley. Or you can visit the **Happy Camp/Oak Knoll Ranger Station** (63822 Hwy. 96, 530/493-2243, www.fs.usda.gov, 8am-4:30pm Mon.-Fri.), about 25 minutes west of Seiad Valley. Both of these offices are fantastic resources for high-quality maps and free handouts with information about hikes, campgrounds, and wildlife in the nearby Trinity Alps, Russian Wilderness, and Marble Mountain Wilderness.

Cellular service is spotty at best in the mountainous canyons east of Seiad Valley. Pay phones are located at **Indian Scotty Campground** (45 minutes south of Seiad Valley on Scott River Road) as well as every 5-10 miles (8-16.1 km) along Highway 96.

Oregon

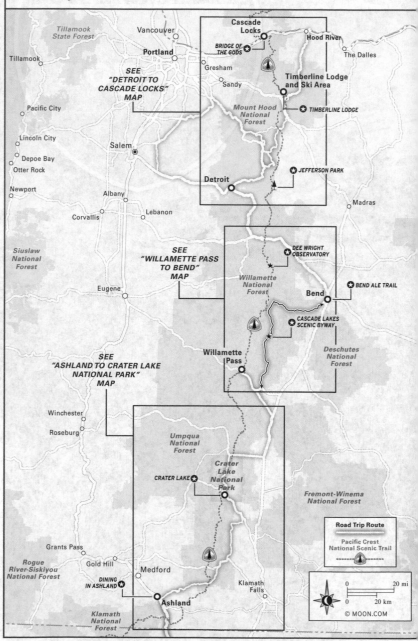

Highlights

★ **Dining in Ashland:** Feast on eclectic world cuisine in the most sophisticated city on the PCT (page 273).

★ **Crater Lake:** Walk along the edge of a giant caldera and gaze into the deepest lake in the nation (page 290).

★ **Dee Wright Observatory:** Climb the stairs to a little lava rock castle overlooking an otherworldly volcanic landscape at McKenzie Pass (page 302).

★ **Cascade Lakes Scenic Byway:** Drive into the heart of Central Oregon's mountains, where the Three Sisters, Broken Top, and Bachelor Butte tower over the road (page 302).

★ **Bend Ale Trail:** Taste the beers that have made Bend's microbreweries famous on this self-guided brewery tour (page 308).

★ **Jefferson Park:** Trek to crystal clear alpine lakes, bask in lush wildflower meadows, and gaze at the craggy, glacier-encrusted slopes of Mount Jefferson (page 316).

★ **Timberline Lodge:** Built in 1938, this gorgeous lodge on the flanks of Mount Hood is renowned for its legendary gourmet buffet (page 320).

★ **Bridge of the Gods:** In the town of Cascade Locks, cross from Oregon into Washington on a historic bridge over the mighty Columbia River (page 332).

Oregon marks the Pacific Crest Trail's official entry into the Pacific Northwest.

Volcanoes tower above tree line, waterfalls tumble over cliffs as rivers cascade out of the mountains, and fields of chunky black lava rocks sprawl among dense conifer forests.

Highways along the eastern side of the Cascade Range offer easy access to the mountains. East of Ashland, Dead Indian Memorial Highway crosses the PCT near Mount McLoughlin, while the Volcanic Legacy Scenic Byway parallels the trail into Crater Lake National Park. Between Crater Lake and Bend, Highway 58 climbs to the top of Willamette Pass, where the PCT crosses the highway near shimmering, swimmable alpine lakes.

Southwest of Bend, the Cascade Lakes National Scenic Byway explores lakes and lava fields before passing between South Sister and Mount Bachelor on its way into the city of Bend. Views are as good as it gets from the McKenzie Pass-Santiam Pass Scenic Byway, northwest of Bend—this route travels over two mountain passes, offering scenic vistas of many Cascade peaks, including the Three Sisters, Mount Washington, and craggy, colorful Three Fingered Jack.

Continuing north from Bend, Forest Road 46 travels through dense low-elevation forests, while the PCT traces the western edge of Mount Jefferson in a rugged alpine area.

East of Portland and north of Mount Jefferson, the Timberline Highway leads to massive Mount Hood, where the PCT ascends to 6,000 feet (1,829 m) as it traces the southern base of the tallest peak in Oregon. Heading north, the Columbia River Gorge awaits. Near Cascade Locks, dozens of hiking trails are accessible along I-84.

Throughout the state, trail towns near the PCT serve regional fare, brew craft beer, and celebrate local art. Ashland, a small city near the California-Oregon border, is famous for its annual Shakespeare Festival and its elegant shops and restaurants. Bend is a sunny outdoor adventure hub on the eastern side of the Cascade Mountains with more than 20 craft breweries. Cascade Locks, less than an hour from Portland, is a riverfront town nestled into the mossy, forested Columbia River Gorge, where hiking trails climb onto the cliffs above the mighty river.

Planning Your Time
Where to Go

With **one week,** you can explore the most scenic mountains, rivers, and lakes of the state. From Ashland, travel northeast through Crater Lake National Park, north into the Three Sisters Wilderness west of Bend, and onto the flanks of Mount Hood before reaching the Columbia River Gorge. Don't miss the sunny city of Bend, where you can explore the forests, peaks, and otherworldly volcanic terrain of the Central Cascades. At the end of the day, reward yourself with a delicious, world-class microbrew from one of Bend's breweries.

For those **short on time**, spend it on Mount Hood, a one-hour drive east from Portland. In addition to showcasing the towering, rocky splendor of the peak itself, the PCT also visits Timberline Lodge, a historic lodge perched at 6,000 feet (1,829 m) on the southern flanks of the volcano.

When to Go

Plan to visit the Oregon section of the PCT between **June and October,** when snow has melted to make trails and roads accessible. Although the state can be rainy, the months of July, August, and September are usually temperate and warm. Winter snowfall starts in October or November and doesn't melt until April or May. Mosquitoes in the alpine areas are vicious during June and July; bring bug repellent.

Day Trips on the PCT

The PCT is only 1-3 hours away from Oregon's busiest cities, and the scenic drive to get there is beautiful, too.

From Bend
Accessible via Cascade Lakes Scenic Byway, hop onto the PCT on the Sisters Mirror Lake Trail to **Koosah Mountain.** Farther north near McKenzie Pass, the PCT twists through a wonderland of volcanic terrain on the **Matthieu Lakes Loop.** Or, head south to **Crater Lake National Park** for a walk along the PCT as it traces the lake's western rim.

From Portland
The PCT traces the western base of Oregon's iconic **Mount Hood** on the way to wildflower-blanketed alpine meadows at **Paradise Park.**

Near vacation destination **Hood River,** hike on the PCT to the top of **Chinidere Mountain.** Or explore the Columbia River Gorge in the town of **Cascade Locks,** where the PCT leads to one of the area's famous waterfalls, **Dry Creek Falls.**

Between **November and April,** highways may close, including the Crater Lake north entrance, Cascade Lakes Scenic Byway southwest of Bend, McKenzie Pass Highway northwest of Bend, and Forest Road 42 between Mount Jefferson and Mount Hood. Popular Rim Drive in Crater Lake National Park is only accessible July-mid-October. Chains may be advised or required on year-round highways including Highway 66 and Dead Indian Memorial Road near Ashland, Highway 58 at Willamette Pass, U.S. 20 at Santiam Pass northwest of Bend, and U.S. 26 and Highway 35 near Mount Hood.

Getting There
Car
I-5 enters Oregon near Ashland and continues north-south through Portland and into Washington. The Pacific Crest Trail is directly accessible off I-5, 12 miles (19.3 km) south of Ashland. From I-5, take exit 6 toward Mount Ashland. Continue south on Old Highway 99 for 1.1 miles (1.8 km) to meet the PCT where it crosses the road.

On the east side of the Cascades, **U.S. 97** parallels I-5 from Klamath Falls north to Bend, extending all the way to the Columbia River Gorge on the border

with Washington. Sandwiched between I-5 and U.S. 97, east-west highways provide a dozen opportunities to hop onto the PCT.

Both I-5 and U.S. 97 are easily accessible year-round. Routes through mountain passes, however, may be hazardous and can close in winter.

For southbound travelers accessing the route from Washington, take I-5 south to Portland. Stay on I-5 into downtown, or hop on I-205 south to avoid potentially crowded freeways, then merge onto I-84 east and follow to Cascade Locks (exit 44) to meet the PCT.

Air
Portland International Airport (PDX, 7000 NE Airport Way, 877/739-4636, www.flypdx.com) is the major airport hub in Oregon. The PCT in Cascade Locks is less than an hour's drive from this airport. If you're planning to start your trip in central or southern Oregon instead, fly into **Eugene Airport** (EUG, 28801 Douglas Dr., 541/682-5544, www. flyeug.com), as opposed to flying into Portland, and save 2-3 hours of driving to Ashland or Crater Lake. Rental cars are available at both airports.

Close to the city of Bend, **Redmond**

OREGON

Best Restaurants

★ **Morning Glory, Ashland:** This place is famous for breakfast and brunch—expect a line on weekends (page 281).

★ **Creekside Pizza, Ashland:** The tables throughout this casual local hangout are fantastic for people-watching (page 283).

★ **Crater Lake Lodge Dining Room, Crater Lake National Park:** The dining room in this national park lodge offers a sweeping panoramic view of the brilliant blue lake and its craggy cliff sides (page 293).

★ **Dogwood Cocktail Cabin, Bend:** This elegant lounge has a distinct urban feel that blends perfectly with the natural, outdoorsy elements for which Bend is known (page 309).

★ **McKay Cottage, Bend:** This place is famous for its delectable breakfasts and brunches (page 311).

★ **Cascade Dining Room, Mount Hood:** A hungry hiker's dream come true, the breakfast and lunch buffets at the Timberline Lodge are legendary (page 323).

★ **pFriem Family Brewers, Hood River:** It's known mostly for its creative brews, but the gourmet food menu makes a visit here incredibly worthwhile even if you don't drink beer (page 327).

★ **Kickstand Coffee & Kitchen, Hood River:** Enjoy craft cocktails and microbrews while locals share stories about their epic days (page 330).

★ **Solstice, Hood River:** Come here for the best pizza in the Columbia Gorge (page 330).

★ **Thunder Island Brewing, Cascade Locks:** Thunder Island offers the best view of any brewery in the Gorge (page 336).

Municipal Airport (RDM, 2522 SE Jesse Butler Circle, Redmond, 541/548-0646, www.flyrdm.com) offers daily direct flights from Denver, Los Angeles, Phoenix, Portland, Salt Lake City, San Francisco, and Seattle.

Train

Amtrak's *Coast Starlight* (800/872-7245, www.amtrak.com) runs north-south along the I-5 corridor with stops in Portland, Oregon City, Salem, Albany, and Eugene. These cities offer access to the central and northern sections of the PCT including the Three Sisters, Mount Jefferson, Mount Hood, and the Columbia Gorge.

Amtrak also has two stations in Chemult and Klamath Falls, which are convenient to the southern parts of the PCT, including Crater Lake and Mount McLoughlin. All train stations are within 50 miles of the PCT, but you'll need a car to get into the mountains.

Bus

Greyhound (800/231-2222, www.greyhound.com, $17-26) offers bus service along the I-5 corridor and has stations in Medford (near Ashland), Portland, and a few cities in between. **BoltBus** (877/265-8287, www.boltbus.com, $17-32) travels between Portland and Seattle with stops in Tacoma.

Best Accommodations

★ **The Ashland Hostel, Ashland:** This PCT-friendly hostel has shared and private rooms plus beautiful communal spaces (page 284).

★ **Callahan's Mountain Lodge, Ashland:** This lodge is a beacon for PCT hikers entering Oregon after hundreds of miles through California (page 284).

★ **Crater Lake Lodge, Crater Lake National Park:** Perched at 7,100-feet on the south rim of the caldera, rooms here offer the best views in the park (page 294).

★ **Diamond Lake Resort, Diamond Lake:** If you're planning to explore Mount Thielsen, take advantage of the rustic, come-as-you-are charm at this 1920s resort (page 295).

★ **Shelter Cove Resort, Crescent Lake:** A popular resupply spot for PCT hikers, this resort has it all (page 300).

★ **McMenamins Old St. Francis School, Bend:** This former Catholic school has been converted into a unique full-service hotel full of quirky amenities (page 313).

★ **Elk Lake Resort, Bend:** A popular stop for PCTers, this resort has glampsites and a restaurant within steps of the trail (page 313).

★ **Breitenbush Hot Springs, Detroit:** This rustic retreat rents primitive cabins with access to natural hot springs (page 318).

★ **Timberline Lodge, Mount Hood:** An overnight stay here offers everything you could want in a historic and elegant mountainside lodge (page 323).

★ **Frog Lake Campground, Mount Hood:** Camp near Timberline Lodge and listen as frogs serenade your site at night (page 324).

★ **Historic Hood River Hotel, Hood River:** This hotel is the best place to stay to explore downtown's restaurants and bars (page 330).

★ **Best Western Plus Columbia River Inn, Cascade Locks:** The most elegant accommodation in town offers a view of the Bridge of the Gods (page 337).

Both bus lines offer multiple departures daily, and buses have Wi-Fi. Advance tickets are recommended, but walk-up fares are sold on an availability basis.

★ Ashland

Both sophisticated and rural, Ashland is a small city set in the Siskiyou Mountains near the Oregon-California border. The town's motto, "As you like it," is a reference to the town's annual Shakespeare festival. The catchphrase also suggests that there's something for everyone in Ashland, and it's true: great restaurants, terrific shopping, world-class theatre, beautiful parks, relaxing spa experiences, and easy access to outdoor activities in the surrounding mountains.

The Pacific Crest Trail enters Oregon near 7,500-foot Mount Ashland, a prominent peak in the mountains southwest of town, then makes its way along the ridgelines southeast of town before tracing the

OREGON

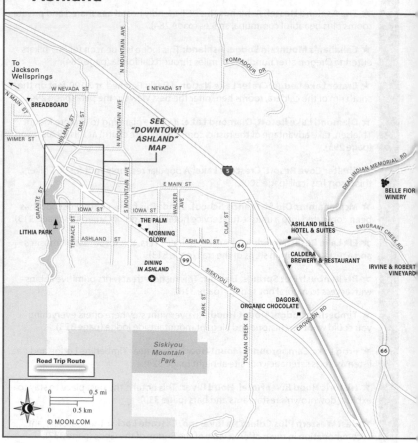

Ashland

To Jackson Wellsprings

BREADBOARD

W NEVADA ST   E NEVADA ST

POMPADOUR DR

N MOUNTAIN AVE

WIMER ST

HELMAN ST

OAK ST

SEE "DOWNTOWN ASHLAND" MAP

N MOUNTAIN AVE

DEAD INDIAN MEMORIAL RD

BELLE FIOR WINERY

E MAIN ST

GRANITE ST

TERRACE ST

IOWA ST

ASHLAND ST

S MOUNTAIN AVE

IOWA ST

WALKER AVE

E MAIN ST

LITHIA PARK

THE PALM

MORNING GLORY

ASHLAND ST

CLAY ST

66

ASHLAND HILLS HOTEL & SUITES

EMIGRANT CREEK RD

CALDERA BREWERY & RESTAURANT

IRVINE & ROBERT VINEYARD

DINING IN ASHLAND

99

SISKIYOU BLVD

PARK ST

DAGOBA ORGANIC CHOCOLATE

TOLMAN CREEK RD

CROWSON RD

66

Siskiyou Mountain Park

Road Trip Route

0   0.5 mi
0   0.5 km

© MOON.COM

base of Mount McLoughlin, Oregon's southernmost volcano.

Getting There

Ashland is located along I-5, about 10 miles (16.1 km) north of the Oregon-California border. From Seiad Valley in California, take Highway 96 east for 45 miles (72 km), merging onto I-5 north. Continue 27 miles (43 km) north into Ashland. The closest PCT trailhead is 7.5 miles (12.1 km) north of the state line, near exit 6 on I-5.

Sights

Ashland's downtown borders **Lithia Park** (Winburn Wy., Fork St., and Glenview Dr.), a 93-acre forested area centered along Ashland Creek with wooded hiking trails, lush grassy lawns, picnic areas, and beautifully manicured gardens. The **Oregon Shakespeare Festival** (www. osfashland.org, Mar.-Oct.) is held at one outdoor stage and three indoor theaters near the northern tip of the park. To identify the park's plants and trees, pick up a *Lithia Park Trail Guide* at the information kiosk on the **Plaza** (between N. Main and E. Main Sts. and Winburn Way).

Next to the kiosk, take a drink from the old-timey **Lithia Fountains,** bubbling with mineral-rich water piped in from nearby springs. Land developers in the early 1900s had designs for a mineral springs-themed resort, but when plans fell through, the water was piped downtown to provide free access to the public. Lithia, also known as lithium oxide, isn't the only mineral in this water—calcium, potassium, magnesium, and sodium bicarbonates also appear in trace amounts. The water has a distinct salty taste to it, and a pungent sulfur-rich smell.

Scenic Drives
Mount Ashland Ski Road

The Pacific Crest Trail and **Mount Ashland Ski Road** (Forest Rd. 20 and Siskiyou Summit Rd.) run side-by-side for 21 miles (34 km) through the Mount Ashland area. This road climbs 3,500 feet (1,067 m) from the I-5 corridor to the top of 7,500-foot Mount Ashland. The 360-degree views from the top include snowcapped Mount Shasta, the city of Ashland, and an endless expanse of Cascade and Siskiyou peaks on every horizon.

Start at the PCT trailhead on Old Highway 99 and follow Mount Ashland Ski Road west for 12 miles (19.3 km) as it twists and turns its way to the very top of Mount Ashland. The road is paved for the first 9 miles (14.5 km) before reaching the base of Mount Ashland Ski Area. There is a parking lot here, and a day lodge open during ski season. In the winter, your drive ends here, as the road is not plowed after this point. During the warmer months (approx. Apr.-Nov.), you may choose to continue driving for 2.8 more miles (4.5 km) to the summit of Mount Ashland along Forest Road 20, a nicely graded dirt road suitable for all vehicles.

From the ski area, continue west for 1.5 miles (2.4 km), then take the right fork to drive north up the hill to the summit. From the top of Mount Ashland, you can gaze down on the cities of Ashland and Medford, and into the Siskiyou and Cascade Mountains, and you'll even spy 14,180-foot Mount Shasta across the California border. Forest Road 20 continues to trace the PCT's path west of Mount Ashland; to extend your scenic drive, return from the summit and make a sharp right onto Forest Road 20, heading west for another 9 miles (14.5 km) to Observation Gap. You'll cross the PCT multiple times and have plenty of opportunities to soak up more views of the Siskiyous, Klamath National Forest, and Mount Shasta.

Mount Ashland Ski Road begins near the PCT trailhead on Old Highway 99, about 11 miles (17.7 km) south of Ashland. Drive south on I-5 to exit 6 and continue straight onto Old Highway 99, following signs for Mount Ashland. This road is open year-round, but chains may be advised or required during winter months.

Green Springs Loop

The **Green Springs Highway** (Rte. 66) curves east out of Ashland into golden, grassy hills before entering the Cascade-Siskiyou National Monument, an area preserved specifically for its biodiversity.

From Ashland, the road twists 17 miles (27 km) southeast before crossing the PCT near Soda Mountain Road. Continue for 1.8 miles (2.9 km) to Green Springs Inn & Cabins, a woodsy resort with accommodations and a restaurant, and a small **visitors center** (www. cascadesiskiyou.org, daily in summer). Rangers are available on weekends to answer questions about the Cascade-Siskiyou National Monument.

From Green Springs, head north on Hyatt Lake Road for 3 miles (4.8 km) and turn left to stay on Hyatt Dam Road. Continue north for the next 10 miles (16.1 km), enjoying shoreline views of Hyatt Lake and Howard Prairie Reservoirs.

(The name of the road changes to Hyatt Prairie Road near Hyatt Lake Resort, a small resort with cabin rentals and a general store about 4.5 miles/7.2 km north of Green Springs.) Both lakes are important stops on the Pacific Flyway for migratory birds. Waterfowl including white pelicans, sandhill cranes, and Caspian terns are among the most captivating.

Dead Indian Memorial Road intersects with Hyatt Prairie Road 13.5 miles (21.7 km) north of Green Springs. To make a scenic loop back to Ashland, turn left to head west on Dead Indian Memorial Road for 17 miles (27 km), where you rejoin Highway 66. This stretch of highway is a twisty descent that leads out of Ashland's eastern hills and back down into the valley.

Allow about 90 minutes for this 45-mile (72-km) drive, more if you plan to stop along the way. Highway 66 and Dead Indian Memorial Road are subject to winter weather; traction tires or chains may be advised or required December-April.

Hiking
Pilot Rock 🄫

Distance: 8.6-9.4 mi/13.8-15.1 km round-trip
Duration: 4 hours
Elevation change: 1,400-2,000 ft/427-610 m
Effort: Moderate
Trailhead: Mount Ashland Ski Road

Hike to the base of Pilot Rock, an iconic basalt formation near the Oregon-California border (and summit the rock itself if you're a climber). In the spring, this part of the Pacific Crest Trail is lush and green; in late summer, the meadows turn golden. From the trailhead on Old Highway 99 South, the Pacific Crest Trail heads west through grasses and brushy trees for 1.1 miles before making a sharp bend to the south.

Continue south, hiking uphill through sparsely forested meadows until the PCT crosses two dirt roads at 2.4 and 2.6 miles. The trail continues to climb, reaching 5,200 feet (1,585 m) at 4 miles,

then descending for 0.3 mile to a saddle between Pilot Rock and a neighboring butte to its west.

Turn around here for an 8.6-mile round-trip hike, or to summit 5,800-foot Pilot Rock, continue west on the northbound PCT for 0.2 mile and look for the spur trail on the south side of the PCT. This climber's trail leads to the top of the rock formation, where Mount Shasta is on display among the Cascade Range and Klamath Mountains.

To make this a longer hike, continue west on the northbound PCT past Pilot Rock toward Hobart Bluff.

Getting There

This trailhead is located on Old Highway 99 South, 0.5 mile south of the intersection of Old Highway 99 and Mount Ashland Ski Road. From Ashland, follow I-5 south and take exit 6 toward Mount Ashland. Continue south on Old Highway 99 for 1.2 miles (1.9 km). Look for the PCT crest on the east side of the road.

Hobart Bluff 🄫

Distance: 2.5 mi/4 km round-trip
Duration: 1.5 hours
Elevation change: 440 ft/134 m
Effort: Easy
Trailhead: Hobart Bluff

The walk to Hobart Bluff showcases the grassy hillsides of the Cascade-Siskiyou National Monument and ends at a cliff overlooking Ashland. From the Hobart Bluff parking area, follow the Pacific Crest Trail northeast past tall grasses, pines, oaks, and junipers. Enjoy panoramic east-facing views and pockets of forest before meeting the spur trail to Hobart Bluff at 0.9 mile. Turn west onto the spur trail and climb 0.3 mile to explore the various vantage points along the edge of the bluff. To the southwest, Pilot Rock and Mount Ashland stand out on the horizon. See the city of Ashland spread out in the valley to the northwest.

Getting There

Hobart Bluff is 20 miles (32 km) southeast of Ashland, about a 40-minute drive. Follow Highway 66 east out of town to Soda Mountain Road (about 16 mi/26 km), then turn right to head south for 4 miles (6.4 km). The trailhead is located at the north edge of the parking area.

Mount McLoughlin 〔PCT〕

Distance: 9.2 mi/14.8 km round-trip
Duration: 8 hours
Elevation change: 3,300 ft/1,006 m
Effort: Strenuous
Trailhead: Mount McLoughlin
Pass/Fee: Northwest Forest Pass

The hike to the top of 9,500-foot Mount McLoughlin isn't technical, but it isn't easy either. The up-close views of Mount McLoughlin itself, a dormant stratovolcano, are just as impressive as the panoramic view from the peak. While the Pacific Crest Trail skirts the eastern edge of the mountain, you'll get a much better lay of the land by climbing to the rocky top.

Begin your hike walking 1 mile northwest through a mixed conifer forest on the Mount McLoughlin Trail before intersecting with the Pacific Crest Trail. Turn right to walk north on the PCT for 0.4 mile to a signed junction where the Mount McLoughlin Trail departs from the PCT. Turn left to head west on the Mount McLoughlin Trail. The fir, pine, and cedar trees along this section are enormous! The steepness increases at 2.5 miles as you enter a rocky patch of manzanita bushes. This is the edge of the steep-sided peak—trees thin, the trail becomes rockier, and vistas of the surrounding lakes start to appear. Four Mile Lake and Klamath Lake are visible from the rocky outcrop at 3.2 miles.

By 3.7 miles, the only remaining trees are bonsai-like limber pines, which only

From top to bottom: PCT sign near Green Springs; Hobart Bluff; craggy terrain on the Mount McLoughlin trail.

grow at high elevation. Look south to spy Lake of the Woods as you continue to ascend amid boulders and lava rock. Around 4 miles, look for pink ribbons on trees and arrows painted on rocks that help distinguish the trail from the surrounding terrain. The remaining 0.6 mile is pure volcanic wonder, with colorful rocks and hoodoo towers on the north side of the peak. The summit at 4.6 miles is unmistakable: There's a giant American flag waving in the wind. Take in the 360-degree views of southern Oregon, including Mount Shasta (in California), Klamath Lake, and the peaks surrounding Crater Lake. You can even see the Three Sisters on a clear day.

Getting There

Mount McLoughlin trailhead is 45 miles (72 km) northeast of Ashland, about an hour's drive. From downtown Ashland, take East Main Street east out of town for 3 miles (4.8 km). Turn left onto Dead Indian Memorial Road and follow it east for 37 miles (60 km) (crossing the PCT near the Pederson Trailhead & Sno-Park). At Lake of the Woods, turn left and follow the lakefront road for 1.4 miles (2.3 km), following signs for Highway 140. Make another left onto Highway 140 westbound, heading west for 0.6 mile, then turn right to head north on Four Mile Lake Road. Continue north for 3 miles (4.8 km) to the intersection with Forest Road 3650. Turn left to head south on Forest Road 3650. The trailhead parking area is on the west side of the road in 0.2 mile.

Sports and Recreation
Skiing

Mount Ashland Ski Area (11 Mt. Ashland Ski Rd., 541/482-2897, www.mtashland. com, 9am-4pm Thurs.-Mon. early Dec., 9am-4pm daily late Dec.-early Jan., 9am-9pm Thurs.-Fri., 9am-4pm Sat.-Mon. Jan.-Mar., $38-52) is a small, local ski area atop 7,500-foot Mount Ashland with four chairlifts and 23 runs. On sunny days, gorgeous views from the ski slopes include Mount Shasta, the Klamath Mountains, and the valley where the city of Ashland sits. Ski, snowboard, and accessory **rentals** ($20-29) are available in the lodge. The historic lodge has a café and bar, plus a lovely outdoor deck overlooking the slopes.

Getting There

Mount Ashland is about a 30-minute drive south of Ashland. Take I-5 south to exit 6 and follow signs for Mount Ashland. If you prefer not to drive to the top of the mountain, take the **Snow Bus** (www.mtashland.com/snowbus, Sat.-Sun. Dec.-Mar. with daily service during winter and spring break, free). There are seven departures daily from Ashland Hills Hotel & Suites. This first-come, first-served shuttle is only available for skiers and snowboarders (no sightseers).

Spa

For a small day-use fee, you can soothe your tired hiking muscles in the hot pool at **Jackson Wellsprings** (2253 Hwy. 99, 541/482-3776, www.jacksonwellsprings. com, 8am-11:45pm Tues.-Sun., 6pm-11:45pm Mon., $10). Enjoy a hot shower and take advantage of the essential-oil-scented soap in the bathrooms. In warm weather, the large cooler pool (adjacent to the hot pool) is lovely for swimming or relaxing. A statue of Ganesh, a Hindu deity, overlooks the pool. Clothing is optional after dark (approx. 9pm summer, 5pm winter), and only guests 18 and older are allowed. Massage services, facials, and other body treatments are available.

Overnight **camping** (June-Oct.) is allowed on a meadow adjacent to the spa building; accommodation options include tent sites ($25/night), RV sites ($35/night), and tepee rentals ($40/night), and the price of admission to the spa is included.

Entertainment and Events
Breweries and Wine-Tasting

With a glimmering purple-tiled fireplace, thousands of beer bottles lining the cavernous walls, and more than 40 house-brewed beers on tap, **Caldera Brewery & Restaurant** (590 Clover Ln., 541/482-4677, www.calderabrewing.com, 11am-9pm daily, $11-24) is unquestionably impressive. Neapolitan-style pizzas are made with baked-from-scratch crusts, and the menu includes recommended beer pairings as well as appetizers, salads, sandwiches, burgers, and entrées. Cozy up in one of the purple booths or dine at the picnic tables outside, and feel the wind in your hair as you gaze out over Ashland's golden hillsides.

While roaming the urbane streets of downtown Ashland, it's easy to forget that the rural farmlands of the Rogue Valley are just outside of town. **Standing Stone Brewery** (101 Oak St., 541/482-2448, www.standingstonebrewing.com, 11am-midnight daily, $13-22, tasting flight $5) is known for a delectable food menu that features ingredients from its very own 260-acre farm, One Mile Farm, which is just one mile from the brewery. The menu includes shareable appetizers, wood-fired pizzas, and globally inspired dishes. As for beers, the expertly crafted pilsners, ales, IPAs, and rotating seasonal brews pair beautifully with the food. The entire restaurant runs on solar power, and the large outdoor deck is popular during Ashland's warm summers. Inside, watch the chefs prepare food in the open kitchen; high ceilings with exposed wooden beams give the space an industrial-chic feel.

Southern Oregon is home to more than 120 wineries. **Belle Fiore Winery** (100 Belle Fiore Ln., 541/552-4900, www.bellefiorewine.com, noon-4pm Mon.-Tues., noon-7pm Wed. and Sun.,

From top to bottom: downtown Ashland; tasting flight at Caldera Brewery & Restaurant; Standing Stone Brewery.

noon-8pm Thurs.-Sat., $15-17) hosts tastings in a delightfully ornate pavilion. The property is also home to a huge chateau that functions as a private event venue. The winery hosts live music acts 5pm-7:30pm Wednesday-Sunday.

Irvine & Roberts Vineyards (1614 Emigrant Creek Rd., 541/482-9383, www.irvinerobertsvineyards.com, noon-6pm daily May-Oct., noon-6pm Wed.-Sun. Nov.-Apr., $12) makes pinot noir, pinot meunier, and chardonnay. The tasting room has floor-to-ceiling windows and an outdoor deck with glass-encased fireplaces and views of Ashland's golden hills. Both wineries are 5 miles (8 km) east of downtown Ashland near Dead Indian Memorial Road.

To learn more about the vineyards and tasting rooms near Ashland, visit www.visit.oregonwine.org.

Festivals and Events

Ashland's **Oregon Shakespeare Festival** (15 S. Pioneer St., 800/219-8161, www.osfashland.org, Tues.-Sun. Mar.-Oct., $40-120) draws more than 100,000 people every year. Eleven plays and 300 shows occur throughout three theaters near downtown's Lithia Park. Shows start around noon and continue into the evening. Although some tickets may be available day-of, advance ticket purchase is recommended. Performances at the **Green Show** (S. Pioneer St. between E. Main and Hargadine Sts., Wed.-Sat. evening June-Sept., free) occur on an outdoor stage, and artists here aren't limited to the Shakespeare theme. Expect to see an array of acts including dance, live music, and more. This festival can bring crowds to Ashland—hotels and restaurants may book up in advance.

Foodies won't want to miss **A Taste of Ashland** (541/488-0178, www.atasteofashland.com, noon-4pm Sat.-Sun. late Apr., $45-65), a self-guided tour of 17 galleries, each hosting one of the city's best restaurants. Small bites are served with wine pairings from local

performers at the Oregon Shakespeare Festival

vineyards. This combination of gourmet cuisine, southern Oregon wine, and local art is a fantastic way to learn about Ashland's unique culture. Most galleries are within walking distance of each other, and free shuttle service is offered for those on the outskirts of town. Tickets are limited; advance purchase is recommended. If any day-of tickets are available, they can be purchased at the **Plaza kiosk** (between N. Main and E. Main Sts. and Winburn Way) between 11am and 4pm.

Shopping

Ashland's downtown is quaint and compact. The city's best shops and restaurants are all within a few minutes' walk, and the sidewalks are a pleasant place to get a taste of Ashland's culture.

Bloomsbury Books (290 E. Main St., 541/488-0029, www.bloomsburyashland. com, 8:30am-9pm Mon.-Fri., 9am-9pm Sat., 10am-6pm Sun.) is a bright, airy boutique bookstore with a great selection of novels, nonfiction, local area guidebooks, and, unsurprisingly, a large selection of books on the performing arts. Toys and locally made goods for sale make great gifts. The staircase in the center of the shop climbs to **Bloomsbury Coffee House** (541/482-6112, 9am-5pm Mon.-Sat., 10am-5pm Sun., $4-8), a cozy café with organic bakery items and espresso—a lovely spot to relax with a good book.

Hand-crafted home goods, jewelry, puzzles, books, maps, and kitchen items are just some of the items on display at **Northwest Nature Shop** (154 Oak St., 877/482-3241, www. northwestnatureshop.com, 10am-6pm daily), an outdoor-themed shop with a wide array of both practical items and whimsical gifts. Those interested in outdoor living or gardening will want to visit. The shop also has a large selection of children's maps, books, and educational toys.

Chocolate-lovers won't want to miss **Dagoba Organic Chocolate** (1105 Benson Way, 541/482-2001, www. dagobachocolate.com, 10am-4pm Mon.-Fri., $3-10), where a tiny little gift shop is located inside the chocolate factory. While you can't tour the factory itself, you can peek at it through a window in the gift shop, where there are free samples of every chocolate bar for sale. The Dagoba factory is 3 miles (4.8 km) southeast of downtown Ashland.

Food

Because so many of the rural towns near the PCT are tiny, food and dining options are quite limited. Hikers who have grown tired of the same old American-style diner fare find the Ashland food scene a thrill. Fresh seafood, worldly spices, and unusual ingredients are abundant on this sophisticated city's creative and diverse menus.

Located in a historic craftsman house, ★ **Morning Glory** (1149 Siskiyou Blvd., 541/488-8636, www.morningglorycafe.

Downtown Ashland

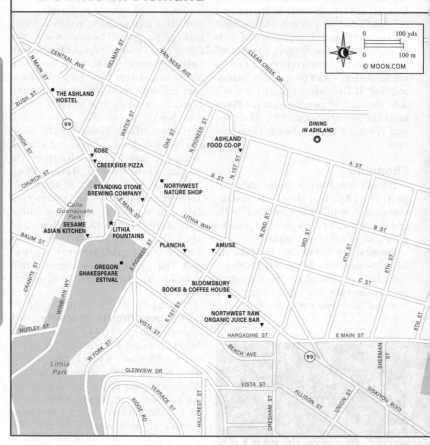

0 100 yds
0 100 m
© MOON.COM

THE ASHLAND HOSTEL

99

KOBE
CREEKSIDE PIZZA

STANDING STONE BREWING COMPANY

NORTHWEST NATURE SHOP

Calle Guanajuato Park

SESAME ASIAN KITCHEN
LITHIA FOUNTAINS

OREGON SHAKESPEARE ESTIVAL

PLANCHA
AMUSE

BLOOMSBURY BOOKS & COFFEE HOUSE

NORTHWEST RAW ORGANIC JUICE BAR

ASHLAND FOOD CO-OP

DINING IN ASHLAND

Lithia Park

org, 8am-1:30pm daily, $10-15) serves a delectable menu of omelets with gorgonzola and grilled onions, crispy risotto and kale cakes with poached eggs, and sourdough-blueberry pancakes with lemon butter. All the breakfast basics are here, too. Walls in the cozy, small indoor space are painted in vibrant colors, and flowers decorate every table. Outdoor tables are a lovely place to enjoy a meal during the warm summer months. No reservations are accepted—expect to wait 15-45 minutes for a table on busy weekend mornings.

The deck at **The Breadboard** (744 N. Main St., 541/488-0295, www.breadboardashland.com, 7am-2pm daily, $8-13) might look familiar if you've seen the movie *Wild*. Reese Witherspoon dined here while playing Cheryl Strayed in the film. For breakfast, this casual eatery serves omelets, scrambles, burritos, waffles, and pancakes, as well as house-baked pastries. Lunchtime options include hearty salads, grilled sandwiches, and soups. Tables on the outdoor deck offer nice views of the golden hillsides east of Ashland.

Amuse (15 N. 1st St., 541/488-9000, www.amuserestaurant.com, 5:30pm-8pm Sun. and Wed.-Thurs., 5:30pm-9pm Fri.-Sat., $22-36) is an elegant French restaurant with a menu that highlights organic, seasonal Pacific Northwest ingredients. The menu features soups, salads, seafoods, handmade pastas, expertly grilled meats, gourmet cheeses, and delicate desserts. Reservations are recommended during Shakespeare season, and are accepted up to two months in advance.

Located across the street from Lithia Park, the sleek and stylish dining room at **Sesame Asian Kitchen** (21 Winburn Way, 541/482-0119, www.sesameasiankitchen.com, 11:30am-9pm daily, $12-19) looks onto the park's lovely lawn. The menu includes an array of expertly spiced and seasoned noodles, curries, salads, veggies, seafood, and meat dishes. Minimalist decor in the restaurant is accented by brightly colored curtains and furniture. Outdoor tables on the charming back patio are shaded by hardwoods and bordered by babbling Ashland Creek.

Kobe (96 N. Main St., 541/488-8058, www.kobeashland.com, 5pm-10pm Sun., 5pm-11pm Mon.-Sat. Memorial Day-Labor Day, 5pm-10pm Sun.-Thurs., 5pm-11pm Fri.-Sat. Labor Day-Memorial Day, $11-30) is a sushi restaurant that perfectly balances Japanese classics with modern creativity. The chef's daily selection of fresh fish is available as an appetizer or platter. Soups, salads, grilled meats, stir-fried veggies, and fried chicken are on the menu, too.

Colorful **Plancha** (165 E. Main St., 541/708-0883, www.planchamex.com, noon-3pm and 4pm-8pm Tues.-Sun., $7-20) serves flavorful and modern Mexican cuisine with more than 40 tequilas behind the bar. Beautifully prepared dishes include tacos, chimichangas, steak entrées, and huevos rancheros with roasted vegetables, grilled meats, chipotle crema, house-made salsa, and fresh tortillas. The colorful, artistic, and playful aesthetics make the dishes here as visibly enjoyable as they are delicious.

Tucked into a historic building along Ashland Creek, ★ **Creekside Pizza** (92 1/2 N. Main St., 541/482-4131, www.creeksidepizza.com, 11am-1am daily, $7-20) attracts a diverse array of customers for its delicious pizza. Inside you'll find stained-glass light fixtures, rotating art installations lining the wood-paneled walls, and windows overlooking the creek. Order a whole pie (gluten-free crust available) or the featured slice of the day (meat or veggie) and wash it down with a pint of locally brewed beer or a cocktail from the full bar while enjoying the view.

For fantastic food without the fancy restaurant atmosphere (or prices), the **Ashland Food Co-Op** (237 1st St., 541/482-2237, www.ashlandfood.coop, 7am-9pm daily) is a big, beautiful grocery store with organic produce, a wide selection of bulk items, and a deli serving espresso, smoothies, salads, tacos, burritos, and sandwiches. Entrées and sides at the hot bar rotate daily. Bring your own durable plate or bowl to save $0.15.

Get a delicious dose of fresh fruits and veggies at **Northwest Raw Organic Juice Bar** (370 E. Main St., 541/708-6363, www.nwraw.com, 7am-7pm daily, $6-8). Fresh-pressed juices and smoothies are paired with vegan soups, snacks, smoothie bowls, toasts, granola, salads, and treats. The sleek, modern space has high ceilings and a cozy fireplace to cuddle up to on chilly mornings.

Accommodations and Camping
Ashland
Close to downtown restaurants, **The Palm** (1065 Siskiyou Blvd., 541/482-2636, www.palmcottages.com, $80-160) is an affordable, centrally located option with beautiful gardens and a heated saltwater pool. Rooms and cottages vary in size and amenities; some include vaulted ceilings, breakfast nooks, fireplaces, and patios. The eco-friendly property prides itself

on utilizing LED lighting and comprehensive recycling. Wi-Fi is fast and free across the property.

Located on the north end of downtown, ★ **The Ashland Hostel** (150 N. Main St., 541/482-9217, www. theashlandhostel.com, $64-139 private rooms, $31 shared) is a PCT-friendly accommodation with a beautiful shared kitchen space, a comfy living room with fluffy couches, and a large front porch with picnic tables. Rooms vary in size, offering private rooms and shared dorm-style rooms. Female- and male-specific dorm rooms are available.

Ashland Hills Hotel & Suites (2525 Ashland St., 541/482-8310, www. ashlandhillshotel.com, $100-170) is a renovated property with a retro design, located on the east edge of town near Ashland's wineries. Rooms include coffee, refrigerators, and microwaves. Free high-speed Wi-Fi is available throughout the property, and overnight stays include continental breakfast. Guests can also take advantage of the hotel's orange cruiser bikes to explore downtown Ashland and the surrounding areas. The on-site restaurant **Luna Café** (8am-9pm Sun.-Thurs., 8am-10pm Fri.-Sat.) serves American lunch, dinner, and weekend brunch.

South of Ashland

★ **Callahan's Mountain Lodge** (7100 Old Hwy. 99 S., 541/482-1299, www. callahanslodge.com, $175-280) is an impressive wooden lodge situated in the forest on the eastern base of Mount Ashland, about a mile northeast of the PCT trailhead at Mount Ashland Ski Road. Elegant hotel rooms feature woodsy details and decor with wood-burning fireplaces, microwaves, mini-fridges, coffeemakers, and jetted spa tubs for two. Wi-Fi is complimentary throughout the property, and your stay includes free breakfast. The on-site **restaurant** (8am-9pm daily, $12-36) serves upscale American fare and features live music nightly at 6pm.

Callahan's is 10 miles (16.1 km) south of Ashland.

East of Ashland

East Ashland is a popular getaway for locals. **Green Springs Inn & Cabins** (11470 Hwy. 66, 541/890-6435, www. greenspringsinn.com, $105-135 rooms, $225-275 cabins) is an expansive, forested property located within the Cascade-Siskiyou National Monument. There are eight simply furnished lodge rooms with microwaves, coffeemakers, and mini-fridges. Some rooms have large jetted spa tubs, private decks, or fireplaces. Nine large, luxurious cabins on the property with full kitchens, hot tubs, and outdoor decks can accommodate groups of six or more. Pet-friendly and pet-free options are available. Wildlife is frequently spotted near the lodge and cabins (along with chickens who live on the property). The casual on-site **café** (9am-8:30pm daily, $10-23) serves American-style breakfast, lunch, and dinner, featuring grass-fed beef from a neighboring farm. Green Springs is 20 miles (32 km) east of Ashland.

On the west side of Hyatt Lake, a popular bird-watching destination, rental cabins at **Hyatt Lake Resort** (7900 Hyatt Prairie Rd., 541/482-3331, www. hyattlake.com, $99-169) are cozily arranged around a small general store and casual **café** (9am-6pm Sun.-Thurs., 9am-7pm Fri., 9am-8pm Sat., $8-18) serving salads, soups, from-scratch pizzas, and house-made berry cobbler. Most cabins are small and designed for just two guests; some of the cabins can accommodate four or six people. All rentals have full kitchens and baths. A few cabins include hot tubs and outdoor decks. Hyatt Lake Resort is 23 miles (37 km) east of Ashland.

The campsites at **Klum Landing Park** (Howard Prairie Dam Rd., 541/774-6301, www.jacksoncountyor.org, Apr.-Sept., $20) are bordered by Howard Prairie Lake and the PCT. The 30 sites

Ashland to Crater Lake National Park

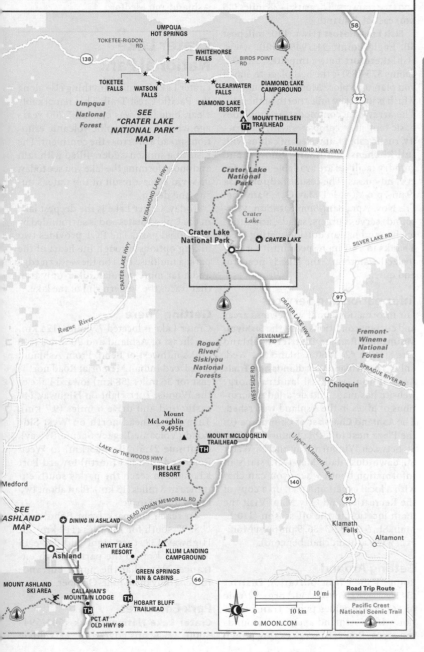

UMPQUA HOT SPRINGS

TOKETEE-RIGDON RD

WHITEHORSE FALLS

BIRDS POINT RD

TOKETEE FALLS

WATSON FALLS

CLEARWATER FALLS

DIAMOND LAKE CAMPGROUND

DIAMOND LAKE RESORT

MOUNT THIELSEN TRAILHEAD

Umpqua National Forest

SEE "CRATER LAKE NATIONAL PARK" MAP

E DIAMOND LAKE HWY

W DIAMOND LAKE HWY

Crater Lake National Park

Crater Lake

Crater Lake National Park

CRATER LAKE

CRATER LAKE HWY

SILVER LAKE RD

Rogue River

Rogue River-Siskiyou National Forests

SEVENMILE RD

CRATER LAKE HWY

Fremont-Winema National Forest

SPRAGUE RIVER RD

Chiloquin

WESTSIDE RD

Mount McLoughlin 9,495ft

MOUNT MCLOUGHLIN TRAILHEAD

Upper Klamath Lake

LAKE OF THE WOODS HWY

FISH LAKE RESORT

Medford

SEE "ASHLAND" MAP

DINING IN ASHLAND

DEAD INDIAN MEMORIAL RD

Klamath Falls

Altamont

Ashland

HYATT LAKE RESORT

KLUM LANDING CAMPGROUND

GREEN SPRINGS INN & CABINS

MOUNT ASHLAND SKI AREA

CALLAHAN'S MOUNTAIN LODGE

HOBART BLUFF TRAILHEAD

PCT AT OLD HWY 99

0   10 mi

0   10 km

Road Trip Route

Pacific Crest National Scenic Trail

© MOON.COM

are first-come, first-served. Amenities include picnic tables, fire rings, restrooms, and free showers. The park is 28 miles (45 km) east of Ashland.

Fish Lake Resort (Hwy. 140, milepost 30, Eagle Point, 541/949-8500, www.fishlakeresort.net, campsites $22-32, cabins $75-185) is the best place to stay if you plan to explore Mount McLoughlin, which is just a few miles north of the lake. The array of accommodations includes basic tent sites, campsites with electricity, rustic cabins, and elegant cabins with full kitchens and linens. Shower and laundry facilities are available for campers and guests. The casual **Tadpole Café** (9am-7pm Mon.-Fri. May-Oct., 9am-7pm Fri. Nov.-Apr., 8am-8pm Sat.-Sun. year-round) serves burgers, salads, and sandwiches and has an outside seating area. Thanks to a 10-mph speed limit for motorized watercraft, the lake is peaceful and quiet.

Information and Services

For information about wilderness areas and current conditions, visit the **Siskiyou Mountains Ranger District** (Ashland Fire Station #2, 1860 Ashland St., Wed. only). The **Ashland Woodlands and Trails Association** (www.ashlandtrails.org) website has maps and detailed descriptions of hikes in the Ashland watershed. The **Ashland Chamber of Commerce** (in the Plaza next to Lithia Fountain, Main St. between Winburn Way and N. Water St., dawn-dusk daily May-Oct.) staffs an information booth where you can chat with a local expert and pick up a copy of the Recreation and City Map. Visit the main location in the off-season (110 E. Main St., 541/482-3486, 9am-5pm Mon.-Fri., www.ashlandchamber.com).

Getting Around

Rogue Valley Transportation District (541/779-5821, www.rvtd.org, $2/ride or $6/day) provides public transportation within Ashland and the surrounding areas. Route 10 services downtown Ashland, with stops along Siskiyou Boulevard, and also travels between Ashland and Medford.

Crater Lake National Park

Crater Lake is unlike anything else along the Pacific Crest Trail. This remarkably clear, blue lake was created 7,700 years ago when a catastrophic volcanic eruption spread ash across the continent. The resulting sunken caldera filled with rain and snow, forming the lake you see today, its vivid color a result of the water's purity and depth.

Today, Crater Lake is the deepest lake in the United States and is surrounded by a national park. The PCT provides two hiking options through the heart of the park: a multiuse trail on the western edge and a far more popular, hiker-only trail that traces the western rim of the lake.

Getting There

Crater Lake is located 77 miles (124 km) northeast of Ashland and 90 miles (145 km) southwest of Bend. From Ashland, take Dead Indian Memorial Road northeast for 36 miles (58 km) toward Lake of the Woods. Turn right on Highway 140 eastbound and drive 6 miles (9.7 km). Turn left to head north on West Side Road (Volcanic Legacy Scenic Byway). Continue 21.5 miles (35 km) to Weed Road and turn left (north) toward Fort Klamath to reach the park's south entrance in 8 miles (13 km). Plan about two hours for the drive.

To reach the park from Bend, take U.S. 97 south for 74 miles (119 km). At Highway 138, turn right and drive 15 miles (24 km) to the park's north entrance. Note that the north entrance route is only open June-October.

Park Entrances

Crater Lake National Park (541/594-3000, www.nps.gov/crla, $25/vehicle

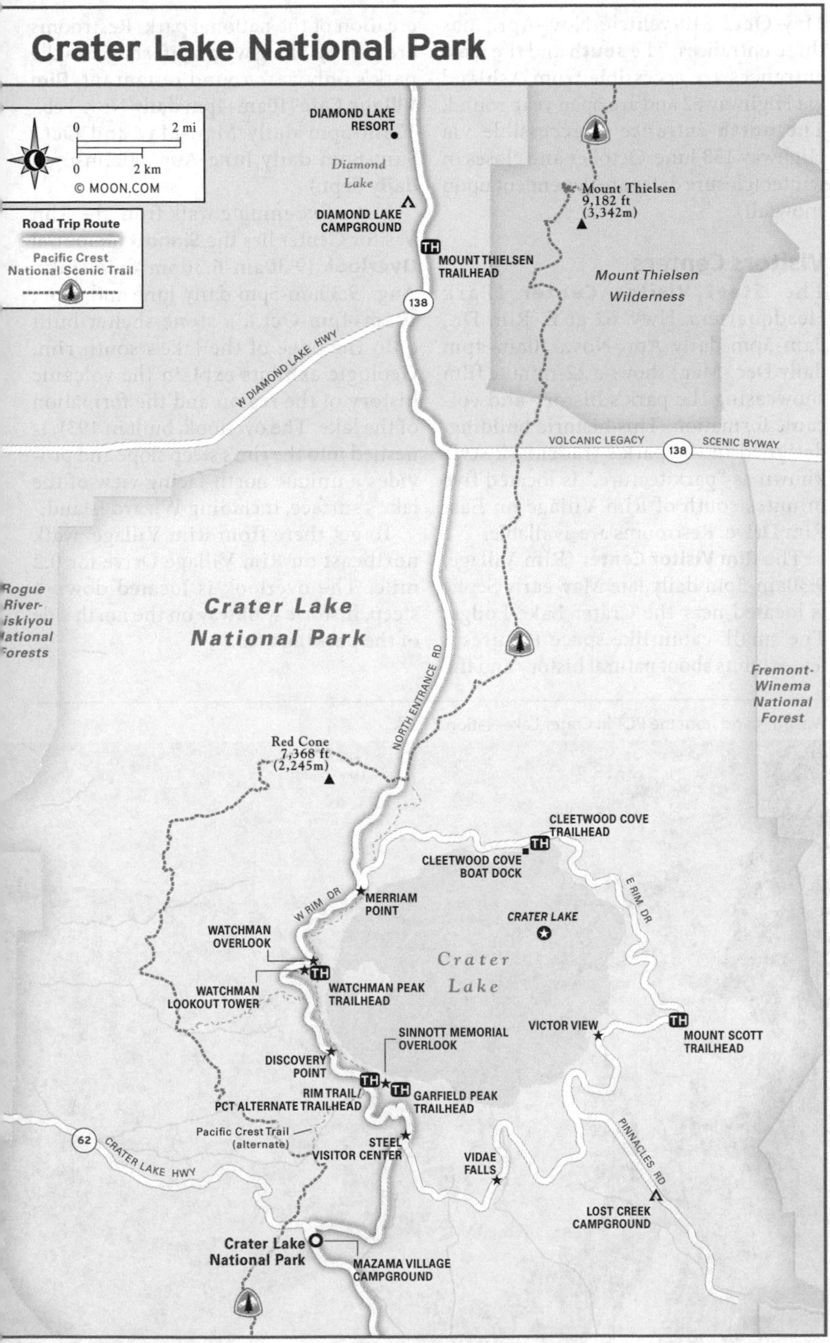

Crater Lake National Park

0   2 mi
0   2 km
© MOON.COM

Road Trip Route

Pacific Crest National Scenic Trail

DIAMOND LAKE RESORT

Diamond Lake

DIAMOND LAKE CAMPGROUND

Mount Thielsen
9,182 ft
(3,342m)

MOUNT THIELSEN TRAILHEAD

Mount Thielsen Wilderness

138

W DIAMOND LAKE HWY

VOLCANIC LEGACY   SCENIC BYWAY   138

Rogue River-iskiyou National Forests

Crater Lake National Park

NORTH ENTRANCE RD

Fremont-Winema National Forest

Red Cone
7,368 ft
(2,245m)

CLEETWOOD COVE TRAILHEAD

CLEETWOOD COVE BOAT DOCK

W RIM DR

MERRIAM POINT

WATCHMAN OVERLOOK

WATCHMAN LOOKOUT TOWER

WATCHMAN PEAK TRAILHEAD

CRATER LAKE

Crater Lake

E RIM DR

SINNOTT MEMORIAL OVERLOOK

VICTOR VIEW

MOUNT SCOTT TRAILHEAD

DISCOVERY POINT

RIM TRAIL/ PCT ALTERNATE TRAILHEAD

GARFIELD PEAK TRAILHEAD

Pacific Crest Trail (alternate)

STEEL VISITOR CENTER

62   CRATER LAKE HWY

VIDAE FALLS

PINNACLES RD

LOST CREEK CAMPGROUND

Crater Lake National Park

MAZAMA VILLAGE CAMPGROUND

OREGON

May-Oct., $10/vehicle Nov.-Apr.) has three entrances. The **south** and the **west** entrances are accessible from Ashland via Highway 62 and are open year-round. The **north** entrance is accessible via Highway 138 June-October and closes in winter (closure dates are dependent upon snowfall).

Visitors Centers

The **Steel Visitor Center** (Park Headquarters, Hwy. 62 at E. Rim Dr., 9am-5pm daily Apr.-Nov., 10am-4pm daily Dec.-Mar.) shows a 22-minute film showcasing the park's history and volcanic formation. This historic building, designed in the park's trademark style known as "parkitecture," is located five minutes south of Rim Village on East Rim Drive. Restrooms are available.

The **Rim Visitor Center** (Rim Village, 9:30am-5pm daily late May-early Sept.) is located near the Crater Lake Lodge. The small, cabin-like space features a few exhibits about natural history and the creation of the national park. Restrooms are nearby, along with a gift shop and the park's only year-round restaurant, **Rim Village Café** (10am-4pm daily Nov.-Feb., 10am-5pm daily Mar.-May and Oct., 9am-8pm daily June-Aug., 10am-6pm daily Sept.).

Just a five-minute walk from the Rim Visitor Center lies the **Sinnott Memorial Overlook** (9:30am-6:30pm daily July-Aug., 9:30am-5pm daily June and Sept., 10am-4pm Oct.), a stone shelter built onto the edge of the lake's south rim. Geologic exhibits explain the volcanic history of the region and the formation of the lake. The overlook, built in 1931, is nestled into the rim's steep slope and provides a unique north-facing view of the lake's surface, including Wizard Island.

To get there from Rim Village, walk northeast on Rim Village Drive for 0.2 mile. The overlook is located down a steep, historic walkway on the north side of the parking area.

Wizard Island from the PCT in Crater Lake National Park

Seasons

Visit during the summer for access to roads and trails throughout the park. **July, August,** and **September** are the best months for hiking (though rain, hail, and snow can make an appearance).

Crater Lake lies at an elevation of 6,200 feet (1,890 m), and the 7,100-foot rim that encircles it experiences significant snowfall every year—an average of 43 feet. Rim Drive is open during summer months and closes in winter. Highway 62 to Park Headquarters is open year-round; the road to Rim Village is open when plowed, allowing for periodic visitation to the rim in winter. Should you choose to visit in winter, sign up for a ranger-led two-hour snowshoe walk (541/594-3100, Sat.-Sun. Nov. 15-Apr. 15, free).

Permits and Regulations

A backcountry permit is required for overnight camping anywhere outside of the park's two designated campgrounds. Permits are free, and must be obtained in person at the **Steel Visitor Center** (9am-5pm daily Apr.-Nov., 10am-4pm daily Dec.-Mar.) or **Canfield Ranger Station** (8am-5pm daily June-Sept., 8am-4pm Thurs.-Sun. Oct.-May), both located at Park Headquarters (Hwy. 62 at E. Rim Dr., 541/594-3060).

Scenic Drive

The Rim Drive (open summer and early fall) makes a 32-mile (52-km) loop around Crater Lake with frequent opportunities to stop and admire the lake's rocky, pumice-crusted edges. This road may be quite busy with cars in summer; allow at least one hour for the drive. Consider driving the rim in September when crowds have thinned but the snow hasn't started.

Start at Rim Village and drive clockwise around the lake. The Rim Drive parallels the popular PCT alternate trail as it follows along the western rim. **Discovery Point** (mile 1.3) is a great place to park and gaze down the steep sides of the rim into the lake.

Continue northbound and stop at the **Watchman Overlook** (mile 4) for an up-close view of Wizard Island, the cone-shaped island on the western edge of the lake. The Watchman Lookout Tower sits atop Watchman Peak, just south of the parking area. Hike the 1.8-mile round-trip trail to the top to see the historic lookout tower and enjoy 360-degree views of the national park and its surrounding terrain.

Continue north on Rim Drive to **Merriam Point** (mile 6). The south-facing vantage includes Wizard Island, Crater Lake Lodge, Mount Scott, and 9,500-foot Mount McLoughlin on the southern horizon. Stay right after Merriam Point to head east on Rim Drive.

At the **Cleetwood Picnic Area** (mile 10), you can look down onto the boat dock 700 feet below. The Cleetwood Cove Trail (1.1 mi/1.7 km one-way, difficult) provides the only access to the lake's surface. The trailhead parking area is located at mile 10.5 on the north side of the road.

The Rim Drive begins to bend southeast, then south, reaching the **Mount Scott trailhead** (mile 17) where you can hike 2.5 miles to the top of 8,800-foot Mount Scott, the highest point in the park.

At mile 18, stop at **Victor View** for a peek at the Phantom Ship, a jagged rock formation in the lake that resembles an old pirate ship.

The twisty road begins to depart from the lake's rim as it continues south and bends west. Pass **Pinnacles Road** (mile 21) or turn left to head south for 5.5 miles (8.9 km) and check out the unique geologic features of the pumice spires.

Rim Drive continues southwest to **Vidae Falls** (mile 26), a waterfall tumbling from Applegate Peak, one of the formations on the rim.

Reach the Park Headquarters at mile 29. Stop here to explore Steel Visitor Center or head north on Rim Drive to return to Rim Village at mile 32.

Wizard Island

Wizard Island is a volcanic cinder cone in the middle of Crater Lake. It may appear small when viewed from the rim, but it actually extends 700 feet above the surface of the lake. This dormant volcano was formed during a series of smaller eruptions after Mount Mazama's major eruption 7,700 years ago (which created the giant caldera we now know as Crater Lake).

A hiking trail on the island leads to the top of the cone, where visitors can look down into the 90-foot crater. The best place to view Wizard Island from the rim is at the **Watchman Overlook.** The only way to explore the island up close is to arrive by boat. Boat tours depart daily from **Cleetwood Cove** during the summer.

Boat Cruise

There's no better way to experience the scale and magnitude of Crater Lake than by hopping into a boat and motoring around the water's surface. **Volcano Boat Cruises** (www.travelcraterlake.com, late June-early Sept., $32-57) depart from Cleetwood Cove daily all summer, whisking passengers around the lake's edges while volunteer tour guides share tidbits about the lake's history and unique geology. Some cruises stop at Wizard Island, where you can hop off the boat and hike around for three hours. Boat cruises have a tendency to sell out weeks or months in advance, so book early. You might get lucky with a day-of ticket at the Cleetwood Cove parking lot if there was a last-minute cancellation. Cleetwood Cove is located on the north side of the lake.

From Rim Village, head northwest on Rim Drive and follow for 6 miles (9.7 km). Veer right to stay on East Rim Drive at Merriam Point. The Cleetwood Cove parking area is on the north side of the road in 4.5 miles. Allow at least 20 minutes to arrive at the parking area from Rim Village.

Hiking
★ Crater Lake Rim
Distance: 6 mi/9.7 km one-way
Duration: 3 hours
Elevation change: 1,000 ft/305 m
Effort: Moderate
Trailhead: Rim Trail/PCT alternate at Rim Village
Pass/Fee: National park pass

Although the official Pacific Crest Trail is plotted through the western part of the park, far from Crater Lake itself (and without any views of the water's surface), most hikers opt to see the lake by hiking a popular PCT alternate that follows the western rim for 6 miles. Depart from Rim Village, or hop onto this north-south trail

Crater Lake Rim Trail

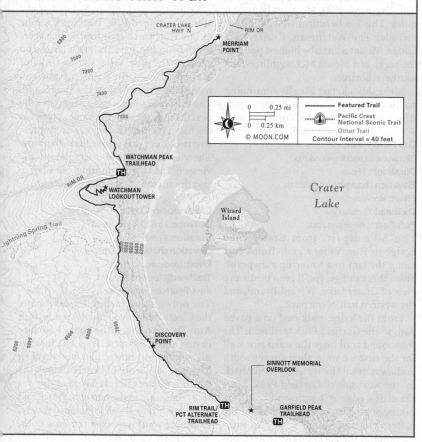

at a scenic roadside parking area to see the lake and its craggy cliff sides up close.

Starting from Rim Village, walk 1 mile northwest on the signed Rim Trail to Discovery Point. This section of trail isn't exactly flat—the ups and downs can feel a bit like a roller coaster as the trail twists through whitebark pines near the steep rim of the lake. Continue as the trail climbs uphill to the base of Watchman Peak at 2.5 miles. The trail bends west away from the rim for 0.5 mile, then bends east and intersects with the Watchman Trail at 3.2 miles.

To climb to the top of Watchman Peak (1 mile round-trip from this junction), make a hard right and walk southeast up the hill, or continue northeast on the Rim Trail/PCT alternate. Pass the Watchman Overlook and parking area at 3.6 miles and enjoy close-up views of Wizard Island below. Reach the highest point of this 6-mile stretch—7,740 feet (2,359 m)—at 4 miles, on the western edge of Hillman Peak, a prominent formation on the rim just north of Watchman Peak. Should you choose to continue north, it's all downhill from here.

The Rim Trail continues northeast along the rim, paralleling the route of Rim Drive, reaching Merriam Point at 6 miles. This is a beautiful viewpoint that includes The Watchman, Crater Lake Lodge, Mount Scott (the highest point in the park), and Mount McLoughlin on the southern horizon.

Make this a longer hike by continuing north on the PCT when it departs from Rim Drive near Merriam Point.

Garfield Peak

Distance: 3.1 mi/5 km round-trip
Duration: 1.5 hours
Elevation change: 1,000 ft/305 m
Effort: Moderate
Trailhead: Garfield Peak
Pass/Fee: National park pass

This hike departs from Crater Lake Lodge in Rim Village and climbs east along the rim to a towering viewpoint. From this vantage, you'll get a bird's-eye view of Crater Lake, Wizard Island, and the western half of the park.

From the lodge, walk east on a paved path to the Garfield Peak trailhead. The westbound trail hugs the steep rim wall for the first 0.6 mile, then curves south and away from the water to switchback up the west side of Garfield Peak. Meet the cliff's edge at 1 mile and continue hiking southeast, taking in views of the eastern rim and Mount Scott (the highest point in the park) on the eastern horizon. Enjoy views of the lodge and Rim Drive at 1.4 miles before arriving at the smooth, rounded top of the peak at 1.6 miles. This is a great place to picnic and enjoy the 360-degree views before heading back down the way you came.

The Watchman

Distance: 1.8 mi/2.9 km round-trip
Duration: 1 hour
Elevation change: 400 ft/122 m
Effort: Easy
Trailhead: Watchman Overlook
Pass/Fee: National park pass

This walk to the top of The Watchman leads to a lookout tower sitting atop a dramatic cliff on the lake's western rim.

From the parking area, head south along the signed Rim Trail for 0.4 mile to The Watchman spur trail, which veers south from the main trail as it climbs up a hill. In 0.5 mile, spy 9,500-foot Mount McLoughlin on the southern horizon with spiky Union Peak in the foreground. The trail switchbacks eight times over the next 0.4 mile to reach the lookout tower at the top. The historic tower is an impressive two-story, stone masonry structure. The viewing platform offers panoramic views of the lake's stunning blue surface and the surrounding volcanic terrain.

Cleetwood Cove

Distance: 2 mi/3.2 km round-trip
Duration: 1 hour
Elevation change: 600 ft/183 m
Effort: Moderate
Trailhead: Cleetwood Cove
Pass/Fee: National park pass

The only official path to the lakeshore, the Cleetwood Cove Trail descends from Rim Drive to reach the water's surface in one mile. Of course, it's a much easier hike on the way down than it is climbing back up, but plenty of benches along the way offer places to rest. Once at the water's edge, walk to the end of the dock and gaze down into the crystal clear waters. Continue southwest past the boat dock, where there's a great cliff for jumping off into the freezing water. Cleetwood Cove is also the departure point for Volcano Boat Cruises, and is a popular fishing spot.

Mount Thielsen

Distance: 11.8 mi/19 km round-trip
Duration: 6-8 hours
Elevation change: 2,100 ft/640 m
Effort: Moderate
Trailhead: Mount Thielsen
Pass/Fee: Northwest Forest Pass

Mount Thielsen is a sight to behold, an impossibly spiky peak located outside the national park boundaries. The mountain is an ancient, extinct volcano; all that remains of it today is its colorful, eroded core. There are two ways to explore the peak: a hike to the incredibly pointy top or a walk on the Pacific Crest Trail along the mountain's western flanks. For either option, start at the Mount Thielsen trailhead.

Follow the Mount Thielsen Trail east out of the parking area. The trail climbs steadily through mixed conifer forest and meets the Spruce Ridge Trail at 1.7 miles. Stay right to continue on the Mount Thielsen Trail as it continues to climb. The pointy peak comes into full view just before the path meets the Pacific Crest Trail at 3.7 miles.

From this intersection, there are two options.

To continue to the summit of **Mount Thielsen** (9.5 mi/15.3 km, 3,900 ft/1,189 m, strenuous), cross the PCT and stay straight on the Mount Thielsen Trail as it travels east and begins a sharp ascent. Although it's only one more mile to the top, the remaining 1,800-foot elevation gain is slow and grueling. This part of the trail is incredibly steep, rocky, and sandy in places, but expert hikers will find the territorial views incredibly rewarding. The top of Mount Thielsen is the only place outside the national park where the surface of Crater Lake is visible. The trail ends 80 feet below the actual summit. Some climbers choose to ascend the remaining rocks with safety equipment, while other hikers are satisfied with the panoramic views at the trail's end.

The other option is easier: visit **Thielsen Creek** (11.8 mi/19 km, 2,100 ft/640 m, moderate) instead of climbing to the top. From the Mount Thielsen Trail junction with the PCT, head north on the PCT for 2.3 miles. This stretch of trail really showcases the colorful striations in the peak's western rock faces. You'll get sweeping territorial views of Diamond Lake, far less pointy Mount Bailey rising over the western horizon, and craggy Diamond Peak to the northwest. Arrive at babbling Thielsen Creek at 5.9 miles and snap a picture of Thielsen's dramatic, rocky summit towering over the creek bed. Return the way you came.

Getting There

Mount Thielsen trailhead is on Highway 138, 5 miles (8 km) north of the national park's north entrance station.

Fishing

Fishing for kokanee salmon and rainbow trout is allowed (and encouraged!) in Crater Lake. Access the lake by hiking to **Cleetwood Cove;** the boat dock and surrounding rocks make great fishing spots. Fishing is also available on Wizard Island, accessible via tour boat. No license is required and there's no catch limit; however, only artificial lures and flies are permitted.

Food

There are two places to get food in Rim Village on the south rim near Crater Lake Lodge.

Built into the east end of the historic lodge, the rustic yet elegant ★ **Crater Lake Lodge Dining Room** (www.travelcraterlake.com, 7am-10am, 11am-3pm, and 5pm-9pm daily May and Oct., 7am-10am, 11am-3pm, and 5pm-9:30pm daily June-Sept., $8-15 breakfast and lunch, $26-40 dinner) is adorned with a beautiful stone hearth and giant pine beams. The menu highlights Oregon-grown ingredients like marionberries, hazelnuts, wild mushrooms, smoked salmon, and grass-fed, pasture-raised meats. Reservations (541/594-2255 ext. 3217, www.zomato.com) are accepted for dinner. The breakfast and lunch menu is priced reasonably, despite the fancy nature of the place.

Ultra-casual **Rim Village Café** (541/594-2255, www.travelcraterlake.com, 10am-4pm daily Jan.-early Mar. and Nov.-Dec., 10am-5pm daily mid-Mar.-mid-May and Oct., 10am-6pm daily mid-May-early June and Sept., 9am-8pm

daily mid-June-Aug., $5-12) shares a building with a gift shop near the visitors center, about 0.3 mile west of Crater Lake Lodge. The café serves sandwiches, salads, snacks, and seasonal soup. Some items are prepackaged to grab and go while others are made to order. There's a nice outside seating area. This is the only restaurant open in the winter.

Mazama Village (late May-Sept.) is located near the south and west entrance stations and has a small **grocery store** (10am-5pm daily late May-mid-June, 7am-9pm daily mid-June-Aug., 8am-8pm daily Sept.). The **Annie Creek Restaurant** (www.travelcraterlake.com, 8am-10:30am, 11am-4pm, and 5pm-8pm daily late May-mid-June and Sept., 7am-10:30am, 11am-4pm, and 5pm-9pm daily mid-June-Aug., $11-17) serves breakfast, lunch, and dinner in an airy space with high ceilings and a huge stone hearth. The menu includes American favorites like omelets, pancakes, soups, burgers, sandwiches, and fish-and-chips, with a few upscale items like maple-Dijon pork loin and herb-baked chicken. Vegetarian and vegan items are also available. Hours are limited in early June and late September.

Accommodations and Camping
Inside the Park
Rim Village

Built in 1915, ★ **Crater Lake Lodge** (565 Rim Dr., 866/292-6720, www.travelcraterlake.com, late May-mid-Oct., $201-268) overlooks the lake from a 7,100-foot perch on the south rim. The grand lodge features beautiful stonemasonry on the ground level, with enormous wooden beams throughout. Inside, the spacious lobby offers comfy seating around a giant stone hearth, while outside, chairs on the north-facing deck overlook the water. A miniature museum

From top to bottom: Wizard Island from Crater Lake Lodge; Mount Thielsen trail; Crater Lake Lodge.

on the 1st floor details the story of the lodge's construction and maintenance over the years. Half of the 71 rooms face the lake, while the remaining rooms offer views of the park's forested terrain. Simply furnished rooms include king or queen beds and free access to Wi-Fi. Some rooms have small desks. Don't expect to find TVs or telephones in the cozy, historic rooms—you might not get a shower either (all rooms do have bathtubs, though). The elegant on-site dining room serves three meals daily.

The Crater Lake area is notorious for severe weather, and storms can occur even in summer. If it's too cold for camping, opt instead for one of the 40 hotel rooms at the **Cabins at Mazama Village** (569 Mazama Village Dr., 866/292-6720, www.travelcraterlake.com, mid-May-late Sept., $165). Mazama Village sits at a lower elevation and is often much warmer. The rustic cabins have soft, comfy beds and private baths, but no TVs or phones, and are a short walk from the on-site restaurant and campground.

Mazama Village

Almost everybody who camps in the national park stays in **Mazama Village Campground** (866/292-6720, www.travelcraterlake.com, June-Sept., $23-32). The 214 sites are organized in paved loops with water spigots placed throughout. Amenities include bathrooms with running water, pay showers, and laundry facilities. The nearby Mazama Village store is a one-stop shop for groceries and camping supplies. Sites are available on a first-come, first-served basis in June; reservations are recommended July-September.

Far less popular than Mazama Village and therefore more peaceful, **Lost Creek Campground** (866/292-6720, www.travelcraterlake.com, July-Oct., $5) is a small, tent-only campground in the southeast corner of the park. While it's not as convenient for hopping on the PCT, this is the place to be if you're hoping for a relaxing backcountry vibe. Amenities are limited to picnic tables, bear-proof food storage lockers, and pit toilets, so bring plenty of water for drinking, cooking, and washing. Sites are first-come, first-served, and all 16 sites are often occupied by mid-afternoon during July and August.

Lost Creek Campground is 14 miles (22.5 km) southeast of Rim Village (a 30-minute drive) at the intersection of Pinnacles and Grayback Drives. From Park Headquarters, take East Rim Drive to Pinnacles Road, then turn right to head south to Grayback Drive.

Outside the Park

Five miles (8 km) north of Crater Lake, Diamond Lake is a large natural lake west of Mount Thielsen. The Pacific Crest Trail skirts the western flank of the mountain, and the Mount Thielsen trailhead (located across the highway from the lake) provides access to the PCT.

★ **Diamond Lake Resort** (350 Resort Dr., Diamond Lake, 541/793-3333, www.diamondlake.net, $94-106 rooms and studios, $224-276 cabins) is a no-frills, year-round waterfront village that was built in the 1920s. Lodging options range from 1950s vintage-style cabins to standard motel rooms to kitchenette studios with stoves and ovens. Although the furnishings and decor may be outdated, the amenities make a stay here a great value: There's a public dock for swimming and boating, boat rentals, a general store with camping supplies, a horse corral (horse rides offered daily), and a lovely lakefront path for walking and biking. Grab a burger or a sandwich at the casual on-site **restaurant** (6am-9pm daily May-Sept., 7am-9pm daily Oct.-Apr., $9-20). The waterfront space looks out over the lake at 8,300-foot Mount Bailey.

Less than 2 miles (3.2 km) south of the resort, **Diamond Lake Campground** (Diamond Lake Loop, 541/498-2531, www.fs.usda.gov) offers 238 campsites, some with lakefront views and others that are set back a bit. **Reservations** (877/444-6777, www.recreation.gov, $16-27) are recommended at this popular campground.

Information and Services

Check the park website (www.nps.gov/crla) for up-to-date information about weather, road closures, and webcams that show whether the lake is visible on a foggy or cloudy day. Inside the park, most services are located at Mazama Village, which has a gas station, RV dump station, coin-op showers, and laundry.

The small **Mazama Village General Store** (10am-5pm daily late May-mid-June, 7am-9pm daily mid-June-Aug., 8am-8pm daily Sept.) sells groceries, camping supplies, and firewood.

Willamette Pass

Sixty miles (97 km) north of Crater Lake, Willamette Pass is a high mountain pass in the Central Cascades, a year-round hub for recreation with hiking trails, lakefront camping, and a ski area. The Pacific Crest Trail crosses Highway 58 here, tracing the edge of gorgeous Odell Lake. The beauty of this lake-studded region does come at a price, when swarms of vicious mosquitoes attack every summer. If you're visiting in June or July, bring bug repellent and be prepared to use it.

Getting There

The fastest route between Crater Lake and Willamette Pass follows three high-speed highways and takes about 75 minutes. Exit the park through the north entrance station and take Highway 138 east for 15 miles (24 km) to U.S. 97. Turn left to head north on U.S. 97 for 18 miles (29 km) to the exit for Highway 58 west toward Eugene. Arrive at Willamette Pass 24 miles (39 km) later, just after passing Odell Lake on the south side of the highway.

If the Crater Lake north entrance station is closed, take Highway 62 south out of the park to Highway 422 toward Chiloquin, which connects to U.S. 97 north.

Option: Forest Road 60

To more closely follow the path of the PCT through the mountains, take this two-hour route past Diamond Lake and Windigo Pass. Exit the national park through the north entrance station and drive north on westbound Highway 138 for 12 miles (19.3 km). When the highway bends left, stay right to continue north onto Forest Road 60. This road curves through the mountains before intersecting with Highway 58. Turn left to travel west for 15 miles (24 km), past Odell Lake to Willamette Pass.

Sights

Salt Creek Falls (May-Nov., weather permitting) is the second-highest waterfall in Oregon, a state famous for its waterfalls, and this 286-foot drop is impressive, to say the least. The magnificent cascade is framed by lush, Pacific Northwest greenery: ferns, moss, and towering evergreen trees. From the parking area, a one-minute stroll on a paved path leads you to a viewing platform above the falls. Vibrant green moss covers the boulders around the waterfall, and ferns sprout directly out of the vertical rock faces on either side of the cascade. Beyond the viewing platform, a set of steep stairs leads down to the base of the falls, where you can feel the spray of the water on your face.

Getting There

Salt Creek Falls is 5.5 miles (8.9 km) west of Willamette Pass on Highway 58. Look for the entrance to the parking area on the south side of the highway. A Northwest Forest Pass is required to park here.

Willamette Pass to Bend

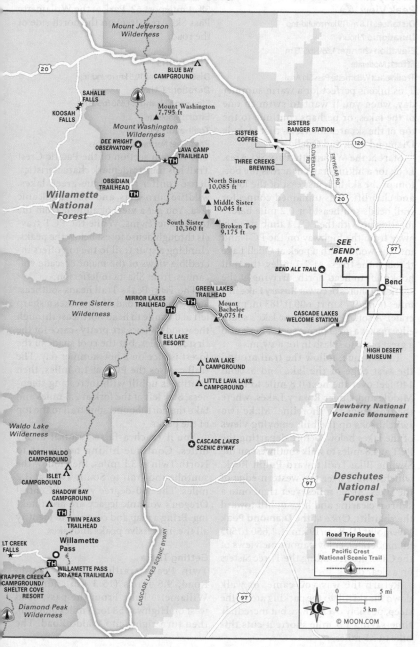

Mount Jefferson Wilderness

BLUE BAY CAMPGROUND

SAHALIE FALLS

KOOSAH FALLS

Mount Washington 7,795 ft

Mount Washington Wilderness

DEE WRIGHT OBSERVATORY

LAVA CAMP TRAILHEAD

SISTERS RANGER STATION

SISTERS COFFEE

THREE CREEKS BREWING

CLOVERDALE RD

126

OBSIDIAN TRAILHEAD

North Sister 10,085 ft

Middle Sister 10,045 ft

South Sister 10,360 ft

Broken Top 9,175 ft

20

Willamette National Forest

SEE "BEND" MAP

97

BEND ALE TRAIL

Bend

FRYREAR RD

MIRROR LAKES TRAILHEAD

GREEN LAKES TRAILHEAD

Mount Bachelor 9,075 ft

CASCADE LAKES WELCOME STATION

Three Sisters Wilderness

ELK LAKE RESORT

HIGH DESERT MUSEUM

LAVA LAKE CAMPGROUND

LITTLE LAVA LAKE CAMPGROUND

Newberry National Volcanic Monument

Waldo Lake Wilderness

NORTH WALDO CAMPGROUND

ISLET CAMPGROUND

SHADOW BAY CAMPGROUND

CASCADE LAKES SCENIC BYWAY

Deschutes National Forest

97

TWIN PEAKS TRAILHEAD

LT CREEK FALLS

Willamette Pass

WILLAMETTE PASS SKI AREA TRAILHEAD

TRAPPER CREEK CAMPGROUND/ SHELTER COVE RESORT

Diamond Peak Wilderness

CASCADE LAKES SCENIC BYWAY

97

Road Trip Route

Pacific Crest National Scenic Trail

0   5 mi
0   5 km

© MOON.COM

Hiking
Rosary Lakes to Diamond Peak View PCT

Distance: 11.8 mi/19 km round-trip
Duration: 6-7 hours
Elevation change: 1,650 ft/503 m
Effort: Moderate
Trailhead: Willamette Pass Ski Area

This hike is perfect for a warm summer day, when you'll want to swim in one of the lakes, or perhaps continue to the top of the ski area for views that include Diamond Peak and Odell Lake.

Start at the Willamette Pass Ski Area. Look for a hiking trail cut across the bottom of the ski hill, just east of the lodge and chairlift. This unnamed connector trail heads southeast for 0.2 mile before meeting up with the PCT. Climb steadily away from the highway on the PCT and into the woods with a peek at Odell Lake through the trees. At 2.3 miles, the trail hooks left to head north, arriving at the sparkling shores of **Lower Rosary Lake** in 3 miles (6 mi/9.7 km rt, 600 ft/183 m, moderate). A soft, flat spot on the lake's south edge makes a great picnic spot. This is also a great place to splash in for a swim.

To continue, follow the trail around the east edge of the lake and ascend 140 feet over the next 0.8 mile to reach Middle and Upper Rosary Lakes, where the trail hugs the shoreline. Make two switchbacks up the hill, enjoying views of the lakes below, before departing the PCT at 4.8 miles to walk southwest on the Skyline Bike Trail toward Pulpit Rock, which towers over the western edge of the lakes. At 5.5 miles, veer right onto a ski-run clearing and hike uphill toward the chairlift. Once at the **Diamond Peak Viewpoint** (11.8 mi/19 km rt, 1,650 ft/503 m, moderate), enjoy panoramic views of the Cascades, including the Three Sisters on a clear day.

Return the way you came, or walk down the ski hill to the parking area—the steep, possibly overgrown, but incredibly time-saving 1.5-mile shortcut cuts this hike to 7.5 miles.

Getting There

Willamette Pass is located on Highway 58 at milepost 62. Park at the Willamette Pass Ski Area (free) on the north side of the road.

The Twins

Distance: 6.5 mi/10.5 km round-trip
Duration: 3-4 hours
Elevation change: 1,650 ft/503 m
Effort: Moderate
Trailhead: Twin Peaks
Pass/Fee: Northwest Forest Pass

The Oregon section of the Pacific Crest Trail has four trademark characteristics: dense conifer forest, blue-green lakes, wildfire burn scars, and bizarre volcanic lava. You get a view of all four from the top of The Twins. While the PCT travels through dense forest below the peaks, climbing a spur trail to the top offers incredible views of the major cascade volcanoes, from Shasta to Jefferson.

The Twin Peaks Trail heads southeast away from the road, then makes a sharp left at 0.1 mile to head northeast through the woods. Views are pretty scarce for the first few miles, but the cool shade of the forest is nice on a hot summer day. The trail crosses the PCT at 1.6 miles, then continues uphill with increasing steepness. Stay left at the fork at 2.5 miles and take the northbound spur trail to the top of the peaks.

You'll reach a false summit at 2.9 miles. Continue hiking northeast to North Twin at 3.1 miles, then follow the southbound trail to South Twin at 3.2 miles. The 360-degree views of Central Oregon's volcanic legacy are breathtaking. Bring a map and compass to identify all the impressive peaks and lakes.

Getting There

Twin Peaks trailhead is on Waldo Road, 9.5 miles (15.3 km) north of Willamette Pass. From the pass, head west on Highway 58 for 3 miles (4.8 km), then turn right onto Waldo Road. The

◈ Side Trip: North Umpqua Waterfalls

Oregon is famous for its dramatic waterfalls that tumble out of the forested, fern-filled Cascade Mountains. Experience four distinct waterfalls along this 15-mile (24-km) stretch of the North Umpqua Highway, then visit Umpqua Hot Springs, which are built into the side of a steep, wooded river canyon. Plan to spend three hours on this 64-mile (103-km) (round-trip) detour, allowing time to marvel at the waterfalls and soak in the hot springs. You will need a Northwest Forest Pass to park at these trailheads and viewing areas.

Toketee Falls

Starting at the Crater Lake National Park north entrance station, head north out of the park and continue north onto Highway 138. Pass Diamond Lake Resort and arrive at **Clearwater Falls** near Highway 138 milepost 69.5. This 30-foot waterfall tumbles over moss-covered rocks to a crystal clear pool below. The driveway and parking area for the falls is on the south side of the highway, on Forest Road 4785.

To see **Whitehorse Falls,** a 15-foot punchbowl waterfall, enter the Whitehorse Falls Campground at milepost 65.9. The parking area is on the north side of the highway on Forest Road 4770.

At 272 feet tall, breathtaking **Watson Falls** is the third-highest waterfall in Oregon. Look for the parking area on the south side of the highway near milepost 60.5. Follow the steep 0.3-mile trail south out of the parking lot to a wooden bridge over Watson Creek to get the best views of the water as it tumbles over a mossy basalt cliff.

A view of **Toketee Falls** requires a short hike, but it's well worth it. The river blasts through a narrow canyon, visible from the hiking trail, before pouring out of a gap in otherworldly columnar basalt. The waterfall can be seen from a wooden viewing platform at the end of the trail. Look for a signed parking area on the north side of the highway near milepost 58.6, then follow the 0.4-mile trail to the viewing platform.

Cap off your waterfall odyssey with a soak in **Umpqua Hot Springs,** where a set of pools has been built into a steep hillside above the North Fork of the Umpqua River. To get there from Toketee Falls, exit the parking area and turn left to head northeast on Toketee-Rigdon Road for 2.2 miles (3.5 km). Veer right and continue east onto Forest Road 3401/North Umpqua Road. The trailhead parking area is on the north side of the road in 2 miles (3.2 km). To reach the hot springs, follow the Umpqua Hot Springs Trail north out of the parking area for 0.3 mile.

trailhead is on the right side of the road at milepost 6.5.

Skiing

Willamette Pass Ski Area (541/345-7669, www.willamettepass.com, 9am-4pm Fri.-Sun. early Dec., 9am-4pm daily during Dec. holidays, 9am-4pm Wed.-Sun. Jan.-Mar., $30-60, credit cards only) is a 555-acre ski resort with four chairlifts. The locally owned and operated ski area boasts the steepest ski run in Oregon, a 52-degree slope known as "RTS." There are also 20 kilometers of groomed Nordic ski trails within the resort's boundaries. Rentals are available ($30-45) on the 1st floor of the lodge. A small café and a full liquor bar are also located inside the lodge. Note that this resort does not accept cash—credit and debit cards are the only accepted forms of payment.

Food and Accommodations

★ **Shelter Cove Resort** (27600 W. Odell Lake Rd., Hwy. 58, Crescent Lake, 541/433-2548, www.highwaywestvacations.com, 8am-8pm Sun.-Thurs., 7am-8pm Fri.-Sat., $115-250) is a beautiful waterfront property on Odell Lake. This resort has it all: a general store (with PCT resupply), shower facilities, guest laundry, and a gorgeous lakefront location. Luxurious, pet-friendly cabins come with kitchens, gas fireplaces, lake views, and private docks. The counter-service restaurant, **Hook & Talon** (7am-10am and 11am-7pm daily May-Oct., $5-12), serves burgers, hot dogs, pizza, salads, and sandwiches made with house-smoked pork and chicken. Hearty breakfast burritos come with potatoes, sausage, and eggs. The full espresso bar is the only place for miles around to get a latte or a cappuccino.

West of Shelter Cove, **Trapper Creek Campground** (Forest Rd. 5810, www.fs.usda.gov, June-Oct.) has 32 sites nestled into the woods on the lakeshore. Sites include fire rings, picnic tables, and access to potable water as well as four restrooms with full plumbing. **Reservations** (877/444-6777, www.recreation.gov, $16-18) are available for all the sites except the 10 lakefront spots, which are first-come, first-served.

There are three camping options on beautiful **Waldo Lake** (www.fs.usda.gov, June-Oct.), 12 miles (19.3 km) north of Willamette Pass. Shadow Bay Campground is located at the south end of the lake, close to the Twin Peaks trailhead; North Waldo and Islet Campgrounds are located at the north end.

While some walk-up sites may be available, **reservations** (877/444-6777, www.recreation.gov, $24) are recommended for these popular campgrounds, especially on busy summer weekends. Waldo Lake is farther from busy Highway 58 than Odell Lake and gasoline-powered motors are not allowed, so it's much quieter.

Bend

With 80,000 residents (and counting), Bend is the biggest city on this road trip. There is truly something for everyone in this sunny, high desert destination: delicious cuisine, craft beer, shopping, nightlife, beautiful scenery, and hundreds of trails into the Central Cascades.

The Pacific Crest Trail travels right through the Cascade peaks that make Bend's western horizon such a dazzling delight: the Three Sisters, Broken Top, Mount Washington, Three Fingered Jack, and Mount Jefferson. Sisters, a smaller town northwest of Bend, is even closer to the mountains, and makes a great jumping-off point for hikes.

Getting There

Bend is located on U.S. 97 in Central Oregon, 70 miles (113 km) northeast of Willamette Pass and 90 miles (145 km) northeast of Crater Lake. From Willamette Pass, head east on Highway 58 to U.S. 97 north. From Crater Lake, follow Highways 62 or 138 east out of the park to U.S. 97 north. It's about a 90-minute drive from either location.

Summer Option: Cascade Lakes Scenic Byway

The **Cascade Lakes Scenic Byway** (www.oregon.gov/odot, May-Nov.) is a beautiful journey through lodgepole pine forests, lava fields, and some of Central Oregon's most prominent peaks. From Willamette Pass, travel southeast on Highway 58 for 10 miles (16.1 km), then turn left to head northeast on Crescent Cutoff Road for another 3 miles (4.8 km). Make a left to head north on Cascade Lakes Scenic Byway and follow for 66 miles (106 km) into Bend.

Bend

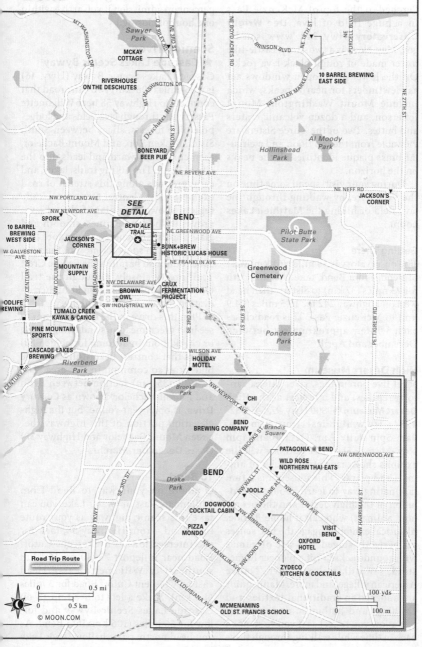

© MOON.COM

Road Trip Route

Sights
★ Dee Wright Observatory

Perched at the top of McKenzie Pass in a huge field of lava, **Dee Wright Observatory** (Hwy. 242, www.fs.usda. gov, May-Nov.) is a two-story, castle-like tower made of rough black lava rocks. On the lower level, open windows act as viewfinders for nearby peaks, which include Mount Washington, Mount Jefferson, and a dozen volcanic craters and buttes. Two of the Three Sisters are viewable from the top floor, and a circular brass plaque identifies all the peaks on the horizon.

During your visit, spend some time on the PCT here, by walking through the lava field or hiking the **Matthieu Lakes Loop.**

Getting There

The observatory is 38 miles (61 km) west of Bend. From Bend, take U.S. 20 north for 23 miles (37 km) to Sisters, then head west on Highway 242 for 15.5 miles (24.9 km) to McKenzie Pass. This road closes each winter, approximately between December and April.

High Desert Museum

Meet live porcupines, river otters, raptors, reptiles, and a bobcat at the **High Desert Museum** (59800 Hwy. 97, 541/382-4754, www.highdesertmuseum.org, 9am-5pm daily Apr.-Oct., 10am-4pm Nov.-Mar., $15), where outdoor wildlife exhibits showcase native species of animals and plants. This museum is a fun, fascinating way to learn about the evolution of the high desert and the people (and animals) who call it home. Inside, historical exhibits engage the five senses via perfectly staged, life-size dioramas with soundtracks. Visit a pioneer homestead, sawmill, railroad town, Native American village, and more. Mannequins are adorned in traditional textiles and clothing, and authentic architectural sets allow you to feel as if you've stepped back in time while walking through these exhibits. (Although you could easily spend hours exploring the place, save 30 percent on admission if you arrive within one hour of closing.)

Scenic Drives
★ Cascade Lakes Scenic Byway

Cascade Lakes Scenic Byway (Hwy. 46) is a 66-mile (106-km) two-lane road that connects to Highway 58 near Willamette Pass, twists through lava fields and lodgepole pine forests, slices between South Sister, Broken Top, and Mount Bachelor, then curves eastward and leads into the city of Bend. The hiking trails, lakes, and campgrounds along this stretch of road exemplify the Central Oregon Cascade region, showcasing giant fields of lava, groves of lodgepole pines, smooth and glassy lakes, and colossal volcanoes that are covered in snow for most of the year. This route also parallels the Pacific Crest Trail pretty closely, although the trail travels through the region at higher elevation to the west of the highway.

Plan this drive in the **early summer** to see lush green meadows and wildflowers, or check it out in **autumn** for golden fall colors that contrast beautifully with the blue skies so common in this area. The 22-mile (35-km) section between Bend and Mount Bachelor, known as **Century Drive,** is open year-round, but the high-elevation portion of this highway (between Mount Bachelor and Highway 58) closes **December-March.**

To Bend

If you're on your way to Bend from Willamette Pass or Crater Lake, you can take this scenic highway as your route into Bend. From Highway 58, look for the intersection with Crescent Cutoff Road near milepost 73 (10 mi/16.1 km southeast of Willamette Pass). Head east on Crescent Cutoff Road for 3 miles (4.8 km). Make a left to head north on Cascade Lakes Scenic Byway and follow for 66 miles (106 km) into Bend. As you head north, pass shallow **Davis Lake** on the west side of the highway before the road twists through a field of huge, chunky black lava rocks. Next, pass **Crane Prairie Reservoir, Lava Lake,** and **Little Lava Lake,** all on the east side of the highway. Enter Lava Lake Campground and park near the lakeshore to soak up some spectacular mountain views of South Sister and Broken Top.

Continuing north on the highway, pass **Elk Lake Resort** on the east side of the road, a popular resupply stop for PCT hikers. Two trailheads on the west side of the road provide access to the PCT: Elk Lake trailhead and Sisters Mirror Lake trailhead.

South Sister rises high above the highway near **Devils Lake,** where the road makes a big bend to travel east. The Green Lakes trailhead is on the north side of the road near Sparks Lake. As you pass through a valley between Broken Top and Bachelor Butte, turn around to get another great view of South Sister.

Allow 90 minutes to make the drive between Highway 58 and Bend (more if you stop to enjoy the views).

From Bend

If you are already in Bend, turn this drive into a scenic 80-mile (129-km) loop. Starting in Bend, head west on Cascade Lakes Scenic Byway (Century Drive). After passing Mount Bachelor and South Sister, the highway bends, heading south.

Pass Elk Lake, Lava Lake, and Little Lava Lake, turn left onto Upper Deschutes Road and head east for 26 miles (42 km) to **Sunriver,** a resort community with restaurants and tourist activities. From Sunriver, it's a 15-mile (24-km) drive north to Bend on U.S. 97.

Allow two hours for this loop (more if you stop along the way).

McKenzie Pass-Santiam Pass Scenic Byway

The scenery on the McKenzie Pass-Santiam Pass Scenic Byway is truly something else. This loop shows off some of the most dramatic volcanic terrain in the state as it travels through lava fields peppered with impossibly pointy peaks and dozens of craters. West of the Cascade Crest, waterfalls along the McKenzie River are some of Oregon's best.

Start the drive in **Sisters,** heading northwest on U.S. 20 toward Santiam Pass and crossing the PCT between Mount Washington and Three Fingered Jack. Turn south onto Highway 126 (also known as the McKenzie River Highway) and stop at **Sahalie Falls** to see the thundering 75-foot waterfall plunge into a beautiful pool below. **Koosah Falls,** another spectacular waterfall downstream, is a short hike (2.6 mi/4.2 km round-trip) along the McKenzie River Trail, which parallels the river and the highway.

Continue south on Highway 126 to **Belknap Springs,** then turn east onto Highway 242 (also known as McKenzie Pass Highway). This narrow, winding road leads to an astonishing volcanic landscape at **McKenzie Pass,** where Mount Washington, North Sister, and Middle Sister are on display. On a clear day, Mount Jefferson makes an appearance on the skyline. Stop at the **Dee Wright Observatory,** where a brass plaque identifies all the peaks in view.

McKenzie Pass Highway is closed **November-June,** so this drive is limited to the summer months. Allow 3-5 hours, depending on how often you stop for photos.

Hiking
Green Lakes

Distance: 9.3 mi/15 km round-trip
Duration: 5 hours
Elevation change: 1,200 ft/366 m
Effort: Moderate
Trailhead: Green Lakes
Pass/Fee: Northwest Forest Pass

This trail offers hikers incredible views of South Sister and Broken Top, following the path of Fall Creek as it flows between the two peaks.

From the parking area, walk north

on the gently graded Green Lakes Trail as it climbs steadily through the forest. You'll see your first waterfall at 0.6 mile. As the trail hugs the western edge of the creek, you'll pass another, larger waterfall at 1.4 miles. Come to a junction with the Moraine Lake Trail at 2 miles and stay right to continue north. At 2.2 miles, catch a glimpse of Broken Top to the east, then cross Fall Creek at 2.4 miles and watch for your first view of South Sister at 2.7 miles. The Broken Top Trail cuts sharply to the right at 4.3 miles as the craggy peak comes into full view. Stay straight on the Green Lakes Trail, heading north, for the best view of South Sister. Hike to the water's edge where a peninsula offers a perfect place to picnic. This is a popular backpacking destination, with spur trails to the top of South Sister and Broken Top.

Getting There

Green Lakes trailhead is 26 miles (42 km) west of Bend on Cascade Lakes Scenic Byway. Look for the signed trailhead parking lot on the north side of the road.

Sisters Mirror Lake and Koosah Mountain 🅿🅲🆃

Distance: 10.5 mi/16.9 km round-trip
Duration: 4-6 hours
Elevation change: 1,200 ft/366 m
Effort: Moderate
Trailhead: Mirror Lakes
Pass/Fee: Northwest Forest Pass

This hike from the Cascade Lakes Scenic Byway leads to the PCT where you'll catch a glimpse of South Sister reflected in a shallow trailside lake.

From the parking area, hike west on the relatively flat Mirror Lakes Trail for 0.6 mile before crossing the Elk Devils Trail. Stay straight, continuing west. From here, the trail increases in steepness as it climbs to a tiny lake below Kokostick

From top to bottom: volcano views from the PCT near Matthieu Lakes; view of South Sister from Koosah Mountain; Obsidian Falls.

Butte, reached at 1.3 miles. The ascent mellows out as the trail continues northwest past some chunky lava rocks and through a mixed conifer forest. Meet the Pacific Crest Trail at 3.5 miles and walk southbound on the PCT for 0.1 mile before taking a westbound spur trail to the shore of **Sisters Mirror Lake** (7.5 mi/12.1 km rt, 700 ft/213 m, easy/moderate). This shallow lake is warm in summer, when it becomes a popular splash-in spot for sweaty hikers.

For a high-elevation view, continue south past Sisters Mirror Lake on the PCT for 1.5 miles as the trail climbs onto **Koosah Mountain** (10.5 mi/16.9 km rt, 1,200 ft/366 m, moderate). Views from this east-facing crag showcase Bachelor Butte, South Sister, and Broken Top.

Getting There

The Mirror Lakes trailhead is 29 miles (47 km) west of Bend, a 45-minute drive. From the intersection of Wall Street and Colorado Avenue, take Colorado Avenue southwest for 1.5 miles (3 km). Continue southwest at the traffic circle, when the name of the road changes to Century Drive/Cascade Lakes Scenic Byway. The trailhead is on the west side of the road 2 miles (3 km) past Devils Lake.

The trailhead is only accessible **April-November** when the Cascade Lakes Scenic Byway is open.

Matthieu Lakes Loop

Distance: 6.1 mi/9.8 km round-trip
Duration: 4 hours
Elevation change: 900 ft/274 m
Effort: Moderate
Trailhead: Lava Camp
Pass/Fee: Northwest Forest Pass

Hike to two lovely, high-elevation lakes on the Pacific Crest Trail and enjoy views of the McKenzie Pass lava fields on your way back down.

From the Lava Camp parking area, walk south on the Lava Lake Camp Trail for 0.2 mile to meet up with the PCT and continue southbound. You'll spend the next mile walking through the charred remains of the devastating 2017 Milli Fire. At 0.6 mile, the trail departs from the PCT, forking right onto the North Matthieu Lake Trail. It starts to get a little greener as you climb; by 1.4 miles, you're back in the lush, green forest. At 1.8 miles, arrive at North Matthieu Lake, a sparkling turquoise beauty, then continue climbing south. The trail rejoins the PCT southbound at 2.6 miles; turn right and arrive at Matthieu Lake in 0.1 mile. Follow the nice loop trail around the lake, then return to the PCT, this time heading north and away from the lake. At the Matthieu Lake Trail junction, stay right to turn this into a loop. Views from the exposed ridgeline are spectacular on the way down: The lower lake comes into view, along with Cascade peaks including Middle and North Sister, Mount Washington, and Three Fingered Jack. The trail reenters the burn zone at around 3.4 miles. Stay right at the Matthieu Lakes Trail junction to return to the parking area.

Option: Make this a longer hike by starting at the PCT trailhead 0.5 mile west of the Dee Wright Observatory, turning this into an 8.9 mile hike (1.4 additional miles each way) that takes you through the lava fields, showcasing the fascinating and unique geology of McKenzie Pass. Note that although this chunky, rough, black lava rock is quite intriguing to walk through, it can be tough on the ankles and feet. Make sure you've got sturdy boots or trail shoes.

Getting There

The Lava Camp trailhead is on Highway 242, 38 miles (61 km) northwest of Bend. From Bend, take Highway 97 north for 3 miles (5 km). Take exit 135A to merge onto Highway 20 west toward Sisters. In 20 miles (32 km), turn left (south) onto Hood Avenue, following signs for McKenzie Pass, then turn right onto Highway 242 west. The trailhead and parking area are on the south side of

Highway 242 in 14 miles (23 km). Allow about 80 minutes for the drive.

This trailhead is only accessible **June-November** when the McKenzie Pass Highway is open.

Obsidian Trail

Distance: 11.8 mi/19 km round-trip
Duration: 6-7 hours
Elevation change: 2,100 ft/640 m
Effort: Strenuous
Trailhead: Obsidian
Pass/Fee: Limited-entry permit required Memorial Day weekend-Oct. 31 ($6)

Hike into a wondrous field of obsidian—a dark, glassy volcanic rock caused by the rapid cooling of liquid lava—with a waterfall and fantastic views of the surrounding volcanic terrain.

From the parking lot, the Obsidian Trail heads southeast, steadily gaining elevation over the first 2 miles as it meanders through the woods. Walk along the northern edge of a lava flow (between 2.1 and 2.5 miles) before the trail curves north into the woods, then bends south and enters the lava bed at 3.1 miles. Views of Middle and North Sister's glaciers start to get really good. The trail reenters the forest at 3.7 miles and veers left on the eastbound Glacier Way Trail. At 4.5 miles, follow the PCT north for 0.1 mile to check out Glacier Creek, then turn around and head south on the PCT to reach **Obsidian Falls** at 6 miles. Obsidian Creek tumbles 30 feet into a plunge pool lined with the shiny black rocks that give the trail its name. To complete the loop, walk south on the PCT for 0.1 mile, then turn right to head west on the Obsidian Trail. Stay left at the Glacier Way Trail junction to cross back over the lava flow and return to the parking area.

This area is popular. The Forest Service limits daily entry to 30 day hikers and 40 overnight backpackers. A **permit** (877/444-6777, www.recreation.gov, $6) is required and can be purchased online or picked up in person at the ranger station in Sisters (U.S. 20 and S. Pine St.,

Sisters, 541/549-7700). Reserve your permit in advance to guarantee entry.

Getting There

The Obsidian trailhead is on Highway 242 45 miles (72 km) northwest of Bend. From Bend, take Highway 97 north for 3 miles (5 km). Take exit 135A to merge onto Highway 20 west toward Sisters. In 20 miles (32 km), turn left (south) onto Hood Avenue, following signs for McKenzie Pass, then turn right onto Highway 242 west. The trailhead and parking area are on the east side of Highway 242 in 21.5 miles (35 km). Allow 85 minutes for the drive.

This trailhead is only accessible **June-November** when the McKenzie Pass Highway is open.

Recreation
Mount Bachelor

Mount Bachelor (13000 SW Century Dr., 541/382-1709, www.mtbachelor.com) is one of the biggest draws in the region—a 9,000-foot butte near Broken Top and South Sister with a ski resort on its north flanks. This mountain, so named because it stands apart from the Three Sisters, is a popular destination for outdoor recreation year-round.

Mount Bachelor is covered with snow in the winter, and downhill skiers from all over Oregon flock here to hit the slopes. Eleven chairlifts provide access to terrain on the north side of the peak. Lift tickets ($96) can be purchased online or on-site, and rentals are available in the Mountain Gateway building at West Village. Cross-country skiing ($21) is also popular on a 56-kilometer trail network connected to the ski area. At the **Nordic Center** (located in the northeast corner of West Village, 541/693-0909), take a one-hour lesson ($55-80) with skilled instructors who can show you the ropes. Cross-country ski rentals are available inside the Nordic Center.

In the summer, the ski slopes are converted into a **mountain bike park** ($42).

Trails of varying difficulties are spread out across the mountain. Take advantage of the chairlifts to take you up the hill and then coast back down. Bike rentals ($55-75) are also available from the rental center inside the Mountain Gateway building at West Village.

Just want to enjoy the views? Take a scenic **chairlift ride** (11am-5pm daily June-Aug., 11am-5pm Fri.-Sun. Sept.-Oct., $20) to the Pine Marten Lodge, a large lodge perched at 7,700 feet (2,347 m) with an outdoor deck. This is a great place to enjoy a snack or lunch while gazing out over the Cascades and Central Oregon's high desert.

A **disc golf course** with 18 holes starts at the top of the Pine Marten chair and concludes near the parking lot. There's no fee to play; bring your own discs and purchase a valid chairlift ticket for access.

Mount Bachelor is a 30-minute drive from downtown Bend. To get there, head west on Century Drive, also known as Cascade Lakes Scenic Byway, for 21 miles (34 km).

Mountain Biking
Mountain biking is incredibly popular in Bend, and a wide network of trails is easily accessible west of town. For a comprehensive mountain biking map complete with trailheads, visit www.bendtrails.org.

Need to rent a bike? **Pine Mountain Sports** (225 SW Century Dr., 541/385-8080, www.pinemountainsports.com, 10am-6pm Mon.-Fri., 9am-6pm Sat.-Sun., $25-75) is near trails. The experts at the store are happy to consult with you about gear.

Deschutes River Float
The Deschutes is Oregon's longest river, with headwaters in Little Lava Lake on the Cascade Lakes Scenic Byway and a 252-mile journey through Central Oregon to the Columbia. The lifeblood of the communities in this dry, sunny high desert region, the Deschutes flows right through the center of Bend.

On a hot summer day, there is no better way to cool off than by floating on a tube along the Deschutes. Rent a tube at **Tumalo Creek Kayak & Canoe** (Riverbend Park, 799 SW Columbia St., 541/317-9407, www.tumalocreek.com, 10am-3:30pm daily June-Sept., $15 for 2 hours, $30 for full day) and float the river through town, enjoying views of downtown's beautiful craftsman homes and the lush green lawns of the city's riverfront parks on this flat, calm stretch of river.

Start your float at Riverbend Park, then let the river carry you to McKay Park or farther downstream to **Drake Park.** Both McKay Park and Drake Park have shuttle bus stops, where you can climb aboard and get a ride back to Riverbend Park.

Entertainment and Events
Bend is famous for its microbreweries. Get a taste of the local beer culture at **Bend Brewfest** (Les Schwab Amphitheater, 344 SW Shevlin Hixon Dr., 541/312-8510, www.bendbrewfest.com, noon-8pm Thurs.-Sat. 3rd weekend in Aug., free), an annual beer celebration at a beautiful riverfront venue. More than 60 craft breweries from all over the state are in attendance, pouring their best beers, along with plenty of food carts dishing up artisan cuisine. Pick up a guide at the entrance to navigate the event by brewery or type of beer. Admission is free, but you'll need to buy a mug ($20, includes 5 tasting tokens) to drink any of the beers.

Central Oregon Beer Week (www.centraloregonbeerweek.com, last week in May) is a weeklong celebration of beers brewed in the Central Oregon communities of Bend, Redmond, Sunriver, Sisters, and Prineville. Events are held throughout the week at various breweries and locations. Advance tickets are not required; just check the website for a listing of events and locations.

For more information about local events and festivals, check out www.visitbend.com.

★ Bend Ale Trail

The **Bend Ale Trail** (www.visitbend.com) is a self-guided tour of more than 20 craft breweries in Bend, Sisters, Sunriver, and Redmond. Grab a trail passport at any taproom and get it stamped at each brewery as you visit; you'll earn a souvenir Silipint, a travel-friendly silicone pint glass. (No purchase is required to get a stamp; just show up with your printed passport or your app.) For those trying not to break the bank, most breweries offer happy hours (approx. 4pm-6pm Mon.-Fri.) with discounts on beer and food.

Famous for their IPAs, **Boneyard Beer** (1955 NE Division St., 541/241-7184, www.boneyardbeer.com, 11am-10pm daily, $11-18) opened this swanky brewpub after spending their first decade in a garage. Despite their humble beginnings, the Boneyard RPM IPA is famous worldwide and is one of the most popular beers in Oregon. Tasting flights include five beers, with bottles for sale in addition to beers on tap. The eclectic food menu offers Asian and Latin American fusion fare, a welcome change from standard pub grub.

Location is part of what makes **Crux Fermentation Project** (50 SW Division St., 541/385-3333, www.cruxfermentation.com, 4pm-9pm Mon., 11:30am-9pm Tues.-Thurs. and Sun., 11:30am-10pm Fri.-Sat., $8-14) a unique brewery. Located at the end of a dead-end street, this expansive space with a huge lawn is a popular summer hangout for locals and visitors to eat, drink, and play lawn games. The tasting room is built right into the middle of the brewery operations; the shiny steel and copper brew kettles give the space an elegant yet industrial vibe. The food is a blend of fancy finger foods and gourmet sandwiches, with a rotating circuit of local food trucks

From top to bottom: Drake Park; tasting flight at Boneyard Beer; appetizer at Crux Fermentation Project.

in the parking area during the summer. Free 45-minute **tours** are offered on Saturday afternoons—reserve your spot in advance (www.cruxfermentation.com/book-a-tour).

Established in 1995, **Bend Brewing** (1019 NW Brooks St., 541/383-1599, www.bendbrewingco.com, 11:30am-10pm daily, $13-15) is the second-oldest brewery in town. The beers here come with a view, enjoyed from inside through the floor-to-ceiling windows or on a big outdoor deck, with picnic tables next to the riverfront lawn. The food menu offers hearty, satisfying cuisine (think poutine, mushroom meatloaf, braised Reubens) as well as some lighter fare and salads.

Grab a pint and gather around the fire pit on the outside patio at **10 Barrel Brewing,** where classic and creative beers are paired with a hearty menu that includes burgers, pastas, sandwiches, and pizzas. The brewery's bright and airy **westside pub** (1135 NW Galveston Ave., 541/678-5228, www.10barrel.com, 11am-11pm Sun.-Thurs., 11am-midnight Fri.-Sat., $12-20) is set in a historic neighborhood amid the lovely craftsman homes of Old Bend. Indoor seating retains the rustic vibe with rough-cut wooden details in the decor. Many locals prefer the **eastside location** (62950 NE 18th St., 541/241-7733, www.10barrel. com, 11am-11pm Sun.-Thurs., 11am-midnight Fri.-Sat., $12-20), which has a darker, sleek industrial design.

Shopping

Spend more than a few minutes in Bend and you're sure to see someone sporting a Patagonia jacket, vest, or hat. **Patagonia @ Bend** (1000 NW Wall St., 541/382-6694, www.patagoniabend.com, 10am-7pm Mon.-Sat., 10am-6pm Sun.) is a locally owned store that carries most of the Patagonia outdoor clothing line, known for being equal parts style, comfort, and function.

South of downtown, **Mountain Supply** (834 NW Colorado Ave., 541/388-0688,

www.mountainsupplybend.com, 10am-6pm Mon.-Sat., 10am-5pm Sun.) has an impressive selection of clothing, footwear, backpacks, accessories, and outdoor equipment. The friendly local staffers are keen to hear about your adventure and outfit you for success.

REI (380 SW Powerhouse Dr., 541/385-0594, www.rei.com, 10am-8pm Mon.-Sat., 10am-6pm Sun.) is a comprehensive outdoor retailer in the Old Mill District. The vast, two-level store is packed with clothing, equipment, gear, footwear, accessories, guidebooks, packaged snacks, and anything else you need for an outdoor adventure.

Spice up your picnic menu with fresh, seasonal produce from the **Bend Farmer's Market** (Brooks Alley, 2pm-6pm Wed. May.-Oct.). You'll also find great trail snacks like sweet sriracha almonds, craft kombucha, from-scratch pastries, artisan toffee, handmade jellies, and bean-to-bar chocolates. Booths are set up in charming Brooks Alley next to the lovely waterfront lawns of Drake Park.

Food

There's always a line at **Spork** (937 NW Newport Ave., 541/390-0946, www.sporkbend.com, 11am-9pm Sun.-Thurs., 11am-10pm Fri.-Sat., $10-15), but don't worry, they'll take your drink order while you wait and the line moves quickly. This Asian-Latin American fusion restaurant serves spicy, eclectic cuisine with artisan cocktails. Stepping inside feels like teleporting to a different place on the planet, although the various world influences make it hard to pinpoint exactly where. After you order, grab one of the oddly charming circle-framed booths against the wall or a regular table amid the bustle.

★ **Dogwood Cocktail Cabin** (147 NW Minnesota Ave., 541/706-9949, www.thedogwoodcocktailcabin.com, 5pm-midnight Tues.-Sun., $11-20) is the kind of place you could easily find in one of the Pacific Northwest's biggest cities.

Post-Hike Brews

Hikers returning from Mount Bachelor, Broken Top, or South Sister will encounter two breweries on Century Drive, also known as Cascade Lakes Scenic Byway.

tasting flight at Three Creeks Brewing

The first is **Cascade Lakes Brewing** (1441 SW Chandler Ave., 541/388-4998, www.cascadelakes.com, 11am-10pm daily, $12-15), which serves satisfying, flavorful salads and upscale American-style pub fare like burgers and tacos, plus a couple of global twists like *yakisoba* and steak with chimichurri. In addition to six year-round beers, the wide array of seasonal brews, including pumpkin ale, pineapple IPA, and salted caramel porter, are delightful.

The second is **Goodlife Brewing** (70 SW Century Dr., 541/728-0749, www.goodlifebrewing.com, noon-10pm Fri.-Tues., $10-14), a bierhall and tasting room with a full liquor bar and windows looking onto the brewery operations. Try their flagship Sweet As Pacific Ale, a beer brewed with New Zealand and Australian hops. Other house-brewed beers span the spectrum, from pilsners to stouts. The food menu includes salads, sandwiches, nachos, wings, and fancy hot dogs. Between June and October, an outdoor beer garden is open with picnic tables and lawn games.

After hiking near McKenzie Pass or Three Fingered Jack, stop in the town of Sisters at **Three Creeks Brewing** (721 S. Desperado St., Sisters, 541/549-1963, www.threecreeksbrewing.com, 11:30am-9pm Sun.-Thurs., 11:30am-10pm Fri.-Sat., $11-17). Beers here are straightforward, traditionally brewed, and delicious. The Five Pine Chocolate Porter is popular in restaurants statewide. The food menu is pretty basic—pizza, fish-and-chips, burgers, and sandwiches—but it does a fantastic job of satisfying hiker hunger.

Prohibition era-influenced cocktails are infused with house-made syrups and served in exquisite glasses. The small plates menu is upscale yet approachable, with everything from chicken wings and fried mac and cheese to almond-stuffed chorizo and peel-and-eat shrimp. Weeknights are mostly mellow, but on the weekends when DJs play live music, the place is one of downtown Bend's trendiest nightlife joints.

It's all in the details at **Chi** (70 NW Newport Ave., 541/323-3931, www.bendchi.com, 4pm-9pm Tues.-Sun., $13-18), a pan-Asian restaurant with a beautiful white-marble bar and floor-to-ceiling windows overlooking the Deschutes River. The menu includes both sushi and traditional Chinese cuisine, expertly spiced, seasoned, garnished, and served in delightfully ornate dishes. Seating on the deck doubles the restaurant's capacity and is downright lovely on a sunny summer day.

If you usually order pad Thai, be prepared to try something new at **Wild Rose Northern Thai Eats** (150 NW Oregon Ave., 541/382-0441, www.wildrosethai.com, 11am-9pm Sun.-Thurs., 11am-10pm Fri.-Sat., $10-18), where traditional family recipes inform every menu item and many dishes are virtually unknown in the United States. The cozy, stylish dining room is at once modern and traditional, embodying the rose theme with floral tablecloths and dried rose bouquets lining the rafters. Try the chili paste flight served with sticky rice, veggies, and crispy pork to get a multisensory experience of Northern Thai flavors.

Find traditional Middle Eastern foods like tahini, tzatziki, grape leaves, and harissa alongside Oregon-grown vegetables, lamb, chicken, and beef at **Joolz** (916 NW Wall St., 541/388-5094, www.joolzbend. com, 4:30pm-9pm Mon.-Sat., $13-27), where "the Middle East meets the Wild West." Small plates, entrées, and warm sandwiches explode with flavor, perfectly spiced and incredibly satisfying. The chef was raised in Beirut with an Oregonian mom and a Lebanese dad, and both his expertise in the cuisine and his passion for supporting Oregon agriculture are apparent in the menu. The space is unpretentious, but the colorful decor and creative menu make for an exotic dining experience.

A popular date spot, **Zydeco** (919 NW Bond St., 541/312-2899, www. zydecokitchen.com, 11:30am-9pm Mon.-Thurs., 11:30am-10pm Fri., 5pm-10pm Sat., 5pm-9pm Sun., $17-38) blends the cuisine of the Pacific Northwest with famous dishes and ingredients from the Southeast. Roasted duck breast and rack of lamb share space on the menu with Cajun classics like jambalaya and blackened redfish. Despite the fine cuisine and sleek, urban design, the service and overall vibe in the place is down-to-earth and friendly. The bar is known for its martinis and fancy cocktails.

A timeless favorite among locals and visitors, **Mondo Pizza** (811 NW Wall St., 541/330-9093, www. pizzamondobend. com, 11am-9:30pm Mon.-Thurs., 11am-10pm Fri.-Sat., 11:30am-9:30pm Sun., $5-10) is a casual pizza joint downtown with hand-tossed pies, calzones, and salads. While many of the neighboring restaurants are a little more upscale, this is a great place to grab some quick grub

without having to change out of your hiking clothes—the after-mountain special, Mondo's version of happy hour, includes two slices and a pint of beer for $8.

It doesn't get any woodsier than **Brown Owl** (550 SW Industrial Way, 541/797-6581, www.brownowlbend.com, 11am-11pm daily, $9-13). Step inside a lofted log cabin where the decor goes beyond the usual wood paneling with a crosscut mural, a chandelier built into a canoe, and giant stumps on the outside patio for seating. The snacks, salads, sandwiches, and entrées on the food menu put creative twists on classics: mac and cheese with garlic confit, BLT with fig jam, and steak salad with pear tomato relish. Hand-crafted cocktails are innovative and delicious, and more than 13 rotating taps feature local beers and ciders.

★ **McKay Cottage** (62910 O. B. Riley Rd., 541/383-2697, www. themckaycottage.com, 7am-2pm daily, $10-15) serves plates that are equally pleasing for the eyes as they are for the belly. Sumptuous, fresh fruits top perfectly cooked waffles and pancakes, and expertly crisped potatoes accompany rich, satisfying omelets and eggs Benedicts. The menu changes seasonally, highlighting the produce and spices that each season is known for. Built into a 1916 craftsman house, the space itself is charming and welcoming, although many diners choose to eat on the outdoor patio during Bend's beautiful summer months.

Specializing in local, seasonal fare with an emphasis on sustainability, **Jackson's Corner** (845 NW Delaware Ave., 541/647-2198, www.jacksonscornerbend.com, 7am-9pm daily, $8-13) is a bright, airy bakery and deli-style restaurant. Fresh, flavorful salads are paired with handmade pastas, sandwiches on house-baked breads, and artisan pizzas with gourmet toppings. The space is welcoming, featuring an open kitchen with all the colorful ingredients spread before your eyes while you order. Visit the **original location**

(1500 NE Cushing Dr., 541/382-1751, 7am-9pm Sat.-Thurs., 7am-10pm Fri.) on the east side of town.

An airy and spacious pinewood café, **Sisters Coffee** (273 W. Hood Ave., Sisters, 541/549-0527, www.sisterscoffee.com, 6am-6pm daily, $3-8) is a great place to grab an espresso and a breakfast sandwich before heading out on the trail. With high ceilings, an upstairs seating area, and a giant hearth to cozy up to, it makes a great place to relax any time of day. This family-owned coffee roaster has been in business since 1989 and also has a café in downtown Portland.

Accommodations
Under $150
On the east side of U.S. 97, **Holiday Motel** (880 SE 3rd St., 541/382-4620, www.holidaymotelbendor.com, $45-90) is a renovated motor lodge with a charming vintage sign. There are 25 guest rooms with mini-fridges, coffeemakers, and microwaves. Rooms with queen beds are available, but spring for a king if you can—these rooms have surprisingly modern, luxurious interiors.

Bunk+Brew Historic Lucas House (42 NW Hawthorne Ave., 458/202-1090, www.bunkandbrew.com, $33-90) is a hostel geared toward adventure travelers. Access to the big beautiful kitchen includes complimentary bread, fruit, eggs, waffles, and non-alcoholic beverages like coffee, tea, juice, and milk. Guests are also welcome to relax in the dining room, lounge, and sunroom. As for overnight accommodations, private rooms and dorm-style hostel rooms are available. Guest laundry is also in the building. In the summer, the large backyard is home to hammocks, an outdoor fire pit, and a gas barbecue grill. During the winter, Bunk+Brew provides shuttle access to Mount Bachelor.

From top to bottom: outdoor patio at McKay Cottage; Little Lava Lake; Elk Lake Resort.

Over $150

McMenamins is a unique Pacific Northwest phenomenon: a brewery-based hospitality business that turns old buildings or city spaces into quirky, somewhat lavish restaurants, hotels, and resorts. The name gives it away at ★ **McMenamins Old St. Francis School** (700 NW Bond St., 541/382-5174, www.mcmenamins.com, $165-250), a historic downtown building converted from a Catholic school into a full-service hotel with four food and drink outlets, a theater, and an ornate soaking pool. Wood-paneled guest rooms are outfitted with the eclectic, artsy decor McMenamins is known for: funky-patterned curtains, hand-painted headboards, and wacky textiles. In addition to on-site food options and amenities, this building is within steps of downtown Bend's best restaurants and shops. The beautifully tiled **soaking pool** (11am-8pm daily, $5) is open to the public and makes a fantastic, relaxing post-hike destination, even if you're staying elsewhere.

The luxurious **Oxford Hotel** (10 NW Minnesota Ave., 541/382-8436, www.oxfordhotelbend.com, $185-400) is within steps of the city's best restaurants. Rooms are furnished with plush bathrobes, mini-fridges, microwaves, hair dryers, and premium organic bath products. Some of the 59 rooms are kitchen suites with sleek wood finishes, granite countertops, and brushed steel appliances. Amenities include a Jacuzzi spa and steam room, free cruiser bikes to explore the city, room service from 6:30am-10pm, complimentary washer and dryer, and a state-of-the-art fitness facility.

Two miles north of downtown Bend, the **Riverhouse on the Deschutes** (3075 N. Hwy. 97, 866/453-4480, www.riverhouse.com, $130-300) overlooks the Deschutes River. Rooms are sleek and simple, with a luxurious design, and come with microwaves, refrigerators, and coffeemakers; some rooms have views of the river. Wi-Fi is free throughout, and

coin-op laundry is on-site. Despite the refined nature of the property, the staff is down to earth and the whole place is quite welcoming.

Camping
Southwest of Bend

Little Lava Lake is home to the headwaters of the Deschutes River, and the shallow lake is a favorite among anglers. Larger, deeper Lava Lake is popular among paddle and oar boats. Campsites at **Lava Lake** and **Little Lava Lake Campgrounds** (Cascade Lakes Scenic Byway and Lava Lake Rd., www.fs.usda.gov) offer views of the lake and surrounding volcanoes through lodgepole pine forests, and some of the 44 sites are right on the lakeshore; all have fire rings and picnic tables. While some sites are available on a first-come, first-served basis, make **reservations** (877/444-6777, www.recreation.gov, Apr.-Oct., $16) at this popular summer campground to guarantee a spot. Popular trailheads including Elk Lake, Sisters Mirror Lake, and Green Lakes are within a 10-20-minute drive on the Cascade Lakes Scenic Byway.

A popular resupply and rest stop for PCT hikers, ★ **Elk Lake Resort** (Cascade Lakes Scenic Byway and Elk Lake Resort Loop, 541/480-7378, www.elklakeresort.net, $70 cabins, $99 glamping tents, $25-35 campsites) is just one mile east of the national scenic trail. Rustic, heated log "camping cabins" sleep four people—bring your own sleeping bag. Glamping tents have heavy-duty canvas walls with futons set up inside, and soft bedding is included with your stay. The waterfront **restaurant** (11am-8pm Mon.-Thurs., 11am-9pm Fri., 9am-8pm Sat., 9am-7pm Sun. May-Sept., hours vary off-season, $8-16) has a nice deck overlooking the lake. The menu includes burgers, sandwiches, salads, and soups, along with traditional American breakfast items.

Northwest of Bend

Suttle Lake is west of Sisters on U.S.

20 and is the best place to camp if you plan to explore Three Fingered Jack or the McKenzie Pass-Santiam Pass Scenic Byway. Beautiful **Blue Bay Campground** (SW Suttle Lake Loop, 541/338-7869, www.fs.usda.gov) is a lakeshore campground in a mixed conifer forest. Campsites have fire rings and picnic tables, as well as easy access to vault toilets and potable water. **Reservations** (877/444-6777, www.recreation.gov, May-Sept., $16) are recommended. If Blue Bay is booked, check out Link Creek and Scout Lake Campgrounds, two less popular spots within a mile of the lake.

Information and Services

The chamber of commerce office at **Visit Bend** (750 NW Lava Rd., Bend, 541/382-8048, www.visitbend.com, 9am-5pm Mon.-Fri., 10am-4pm Sat.-Sun.) is your one-stop shop for information about food and drink, accommodations, activities, and tours. Friendly locals can steer you in the right direction during your visit.

Stop by the **Cascade Lakes Welcome Station** (18500 Cascade Lakes National Scenic Byway, 541/383-5300, www.fs.usda.gov, 8am-4pm daily June-Aug., 8am-4pm Thurs.-Mon. Sept., 10am-4pm Fri.-Sun. Oct.-Nov., 8am-4pm Sat.-Sun. Mar.-May) for information about the surrounding Mount Bachelor and South Sister area. Rangers provide helpful advice about trail conditions, closures, and potential seasonal highlights such as wildflower blooms.

If you're planning to visit McKenzie Pass or Three Fingered Jack, **Sisters Ranger Station** (Hwy. 20 and S. Pine St., Sisters, 541/549-7700, www.fs.usda.gov, 8am-4:30pm Mon.-Fri.) is a convenient place to stop for up-to-date trail info and conditions. Pick up printed maps and materials and find out about any closures or hazardous conditions before heading into the wilderness.

Getting Around

Rent a set of wheels from **Zagster** (202/999-3924, www.zagster.com/osucascades, $3/hour), a public bikeshare organization with eight self-service rental stations conveniently located around Bend. To reserve a bike, visit the Zagster website to download the app. You'll be prompted to join and provide payment info. The app will provide you with a detailed map of rental stations so you can find the nearest one; when you're done riding, you can return the bike to any station regardless of where you rented it.

◈ Side Trip: Mount Jefferson

Adventurous travelers won't want to miss Mount Jefferson. The Pacific Crest Trail traces the western base of this notoriously rugged and beautiful volcano. This remote area sees far fewer visitors than popular destinations like Crater Lake, the Three Sisters, and Mount Hood. Travel on dirt roads is required, but the hikes in this area can be accessed in any passenger vehicle (if you don't mind a bumpy ride).

The area surrounding Mount Jefferson is pretty remote, but the tiny town of **Detroit** is nearby. It has a couple of restaurants, a gas station, and a mini-mart. Most businesses in town close early and the selection is limited; do your shopping and resupplying in Bend or Sisters.

Getting There

From Bend, take U.S. 20 north for 24 miles (39 km) to the town of Sisters. Continue northwest on U.S. 20 for 20 more miles (32 km). West of Lost Lake, veer north onto Highway 22 and continue 30 miles (48 km) north to the town of Detroit.

It's also possible to reach Detroit from the west. From I-5 in Salem, follow Highway 22 east for 52 miles (84 km).

Detroit to Cascade Locks

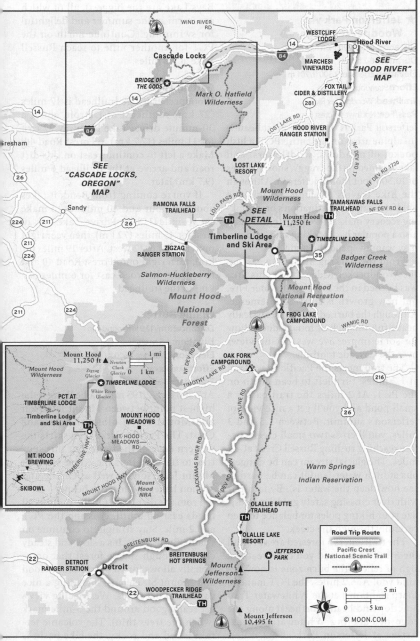

WIND RIVER RD

WESTCLIFF LODGE

Hood River

14

84

Cascade Locks

MARCHESI VINEYARDS

SEE "HOOD RIVER" MAP

BRIDGE OF THE GODS

Mark O. Hatfield Wilderness

FOX TAIL CIDER & DISTILLERY

281

35

14

84

LOST LAKE RD

HOOD RIVER RANGER STATION

NF DEV RD 17

Gresham

SEE "CASCADE LOCKS, OREGON" MAP

LOST LAKE RESORT

NF DEV RD 1720

26

LOLO PASS RD

Mount Hood Wilderness

TAMANAWAS FALLS TRAILHEAD

NF DEV RD 44

Sandy

RAMONA FALLS TRAILHEAD

TH

SEE DETAIL

Mount Hood 11,250 ft

TH

224

211

26

ZIGZAG RANGER STATION

Timberline Lodge and Ski Area

TIMBERLINE LODGE

211

224

Salmon-Huckleberry Wilderness

35

Badger Creek Wilderness

211

224

Mount Hood National Forest

Mount Hood National Recreation Area

FROG LAKE CAMPGROUND

WAMIC RD

Detail inset:

Mount Hood 11,250 ft

0   1 mi

0   1 km

Newton Clark Glacier

Mount Hood Wilderness

Zigzag Glacier

TIMBERLINE LODGE

PCT AT TIMBERLINE LODGE

White River Glacier

Timberline Lodge and Ski Area

TH

MOUNT HOOD MEADOWS

MT. HOOD BREWING

MT. HOOD MEADOWS RD

SKIBOWL

TIMBERLINE HWY

MOUNT HOOD HWY

WAMIC RD

Mount Hood NRA

Main map (continued):

OAK FORK CAMPGROUND

NF DEV RD 58

TIMOTHY LAKE RD

SKYLINE RD

26

216

CLACKAMAS RIVER RD

NF DEV RD 4690

Warm Springs Indian Reservation

OLALLIE BUTTE TRAILHEAD

TH

BREITENBUSH RD

OLALLIE LAKE RESORT

Road Trip Route

Road Trip Route

Pacific Crest National Scenic Trail

22

DETROIT RANGER STATION

Detroit

BREITENBUSH HOT SPRINGS

JEFFERSON PARK

Mount Jefferson Wilderness

22

WOODPECKER RIDGE TRAILHEAD

TH

Mount Jefferson 10,495 ft

0   5 mi

0   5 km

© MOON.COM

Hiking

★ Jefferson Park via Woodpecker Ridge (PCT)

Distance: 12.5 mi/20.1 km round-trip
Duration: 6-7 hours
Elevation change: 2,300 ft/701 m
Effort: Strenuous
Trailhead: Woodpecker Ridge
Pass/Fee: Northwest Forest Pass

Jefferson Park is one of the most beautiful alpine areas on the entire PCT, a lush pocket of meadows, wildflowers, and lakes framed by the craggy, snowy slopes of 10,500-foot Mount Jefferson. Although the hike travels through a blackened wildfire scar, the destination's breathtaking scenery makes it well worth it. This is also a popular backpacking spot, and you may want to spend the night.

From the parking area, hike east up the Woodpecker Ridge Trail. This area was burned in the 2017 Whitewater Fire, but new growth is starting to emerge. Although the burned area isn't classically beautiful, the lack of foliage does allow for some impressive west-facing views over the Cascade foothills.

The trail meets the Pacific Crest Trail at 1.7 miles; turn left to head north on the PCT. At 2 miles the trail passes a small pond and you'll get a nice view of Jefferson's summit. Between 2.5 and 3 miles, you'll cross two small creeks before reaching rushing Russell Creek at 4.2 miles. The glacial stream can be dangerous at high water (and it can be hard to see how deep the water is). Be familiar with river crossing safety guidelines; utilize your hiking poles for balance to step carefully through the creek.

The trail enters a forested area around the 5-mile mark and you can breathe a sigh of relief—the burn zone is now behind you! At 5.2 miles, the PCT makes a sharp right turn at the Whitewater Trail junction and heads northeast along the edge of babbling Whitewater Creek. Arrive at Jefferson Park at 6.2 miles,

where a network of trails surrounds five lakes! Explore the lakes (**Scout Lake** and Bays Lake are the biggest), all of which are warm in the summer and delightful for swimming! Continue north on the PCT for another mile to reach Russell Lake at 7.2 miles.

Getting There

Woodpecker Ridge trailhead is 17 miles (27 km) southeast of Detroit, about a 30-minute drive. Take Highway 22 east for 11 miles (17.7 km) to Forest Road 40. Make a left to continue east on this dirt road and arrive at the trailhead 6 miles (9.7 km) later.

If you're coming from Bend, it takes about an hour and 40 minutes to make the 73-mile (118-km) drive. Take U.S. 20 west for 45 miles (72 km), then veer right onto Highway 22 west. After 19 miles (31 km), turn right onto Forest Road 40 and follow the dirt road east for 6 miles (9.7 km) to the trailhead.

Olallie Butte

Distance: 8 mi/12.9 km round-trip
Duration: 4-5 hours
Elevation change: 2,600 ft/792 m
Effort: Strenuous
Trailhead: Olallie Butte

At 7,200 feet (2,195 m), Olallie Butte is the highest point between Mount Jefferson and Mount Hood along the Cascade Crest. The Pacific Crest Trail skirts the western edge of the butte, but this spur trail to the top offers incredible views of Mount Jefferson, as well as Olallie and Monon Lakes in the basin below.

From the dirt road, Olallie Butte Trail heads east up a hill, crossing the PCT at 0.2 mile. Stay straight to continue on Olallie Butte Trail. It's a slow and steady climb through sparse forest that occasionally allows for views of Mount Hood and Mount St. Helens, including a nice vantage at 2.9 miles. West-facing views get really good around the 3-mile mark (when the trees thin). The volcanic terrain is red and rocky, the lake basin is

Jefferson Park via Woodpecker Ridge

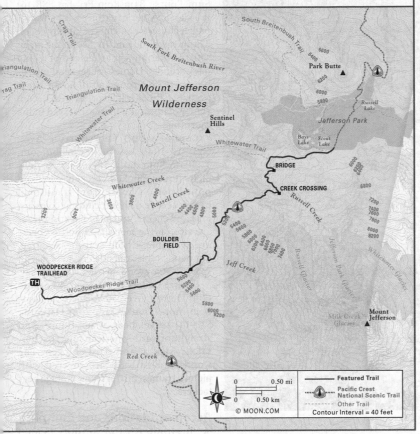

Craig Trail

South Breitenbush Trail

South Fork Breitenbush River

South Breitenbush Trail

6600
6400

Park Butte

6200

Triangulation Trail

6000
5800

Russell Lake

Triangulation Trail

**Mount Jefferson
Wilderness**

Jefferson Park

Whitewater Trail

Sentinel
Hills

Bays
Lake

Scout
Lake

Whitewater Trail

BRIDGE

Whitewater Creek

Russell Creek

6600
6400

CREEK CROSSING

6800

Russell Creek

3800

4200
4400
4600

7200
7400
7600
7800

3800

3400

3200

4000

4800
5000

5200
5400
5600
5800
6000
6200
6400
7000
7400

8000
8200

Whitewater Glacier

**BOULDER
FIELD**

Jeff Creek

Russell Glacier

Jefferson Park Glacier

**WOODPECKER RIDGE
TRAILHEAD**

TH

5000
5200
5400
5600

Woodpecker Ridge Trail

5800
6000
8200

Milk Creek
Glacier

**Mount
Jefferson**

Red Creek

| | 0 | 0.50 mi | | **Featured Trail** |

0

0.50 km

© MOON.COM

Pacific Crest
National Scenic Trail

Other Trail

Contour Interval = 40 feet

visible below, and Mount Jefferson is larger than life. Reach the summit at 4 miles and enjoy sweeping territorial views that showcase the dramatic differences between Oregon's woodsy western and arid eastern sides.

Getting There

Olallie Butte is 34 road miles (55 km) northeast of Detroit, about an hour's drive, and near Olallie Lake Resort. This trip requires travel on dirt roads, but they are well-graded and suitable for all passenger vehicles. From Detroit, take Breitenbush Road (Forest Road 46) northeast for 23 miles (37 km), then turn right onto Forest Road 4690, following signs for Olallie Lake. Stay left on Forest Road 4690 at the fork at 3.7 miles (6 km). At the intersection at 3.4 miles (5.5 km), turn right onto Oregon Skyline Road (Forest Road 4220). The trailhead is 2.7 miles (4.3 km) south on this road on the left, at the southern edge of the power lines.

Food

Restaurants in the tiny Detroit community serve simple, hearty American

fare at good prices. **Korner Post** (100 Detroit Ave., 503/854-3735, 8am-7pm Sun.-Thurs., 8am-8pm Fri.-Sat., $8-16) is a classic American diner with a wood-paneled interior and lots of kitschy decor. The burgers and sandwiches on the menu satisfy hiker hunger at the end of a long day outdoors. Domestic beers and micro-brews are on tap, and a full liquor bar is available. Breakfast favorites with bacon, eggs, potatoes, and toast are served in the morning.

Connor's BBQ (195 Detroit Ave., 503/913-1040, www.connorbbq.com, 11:30am-9pm daily, $8-16) serves deli-cious house-smoked chicken, ribs, and pulled pork. Choose from traditional barbecue side dishes including coleslaw, mac and cheese, and baked beans. Pizzas are also on the menu, and bottled beers are available. Inside seating is scarce, but picnic tables outside create plenty of space to enjoy food on a hot summer day.

Casual **Cedars Restaurant & Lounge** (200 Detroit Ave., 503/854-3636, 8am-8pm Mon.-Thurs., 7am-9pm Fri.-Sun., $10-14) serves beer, wine, liquor, and straightforward American food: nachos, salads, steaks, and fried chicken. The wood-paneled walls are covered with picture frames, mirrors, and vintage beer tackers.

Accommodations and Camping

★ **Breitenbush Hot Springs** (53000 Breitenbush Rd. SE, Detroit, 503/854-3320, www.breitenbush.com, $75-100 lodge rooms, $120-170 cabins, $70 tents, $38 day use) is a rustic retreat cen-ter nestled in the woods where natural hot springs are piped into beautifully crafted stone pools. While private re-treats focused on well-being are ongo-ing year-round, the property is open to the public. Reservations are required for both day use and overnight stays. Cabins

From top to bottom: the PCT south of Jefferson Park; Scout Lake at sunset; Olallie Lake Resort.

are equipped with geothermic heat, and beds are covered with fitted sheets, but you'll want to bring your own sleeping bag or bedding. Some cabins have plumbing with sinks and flush toilets; others do not have plumbing, but are located near bathhouses with toilets, sinks, and showers. There are two rooms in the main lodge with beds, desks, and windows. Additionally, you can bring your own tent, or rent a large platform tent (a tent set up on a flat wooden platform). Delicious vegetarian meals are included with overnight stays.

The Pacific Crest Trail passes right through **Olallie Lake Resort** (4 Forest Rd. 4220, 503/853-3481, www.olallielakeresort.com, June-Sept., $65-110 cabins/yurts, $15 campsites), a casual lakefront resort with 10 cabins, two yurts, picnic tables, a dock, and a small store. Views of Mount Jefferson from the lake and the northern shoreline are incredible. The rustic cabins are not equipped with electricity or plumbing, but they do include beds, countertops and shelving, dining tables and chairs, and woodstoves for heat. Yurts include beds and dining tables with chairs. Bring your own bedding. If you prefer to camp, the resort manages four campgrounds in Olallie Lake Scenic Area, all within four miles of the resort. All 97 campsites are first-come, first-served and include fire rings, picnic tables, and access to pit toilets.

Information and Services

Stop at the **Detroit Ranger Station** (44125 N. Santiam Hwy., 503/854-3366, www.fs.usda.gov, 8am-4:30pm Mon.-Fri.) to pick up hiking maps and find out about trail conditions.

Mount Hood

At 11,250 feet (3,429 m), Oregon's tallest volcano looms over the surrounding landscape, dominating the eastern horizon of nearby Portland and showcasing its glistening glaciers to a number of smaller cities near its base. The mountain is a year-round mecca for hikers, climbers, and skiers. The Pacific Crest Trail ascends out of the forest to 6,000 feet (1,829 m) on the southern side of the volcano, then traces the western edge of the mountain along the tree line.

South of Mount Hood, the PCT traces the eastern edge of Timothy Lake, a popular summer camping destination. Government Camp is a tiny town with restaurant and services, located 5 miles (8 km) west of the Pacific Crest Trail on U.S. 26. The nearest ranger station is located another 11 miles (17.7 km) west in Zigzag.

Getting There
From Mount Jefferson

Timberline Lodge is 60 miles (97 km) north of Detroit, about a two-hour drive. From Detroit, take Forest Road 46 north for 28 miles (45 km). Turn right onto Forest Road 42 and drive 26 miles (42 km) north to the junction with U.S. 26. Turn left to head north on U.S. 26 west for 11 miles (17.7 km) to Government Camp and the spur road to Timberline Lodge. The narrow, winding roads are paved and suitable for all passenger vehicles.

Forest Road 42 closes during the winter (approx. Dec.-Apr.) due to heavy snowfall. To reach Mount Hood, head west on Highway 22 to I-5 and travel north to Portland, or head east on Highway 22 and U.S. 20 to Bend.

From Bend

From Bend, you can skip Mount Jefferson and go straight to Mount Hood. Follow U.S. 97 north for 43 miles (69 km) to the town of Madras. Continue north as U.S. 97 becomes U.S. 26 west and arrive in Government Camp in 62 miles (100 km). The drive takes about two hours. Both highways are open year-round, but traction tires or chains may be advised or required on U.S. 26 between December and March.

From Portland

Timberline Lodge is a fantastic day-trip destination from Portland. From downtown, head east on U.S. 26 (also known as Powell Boulevard) for about 50 miles (81 km). This trip takes about 75 minutes without traffic.

Alternatively, take I-84 east to exit 16 and turn right to head south on NE 238th Drive. Continue south as the road becomes NE 242nd Drive. After 2.8 miles, turn left to continue south on NE Burnside Road, then stay straight onto U.S. 26 east, following signs for Mount Hood. This trip takes 65-75 minutes without traffic.

Sights

★ Timberline Lodge

Built in 1938, world-famous Timberline Lodge draws almost two million visitors a year. The stone and wooden structure is built into the southern side of Mount Hood at 6,000 feet (1,829 m), and the surrounding scenery is stunning. You can see the craggy summit of Mount Hood, the year-round icy sheen of the Palmer Glacier stretching up the slopes, and even Mount Jefferson on the southern horizon.

Perhaps the most breathtaking part of the building is the main lobby: a warm and cozy space with 50-foot ceilings; an enormous, circular stone hearth; and huge, hexagonal wooden beams holding it all together. Design details throughout the entire building are fascinating, too. Mosey your way through the halls to find a mosaic featuring local wildlife on the 1st floor, carved wooden panels and staircase railings, and expert stonemasonry.

Hiking

Ramona Falls Loop 🅿ᴄᴛ

Distance: 7.5 mi/12.1 km round-trip
Duration: 3-4 hours
Elevation change: 1,100 ft/335 m
Effort: Easy/Moderate
Trailhead: Ramona Falls/Sandy River #770
Pass/Fee: Northwest Forest Pass

This loop hike along the Sandy River to a

rocky waterfall showcases Mount Hood's glaciated western slopes and the thick, mossy forest beneath.

The wide Sandy River Trail travels east out of the parking area through a sparse conifer forest for the first mile before crossing the Sandy River. (While there may be a makeshift log bridge across the river here, this crossing can be dangerous in early summer when snowmelt is in full effect—review the Forest Service's "River Crossing Safety Guidelines" on the trailside signs at 0.3 and 0.8 mile.) Views of 11,250-foot Mount Hood from the dry riverbed on the north shore are spectacular, especially in afternoon light. Meet the Pacific Crest Trail at 1.6 miles and stay right to walk southbound toward Ramona Falls.

At 2.5 miles, the scenery abruptly shifts from sparse and sandy to dense and lush forest. When the trail forks at 3.1 miles, stay left, departing from the PCT, and walk west uphill. The trail gets a little steeper before arriving at 120-foot Ramona Falls at 3.5 miles, where Ramona Creek cascades over chunky black stones. Cross the bridge below the falls to complete the loop, following the creek. The clear, babbling brook is lovely to walk alongside; some exposed cliffs between 4.2 and 4.6 miles make for interesting volcanic scenery. The trail transitions from thick forest back to sand at 4.9 miles.

Meet the PCT at 5.4 miles and turn left to travel southbound, crossing Ramona Creek on a sturdy bridge at 5.8 miles. Arrive back at the Sandy River Trail at 5.9 miles and turn right to walk west back toward the parking area.

Getting There

Ramona Falls trailhead is 18 miles (29 km) northwest of Government Camp, about a 30-minute drive. Follow U.S. 26 west for 10 miles (16.1 km), then turn right to head north on Lolo Pass Road. In 4 miles (6.4 km), turn right to drive east on Muddy Fork Road. Following signs for the Ramona Falls trailhead, stay right when the road forks at 0.7 mile and continue east on Muddy Fork Road/ Forest Road 1825 for another 1.7 miles (2.7 km). The large parking area is on the north side of the road.

Paradise Park

Distance: 12.4 mi/20 km round-trip
Duration: 6-7 hours
Elevation change: 2,720 ft/829 m
Effort: Strenuous
Trailhead: Pacific Crest Trail at Timberline Lodge

The meadows in Paradise Park are colorful throughout hiking season: Lush green grasses are speckled with wildflowers in June and July, then ablaze with reds and yellows in the autumn, and always framed by the rocky outcroppings of Mount Hood's summit. Along the southwest flanks of Mount Hood, the Pacific Crest Trail shares 13 miles with the 40-mile **Timberline Trail,** which circles the mighty volcano. This hike to Paradise Park explores the scenery and terrain of this part of the mountain.

Starting at Timberline Lodge, walk north uphill for 0.1 mile to meet the well-signed Pacific Crest Trail. Turn left to head west on the northbound PCT. The trail descends west away from the lodge, crossing sandy, rocky Little Zigzag Canyon at 1.1 miles. At 2.4 miles, stand atop the eastern rim of **Zigzag Canyon** (4.8 mi/7.7 km rt, 900 ft/274 m, moderate) 500 feet above the Zigzag River with Mount Hood's summit in clear view.

To continue to **Paradise Park** (12.4 mi/20 km rt, 2,720 ft/829 m, strenuous), head northwest down the switchbacks into Zigzag Canyon and cross the Zigzag River with caution. (While there may be a makeshift log bridge across the river here, this crossing can be dangerous in early summer when snowmelt is in full effect—review the Forest Service's "River Crossing Safety Guidelines" on the

From top to bottom: Timberline Lodge; bridge over Ramona Falls Loop; Zigzag Canyon.

trailside signs near Timberline Lodge.) Ascend out of the canyon to a trail junction at 3.9 miles with the Paradise Park Loop Trail. Stay left to continue north on the Pacific Crest Trail (you will return to this location via Paradise Park Loop). Stop for a scenic south-facing vista of Zigzag Canyon and Mount Jefferson at 4.3 miles, then continue north on the PCT, staying straight at the junction with Paradise Park Trail at 4.4 miles. Cross small streams Lost Creek at 5.1 miles and Rushing Water Creek at 5.7 miles. At 6.2 miles, make a hard right to head south on the Paradise Park Loop Trail. Views during the next mile are superb, including everything on the horizon from Mount Jefferson 50 miles to the south and both Mount St. Helens and Mount Adams, 60 miles to the north. During July and early August, this section of trail is also a delightful walk of wildflowers in shades of purple, red, pink, yellow, and white. Cross Lost Creek again at 7.4 miles and gaze up to get a good look at Mount Hood's Mississippi Head, a rocky outcropping west of the Zigzag Glacier.

Descend between miles 7.7 and 8.7 before rejoining the Pacific Crest Trail and turning left to walk southeast back toward Zigzag Canyon. Return to Timberline Lodge on the PCT.

Getting There

This hike begins at Timberline Lodge, 6 miles (9.7 km) northeast of Government Camp on the Timberline Highway.

Tamanawas Falls

Distance: 3.4 mi/5.5 km round-trip
Duration: 1.5-2 hours
Elevation change: 600 ft/183 m
Effort: Easy
Trailhead: Tamanawas Falls
Pass/Fee: Northwest Forest Pass

This short hike to a thundering waterfall is a must-do for anyone traveling on Highway 35 between Timberline Lodge and Hood River. Depart from the parking area and head north on the East Fork

Trail for 0.5 mile, paralleling the highway and the East Fork of the Hood River. Turn left to head west on the Tamanawas Falls Trail and begin to climb into a conifer forest as the trail follows the edge of Tamanawas Creek. Arrive at the falls at 1.7 miles, a 40-foot-wide cascade tumbling 100 feet over a cliff into a plunge pool. Behind the falls, a large dry cave looms, begging to be explored. The rocks near the falls can be slippery—if you explore the cave, wear shoes with good traction.

Getting There

The Tamanawas trailhead is on Highway 35, 17.5 miles (27 km) northeast of Government Camp and 25 miles (40 km) south of Hood River. From Government Camp, take Highway 26 east for 2 miles (3 km) to the junction with Highway 35. Follow Highway 35 for 15 miles (24 km). The trailhead is on the west side of the road.

Recreation
Skiing

When the winter snows have melted at all the other North American resorts, Timberline is still frozen. Spring skiing continues well into June (and depending on the snow that season, all year long!) at **Timberline Ski Area** (27500 Timberline Rd., 503/272-3311, www.timberlinelodge.com, $70). Professional athletes train on the perpetually frozen Palmer Glacier, the giant snowfield visible from Timberline Lodge. Views from this ski area on a clear day are incredible: Not only is Mount Hood a sight to behold up close, but Mount Jefferson and the Three Sisters are in sight on the southern horizon.

Ski Bowl (87000 Hwy. 26, Government Camp, 503/272-3206, www.skibowl.com, 3pm-10pm Mon.-Thurs., 9am-11pm Fri.-Sat. and daily during holiday break, 9am-10pm Sun., approx. Dec.-Mar., $36-59) is another ski area with 65 downhill runs and a tubing park.

Mountain Biking

Mount Hood National Forest is home to 140 miles of bike-friendly trails, and some of the conifer forests here have maintained old-growth status. Stop by the **Zigzag Ranger Station** (70220 Hwy. 26, Zigzag, 503/622-3191, www.fs.usda. gov, 8am-noon and 1pm-4pm daily) to pick up a map of trails in the area, or visit **Mountain Bike Park at Ski Bowl** (87000 Hwy. 26, Government Camp, 503/272-3206, www.skibowl.com, 9am-5pm Sat.-Sun. June and Sept., 9am-5pm daily July-Aug., $30-40). Mountain bike rentals are available ($15-45) by the hour or all day.

Entertainment and Events

Just a few miles west of Timberline, **Mt. Hood Brewing Co.** (87304 Government Camp Loop, Government Camp, 503/272-3172, www.mthoodbrewing. com, 11am-9pm daily, $12-26) makes ales with pure glacial water from the flanks of its namesake volcano. The brewery is spacious and sleek, with bright and clean design and a big window looking into the brewhouse operations. An ice-rail rimming the bar keeps beers cold while you share snacks or trail stories. On the menu, American classics like hand-tossed pizzas and sandwiches accompany worldly shared plates like Korean barbecue ribs and house-made *labneh* (yogurt cheese). The brewery began in 1991, long before the explosion of Oregon craft breweries, and has kept itself small intentionally—beers are only distributed within the state.

Food

The legendary buffets at the ★ **Cascade Dining Room** (Timberline Lodge, 27500 E. Timberline Rd., 503/272-3104, www. timberlinelodge.com, 7:30am-10am and 11:30am-2pm Mon.-Fri., 7:30am-10:30am and 11:30am-3pm Sat.-Sun., $18 breakfast, $25 lunch) leave no culinary stone unturned. You'll find whatever you're in the mood for, whether it's eggs and bacon, waffles, French toast, fresh fruit, sliced meats, pastas, mixed greens, grain and bean salads, cheeses, grilled veggies, or decadent desserts. The best part: There's no limit on how many times you can fill your plate. During **dinner** (6pm-8pm Sun.-Fri., 5:30pm-8pm Sat., $28-48), the restaurant offers table service and made-to-order items featuring local produce and artisan meat, seafood, and vegetarian entrées.

The lodge also has more casual dining options, including the **Ram's Head Bar & Restaurant** (503/272-3311, 2pm-11pm Mon.-Thurs., 10:30am-11pm Fri.-Sun., $8-26) on the 3rd-floor circular balcony. Tables overlook the huge stone hearth and cozy lounge area below. In addition to classy snacks like spiced nuts and charcuterie boards, the menu includes a few upscale sandwiches, soups, and entrées like duck cassoulet and beef short ribs. If you're in the mood for a fancy drink, you'll want to check out the Prohibition-inspired cocktails on the menu, too.

Tucked into a tiny space behind the main lobby, the **Blue Ox Bar** (503/272-3391, noon-8pm daily May-Sept., Thanksgiving weekend, and mid-Dec.-early Jan., $15-18) is a cozy wooden bar with hand-tossed pizzas and Mt. Hood Brewing beers on tap.

Accommodations

The four-story ★ **Timberline Lodge** (27500 E. Timberline Rd., 503/272-3311, www.timberlinelodge.com, $150-300) was constructed in the 1930s and is just as magnificent as the towering mountain it sits upon. You may recognize the wood and stone exterior from the movie *The Shining* (although a different lodge was used for interior scenes). Skiers flock to Timberline Lodge in the winter; the lodge sits at the base of Timberline Ski Area. In the summer, hiking opportunities abound on the Pacific Crest Trail, the Timberline Trail, and many other hiking trails.

⚑ Side Trip: The Fruit Loop

The fertile Hood River Valley stretches south from downtown Hood River toward Mount Hood. Dozens of orchards, farms, and wineries are located along the **Fruit Loop** (www.hoodriverfruitloop.com), a 35-mile (56-km) route of byways that can be experienced as a scenic drive or a bike ride. Views of Mount Hood along this loop are larger-than-life as the pointy, snowcapped volcano towers over fields of fruit trees. During the sunny summer months, peaches, plums, apricots, and berries are abundant. Apples and pears make their appearance in the fall. Allow at least an hour to make the drive, more if you plan to stop for snacks and tastes.

Visit the website to download a map of the route, including almost 30 farms, bakeries, u-pick orchards, cideries, and wineries. Some locations are open for year-round visitation while others close during the cold winter months.

Inside, a giant hearth sits in a six-sided stone chimney, surrounded by astonishingly large wooden beams. Perfectly appointed guest rooms are small, featuring a rustic alpine decor and luxurious linens. Guests get playful in the downstairs game room, filled with Ping-Pong tables, shuffleboard, and dozens of board games. Wi-Fi is free throughout the lodge, and although the TVs in the rooms don't offer premium channels, there is a wide selection of DVDs available for rent at the front desk.

Rooms are located on the 2nd, 3rd, and 4th floors; restaurants are on the 2nd and 3rd floors. A heated outdoor swimming pool is open year-round, as is an outdoor hot tub. The sauna offers a wonderful treat for tired hiking muscles. The on-site **Cascade Dining Room** (7:30am-10am and 11:30am-2pm Mon.-Fri., 7:30am-10:30am and 11:30am-3pm Sat.-Sun., 6pm-8pm Sun.-Fri., 5:30pm-8pm Sat.) is renowned for its buffet.

Camping

If you'd like to camp near Timberline Lodge, ★ **Frog Lake Campground** (U.S. 26 and Frog Creek Rd., www.fs.usda. gov, May-Sept.) offers an incredibly convenient location. True to its name, frogs can be heard during the evening hours when highway traffic quiets down. All 12 campsites have fire rings and picnic tables, as well as access to potable water and pit toilets. The PCT crosses the highway just north of the campground, so it's common to see thru-hikers here late July-early September. (If they're headed for the buffet at Timberline Lodge, they may not feel like chatting.) This small campground can fill on weekends; **reservations** (877/444-6777, www. recreation.gov, $22) are recommended. Frog Lake is 8 miles (12.9 km) south of Government Camp on U.S. 26.

South of Mount Hood, the PCT traces the eastern shore of beautiful **Timothy Lake,** one of the best places in the area to view snowcapped Mount Hood as it towers over an endless green forest. A mostly flat, 15-mile trail circles the lake, overlapping with the PCT for 6 miles.

Oak Fork Campground (Forest Rd. 57, www.fs.usda.gov, June-Oct.) is located on a peninsula in the southeast corner of the lake; the lakeside trail is just steps away. This waterfront campground has 26 drive-in campsites, six cabins, and eight hike-in sites with easy access to the lakeshore. Make **reservations** (877/444-6777, www.recreation.gov, $16 sites, $45 cabins) to guarantee a spot at this gorgeous campground.

Getting There: Timothy Lake is 21 miles (34 km) south of Government Camp, about a 30-minute drive. Follow U.S. 26 east for 11 miles (17.7 km) to Oregon Skyline Road (also known as Forest Road 42) and turn right to head south. Continue for 10 miles (16.1 km), crossing the PCT at Joe Graham Horse

Camp, and veer right onto Forest Road 57.

Information and Services

The closest ranger station is in the community of **Zigzag** (70220 Hwy. 26, Zigzag, 503/622-3191, www.fs.usda.gov, 8am-noon and 1pm-4pm daily), which is frequented by Portland day-trippers. Stop here for current updates about trail conditions and closures and to pick up area maps.

Getting Around

The **Mount Hood Express Route** (www.mthoodexpress.com, 5:15am-7:15pm daily year-round, $2-5) runs a public bus service from the operations center in Sandy, Oregon (16610 Champion Way) to Timberline Lodge. The 35-mile (56-km) trip takes 75 minutes each way.

Hood River

Nestled in the Columbia River Gorge between two massive, majestic volcanoes, Hood River is one of the most scenic towns in Oregon. Outdoor athletes flock to the Gorge for mountain biking, skiing, and kiteboarding, and their sporty spirit is evident in the arts, shopping, and restaurant scenes. The area's natural beauty and multitude of outdoor activities aren't the only wow factors; the historic downtown is cute, with shops, restaurants, and accommodations.

Southwest of Hood River, the Pacific Crest Trail traces the western edge of Mount Hood on its way to the Columbia Gorge. There aren't any driving routes that parallel the path of the PCT, but scenic Highway 35 takes road-trippers around the eastern base of the mighty mountain before arriving in Hood River.

Getting Around

Hood River is 40 miles (64 km) northeast of Timberline Lodge, about a 50-minute drive on Highway 35. From Timberline

Lodge, take U.S. 26 east for about 2 miles (3.2 km) and exit onto Highway 35 north. Continue on Highway 35 north for 40 miles (64 km) to Hood River.

To reach Hood River from Portland, take I-84 east to exit 63. This drive takes about an hour.

Hiking
Chinidere Mountain

Distance: 4 mi/6.4 km round-trip
Duration: 2 hours
Elevation change: 1,200 ft/366 m
Effort: Moderate
Trailhead: Wahtum Lake Campground
Pass/Fee: Northwest Forest Pass

This loop hike travels around the shores of Wahtum Lake to the top of Chinidere Mountain, a popular picnic spot where Mount Hood looms large, three of Washington's volcanoes are in view, and endless green mountains sprawl in every direction.

Start the hike from the bulletin board at Wahtum Lake Campground. Follow the Wahtum Express Trail northwest downhill for 0.1 mile, away from the parking area toward the lake. The Wahtum Express Trail descends 200 stairs to meet the Pacific Crest Trail. Turn left onto the PCT and continue hiking clockwise, heading west on the southbound PCT for 0.2 mile. Veer right onto Eagle Creek Trail for 0.1 mile, then make another right onto Chinidere Cutoff Trail and hike north over the western outlet of the lake. The Chinidere Cutoff Trail makes a steep westbound ascent between 0.6 and 1.2 miles where it rejoins the PCT.

Follow the northbound PCT west for 0.1 mile, then look for a steep, narrow trail that splits off to the right; take this trail to head north to the top of Chinidere. The trail zigzags up the side of the mountain for 0.4 mile before reaching the incredible viewpoint at 1.6 miles. Giant volcanoes line the horizon and you'll notice a large swath of burned forest, a scar from the devasting 2017 Eagle Creek Fire.

OREGON

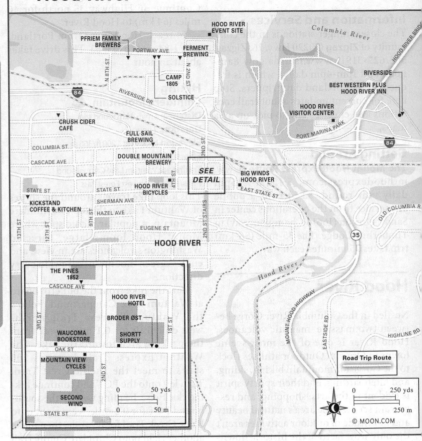

Hood River

HOOD RIVER
EVENT SITE

Columbia River

PFRIEM FAMILY
BREWERS

PORTWAY AVE.

FERMENT
BREWING

N 2ND ST.

N 8TH ST.

CAMP
1805

SOLSTICE

RIVERSIDE DR.

84

RIVERSIDE

BEST WESTERN PLUS
HOOD RIVER INN

HOOD RIVER
VISITOR CENTER

PORT MARINA PARK

84

CRUSH CIDER
CAFÉ

FULL SAIL
BREWING

COLUMBIA ST.

CASCADE AVE.

DOUBLE MOUNTAIN
BREWERY

2ND ST.

OAK ST.

**SEE
DETAIL**

BIG WINDS
HOOD RIVER

STATE ST.

STATE ST.

HOOD RIVER
BICYCLES

4TH ST.

EAST STATE ST.

OLD COLUMBIA R

KICKSTAND
COFFEE & KITCHEN

SHERMAN AVE.

HAZEL AVE.

9TH ST.

13TH ST.

12TH ST.

EUGENE ST.

2ND ST. STAIRS

35

HOOD RIVER

Hood River

MOUNT HOOD HIGHWAY

EASTSIDE RD.

HIGHLINE RD

THE PINES
1852

CASCADE AVE.

HOOD RIVER
HOTEL

BRODER ØST

3RD ST.

WAUCOMA
BOOKSTORE

OAK ST.

SHORTT
SUPPLY

1ST ST.

Road Trip Route

MOUNTAIN VIEW
CYCLES

SECOND
WIND

2ND ST.

STATE ST.

| 0 | 50 yds |
| 0 | 50 m |

| 0 | 250 yds |
| 0 | 250 m |

© MOON.COM

Make your way back down by returning to the PCT and continuing east at 2.1 miles rather than taking the steep cutoff trail you hiked up. Follow the southbound PCT as it curves northeast past the Herman Creek Trail at 2.2 miles. The PCT then transitions east as it descends through thick forest on the edge of the lake. Afternoon views of the sparkling lake are beautiful in this section. At 3.9 miles, you'll reach the staircase you descended earlier; take this back up or make a sharp left to opt for a gently sloping 0.3-mile path back to the parking lot.

Getting There

Wahtum Lake is 26 miles (42 km) southwest of Hood River, about a 50-minute drive. Take Highway 281 south out of town for 11 miles (17.7 km), following signs for Odell and Parkdale as the road makes several left and right turns. In Dee, turn right onto Lost Lake Road and drive southwest for 5 miles (8 km). Make a right onto Forest Road 13, heading northwest for 10 miles (16.1 km) to Wahtum Lake.

Recreation
Mountain Biking

Mountain biking is one of the most popular outdoor activities in the Hood River area. Trails on both sides of the Columbia River stretch into forested hills, across grassy prairies, and onto exposed ridgelines with views of the mighty river. There are trails for riders of every level, from beginner to expert. Rent a bike at **Mountain View Cycles** (205 Oak St., 541/386-2453, www.mtnviewcycles.com, 10am-6pm Mon.-Sat., $75) or **Hood River Bicycles** (208 4th St., 541/387-3276, www. hoodriverbicycles.com, 9am-5pm Wed.-Sun., $60-100). Experts at these shops can provide you with trail maps and details about the area's best rides.

Kiteboarding and Windsurfing

The Columbia Gorge is an incredibly windy place in the summer, a result of cool air from Portland rushing through the river valley toward the hot desert air on the eastern side of the state. This phenomenon has turned Hood River into a world-class kiteboarding and windsurfing destination. Most kiteboarders launch at the **Hood River Event Site** (Portway Ave., 541/386-1645, www. portofhoodriver.com, 7am-11pm daily May-Oct., $8/day parking fee), a large beach on the north side of the interstate near exit 63. Rent equipment or sign up for lessons at **Big Winds** (207 Front St., 541/386-6086, www.bigwinds.com, 9am-5pm daily). This large shop has both kiteboarding and windsurfing equipment, along with stand-up paddleboards, clothing, and all the outdoor accessories you may need to stay comfortable and safe. Lessons ($90-150) include all equipment and gear.

Skiing

When the temperatures drop, the wind dies down, and the winter sun slides across the southern sky, Hood River athletes hit the slopes. **Mount Hood Meadows** (14040 Hwy. 35, Mt. Hood, 503/337-2222, www.skihood.com, 9am-4pm Mon.-Tues., 9am-9pm Wed.-Sun. Dec.-Mar., $49-89), a ski resort on the eastern flanks of Mount Hood, has 2,150 acres of skiable terrain and lifts scaling the mountain at elevations up to 7,300 feet (2,225 m). Known locally as simply "Meadows," the resort has two lodges with sports shops and restaurants. Equipment rentals ($40-50) can be reserved in advance on the website or obtained day-of at the rental center.

Mount Hood Meadows is 35 miles (56 km) south of Hood River on Highway 35, about a 45-minute drive.

Entertainment and Events
Breweries

Oregon is famous for its microbreweries, and the Columbia Gorge is no exception. Hood River is home to multiple breweries whose personalities couldn't be more different from each other.

Even though **Double Mountain Brewery** (8 4th St., 541/387-0042, www. doublemountainbrewery.com, 11am-11pm daily, $9-15) is a big space, it manages to be cozy and warm with a pub-like feel. The brewery makes four year-round beers, a half dozen seasonal beers, and one-off experimental brews throughout the year. The hoppy, resinous IPAs are popular. Two house-brewed non-alcoholic options are on tap, too: root beer and ginger. As for food, the brewery serves delicious brick-oven pizza alongside salads, shareable appetizers, and sandwiches. A downstairs stage hosts live music on Tuesdays.

Located in a trendy waterfront neighborhood, ★ **pFriem Family Brewers** (707 Portway Ave., 541/321-0490, www. pfriembeer.com, 11:30am-9pm daily, $12-15) brews traditional styles like IPAs, pales, stouts, and lagers, but it's best known for its more creative beers: golden coffee pale, Belgian strong blonde, frambozen, and fest bier, to name a few. The unusual beers are a draw. Expect to wait for a table during the summer or on

busy weekends. While you wait, enjoy the gorgeous scenery around the Hood River waterfront park.

Climb the stairs to **Ferment Brewing** (403 Portway Ave., 541/436-3499, www.fermentbrewing.com, 11am-9pm Sun.-Thurs., 11am-10pm Fri.-Sat., $11-14), where you'll find creative microbrews like saisons and barrel-aged ales paired with house-made pickles, rotisserie meats, and locally baked breads. The menu's heavy Middle Eastern influence is showcased in dishes with lamb, falafel, hummus, and harissa—but you can order a burger if you're in the mood for something more classic American. The huge, lofty space has big, exposed beams and floor-to-ceiling windows overlooking the river and the mountains on the Washington side of the Columbia River.

Full Sail Brewing (506 Columbia St., 541/386-2247, www.fullsailbrewing.com, 11am-9pm daily, $9-16) is the largest brewery in Hood River, and its enormous building can be seen from the freeway. This brewery's most famous beer is the Session lager.

Still thirsty? Take the self-guided **Breweries in the Gorge** (www.breweriesinthegorge.com) tour to experience all 13 breweries in the region. Collect stamps at each one to earn a pint glass.

Wine-Tasting

Marchesi Vineyards (3955 Belmont Dr., 541/386-1800, www.marchesivineyards.com, 11am-6pm daily) is a beautiful property in west Hood River, set back from the busy downtown area on a quiet country road. Sip Italian-style wines from grape varietals like Barbera, Dolcetto, and Pinot Nero inside the tasting room's warm and cozy interior or on the breezy patio overlooking the vineyards and the Hood River Valley.

Taste estate-grown wines at **The Pines**

From top to bottom: Hood River apple orchards; Broder Øst; cabin at Lost Lake Resort.

1852 (202 Cascade Ave., 541/993-8301, www.thepinesvineyard.com, noon-5pm Mon.-Wed., noon-7pm Thurs. and Sat.-Sun., noon-10pm Fri.). This winery is known for its big reds—cab, merlot, zinfandel—but their chardonnay, gewürztraminer, and pinot gris are equally delightful, and the sparkling wine is a treat. The simple tasting room is bright and classy, and within steps of downtown restaurants and shops.

Ciders and Spirits

In the Northwest, craft cider is making a name for itself along with an explosion in microbreweries. **Crush Cider Café** (1020 Wasco St., 541/399-9585, www.crushcidercafe.com, 3pm-8pm Mon. and Wed.-Thurs., noon-10pm Fri.-Sat., noon-8pm Sun., $4-12) is a downtown café whose rotating taps feature their own ciders alongside those from other regional cideries. Order a flight of three or six ciders, served with detailed tasting notes, or a full pint. Fresh apple juice from Hood River apples, flatbreads, soups, and warm pretzels are also available. The small space has a few seats at the bar, a couple of wooden tables, and two picnic tables outside.

Nestled in the apple orchards of the Hood River Valley, **Foxtail Cider & Distillery** (2965 Ehrck Hill Dr., 541/716-0093, www.foxtailcider.com, 11am-6pm daily June-Sept., 11am-5pm Fri.-Mon. Oct.-May) has a tasting room housed in a big red barn. Its proprietary ciders are served as samples, flights, pints, or in growlers. This is a great spot to enjoy a refreshing beverage on a hot summer day. It's located south of town and is one of the stops on the Fruit Loop, a 35-mile (56-km) scenic drive or bike ride through the orchards and fields of Hood River Valley.

In an area dominated by microbreweries, **Camp 1805 Distillery and Bar** (501 Portway Ave., 541/386-1805, www.camp1805.com, 3pm-10pm Mon.-Thurs., 3pm-11pm Fri., noon-11pm Sat., noon-9pm Sun., $12-15) offers a unique experience. Craft cocktails utilize house spirits along with the best liquors from around the world. Most of the seating is inside, where patrons can gaze through giant windows into the distillery operations. Tables outside look out onto Hood River's waterfront park and are great for people-watching.

Festivals and Events

Hood River Hops Fest (Columbia Lot, 5th Ave. and Columbia St., 541/386-2000, www.hoodriver.org, noon-8pm 3rd Sat. in Sept., $10-20) is a celebration of Oregon-brewed beer. This outdoor gathering is held in downtown Hood River near some of the town's best restaurants and breweries. Beers at the event hail from all over the state: Oregon Coast, Portland area, Central Oregon, and the Columbia Gorge. (A Seattle brewery may even make an appearance.) Local live music acts play all day. Children and underage attendees are welcome before 5pm.

There is metered street parking only. Shuttle service (www.columbiagorgeexpress.com, $5-15) is provided between Hood River, Cascade Locks, and Portland.

Shopping

Originally focused on running, **Shortt Supply** (116 Oak St., 541/386-5474, www.shorttsupply.com, 10am-6pm Mon.-Fri., 10am-5pm Sat., 11am-4pm Sun.) is an outdoor apparel store with clothing, footwear, accessories, and snacks for running, hiking, camping, and swimming. Merchandise isn't cheap, but it's high-quality, and store associates are expert shoe fitters.

Second Wind (202 State St., 541/386-4464, www.2ndwind-sports.com, 10am-6pm Mon. and Wed.-Sat., 2pm-6pm Tues., 11am-5pm Sun.) offers both new and second-hand items for hiking, camping, and the wind sports that are popular in the Columbia Gorge. This is the best place in town for backpacking accessories like ultralight stoves and trekking poles, and the clothing selection is solid as well.

Locally grown produce, artisan food products, and handcrafted home goods are on display every weekend at the outdoor **Hood River Farmers Market** (5th Ave. and Columbia St., 9am-1pm Sat. May-Nov.). In addition to the bounty of fresh fruits and vegetables from nearby orchards, find local meats, cheeses, jams, sauces, and other accoutrements. There are also booths with unique gifts including hats, jewelry, accessories, and artwork.

Waucoma Bookstore (212 Oak St., 541/386-5353, www.waucomabookstore. com, 10am-6pm Mon.-Fri., 9:30am-6pm Sat.-Sun.) is a cozy downtown bookshop packed with books, cards, gifts, and toys. Locally made artwork and jewelry is for sale, along with calendars, kitchen gadgets, coloring books, and clothing. There's also a nice selection of maps and local guides.

Food

There's no better place to get a taste of Hood River culture than at ★ **Kickstand Coffee & Kitchen** (1235 State St., 541/436-0016, www.kickstandcoffee. net, 7am-10pm daily, $8-20), a coffee shop, restaurant, and bar with an outdoor patio and year-round fire pit that's ultra-popular among mountain bikers and kiteboarders. Espresso and handmade pastries are popular in the early hours, along with breakfast sandwiches and burritos. For lunch and dinner, sandwiches, burgers, and salads are the highlights, and there are a few worldly items peppered in like kimchi fried rice and spicy ahi tuna poke.

Broder Øst (102 Oak St., 541/436-3444, www.brodereast.com, 7am-2pm Mon.-Fri., 7am-3pm Sat.-Sun., $7-14) is a Scandinavian-themed breakfast and lunch joint on the first level of the Historic Hood River Hotel. Order a Swedish breakfast with smoked trout, soft-boiled egg, rye toast, and yogurt parfait, or opt for the more American baked-egg dishes. The Danish pancakes and Norwegian potato cakes are also popular. The bright, airy space features high ceilings, hardwood details, and floor-to-ceiling windows that look out onto downtown Hood River's busy sidewalk.

★ **Solstice** (501 Portway Ave., 541/436-0800, www.solsticewoodfirecafe.com, 11am-9pm Wed.-Mon., $13-21) is located in a trendy waterfront neighborhood across from a park. Perfectly crisp pizzas are topped with fresh, local veggies and artisan meats and cheeses. The sumptuous salads are popular, too. Expect to wait up to an hour for a table on busy, sunny days.

Hood River's only waterfront deck dining, **Riverside** (1108 E. Marina Dr., 541/386-4410, www.riversidehoodriver. com, 6am-9:30pm Sun.-Thurs., 6am-10pm Fri.-Sat. June-Sept., 6am-9pm daily Oct.-May, $12-28) draws just as many locals as visitors, even during the busy tourist season. The menu lists a blend of American favorites and traditional Italian pastas. Happy hour in the bar (4pm-6pm Mon.-Fri.) is a great way to enjoy this upscale spot with a lower price tag.

Accommodations and Camping

Hood River's population doubles during the summer, when the sleepy town becomes a bustling hub for both visitors and locals. This is where Oregonians and global travelers alike come to recreate and relax. Accommodations are expensive and competitive June-September, which makes reservations critical. But don't let this deter you from visiting. The fancy-free vacation vibes are intoxicating.

★ **Historic Hood River Hotel** (102 Oak St., 541/386-1900, www.hoodriverhotel. com, $120-220) may be the oldest hotel in town, but the updated rooms are furnished with decor that perfectly blends vintage charm, modern comfort, and hip design. Windows look out onto downtown Hood River or toward the mountains on the Washington side. Some suites feature microwaves and coffeemakers (specify, if that's important to you).

In operation since 1967, the **Best Western Hood River Inn** (1108 E. Marina Dr., 541/386-2000, www.bestwestern. com, $120-250) is a waterfront hotel with fantastic views of the Columbia River and Hood River Bridge. Remodeled rooms are sleek and modern, with microwaves, fridges, and coffeemakers, and Wi-Fi is complimentary throughout the property. On a hot and windy summer day, there's nowhere more luxurious to cool off than at the hotel's outdoor pool. Your stay includes a free breakfast at the popular on-site restaurant, **Riverside** (541/386-4410, www.riversidehoodriver.com, 6am-9:30pm Sun.-Thurs., 6am-10pm Fri.-Sat. June-Sept., 6am-9pm daily Oct.-May).

Perched on a north-facing bluff at the west end of town, **Westcliff Lodge** (4070 Westcliff Dr., 541/386-2992, www. westclifflodge.com, $140-240 summer, $90-120 winter) is a great value. It's a few miles west of Hood River's bustling downtown, so the rooms are less expensive and there's plenty of parking. Most of the 57 rooms offer spectacular views of the Columbia River and Underwood Mountain on the Washington side.

The picture-perfect postcard views of Mount Hood from **Lost Lake Resort** (9000 Lost Lake Rd., 541/386-6366, www. lostlakeresort.org, $27-32 campsites, $80-170 cabins) have turned this popular resort into one of the most photographed places in Oregon. There's something for everyone at this family-friendly getaway: boat rentals, hiking trails, a restaurant, cabins, campsites, and hotel rooms in a gorgeous wooden lodge. While you shouldn't expect solitude at this forested hot spot, you can expect a celebration among everyone about soaking up the sunshine in this beautiful place.

Getting There: Lost Lake is 25 miles (40 km) southwest of Hood River, about a 45-minute drive. Take Highway 281 south out of town (known as 13th Street within city limits) for 11 miles (17.7 km) to Lost Lake Road, then turn right and continue another 14 miles (22.5 km) to the resort.

Information and Services

For wilderness information, including trail and weather conditions, visit the **Hood River Ranger Station** (6780 Hwy. 35, 541/352-6002, www.fs.usda.gov, 8am-4:30pm Mon.-Sat.), where you can also pick up maps and brochures. Rangers offer status updates about any wildfires or trail closures in the area and are knowledgeable about the best places to go.

The **Hood River Visitor Center** (720 E. Port Marina, 541/386-2000, www. hoodriver.org, 9am-5pm Mon.-Fri., 10am-4pm Sat.) is located on the downtown waterfront near the Hood River Bridge. The office is staffed by the chamber of commerce and is the best source of information.

Getting Around

Columbia Area Transit (541/386-4202, www.cattransit.org, $1) offers weekday bus service between Hood River (224 Wasco Loop) and Cascade Locks (Columbia Market, 450 Wa Na Pa St.). There's also a weekday commuter route ($10) with Portland departure times between 5:45am and 7:15am, with an 8:15am arrival in Hood River. The same bus departs Hood River at 5:15pm for the return to Portland. Pay your fare in cash (make sure you've got exact change) or download the Hopthru app (www. hopthru.com) on your smartphone to pay your fare digitally.

Cascade Locks

Cascade Locks is an iconic destination on the PCT—the place where Oregon meets Washington in the dramatic Columbia River Gorge. Located less than an hour drive from Portland, it's also a popular

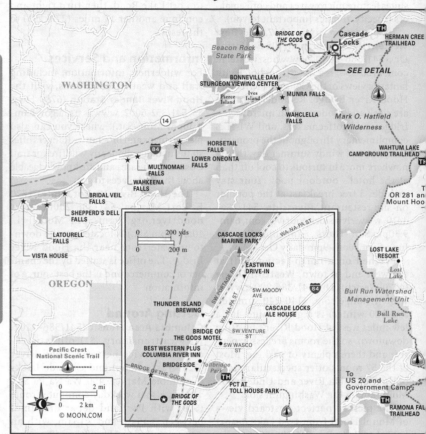

Cascade Locks, Oregon

destination for urbanites eager to escape the city and enjoy some of the best natural scenery in the state. Nearby hikes lead to waterfalls that tumble hundreds of feet over thickly forested cliffs on their way to the Columbia River.

The town of Cascade Locks offers a handful of casual but satisfying eating options, a terrific microbrewery, and comfortable places to spend the night.

Getting There

Cascade Locks is located in the heart of the Columbia River Gorge. From Hood River, take I-84 west for 20 miles (32 km) (about a 25-minute drive). From Portland, take I-84 east to exit 44 in Cascade Locks; the drive takes about 45 minutes without traffic.

Sights

★ Bridge of the Gods

The Columbia River begins in the Canadian Rockies, flows south through central Washington, then turns and cuts through the Cascade Range, forming the dramatic Columbia Gorge on the Oregon-Washington border. Built in 1926, the **Bridge of the Gods** (Wa Na Pa St., Cascade Locks, $1 pedestrian toll, $2 auto toll) is one of only two Columbia River crossings in the mountainous 80-mile (129-km) stretch between Portland and The Dalles. The bridge is named after a natural bridge that was formed by a catastrophic landslide on the north shore of the river. Evidence of the slide can be seen in the pointy, sheared rock faces of Greenleaf Peak and Table Mountain—both visible from the bridge and from the town of Cascade Locks. Check out the mural under the bridge on Wa Na Pa Street, painted onto one of the bridge's cement support structures, to see an artist's rendition of the natural bridge.

The Bridge of the Gods also serves as the Pacific Crest Trail's official crossing between Oregon and Washington. If you've read *Wild* or seen the movie, you'll remember this bridge from the final scene of Cheryl Strayed's story. PCT hikers walk across the steel truss cantilever bridge, the mighty river visible through the grated bridge deck 140 feet below. There are no sidewalks, so pedestrians share the entire length of the bridge (1,110 feet from shore to shore) with cars and trucks. If you're afraid of heights, driving across is the way to go. Prefer to walk? Park in the lot on Wa Na Pa Street underneath the bridge, then cross the street and walk south to the tollbooth. The bridge leads to a forested patch of Highway 14 in Washington, where the northbound PCT continues.

Cascade Locks Marine Park

Before the Bonneville Dam drowned the nearby rapids, steamboats used locks for safe passage through a dangerous stretch of river. **Cascade Locks Marine Park** (395 Portage Rd., 541/374-8619, www.portofcascadelocks.com) is the best place to enjoy the extraordinary scenery of the Columbia Gorge. The waterfront park includes plenty of grassy space with picnic tables, barbecues, and walking paths. The west end of the park is a popular fishing spot, while the east edge has a nice swimming beach. Be sure to check out Thunder Island, which was carved out of the mainland in 1890 to create a canal. This small island, which can be accessed via a footbridge over the defunct locks canal, is landscaped with a mix of trees and lush green lawns. Views of the Columbia River and the Bridge of the Gods are spectacular from the island's edges.

Hiking
Dry Creek Falls

Distance: 4.4 mi/7.1 km round-trip
Duration: 2 hours
Elevation change: 800 ft/244 m
Effort: Moderate
Trailhead: Pacific Crest Trail at Tollbridge Park
Pass/Fee: Northwest Forest Pass

Waterfalls in the Columbia Gorge have made the region a famous photography destination. This meander along the Pacific Crest Trail showcases a beautiful 75-foot cascade.

Start at Tollbridge Park and find the PCT trailhead on the south side of the parking area. Walk underneath the I-84 freeway and cross Moody Avenue, where the trail enters the woods. This forest was scorched in the 2017 Eagle Creek fire, but thanks to the wet, rainy winters in Cascade Locks, new plant life and lush greenery are reestablishing their reign. The path climbs steadily away from the interstate and onto the lumpy basalt cliffs characteristic of the region. At 1.1 miles, hike under a set of power lines and then, at around 1.3 miles, look through the trees to see the Columbia River Gorge. You'll find yourself under the towering basalt cliffs at 1.5 miles. Reach a bridge at 1.9 miles where Dry Creek rushes below. Turn right to walk south up a steep hill for 0.3 mile to arrive at the long, lacy waterfall at 2.2 miles.

Indian Point Loop

Distance: 8 mi/12.9 km round-trip
Duration: 4-5 hours

Elevation change: 2,900 ft/884 m
Effort: Strenuous
Trailhead: Herman Creek
Pass/Fee: Northwest Forest Pass

Climb onto the high, forested bluffs east of Cascade Locks and immerse yourself in the Columbia Gorge's rugged terrain, stopping halfway at an incredible viewpoint to soak in the stunning scenery. The vast network of trails in this area means that you'll encounter a number of trail junctions; pay close attention to avoid any wrong turns.

From the Herman Creek parking area, walk south on Herman Creek Trail #406 for 0.4 mile. At a trail junction, the Herman Creek Cutoff Trail forks off to the right—you want to stay left. Another trail junction appears in 0.7 mile; stay right this time, then continue straight. At 1.3 miles, head east onto Gorton Creek Trail #408, which climbs along the river-facing bluff. The Gorge Trail #400 veers off to the left here—stay straight on Gorton Creek Trail #408. At 3.8 miles, look for the Indian Point spur trail on the east side of the trail. Follow this spur down the hill for 0.2 mile for a fantastic view of the Columbia River and Wind Mountain as it rises from the river like a rounded pyramid. Then return to the main trail and walk southwest on Ridge Cutoff Trail #437. The trail meets Nick Eaton Trail #447 at 4.8 miles; turn right and walk west along the ridgeline. It's all downhill from here. Continue west to 6.6 miles where you'll rejoin the Herman Creek Trail and arrive back at the parking area at 8 miles.

Getting There

Herman Creek trailhead is 3 miles (4.8 km) east of Cascade Locks. Take Wa Na Pa Street east for 1 mile (1.6 km), pass under I-84, and continue south onto Frontage Road. The road bends to the left, traveling east for 1.7 miles (2.7 km) to Herman Creek Road. The trailhead parking area is on the south side of Frontage Road.

Entertainment and Events

PCT Days (Cascade Locks Marine Park, 355 Wa Na Pa St., www.pctdays.com, 3rd weekend in Aug., free) is an annual hiker festival and gear expo with a raffle, food vendors, beers from Thunder Island Brewing, and a PCT film festival under the stars (Sat.). Many PCT hikers attend the event as part of their thru-hike (it's timed to overlap with the thru-hike schedule), but the weekend activities are geared toward anyone who loves hiking. The outdoor venue couldn't be more beautiful: forested bluffs surround a lush green lawn on the southern banks of the Columbia River. Sponsors and gear vendors donate raffle prizes like overnight packs, outdoor clothing, hiking accessories, and snacks. Overnight camping ($20, cash only) is available on Thunder Island, the park's beautifully landscaped man-made island. If you're thinking about hiking the PCT, don't miss this inspiring event—in addition to being an incredibly fun networking activity, it's a fantastic opportunity to talk with hikers and wilderness experts who are passionate and knowledgeable about long-distance hiking.

Hundreds of runners dash across the Bridge of the Gods in the annual **Bridge of the Gods Run** (www.bridgeofthegodsrun. com, 2nd Sun. in Aug., $50-95). The run starts on the Washington side of the Columbia River and continues out of Cascade Locks along the Columbia River Highway State Park Trail, which parallels I-84 through the mountains. There are three run options (5K, 10K, or half marathon), all of which end on Thunder Island, where contestants celebrate with a big party and plenty of beer, food, and live music. Register early to ensure the best price; entry fees are more expensive closer to the event date.

Food

Bridgeside (745 NW Wa Na Pa St., 541/374-8477, www.bridgesidedining. com, 6:30am-8pm daily, $9-18) is a classy

I-84 and Hwy. 30: Waterfall Alley

Along the southern walls of the Columbia Gorge, more than a dozen waterfalls plummet over basalt cliffs toward the Columbia River. This area is a temperate rainforest, which means it's green year-round, covered in moss, ferns, and dense undergrowth. Watching water surge out of the mountains into this misty, mossy forest is a unique and worthy experience, not to be missed. Some waterfalls require hikes to see, while others are just a few steps from the parking area.

Allow at least 90 minutes for this 50-mile (81 km) out-and-back detour, more if you plan to picnic, hike, or linger at any of the waterfalls. From Cascade Locks, head west on I-84 for 9 miles (14.5 km) to exit 35 and continue west onto Historic Highway 30.

The first waterfall you'll encounter is **Horsetail Falls**, a 176-foot cascade. Continue west on Highway 30 for 0.5 mile to the Oneonta Creek Trail, where a 0.7-mile trail leads to lower **Oneonta Falls**, a 100-foot thread of water pouring over a cliff. Your next destination is the grandest falls of them all, 620-foot **Multnomah Falls** (2 mi/3.2 km west of Oneonta on Hwy. 30). Expect to share this beautiful sight with hundreds of other visitors, especially during the summer. To avoid the crowds, visit in the early morning or during the shoulder season. There is a visitors center at the base of the falls in a historic lodge that has restrooms and a café.

Next, drive 0.7 mile west on Highway 30 to the base of **Wahkeena Falls,** a 242-foot waterfall that can be enjoyed from a viewing platform, an easy 0.5-mile walk from the parking area. More waterfalls await you to the west.

Drive west on Highway 30 for 3 miles (4.8 km) to **Bridal Veil Falls**, a 120-foot cascade accessible on a 0.6-mile round-trip paved path. To see **Shepherd's Dell Falls,** 1 mile west of Bridal Veil Falls, drive west on Highway 30 and walk on the 0.1-mile paved trail from the parking area to a bridge overlooking the 220-foot waterfall. **Latourell Falls** is a two-level waterfall located 1.2 miles (1.9 km) west of Shepherd's Dell; the 225-foot lower falls can be seen from the parking area, while the 130-foot upper falls requires a 2-mile loop hike into a dramatic river gorge.

Cap your waterfall odyssey with a visit to the **Vista House** (40700 E Historic Columbia River Hwy., 503/344-1638, 9:30am-6pm daily), a museum perched atop a steep cliff at Crown Point. This hexagonal building resembles a cathedral, and its location at Crown Point allows for sweeping views of the Columbia River Gorge Scenic Area. From Latourell Falls, head west on Highway 30 for 2.5 miles (4 km) to arrive at the Vista House.

To return to Cascade Locks, depart from the Vista House and head west on Highway 30 for 2.5 miles (4 km) to the town of Corbett. Follow signs for I-84 and turn right to head north on NE Corbett Hill Road for 1.5 miles (2.4 km), merging onto I-84 east. On your way to Cascade Locks, take exit 40 and stop at the **Bonneville Dam Sturgeon Viewing Center** (70543 NE Herman Loop, Cascade Locks, 541/374-8393, 7am-8pm daily Mar.-Oct., 7am-5pm daily Nov.-Feb., free) to see Herman, a 500-pound, 80-year-old live sturgeon that is almost 11 feet long! Two more waterfalls, **Wahclella Falls** and **Munra Falls,** are both accessible on a 1.8-mile loop hike along the Wahclella Falls Trail. The trailhead is located on the south side of the interstate at exit 40.

Visit www.gorgefriends.org to learn more about Columbia Gorge waterfalls and hikes.

counter-service restaurant with a killer view of the Bridge of the Gods. The 1960s building retains its retro charm with a high, slanted ceiling and 10-foot-tall, north-facing windows that showcase the woodsy river gorge at its narrowest point. The breakfast menu includes standard American fare like eggs, bacon, French toast, and biscuits. Lunch and dinner items are casual and satisfying: burgers, sandwiches, hearty soups, and a salad bar with enough delicious fixings to piece together a full meal.

There's always a line outside **Eastwind Drive-In** (395 Wa Na Pa St., 541/374-8380, 7am-7pm Mon.-Fri., 7:30am-7pm Sat.-Sun., $4-8), an old-school fast-food stand located on the main drag. The food is nothing fancy—bacon cheeseburgers, hamburgers, fishwiches, fry baskets, and giant, swirly ice cream cones—but the retro vibe of the place, including 1950s-style architecture, old-fashioned plastic lettering on the menu boards, and a neon sign with a penguin holding an ice cream cone, is charming. There are a few barstools for seating inside at a red countertop; outdoor picnic tables can be hard to come by on busy summer afternoons. Take advantage of the drive-thru, or walk up and get your food to go to enjoy a grassy picnic at the Marine Park (a five-minute walk under the railroad tracks, toward the river).

★ **Thunder Island Brewing** (515 NW Portage Rd., 971/231-4599, www.thunderislandbrewing.com, 11am-9pm Sun.-Thurs., 11am-10pm Fri.-Sat., $10-15) is perched on the Columbia River right next to the Bridge of the Gods. Choose from upscale sandwiches, giant salads with house-made dressing, and hearty, shareable appetizers. House-brewed beers are on tap, along with guest taps featuring other Gorge breweries, ciders, and both red and white wines. Customize your flight with tastings from four or eight taps. At the outdoor picnic tables, feel the wind in your hair as you gaze over the river to 3,500-foot Table Mountain on the opposite side. (Note: These guys plan to move to a new location on Wa Na Pa Street).

Bridge of the Gods

Cascade Locks Alehouse (500 Wa Na Pa St., 541/374-9310, www.cascadelocksalehouse.com, noon-9pm Wed.-Mon., $9-15) is a casual, family-friendly pub that serves soups, salads, pizzas, sandwiches, and burgers. Cedar shingles on the walls and a big stone fireplace give the place a woodsy, cabin-like feel. With more than 20 beers and ciders on tap and a large, grassy outdoor seating area in back, it's a pleasant place to relax and recharge after a long day of hiking.

Accommodations and Camping

Cascade Locks is one of the most beautiful places in Oregon; however, it's not the quietest. The small community is sandwiched between I-84 and a busy set of train tracks. Expect to hear cars and trains at all hours of the day and night. Bring earplugs if you're a light sleeper.

The ★ **Best Western Plus Columbia River Inn** (735 Wa Na Pa St., 541/374-8777, www.bestwestern.com, $130-250) overlooks the Bridge of the Gods and the Columbia River. The pet-friendly rooms include coffeemakers, microwaves, and refrigerators. Guests enjoy access to a heated indoor pool and lovely outdoor deck, free Wi-Fi, and complimentary breakfast at the **Bridgeside** restaurant, next door.

Bridge of the Gods Motel (630 Wa Na Pa St., 541/374-8628, www.bridgeofgodsmotel.com, $80-160 rooms, $150-170 cabins) is a life-size Lincoln Log cabin. Rooms feature comfy memory foam beds, and two rooms have kitchenettes; some rooms are pet-friendly. Amenities include free Wi-Fi and laundry facilities. If you prefer not to share walls, opt for a cabin, which come with a kitchenette and a jetted tub.

Information and Services

The visitors center in the **Port of Cascade Locks Marine Park** (395 Portage Rd., 10:30am-6pm daily May-Oct.) has information about area history and recreation. The facility is staffed with friendly, knowledgeable locals who love to share information about hiking trails and things to do in their beautiful hometown.

Take advantage of the laundromat at the **Bridge of the Gods Motel** (630 Wa Na Pa St., 541/374-8628, www.bridgeofgodsmotel.com).

You'll need a Northwest Forest Pass ($5/day or $30/year) to park at area trailheads. Pick one up at the **Columbia Market** (450 Wa Na Pa St., 541/374-8425, 7am-9pm Sun.-Thurs., 7am-10pm Fri.-Sat.). This supermarket is also the only place in town to get groceries and camping supplies.

Getting Around

Columbia Area Transit (541/386-4202, www.cattransit.org, $1) offers weekday bus service between Hood River (224 Wasco Loop) and Cascade Locks (Columbia Market, 450 Wa Na Pa St.). Pay your fare in cash (make sure you've got exact change) or download the Hopthru app (www.hopthru.com) on your smartphone to pay your fare digitally.

Washington

Washington

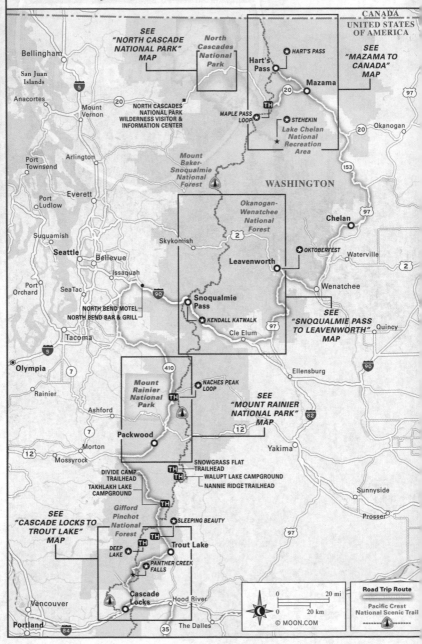

CANADA
UNITED STATES
OF AMERICA

SEE
"NORTH CASCADE
NATIONAL PARK"
MAP

North
Cascades
National
Park

SEE
"MAZAMA TO
CANADA"
MAP

☆ HART'S PASS

Hart's
Pass

Mazama

Bellingham

San Juan
Islands

Anacortes

Mount
Vernon

NORTH CASCADES
NATIONAL PARK
WILDERNESS VISITOR &
INFORMATION CENTER

MAPLE PASS
LOOP

☆ STEHEKIN

Lake Chelan
National
Recreation
Area

Okanogan

Port
Townsend

Arlington

Everett

Mount
Baker-
Snoqualmie
National
Forest

WASHINGTON

Port
Ludlow

Suquamish

Skykomish

Okanogan-
Wenatchee
National
Forest

Chelan

Seattle

Bellevue

☆ OKTOBERFEST

Waterville

Issaquah

Leavenworth

Port
Orchard

SeaTac

Wenatchee

NORTH BEND MOTEL
NORTH BEND BAR & GRILL

Snoqualmie
Pass

SEE
"SNOQUALMIE PASS
TO LEAVENWORTH"
MAP

Quincy

Tacoma

☆ KENDALL KATWALK

Cle Elum

Olympia

Ellensburg

Rainier

Mount
Rainier
National
Park

☆ NACHES PEAK
LOOP

SEE
"MOUNT RAINIER
NATIONAL PARK"
MAP

Ashford

Packwood

Yakima

Morton

Mossyrock

SNOWGRASS FLAT
TRAILHEAD

WALUPT LAKE CAMPGROUND

NANNIE RIDGE TRAILHEAD

DIVIDE CAMP
TRAILHEAD

TAKHLAKH LAKE
CAMPGROUND

Sunnyside

SEE
"CASCADE LOCKS TO
TROUT LAKE"
MAP

Gifford
Pinchot
National
Forest

☆ SLEEPING BEAUTY

Prosser

DEEP
LAKE ☆

Trout Lake

☆ PANTHER CREEK
FALLS

Vancouver

Cascade
Locks

Hood River

Portland

The Dalles

Road Trip Route

Pacific Crest
National Scenic Trail

0   20 mi

0   20 km

© MOON.COM

Highlights

★ **Panther Creek Falls:** Deep in the fern-filled forest of southern Washington, water pours over basalt cliffs on its way to the Columbia River (page 346).

★ **Deep Lake:** Feast on sweet and tangy huckleberries on this hike in the mountainous Indian Heaven Wilderness (page 354).

★ **Sleeping Beauty:** Climb to the top of an ancient volcanic basalt flow to get a bird's-eye view of the southern Washington Cascade Range, including a spectacular view of Mount Adams (page 354).

★ **Naches Peak Loop:** Get up close and personal with the biggest volcano in the Cascade Range at Mount Rainier National Park (page 365).

★ **Kendall Katwalk:** Climb out of the woods and onto a rocky, narrow strip of trail on the impossibly steep side of a granite peak (page 374).

★ **Oktoberfest:** Sip a German bier and sink your teeth into a wurst in the charming Bavarian town of Leavenworth (page 381).

★ **Stehekin:** Take a ferry across Lake Chelan to a peaceful lakefront town with a famous bakery, a 300-foot waterfall, and no roads to the outside world (page 385).

★ **Maple Pass Loop:** Get a peek at the glacier-encrusted peaks of North Cascades National Park on this loop hike around a sparkling tarn (page 394).

★ **Harts Pass:** Golden larches light up the steep mountainsides at Hart's Pass, a campground and hiking area at the end of Washington's highest road (page 396).

Glacier-encrusted volca-noes, moss-covered groves of enormous old-growth trees, and panoramic mountain vistas are hallmarks of this state.

The Washington section of the Pacific Crest Trail is remote. Similar to the High Sierra, much of the Northern Cascades interior is too treacherous to be reached by car. Luckily, a handful of highways snake through mountain passes and give road-trippers a peek into this spectacular alpine landscape.

The Pacific Crest Trail follows the Cascade Range from south to north through the state, dividing Washington into east and west halves.

From the south, the trail departs from Cascade Locks, Oregon, and enters Washington on the Bridge of the Gods near Stevenson. After climbing out of the Columbia River Gorge on the Wind River Highway, the Carson-Guler Road stretches northeast between Carson and Trout Lake, providing access to lush and densely wooded sections of the PCT.

North of Trout Lake, the Pacific Crest Trail nears Mount Adams. Exploration on the western edge of this massive volcano requires travel on unpaved forest roads, but your efforts are rewarded with epic views of mountains and meadows, waterfalls and wildlife.

Between Trout Lake and Mount Adams, Forest Road 23 travels through dense, lowland woods. The PCT parallels the driving route but at much higher elevation, traversing the Goat Rocks Wilderness, which is a roadless area accessible only by hiking.

The PCT intersects with the east side of Mount Rainier National Park, where Highways 123 and 410 access trailheads for some of the most beautiful day hikes in the park. As you drive north from Rainier, the forested foothills of southern Washington give way to the steep granite mountainsides of the North Cascades.

An hour east of Seattle, I-90 crosses the PCT at Snoqualmie Pass in the Alpine Lakes Wilderness. This area is a popular hiking destination for urban dwellers.

North of Snoqualmie Pass, there are only three places to access the Washington PCT by car: on U.S. 2 just west of Leavenworth, in North Cascades National Park at Rainy Pass, and at remote Hart's Pass near Mazama.

North Cascades National Park marks the end of the PCT in Washington, at least the portion that's accessible by car. From here, our road trip heads west to return to the scenic coast at Bellingham. With passport in hand, adventurous travelers can head north across the Canadian border to the northern terminus monument in Manning Park, BC.

Planning Your Time
Where to Go

With **one week,** you can explore the best parts of the state. Start at the Columbia River Gorge and travel north past the Mount Adams and Mount Rainier volcanoes, through the Alpine Lakes Wilderness east of Seattle, and into the North Cascades. Mount Rainier National Park is a must-see, and the hulking volcano is only one aspect of the park's splendor. Wildflowers light the surrounding hillsides in summer and are a major attraction.

If your time is limited, spend it in the remote North Cascades; though it requires a long drive from urban areas, the vast and astonishing beauty is beyond impressive and the drive along the North Cascades Highway is worth the trip.

When to Go

Summer is the only time to travel the PCT. Although Washington is known for rain, the mountains see a lot of sun

Day Trips on the PCT

Leave the hustle and bustle of the big city for the day, and drive 1-3 hours to scenic mountaintop hikes on the PCT.

From Portland

Near the town of **Carson,** hike along the PCT to **Red Mountain Fire Lookout,** where you can see five snowcapped Cascade volcanoes. Or start at the base of **Mount Adams** to see pink and purple wildflower blooms light up the fields near **Killen Creek Meadows.**

From Seattle

Mount Rainier National Park is just 70 miles (113 km) southeast of the city, where the **Naches Peak Loop** follows the PCT through the scenic east edge of the park. Step onto the PCT at **Snoqualmie Pass** for a hike to dramatic **Kendall Katwalk** in the Alpine Lakes Wilderness.

Or head to **Stevens Pass,** where the PCT leads to the top of **Big Chief Mountain,** offering endless vistas of craggy peaks on all horizons.

---

in **July, August,** and **September.** Harsh winter conditions keep the hiking season short—snowfall starts in October and doesn't melt until May or June. Mosquitoes in the alpine areas are vicious during June and early July snowmelt. Bring bug repellent in June, or schedule your PCT trip during August and September.

Between **November and June,** several **highways close,** including the North Cascades Scenic Byway, Highways 410 and 123 near Mount Rainier, and roads in the heavily wooded Gifford Pinchot National Forest between the Columbia River and U.S. 12 (although the town of Trout Lake is accessible year-round).

Getting There

Car

From Portland, Oregon

Take I-5 north for 9 miles (14.5 km) to Vancouver, Washington. In Vancouver, head east on scenic Highway 14 for 40 miles (64 km). The road follows the northern shore of the Columbia River Gorge to connect with the PCT at the Bridge of the Gods near Stevenson.

Following the PCT in Oregon, you'll end up in Cascade Locks at the Bridge of the Gods. You can walk or drive north across the bridge in less than 1 mile, entering Washington at Highway 14 about 3.2 miles (5.1 km) west of Stevenson.

From Seattle

The PCT is most easily accessed at Snoqualmie Pass. Take I-90 east for 52 miles (84 km) to Snoqualmie Pass. Or, to begin your northbound road trip at the Oregon-Washington border, take I-5 south from Seattle for 165 miles (265 km) to Vancouver, Washington, then head east on Highway 14 for 40 miles (64 km) to the Bridge of the Gods.

Air

Fly into **Portland International Airport** (PDX, 7000 NE Airport Way, Portland, OR, 877/739-4636, www.pdx.com) to explore the southern part of the PCT, including the Columbia River Gorge and Mount Adams. Stevenson, Carson, and Trout Lake are a 1-2 hour drive from the airport.

Mount Rainier and the northern PCT are closer to Seattle and the **Seattle-Tacoma International Airport** (SEA, 17801 International Blvd., Seattle, WA, 800/544-1965, www.portseattle.org).

Best Restaurants

★ **Red Bluff Tap House, Stevenson:** Local beers, wines, and ciders complement elegant small plates at this refined restaurant (page 349).

★ **Crosscut Espresso & Deli, Carson:** This lumber-themed coffee shop serves great burritos and sandwiches (page 349).

★ **Trout Lake Country Inn, Trout Lake:** This homey restaurant serves comforting American cuisine in a historic building (page 356).

★ **Cliff Droppers Burgers, Packwood:** Bite into a juicy burger before hitting the slopes or trails near Mount Rainer (page 359).

★ **Paradise Inn Dining Room, Mount Rainier National Park:** Come here for the fanciest food in the national park (page 370).

★ **North Bend Bar & Grill, North Bend:** This is the best place west of Snoqualmie Pass for a post-hike burger and brew (page 376).

★ **Fresh Burger Café, Leavenworth:** Enjoy a perfect post-hike meal at this café, located in a charming Bavarian village (page 383).

★ **Stehekin Pastry Company, Stehekin:** This bakery is famous for enormous, delectable cinnamon rolls that beckon thru-hikers for miles (page 389).

★ **Mazama Store, Mazama:** An epicurean diamond in the rough, this upscale shop serves delectable sandwiches and baked goods (page 397).

Train

Amtrak (800/872-7245, www.amtrak.com) operates train service throughout the state. The *Cascades* route operates north-south along the I-5 corridor, with stops in Portland, Oregon; Seattle, Washington; and Vancouver, British Columbia, with a handful of smaller cities in between. The east-west *Empire Builder* route enters Washington near Spokane to end in Seattle.

Bus

BoltBus (877/265-8287, www.boltbus.com) offers express service between Portland, Seattle, and Bellingham with free onboard Wi-Fi. **Greyhound** (800-231-2222, www.greyhound.com) provides bus service to more than 50 stations throughout the state, including three locations in Seattle.

Stevenson, Carson, and the Columbia River Gorge

Just 4 miles (6.4 km) east of the PCT and the Bridge of the Gods, historic Stevenson is a popular spot for post-hike brews and eats. The town sits on the north shore of the Columbia River, and views of the surrounding peaks are stunning. As the PCT travels north out of the river gorge, it traces the edge of Beacon Rock State Park, a popular hiking destination with trails that showcase the unique geology of what's known locally as "The Gorge." Five miles northeast of Stevenson, the small town of Carson is an ideal jumping-off spot for PCT hikes that showcase mossy, fern-filled forests and beautiful, tumbling waterfalls as creeks and rivers make their way toward the mighty Columbia.

Best Accommodations

★ **Skamania Lodge, Stevenson:** Set on a beautiful, forested property with sweeping views of the Columbia River, this is the busiest resort in the Gorge (page 350).

★ **Takhlakh Lake Campground, Trout Lake:** Overnight stays at this campsite include stunning views of Mount Adams (page 357).

★ **Crest Trail Lodge, Packwood:** A generous (free) breakfast lures PCT hikers to this lodge in Packwood (page 361).

★ **Paradise Inn, Mount Rainier National Park:** It's easy to sacrifice modern amenities for the larger-than-life views of Mount Rainier at this national park lodge (page 370).

★ **Obertal Inn, Leavenworth:** A gourmet breakfast is sure to entice foodies to this inn near Stevens Pass (page 384).

★ **Stehekin Log Cabins, Stehekin:** Next-door access to Stehekin's delicious bakery and a complimentary vehicle for guests makes this the place to stay in the Stehekin Valley (page 390).

★ **Freestone Inn at Wilson Ranch, Mazama:** This luxurious mountain retreat has cabins, plentiful amenities, and stand-out dining (page 398).

★ **Rolling Huts, Mazama:** Equal parts tiny house, cabin, and luxury apartment, these unique "huts" are unlike anything else (page 398).

★ **Ross Lake Resort, North Cascades National Park:** These floating lakefront cabins are accessible only by boat (page 402).

Getting There

From Cascade Locks, Oregon, drive north over the Bridge of the Gods and head east on Highway 14 for 3 miles (4.8 km) to Stevenson.

From Vancouver, Washington, follow Highway 14 east for 45 miles (72 km), about a 50-minute drive.

Carson is 4.5 miles (7.2 km) northeast of Stevenson. From Stevenson, take Highway 14 east for 3.5 miles (5.6 km), then veer left onto the Wind River Highway. Travel north for 1 mile (1.6 km) to arrive in Carson.

Sights

Columbia Gorge Interpretive Center Museum

History buffs shouldn't miss the

Columbia Gorge Interpretive Center Museum (990 SW Rock Creek Dr., Stevenson, 509/427-8211, www.columbiagorge.org, 9am-5pm daily, $10), where captivating exhibits detail the unique geology of the region. Cultural displays span the lives of past and present Gorge inhabitants.

Bonneville Dam

The Columbia River was forever altered by a series of dams built along its passage from Canada to the Pacific Ocean. When it was built in the 1930s, the Bonneville Dam was the largest project of its kind in the entire country. The dam site was selected due to the narrow passage of the Columbia River where the Bridge of the Gods spans the river.

The construction of the dam raised the river level significantly—the Bridge of the Gods was raised to accommodate the higher water levels, and the locks in Cascade Locks, for which the town was named, were drowned. Had this dam not been constructed, PCT hikers would have a very different view of the river from the bridge, one that included rapids so dangerous, safe passage was required through locks near the shoreline.

At the **Bonneville Dam Washington Shore Visitor Center** (Hwy. 14, 5 mi/8 km west of Stevenson, 509/427-4281, www.nwp.usace.army.mil, 9am-5pm daily, free) two outdoor decks are open to public visitation. On the upper deck, watch for ospreys, large birds of prey that like to hunt for fish in the waters below. The lower deck follows the edge of a fish ladder (a river channel designed for upstream and downstream fish travel). The indoor section of the visitors center features exhibits about the history of fishing in the Columbia River, including Native American practices and the development of technologies utilized by settlers. This indoor area, carpeted in rainbow colors for some bizarre reason, also features windows looking into the underwater section of the fish ladder. During the fall (late Aug.-early Nov.), you can watch salmon swimming upstream.

High Bridge

The Columbia Gorge may be the grandest gorge of all, but each of its tributaries in this region carved gorges of their own. The Wind River, with headwaters in the Gifford Pinchot National Forest near the path of the Pacific Crest Trail, is one of them. The PCT crosses the Wind River and the Wind River Highway north of Carson.

The most spectacular part of the river's gorge is actually closer to town at 270-foot-tall Carl Lundy Jr. Bridge, known locally as **High Bridge** (2.5 mi/4 km north of Carson on Wind River Hwy.). Park safely on the south side of the bridge and then walk across it to marvel at the Wind River as it winds through a forested gulch with moss-covered boulders. Keep your eyes peeled for whitewater kayakers—this section of the Wind River is a popular run for expert Class IV and V whitewater boaters.

★ Panther Creek Falls

Panther Creek Falls (www.fs.usda.gov) is a wondrous delight of the Pacific Northwest. Embedded in the fern- and cedar-speckled Gifford Pinchot National Forest, Panther Creek is actually a combination of waterfalls: dozens of natural springs shoot out of a basalt column next to the creek's 20-foot cascade over a neighboring cliff. Some of these springs blast over the moss-encrusted rocks while others barely trickle, forming veils, streams, and threads of white water.

A viewing platform on the south side of the creek overlooks the falls.

Getting There

From the town of Carson, drive north on Wind River Highway for 4.8 miles (7.7 km). Turn right on Old State Road, then take an immediate left onto Forest Road 65, following signs for Panther Creek Campground. Continue on Forest Road 65 for 7.9 miles (12.7 km). The 0.3-mile footpath to the viewing platform is on the north side of the road, about 100 feet west of the parking area (which is on the south side).

Visit between **April and October** to avoid snow, ice, and potentially dangerous winter driving conditions.

Hiking
Beacon Rock

Distance: 1.3 mi/2.1 km round-trip
Duration: 1 hour
Elevation change: 560 ft/171 m
Effort: Moderate
Trailhead: Beacon Rock
Pass/Fee: Discover Pass

Aptly named Beacon Rock is a huge, distinct basalt tower on the north shore of the Columbia River. The climb to the top is on a well-graded cement and wooden path with handrails (built in 1918!).

The hike begins on the north side of the rock next to Highway 14, between two parking areas. Walk on a dirt trail through woods for 0.1 mile before reaching the edge of the rock, where you'll step onto a constructed pathway. The path hugs the western side of the rock for 0.3 mile to where it begins a four-dozen-switchback ascent up the southern edge. There are almost as many places to stop for views are there are switchbacks. From the top, enjoy a unique, bird's-eye perspective of the nearby Bonneville Dam and the dramatic, forested slopes of the Columbia Gorge. Hamilton Mountain is across Highway 14 to the north; the Pacific Crest Trail passes through the area just east of Hamilton.

Across the mighty river, the Oregon community of Warrendale is nestled on the river's shoreline. Many of the Gorge's famous waterfalls lie west.

Hamilton Mountain

Distance: 7.5 mi/12.1 km round-trip
Duration: 4 hours
Elevation change: 2,200 ft/671 m
Effort: Moderate
Trailhead: Hamilton Mountain
Pass/Fee: Discover Pass

This hike inside **Beacon Rock State Park** visits a unique waterfall and showcases the incredible scenery of the Columbia Gorge National Scenic Area, including stunning views of the river gorge and the path of the nearby PCT. (Hamilton Mountain is one mile west of the Pacific Crest Trail as it climbs out of the Gorge.)

Start your hike by walking northeast out of the parking area into the forest on the Hamilton Mountain Trail. After passing under a set of power lines at 0.5 mile, you're back in the forest and climbing steadily. Take the right fork at 1.1 miles to a viewing platform, where Hardy Creek tumbles through a steep canyon. Return to the main trail and continue

northeast, arriving at Pool of the Winds at 1.2 miles, where Hardy Creek blasts through a crevice in the basalt cliff. After the falls, the trail continues east to a fork at 1.4 miles. Stay right and continue east on the Hamilton Mountain Trail to summit Hamilton Mountain. (The left fork is the Hardy Creek Trail, which you'll return on during your descent.) The stretch between 1.5 and 2.1 miles are the steepest of the hike as the trail climbs onto an exposed rock face. The best views of the Gorge and Table Mountain are to the east at 2.4 miles on a rocky outcropping.

After stopping to enjoy the views, continue climbing through a series of switchbacks to reach the summit at 3 miles. The summit is nestled in a thick forest, and while it doesn't offer any views, it does promise relief from any more elevation gain.

To make a loop back down, continue on the trail and stay left at 3.8 miles, heading west. Make another sharp left at 3.9 miles onto the southbound **Hardy Creek Trail.** Rejoin the main trail at 6.2 miles, passing Pool of the Winds on your way down.

Rock Creek Bridge

Distance: 1.5 mi/2.4 km round-trip
Duration: 30 minutes-1 hour
Elevation change: 215 ft/66 m
Effort: Easy
Trailhead: Pacific Crest Trail at Red Bluff Road
Pass/Fee: Northwest Forest Pass

It will take you longer to drive to this hike than it will to walk to the bridge, but if you're seeking solitude, this little-used section of the Pacific Crest Trail through the forest offers just that, plus you'll get to see two beautiful waterfalls on the way to the trailhead. During your hike, Snag Creek and Rock Creek babble nearby as the trail meanders through thick, moss-covered groves of conifers.

From Red Bluff Road, the Pacific Crest Trail departs from the road and heads west. Arrive at Snag Creek at 0.3 mile and cross carefully on boulders or

logs. The path continues westward along a steep embankment with Rock Creek rushing through the valley below. At 0.6 mile, the trail descends to Rock Creek, where a bridge spans the waterway. This is a beautiful place to stop and marvel at the serene woodland surroundings.

To make this a longer hike, continue south on the PCT up out of the Rock Creek drainage and see more of the dense, mossy woods the region is famous for.

Getting There

This 10-mile (16.1-km) drive takes about 30 minutes from Stevenson. From the intersection of Highway 14 and SW Rock Creek Drive in Stevenson, take SW Rock Creek Drive northwest for 0.6 mile, then bear right onto Ryan-Allen Road. Turn right at 0.4 mile to stay on Ryan-Allen Road for another 0.5 mile, then make a left to head northwest on Red Bluff Road and set a trip mileage counter. Keep right just after a small bridge. As the pavement ends, Red Bluff Road becomes CG Road 2000.

At mile 5.7, pass **Steep Creek Falls,** visible from your car on the south side of Rock Creek. At 6 miles (9.7 km), park the car and look for a trail on the south side of the road. A one-minute walk on this path leads to the creek's edge where you can see **Heaven and Hell Falls,** a two-part waterfall that tumbles over rocky basalt outcroppings in the creek bed.

Return to the car and continue west on Red Bluff Road/CG Road 2000 to 8 miles (12.9 km), where you'll turn right on CG Road 2070 (may not be marked). Go about 0.3 mile to reach the PCT crossing (easy to miss). Look for the PCT crest and a white, diamond-shaped reflective panel on a pine tree on the south side of the road.

From top to bottom: Beacon Rock trail; Steep Creek Falls; Backwoods Brewing.

Recreation

Only locals are not astonished by the size and density of the coniferous trees in this part of the Pacific Northwest. Wooden platforms, ladders, and ziplines at **Skamania Lodge Adventures** (1131 Skamania Lodge Way, Stevenson, 509/427-0202, www.zipnskamania. com, $69-99) offer the chance to climb into the trees and sail through them at thrilling speeds. An exhilarating activity for kids (60-plus lbs.) and adults, this zipline course explores the forest high above the ground from the safety of your harness.

Entertainment and Events
Breweries

Backwoods Brewing (1162 Wind River Hwy., Carson, 509/427-3412, www. backwoodsbrewingcompany.com, 11:30am-9pm daily, $11-13) is a local watering hole and brewpub serving pizzas, sandwiches, and homemade desserts served in mason jars. The interior resembles a log cabin, and the lumberjack vibe is homey and welcoming. Typical of Pacific Northwest breweries, there are always at least two IPAs on tap, and the Pecan Pie Porter and Copperline Amber are two of the most popular beers.

With a large, lovely patio adorned in hop vines and shaded by hardwoods, **Walking Man Brewing** (240 1st St., Stevenson, 509/427-5520, www. walkingmanbeer.com, 11:30am-9pm Wed.-Sun. and Labor Day, $8-14) is a beautiful place to enjoy a cold beer after a hike. Tasting flights include five-ounce pours of the 10 house-brewed beers. The brewpub is located in the downstairs of a historic building, with a cozy Irish bar interior set with dark-wood paneling and green leather booths. Pizzas, sandwiches, salads, and appetizers are on the menu.

Festivals and Events

Every summer, Stevenson welcomes 16 craft breweries and hundreds of blues fans to boogie down and drink up at the **Gorge Blues & Brews Festival** (Skamania County Fairgrounds, 710 SW Rock Creek Dr., Stevenson, www. gorgebluesandbrews.com, 3rd weekend in June, $20 advance, $25 at the door). Food vendors specialize in barbecue, Southern specialties, authentic Mexican dishes, and even fruit smoothies. Headliners in previous years include Hillstomp, Patrick Lamb and the Funkified Band, and International Blues Challenge winners Rae Gordon and the Backseat Drivers. Friday evening festivities are free to attend, and Saturday's admission fee includes a commemorative beer mug or wine glass, plus five drink tokens to sample the brews and beverages of the Gorge.

Food

The 16 taps at ★ **Red Bluff Tap House** (256 2nd St., Stevenson, 509/427-4979, www.redblufftaphouse.com, 11am-9pm Sun.-Thurs., 11am-10pm Fri.-Sat., $11-14) feature local beers, wines, and ciders. The space feels natural yet refined, with exposed brick and polished wood. The elegant small plates are great for sharing (the crispy Brussels sprouts and empanadas with chimichurri are heavenly); burgers and heartier entrées are also available.

On the Stevenson waterfront, **Clark and Lewie's** (130 SW Cascade Ave., Stevenson, 509/219-0097, www. clarkandlewies.com, 11:30am-8:30pm Mon. and Wed.-Thurs., 11:30am-9pm Fri., 10am-9pm Sat., 10am-8pm Sun., $8-16) serves soups, salads, sandwiches, and shareable appetizers named after the famous explorers. There's no better deck in Stevenson to enjoy a meal and a view of the Columbia River.

★ **Crosscut Espresso & Deli** (1252 Wind River Hwy., Carson, 509/427-4407, 6am-4:30pm Mon.-Fri., 8am-4:30pm Sat.-Sun, $4-9) is a lumber-themed coffee shop on the north side of town. Hearty, satisfying breakfast burritos and sandwiches are popular among locals and visitors. Lunch sandwiches and wraps are available with gluten-free options or as salads. There's a drive-thru window, plus plenty of seating inside.

Accommodations

★ **Skamania Lodge** (1131 SW Skamania Lodge Way, Stevenson, 509/314-4177, www.destinationhotels.com, $230-300) is the biggest and busiest resort in the Gorge. The lobby is constructed of massive, beautiful logs with a three-story stone fireplace framed by picture windows overlooking the Columbia Gorge. Guest rooms and suites come with mini-fridges, microwaves, and coffeemakers; some have fireplaces or river views. For those seeking privacy, book one of the treehouses nestled in a grove of Douglas firs. Each comes with a fireplace and a deck overlooking the property, and all are set apart from the hustle and bustle of the main building.

Studios at the **Columbia Gorge Riverside Lodge** (200 SW Cascade Ave., Stevenson, 509/427-5650, www. cgriversidelodge.com, $109-129) feature worldly themes—Afrika, the Far East, Calypso—with unique textiles. Studios are built into multi-unit log cabins with gas fireplaces, kitchenettes, and outdoor river-facing decks with shared hot tubs. The beautiful riverfront property offers world-class views of the mighty Columbia River and the dramatic gorge walls.

Built above the steep canyon walls of the Wind River, **Carson Hot Springs Resort** (372 St. Martin's Springs Rd., Carson, 509/427-8296, www. carsonhotspringsresort.com, $179-249) is a rustic resort that dates to the early 1900s. (Some of the buildings are newer.) The quiet rooms are appointed with modern amenities. An on-site spa offers a signature "bath and wrap" experience ($30-35), a 25-minute mineral soak followed by a tight linen fabric body wrap.

Camping

Tucked deep into the forest near the Wind River, **Panther Creek Campground** (8 mi/12.9 km north of Carson, Forest Rd. 65, www.fs.usda.gov, May-Sept., $18-34) offers a shady escape on hot summer days. The PCT meets Panther Creek Road just south of the campground, crossing the creek itself on the east side of the road. The campground gets busy on summer weekends; **reserve** in advance (877/444-6777, www.recreation.gov) to save your spot under the trees.

Information and Services

Stop by the **Skamania County Chamber of Commerce** (167 NW 2nd Ave., Stevenson, 509/427-8911, www.skamania.org, 8:30am-5pm Mon.-Fri., 9am-5pm Sat., 10am-5pm Sun.) to find out about local happenings and pick up area maps, including *The Skamania County Fun Map:* an illustrated guide to the county, which is almost entirely made up of national forest.

Trout Lake and Mount Adams

Trout Lake is a sleepy rural community in a valley south of Mount Adams. The town's view of the second-highest peak in the state (one of five active volcanoes in the Washington Cascades) is larger than life. Trout Lake offers a handful of food and lodging options, but outdoor recreation is what draws visitors to the area: world-class hiking, whitewater boating, mountaineering, fishing, and camping are all within a few miles.

The Pacific Crest Trail passes through huckleberry-laden **Indian Heaven Wilderness,** 15 miles (24 km) west of Trout Lake, and along the western base of Mount Adams, 15 miles (24 km) to the north. While these two high-elevation areas of the PCT are only accessible during the summer, the Trout Lake Valley is a popular cross-country skiing area during the snowy winter months.

Cascade Locks to Trout Lake

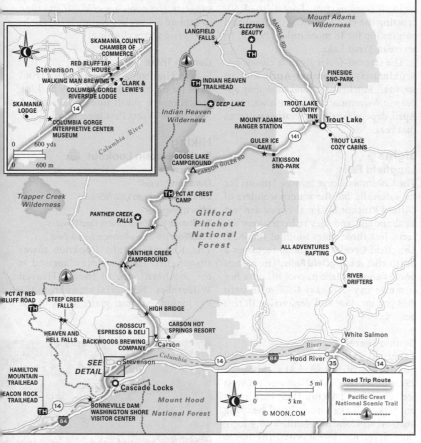

Getting There

Trout Lake lies 38 miles (64 km) north-east of Stevenson. There are two routes to get there.

Highways 14 and 141

This beautiful scenic route follows the northern shore of the Columbia River through the Columbia Gorge National Scenic Area, and is the most popular route between Stevenson and Trout Lake. From Stevenson, follow Highway 14 east for 19 miles (31 km), then turn left on Highway 141 north. Drive 19 miles (31 km) to Trout Lake. There are multiple places to stop and take pictures of the dramatic mountain scenery.

Carson-Guler Road

This remote route more closely follows the path of the Pacific Crest Trail from Stevenson to Trout Lake, through the Cascade foothills between the Columbia River Gorge and the Trout Lake Valley. From Carson, take the Wind River Highway north for 4.8 miles (7.7 km) and turn right onto Old State Road. Make an immediate left to continue north on

Forest Road 65 toward Panther Creek. Continue 11 miles (17.7 km) and turn right to head east on Forest Road 60, crossing the PCT at 2 miles (3.2 km) and continuing for 18 more miles (29 km) to arrive in Trout Lake.

The Carson-Guler Road is closed approximately **December-April** due to snowfall. Patches of ice and snow may appear in November and remain well into April, depending on the weather patterns that year.

Sights
Langfield Falls

The Columbia Gorge may be famous for its waterfalls, but the watery wonders of Gifford Pinchot National Forest are just as abundant, and they're better-kept secrets. Just three miles south of the PCT, Langfield Creek tumbles 60 feet over a basalt cliff at **Langfield Falls.** The plunge pool is a great place to cool off on a hot summer day. An easy 0.25-mile path gets you up close and personal with this beauty.

Getting There

Langfield Falls is 14 miles (22.5 km) northwest of Trout Lake, about a 25-minute drive. Take Highway 141 west for 1.5 miles (2.4 km), then turn right onto Trout Lake Creek Road heading northwest. Continue 4 miles (6.4 km), then drive northwest when the name of the road changes to Forest Road 88. Reach Big Tire Junction 8.5 miles (13.7 km) later. A parking area is on the right, north of the big tire. A Northwest Forest Pass is required.

Guler Ice Cave

Do you know the difference between stalagmites and stalactites? Find both in the **Guler Ice Cave** (May-Nov.), a 650-foot cave formed by lava flows from Mount Adams 15,000 years ago. A wooden staircase leads underground into a giant, dark cavern. With a flashlight, you can see a diverse array of ice formations, some of which stretch all the way from the musty cave's floor to its ceiling. As the name suggests, the caves are cold—if you plan to explore below the ground, bring flashlights and warm clothing.

Getting There

Follow Highway 141 west out of Trout Lake for 6.5 miles (10.5 km). A parking area is on the south side of the road. A Northwest Forest Pass is required.

Hiking
Red Mountain Lookout

Distance: 9.4-10 mi/15.1-16.1 km round-trip
Duration: 5 hours
Elevation change: 1,700 ft/518 m
Effort: Strenuous
Trailhead: Pacific Crest Trail at Crest Camp
Pass/Fee: Self-issue wilderness permit (free)

The Red Mountain Lookout tower sits perched atop a volcanic mound at the southern edge of Indian Heaven Wilderness. Territorial views from the top include all four giant peaks of the area—St. Helens, Rainier, Adams, and Hood—and the forested, glacier-formed valleys between them.

Start your hike at the PCT trailhead on the north side of the road. After filling out your wilderness permit, head north on the PCT through a dense pine, cedar, and hemlock forest. Indian Heaven Wilderness is known for its abundance of lakes, and you'll pass by your first pond at 1.7 miles. Pay close attention to the trail at 2 miles—this is the 2,200-mile point for PCT thru-hikers traveling from Mexico to Canada (you may see this number on the trail, fashioned from rocks or pine cones). The forest opens up into your first of many meadows at 2.1 miles; at 2.7 miles, the lookout tower comes into view on the southwest horizon. At a trail junction at 3.1 miles, turn left to head west on the 0.6-mile Shortcut Trail toward Indian Racetrack. The racetrack is a trail in a meadow that was historically used for horse racing during annual Native

American gatherings in the area. Turn around here for a 9.4-mile hike, or continue to the lookout tower on the steep, southbound Indian Racetrack Trail, which meets the Shortcut Trail on the southwest side of the meadow.

Between miles 3.7 and 4.7, you'll climb 530 feet (162 m) onto Red Mountain. Meet a fire service road at 4.7 miles and continue south for 0.3 mile to the defunct, boarded-up tower. Enjoy views of Mount St. Helens to the northwest, Mount Rainier to the north, Mount Adams to the northeast, Mount Hood to the southeast, and the Gifford Pinchot National Forest's endless valleys of trees.

Return the way you came for a 10-mile round-trip hike, or use the fire access road to shave off a mile. The road makes a sharp turn at the intersection with Indian Racetrack Trail (where you approached). Follow the road south for 3.2 miles to the gated Carson-Guler Road, then turn left to walk west on the road for 0.5 mile back to your car.

Trout Lake and Mount Adams

Getting There

Crest Camp trailhead is 18 miles (29 km) southwest of Trout Lake, about a 35-minute drive. Follow Highway 141 out of Trout Lake west for 18 miles (29 km); stay straight as the name of the road changes to Carson-Guler Road at 6 miles (9.7 km), then to Forest Road 60 at 9.5 miles (15.3 km). The trailhead is on the north side of the road across from Crest Camp.

TOP EXPERIENCE

★ Deep Lake, Lemei Rock, and Lake Wapiki

Distance: 5-10 mi/8-16.1 km round-trip
Duration: 2.5-5 hours
Elevation change: 1,100-2,200 ft/335-671 m
Effort: Moderate/Strenuous
Trailhead: Indian Heaven #33
Pass/Fee: Northwest Forest Pass and self-issue wilderness permit (free)

This hike through the Indian Heaven Wilderness showcases the best scenery of the region and takes you through the area's most abundant huckleberry fields. The price of admission is steep—a 1,110-foot ascent from the trailhead to the high alpine plateau—but the rewards are divine: spectacular mountain views, sparkling alpine lakes, and endless delectable huckleberries.

From the parking area, walk southwest on Indian Heaven Trail, crossing Cultus Creek and immediately beginning the grueling climb. The forest is dense for the first 1.1 miles before you reach a jagged, exposed edge where you can step out and soak up amazing territorial views of the valley between Indian Heaven and Mount Adams. The volcano, of course, is glorious. Look left (north) to see Mount Rainier, the tallest point in Washington, peeking over the horizon. This view alone is worthy of its own hike, but keep walking to reap more rewards. Reach your first meadow at 1.6 miles and look for ripe huckleberries on the bushes nearby. More fantastic views

of Mount Adams lie through the trees at 2.1 miles. The trail meets the Deep Lake spur trail at 2.3 miles; continue straight toward Lemei Rock and Lake Wapiki, or take the 0.1-mile eastbound trail to **Deep Lake** (4.8 mi/7.7 km rt, 1,100 ft/335 m, moderate) to swim, picnic, camp, or turn around for a 5-mile round-trip hike with a 1,110-foot elevation gain.

To carry on toward **Lake Wapiki** (10 mi/16.1 km rt, 2,200 ft/671 m, strenuous), continue south past Cultus Lake for 0.2 mile before meeting the Lemei Trail and turning left to walk east. Pass through a lovely meadow and begin a gentle ascent toward the north side of Lemei Rock, the tallest point between Mount Adams and Mount St. Helens. The trail gets a little steeper at mile 3.6 as it climbs onto the saddle that makes up the eastern side of **Lemei Rock** (8.6 mi/13.8 km rt, 1,600 ft/488 m, moderate). Stop at mile 3.7 to check out Mount Rainier to the north and Mount St. Helens to the northwest. The trail makes a horseshoe bend and descends; take the Lake Wapiki spur trail at 4.6 miles. The lake is 0.4 mile down the trail, nestled into a crater on the east side of Lemei Rock.

Getting There

The Indian Heaven Trail #33 trailhead is located in the Cultus Creek Campground, which is 17 miles (27 km) northwest of Trout Lake. Follow Highway 141 west out of town, continuing straight at 5.8 miles (9.3 km) when the name of the road changes to Carson-Guler Road. At 7.8 miles (12.6 km), turn right onto Forest Road 24 toward Cultus Creek Campground. After 9 miles (14.5 km), turn left into the campground circle and continue to the southern end of the campground loop where there is a parking area for the trailhead.

★ Sleeping Beauty

Distance: 2.3 mi/3.7 km round-trip
Duration: 1.5 hours
Elevation change: 1,300 ft/396 m

Effort: Moderate

Trailhead: Sleeping Beauty

Climb to the top of Sleeping Beauty, an iconic basalt formation towering above Trout Lake and the PCT's route through the woods, to get a better sense of the region.

Begin by hiking north out of the parking area into dense woods. Note: The road continues east after the parking area, but do not walk this way; it dead-ends 0.25 mile later. Right away, the elevation gain begins and doesn't quit. Views of the surrounding terrain don't appear until the forest begins to thin at 1.1 miles and the rocky outcropping known as Sleeping Beauty appears.

Climb for another 0.1 mile to the top of the point, which may be quite windy, and soak up the larger-than-life views of Mount Adams, as well as a sweeping territorial view of the entire area. Once you've reached the high point, continue west over the rocks toward the remains of an old lookout tower. Mount Hood is on the southern horizon and Mount St. Helens is to the west.

Getting There

From Trout Lake, follow Highway 141 west for 1.5 miles (2.4 km), then turn right to continue west onto Trout Lake Creek Road. As the road bends north, continue 5.5 miles (8.9 km), then veer right to travel north on Forest Road 8810. After 6.2 miles (10 km), turn right onto Forest Road 40, following signs for Sleeping Beauty Trail. The parking area is in 0.4 mile.

Killen Creek Meadows

Distance: 10 mi/16.1 km round-trip

Duration: 5 hours

Elevation change: 1,470 ft/448 m

Effort: Moderate

Trailhead: Divide Camp #112

Pass/Fee: Self-issue wilderness permit (free)

This Pacific Crest Trail hike along the northeast base of Mount Adams is known for gorgeous wildflower blooms, waterfalls, and extremely impressive views of the volcano. Note: This hike includes a crossing of Adams Creek, and there is no bridge. Hikers are advised to use trekking poles and cross carefully on logs, rocks, or through the creek itself.

Start hiking on the Divide Camp Trail, which climbs 1,300 feet (396 m) through pine and cedar forest before delivering you to the Pacific Crest Trail. Hear the rushing waters of Adams Creek at 0.8 mile and get a good look at the flow at 1.8 miles when the trail skirts the southern edge of the water. The woods open into a vast, flower-speckled meadow at 2 miles, with Mount Adams and the Adams Glacier as a massive, dramatic backdrop. Continue straight past the Divide Camp spur and meet the PCT at 2.8 miles. Congratulations—you've accomplished the bulk of the climbing!

The Pacific Crest Trail is gently graded during the rest of the hike to Killen Creek Meadows; you'll only climb another 170 feet over the next 2 miles. Follow the PCT northbound through a lava field to the edge of Adams Creek at 3.1 miles. Use caution as you cross the creek, taking your time and finding strong footing with each step. The trail continues northeast, winding through pockets of limber pines, grassy meadows, and fields of wildflowers. On clear days, Mount St. Helens, Mount Rainier, and Goat Rocks (the once-volcanic area between Adams and Rainier) are visible on the western and northern horizons.

Arrive at Killen Creek Meadows at 5 miles. The meadow features two cascading waterfalls as well as a lake, which is located 0.25 mile north of the PCT bridge over Killen Creek. Follow the spur trail out of the creekside campsite to the lakeshore. Look for salamanders in the crystal clear water, and walk to the beach on the northwest shore for a mirrored reflection of the snowy volcano in the water's surface.

Getting There

Divide Camp trailhead is 28 miles (45 km) north of Trout Lake, about an hour's drive. Follow Mount Adams Road north out of town for 1.3 miles (2.1 km), then veer left at the fork onto Forest Road 23 toward Randle, following for 23 miles (37 km). Veer right onto Forest Road 2329 and continue north, then stay right at the fork at 1.2 miles (1.9 km) to stay on 2329. Follow for 2.3 miles (3.7 km) to the trailhead parking lot.

Recreation
Whitewater Rafting

The rapids of the White Salmon River attract whitewater enthusiasts from around the world. For adventure, excitement, and exclusive views of the river's diverse geology and wildlife, hop into a boat with one of the local rafting companies. Beginners and experienced paddlers are equally welcome on these excursions. **River Drifters** (856 Hwy. 141, 509/493-2816, www.riverdrifters.net) offers guided half-day ($65) and full-day ($125, lunch included) trips along this wild and scenic river, or join **All Adventures Rafting** (1256 Hwy. 141, 509/998-8545, www. adventuresrafting.com, $70) for 2.5-hour tours through Class III, IV, and V rapids.

Winter Sports

In the winter, the forests surrounding Trout Lake are transformed into peaceful, pristine, snowy wonderlands. There are many popular snowshoeing and cross-country skiing trails. **Atkisson Sno-Park** (5 mi/8 km west of Trout Lake on Hwy. 141) provides access to 10 miles of ungroomed winter trails. **Pineside Sno-Park** (5 mi/8 km north of Trout Lake), near Mount Adams Wilderness, provides access to 20 miles of groomed winter trails for skiing and snowshoeing. To get to Pineside from Trout Lake, follow

From top to bottom: Red Mountain Lookout; Deep Lake in Indian Heaven Wilderness; Trout Lake Country Inn.

Mount Adams Road north for 3.7 miles (6 km), continuing straight for another 0.9 mile when the road becomes Mount Adams Recreation Area Road. Turn right onto Forest Road 82 and arrive at the sno-park in 400 feet.

Before you head to the Sno-Park, pick up your **Washington State Sno-Park Permit** (www.parks.state.wa.us, required Dec. 1-Mar. 31, $20/day or $40/year) online or at the Mount Adams Ranger Station (2455 Hwy. 141, 509/395-3402, www.fs.usda.gov, 8am-4:30pm Mon.-Sat.).

Food

The Station Café (2376 Hwy. 141, 509/395-2211, 7am-6pm daily, $8-13) serves burgers, comfort food, and hot sandwiches in a tiny, diner-style café with wood-paneled walls. The charming backyard features picnic tables on a lawn next to Trout Lake Creek. Ask about the impressive selection of bottled beers or stop in next door at **Heavenly Grounds Espresso** (2374 Hwy. 141, 509/395-2211, 7am-4pm daily, $3-6) for coffee or a huckleberry milkshake in August (berry-picking season)—it's a must for hikers!

Rustic in every sense of the word, the ★ **Trout Lake Country Inn** (15 Guler Rd., 509/395-3667, www.troutlakecountryinn. net, 5pm-9pm Thurs.-Mon., $13-23) is a homey restaurant located in a historic building constructed in 1904 and painted like a red barn. Inside, tables feature a different collection of chairs with a unique tablecloth, though the front porch is a beautiful place to enjoy a meal as well. A six-seat bar is lit by mason-jar lanterns and hosts locals most nights. Mondays are taco nights; the rest of the week, the eatery serves comforting American favorites with globally inspired spices and sauces.

For hiking snacks, beverages, or camping supplies, visit **Trout Lake Grocery** (2383 Hwy. 141, 509/395-2777, 7am-8pm daily). Breakfast sandwiches are available in the deli case. Pacific Crest Trail hikers hang out on the front porch and the backyard picnic area during August and September, eating ice cream and relaxing after many miles on the trail.

Accommodations

Trout Lake Cozy Cabins (2291 Hwy. 141, 509/395-2068, www.troutlakecozycabins. com, $89-129) are tucked into the woods on the south end of town. The luxurious cabins are well appointed, with huge windows, modern kitchenettes, and hardwood A-frame ceilings; some have views of Mount Adams. Most cabins require a two-night stay during the busy summer months, but the friendly local couple who owns the property might make an exception if you call ahead.

Camping

Camp in town just two blocks from Trout Lake Grocery at **Guler Mount Adams County Park** (18 Trout Lake Park Rd., 509/773-4616, www.klickitatcounty.org, $18-24). Trout Lake Creek runs right though the campground and some sites have creek access. Pine trees throughout the park offer shade on warm days. Coin-op showers are available in the bathrooms.

Goose Lake Campground (13.5 mi/21.7 km west of Trout Lake, Forest Rd. 60, 360/891-5000, www.fs.usda.gov, June-Oct., $10) is a popular tent-only campground on a beautiful lake that's stocked with fish and is fantastic for swimming. Campsites are first-come, first-served and tend to fill on weekends in the summer. Goose Lake is 4.5 miles northeast of the Red Mountain Lookout hike.

The views of Mount Adams from ★ **Takhlakh Lake Campground** (26 mi/42 km north of Trout Lake, Forest Rd. 2329, 360/497-1100, www.recreation.gov, July-Sept., $18-24) are unbeatable. Each site has a picnic table and a fire ring; bring your own water for drinking, cooking, and washing. Vault toilets are in the campground. Four sites are available for advance reservation; the other 50 sites are first-come, first-served. Many campers bring kayaks and canoes, and the lake is a popular fishing spot as well. A walking trail around the lake is great for children. The Divide Camp trailhead, which provides access to the Pacific Crest Trail, is just 2 miles (3.2 km) southeast of the campground.

Getting There: Follow Mount Adams Road north out of town for 1.3 miles (2.1 km). Continue straight onto Forest Road 23 for 23 miles (37 km) toward Randle. Veer right onto Forest Road 2329 and continue north. Stay right at the fork at 1.2 miles (1.9 km) to continue on Forest Road 2329. Drive 0.3 mile to the Takhlakh Loop Road and turn right to enter the campground.

Information and Services

Mount Adams Ranger Station (2455 Hwy. 141, 509/395-3402, www.fs.usda.gov, 8am-4:30pm Mon.-Sat.) is your source for maps and information about Indian Heaven, Mount Adams, and the Gifford Pinchot National Forest. Rangers are up-to-date on campground conditions, fire closures, burn bans, road washouts, wildlife information, and trail conditions.

Packwood and Goat Rocks Wilderness

Packwood is a no-frills mountain town with restaurants, hotels, a gear shop, and a grocery store. It's not uncommon to see an elk in town, grazing on a lawn or crossing the street. Located in a river valley between Goat Rocks and Mount Rainier—two of the Pacific Crest Trail's most iconic Washington destinations—Packwood is your best bet for a hot meal or camping supplies. The Pacific Crest Trail traverses high-elevation terrain southeast of Packwood on its way through the Goat Rocks, the rocky remains of an extinct volcano, before crossing U.S. 12 at White Pass.

Getting There

Packwood is located on U.S. 12, about 65 miles (105 km) east of I-5 and 73 miles (118 km) west of Yakima. U.S. 12 is open year-round, but smaller forest roads in the area close each winter due to heavy snows.

Forest Road 23

Packwood is 58 miles (93 km) north of Trout Lake on Forest Road 23, about a two-hour drive on a slow, twisty road through dense forest and mountainous terrain. This beautiful, remote route is open approximately May-November. From Trout Lake, follow Mount Adams Road north for 1.3 miles (1.6 km). Veer left at the fork onto Forest Road 23 toward Randle and drive 54 miles (87 km) north. Turn right to stay north on Highway 131 for 1 mile (1.6 km), then make a right onto U.S. 12 west. You'll arrive in Packwood in 16 miles (26 km).

Winter Travel

Reaching Packwood from Trout Lake takes about 3.5 hours during the winter when Forest Road 23 is closed. Head south on Highway 141 for 19 miles (31 km), then stay right to veer onto Highway 141 Alt for 2 more miles (3.2 km) to the intersection with Highway 14. Drive west on Highway 14 for 56 miles (90 km). Merge onto I-205 north, then merge onto I-5 north and continue to exit 68. Head east on U.S. 12 for 65 miles (105 km) to arrive in Packwood.

Hiking
Nannie Peak

Distance: 5.8 mi/9.3 km round-trip
Duration: 3 hours
Elevation change: 2,100 ft/640 m
Effort: Strenuous
Trailhead: Nannie Ridge #98
Pass/Fee: Northwest Forest Pass

Nannie Peak, near the southern edge of Goat Rocks Wilderness, offers outstanding territorial views, including Mount Adams, the Goat Rocks massif, extinct volcano Old Snowy, and the path of the PCT through this wilderness.

From the trailhead, the Nannie Ridge Trail climbs steadily, relentlessly, northeast through the forest for 2.3 miles until the trees thin and the surrounding terrain comes into view. Listen for squeaks of picas in the scree fields next to the trail at mile 2.4 and beyond. The Nannie Peak Trail splits from the Nannie Ridge Trail at 2.5 miles; veer left to head north, beginning your ascent to the high point. Walk through patches of rock, meadow, and forest for the remaining 0.4 mile to the top of the peak, where you'll enjoy amazing 360-degree views of the South Washington Cascades.

Getting There

Nannie Ridge trailhead is located at the eastern edge of Walupt Lake Campground, a one-hour drive from Packwood. Follow U.S. 12 west for 3.5 miles (5.6 km), then turn left to go south on Forest Road 21 for 16 miles (26 km). Make a left onto Forest Road 2160 and continue east for 4.5 miles (7.2 km) to the campground.

Snowgrass Flat

Distance: 9.2 mi/14.8 km round-trip
Duration: 5 hours
Elevation change: 1,300 ft/396 m
Effort: Moderate
Trailhead: Snowgrass Flat #96
Pass/Fee: Northwest Forest Pass

The Pacific Crest Trail travels north-south through the Goat Rocks Wilderness, an alpine area formed by the remains of an extinct volcano called Old Snowy. Day hikes to the actual route of the PCT are long and arduous (14-plus miles), but this hike to Snowgrass Flat offers views of some of the rocky, volcanic terrain the Goat Rocks are famous for.

The Snowgrass Flat Trail heads northeast out of the parking area through a pleasant forest of cedar trees covered with old man's beard, a pale green droopy moss. Gain almost no elevation until you

cross the bridge over Goat Creek at 1.8 miles, then begin working your way up a steep, forested slope. Meet the edge of Snowgrass Creek, a tributary to the Cispus River, at 3.3 miles as it tumbles down the hillside in a white waterfall. Continue climbing for 0.6 mile past the signed trail for Bypass Trail #97 (which connects to the PCT in 1 mile, should you choose to explore it), then another 0.7 mile to the junction of Snowgrass Trail and Lily Basin Trail. Views of Mount Adams here are spectacular. Turn around here for a 9.2-mile hike round-trip, or to see more of the Goat Rocks area, walk west on the Lily Basin Trail for 0.5 mile or so.

Getting There

Snowgrass Flat trailhead is 19 miles (31 km) southeast of Packwood, about a 50-minute drive. Follow U.S. 12 west for 2.5 miles (4 km), then turn left to go south on Forest Road 21 for 12 miles (19.3 km). Veer left onto Forest Road 2150, follow for 2 miles (3.2 km), then veer left again, heading northeast. The parking area is on the left after 2 miles (3.2 km).

Recreation
Fishing

The 105-mile Cowlitz River flows right through Packwood, and it's a popular year-round fishing destination. Two fish hatcheries located along the river have bulked up the rainbow trout, coho salmon, and steelhead populations. While much of the river's shoreline is located on private property, **La Wis Wis Campground** (7.5 mi/12.1 km east of Packwood on U.S. 12) provides shoreline access to the Clear Fork of the Cowlitz River.

Mountain Biking

The dense woodlands south of Packwood are home to mountain biking trails of all levels. The 7.5-mile **Valley Trail #270** (accessible via Forest Rd. 28 near North Fork Campground) is an intermediate-level trail that parallels the path of Forest Road 23 and the eastern bank of the Cispus River through a mixed conifer and hardwood forest. High on a ridgeline above the western edge of the river, 5-mile **Tongue Mountain Trail** (accessible via Forest Rds. 2801 and 2904) and the 2-mile **High Bridge Trail** (accessible via Forest Rd. 29) offer stunning views of the Central and South Washington Cascades, including Mount Adams to the south. Up-to-date information about these trails is available on the U.S. Forest Service website (www.fs.usda.gov).

Winter Sports

Located between Packwood and Naches, the **White Pass Ski Area** (48935 Hwy. 12, Naches, 509/672-3100, www.skiwhitepass.com, 9am-9pm Dec.-Apr., $49-66) has eight lifts spread across Pigtail Peak and Hogback Mountain, where the PCT is buried in snow during the winter. The area offers much more than just downhill skiing, including snowshoe tours ($39 including light appetizers), tubing ($13 including tube rental), and a robust Nordic ski area with cross-country trails.

Shopping

White Pass Sports Hut (13020 Hwy. 12, 360/494-7321, 8am-6pm daily) is housed in a wooden A-frame hut and is filled to the brim with ski gear, fishing supplies, climbing equipment, camp stuff, and outdoor accessories for year-round recreation activities. In the winter, rent skis, boots, and poles here before heading up to White Pass Ski Area. The locally crafted hats make great gifts.

Food

Stop by **Mountain Goat Coffee Company** (105 Main St., 360/494-5600, 7am-5pm daily, $3-7) for coffee, espresso, or sweet and spicy chai. The clean and cozy shop has two indoor seating areas on either side of a counter, while the covered outdoor patio is a lovely place to sip your

drink, even in wet weather. Bakery items include savory scones, cinnamon rolls, and muffins and they are fresh, fragrant, and flavorful. Handmade mugs and local goods are available, as are house-roasted coffee beans.

Cruiser's Pizza (13028 Hwy. 12, 360/494-5400, www.cruiserspizza.com, 9am-9pm Mon.-Fri., 8am-10pm Sat., 8am-9pm Sun., $8-25) is popular among hungry hikers and outdoor enthusiasts. The lofty space has exposed wooden beams that give the place a lodge-like vibe despite the tables and chairs that resemble those from a school cafeteria. The menu offers something for everyone: burgers, seafood, chicken and pork entrées, pastas, and sandwiches. Pizzas feature thick, chewy crusts with lots of cheese and your choice of toppings. Breakfast is also served daily.

Blue Spruce Saloon and Grill (13019 Hwy. 12, 360/494-5605, 11am-midnight daily, $9-19) is a quintessential dive bar with a jukebox, pool tables, and dartboards. The extensive menu selection includes sandwiches, burgers, fry baskets, wraps, and salads. Local beers are on tap. The large interior has plenty of table seating and barstools and is a gathering place for locals and outdoor enthusiasts. The saloon is family-friendly until 10pm.

You can't miss the colorful line of vintage alpine skis outside ★ **Cliff Droppers Burgers** (12968 Hwy. 12, 360/494-2055, 11am-7pm Wed.-Mon., $10-12). Juicy burgers are served on toasted brioche buns with all the fixings, including a delectable house sauce. Pescatarians will be pleased to see two fish burgers and a fish basket on the menu; veggie burgers are available, too. Order at the counter and enjoy a cold beer while you wait.

The **Kracker Barrel Store & Service** (48851 Hwy. 12, 509/672-3105, 7am-7pm daily) is a critical resupply point for PCT hikers as they travel between Goat Rocks and Mount Rainier. This convenience store and gas station also has a wide array of sandwiches, a full espresso bar, and hot deli food like burritos, corn dogs, and pizza. Plus, it's the only place to get hot food at the top of the pass during hiking season.

Accommodations

White Pass Travel operates two reputable accommodations in Packwood. Set back from the highway on an enormous lawn, **Cowlitz River Lodge** (13069 Hwy. 12, 888/305-2185, www.whitepasstravel.com, $150-170 May-Sept., $120-140 Oct.-Apr.) is an elegant yet unassuming hotel with comfy leather couches around a stone hearth in the lobby. Rooms have outdoor entrances, coffee, microwaves, TVs, mini-fridges, and air-conditioning. All too appealing for PCT hikers, ★ **Crest Trail Lodge** (12729 Hwy. 12, 800/477-5339, www.whitepasstravel.com, $140-150 May-Sept., $110-120 Oct.-Apr.) offers a free breakfast (7:30am-10am) that includes waffles, scrambled eggs, sausage, and biscuits and gravy. Rooms include TVs, air-conditioning, coffee, microwaves, and mini-fridges. Free Wi-Fi is included in stays at both properties.

Steps from the PCT and White Pass Ski Area are the condos at **White Pass Village Inn** (48933 Hwy. 12, Naches, 509/672-3131, www.staywhitepass.com, $95-320). Each unit varies in size (most accommodate up to eight guests) and include full kitchens; some offer bunk beds or loft floor plans. Units are privately owned, so each one is uniquely decorated. The **Kracker Barrel** (48851 Hwy. 12, 509/672-3105, 7am-7pm daily), a convenience store next to the condo property, has a deli with espresso drinks and sandwiches made fresh each morning.

Camping

Less than 15 minutes from Packwood, **La Wis Wis Campground** (7.5 mi/12.1 km east of Packwood on U.S. 12,

From top to bottom: Goat Rocks Wilderness; Mount Adams from Snowgrass Flat; Mountain Goat Coffee Company.

360/891-5000, www.fs.usda.gov, May-Sept., $20) is a large campground with 100 sites at the confluence of the Ohanapecosh and Cowlitz Rivers and Purcell Creek. Reservations (877/444-6777, www.recreation.gov) are recommended, but a portion of the sites are reserved for walk-up campers throughout the season. Potable water and pit toilets are on-site, and the location is convenient to Packwood, White Pass, and Mount Rainier.

Pacific Crest Trail hikers know Walupt Lake as the southern border to the Goat Rocks Wilderness. The **Walupt Lake Campground** (23 mi/37 km southeast of Packwood, Forest Rd. 2160, 541/338-7869, www.fs.usda.gov, June-Sept., $18) offers fishing, boating, and hiking in a serene and peaceful forest. The 42 campsites are surrounded by thick forest and offer lots of privacy. Trailheads for the Nannie Ridge and Walupt Lake Trails, both of which connect to the PCT, are located at the east edge of the campground. This is a popular spot in the summer, so **reservations** (877/444-6777, www.recreation.gov) are recommended.

Walupt Lake is about an hour's drive from Packwood. From Packwood, follow U.S. 12 west for 3.5 miles (5.6 km), then turn left to head south on Forest Road 21 for 16 miles (26 km). Turn left onto Forest Road 2160 and continue east for 4.5 miles (7.2 km) to the campground.

Information and Services
Cowlitz Valley Ranger Station (10024 Hwy. 12, Randle, 360/497-1103, www.fs.usda.gov, 8am-noon and 1pm-4:30pm Mon.-Sat.) is 20 minutes west of Packwood on U.S. 12. Stop here for maps, information, backcountry resources, and to get the most up-to-date news about wildfires in the area. Rangers are knowledgeable about Gifford Pinchot National Forest (to the south), Goat Rocks Wilderness (to the southeast), and Mount Rainier National Park (to the northeast),

as well as nearby mountainous areas that the PCT doesn't even pass through.

Mount Rainier National Park

Mount Rainier is the largest volcano in the Cascade Range and the tallest point in Washington. Known simply as "The Mountain," its snowcapped peak can be seen from hundreds of miles away. Mount Rainier is surrounded by a huge national park of the same name. The national park encompasses more than 300 square miles and includes peaks, rivers, and valleys on all sides of the mountain.

The Pacific Crest Trail traces the eastern border of the park near Chinook Pass, an area covered in snow for seven months of the year. Although the hiking season is short, it's incredibly rewarding, with stunning views of the national park terrain and famous wildflower blooms each July.

Getting There
Mount Rainier is 10 miles (16.1 km) north of Packwood and 70 miles (113 km) southeast of Seattle.

From Packwood
Follow U.S. 12 northeast for 7.5 miles (12 km). Turn left to head north on Highway 123 and you'll arrive at the Stevens Canyon entrance (open May-Oct.) in 3 miles (4.8 km).

During winter, access the park via the Nisqually entrance by heading west out of Packwood on U.S. 12 to Highway 7 in the town of Morton. Follow Highway 7 north for 16 miles (26 km), then turn right to head east into the park on Highway 706.

From Seattle
Follow I-5 south for 29 miles (47 km) to exit 142A. Head east on Highway 164 for 15 miles (24 km), and continue straight when the road becomes Highway 410 in

Mount Rainier National Park

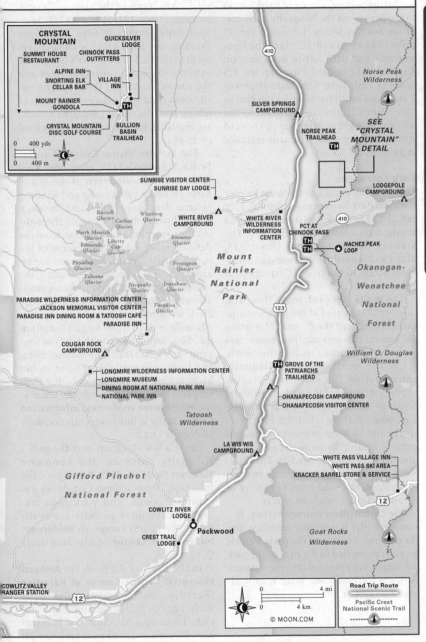

CRYSTAL MOUNTAIN

QUICKSILVER LODGE

SUMMIT HOUSE RESTAURANT

CHINOOK PASS OUTFITTERS

ALPINE INN

SNORTING ELK CELLAR BAR

VILLAGE INN

MOUNT RAINIER GONDOLA

CRYSTAL MOUNTAIN DISC GOLF COURSE

BULLION BASIN TRAILHEAD

0   400 yds
0   400 m

Norse Peak Wilderness

SEE "CRYSTAL MOUNTAIN" DETAIL

SILVER SPRINGS CAMPGROUND

NORSE PEAK TRAILHEAD

LODGEPOLE CAMPGROUND

SUNRISE VISITOR CENTER
SUNRISE DAY LODGE

WHITE RIVER CAMPGROUND

WHITE RIVER WILDERNESS INFORMATION CENTER

PCT AT CHINOOK PASS

NACHES PEAK LOOP

Russell Glacier

Carbon Glacier

Winthrop Glacier

North Mowich Glacier

Edmunds Glacier

Liberty Cap Glacier

Puyallup Glacier

Emmons Glacier

Fryingpan Glacier

Mount Rainier National Park

Okanogan-

Wenatchee

National

Forest

Tahoma Glacier

Nisqually Glacier

Ingraham Glacier

PARADISE WILDERNESS INFORMATION CENTER
JACKSON MEMORIAL VISITOR CENTER
PARADISE INN DINING ROOM & TATOOSH CAFE
PARADISE INN

Paradise Glacier

William O. Douglas Wilderness

COUGAR ROCK CAMPGROUND

LONGMIRE WILDERNESS INFORMATION CENTER
LONGMIRE MUSEUM
DINING ROOM AT NATIONAL PARK INN
NATIONAL PARK INN

GROVE OF THE PATRIARCHS TRAILHEAD

OHANAPECOSH CAMPGROUND
OHANAPECOSH VISITOR CENTER

Tatoosh Wilderness

LA WIS WIS CAMPGROUND

WHITE PASS VILLAGE INN
WHITE PASS SKI AREA
KRACKER BARREL STORE & SERVICE

Gifford Pinchot

National Forest

COWLITZ RIVER LODGE

Packwood

CREST TRAIL LODGE

Goat Rocks Wilderness

COWLITZ VALLEY RANGER STATION

0   4 mi
0   4 km

© MOON.COM

Road Trip Route

Pacific Crest National Scenic Trail

Enumclaw. Arrive at the White River entrance in 37 miles (60 km).

During winter, the only road access to the park is via the Nisqually entrance. From Seattle, follow I-5 south for 39 miles (63 km) to exit 127. Take the freeway exit and turn left to head east on Highway 512 toward Puyallup for 2.5 miles (4 km). Turn right onto Highway 7 and head south for 35 miles (56 km) to Elbe. When Highway 7 veers off to the left, stay straight on Highway 706 toward Ashford. Arrive at the Nisqually entrance in 14 miles (22.5 km).

Park Entrances

There are four entrances to **Mount Rainier National Park** (www.nps.gov/mora), $30/vehicle). The park's eastern entrances are the most convenient to the PCT. The **Stevens Canyon entrance** (Hwy. 123, May-Oct.) is north of Packwood and provides access to the park's Ohanapecosh area.

The **White River entrance** (Hwy. 410, July-Sept.) is located at the park's northeast corner, near the Crystal Mountain Ski Resort. This entrance provides access to the park's Sunrise area from the north.

On the west side, the **Nisqually entrance** (Hwy. 706, year-round) is at the southwest corner of the park. It provides access to the busy and popular Paradise area, where parking is limited. Plan to arrive before 10:30am to avoid traffic congestion; it can take more than one hour just to drive up the road to Paradise. Note that though the entrance is open year-round, the road from Longmire to Paradise closes at night in winter.

The **Carbon River entrance** (Hwy. 165, summer only) is a remote entrance into the northwest corner of the park. Vehicle access is permitted to the edge of the park boundary, but entrance into the national park via Carbon River Road is only allowed on foot or bike.

Visitors Centers

The **Ohanapecosh Visitor Center** (2 mi/3.2 km south of the Stevens Canyon entrance, Hwy. 123, 360/569-6581, 9am-5pm daily May-early Sept., 9am-5pm Fri.-Sun. late Sept.-Oct.) is most convenient to the PCT. The center's interactive exhibits showcase enormous trees and the natural history of the area. The onsite bookshop has a decent selection of hiking and wilderness guides. Restrooms are available, but you won't find any food or drinks.

The **Sunrise Visitor Center** (Sunrise Park Rd., 360/663-2425, 10am-6pm daily July-Sept.) is located west of the White River entrance via the long and winding Sunrise Park Road (July-Oct.). Inside, a handful of exhibits are spaced throughout the roomy log building. Check out the detailed relief map to get a sense of the park's varied terrain. Restrooms are located in a separate building just east of the visitors center. Food and drinks are available at the **Sunrise Day Lodge** (360/663-2574, www.mtrainierguestservices.com, 10am-7pm daily July-Aug., 11am-3pm Sat.-Sun. Sept.), along with loads of souvenirs and gifts. Trail information, maps, and books are available at Sunrise, but backpacking permits are not—the closest place to get an overnight permit is at the **White River Wilderness Information Center** (at the White River entrance, daily May-early Oct.).

Set at a low elevation near the park's Nisqually entrance, the **Longmire Museum** (360/569-6575, 9am-5pm daily July-Sept., 9am-4:30pm Oct.-June) has exhibits, books, and park information. Backcountry permits are available at the nearby **Longmire Wilderness Information Center** (daily May-early Oct.).

In the heart of the park, the **Jackson Memorial Visitor Center at Paradise** (Paradise, 360/569-6571, 10am-7pm daily June-Sept., 10am-5pm Sat.-Sun. Oct., 10am-4pm Sat.-Sun. and holidays Nov.-Dec.) is perched near tree line on the southern edge of Mount Rainier, providing an incredible view. Restrooms are available, as well as a gift shop with clothing, books, and keepsakes. The Paradise Camp Deli serves pizza, sandwiches, hot dogs, soups, and salads, plus espresso drinks and ice cream. Backcountry permits are available at the nearby **Paradise Wilderness Information Center** (daily May-early Oct.). Paradise is 17 miles (27 km) east of the Nisqually entrance and 21 miles (34 km) west of the Stevens Canyon entrance.

Seasons

While the park is open year-round, most **roads close November-May,** making much of the park inaccessible. The Pacific Crest Trail follows the eastern edge of the park at a high elevation and is best experienced **July-September,** when snow has melted and the sun is shining.

Hiking

Day hikes in the park are plentiful. Backcountry **permits** ($20) are required for overnight backcountry stays in the park. Obtain permits at a park ranger station or reserve online in advance (www.nps.gov/mora). Permits allow site-specific camping within the park.

The Pacific Crest Trail passes through the eastern edge of the park from Laughingwater Creek to Chinook Pass. You can access the PCT at Chinook Pass, where the national scenic trail crosses Highway 410. Day hike destinations on the PCT from Chinook Pass include Naches Peak Loop, Sheep Lake, and Dewey Lake.

Just outside the northeastern park boundary, the PCT passes through Crystal Mountain Resort, accessible via Crystal Mountain Boulevard. From here, you can day hike to the top of Norse Peak or hike the Crown Point Loop.

Grove of the Patriarchs Trail

Distance: 1.3 mi/2.1 km round-trip
Duration: 1 hour
Elevation change: 50 ft/15 m
Effort: Easy
Trailhead: Stevens Canyon entrance
Pass/Fee: National park pass

While the PCT traverses a high-elevation section of the park near Chinook Pass, this must-do hike through towering old-growth conifers showcases the Pacific Northwest's awe-inspiring forests.

Park in the designated parking area just north of the Stevens Canyon entrance and walk north on the flat Grove of the Patriarchs Trail. The path follows the western edge of the Ohanapecosh River, named after a historic Native American habitation site that translates to "standing at the edge." Melted glacial ice is responsible for the vibrant blue color of the river. At 0.4 mile, keep right at the junction with the Eastside Trail and cross the river on a suspension bridge. Take either option when the path forks at 0.5 mile; the trail makes a loop through the trees, some of which are 1,000 years old. Cross back over the bridge and return to your car, or to make it a longer hike, opt to walk north on the Eastside Trail along the bank of the Ohanapecosh.

★ Naches Peak Loop

Distance: 3.6 mi/5.8 km round-trip
Duration: 1.5-2 hours
Elevation change: 650 ft/198 m
Effort: Easy
Trailhead: Naches Peak Loop, on south side of Highway 410
Pass/Fee: Northwest Forest Pass

Located on the eastern border of Mount Rainier National Park, this loop hike has it all: waterfalls, wildflowers, alpine lakes, craggy ridgelines, and breathtaking views of Rainier.

Start your hike at the southern end of Tipsoo Lake. Walk south on the Naches Peak Loop Trail, climbing onto the ridgeline between Tipsoo Lake and the Dewey Creek Basin. Avalanche lilies are abundant here during the spring (which actually occurs in July at this elevation). The trail turns east at 0.4 mile onto the southwest arm of Naches Peak. Take in the best views of Mount Rainier around 0.7 mile, then continue east to the **Dewey Lake** viewpoint at 1.1 miles. This is your highest point, around 5,850 feet (1,783 m), and you'll remain at this elevation for the next 0.6 mile before descending. Continue west, stopping in the meadow at 1.5 miles for another great vantage of Rainier, before meeting up with the Pacific Crest Trail at 1.6 miles. Turn left to walk north on the PCT, descending into the meadows east of Naches Peak. Step across five trickling streams and past waterfalls as the trail continues northwest toward Chinook Pass. You may encounter patches of snow on the north-facing slopes, even well into July. At 3.1 miles, stay left at the trail junction to cross Highway 410 on the Mount Rainier National Park bridge.

On the west side of the highway, the PCT turns north; stay straight to continue west toward Tipsoo Lake. The trail leads you down a forested slope to the lakeshore. Follow the trail on the shoreline back to the parking area.

To spread the elevation gain out over 2 miles instead of 1, walk in a clockwise direction. Or, to make this a longer hike, walk south on the PCT to Dewey Lake (rather than turning left to walk north at 1.6 miles).

Sheep Lake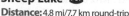

Distance: 4.8 mi/7.7 km round-trip
Duration: 2.5 hours
Elevation change: 600 ft/183 m
Effort: Easy
Trailhead: Pacific Crest Trail at Chinook Pass
Pass/Fee: Northwest Forest Pass

This easy walk along the PCT runs parallel to Mather Memorial Parkway to iconic Sheep Lake just outside the borders of the national park.

Begin at Chinook Pass and walk north on the PCT along the eastern edge of Yakima Peak. At 1.4 miles, the trail makes a left turn and ascends westward, away from the highway. When the trail

forks at 2 miles, take either trail to access the shore of Sheep Lake at 2.4 miles. On calm days, the steep hillside behind the lake is reflected in the water's surface. This subalpine lake is a popular camp spot for backpackers.

For a longer hike, continue past Sheep Lake on the PCT for 1 mile (1.6 km) to Sourdough Gap, where you'll get expansive views of Mount Rainier and the surrounding peaks.

Crown Point Loop

Distance: 7.7 mi/12.4 km round-trip
Duration: 4 hours
Elevation change: 2,200 ft/671 m
Effort: Strenuous
Trailhead: Bullion Basin at Crystal Mountain Resort
Pass/Fee: Northwest Forest Pass

Hike through dense forest and lush meadows on your way to Crown Point, where you'll get fantastic views of Mount Rainier and Crystal Mountain, as well as Mount Adams, Goat Rocks, and the eastern Cascades.

Your journey starts on the Bullion Basin Trail, which is a wide dirt road during the summer months. Climb east away from the ski area buildings and bear left at the trail junction at 0.3 mile to continue northeast on the Bullion Basin Trail. Horses use this trail during the summer, so you'll see evidence of their travels. Cross a dirt road at 0.4 and 0.5 mile, then cross Silver Creek at 0.6 mile. The trail switchbacks to head southeast along Silver Creek for the next 1.5 miles, passing through a grassy, flowered meadow at 2 miles. Get your first views of Rainier's white, snowy top at 2.2 miles as you scale the western edge of Bullion Basin. Meet the Pacific Crest Trail at 2.3 miles, making a sharp right to walk south. Your next mile along the ridgeline is absolutely stunning: Bullion Basin, Crystal Mountain, and Rainier. Wildflowers abound during July and August. Look for bright pink and orange Indian paintbrush, purple lupine, and white avalanche lilies. Your highest point is 6,350 feet (1,935 m) at 3.3 miles; it's all downhill from here.

Walk along the western edge of Crown Point at 3.5 miles before the PCT turns left to head east, then makes a sharp right at 3.8 miles to head west over Pickhandle Gap. Goat Rocks, the remains of an ancient volcano dubbed Old Snowy, is visible to the south, along with Mount Adams. This crest-line section of the trail makes obvious the difference between Washington's western terrain (dense and green) and eastern (sparse and arid). Continue along the PCT to the Bear Gap trail junction at 5.2 miles. Turn right to head north and, after one switchback, meet the Silver Creek Trail. Turn right, walking north toward the ski area lodge and buildings, passing an abandoned mine entrance at 6.9 miles. You'll complete the loop at 7.4 miles, meeting up with the Bullion Basin Trail leading back to the parking area.

Getting There

Crown Point is just east of Crystal Mountain Ski Area. From Packwood, take U.S. 12 northeast for 7.5 miles (12.1 km) to Highway 123. Turn left to head north toward Mount Rainier National Park. Follow for 16 miles (26 km), then continue north onto Highway 410 West for another 8 miles (12.9 km). Turn right on Crystal Mountain Boulevard (Forest Road 7166) and continue for 6 miles (9.7 km). Park in the paved parking lot near the lodge and the Silver Skis Chalet. The trailhead is located on the ski hill behind Silver Skis Chalet and Quicksilver Lodge.

Norse Peak

Distance: 9.2 mi/14.8 km round-trip
Duration: 5 hours
Elevation change: 3,300 ft/1,006 m
Effort: Strenuous
Trailhead: Norse Peak via Crystal Mountain Resort

From top to bottom: PCT crossing Highway 410 at Chinook Pass; Naches Peak Loop; Mount Rainier from Naches Peak Loop.

Pass/Fee: Northwest Forest Pass

Although the Norse Peak Fire destroyed much of the forest in 2017, this wilderness area is absolutely stunning, and views from the summit stretch from Mount Adams to the south to Mount Stuart to the north. See the hulking, icy mass of Mount Rainier up close and personal. Even Puget Sound is visible on a clear day. The elevation gain is substantial, but the trail is graded evenly, which makes this hike very doable with plenty of water and daylight.

Begin your hike on Gold Hill Road, an unmarked dirt road 2 miles north of Crystal Mountain Resort. Walk up the road for 0.2 mile to the trailhead to begin your ascent. Walk through dense woods for 1.5 miles, gaining 1,000 feet (305 m) of elevation. This is where you'll enter a burn zone; much of the trail from here forward was destroyed. Wildflowers like lupine thrive in this environment. Get your first views of Crystal Mountain to the west at 1.8 miles. The road to the ski area, plus the lodge and resort housing, are in sight at 1.9 miles. Mount Rainier comes into view around 2.3 miles, and the views only get better from here as you continue to ascend. Stay straight at 2.8 miles where the Goat Lake Trail splits off to the southeast. Keep climbing, soaking in the Rainier views and the expanding vistas.

Crest a ridgeline at 4.5 miles and get awe-inspiring views of the entire Norse Peak Wilderness, the Snoqualmie summits to the north and the Stuart Range to the northeast. You're almost to the summit! Continue for 0.1 mile up the side of Norse Peak to the scant remains of an old fire lookout. Look down to see the Pacific Crest Trail as it traces the east side of the peak 300 feet below. Turn around here to head back the way you came.

To make it a loop, continue for 0.4 mile to the PCT junction. Follow the Pacific Crest Trail south through a beautiful, unburned area to the Bullion Basin Trail at 6.4 miles. This 1.7-mile trail leads back to Crystal Mountain Resort through thick forest and lush, wildflower-strewn meadows. Arrange a shuttle at the Crystal Mountain parking lot (8.1 total miles from Norse Peak trailhead), or walk the road 2 miles north back to your starting point (10.1 total miles).

Getting There
Norse Peak is just north of Crystal Mountain Ski Area. From Packwood, take U.S. 12 northeast for 7.5 miles (12.1 km) to Highway 123. Turn left to head north toward Mount Rainier National Park. Follow for 16 miles (26 km), then continue north onto Highway 410 West for another 8 miles (12.9 km). Turn right on Crystal Mountain Boulevard (Forest Road 7166) and continue for 4 miles (6.4 km). Park in the gravel parking area on the west side of the highway across from Gold Hill Road (a dirt road). The trailhead is located 0.2 mile up Gold Hill Road on the left.

Crystal Mountain Resort
In addition to the hiking and exploring opportunities within the national park, **Crystal Mountain Resort** (www.crystalmountainresort.com) offers a number of activities summer and winter for enjoying the steep, rugged terrain near Mount Rainier. The resort sits tucked into a forested subalpine valley just outside the park's northeast border, about a 20-minute drive from the White River entrance. The Pacific Crest Trail traces the valley's eastern ridgeline, overlooking the resort's day lodge, hotels, and downhill ski runs on the western slopes. In winter, Crystal Mountain is a popular skiing and snowshoeing destination, while horseback riding, hiking, disc golf, and sightseeing draw visitors June-September. The resort's restaurants and lodging options provide comfort and convenience during multiday stays in an otherwise remote mountain region.

A ride on Crystal Mountain's **Mount Rainier Gondola** (33914 Crystal

Mountain Blvd., 360/663-3050, 10am-5pm Sun.-Fri., 10am-7pm Sat., June-Sept., $25) delivers you to the top of a ski hill (mostly snow-free during the summer months) where unobstructed views of Mount Rainier are unbeatable. Ride the gondola back down after soaking up the views, or hike back down the snow-free slopes through the **Crystal Mountain Disc Golf Course** (June-Sept., free). Pick up a course map at the front desk of any of the resort's hotels (360/663-2262, www.crystalhotels.com) or from the Snorting Elk Cellar Bar (33818 Crystal Mountain Blvd., 360/663-7798).

Horseback rides explore the eastern half of the valley, which is where the PCT is located. Climb onto a gentle, surefooted horse at **Chinook Pass Outfitters** (Parking Lot C, Crystal Mountain Blvd., 509/653-2633, www.chinookpassoutfitters.com, June-Sept., from $40, cash only) for a ride through lush meadows and dense subalpine conifer forests. Rides vary in length from one hour to all day.

The downhill terrain at **Crystal Mountain Ski Area** (33914 Crystal Mountain Blvd., 360/663-3050, www.crystalmountainresort.com, $45-99) is recognized as some of the Pacific Northwest's best. Nine chairlifts in the main ski area provide access to ski runs of varying difficulties, from beginner to expert. The Northway chair provides access to more than 15 black diamond and double black diamond runs.

Guided snowshoe tours (Dec.-Mar., $70-99) are also popular. Starting at 3pm, tours include a chairlift ride, a walk through winter wonderland with an expert guide, and dinner or drinks afterward in the upper level of Crystal Mountain's day lodge. Ticket price includes snowshoe and pole rental.

From top to bottom: Dewey Lake; Mount Rainier from Norse Peak Loop; Indian paintbrush.

Food

There are only three dining options inside the park. Most hikers bring food with them.

The **Sunrise Day Lodge** (Sunrise, 360/663-2574, www. mtrainierguestservices.com, 10am-7pm daily July-Aug., 11am-3pm daily Sat.-Sun. Sept.) is a big, cedar-shingled lodge with a gift shop and a snack bar. Tuned into the needs of hungry hikers (and the dramatic weather variations at the high elevation), the kitchen serves hot chili, soups, sandwiches, and ice cream.

The **Dining Room at National Park Inn** (Longmire, 360/569-2411, 7am-11am and 11:30am-4:30pm daily, 5pm-7:30pm Sun.-Thurs., 5pm-8:30pm Fri.-Sat., $18-30) serves casual American cuisine including standard breakfast fare, burgers, sandwiches, salads, steaks, and seafood. Only famished hikers will find the food anything but ordinary, but the coffee is hot, and the service is friendly and prompt.

The ★ **Paradise Inn Dining Room** (Paradise, 855/755-2275, https:// mtrainierguestservices.com, 7am-9am, noon-2:30pm, and 5:30pm-8pm daily May-Oct., $18-31) is huge, with dozens of tables covered in white linen, big picture windows, and a large stone hearth with a chimney. Lunch and dinner items include burgers with truffle oil, crab cakes, prime rib, and grilled salmon. Vegetarian items are available as well. The breakfast buffet includes eggs, bacon, pastries, fruit, Belgian waffles, and a rotating selection of hot entrées. **Tatoosh Café** (hours vary daily May-Oct., $3-12) is a small coffee shop inside the Paradise Inn with espresso drinks, pastries, grab-and-go items like sandwiches, and beer and wine on tap.

Located outside the park at Crystal Mountain Resort, **Snorting Elk Cellar Bar** (33818 Crystal Mountain Blvd., 360/663-7798, www.crystalhotels.com, 3pm-10pm Mon.-Fri., 2pm-10pm Sat.-Sun. summer, 11am-10pm Sun.-Thurs., 11am-midnight Fri.-Sat. winter, $13-24) serves microbrews, including Snorting Elk Frost, a custom beer from Seattle's Elysian Brewing. Built into a steep hillside at the bottom of the resort's ski runs, this Bavarian-themed bar has cozy tables and booths with windows on one side that overlook a courtyard. Cheesy, satisfying pizza and nachos are highlights of the menu.

Perched atop Crystal Mountain at almost 6,900 feet (2,103 m), the view at **Summit House Restaurant** (33914 Crystal Mountain Blvd., 360/663-3085, www. crystalhotels.com, 10:30am-4:30pm Sun.-Fri., 10:30am-6:30pm Sat. late June-early Sept., 10:30am-4:30pm daily late Sept., $12-20) draws more diners than the food. On Saturdays during the summer, dinner seatings are offered 4pm-4:30pm and 6pm-6:30pm. Humans with canine companions are welcome to dine outside on the "paw-tio." Burgers, sandwiches, and salads are on the food menu, and beverages from a full bar are available. Getting to the Summit House requires a ride on the Mount Rainier Gondola (360/663-3050, $25).

Accommodations

All 121 guestrooms at 100-year-old ★ **Paradise Inn** (Paradise, 360/569-2275, www.mtrainierguestservices.com, May-Sept., $134-341) are cozy and free from the distractions of modern life—you won't find TVs or telephones in these rooms. Instead, you get incredible, larger-than-life views of Mount Rainier, access to some of the best hiking trails in the park, and the Jackson Visitor Center just steps from your door. Wood-paneled rooms in the annex offer private baths, while rooms in the main lodge have shared bathrooms at the end of the hall. Food is available on-site at the **Paradise Inn Dining Room** (7am-9am, noon-2:30pm, and 5:30pm-8pm daily May-Oct., $18-31) and **Tatoosh Café** (hours vary daily May-Oct., $3-12).

In Longmire, 25 rooms at the **National Park Inn** (47009 Paradise

Rd. E., 360/569-2411, www.
mtrainierguestservices.com, $132-277)
are tucked into the second story of a
1911-vintage cabin-style lodge. The furnishings are a bit outdated, but the location is convenient to the park's only
year-round entrance, and the **National
Park Dining Room** (360/569-2411, 7am-
11am and 11:30am-4:30pm daily, 5pm-
7:30pm Sun.-Thurs., 5pm-8:30pm
Fri.-Sat., $18-30) is right downstairs.

Crystal Mountain Hotels (33818
Crystal Mountain Blvd, 888/754-6400,
www.crystalhotels.com, June-Sept. and
Dec.-Apr., $100-260) offers three lodg-
ing options just north of the national
park's White River entrance. Winter is
Crystal's busy season, but the hotels are
available during the summer. Miles of
hiking trails are accessible via the resort,
including the trails to Crown Point and
Norse Peak.

Built in 1964, the signature **Alpine Inn**
is a Bavarian-style lodge adjacent to the
Mount Rainier Gondola. The cozy rooms
are a bit small (the assumption is that
you're there to frolic outside, not hang
out in your hotel room), but some have
mountain views and the **Snorting Elk
Cellar Bar** (3pm-10pm Mon.-Fri., 2pm-
10pm Sat.-Sun. summer; 11am-10pm
Sun.-Thurs., 11am-midnight Fri.-Sat.
winter, $13-24) is right downstairs. The
Village Inn and the **Quicksilver Lodge** are
more modern buildings located across
the road. Rooms here are a bit larger and
feature flat-screen TVs, mini-fridges, microwaves, and free Wi-Fi. Both buildings
have lobbies with seating.

All the Crystal Mountain accommodations are within walking distance to the
valley's hiking trails, the ski hills, and the
Mount Rainier Gondola, which delivers
you to the **Summit House Restaurant**
(33914 Crystal Mountain Blvd., 360/663-
3085, www.crystalhotels.com, 10:30am-
4:30pm Sun.-Fri., 10:30am-6:30pm Sat.
late June-early Sept., 10:30am-4:30pm
daily late Sept., 10:30am-2:45pm daily
Dec.-Apr., $12-20).

Camping
There are three campgrounds within the
national park, as well as two outside the
park's eastern borders near the Pacific
Crest Trail.

Ohanapecosh Campground (Hwy.
123, 877/444-6777, www.recreation.gov,
June-Oct., $20) is nestled among tower-
ing moss-covered, old-growth trees along
the Ohanapecosh River. The huge campground has 191 sites that book quickly.
Although walk-up sites are available, reservations are recommended before Labor
Day. Access the Pacific Crest Trail 16.5
miles (26.6 km) north at Chinook Pass, or
16.5 miles (26.6 km) southwest at White
Pass. Other popular nearby trails include
Grove of the Patriarchs and Silver Falls.

The campground is 4.2 miles (6.8 km)
north of the intersection of U.S. 12 and
Highway 123 near Packwood.

All 112 sites at **White River
Campground** (White River Rd., June-
Sept., $20) are first-come, first-served.
The Wonderland Trail, a 93-mile hiking trail that encircles Mount Rainier,
passes right through the campground.
Campsites have picnic tables, fire rings,
and access to bathrooms with running
water and flush toilets. This campground is convenient to the Sunrise area,
which is 3.5 miles (5.6 km) away on the
Wonderland Trail or a 12-mile (19.3-km)
drive up Sunrise Park Road.

The campground is 5 miles (8 km)
west of the White River entrance on
White River Road.

In the southwest corner of the
park near Longmire, **Cougar Rock
Campground** (Paradise Valley Rd.,
877/444-6777, May-Sept., $20) has 173
sites with picnic tables, fire rings, and
access to bathrooms with running water
and flush toilets. Walk-up sites are available on a first-come, first-served basis,
but reservations are recommended.

The campground is 2.2 miles (3.5 km)
northeast of Longmire on Paradise Valley
Road.

Lodgepole Campground (Hwy.

410, Naches, 509/653-1401, Memorial Day-Labor Day) is on the east side of the Cascade crest in the Okanogan-Wenatchee National Forest, and is likely to be sunnier and warmer than campgrounds inside the park. There are 28 campsites on two loops adjacent to the American River, which is full of trout. **Reservations** (877/444-6777, www.recreation.gov, $18) are recommended.

The campground is 7.5 miles (12.1 km) east of Chinook Pass. During the winter, this campground is only accessible from the east—Highway 410 is closed between Crystal Mountain Boulevard and Morse Creek (about 5 mi/8 km east of Chinook Pass) between November and May each year.

Silver Springs Campground (Hwy. 410 near Crystal Mountain Blvd., 360/825-6585, Memorial Day-Labor Day) is located just outside the national park's White River entrance, and is the most convenient campground to Crystal Mountain Resort. Trailheads to Norse Peak and Crown Point are 15 minutes away by car. All 56 campsites here include fire rings, picnic tables, and access to flush toilets and potable water. The East Fork of the White River, popular for salmon and trout fishing, rushes past nearby. **Reservations** (877/444-6777, www.recreation.gov, $20) are highly recommended at this busy campground.

Snoqualmie Pass and North Bend

Snoqualmie Pass is the southern gateway to the Alpine Lakes Wilderness, a region that is home to more than 700 lakes, ponds, and tarns. The area shows a distinct shift in terrain as the PCT departs the green, forested hills of southern Washington and enters a formidable range of jagged, glacier-encrusted peaks that stretch beyond the northern border of the state. North Bend, a growing town in the foothills 30 minutes west of the

pass, is a convenient stop for groceries, restaurants, gas, and accommodations.

Getting There

The PCT travels due north from Mount Rainier to Snoqualmie Pass, but there are no roads that parallel this route. Road-trippers must make a two-hour detour west toward Puget Sound and then back into the mountains to Snoqualmie Pass.

From the northern boundary of Mount Rainier National Park, take Highway 410 west for 33 miles (53 km) to Enumclaw. In Enumclaw, hop onto Highway 169 north for 15 miles (24 km), merging onto Highway 18 east toward North Bend. Highway 18 meets I-90 east in 12 miles (19.3 km). Turn east on I-90 and drive 29 miles (47 km) to Snoqualmie Pass.

Alternatively, from Seattle take I-90 east for 30 miles (48 km) to North Bend. Snoqualmie Pass is another 25 miles (40 km) east on I-90.

Sights
Goldmyer Hot Springs

Burrowed deep in a mossy, fern-filled forest, **Goldmyer Hot Springs** (Forest Rd. 5620, 206/789-5631, www.goldmyer.org, $20/person) is a magical mountain escape just west of the Alpine Lakes Wilderness. While not technically on the PCT, many hikers opt to visit this rustic, privately operated natural wonder to rest their bones and warm up on chilly autumn evenings.

The easy walk to the springs follows a pedestrian-only road along the north shore of the Middle Fork of the Snoqualmie River. From the parking area, the 5.5-mile walk takes about two hours. At 4.9 miles, look for a signed junction with the narrow, single-file Goldmyer Trail. Turn right to walk south for 0.25 mile and check in with the caretakers before continuing to the clothing-optional pools where hot water emerges from a cave, then cascades into two larger pools of varying temps. A wooden shelter is nearby to hang clothing, change, and

Snoqualmie Pass to Leavenworth

Glacier Peak
Wilderness

Henry M. Jackson
Wilderness

Wild Sky
Wilderness

Lake
Wenatchee

LAKE WENATCHEE
STATE PARK

Mount Baker-Snoqualmie
National Forest

2

SMITHBROOK
TRAILHEAD

Skykomish

PCT AT STEVENS PASS
STEVENS PASS MOUNTAIN RESORT

IRON GOAT
TRAILHEAD

2

SEE
"LEAVENWORTH"
MAP

ALPINE
ADVENTURES

LEAVENWORTH SKI
HILL

Leavenworth

OKTOBERFEST

ICICLE VILLAGE
RESORT

RIVER
RIDERS

Alpine Lakes
Wilderness

ENCHANTMENT
PARK

97

GOLDMYER
HOT SPRINGS

SNOW LAKE
TRAILHEAD

PCT AT SNOQUALMIE PASS
Snoqualmie Pass
SUMMIT TUBING HILL

KENDALL
KATWALK

DENNY CREEK
CAMPGROUND

Kachess
Lake

Okanogan-Wenatchee
National Forest

90

Cle Elum
Lake

Cle Elum

97

0   5 mi
0   5 km

© MOON.COM

90

Road Trip Route

Pacific Crest
National Scenic Trail

store belongings. Visitation is limited to 20 people per day; advance **reservations** are critical. Forested campsites are available on the property ($5/night pp).

Getting There
Goldmyer Hot Springs is 25 miles (40 km) east of North Bend on Forest Road 5620. A Northwest Forest Pass is required to park.

Hiking
★ Kendall Katwalk 🅿️
Distance: 11.5 mi/18.5 km round-trip
Duration: 6-8 hours
Elevation change: 2,600 ft/792 m
Effort: Strenuous
Trailhead: Pacific Crest Trail
Pass/Fee: Northwest Forest Pass

For hikers in search of a shortcut into the colorful and steep terrain of the North Cascades, the trailhead to Kendall Katwalk is just an hour's drive from downtown Seattle. Park in the Pacific Crest Trail parking area just north of Commonwealth Campground. The trail leading out of the parking area is wide and may be heavily trafficked due to its proximity to the interstate. Although the climb through the forest isn't steep, it's unrelenting, and this thins the crowds after the first mile.

Meander through lush old-growth forest to where the trees thin just long enough to reveal a view of Snoqualmie Mountain at 2 miles. Creek crossings around the 3-mile mark can be hazardous in early summer—use trekking poles for balance if you have them, and boots or trail shoes with good tread. Look up when you enter the next clearing to see the rocky ridge you're headed toward. The trail breaks out of the forest at 4.5 miles and climbs onto the western side of Kendall Peak. From this vantage point on an open hillside, take in a bird's-eye view of I-90—where you started—2,000 feet below. To the north, dramatic and craggy Red Mountain stands out from the other granite giants with its ruddy coloring.

Arrive at the Katwalk at 5.7 miles, a narrow, 150-foot stretch of trail blasted into the steep southwest edge of Collar Mountain. Here you're rewarded with expansive views of Gold Creek Basin to the east, Alta Mountain, and the spired, granite slabs characteristic of the Washington Cascades. This is your turnaround point. The PCT continues north into the Alpine Lakes Wilderness.

Getting There
The northbound PCT trailhead is located at exit 52 on I-90, on the north side of the freeway. To get there from North Bend, follow I-90 east for 23 miles (37 km), take exit 52, and turn left onto Highway 906/Forest Road 9041. Follow for 0.1 mile and turn right into the PCT parking area.

Snow Lake and Gem Lake
Distance: 6.4-10 mi/10.3-16.1 km round-trip
Duration: 3-6 hours
Elevation change: 2,600 ft/792 m
Effort: Moderate/Strenuous
Trailhead: Snow Lake
Pass/Fee: Northwest Forest Pass

The rocky ascent to Snow Lake showcases the jagged peaks and sparkling lakes characteristic of the Alpine Lakes Wilderness. Many Pacific Crest Trail hikers opt to take an alternate route into this wilderness, passing Snow Lake and stopping at Goldmyer Hot Springs before reconnecting to the PCT.

Start your hike at the base of 7,000-foot Snoqualmie Mountain, walking northwest above the South Fork of the Snoqualmie River. At 1.7 miles, the trail begins a series of northbound switchbacks up a rocky slope; when it crests the hill at 2.3 miles, **Snow Lake** (6.4 mi/10.3 km rt, 1,700 ft/518 m, moderate) comes into view. Access the lakeshore at 2.8 miles.

To continue toward **Gem Lake** (10 mi/16.1 km rt, 2,600 ft/792 m, strenuous), make a left at the junction at 3.4 miles and head west. More climbing awaits, but the higher you climb, the more surrounding peaks come into view—steep, stunning, and some glaciated. Reach much smaller Gem Lake at 5 miles.

This is an extremely popular trail among Seattle-area hikers and backpackers, and the parking lot fills up on weekends. Arrive early and be prepared to share this beautiful area with many other outdoor enthusiasts.

Getting There

Snow Lake trailhead is located near exit 52 on I-90, on the north side of the freeway. To get there from North Bend, follow I-90 east for 23 miles (37 km), take exit 52, and turn left onto Highway 906/Forest Road 9041. Follow for 1.4 miles (2.3 km) (the name of the road changes to Erste Strasse) and look for the Alpental parking area. The trailhead is on the right on the north side of the parking lot.

Winter Sports

The **Summit at Snoqualmie** (1001 Hwy. 906, 425/434-7669, www.summitatsnoqualmie.com, Dec.-Mar., $50-75) is a busy ski area with 2,000 ski-able acres and 25 lifts. Lights illuminate the slopes for night skiing. Equipment rentals are available ($22-43) for skis, snowboards, Nordic skis, and snowshoes. **Summit Tubing Hill** (Hwy. 906, across from Summit Central parking area, 9am-10pm Fri.-Sun., $24-28) is nearby, along with snowshoe trails and Nordic ski trails. An hour from Seattle, this popular ski area has plenty of parking and more than a dozen restaurants across three day lodges: Summit West, Summit Central, and Summit East.

Food

Red Mountain Coffee (773 Hwy. 906, Snoqualmie Pass, 425/434-7337, 7am-7pm daily, $4-6) is a gift shop serving coffee, hearty breakfast burritos, and hot pizza by the slice. With plenty of

From top to bottom: Goldmyer Hot Springs; Kendall Katwalk; waterfall near Snow Lake.

indoor seating, this cozy café is a wonderful place to warm up on a chilly morning or to fuel up before climbing into the wilderness.

The **Summit Pancake House** (Summit Inn, 603 Hwy. 906, 425/434-6249, Snoqualmie Pass, 7am-9pm daily, $9-23) serves American-style breakfast, lunch, dinner, and surprisingly, teriyaki. The wood-paneled, cabin-like space is filled with cozy booths and a big stone hearth.

Thirty minutes west of the pass, ★ **North Bend Bar & Grill** (145 E. North Bend Way, North Bend, 425/888-1234, www.northbendbarandgrill.com, 8am-midnight daily, $13-24) is a busy restaurant and bar that serves shareable appetizers, hot sandwiches, satisfying salads, fresh seafood, and hearty pastas. Proud of its fresh, local ingredients, the restaurant bakes its own breads and buns, sources in-season local produce, and pours a rotating selection of Pacific Northwest brews. Exposed wooden beams and a fireplace with couch seating make the place feel like a lodge.

Accommodations

The **Summit Inn** (603 Hwy. 906, Snoqualmie Pass, 425/434-6300, www.summitinnwashington.com, $100-180) is the only hotel at the pass. It has free Wi-Fi, microwaves, coffeemakers, and mini-fridges in each room. Coin-op laundry facilities are on-site, along with a sauna and a hot tub. The attached **Summit Pancake House** (425/434-6249, 7am-9pm daily, $9-23) serves breakfast, lunch, and dinner.

The **North Bend Motel** (322 E. North Bend Way, North Bend, 425/888-1121, $90-100) is a quiet, no-frills spot, walking distance to restaurants and coffee shops along the town's main drag. Grocery stores and clothing outlets are a few minutes' drive away. Affordable rooms offer free Wi-Fi, mini-fridges, microwaves, and outdoor entrances. Some rooms have views of the Cascade foothills.

Camping

Denny Creek Campground (Forest Rd. 5800, Snoqualmie Pass, 425/888-1421, Memorial Day-Labor Day) has 24 sites nestled in a large forested gulch between the east- and west-bound lanes of I-90. Although it isn't the quietest campground, it does provide immediate access to the best trails and activities in the Snoqualmie Pass area. The northbound PCT trailhead (which leads to Kendall Katwalk) is just 3 miles (4.8 km) away. The Denny Creek and Franklin Falls trailheads are located within the campground itself. **Reservations** (877/444-6777, www.recreation.gov, $20) are highly recommended.

Information and Services

Rangers at the **Snoqualmie Pass Visitor Center** (69805 SE Snoqualmie Pass Summit Rd., 8am-4pm Tues.-Sun. Memorial Day-Labor Day, 8am-4pm Sat.-Sun. Jan.-Mar.) are knowledgeable about trail conditions, closures, and campsites. The building once housed a snow ranger, and the roof is covered with more than a foot of snow in the winter. Maps are available.

While gas is available at one Chevron station at Snoqualmie, the town of North Bend (25 mi/40 km west of the pass on I-90) has a number of gas stations, as well as two grocery stores and a retail mall.

Leavenworth and Stevens Pass

Leavenworth is an adorable Bavarian village on the eastern edge of the Cascade Mountains with beautiful architecture, fantastic restaurants, lots of hotels, and fun festivals throughout the year. Peaks up to 6,000 feet (1,829 m) tall rise above the ornate rooftops, and the Wenatchee River flows through downtown. Outdoor enthusiasts flock to this busy tourist destination for hiking, rock climbing, whitewater rafting, mountain biking, and skiing. The Pacific Crest Trail at Stevens Pass, the nearest ski area, is a gateway into the stunning, pristine lakes, valleys, and peaks of the Northern Cascades.

Getting There

Leavenworth is on the eastern edge of the Cascade Range, 35 miles (56 km) southeast of Stevens Pass and a 90-minute drive northeast from Snoqualmie Pass.

From Snoqualmie Pass, follow I-90 east for 32 miles (52 km) to exit 85 for Highway 970. Head east on Highway 970 for 10 miles (16.1 km), then turn left to drive north on U.S. 97 for 35 miles (56 km). Turn left onto U.S. 2 west and arrive in Leavenworth in 4 miles (6.4 km).

All of these highways are open year-round, but are subject to harsh winter weather. Cars may be advised or required to carry chains **December-March.** (Plan an extra 30 minutes if you're driving from North Bend to Leavenworth, as North Bend is 25 miles (40 km) west of Snoqualmie Pass on I-90.)

To access Stevens Pass from the Seattle area, take I-405 to exit 23 for Highway 522 east. Continue 14 miles (22.5 km) to the intersection with U.S. 2, then head east on U.S. 2 for 50 miles (81 km) to Stevens Pass.

Sights

Walks through downtown Leavenworth's riverfront parks are incredibly pleasant, especially on a warm summer or autumn day. Start at **Waterfront Park** (8th St. and Commercial St.) and walk south on a bridge over the Wenatchee River to Blackbird Island, where you can watch waterfowl frolic.

You can also reach the island via a bridge from **Enchantment Park** (Enchantment Way), named for The Enchantments, the steep, rocky mountain range towering over Leavenworth's eastern horizon. The parks are minimally landscaped, with plenty of trees and sandy beaches on the northern shore of the Wenatchee River.

Hiking

The Pacific Crest Trail travels right through Stevens Pass, a ski area 35 miles (56 km) northeast of Leavenworth. The southbound PCT enters the Alpine Lakes Wilderness, while the northbound PCT provides access to the Henry M. Jackson and Glacier Peak Wilderness areas. These protected forests offer some of the most rugged, beautiful terrain in the entire state!

The Enchantments is an extremely popular hiking and backpacking area near Leavenworth, famous for its sparkling tarns and formidable granite peaks. Overnight stays are limited to permit-holders who compete in an annual lottery. Stop by the **ranger station** (600 Sherbourne St., Leavenworth, 509/548-2550, www.fs.usda.gov, 8am-4:30pm Mon.-Sat. June-Oct., 8am-4:30pm Mon.-Fri. Nov.-May) to learn more about hiking in The Enchantments.

Lake Valhalla 🅿

Distance: 6.2 mi/10 km round-trip
Duration: 3 hours
Elevation change: 1,300 ft/396 m
Effort: Moderate
Trailhead: Smithbrook
Pass/Fee: Self-issue wilderness permit (free)

This hike along the Pacific Crest Trail takes you to a shimmering alpine lake below Lichtenberg Mountain, an impossibly pointy granite peak.

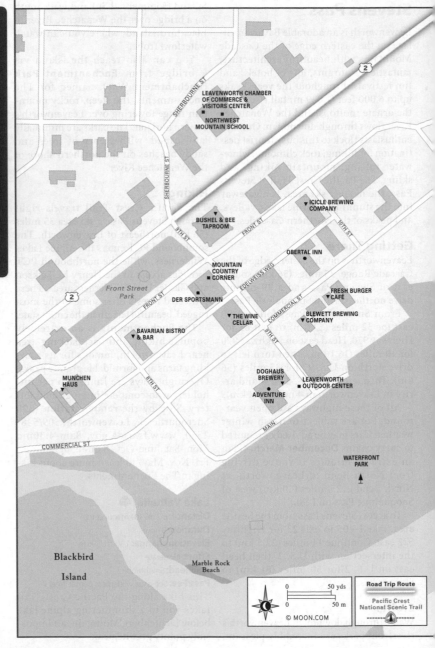

Leavenworth

LEAVENWORTH CHAMBER
OF COMMERCE &
VISITORS CENTER

NORTHWEST
MOUNTAIN SCHOOL

SHERBOURNE ST

SHERBOURNE ST

2

ICICLE BREWING
COMPANY

BUSHEL & BEE
TAPROOM

FRONT ST

9TH ST

10TH ST

OBERTAL INN

EDELWEISS WEG

Front Street
Park

MOUNTAIN
COUNTRY
CORNER

FRESH BURGER
CAFÉ

2

FRONT ST

DER SPORTSMANN

COMMERCIAL ST

BLEWETT BREWING
COMPANY

THE WINE
CELLAR

9TH ST

BAVARIAN BISTRO
& BAR

8TH ST

MUNCHEN
HAUS

DOGHAUS
BREWERY

LEAVENWORTH
OUTDOOR CENTER

ADVENTURE
INN

8TH ST

MAIN

COMMERCIAL ST

WATERFRONT
PARK

Blackbird
Island

Marble Rock
Beach

0   50 yds

0   50 m

© MOON.COM

Road Trip Route

**Pacific Crest
National Scenic Trail**

Starting at Smithbrook trailhead, the trail switchbacks up a forested slope for 0.7 mile before opening up into a meadow below a granite boulder field. Watch for raised, gnarled roots in the trail, and be prepared to climb over a couple of giant Douglas firs that toppled in winter storms. When the Smithbrook Trail meets the PCT at 1.2 miles, turn left to walk south. The elevation continues to gain gently as you walk through hemlocks, firs, cedars, and pines. Catch your first glimpse of Lichtenberg Mountain at 2.1 miles, when the forest gives way to huckleberry and brilliant red-berried Sitka ash bushes. Reach the high point of your hike at 2.7 miles, where the lake comes into view, framed by the jagged peaks and glaciers of the Alpine Lakes Wilderness south of Stevens Pass.

To get to **Lake Valhalla** (6.2 mi/10 km rt, 1,300 ft/396 m, moderate), continue on the PCT down the hill to the lake access trail at 3 miles. In addition to some overnight campsites, there's a lovely day-use peninsula next to the lakeshore (your turnaround point).

If you're eager for a challenge—and breathtaking, 360-degree views of the North Cascades—take the 0.6-mile spur trail departing from the PCT at 3.6 miles on your way back. It climbs 700 feet (213 m) to the top of **Mount McCausland** (8.4 mi/13.5 km rt, 2,000 ft/610 m, strenuous), where you'll get incredible views of the dramatic terrain, including Glacier Peak. Be sure to follow the trail all the way to the northern edge of the peak to find the cache box, where you can record your accomplishment in one of the notebooks inside. The trail is steep; you may want to use your hands while climbing, and trekking poles are helpful for the descent.

Getting There

From Stevens Pass, take U.S. 2 east for 4 miles (6.4 km). Turn left onto Forest Road 6700, heading northwest for 2.7 miles (4.3 km) to the trailhead parking area.

From Leavenworth, take U.S. 2 west for 31 miles (50 km). Turn right onto Forest Road 6700, heading northwest for 2.7 miles (4.3 km) to the trailhead parking area.

Big Chief Mountain, Lake Susan Jane, and Josephine Lake View @

Distance: 4.2-9.7 mi/6.8-15.6 km round-trip
Duration: 2-5 hours
Elevation change: 1,050-2,200 ft/320-671 m
Effort: Moderate
Trailhead: Pacific Crest Trail at Stevens Pass
Pass/Fee: Self-issue wilderness permit (free)

Hike under the chairlifts at Stevens Pass ski area toward two beautiful alpine lakes, soaking up incredible views of craggy Cascade peaks along the way.

Start your trek in the eastern parking area on the south side of U.S. 2. The trailhead isn't terribly obvious—look for the brown hiker icon on the south side of the parking lot and a trail leading sideways up a hill. Your hike begins in the woods, but almost immediately the trail opens into a brushy meadow. Walk underneath a chairlift at 0.4 mile and another at 1.1 miles, enjoying westward views of Cowboy Mountain across the ski area basin. The trail makes a series of switchbacks between 1.2 and 2.1 miles, ducking in and out of patches of trees as it approaches the crest of **Big Chief Mountain** (4.2 mi/6.8 km rt, 1,050 ft/320 m, moderate). Views from the top are spectacular: the Chiwaukum Mountains to the southeast with the Stuart Range and Enchantment Peaks behind them, plus 6,500-foot French Ridge to the south.

Turn around here, or continue along the PCT as it descends underneath another chairlift and a set of power lines above Mill Creek Basin. Cross the ski area boundary at 3.2 miles, step over a mossy creek at 3.6 miles, and reach tiny tarn **Lake Susan Jane** at 4.2 miles (8.4 mi/43.5 km rt, 1,800 ft/549 m, moderate).

To see much grander **Josephine Lake** (9.7 mi/15.6 km rt, 2,200 ft/671 m, moderate), continue up the ridgeline to the PCT's intersection with the Icicle Ridge

Trail at 4.8 miles. To get the best view of the shimmering turquoise lake, walk south on the PCT for 0.1 mile to the overlook.

Recreation

Leavenworth's summers are hot, and there's no better way to cool off than by splashing into the Wenatchee River, which runs right through town. **Leavenworth Outdoor Center** (321 9th St., 509/548-8823, www.leavenworthoutdoorcenter.com, call for hours, $20-40) rents tubes, stand-up paddleboards, and kayaks. Depending on the season, there are options for four-hour or two-hour floats on nearby Icicle Creek and the Wenatchee River. A shuttle drops you off a few miles upstream where you can jump in with your tube and float back down to Waterfront Park. Prefer to stay dry? LOC rents bikes, too, and suggests routes around town depending on your skill level.

Whitewater Rafting

The Wenatchee River is one of Washington's most popular whitewater destinations. Zip into a wetsuit and hop onto a guided raft trip with **Alpine Adventures** (11358 Riverbend Dr., 800/723-8386, www.alpineadventures.com, Apr.-July, $70-80) to splash through the Leavenworth area. **River Riders** (10860 Hwy. 2, 800/448-7238, www.riverrider.com, Apr.-July, $65-95) also offers trips on the Wenatchee in the spring and early summer when the water is high. Trips down the river include areas of exhilarating whitewater as well as sections of smooth sailing over calm waters. While the Wenatchee River's season is short, trips on other nearby rivers are available throughout August and September.

From top to bottom: sunset at Lake Valhalla; fall colors on Big Chief Mountain; truffles and sausage at Icicle Brewing Company.

Rock Climbing

The crags and boulders of Leavenworth attract rock climbers from around the globe. Guides at **Northwest Mountain School** (940 Hwy. 2, 509/548-5823, www.mountainschool.com, Mar.-Nov., $100-200) offer beginners classes, plus specialized courses with instruction in lead climbing, multi-pitch, crack climbing, and sport climbing.

Mountain Biking

During the summer, the slopes at **Stevens Pass** (35 mi/56 km northwest of Leavenworth, U.S. 2, 206/812-4510, www.stevenspass.com, noon-8pm Thurs.-Fri., 10am-6pm Sat.-Sun. late June-Aug., 10am-6pm Fri.-Sun. Sept.) are open for mountain biking ($43), as well as disc golf ($15), scenic chairlift rides ($15), and hiking. The park's downhill bike trails are the only ones in Washington State accessible via chairlift.

More mountain biking trails are accessible at the **Leavenworth Ski Hill** (10701 Ski Hill Dr., 509/548-6975, www.skileavenworth.com). These 5-6-mile loops vary in just a five-minute drive from downtown.

Skiing

A popular ski area for Seattle-area residents, **Stevens Pass** (35 mi/56 km northwest of Leavenworth, U.S. 2, 206/812-4510, www.stevenspass.com, 9am-4pm Mon.-Tues., 9am-10pm Wed.-Sun. and holidays Dec.-Mar., $69-89) sits at 4,000 feet (1,219 m) and has a reputation among Seattle-area residents for great snow. On sunny days, views of the Alpine Lakes Wilderness and the North Cascades from the resort's hilltops are absolutely unbeatable. There are 37 runs, many of which are open for night skiing after 4pm ($45).

Entertainment and Events
★ Oktoberfest

Beer, bratwursts, and nonstop entertainment fill the streets of Leavenworth during the annual **Oktoberfest** (www.leavenworthoktoberfest.com, first three weekends in Oct., $10-20/day). Don your lederhosen and dirndl, and join hundreds of other partygoers dressed in traditional German garb. (Of course, you're welcome to enjoy all the festivities in regular clothes, too.) Local live music acts play 6pm-midnight on Fridays and 1pm-1am on Saturdays across four stages. The mayor performs a traditional keg-tapping ceremony at 1pm every Saturday. The festival is set up on the east end of town near the **Festhalle** (10th and Commercial Sts.). Downtown Leavenworth's restaurants and shops are open to the public and stay quite busy during festival weekends.

Free **shuttle** transportation is offered within Leavenworth; shuttles to and from nearby Wenatchee ($8-18/person) and other towns are also available. It's a good idea to buy tickets online in advance, but tickets are also available at the gate (cash only). Overnight accommodations book up to three months in advance—especially on the weekend.

Breweries

Leavenworth's three breweries couldn't be more different from each other in character. If you love beer, they're all worth checking out.

Icicle Brewing Company (935 Front St., 509/548-2739, www.iciclebrewing.com, 11am-10pm Sun.-Thurs., 11am-11pm Fri.-Sat., $10) is the biggest and busiest brewery in town. Ask the bartender to pour you a beer from a tap handle shaped like a giant icicle, then grab a table in the lovely outdoor seating area or head upstairs to relax overlooking the brewery operations in the basement. Brews span the spectrum, from pilsners to porters with a heavy dose of IPAs in the middle. This brewery has dessert covered, too: the Dark Persuasion, a rich, velvety German chocolate cake ale. Snack plates include meats, cheeses, and nuts, as well as warm pretzels and tomato soup.

Blewett Brewing (911 Commercial St., 509/888-8809, www.blewettbrew.com, noon-9pm Mon.-Thurs., noon-10pm Fri., 11am-10pm Sat., 11am-9pm Sun., $13-18) brews IPAs, lagers, and ales. Their gourmet pizzas include ingredients like aged mozzarella, braised mushrooms, and smoked red onion. Of course, classic cheese and pepperoni is available, too. The modern interior is somehow both rustic and polished, with wooden furniture and copper brew kettles behind the bar.

Located in the basement of the Adventure Inn, **Doghaus Brewery** (321 9th St., 509/393-3134, www.doghausbrewery.com, 3pm-9pm Mon.-Thurs., 1pm-10pm Fri., noon-10pm Sat., noon-6pm Sun., $10) keeps eight beers in rotation and showcases seasonal brews and experimental one-offs. This is Leavenworth's smallest brewery, with just five barstools set around a tiny counter, but the beers are big in personality, and just outside the door is a giant beer garden near the river. Plus, the space is dog-friendly!

Wine-Tasting
Downtown Leavenworth is home to more than 20 tasting rooms featuring wines from local vineyards and winemakers. Tasting fees vary, but are (usually) waived with bottle purchase. Kill six birds with one stone at **The Wine Cellar** (217 9th St., 206/618-2586, 11am-7pm daily), where you can try wines from Basel Cellars, Isenhower Cellars, Obelisco Estate Winery, Patterson Cellars, and Sigillo Cellars. The tasting rooms are downstairs, below sidewalk level.

Shopping
Der Sportsmann (837 Front St., 509/548-5623, www.dersportsmann.com, 9am-7pm daily) is an immaculate, well-stocked outdoor store specializing in equipment for hiking, climbing, mountain biking, and cross-country skiing. The store also stocks fishing gear, accessories for

Leavenworth

hunting, backpacking food, and a wide array of outdoor recreation guidebooks.

If you're looking for Bavarian-themed gifts, check out **Mountain Country Corner** (843 Front St., 509/548-5312, 9am-9pm Mon.-Sat., 9am-8pm Sun. May-Oct. and Dec., 9am-7pm daily Nov. and Jan.-Apr.), a small retail store packed to the brim with a wide array of clothing, gifts, souvenirs, knives, hats, leather goods, and sunglasses.

Food

Find quite possibly the most perfect post-hike food (a burger, of course) at ★ **Fresh Burger Café** (923 Commercial St., 509/548-3300, www.freshburgercafe. com, 11am-8pm daily, $9-13), a casual, counter-service café serving juicy, satisfying burgers to hungry outdoor enthusiasts. Choose from one of their signature burgers, or design your own from a list of fresh ingredients. Seating inside is limited, but there are plenty of tables on the front porch and back patio.

South (913 Front St., 509/888-4328, www.southrestaurants.com, 11:30am-9pm Mon.-Thurs., 11:30am-11pm Fri., 11am-11pm Sat., 11am-9pm Sun., $11-18) serves creative Latin and Mexican fare busting with flavor. The delightfully colorful space features painted longhorn skulls on the wall and bright lights in the bar. Sit in the charming outdoor patio beneath a wall of grapevines.

For a fancy drink with dinner, climb the stairs to the cozy yet elegant **Bavarian Bistro & Bar** (801 Front St., 509/548-5074, www.bavarianbistrobar.com, 11am-10pm Sun.-Wed., 11am-11pm Thurs., 11am-midnight Fri.-Sat., $11-15). An extensive beverage list features unusual (and delicious!) cocktails, as well as wine and beer. The menu offers a balance of German, American, and globally inspired items such as schnitzels, burgers, salads, pretzels, charcuterie, and fries. Food is available until 10pm, after most restaurants in town have closed.

Choose from more than 16 artisan mustards at **Munchen Haus** (709 Front St., 509/548-1158, www.munchenhaus. com, 11am-10pm Sun.-Thurs., 11am-1am Fri.-Sat., $7-10), a casual wiener joint with outside seating in a sausage garden. Locally made European sausages and wursts are utterly delicious. Beers from Leavenworth's own Icicle Brewing are on tap at the bar, around the corner from the order window. Enjoy live music (6pm-9pm Thurs.-Sat.) in the garden during summer and outdoor fireplaces on chilly evenings.

Get world-famous Washington apples at the **Leavenworth Farmers Market** (696 Hwy. 2, 4pm-8pm Thurs. June-Oct.), along with peaches, plums, berries, vegetables, and locally made goods. You'll definitely want to check this out if you're shopping for unique gifts. Booths are set up in Lions Club Park in downtown Leavenworth during summer.

Accommodations

October is the busiest month in Leavenworth, thanks to the Oktoberfest celebrations. Accommodations on festival weekends are at a premium, so book early (three or more months in advance) to guarantee a room. If the festival doesn't interest you, September is an ideal month to visit: The weather is lovely, prices are low, and the whirlwind of summer tourism has settled.

Owned and operated by a family of self-proclaimed "foodies," the ★ **Obertal Inn** (1414 Commercial St., 509/548-5204, www.obertal.com, $99-329) serves a complimentary breakfast that is exquisite: fresh fruit salad with nuts and seeds, a waffle bar with gourmet sauces and compotes, veggie-bacon scrambles, and premium Italian coffee. The 27 rooms include outdoor entrances, fireplaces, and cozy bathrobes; some rooms have spa tubs with jets. Downtown restaurants and shops are steps away from this pet-friendly inn.

The Adventure Inn (321 9th St., 509/548-5250, www.adventureinnleavenworth.com, $89-219) is a casual hotel geared toward outdoor enthusiasts. The nine rooms are designed as studio, one-bedroom, and two-bedroom suites. The inn is located on the 3rd floor of the historic Cascade Sanitarium, where the 1st floor houses the Leavenworth Outdoor Center (river tube rentals are available). A tiny microbrewery has a tasting room set up in the basement next to the Leavenworth Beer Garden.

Located on the west edge of town next to the Wenatchee River, **Icicle Village Resort** (505 Hwy. 2, 509/548-7000, www.iciclevillage.com, $139-275) boasts a seasonal pool, a spa, a restaurant, and a mini golf course. The rustic yet elegant rooms are appointed with microwaves, mini-fridges, coffeemakers, and free Wi-Fi; many feature mountain views. A complimentary breakfast buffet is served 7am-10am.

Many visitors choose to stay in cabins and vacation rentals. **Destination Leavenworth** (940 Hwy. 2, 509/548-4230, www.destinationleavenworth.com, from $200) manages 38 properties within 30 minutes of town, including downtown condos, modest homes, and riverfront palaces.

Camping

Lake Wenatchee State Park (21588 Hwy. 207, 509/763-3101, www.parks.state.wa.us, Apr.-Oct., $32-40) has 155 campsites with picnic tables, fire rings, and access to heated bathrooms with plumbing. Glacier-fed Lake Wenatchee sits just below Grizzly Peak, one of the few places where the path of the PCT actually summits a mountain instead of skirting the side. The park has eight miles of hiking trails, including a lakeshore loop, and provides access to the Nason Ridge, Hidden Lakes, and Heather Lake trailheads.

Information and Services

Stop for maps and information at the **Leavenworth Ranger Station** (600 Sherbourne St., 509/548-2550, www.fs.usda.gov, 8am-4:30pm Mon.-Sat. June-Oct., 8am-4:30pm Mon.-Fri. Nov.-May). Ask rangers for up-to-date trail conditions and closures, as well as wildfire activity.

The Leavenworth Chamber of Commerce staffs a **visitor center** (940 Hwy. 2, 509/548-5807, www.leavenworth.org, 8am-6pm Mon.-Thurs., 8am-8pm Fri.-Sat., 8am-4pm Sun.) with detailed information about lodging, restaurants, festivals, and town happenings.

⬥ Side Trip: Skykomish

Skykomish is a tiny community 16 miles (26 km) west of Stevens Pass on U.S. 2. Rooted in the construction of a railroad, the town is often visited by PCT hikers.

Getting There

Skykomish is 50 miles (81 km) west of Leavenworth on U.S. 2. This highway is open all year, but is subject to winter snowstorms. Vehicles may be advised or required to carry chains **December-March.**

Hiking

A hike on the **Iron Goat Trail** (9 mi/14.5 km one-way with options for shorter hikes, 1-6 hours) offers a fascinating glimpse into the history of mountain travel. Through interpretive signage and relics of old railroad tracks, you can learn about the unlikely construction and operation of the railroad through Stevens Pass in the 1890s. Travel through this mountain pass was dangerous, and fraught with accidents and difficulties related to the area's harsh weather and rugged terrain, but railroad tracks were built anyway, and passengers made the risky trip on a regular basis.

Railroads are still functional in this area today, although some of the tracks have been rerouted through safer tunnels and corridors. The Iron Goat Trail is built along defunct railroad tunnels and tracks cut in the hillside, and the wooded hiking trail follows the old railroad grade. A great trail for kids due to its easy elevation profile, this hike is also a must-do for history buffs. While the trail in its entirety is 9 miles long from end to end, many of the tunnels and main historical attractions are accessible via a 3-mile loop hike from the parking area.

Getting There

The trailhead is 10 miles (16.1 km) east of Skykomish on U.S. 2, about a 10-minute drive. The parking area is well signed and easy to find on the north side of the highway. Restrooms are available.

Food and Accommodations

Built in 1922, the historic **Cascadia Inn** (210 E. Railroad Ave., 360/677-2030, www.historiccascadia.com, $70-105)

has 14 hotel rooms and a casual restaurant. All but three rooms are TV-free, encouraging guests to relax in the peace and antiquity of the property. The **café** (10am-5pm Mon.-Wed., 10am-7pm Thurs., 8am-9pm Fri.-Sat., 8am-7pm Sun., $8-15) has been serving homestyle favorites since opening day in 1922; choose from bacon and eggs, sandwiches, and soups to burgers and steaks. The **Caboose Room Lounge** (5pm-9pm Sun.-Mon. and Thurs., 5pm-10pm Fri.-Sat.) is a favorite watering hole of both locals and travelers on their way over Stevens Pass.

Whistling Post (116 E. Railroad Ave., 360/677-2111, 11am-11pm Mon.-Thurs., 11am-2am Fri.-Sun., $6-12) is a snazzy sports bar that was built in 2013, but designed to look like an original 1897 Skykomish tavern that existed in the same location. In the 1920s, the original tavern (in operation from 1897-2010 under one name or another) survived Prohibition by calling itself Maple Leaf Confectionery while quietly still operating a card room and a dance hall. Thoroughly modern, it now features big-screen TVs and pool tables, with historical architectural touches.

★ Stehekin

TOP EXPERIENCE

Almost 60 miles (97 km) from Leavenworth, U.S. 2 and U.S. 97 climb north to Chelan, a sunny vacation town on the southern shore of a 50-mile natural lake. At the northern tip of the lake, accessible only by hiking trails or by boat from Chelan, sits a tiny village nestled in a mountainous river valley. (Stehekin means "the way through.") The valley was once used for foot travel through the wild and rugged North Cascades, which border the lake on both sides. Peaceful and isolated, Stehekin offers a wild yet luxurious escape from modern life, with delicious food, well-appointed accommodations, copious camp spots, and miles of hiking trails into the mountains. The Pacific Crest Trail skirts the northern edge of the Stehekin River Valley between Glacier Peak Wilderness and North Cascades National Park.

Getting There

Chelan is about 60 miles (97 km) northeast of Leavenworth, and the Lady of the Lake boat dock in Chelan is about an hour's drive. From Leavenworth, follow U.S. 2 east for 19 miles (31 km) toward Wenatchee. Following signs for Chelan, take U.S. 97 Alternate north for 43 miles (69 km) to Chelan.

Stehekin has **no roads** to the outside world, which means there are only two ways of getting there from Chelan: by boat or on foot (see *Getting Around*).

Sights
Stehekin Landing

More than 50 miles long, Lake Chelan is the largest natural lake in the state, with the craggy splendor of the North Cascades viewable from the public dock at **Stehekin Landing.** On calm days, the mountains reflect in the lake's glassy surface—there's nowhere better to get a sense of the place than from this waterfront location. Stehekin Landing is a hub for travelers, home to the boat dock and the North Cascades Lodge at Stehekin, which houses a restaurant and a small general store. This is where the red shuttle buses depart from, and where *Lady of the Lake* boats—the only means of motorized access here—arrive and depart. You'll also find a visitors center, a campground, and a building housing public showers, coin-operated laundry, and a pay phone.

Rainbow Falls

The Stehekin Valley is nestled between ridgelines with peaks exceeding 5,000 feet (1,524 m). As snow-fed creeks and streams make their way down the mountain slopes, the water surges over cliffs and rock faces on its way toward the Stehekin River.

At **Rainbow Falls,** a 300-foot waterfall splashes into a vivid plunge pool before cascading further over a series of smaller rocks and boulders. From Stehekin Valley Road, follow the short path to the lower viewpoint, where the waterfall is visible in its entirety. A higher viewpoint (left of the falls) offers a closer view of the white ribbon of water.

Rainbow Falls is 3.5 miles (5.6 km) north of Stehekin Landing (or 1.7 mi/2.7 km north of Stehekin Pastry Company) on Stehekin Valley Road. The red shuttle bus makes a stop here, or you can walk or ride a bike to this trailhead.

High Bridge

At the end of Stehekin Valley Road, **High Bridge** stretches over the Stehekin River and the nearby tributary of Agnes Creek. Walk across the bridge for a view of the icy, turquoise Stehekin River as it rushes over smooth, granite boulders in a dramatic, lichen-speckled gorge. The bridge isn't terribly tall, nor is the structure itself much to marvel at, but it does provide passage into wild, rugged North Cascades National Park. Half a dozen hiking trails depart from this area, including the Pacific Crest Trail; in fact, High Bridge is part of the PCT itself. The nearby High Bridge ranger station was constructed in the 1930s during the New Deal era, when many national forests were developed to increase use and tourism.

The bridge is 11 miles (17.7 km) northwest of Stehekin Landing.

Hiking
Agnes Gorge

Distance: 5 mi/8 km round-trip
Duration: 2 hours
Elevation change: 500 ft/152 m
Effort: Easy
Trailhead: Agnes Gorge

While the PCT follows the southern side of Agnes Creek, the views of the mountains and the gorge are far superior on the northern side along the Agnes Gorge

Stehekin

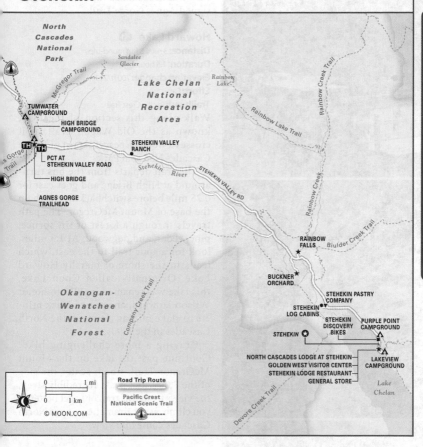

Trail. Follow this easy trail to catch a great glimpse of Agnes Peak and end at a dramatic, turquoise waterfall.

Begin your hike on the Agnes Gorge Trail by walking south through a forest of both coniferous and deciduous trees, glancing behind you to behold Mount McGregor, one of Stehekin Valley's most prominent peaks. The trail follows Agnes Creek, and though you'll hear its rushing waters in the gorge below, you won't see it yet. The trail enters Glacier Peak Wilderness at 1.2 miles; the rugged and famously remote wilderness area is south

of North Cascades National Park. Agnes Peak and its glacier come into view as the trees thin at 1.5 miles. A few tributary streams cross the trail between 2 and 2.2 miles, but at 2.5 miles is the best waterfall of them all: Agnes Creek enters a narrow gorge and tumbles over boulders into a turquoise pool. The trail ends at the waterfall; return the way you came.

Getting There

Take the red bus to High Bridge, the bus turnaround. Cross High Bridge, entering North Cascades National Park, then

follow the dirt road for 0.25 mile past the PCT trailhead and up the hill to the well-signed Agnes Gorge Trail.

Howard Lake
Distance: 3 mi/4.8 km round-trip
Duration: 1.5 hours
Elevation change: 700 ft/213 m
Effort: Easy
Trailhead: Pacific Crest Trail

Walk along this section of the PCT, known as the Old Wagon Trail, as it crosses a woodsy, peaceful part of North Cascades National Park.

The trail departs from the bus turn-around at High Bridge and goes east for 0.25 mile before switchbacking north up the base of Mount McGregor. The path travels through a forest of fir, spruce, pine, cedar, and dogwood. At 1.3 miles, look for a spur trail to the east, which leads to the shore of marshy Howard Lake. Originally called Coon Lake, this lake was renamed in 2015 to honor Wilson Howard, one of two black miners to stake mining claims in the North Cascades in the 1890s.

Craving a more challenging hike? Continue past the lake on the Mount McGregor Trail, which scales the side of the 8,000-foot peak. Incredibly steep, the views from this trail only get better as you climb, as the dramatic, rugged North Cascades come into view.

Getting There
Take the red bus to High Bridge, the bus turnaround. The northbound PCT departs from the bus turnaround area.

Recreation
Horseback Riding
Climb onto a beautiful, black-and-tan Norwegian Fjord Horse for a ride along one of Stehekin's peaceful hiking trails. The sure-footed horses know the local trails well. **Stehekin Outfitters**

From top to bottom: *Lady of the Lake* at Stehekin Landing; Rainbow Falls; High Bridge.

(Stehekin Valley Rd., 9 mi/14.5 km from the landing, 509/682-7742, www.stehekinoutfitters.com, $65-140) provides helmets, saddles, and basic instruction on horse handling. During half-day or full-day rides, guides lead you and your horse along the trail, stopping to admire nearby peaks, glaciers, and unique natural features.

Kayaking

To experience Stehekin's beauty from the surface of the lake, rent a kayak at the **General Store** (next to the Stehekin Lodge Restaurant, 9am-6pm daily May-Oct., $20/hour). Paddle across Lake Chelan to see ancient pictographs on the south shore's cliffs and soak up views of the area's highest peaks: The Castle, Mount McGregor, and the Boston Glacier.

Biking

Scenic Stehekin Valley Road runs along the northern edge of Lake Chelan, then follows the shore of the Stehekin River. Bring your own bike or rent one from **Stehekin Discovery Bikes** (Stehekin Valley Rd., 0.25 mi from the landing, www.stehekindiscoverybikes.com, $5/hour, $25/day) to explore 12-mile (19.3-km) Stehekin Valley Road and 2.3-mile (3.7 km) Company Creek Road, a shorter road running along the other side of the river north of the Harlequin Bridge. Both roads are lightly traveled by car, and local drivers are friendly to pedestrians and bicyclists. Another bonus of traveling by bike: You can ride to the Stehekin Pastry Company—much faster than walking or waiting for the next red bus.

Entertainment and Events

Stehekin homesteaders in the 1910s dug canals from nearby Rainbow Creek to their orchards to irrigate apple trees. See these (still-functional) canals and the beautiful grove they sustain at **Buckner Orchard Harvest Fest** (Stehekin Valley Rd. and Buckner Ln., www.bucknerhomestead.org, first weekend in Oct., free). Enjoy a peaceful walk around the homestead, and stay for apple-picking, cider-making, live music, a community potluck, and even a poetry night. Bring your own container to take cider with you!

The festival is held at Buckner Orchard, 3 miles (4.8 km) north of the landing. Walk, ride a bike, or take the red bus to the Rainbow Falls stop. The orchard is on the south side of the road.

Food

The enormous, delectable cinnamon rolls at ★ **Stehekin Pastry Company** (Stehekin Valley Rd., 509/682-7742, www.stehekinpastry.com, 7:30am-5pm daily mid-June-mid-Oct., 8am-3pm Wed.-Sun. May mid-June and late Oct., $5-9) entice hikers and visitors for days leading up to their arrival in Stehekin. The bakery, famous for its quality and variety, is set in a giant log cabin 2 miles (3.2 km) north from the landing. Inside the spacious yet cozy place is a pastry case overflowing with pies, tarts, muffins, cookies, buns, cakes, and those famous cinnamon rolls. In addition to sweets, you'll find savory home-style pizzas, sandwiches, and soups that are both hearty and satisfying. Stehekin-themed gifts such as sweatshirts and stickers are also for sale.

The building itself may not look fancy, but the **Stehekin Lodge Restaurant** (509/682-4494, www.lodgeatstehekin.com, breakfast, lunch, and dinner daily May-Oct., hours vary seasonally Nov.-Apr., $10-25) serves artful, upscale cuisine. Classic breakfast items include scrambles, waffles, and biscuits and gravy, while lunch is limited to grilled ciabatta sandwiches. Dinner entrées include seafood, meat, and vegetarian options—the bacon-wrapped meatloaf is a hiker favorite. Local wines and a variety of bottled beers are also available. Eat inside the café-like setting or enjoy the lakefront scenery on the outside deck.

Groceries are almost nonexistent in Stehekin, but the organic fruits and veggies at **The Garden** (995 Stehekin Valley Rd., www.stehekingarden.com, 8am-5pm daily late May-Oct.) couldn't be fresher. The colorful garden teems with life, filled with blossoming fruit trees, vegetable plants, and bees buzzing about. The gardener, Karl, married his wife in Stehekin in 1977 and purchased the property one year later. Watch as he pulls your carrots from the earth, meet the goats responsible for the delicious goat cheese, and taste raw honey made from the garden's bees.

Accommodations

Located next to the landing, **North Cascades Lodge at Stehekin** (Stehekin Valley Rd., 509/682-4494, www. lodgeatstehekin.com, $145-250) offers charming, woodsy guest rooms and cabins that are warm and cozy; many feature views of the lakeshore, the marina, and the rugged peaks across the water. The 20 seasonal guest rooms in the Alpine House and Swissmont (the main lodge buildings) are only available May-September when the restaurant is open. The rest of the year, five cabins with kitchenettes are available. (The lodge advises that guests bring their own food.) **Reservations** (855/685-4167) are recommended, especially in late September and early October when Stehekin's Buckner Orchard hosts the Harvest Fest.

Fully furnished ★ **Stehekin Log Cabins** (Stehekin Valley Rd., 2 mi/3.2 km from the landing, 509/682-7742, www. stehekinpastry.com, $240) not only provide you with momentary access to the famous bakery, but your stay also includes a vehicle with which to explore the 20 miles of roads in the Stehekin Valley—no need to rely on the red shuttle bus! Cabins are located on a lush lawn behind the bakery and next to a horse pasture thick with chickens roaming. One cabin accommodates nine guests, the other accommodates five guests. The two-story cabins are designed with kitchen and living areas on the 1st floor and bedrooms on the 2nd floor. Views include the rugged mountain peaks on either side.

Peaceful and secluded, **Stehekin Valley Ranch** (Stehekin Valley Rd., 9 mi/14.5 km from the landing, 800/536-0745, www. stehekinvalleyranch.com, $105-140 pp) is a gorgeous property under Mount McGregor, Stehekin's most prominent peak. Accommodations include a cabin, tent cabin, or gypsy wagon (a wagon-themed tiny house). Cabins and wagons have their own bath; guests in tent cabins share a common bathroom and shower house less than 250 feet away. Gourmet meals are included with your stay and are served family-style in a great hall with beautifully hewn log tables and a wood-burning stove. Transportation on the red shuttle bus is also included in the rate.

Camping

Camping is free in Stehekin. Backcountry permits are required and can be obtained at the **Golden West Visitor Center** (509/699-2080 ext. 14, 8:30am-5pm daily May-Oct.) near the landing. While reservations are not required, requests for advance reservations can be submitted as early as March 15 for camping between May 15 and September 30.

There are two campgrounds within a short walk of the boat landing that enjoy most of the village's amenities. **Purple Point Campground** (Stehekin Valley Rd., 0.25 mi from the landing) has six small tent sites built into a steep, rocky hillside. **Lakeview Campground** (on the hill behind the visitors center) has 10 tent sites. Bear-proof food storage containers are on-site at both campgrounds. Each has bathrooms with a flush toilet, potable water, and a dishwashing sink.

At the end of the Stehekin Valley Road lie two primitive campgrounds geared toward backpackers: **High Bridge** and **Tumwater Campgrounds** (Stehekin Valley Rd., 12 mi/19.3 km from the landing)—remote, isolated, and peaceful. The campgrounds offer the best access to the hiking trails in North Cascades National

Park and Glacier Peak Wilderness, including the PCT, the Mount McGregor Trail, and the Agnes Gorge Trail. These camps are small, with just two sites each, and geared toward backpackers. Picnic tables, fire rings, and pit toilets are on-site; potable water is not, so bring plenty of your own for cooking and drinking. To get there, ride the red shuttle bus to the High Bridge bus turnaround and walk across High Bridge. Campgrounds are well-signed.

Information and Services

Located on a hill south of Stehekin Landing, the **Golden West Visitor Center** (509/699-2080 ext. 14, www.nps.gov, 8:30am-5pm daily May-Oct.) provides information about camping options and hiking trails, and can advise on trail closures due to wildfire, an annual occurrence. If you're camping in the Stehekin area, obtain a free backcountry permit here. A detailed relief map of the national park displays and names the park's major peaks, glaciers, and trails.

One building (0.1 mi north of the landing) houses public showers, coin-operated laundry, and—because cell phone reception in Stehekin is nonexistent—a pay phone.

Getting Around

There are only two ways of getting here: by boat or by hiking trail.

Within the Stehekin Valley, all businesses, hikes, and attractions are located along 20 miles of road that can be accessed on foot, by bicycle, or via a red shuttle bus operated by the park service.

By Boat

Most travelers visit Stehekin by boat on the *Lady of the Lake* (1418 W. Woodin Ave., Chelan, 509/682-4584, www.ladyofthelake.com, $40-61 round-trip). From the southern end of Lake Chelan,

From top to bottom: Lake Chelan; Stehekin Pastry Company; Stehekin Lodge Restaurant.

the boats motor north up the 50-mile lake in 2.5-4 hours. Two boats—the *Lady II* and the *Lady Express*—offer indoor and outdoor seating options. During your trip, views showcase the dramatic climate shift from dry, arid eastern Washington to the rugged, high-elevation North Cascades. The captain may even jump on the microphone to share interesting geographical and historical facts about the region.

Both boats operate year-round, although the off-season schedule is less robust with departures only three days per week. During high season (May 1-Oct. 15), both boats depart daily at 8:30am from Chelan and dock at Stehekin Landing, next to the lodge, restaurant, gift shop, and marina. Overnight visitors leave their cars at the parking lot in Chelan (across the street from the dock) for a $7 fee per vehicle.

On Foot

There aren't any short, easy ways to hike into Stehekin, but it can certainly be done. The following options end at High Bridge, at the western edge of Stehekin Valley Road. From here, you can catch a red bus into town.

The shortest, most direct hiking route into Stehekin starts at Rainy Pass on Highway 20 (35 mi/56 km west of Winthrop). Hike south on the **Pacific Crest Trail** for 18 miles (29 km) to reach High Bridge. (This section of the PCT is also known as Bridge Creek Trail and Old Wagon Trail.) Views of the surrounding territory are slim-to-none; you'll spend most of the hike in the forest.

Alternatively, from the Cascade Pass parking area (23 mi/37 km east of Marblemount), you can reach Stehekin by hiking over **Cascade Pass,** through Horseshoe Basin, and along the old Stehekin Valley Road to High Bridge. This scenic 23-mile trek showcases some of the most stunning terrain in North Cascades National Park.

By Bus

Most Stehekin visitors get around on the vintage-style **red buses** (four trips daily July-Sept., two trips daily May and Oct., $8 one-way), which have see-through windowpanes on the ceiling for optimal sightseeing. The route along Stehekin Valley Road begins at the Stehekin Landing and travels all the way to the end of the road at High Bridge, stopping along the way at the bakery, Harlequin Bridge, and Stehekin Valley Ranch. The bus schedule is coordinated with the arrivals of *Lady of the Lake* boats at the landing. Pick up a schedule on the boat or at the Golden West Visitor Center.

Mazama and Winthrop

Mazama is a tiny community just outside the eastern edge of North Cascades National Park. Highway 20, the North Cascades Scenic Byway, follows the path of the Methow River as it flows peacefully through Mazama and a Western-themed town called Winthrop. With restaurants, services, and accommodations, these two towns make perfect base camps for exploring the eastern side of the national park. The Pacific Crest Trail crosses the highway at Rainy Pass on its way from Stehekin to the Canadian border.

Getting There

Winthrop is 60 miles (97 km) north of Chelan, about an hour's drive, and Mazama is 13 miles (20.9 km) west of Winthrop on Highway 20. From Leavenworth, Wenatchee, or Chelan, follow U.S. 97 north to Highway 153 (at Pateros), then turn left to head northwest on Highway 153 for 30 miles (48 km). Take Highway 20 west for 11 miles (17.7 km) to Winthrop, or 24 miles (39 km) to Mazama.

Alternatively, between May and October, you can reach Mazama and Winthrop from the west. From I-5, take

Mazama to Canada

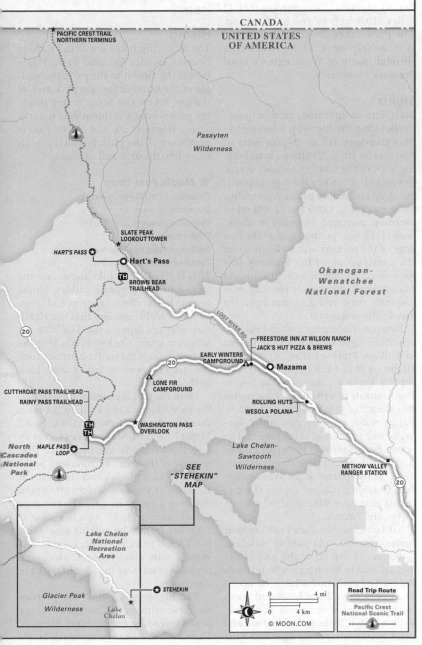

PACIFIC CREST TRAIL
NORTHERN TERMINUS

CANADA
UNITED STATES
OF AMERICA

Pasayten
Wilderness

SLATE PEAK
LOOKOUT TOWER

HART'S PASS

Hart's Pass

BROWN BEAR
TRAILHEAD

Okanogan-
Wenatchee
National Forest

LOST RIVER RD

FREESTONE INN AT WILSON RANCH
JACK'S HUT PIZZA & BREWS

EARLY WINTERS
CAMPGROUND

Mazama

LONE FIR
CAMPGROUND

CUTTHROAT PASS TRAILHEAD
RAINY PASS TRAILHEAD

ROLLING HUTS
WESOLA POLANA

North
Cascades
National
Park

MAPLE PASS
LOOP

WASHINGTON PASS
OVERLOOK

Lake Chelan-
Sawtooth
Wilderness

METHOW VALLEY
RANGER STATION

SEE
"STEHEKIN"
MAP

Lake Chelan
National
Recreation
Area

STEHEKIN

Glacier Peak
Wilderness

Lake
Chelan

| 0 | 4 mi |
| 0 | 4 km |

Road Trip Route

Pacific Crest
National Scenic Trail

© MOON.COM

exit 230 toward Burlington and head east on Highway 20 for 120 miles (193 km) to Mazama. Continue another 13 miles (20.9 km) to reach Winthrop. The drive takes about 2.5 hours and is incredibly scenic as the road twists through some of Washington's most dramatic mountains.

Sights

Built onto an enormous granite massif overlooking the highway, **Washington Pass Overlook** (17 mi/27 km west of Mazama on Hwy. 20) offers a breathtaking view of the North Cascades Scenic Byway as it meanders through impossibly steep and pointy peaks. Mountains, some exceeding 8,000 feet (2,438 m) in elevation, surround the entire overlook. Stop at the interpretive signs at the east edge of the parking area to learn about the construction of the highway (the high-elevation stretch took 10 summers to complete!), then follow the 0.25-mile loop onto the overlook to gaze upon the area's natural splendor.

Between Washington Pass and Pateros, porcelain signs containing the poems of **William Stafford** line 70 miles of Highways 20 and 153. In the early 1990s, the U.S. Forest Service asked the former Poet Laureate to write lines of poetry for this stretch of scenic highway; Methow Valley residents were pleasantly surprised when he agreed to the project. The poems evoke a sense of place that expository wildlife descriptions simply cannot. Look for two poems at the Washington Pass Overlook; the rest appear at viewpoints east near Mazama, Winthrop, Twisp, and Pateros.

At Hart's Pass, the **Slate Peak Lookout Tower** (closed to the public) stands at 7,400 feet (2,256 m) at the end of the highest road in Washington State. From the Hart's Pass Guard Station on Forest Road 5400, drive 2.5 miles (4 km) north to the gate below the tower and park. Walk 0.25 mile to the end of the road and check out the interpretive signs under the

lookout tower that display historical information and diagrams of the surrounding peaks.

Hiking

The following hikes are found outside North Cascades National Park. Maple Pass is the closest to the park; the middle of the trail borders the park and, at the top, hikers can actually step inside the park border. Cutthroat Pass is north across Highway 20, and Hart's Pass is northeast of the park boundary, with views into the park and its peaks.

★ Maple Pass Loop

Distance: 6.7 mi/10.8 km round-trip
Duration: 3.5 hours
Elevation change: 2,200 ft/671 m
Effort: Strenuous
Trailhead: Rainy Pass/Lake Ann/Maple Pass
Pass/Fee: Northwest Forest Pass

This fantastic loop hike showcases the jagged peaks, gigantic valleys, shimmering lakes, vibrant flowers and trees, and formidable glaciers that the North Cascades are famous for. The hike description routes clockwise, reaching the highest point of the trail at 2.9 miles, then gradually descending for 3.8 miles back to the trailhead.

From the parking area, walk south on the paved Rainy Lake Trail for 0.4 mile, then take the right fork onto the unpaved Maple Pass Trail. Make a steep ascent up a forested hillside, catching your first glimpse of the area's surrounding peaks at 1 mile. Rainy Lake comes into view at 1.2 miles as the switchbacks straighten out onto a ridgeline between two lake basins. Smaller Lake Ann is visible at 1.8 miles, framed by hulking mountains Black Peak and Corteo Peak. From this vantage point, almost the entire loop trail is visible as it traces the edge of the Lake Ann basin.

The higher you climb, the prettier the views with an endless sea of craggy peaks spreading out on every horizon. Vegetation thins as you approach Maple

Pass at mile 2.5, but larch trees—known for their golden yellow needles in the autumn—sprinkle the hillside. Reach 6,970-foot Maple Pass, the high point of the hike, at 2.9 miles, where you'll find yourself gazing into the interior of North Cascades National Park. Glacier Peak, the most remote volcano in Washington, stands tall among its glaciated neighbors. This view lingers for the next 0.5 mile as you traverse the southern edge of the lake basin. Begin your gradual descent past Heather Pass at 4.3 miles and enjoy close-up views of Lake Ann.

Getting There
Rainy Pass is 23 miles (37 km) west of Mazama on Highway 20. The large parking area is located on the south side of the highway.

Cutthroat Pass 🅿ꜩ
Distance: 10 mi/16.1 km round-trip
Duration: 5 hours
Elevation change: 2,000 ft/610 m
Effort: Strenuous
Trailhead: Rainy Pass/Pacific Crest Trail
Pass/Fee: Northwest Forest Pass

Cutthroat Pass is a high point, both literally and figuratively, for PCT hikers, with spectacular views of the area's peaks and vibrant fall foliage.

The trail departs from the northwest corner of the parking lot, and climbs steadily through dense forest for the first 1.9 miles before crossing Porcupine Creek. This creek can be swift at high water during early summer; trekking poles are helpful. The trail switchbacks twice as it climbs onto the eastern edge of Porcupine Peak and ascends through a glacier-carved basin. The forest thins around 3.5 miles as larch trees begin to appear with golden yellow needles in the fall.

Views are superb for the next 1.5 miles

From top to bottom: Washington Pass Overlook above Highway 20; Lake Ann from Maple Pass; view from the top of Cutthroat Pass.

to the crest of the pass, with more and more peaks appearing on the horizon as you climb. Reach the pass at 5 miles and enjoy a panoramic scene of endless mountains in all directions, including Tower Mountain and The Needles to the north; Cutthroat Peak to the south; Corteo Peak, Frisco Mountain, and Black Peak to the southwest; and Liberty Bell to the southeast.

Getting There
Rainy Pass is 23 miles (37 km) west of Mazama on Highway 20. A large parking area is located on the north side of the highway.

★ Hart's Pass to Tatie Peak
Distance: 5.4 mi/8.7 km round-trip
Duration: 2 hours
Elevation change: 900 ft/274 m
Effort: Easy
Trailhead: Brown Bear
Pass/Fee: Northwest Forest Pass

You could hike out of Hart's Pass in any direction, on any trail, and be supremely rewarded with stunning views of the craggy, weathered terrain. This Pacific Crest Trail hike is one way to experience the wild and dazzling beauty of the area.

Starting from the Brown Bear trailhead, walk west out of the parking area for 0.1 mile to meet the PCT, then turn left to head south. Right away, pop out of the woods into a patch of huckleberry bushes, fiery red during late summer and early fall. The trail passes through a scree field next; listen for the "squeaky-toy" sound of picas that live in the rocks. At 0.8 mile, the trail makes a sharp bend to head west along the inside of a steep valley wall above Trout Creek. Peaks on the southern horizon include The Needles, Tower Mountain, and Mount Hardy. In the autumn, the vibrant yellow needles of larch trees light up the hillsides.

Continue west onto a ridge at 1.8 miles, overlooking Ninetynine Basin to the north and Slate Peak with its lookout tower. The trail bends south along the side of Tatie Peak before arriving in another saddle at 2.7 miles, where you can gaze west toward Mount Ballard, Cady Pass, and the peaks within North Cascades National Park. Turn around here, or continue south toward Grasshopper Pass.

Shorten or lengthen this hike according to your preferences. The scenery at mile 1 is equally stunning as it is at mile 10.

Getting There
Hart's Pass is 20 miles (32 km) northwest of Mazama, about a 50-minute drive on a sometimes bumpy dirt road. The road is suitable for all passenger vehicles, although it may require slow speeds at times. No trailers are allowed.

From Mazama, follow Lost River Road northwest for 8.5 miles (13.7 km). Make a sharp right onto Forest Road 5400, following signs for Hart's Pass. The road continues for 9.5 miles (15.3 km) to Hart's Pass Guard Station. To reach the trailhead, turn left to head south on Forest Road 500 toward Meadows Campground and continue for 1.7 miles (2.7 km) to the trailhead parking area.

Recreation
Rock Climbing
The steep granite walls of the North Cascades are popular among rock climbers of all skill levels. Destinations near Mazama include **Goat Wall** (on the north side of Lost River Road, 2.5 mi/4 km northwest of Mazama Store), as well as spires on Silver Star Mountain and **Liberty Bell** (13-15 mi/20.9-24 km west of Mazama on Hwy. 20). Try a half-day or full-day guided climb with **North Cascades Mountain Guides** (48 Lost River Rd., Mazama, 509/996-3194, www.ncmountainguides.com, 9am-5pm daily June-Oct., 9am-5pm Mon.-Fri. Nov.-May, $80-350).

Nordic Skiing
When the Methow River Valley is blanketed in snow between December and

March, it's a haven for cross-country skiers. **Methow Trails** (309 Riverside Ave., Winthrop, 509/996-3287, www.methowtrails.org) maintains more than 120 miles of nonmotorized winter trails near Mazama, Winthrop, and Twisp. Daily passes ($5 snowshoe, $24 ski) and three-day ski passes ($60) are available at vendors in each of the three towns.

Food and Accommodations

The ★ **Mazama Store** (50 Lost River Rd., Mazama, 509/996-2855, www.themazamastore.com, 7am-6pm daily) is an unexpectedly upscale little shop with food, clothing, gifts, and a deli counter with espresso drinks. The deli makes delectable sandwiches to order (and a few are always available in the cold case for grab-and-go). Fresh-baked bagels, pies, and pastries at the counter accompany an array of luxury grocery items on the shelves, and an impressive selection of local produce from the Methow Valley is in the back.

Wesola Polana (18381 Hwy. 20, Winthrop, 509/996-9804, www.woodstoneatwesola.com, 8am-9:30pm Thurs.-Mon., $10-18) has an eclectic menu with local ingredients and European influences: salads with beets and grapefruit, giant Greek white beans, charcuterie, and pizzas with gourmet toppings. German, Polish, Czech, and Belgian beers are on tap, available in pints or pitchers. In addition to the creative menu, the sleek urban design sets this restaurant apart from other more traditional eateries in the Methow Valley.

Mazama Country Inn (15 Country Rd., Mazama, 509/996-2681, www.mazamacountryinn.com, year-round) is a rustic lodge with a roomy dining area, complete with rough-hewn log beams and a giant river stone hearth. The **restaurant** (7:30am-11am daily, 5:30pm-9pm Thurs.-Sun., $10-25) serves grains, griddlecakes,

From top to bottom: Slate Peak Lookout Tower at Hart's Pass; Tatie Peak; Mazama Store.

and egg dishes in the morning, while the dinner menu features American favorites like meatloaf, crab cakes, and burgers, plus some hearty salads and vegetarian options. The log cabin-style lodge offers cozy rooms ($115-180) as well as 15 cabin rentals ($88-350) in the Methow Valley. All lodge rooms have basic amenities (air-conditioning, Wi-Fi, coffee and tea, private baths, access to the hot tub and seasonal pool); some rooms have kitchenettes and private decks.

★ **Freestone Inn at Wilson Ranch** (31 Early Winters Dr., Mazama, 509/996-3906, www.freestoneinn.com, $130-370) is a luxurious mountain retreat established in the 1940s by a husband-and-wife homesteading team. Rooms feature fireplaces, elegant decor, coffeemakers, mini-fridges, fluffy linens, and free Wi-Fi (spotty in the guest rooms, but reliable in the great hall). Fifteen cabins are also peppered across the property, and there is a seasonal pool. A complimentary breakfast is included, served in the log cabin-style great hall. There are two restaurants on-site. **Jack's Hut Pizza & Brews** (noon-7pm daily, $9-16) is a classy bar serving (you guessed it) pizza and beer, plus salads and desserts. **Sandy Butte Bistro** (3pm-9pm Wed.-Sun. June-Aug., 4pm-9pm Thurs.-Sat. Sept.-May) is a cut above Jack's, with fancy cheese, seafood, sautéed veggies, pastas, and ribs on the dinner menu.

Grouped together in a herd, the ★ **Rolling Huts** (18381 Hwy. 20, Winthrop, 509/996-4442, www.rollinghuts.com, $145) offer a sprinkling of sleek urban design in the rugged natural beauty of the Methow Valley. Each hut is set up like a studio, with a kitchenette, a sleeping platform, furnished living room, and an adjacent portable toilet. Shared drinking faucets are outside in the lawn; full bathrooms with showers are located in a nearby barn.

Camping

Convenient to Cutthroat Lake, Rainy Pass, and the PCT, campsites at **Lone Fir Campground** (11 mi/17.7 km west of Mazama, Hwy. 20, 509/996-4000, www.fs.usda.gov, $12) showcase the stunning 7,000-foot mountains. All sites are first-come, first-served and have access to drinking water, pit toilets, picnic tables, and fire rings. This popular campground fills on sunny summer weekends.

Early Winters Campground (2.5 mi/4 km west of Mazama, Hwy. 20, 509/996-4003, www.fs.usda.gov, Apr.-Oct., $8) is named after the dramatic spires at nearby Washington Pass. The first-come, first-served sites line both sides of the highway; each site has a picnic table and fire ring, and potable water is on-site. Located east of the crest and lower in elevation, this campground is likely to be warmer and drier than those within North Cascades National Park. It's close to food and services in Mazama.

Information and Services

There is no gas available along Highway 20 between Mazama and Marblemount (75 mi/119 km to the west). Fill up at the **Mazama Store** (50 Lost River Rd., Mazama, 509/996-2855, www.themazamastore.com, 7am-6pm daily) or **Chevron** (900 Hwy. 20, Winthrop).

North Cascades National Park

North Cascades National Park (360/854-7200, www.nps.gov/noca) encompasses the most rugged, glaciated mountains of Washington's northern peaks. The park is bordered by Canada on the north side, volcanoes Mount Baker and Glacier Peak to the west and south, respectively, and the Pasayten Wilderness to the east.

The Pacific Crest Trail barely scratches the surface of the park, tracing the park's southeast boundary for less than 20 miles (32 km) between Stehekin and Rainy Pass. Mountains and ridgelines of equal splendor border the park's peaks, so although the path of the PCT departs from the park as it continues toward Canada, the breathtaking scenery is absolutely captivating.

Eight months of winter and summer thunderstorms make this area volatile, weather-wise. Sunshine is plentiful during July, August, and September, but there are no guarantees. A successful visit to the North Cascades requires equal parts planning, adaptability, and luck.

Getting There

Only one road enters the North Cascades—Highway 20—and technically, it doesn't actually enter the park. National recreation areas border both sides of the east-west highway, splitting the national park into northern and southern halves. The park itself is virtually roadless (Cascade Pass Road is the only exception), an intentional decision during the park's creation to preserve the wild, rugged environment.

There is no fee to enter North Cascades National Park. Highway 20 is closed **November-May** between milepost 134 (at Diablo Overlook) and milepost 171 (14 mi/22.5 km west of Mazama). In winter, entrance to the park is only accessible via the west.

From the East

From Leavenworth, Wenatchee, or Chelan, follow U.S. 97 north to Highway 153 (at Pateros). Head northwest for 32 miles (52 km) to Twisp, and continue west onto Highway 20, also known as the North Cascades Scenic Byway. Another 39 miles (63 km) northwest on Highway 20 delivers you to the eastern edge of the North Cascades. This route is accessible **June-October.**

From the West

From Seattle/Everett or anywhere on the west side of the Cascade Range, follow I-5 north to exit 230 and head east toward Sedro-Woolley. Follow Highway 20 east for 45 miles (72 km) to Marblemount. To access the Pacific Crest Trail, continue east for another 52 miles (84 km) to reach Rainy Pass, where the PCT crosses the highway.

Visitors Centers

The PCT and other hiking trails are located at the eastern edge of the park, more than 50 miles from the national park visitors centers on the west side. If approaching the area from the east, the **Methow Valley Ranger Station** (24 W. Chewuch Rd., Winthrop, 509/996-4003, 8am-4:30pm daily July-Sept., 8am-4:30pm Mon.-Fri. Oct.-June) is the most convenient place for information about the area. The station is jointly staffed by U.S. Forest Service and National Park Service rangers. Backcountry permits are available, along with area maps and guides.

If you're entering the park from the west via Marblemount and Newhalem, stop at the **North Cascades Visitor Center** (Hwy. 20 at milepost 120, Newhalem, 206/386-4495 ext. 11, www.nps.gov, 9am-5pm daily May-Sept.). This family-friendly visitors center has multimedia exhibits to captivate potentially restless travelers, and a theater with a short film about the park. Inside, a detailed

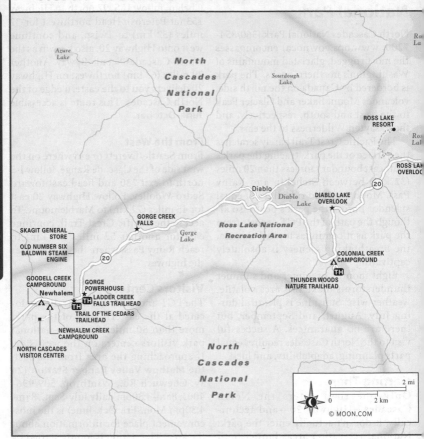

North Cascades National Park

Azure Lake

North Cascades National Park

Sourdough Lake

ROSS LAKE RESORT

Ross Lake

ROSS LAKE OVERLOOK

Diablo

Diablo Lake

DIABLO LAKE OVERLOOK

Ross Lake National Recreation Area

Gorge Lake

GORGE CREEK FALLS

SKAGIT GENERAL STORE

OLD NUMBER SIX BALDWIN STEAM ENGINE

GOODELL CREEK CAMPGROUND

Newhalem

GORGE POWERHOUSE

LADDER CREEK FALLS TRAILHEAD

TRAIL OF THE CEDARS TRAILHEAD

NEWHALEM CREEK CAMPGROUND

NORTH CASCADES VISITOR CENTER

COLONIAL CREEK CAMPGROUND

THUNDER WOODS NATURE TRAILHEAD

North Cascades National Park

0 — 2 mi
0 — 2 km

© MOON.COM

relief map of the park showcases the area's peaks, valleys, and rivers. Gifts and books are also for sale.

Backpackers entering the park from the west will want to visit the **Wilderness Information Center** (7280 Ranger Station Rd., Marblemount, 360/854-7245, www. nps.gov, 8am-5pm daily May-June and Sept.-Oct., 7am-6pm daily July-Aug.) to get the scoop on trail closures, fire conditions, and other backcountry details. Get a camping permit here as well; backcountry campsites are limited in the park.

Seasons

Plan to visit between **July** and **September,** when the roads are open, the sun is shining, and the trails are accessible. Thanks to its high elevation, the North Cascades experience long winters. Snow starts falling in late October and doesn't melt completely until July. Highway 20 closes every November between Diablo Overlook and Mazama, usually opening again in June. Summer visits are optimal, but be aware of mosquitoes and wildfire risks. During snowmelt (May-July), mosquitoes are downright vicious, and lightning strikes during summer thunderstorms start wildfires, which affect air quality and close some areas of the park every year.

Permits and Regulations

Free backcountry permits are required for overnight backpacking trips and can be obtained at any visitors center or ranger station. Some trailheads may require free self-issue permits for day hikes; complete these upon arrival at the trailhead.

Sights

The Skagit River is dammed in three places near Highway 20, each creating a beautiful lake surrounded by forested ridgelines and peaks up to 9,000 feet (2,743 m) tall. A scenic drive along this highway offers the chance to see the sparkling lakes and their incredible alpine backdrops. To uphold the national park's definition of wilderness, these lakes (and the highway) lie inside Ross Lake National Recreation Area, which is adjacent to the national park.

Ross Lake

An overlook on Highway 20 provides a view of 23-mile-long **Ross Lake,** the biggest of the three reservoirs. This lake extends across the U.S. border into Canada. Snowcapped peaks up to 9,000 feet (2,743 m) tall surround the lake, including Hozomeen Mountain, Desolation Peak, Mount Prophet, and Jack Mountain. Stop to marvel at the sparkling reservoir at an overlook near milepost 135. There are no services here, just a parking area on the north side of the road.

Diablo Lake

Near milepost 132, an overlook on the south shore of **Diablo Lake** showcases this famous North Cascades destination. The water's vibrant green hue is a result of glacial sediment carried into the lake by creeks flowing down from the icy peaks nearby. Thick forests surround the lake on all sides, with craggy peaks rising up

behind the wooded ridgelines. This awe-inspiring reservoir, a result of the Diablo Dam, is one of the most photographed places in the national park. Restrooms are available at this overlook.

Colonial Creek

The picnic area, campground, and interpretive trail at **Colonial Creek** (1.5 mi/2.4 km west of Diablo Lake Overlook) are worthy of a stop. Towering old-growth trees surround the campground, which sits on the western shore of Diablo Lake's Thunder Arm. Stretch your legs during a walk along the 0.9-mile Thunder Woods Nature Trail, with a trailhead near the amphitheater. Ranger programs are held daily at the amphitheater during the summer months—pick up a program schedule at a visitors center or ranger station.

Gorge Creek Falls

Stop at **Gorge Creek Falls** (8.5 mi/13.7 km west of Diablo Lake Overlook) to get great views of a narrow waterfall as it tumbles toward the Skagit River Gorge. While you can see the falls from your car, the best views are had with a walk across the bridge where Highway 20 crosses Gorge Creek. There are parking areas on Highway 20 on both east and west sides of Gorge Creek. South of the highway lies the Gorge Dam. Follow the 0.5-mile Gorge Overlook Trail (departing from the western parking area) to get a closer look at Gorge Lake and the dam that created it.

Newhalem

Newhalem is the western gateway to North Cascades National Park and Ross Lake National Recreation Area. A tiny settlement with a convenience store and a visitors center, the homes here are inhabited by employees of Seattle City Light and Skagit Hydroelectric Project. This is a great place to explore the influence of hydroelectric power on the Skagit River Valley—its history and its incredible

impact on the residents of the Puget Sound region.

Walk into the **Gorge Powerhouse Visitor Gallery** (9am-4pm daily May-Sept.) to learn the details about how hydroelectric power is created. A diagram inside demonstrates how the Ross, Diablo, and Gorge Dams interface with the Skagit River. Park in the small lot by the suspension bridge at the northern tip of Newhalem. Walk across the bridge and up the stairs behind the powerhouse. Before the construction of Highway 20, a steam engine transported employees and visitors from Rockport to Newhalem. The Old Number Six, a Baldwin steam engine, has been restored and is on display in Newhalem just north of the Skagit General Store.

See Newhalem's natural beauty while you're there on a walk along the 0.4-mile **Ladder Creek Falls Trail.** This paved loop trail displays glacier-fed Ladder Creek as it tumbles over multiple rocky outcroppings, forming a staircase-like waterfall. The trail begins in the parking lot on the north end of Newhalem near the suspension bridge. The **Trail of Cedars** nature walk also includes a suspension bridge that crosses the Skagit River near Main Street in Newhalem. This 0.3-mile trail through old-growth conifer forest follows the edge of the river.

Accommodations

Floating lakefront cabins at ★ **Ross Lake Resort** (503 Diablo St., Rockport, 206/386-4437, www.rosslakeresort.com, June-Oct., $205-385) range in size, with accommodations for 2-6 people depending on availability. Some cabins have picture windows facing the lake and include views of Colonial and Pyramid Peaks. Completely furnished with full kitchens, wired for electricity, and with hot running water, these luxurious cabins are the

From top to bottom: the North Cascades terrain; Ross Lake; Diablo Lake from the Diablo Lake Overlook.

only accommodations of their kind in the recreation area.

Getting There

Ross Lake Resort is only accessible by boat or hiking trail. Boats ($20/person) depart daily at 8:30am and 3pm from the Ross Lake Resort parking area near Diablo Dam. This boat ride takes you to the end of Diablo Lake where you'll step off the boat and climb into a resort truck ($8/person) that takes you to Ross Lake Resort. You can hike in if you're backpacking, or if you can easily carry all your overnight gear on a brief walk. Park at the Ross Dam trailhead and hike down a steep trail to Ross Dam, where you'll find a telephone with which to dial Ross Lake Resort. Someone will come pick you up with a motorboat ($2/person).

Check out www.rosslakeresort.com/mapsanddirections for more details about transportation.

Camping

Colonial Creek Campground (Hwy. 20 at milepost 130, 877/444-6777, www.recreation.gov, $16) is located in a woodsy valley on Diablo Lake's Thunder Arm. Reservations are available May-September, but some sites are available on a first-come, first-served basis throughout the year. All 135 campsites have picnic tables (some with lake views), fire rings, and access to potable water, flush toilets, and hot running water. The lakefront section of this campground is open year-round—there is no fee to camp here during the off-season (Oct.-Apr.) when no water or services are available.

There are two campgrounds in Newhalem, convenient to the visitors center and a number of hiking trails near the Skagit River Gorge. All 19 sites are first-come, first-served at **Goodell Creek Campground** (Hwy. 20 at milepost 119, www.nps.gov, $16), located on the north side of the highway, near the Skagit River in a lush, old-growth forest. Campsites include picnic tables, fire rings, and

access to potable water and flush toilets. During the off-season (Nov.-May), this campground is open with no water, services, or fees.

Larger **Newhalem Creek Campground** (Hwy. 20 at milepost 119, 877/444-6777, www.recreation.gov, $16) has 107 sites that can be reserved in advance. Sites have fire rings, picnic tables, and access to potable water and flush toilets.

Services

In Newhalem, the small **Skagit General Store** (502 Newhalem St., Rockport, 7:30am-5pm Mon.-Fri., 10am-5pm Sat.-Sun. Nov.-May) has convenience items including snacks, a small inventory of camping and picnic supplies, and a few grocery items. A deli inside the store also serves soups, sandwiches, hot dogs, coffee, and fudge.

There are no gas stations available on the 75-mile (121-km) stretch of Highway 20 between Mazama and Marblemount. Marblemount (15 mi/24 km west of Newhalem) has two gas stations, as well as three restaurants and a post office.

End of the Road

From Stehekin and the North Cascades, the road truly ends. The remaining section of the PCT continues north from Hart's Pass for 31 miles (50 km), crossing the border into Canada where it ends at Manning Park. This remote section is only navigable by foot. Road-trippers must head west to I-5 to conclude their trip or grab their passport and enter Canada.

Return to Seattle

From Mazama, head west on Highway 20 for 120 miles (193 km), crossing through Ross Lake National Recreation Area, to reach the town of Burlington and the junction with I-5. To return to Seattle and catch a flight home, follow I-5 south for 82 miles (132 km).

◈ Manning Provincial Park, British Columbia

The Cascade Mountains continue north into British Columbia, Canada. **Manning Provincial Park,** located on the eastern side of the mountains, is a popular destination for outdoor recreation year-round. The northern terminus of the 2,650-mile Pacific Crest National Scenic Trail is located near Manning Park Resort, where long-distance hikers receive a warm welcome at the beginning or end of their journey.

PCT to Monument 78 🔲

The PCT ends in the forest, miles away from the nearest road, at **Monument 78,** a four-foot-tall metallic tower, one of 17 that were erected between 1906 and 1907. Northbound long-distance hikers reach the monument by way of a 30-mile trek through the Pasayten Wilderness from Hart's Pass.

More important is the **PCT Monument,** a four-column wooden tower embossed with the PCT crest. A matching tower exists in Campo at the trail's southern terminus. These monuments bookend life-changing experiences for hikers who spend up to six months backpacking the PCT.

Monument 78 is 8.5 miles south of Manning Park Resort and can only be reached on foot. From the resort, follow the Windy Joe Trail for approximately 3.5 miles to a fork with the Pacific Crest Trail, then continue south on the PCT for 5 miles. The hike from Manning Park Resort to the monument is 17 miles round-trip; backpackers may spend the night at **Monument Camp** (0.25 mi from the monument).

Manning Park Resort

Manning Park Resort (7500 BC-3, 604/668-5922, www.manningpark.com) is a four-season resort with accommodations, a restaurant, and an array of outdoor activities. Hiking is a huge draw during the summer, as is boating the Similkameen River, which flows through the middle of the park. West of the resort, Lightning Lake has a boat launch, fishing docks, and swimming beaches. Winter brings snowshoeing and skiing to the area. In addition to a wide network of cross-country ski trails, there's a downhill ski area with four lifts and 140 skiable acres.

Resort accommodations include lodge rooms ($149), cabins ($249), and chalets ($349) with pet-friendly options. Inside the lodge, the **Pinewoods Dining Room** (604/668-5933, 8am-8pm Sun.-Thurs., 8am-9pm Fri.-Sat., $12-34) serves breakfast, lunch, and dinner daily.

Getting There

The 185-mile journey to Manning Park from North Cascades National Park takes 3.5-4 hours to drive. Sumas is the best place to cross the U.S.-Canada border if heading into Manning Park. From Newhalem, take Highway 20 west for 39 miles (63 km) to Highway 9 in Sedro Woolley. Turn right and head north on Highway 9 for 40 miles (64 km) through Deming, Nugent's Corner, and Everson, following signs for Sumas. Allow two hours for this part of the drive.

From Sumas, it's 1 hour and 40 minutes to Manning Park. Head north from the border on Sumas Way for 2 miles (3.2 km), then merge onto Trans-Canada Highway/BC 1 east toward Hope. In 48 miles (77 km), stay right to continue east on BC 3 for 42 miles (68 km).

Entering Canada

To enter Canada, you'll need both proof of citizenship and proof of identity. For U.S. citizens, this means a valid **passport** or passport card. Wait times at the border vary and can be affected by weekend or holiday traffic. Check online (www.wsdot.wa.gov/traffic/border) for wait times.

entrance to Manning Provincial Park on British Columbia Highway

North to Canada

From Burlington, I-5 heads north for 48 miles (77 km) to the **Peace Arch** on the Canadian border. A valid passport is required to enter Canada from the United States. Wait times at this border crossing vary and can be impacted by holiday weekends and rush hour. You may cross at any time—the border crossing is always open. For more information about entry into Canada, visit www.cbsa-asfc. gc.ca.

Essentials

Getting There

San Diego
Air

San Diego International Airport (SAN, 3225 N. Harbor Dr., 619/400-2404, www.san.org) is the most convenient major airport to the southern terminus of the trail, with flights from 17 airlines, including Alaska, Air Canada, American, British Airways, Frontier, Hawaiian, JetBlue, Southwest, and United. The airport is located on the northwest side of downtown San Diego.

Pick up your rental car at the **rental car center** (3355 Admiral Boland Way), where rentals from more than a dozen agencies are available—free, frequent shuttles run between the terminals and the center.

Airport Transportation

Taxis pick up passengers at both terminals in designated taxi zones on the Arrivals/Baggage Claim level.

City buses service the airport on **Metropolitan Transit System** (MTS, www.sdmts.com/schedules-real-time/trip-planner). Route 992 stops every 15-20 minutes outside both terminals. The **San Diego Trolley** (www.san.org/to-from) also services the airport via the Sycuan Green Line. Take a free rental car shuttle and notify the driver to drop you off at the northeast end of the airport, near Middleton Station.

Train

Amtrak (800/872-7245, www.amtrak.com) offers rail service to the downtown Santa Fe Station (1050 Kettner Blvd.). The *Pacific Surfliner* route connects north to coastal cities including Los Angeles, Santa Barbara, and San Luis Obispo.

Bus

Greyhound (800/231-2222, www.greyhound.com) offers bus service to San Diego (1313 National Ave., 619/515-1100).

You can also take a **FlixBus** (855/626-8585, www.flixbus.com) between San Diego and Bakersfield, Fresno, Los Angeles, Ontario, Palm Springs, Reno, Riverside, San Bernardino, Victorville, and many other cities.

Los Angeles
Air

Los Angeles International Airport (LAX, 1 World Way, 855/463-5252, www.flylax.com) is located about 10 miles (16 km) south of the city of Santa Monica. If you're coming in from another country or from across the continent, you're likely to find your flight coming into this endlessly crowded hub. If you're flying home from LAX, plan plenty of time to get through security and the check-in lines, up to three hours for a domestic flight on a holiday weekend.

To miss the crowds, consider flying into one of the many suburban airports: **Hollywood Burbank Airport** (BUR, 2627 N. Hollywood Way, Burbank, 818/840-8840, http://hollywoodburbankairport.com), **John Wayne Airport** (SNA, 18601 Airport Way, Santa Ana, 949/252-5200, www.ocair.com), and **Long Beach Airport** (LGB, 4100 Donald Douglas Dr., Long Beach, 562/570-2600, www.lgb.org).

Located 38 miles (61 km) east of downtown LA, **Ontario International Airport** (ONT, 909/544-5300, www.flyontario.com) is convenient to destinations on the Pacific Crest Trail—it's about a 90-minute drive from Idyllwild or Big Bear, and under an hour's drive to Wrightwood. With flights from Alaska, American, China Airlines, Delta, Frontier, JetBlue, Southwest, and Volaris, this relatively small airport is far preferable to any of the larger Los Angeles options. Rental cars are available, and free shuttle service is provided between the terminals and the consolidated **rental car center** (3450 E. Airport Dr., near Haven Ave.).

On the eastern side of Southern California's mountain ranges, the **Palm Springs International Airport** (PSP,

3400 E. Tahquitz Canyon Way, 760/318-3800, www.palmspringsca.gov) is serviced by Air Canada, Alaska, Allegiant, American, Delta, Flair, Frontier, JetBlue, Sun Country, United, and West Jet. The airport is about an hour's drive from the town of Idyllwild. Rental cars are available at the airport, along with taxi and shuttle service to destinations within Palm Springs.

Airport Transportation
From LAX, free shuttle buses provide service to **Metro Rail** (323/466-3876, www.metro.net, $1.75), accessible at the Green Line Aviation Station. Metro Rail trains connect Long Beach, Hollywood, North Hollywood, downtown Los Angeles, and Pasadena. Passengers should wait under the blue "LAX Shuttle Airline Connection" signs outside the lower-level terminals and board the "G" shuttle. Passengers may also take the "C" shuttle to the **Metro Bus Center** (323/466-3876, www.metro.net), which connects to city buses that serve the entire L.A. area.

Shared-ride shuttle services are also available. **Prime Time Shuttle** (800/733-8267, www.primetimeshuttle.com) and **SuperShuttle** (800/258-3826, www.supershuttle.com) serve the Los Angeles area from LAX. These vans can be found on the lower/arrivals deck in front of each terminal, under the orange "Shared Ride Vans" signs.

Taxis can be found on the lower/arrivals level islands in front of each terminal, below the yellow "Taxi" signs. Only licensed taxis are allowed into the airport; they have standard rates of about $40 to downtown and $30 to West Los Angeles. Use your cell phone to access ride-sharing services **Lyft** (www.lyft.com) or **Uber** (www.uber.com), which charge $25-30 for a ride from LAX to downtown.

Train
Amtrak (800/872-7245, www.amtrak.com) travels to Los Angeles' Union Station (800 N. Alameda St., www.unionstationla.com), though there are other stops, in Glendale (400 W. Cerritos Ave.), Anaheim (2626 E. Katella Ave.), and Santa Ana (1000 E. Santa Ana Blvd.). Both of the train's classic *Coast Starlight* (Seattle to Los Angeles) and *Pacific Surfliner* (San Luis Obispo to San Diego) routes stop in Los Angeles.

Bus
Greyhound (800/231-2222, www.greyhound.com) provides cheap transportation to Los Angeles and many of the surrounding communities. There's the Los Angeles Station (1716 E. 7th St., 213/629-8401) along with other stations including Long Beach (1498 Long Beach Blvd., 562/218-3011), North Hollywood (11239 Magnolia Blvd., 818/761-5119), and Anaheim (2626 E. Katella Ave., 714/999-1256).

BoltBus (877/265-8287, www.boltbus.com) serves Los Angeles from Barstow, Fresno, Oakland, San Francisco, and San Jose. **FlixBus** (855/626-8585, www.flixbus.com) provides another inexpensive bus seat between the Los Angeles area and destinations convenient to the PCT farther north, including Bakersfield, Fresno, Sacramento, and Reno.

San Francisco
Air
The **San Francisco International Airport** (SFO, off U.S. 101, 650/821-8211 or 800/435-9736, www.flysfo.com) is located approximately 13 miles (20.9 km) south of the city. Plan to arrive at the airport up to three hours before your flight leaves. Airport lines, especially on weekends and holidays, are notoriously long, and planes can be grounded due to fog.

To avoid the crowds, consider booking a flight into one of the Bay Area's less crowded airports. **Oakland International Airport** (OAK, 1 Airport Dr., Oakland, 510/563-3300, www.oaklandairport.com) serves the East Bay with access to San Francisco via the Bay Bridge and commuter trains. **Mineta San José Airport** (SJC, 1701 Airport Blvd., San Jose, 408/392-3600, www.flysanjose. com) is 45 miles (72 km) south of San Francisco. These airports are quite a bit smaller than SFO, but service is frequent from many U.S. destinations.

Airport Transportation

Several public and private transportation options can get you into San Francisco. **Bay Area Rapid Transit** (BART, 415/989-2278, www.bart.gov) connects directly with SFO's international terminal, providing a simple and relatively fast (under one hour) trip to downtown San Francisco. A BART station is an easy walk or a free shuttle ride from any point in the airport.

BART trains also connect Oakland Airport to the city of San Francisco. Both BART and **Caltrain** (800/660-4287, www.caltrain.com) connect Mineta San José Airport to San Francisco. To access Caltrain from the airport, you must first take BART to the Millbrae stop, where the two lines meet. This station is designed for folks jumping from one line to the other. Caltrain tickets vary in price depending on your destination.

Shuttle vans are another cost-effective option. From the airport to downtown San Francisco, the average one-way fare is $17-25 per person. Shuttle vans congregate on the second level of SFO above the baggage claim area for domestic flights, and on the third level for international flights. Advance reservations guarantee a seat, but aren't required and don't necessarily speed the process.

Some companies to try include **Quake City Shuttle** (415/255-4899, www. quakecityshuttle.com) and **SuperShuttle** (800/258-3826, www.supershuttle.com).

For taxis, the average fare to downtown San Francisco is around $40. Use your cell phone to access ride-sharing services **Lyft** (www.lyft.com) or **Uber** (www.uber.com), which charge $29-45 for a ride from the airport to downtown.

Train

The closest **Amtrak** (800/872-7245, www. amtrak.com) is in Emeryville (5885 Horton St.). Fortunately, coach buses ferry travelers from the Emeryville Station to downtown San Francisco. The *California Zephyr* route runs from Chicago and Denver, while the *Coast Starlight* travels down the West Coast from Seattle and Portland as far as Los Angeles.

Bus

The **Greyhound** (800/231-2222, www. greyhound.com) San Francisco Station (200 Folsom St., 415/495-1569) is a hub for bus lines. Another option is **Megabus** (http://us.megabus.com), which has stops in San Francisco and San Jose.

How about going to sleep in San Francisco and waking up in Los Angeles? That's the idea behind **Cabin** (www. ridecabin.com), a charter bus with sleeping pods that leaves from San Francisco's Bayside Lot (1 Bryant St.) at 11pm and arrives at 7am at Santa Monica's Palisades Park (Palisades Park at Ocean Ave. and Arizona Ave.).

Portland
Air

Portland International Airport (PDX, 7000 NE Airport Way, 877/739-4636, www.flypdx.com) is the major airport hub in Oregon, located 11 miles (18 km) northeast of downtown. The PCT in Cascade Locks is less than an hour's drive away on I-84. Fifteen airlines service PDX, including Air Canada, Alaska, American, Delta, Frontier, Hawaiian, JetBlue, Southwest, and United.

If starting your trip in central or southern Oregon, fly into **Eugene Airport** (EUG, 28801 Douglas Dr., 541/682-5544, www.flyeug.com), which is closer to Ashland and Crater Lake. Rental cars are available at both airports.

Close to the city of Bend, **Redmond Municipal Airport** (RDM, 2522 SE Jesse Butler Circle, Redmond, 541/548-0646, www.flyrdm.com) offers daily direct flights from Denver, Los Angeles, Phoenix, Portland, Salt Lake City, San Francisco, and Seattle.

Airport Transportation

Transportation to and from the airport is easy on the MAX (Portland's rapid transit train) Red Line, which travels between PDX and downtown with stops in northeast Portland along the way. Taxis and rideshares including Lyft (www.lyft.com) and Uber (www.uber.com) pick passengers up outside the baggage claim, with fares averaging $25-30 to downtown Portland. Car rentals are available on level 1 of the short-term parking garage.

Train

Amtrak's *Coast Starlight* (800/872-7245, www.amtrak.com) runs north-south along the I-5 corridor with stops in Portland at Union Station (800 NW 6th Ave), Oregon City, Salem, Albany, and Eugene. The east-west *Empire Builder* travels through the Columbia River Gorge on its way between Portland and Chicago, with stops along the way. Amtrak also has two stations in Chemult (Palmer/Kranz St. and Depot St.) and Klamath Falls (1600 Oak Ave.), which are convenient to the southern parts of the PCT.

Bus

Greyhound (800/231-2222, www.greyhound.com) offers bus service along the I-5 corridor and has stations in Medford (220 S. Front St.), Portland (2846 NE 8th Ave.) and a few cities in between. **BoltBus** (877/265-8287, www.boltbus.com) travels between Portland and Seattle with stops in Albany and Eugene. Both bus lines offer multiple departures daily, and buses have Wi-Fi. Advance tickets are recommended.

Seattle
Air
The **Seattle-Tacoma International Airport** (SEA, 17801 International Blvd., 800/544-1965, www.portseattle.org/seatac) offers the most convenient air access to Mount Rainier, Leavenworth, and the North Cascades. More than 30 airlines operate in this busy international hub. SeaTac is 14 miles (22.5 km) south of downtown Seattle—traffic along this corridor is some of the worst in the country, so plan extra time for this drive, especially during rush hour.

Airport Transportation

Avoid traffic by taking the **Link light rail** (www.soundtransit.org, station located on the northeast side of the short-term parking garages). Rental cars are available at the off-site **rental car** (3150 S. 160th St.) facility with 24-hour shuttle service from the airport baggage claim area. Taxis and rideshare options including **Lyft** (www.lyft.com) and **Uber** (www.uber.com) pick passengers up here as well, with fares averaging $35-40 to downtown Seattle.

Train

Amtrak (800/872-7245, www.amtrak.com) operates the *Cascades* route along the I-5 corridor, with stops in Portland, Oregon, and Seattle, Washington, and Vancouver, British Columbia, with a handful of smaller cities in between. The east-west *Empire Builder* travels across the center of the state, passing through Stevens Pass and Leavenworth on its way between Seattle and Chicago. Catch your train at King Street Station (303 S. Jackson St.) in downtown Seattle.

Bus

Greyhound (800/231-2222, www.greyhound.com) provides bus service to more than 50 stations throughout the state, including downtown Seattle (503 S. Royal Brougham Way). **BoltBus** (877/265-8287, www.boltbus.com) offers express service between Portland, Seattle, and Bellingham with free on-board Wi-Fi.

The History of the PCT

Nobody knows for sure who first envisioned the wilderness trail stretching from Mexico to Canada, but we do know of some highly influential people who, together, made the dream a reality. Before the Pacific Crest Trail, there was the John Muir Trail through the High Sierra, conceptualized, scouted, and mapped by Theodore Solomans in the 1890s (although it didn't earn its name until 1915, when a bill was passed to fund the construction of the trail just four weeks after the death of John Muir, the Sierra Nevada's most dedicated advocate). Next came the Oregon Skyline Trail. Forest Service employee Fred Cleator blazed this path in the 1920s while scouting a route for a trans-Cascades highway across Oregon's crest. At the end of the project, he and his team declared the country much too beautiful, in their opinions, to build a road through; alas, the highway was never built.

Catherine Montgomery, an educator and avid outdoorswoman in Bellingham, Washington, is often referred to as "the mother of the PCT." Her 1926 proposition for a border-to-border wilderness trail is the first one we see in any written record. Her idea made its way south to California, where a wealthy hiker, writer, and businessman named Clinton Clarke became its biggest proponent. He drew up maps for a high country route through the most rugged mountains of California, Oregon, and Washington, and trail construction began in the 1930s. This was revolutionary—routes through the Sierra Nevada and the Cascades had previously only been practical (or desirable) as east-west routes focused on quick passage across the range, rather than continuously through them simply for leisure and sightseeing. Photographer Ansel Adams made sections of the Sierra Nevada (and the Pacific Crest Trail) famous in breathtaking photography during the 1920s, '30s, and '40s. Although Adams was sometimes criticized for the lack of human beings or animals in his photos, he was a passionate conservationist who utilized his talent to showcase the raw beauty of the wilderness in hopes of preserving it for future generations.

In 1968, under the direction of President Lyndon B. Johnson, both the PCT and the Appalachian Trail received National Scenic Trail designation. This meant the trail would be protected and supported for its scenic, natural, historical, and cultural qualities. The Pacific Crest Trail gained popularity slowly but steadily among outdoor enthusiasts over the next four decades.

It wasn't until Cheryl Strayed's memoir *Wild* hit bookshelves in 2012 that the PCT became a household name. In 2017, more than 4,990 people applied to the PCTA for thru-hike permits (compared to 1,050 in 2013). Only about 60 percent of those hikers actually complete a border-to-border thru-hike. But the Pacific Crest Trail is not reserved only for long-distance hikers—day hikers and section hikers comprise a huge portion of the people who enjoy the PCT on a regular basis, reveling in its uncompromised beauty and adventure.

Road Rules

Car Rental

Most car rental companies are located at each of the major airports. To reserve a car in advance, contact **Budget Rent A Car** (U.S. 800/218-7992, outside U.S. 800/472-3325, www.budget.com), **Dollar Rent A Car** (800/800-5252, www.dollar.com), **Enterprise** (855/266-9289, www.enterprise.com), or **Hertz** (U.S. and Canada 800/654-3131, international 800/654-3001, www.hertz.com).

To rent a car, drivers in California, Oregon, and Washington must be at least 21 years of age and have a valid driver's license. All three state laws also require that all vehicles carry liability insurance. You can purchase insurance with your rental car, but it generally costs an additional $10-30 per day, which can add up quickly. Most private auto insurance will also cover rental cars. Before buying rental insurance, check your car insurance policy to see if car rental coverage is included.

The average cost of a rental car is $50-80 per day or $300-500 per week; however, rates vary greatly based on the time of year and distance traveled. Weekend and summer rentals cost significantly more. Generally, it is more expensive to rent from car rental agencies at an airport. To avoid excessive rates, first plan travel to areas where a car is not required, then rent a car from an agency branch in town to further explore more rural areas. Most major rental agencies occasionally allow vehicle drop-off at a different location from where it was picked up, but they'll charge an additional fee.

Before renting, find out if mileage restrictions will apply. Map your planned route to determine how many miles you expect to travel, and ensure your rental agreement is accommodating. Inquire about tolls as well—these days, many tolls are automated with cameras, rather than staffed by humans in booths, so determine whether your rental is compatible with these automated systems and how to handle tolls if not.

RV Rental
Renting an RV means you won't have to worry about camping or lodging options, and many facilities, particularly farther north, accommodate RVs. However, RVs are difficult to maneuver and park, limiting your access to metropolitan areas. They are also expensive, both in terms of gas and the rental rates. Rates during the summer average $1,300 per week and $570 for three days, the standard minimal rental.

Cruise America (800/671-8042, www.cruiseamerica.com) has branches in California, Portland, Oregon, and western Washington. **El Monte RV** (800/337-2214, www.elmonterv.com) operates out of San Francisco and Los Angeles. Many individual owners choose to rent their RVs to travelers while they aren't using them (like AirBnB, for RVs). Browse listings for California, Oregon, and Washington on the **RVshare** website (www.rvshare.com).

Jucy Rentals (800/650-4180, www.jucyrentals.com) rents minivans with pop-up tops. These colorful vehicles are smaller and easier to manage than large RVs, but still come equipped with a fridge, a gas stove, a sink, a DVD player, and two double beds. Rental locations are in San Francisco, Los Angeles, and Las Vegas. **PacWesty** (844/817-0463, www.pacwesty.com) rents Volkswagen Vanagons near Seattle, offering renters the option to travel in Westfalia-outfitted vans throughout the Cascades to destinations on and near the PCT.

Driving Rules
Speed limits in California, Oregon, and Washington vary greatly and will range between 25 miles per hour in small towns to 70 miles per hour on the interstate. Seat belts are required at all times for all passengers. State law in all three states also prohibits the delay of five or more vehicles; roads provide slow vehicle turnouts to let other cars pass. When two or more lanes are present, stay right except to pass.

Note that California, Oregon, and Washington have laws against using handheld cell phones while driving. Don't risk the hefty fine or the potentially terrible accident.

Road and Weather Conditions
In an emergency, dial 911 from any phone. The **American Automobile Association** (AAA, 800/222-4357, www.aaa.com) offers roadside assistance—free to members; others pay a fee. Be aware of your car's maintenance needs while on the road. Keep in mind that at times during this road trip, you'll be traveling on remote routes through the mountains where cell phone coverage is slim to none—911 and AAA can

only assist you if you can reach them by phone. Keeping your car properly fueled and maintained with regular oil services every 3,000 miles will minimize your risk of an auto emergency in a remote location.

The most frequent maintenance needs result from summer heat. If the car gets hot or overheats, stop for a while to cool it off. Never open the radiator cap if the engine is steaming. After the engine cools, squeeze the top radiator hose to see if there's any pressure in it; if there isn't, it's safe to open. Never pour water into a hot radiator because it could crack the engine block. If you start to smell rubber, your tires are overheating, and that's a good way to have a blowout. Stop and let them cool off.

During winter in the high country, a can of silicone lubricant such as WD-40 will unfreeze door locks, dry off humid wiring, and keep your hinges in shape. Some mountain routes will still have snow on the road during the winter and spring (possibly even into June or July, depending on the weather patterns that year). For winter travel, choose high-quality traction tires. Carry chains and a snow shovel, and familiarize yourself with how to use them. Many winter travelers choose to pack extra clothing, snacks, and blankets in case of a weather or auto emergency.

Roads at high elevations, especially those crossing mountain passes, may close during the winter (for the entire season or temporarily during harsh weather conditions). Find out what's going on before you travel by visiting **TripCheck** (www.tripcheck.com), a website with detailed, real-time information about roads in Oregon, as well as basic up-to-date info about California and Washington road conditions.

Fuel

Fuel is expensive in California. As a general rule, fueling up in tiny, remote mountain towns will cost you more than

North Cascades Scenic Byway

in cities or suburbs. This is especially true along U.S. 395. If you see a good deal on gas, take advantage of it.

Until 2018, it was illegal for drivers to pump their own gas in Oregon. State laws have relaxed somewhat: In counties of less than 40,000, self-service may be allowed. Many stations still staff attendants between the hours of 6am and 6pm. When you find yourself at a gas station in a rural area, pull up to the pump and wait for an attendant to approach. You may pump your own gas if no attendant is present.

The Washington portion of your road trip is the most remote—gas stations may be few and far between, especially in the North Cascades. Fuel up in advance before heading over a mountain pass.

International Drivers Licenses

If you are visiting the United States from another country, you need to secure an International Driving Permit from your home country before coming to the

United States. It can't be obtained once you're here. You must also bring your government-issued driving permit.

Visitors from outside the United States should check the driving rules of the states they will visit at www.usa.gov/Topics/Motor-Vehicles.shtml. Among the most important rules is that traffic runs on the right side of the road in the United States.

Maps and Visitor Information

The best maps for road-trippers are state-specific **DeLorme Atlas & Gazetteers** (www.buy.garmin.com), which include detailed road maps and comprehensive guides to campgrounds, recreation sites, and noteworthy sights. The American Automobile Association, better known as **AAA** (www.aaa.com), offers free maps to its members. Almost all gas stations and drugstores sell maps.

As for hiking maps, **Green Trails** (www.greentrailsmaps.com) and **National Geographic Trails Illustrated** (www.natgeomaps.com) maps do an excellent job of showcasing the PCT among other hiking trails, campsites, roads, campgrounds, and recreation sites. The waterproof, tear-resistant, ultralight maps are critical companions for hiking trips.

When visiting California, rely on local, regional, and national park visitors centers, which are usually staffed by rangers or volunteers who feel passion and pride for their locale. The **Golden State Welcome Centers** (www.visitcalifornia.com) scattered throughout the state are less useful, but can be a good place to pick up maps and brochures. The state's California Travel and Tourism Commission (916/444-4429, www.visitcalifornia.com) also provides helpful and free tips, information, and downloadable maps and guides.

Oregon also staffs **state welcome centers** (www.traveloregon.com) in Klamath Falls and Oregon City, as well as five other locations farther from the

PCT. The Travel Oregon website (www. traveloregon.com) offers free travel guides and countless articles with information about the diverse array of things to do in the state.

Visitors in Washington can find a comprehensive list of local visitors centers and chambers of commerce at **Experience Washington** (www. experiencewa.com/wa/visitor-centers) as well as a Washington visitors guide available for download.

California, Oregon, and Washington are in the Pacific time zone (PST and PDT) and observe daylight saving time March-November.

Visas and Officialdom

Passports and Visas

If visiting from another country, you must have a valid passport and a visa to enter the United States. If you hold a current passport from one of the following countries, you may qualify for the Visa Waiver Program: Andorra, Australia, Austria, Belgium, Brunei, Chile, Czech Republic, Denmark, Estonia, Finland, France, Germany, Greece, Hungary, Iceland, Ireland, Italy, Japan, Latvia, Liechtenstein, Lithuania, Luxembourg, Malta, Monaco, the Netherlands, New Zealand, Norway, Portugal, San Marino, Singapore, Slovakia, Slovenia, South Korea, Spain, Sweden, Switzerland, and the United Kingdom. To qualify, you must apply online with the **Electronic System for Travel Authorization** (www. cbp.gov) and hold a return plane or cruise ticket to your country of origin dated less than 90 days from your date of entry. Holders of Canadian passports don't need visas or visa waivers.

In other countries, the local U.S. embassy should be able to provide a tourist visa. The application fee for a visa is US$160, although you will have to pay an issuance fee as well. While a visa may be processed in as little as 24 hours

upon request, plan for at least a couple of weeks, as there can be unexpected delays, particularly during the busy summer season (June-Aug.). For information, visit http://travel.state.gov.

Consulates

San Francisco, Portland, and Seattle are home to consulates from many countries around the globe. If you should lose your passport or find yourself in some other trouble while visiting, contact your country's offices for assistance. The website of the U.S. State Department (www.state.gov) lists the websites for all foreign embassies and consulates in the United States. A representative will be able to direct you to the nearest embassy or consulate.

The **British Consulate** (www.gov.uk) has offices in San Francisco (1 Sansome St., Ste. 850, 415/617-1300) and Seattle (900 4th Ave., Ste. 3100, 206/622-9255).

The **Australian Consulate** (www. usa.embassy.gov.au) has offices in Los Angeles (2029 Century Park E, 310/229-2300) and San Francisco (575 Market St., Ste. 1800, 415/644-3260).

The **Consulate General of Canada** has an office in San Francisco (580 California St., 14th Fl., 415/834-3180) and one in Seattle (1501 4th Ave., 206/443-1777).

Customs

Before you enter the United States from another country by sea or by air, you'll be required to fill out a customs form. Check with the U.S. embassy in your country or the Customs and Border Protection website (www.cbp.gov) for an updated list of items you must declare.

If you require medication administered by injection, you must pack your syringes in a checked bag; syringes are not permitted in carry-ons coming into the United States. Also, pack documentation describing your need for any narcotic medications you've brought with you. Failure to produce documentation for narcotics upon

The Ten Essentials

When hitting the trail, you're likely to share the path with other outdoor enthusiasts. Ensure the best experience for everyone by following some simple trail etiquette guidelines. Always yield to horses and those climbing uphill (or anyone hiking faster than you)—simply step aside and let them pass. If you listen to music while hiking, wear headphones; it allows other hikers to experience the peace and quiet of the trail. Leave nothing but footprints and take nothing but photographs. Familiarize yourself with the principles of Leave No Trace (www.lnt.org) before heading into the wilderness.

Follow the National Park Service's advice to pack the Ten Essentials whenever you travel:

♦ **Navigation:** Bring printed maps. Cell service can be spotty in mountainous areas and paper maps are more reliable than online options. Keep a road atlas in the car.

♦ **Sun protection:** Pack sunscreen, sunglasses, a hat, and layered clothing. This is especially critical in Southern California and the High Sierra.

♦ **Insulation:** Temperatures along the Pacific Crest Trail can drop below freezing. Bring extra layers, socks, hats, and gloves in case you end up spending the night somewhere colder than expected.

♦ **Illumination:** Headlamps and flashlights are critical for hiking and camping. Pack extra batteries.

♦ **First-Aid Supplies:** Pack a comprehensive travel kit with first-aid supplies, and familiarize yourself with how to use them in the case of injury or emergency.

♦ **Fire:** Matches, fire starters, and lighters can be helpful in an emergency.

♦ **Repair Kit and Tools:** Bring a few basic tools and supplies to repair your gear: duct tape, scissors, and a screwdriver or multi-tool. In your vehicle, carrying jumper cables, chains, and an ice scraper.

♦ **Nutrition:** Always carry more food than you think you need in case of an emergency and for strenuous hikes, outside overnights, and long drives.

♦ **Hydration:** Nothing ruins an outdoor adventure faster than a case of dehydration. Bring plenty of water (one liter of water for every four miles you hike) and keep an extra gallon in the car. If you plan to drink water from streams or lakes, bring a filter or other form of water treatment.

♦ **Emergency Shelter:** Pack extra blankets in your vehicle and carry an emergency blanket in your backpack.

request can result in severe penalties in the United States.

If you're driving into California along I-5 or another major highway, prepare to stop at agricultural inspection stations a few miles inside the state line. You don't need to present a passport, a visa, or even a driver's license; instead, you must be prepared to present all your fruits and vegetables. California's largest economic sector is agriculture, and a number of the major crops grown here are sensitive to pests and diseases. In an effort to prevent known pests from entering the state and endangering crops, travelers are asked to identify all produce they're carrying in from other states or from Mexico. If you've got produce, especially home-grown or from a farm stand, it could be infected by a known problem pest or disease. Expect it to be confiscated on the spot.

If you're driving across the border into Canada, expect similar questions and prohibitions on produce. Upon entry into the United States via plane or boat, you'll also be asked about fruits and veggies on your U.S. Customs form, which you'll fill out on the airplane or ship before you reach the United States. Although marijuana is legal in Canada, crossing the border with it is not legal, whether entering or exiting. Marijuana products will be confiscated, and your entry into Canada may be denied.

Travel Tips

Conduct and Customs

The **legal drinking age** in the United States is 21. Expect to have your ID checked if you look under age 30, especially in bars and clubs, but also in restaurants and wineries. Most bars and clubs that serve alcohol close at 2am.

Smoking has been banned in many places throughout the region. Don't expect to find a smoking section in any restaurant or an ashtray in any bar. Smoking is illegal in all bars and clubs, but your new favorite watering hole might have an outdoor patio where smokers can huddle. Taking the ban one step further, many hotels, motels, and inns are strictly nonsmoking, and you'll be subject to fees of hundreds of dollars if your room smells of smoke when you leave. There's no smoking in any public building, and even some parks don't allow cigarettes. There's often good reason for this; the fire danger is extreme in the summer, and one carelessly thrown butt can cause a catastrophe.

As of 2016, **recreational marijuana** is legal and decriminalized in California, Oregon, and Washington. Stores throughout all three states vend weed products for smoking and eating. That said, many public places (and almost all businesses) still prohibit the use of marijuana. Driving under the influence is a serious crime, and the drug is still illegal under federal law. If you choose to smoke at your campsite or on the trail, use discretion and be respectful of those around you—although it's legal, there are plenty of people who would rather not interact with it.

Money

California, Oregon, and Washington use the **U.S. dollar ($).** Most businesses also accept the major credit cards Visa, MasterCard, Discover, and American Express. ATM and debit cards work at many stores and restaurants, and ATMs are available throughout the region.

You can change currency at any international airport. Currency exchange points also crop up in most major cities and at some of the business hotels in urban areas.

For travelers entering Canada, stop at the currency exchange at the border crossing to exchange your U.S. dollars for Canadian dollars.

Tipping is expected and appreciated, and a 15-20 percent tip for restaurants is the norm. When ordering in bars, tip the bartender or waitstaff $1 per drink. Cafés and coffee shops often have tip jars out. There is no consensus on what is appropriate when purchasing a $3 beverage. Often $0.50 is enough, depending on the quality and service. For taxis, plan to tip 15-20 percent of the fare.

California sales tax varies by city and county, but the base rate is 7.25 percent. **Washington sales tax** varies from 6.5 to 10.4 percent, with higher taxes in the dense urban areas.

All goods are taxable with the exception of food not eaten on the premises.

For example, your bill at a restaurant will include tax, but your bill at a grocery store will not.

There's **no sales tax in Oregon,** so it's a great place to shop, especially for high-priced outdoor gear and clothing items.

State lodging tax is another unexpected added expense to traveling in California, Oregon, and Washington. Most cities have enacted a **hotel room tax** largely to make up for budget shortfalls. As you would expect, these taxes are higher in areas more popular with visitors.

Communications and Media
Cell phone reception is good in most populated areas, as is internet access. The bigger cities are well wired, but even in small towns you can log on either at a library or in a café with a computer in the back. Be prepared to pay a per-minute usage fee or purchase a drink. Don't expect any cell phone coverage on hiking trails, especially those in the High Sierra, Northern California, Oregon, and Washington. In fact, some of these areas are so remote, you'll lose coverage during the drive to the trailhead. If you're using online maps or guides, download all the necessary information in town before heading out onto the trail. Remote campgrounds will also lack cell phone coverage.

The main newspapers in California are the *San Francisco Chronicle* (www.sfchronicle.com) and the *Los Angeles Times* (www.latimes.com). Oregon's biggest newspaper is the *Oregonian* (www.oregonlive.com) and Washington's is the *Seattle Times* (www.seattletimes.com). Most major cities also have a free weekly newspaper with comprehensive arts and events coverage. Of course, there are other regional papers that may offer some international news in addition to the local color.

There are some radio news stations on the FM dial. In most regions, you can find a **National Public Radio** (NPR, www.npr.org) affiliate. While they will all offer some NPR news coverage, some stations will be geared toward local concerns.

Accessibility
Most California attractions, hotels, and restaurants are accessible for travelers with disabilities. State law requires that public transportation must accommodate travelers with disabilities. Public spaces and businesses must have adequate facilities with equal access. This includes national parks and historic structures, many of which have been refitted with ramps and wider doors. Many hiking trails are also accessible to wheelchairs, and most campgrounds designate specific campsites that meet the Americans with Disabilities Act standards. The state of California also provides a free telephone TDD-to-voice relay service; just dial 711.

If you are traveling with a disability, there are many resources to help you plan and enjoy your trip. For those who are blind or permanently disabled, the **Access Pass** (www.store.usgs.com) allows free entry to designated federal recreation areas including parks, monuments, BLM lands, and U.S. Fish & Wildlife Service sites. **Access Northern California** (http://accessnca.org) is a nonprofit organization that offers general travel tips, including recommendations on accommodations, parks and trails, transportation, and travel equipment. **Gimp-on-the-Go** (www.gimponthego.com) is another travel resource. The message board on the **American Foundation for the Blind** (www.afb.org) is a good forum to discuss travel strategies for the visually impaired. **Wheelchair Getaways** (800/642-2042, www.wheelchairgetaways.com) in San Francisco (800/638-1912) and Los Angeles (800/638-1912) rent wheelchair-accessible vans and offer pickup and drop-off service from airports ($100-300). **Avis Access** (888/879-4273, www.avis.com) rents cars, scooters, and other products to make traveling with a disability easier; click on the "Services" link online.

Adventures Without Limits (503/359-2568, www.awloutdoors.org) is an Oregon-based company that offers kayaking, canoeing, stand-up paddleboarding, rock climbing, rafting, and cross-country skiing trips. **Accessible Nature** (www.accessiblenature.info) lists trails classified as very easy or wheelchair accessible in Pacific Northwest regions including Crater Lake, Mount Hood, the Columbia Gorge, and the North Cascades.

Traveling with Children

Well-marked and never too steep, the Pacific Crest Trail is a fantastic trail for little hikers. Certain sections come with precautions for sensitive kiddos: The desert grows dangerously hot in the summer, so visit with kids during the spring when temperatures are mild and cactus flowers are blooming; snowmelt at high elevations results in mosquitoes in June and July; and temperatures in Washington can dip into the 40s even in midsummer. Extra water, snacks, clothing, and bug spray may allay these issues.

Some kids get carsick in the backseat on winding mountain roads. Encourage your kids to look at objects outside the car in the distance, rather than screens or books inside the moving vehicle, or offer this as a time to nap. Dramamine is approved for kids over two and helps alleviate motion sickness symptoms.

Senior Travelers

Senior discounts are available nearly everyplace you go, including restaurants, golf courses, major attractions, and even some hotels. The minimum age ranges 50-65. Ask about discounts and be prepared to produce ID if you look younger than your years. You can often get additional discounts on rental cars, hotels, and tour packages as a member of **AARP** (888/687-2277, www.aarp.org). If you're not a member, its website can offer helpful travel tips and advice.

Road Scholar (800/454-5768, www.roadscholar.org) is another great resource for senior travelers. Dedicated to providing educational opportunities for older travelers, Road Scholar provides package trips to beautiful and interesting destinations. Called "Educational Adventures," these trips are generally 3-9 days long and emphasize nature, history, art, and music.

Gay and Lesbian Travelers

California, Oregon, and Washington are three of the most LGBTQ-friendly states in the entire nation. As with much of the country, the farther you venture into rural and agricultural regions, the more likely you are to encounter intolerance. However, thanks in part to the diverse array of backpackers who trek the PCT every year and visit the small towns near the trail, residents of these rural areas tend to be incredibly open-minded, welcoming, and warm-hearted. The **International Gay and Lesbian Travel Association** (www.iglta.org) has a directory of gay- and lesbian-friendly tour operators, accommodations, and destinations. Based in the Seattle area, **OutVentures** (www.outventures.org) is a volunteer-driven outdoor event company with LGBTQ-friendly trips to many destinations on or near the PCT, including Mount Hood, Crater Lake, Mount Rainier, and more.

Health and Safety

Medical Services

In an emergency, dial 911. In urban and suburban areas, full-service hospitals and medical centers abound, but in more remote regions, help can be hours away. If you plan to spend any time in the backcountry, you may want to invest time in a Wilderness First Aid course through the **National Outdoor Leadership School** (www.nols.edu). These two-day courses prepare you for medical emergencies in remote places.

If you are experiencing a medical emergency in the wilderness, find out if anyone in the area is certified in wilderness medicine. Don't be afraid to ask for help from other hikers on the trail. Send someone in your party for help if you need to. No matter what, never venture off-trail, even if you think there's a shortcut—hikers who stay on the trail are exponentially more likely to get home safe and/or be successfully rescued.

Wilderness Safety

If you're planning a backcountry expedition, follow all rules and guidelines for obtaining wilderness permits and for self-registration at trailheads. These are for your safety, letting the rangers know roughly where you plan to be and when to expect you back. National park and state park visitors centers can advise in more detail on any health or wilderness alerts in the area. Also let someone outside your party know your route and expected date of return.

Heat Exhaustion and Heatstroke

Being out in the elements can present its own set of challenges. Heat exhaustion and heatstroke can affect anyone during the hot summer months, particularly during a long, strenuous hike in the sun. Common symptoms include nausea, lightheadedness, headache, or muscle cramps. Dehydration and loss of electrolytes are the common causes of heat exhaustion. (The risks are even higher in the desert regions.) If you or anyone in your group develops any of these symptoms, get out of the sun immediately, stop all physical activity, and drink plenty of water. Heat exhaustion can be severe, and if untreated can lead to heatstroke, a condition in which the body's core temperature reaches 105°F. Fainting, seizures, confusion, and rapid heartbeat and breathing can indicate the situation has moved beyond heat exhaustion. If you suspect this, call 911 immediately.

Hypothermia

Hypothermia is caused by prolonged exposure to cold water or weather. This can happen on a rainy hike or backpacking trip without sufficient rain gear, or by staying too long in the ocean or another cold body of water without a wetsuit. Symptoms include shivering, weak pulse, drowsiness, confusion, slurred speech, or stumbling. To treat hypothermia, immediately remove wet clothing, cover the person with blankets, and feed him or her hot liquids. If symptoms don't improve, call 911.

Altitude Sickness

Hikes at high elevations, especially those above 10,000 feet (3,048 m), may result in altitude sickness. Symptoms include headache, nausea, tiredness, and dizziness—all signs of rapid exposure to reduced amounts of oxygen. Even highly experienced, very fit hikers can suffer from these symptoms. The best way to prevent altitude sickness is to ascend slowly. For example, if you're planning to hike in the High Sierra two days from now, spend tonight above 7,000 feet (2,134 m). Tomorrow night, sleep at 9,000 feet (2,743 m). Your body will be less likely to respond poorly if it has a chance to gradually adjust to the reduction in oxygen. If you find yourself suffering from altitude sickness, your best bet is to descend. Symptoms generally fade away within hours of returning to the altitude your body is accustomed to. If symptoms don't improve within a day or two, seek medical attention.

Ticks

Ticks live in many of the forests and grasslands throughout California, as well as eastern Oregon and Washington, but they are not common at higher elevations. If you are hiking through brushy, low-elevation areas, wear pants and long-sleeve shirts. Ticks like to crawl to warm, moist places (armpits are a favorite) on their host. If a tick is engorged, it can be difficult to remove. There are two main types of ticks: dog ticks and deer ticks. Dog ticks are larger, brown, and have a gold spot on their backs, while deer ticks are small, tear-shaped, and black. Deer ticks are known to carry Lyme disease. While Lyme disease is relatively rare on the West Coast, it is very serious. If you get bitten by a deer tick and the bite leaves a red ring, seek medical attention. Lyme disease can be successfully treated with early rounds of antibiotics.

Poison Oak

Poison oak can cause an adverse reaction in humans if you touch the leaves or stems. The common shrub has a characteristic three-leaf configuration, with scalloped leaves that are shiny green in the spring and then turn yellow, orange, and red in late summer-fall. In fall, the leaves drop, leaving a cluster of innocuous-looking branches. The oil in poison oak is present year-round in both the leaves and branches. Your best protection is to wear long sleeves and long pants when hiking, no matter how hot it is. If your skin comes into contact with poison oak, expect a nasty rash known for its itchiness and irritation. Poison oak is also extremely transferable, so avoid touching your eyes, face, or other parts of your body to prevent spreading the rash. A product called Tecnu is available

at most drugstores; if you are worried that you may have come into contact with poison oak, wash thoroughly with Tecnu and cool water as soon as possible to remove the oils from your skin. If and when a rash develops, calamine lotion can help, and in extreme cases a doctor can administer cortisone to help decrease the inflammation. Whatever you do, don't moisturize the rash—this only worsens the reaction.

Wildlife
Bears

Use precautions with regard to wildlife. Black bears are often seen in the mountains foraging for food in the spring, summer, and fall. If a bear sees you, identify yourself as human by waving your hands above your head, speaking in a calm voice, and backing away slowly. If a bear charges, do not run, and never get between a bear and her cub. One of the best precautions against an unwanted bear encounter is to keep a clean camp: Store all food in airtight, bear-proof containers, and strictly follow any guidelines given by the park or rangers.

Mountain Lions

Mountain lions can be found in the mountains as well as in grasslands and forests. Because of their solitary nature, it is unlikely you will see one, even on long trips in the backcountry. Still, there are a couple things to remember. If you come across a kill (probably a large, partly eaten deer), leave immediately. If you see a mountain lion and it sees you, do not run (running triggers its hunting instincts). Identify yourself as human and make your body appear as large as possible. If a mountain lion attacks, fight back; cats don't like to get hurt.

Rattlesnakes

Rattlesnakes are often found in summer in hot and dry areas from the coast to the Sierra Nevada. When hiking in this type of terrain (many parks will indicate if rattlesnakes are a problem in the area), keep your eyes on the ground and an ear out for the telltale rattle. Snakes like to warn you to keep away. The only time this is not the case is with baby rattlesnakes that have not yet developed their rattles. Unfortunately, they have developed their fangs and venom, which is particularly potent. Should you be bitten, seek immediate medical help.

Internet Resources

AllTrails
www.alltrails.com
Get detailed maps for trails across all three states, complete with elevation profiles, GPS coordinates, directions to the trailhead, and weather forecasts.

Guthook Guides
https://atlasguides.com
Guthook offers a smartphone-compatible PCT guide that utilizes GPS to plot your location along the trail, offering elevation profiles and detailed waypoint information.

Halfmile's PCT Maps
www.pctmap.net
Thru-hikers and section hikers rely on Halfmile's downloadable, mobile-friendly PCT maps, which detail topographic features, water sources, campsites, road crossings, and PCT mileage points.

National Park Service
www.nps.gov
The website has lots of great information for trip planning for travel in all the national parks, including an overview of park features, write-ups on trails, and the latest road conditions.

Pacific Crest Trail Organization
www.pcta.org
The PCTA is your go-to source for all info PCT-related, including current trail closures, in-depth history, advice for hikers, and opportunities to volunteer or donate to the organization.

U.S. Forest Service
www.fs.fed.us
Most campgrounds, wilderness areas, rivers, and trails have corresponding info pages on the Forest Service website.

California

California Outdoor and Recreational Information
www.caoutdoors.com
This recreation-focused website includes links to maps, local newspapers, festivals, and events as well as a wide variety of recreational activities throughout the state.

California State Parks
www.parks.ca.gov
The official website lists hours, accessibility, activities, camping areas, fees, and more information for all parks in the state system.

Caltrans
www.dot.ca.gov
Check the California Department of Transportation website for state map and highway information before planning a road trip.

Visit California
www.visitcalifornia.com
Visit the official tourism site of the state of California.

Oregon

ODOT
www.oregon.gov/odot
Find travel resources including maps, guides to Oregon's scenic byways, and other trip planning tools on the Oregon Department of Transportation website.

Oregon Hikers
www.oregonhikers.org
Find trip reports (and hike descriptions

in the Field Guide section) on this popular hikers' forum.

Travel Oregon
www.traveloregon.com
Visit Oregon's official tourism site to get more details about the beauty and adventure Oregon has to offer.

Washington
Experience Washington
www.experiencewa.com
The official tourism site of Washington offers helpful resources for trip planning as well as travel advisories.

Washington Trails Association
www.wta.org
Read detailed hiking descriptions for hiking trails in Washington, many of which include recent trip reports with up-to-date info about road conditions, bugs, and trail conditions.

WSDOT
www.wsdot.wa.gov
The Washington State Department of Transportation offers live updates on traffic conditions, road closures, mountain passes, weather warnings, and road construction in Washington.

INDEX

LIST OF MAPS

PHOTO CREDITS

ACKNOWLEDGMENTS

The Pacific Crest Trail changed my life when I hiked it in 2014, but I never imagined I'd find myself writing a book about it four years later. I am incredibly grateful to the people who made it possible for me to experience another fun, challenging, and humbling adventure on the PCT.

Huge thanks to the acquisitions team at Moon Travel, specifically Nikki Ioakimedes and Grace Fujimoto, who saw potential in me and chose me as the author for this guide. Thank you to my editor, Sabrina Young, for your unending patience with me as a first-time guidebook author and for your expertise, support, flexibility, and assistance during this monumental project. To copyeditor Ann Siefert, who reviewed my monstrous manuscript with a fine-toothed comb, thank you for making sure my mistakes and inconsistencies didn't make it into the final draft. To Suzanne Albertson in graphics and Albert Angulo in cartography: Thank you for creating a beautiful guide I'm proud to put my name on.

To my parents, Peter and Gaye, and my brother, Cody, who believed wholeheartedly in me even when I had my doubts: Thank you for being my biggest fans.

And to my wonderful boyfriend David, who accompanied me on every research trip, took fantastic photos, kept me laughing, and helped me find the perfect adjectives to write about everything afterward: Thank you for being the best adventure partner I could ever wish for.

MORE ROAD TRIP GUIDES FROM MOON

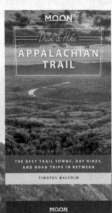

MOON

Drive & Hike
APPALACHIAN TRAIL

THE BEST TRAIL TOWNS, DAY HIKES,
AND ROAD TRIPS IN BETWEEN

TIMOTHY MALCOLM

MOON

BLUE RIDGE PARKWAY
Road Trip

INCLUDING SHENANDOAH & GREAT SMOKY
MOUNTAINS NATIONAL PARKS

JASON FRYE

MOON

CALIFORNIA
Road Trip

SAN FRANCISCO, YOSEMITE, LAS VEGAS,
GRAND CANYON, LOS ANGELES,
& THE PACIFIC COAST HIGHWAY

STUART THORNTON

MOON

NASHVILLE TO NEW ORLEANS
Road Trip

NATCHEZ TRACE PARKWAY • MEMPHIS •
TUPELO • MISSISSIPPI BLUES TRAIL

MARGARET LITTMAN

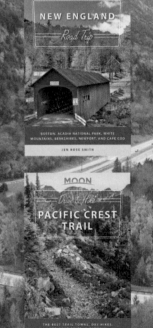

MOON

NEW ENGLAND
Road Trip

BOSTON, ACADIA NATIONAL PARK, WHITE
MOUNTAINS, BERKSHIRES, NEWPORT, AND CAPE COD

JEN ROSE SMITH

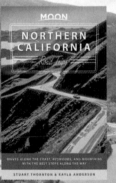

MOON

NORTHERN CALIFORNIA
Road Trip

DRIVES ALONG THE COAST, REDWOODS, AND MOUNTAINS
WITH THE BEST STOPS ALONG THE WAY

STUART THORNTON & KAYLA ANDERSON

MOON

PACIFIC COAST HIGHWAY
Road Trip

CALIFORNIA,
OREGON & WASHINGTON

IAN ANDERSON

MOON

Drive & Hike
PACIFIC CREST TRAIL

THE BEST TRAIL TOWNS, DAY HIKES,
AND ROAD TRIPS IN BETWEEN

CAROLINE HINCHLIFF

MOON

PACIFIC NORTHWEST
Road Trip

SEATTLE, VANCOUVER, VICTORIA,
THE OLYMPIC PENINSULA, PORTLAND,
THE OREGON COAST & MOUNT RAINIER

ALLISON WILLIAMS

MOON.COM | @MOONGUIDES

If you enjoyed this book, keep an eye out for more from Moon's Road Trip and Drive & Hike travel guide series!

Road Trip USA

Covering more than 35,000 miles of blacktop stretching from east to west and north to south, *Road Trip USA* takes you deep into the heart of America.

This colorful guide covers the top road trips including historic Route 66 and is packed with maps, photos, illustrations, mile-by-mile highlights, and more!

MAP SYMBOLS

Expressway	○ City/Town	ⓘ Information Center	♣ Park
Primary Road	◉ State Capital		⚲ Golf Course
Secondary Road	⊛ National Capital	🅿 Parking Area	✦ Unique Feature
Unpaved Road	✪ Highlight	⛪ Church	🖋 Waterfall
Trail	★ Point of Interest	🍇 Winery/Vineyard	⛺ Camping
Ferry	• Accommodation	🚩 Trailhead	▲ Mountain
Railroad	▼ Restaurant/Bar	🚉 Train Station	🎿 Ski Area
Pedestrian Walkway	■ Other Location	✈ Airport	🌊 Glacier
Stairs		✗ Airfield	

CONVERSION TABLES

°C = (°F - 32) / 1.8
°F = (°C x 1.8) + 32
1 inch = 2.54 centimeters (cm)
1 foot = 0.304 meters (m)
1 yard = 0.914 meters
1 mile = 1.6093 kilometers (km)
1 km = 0.6214 miles
1 fathom = 1.8288 m
1 chain = 20.1168 m
1 furlong = 201.168 m
1 acre = 0.4047 hectares
1 sq km = 100 hectares
1 sq mile = 2.59 square km
1 ounce = 28.35 grams
1 pound = 0.4536 kilograms
1 short ton = 0.90718 metric ton
1 short ton = 2,000 pounds
1 long ton = 1.016 metric tons
1 long ton = 2,240 pounds
1 metric ton = 1,000 kilograms
1 quart = 0.94635 liters
1 US gallon = 3.7854 liters
1 Imperial gallon = 4.5459 liters
1 nautical mile = 1.852 km

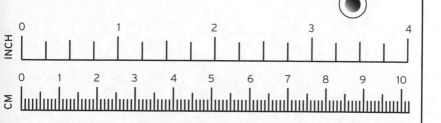

**MOON DRIVE & HIKE
PACIFIC CREST TRAIL**
Avalon Travel
Hachette Book Group
1700 Fourth Street
Berkeley, CA 94710, USA
www.moon.com

Editor and Series Manager: Sabrina Young
Acquiring Editor: Nikki Ioakimedes
Copy Editor: Ann Seifert
Production and Graphics Coordinator:
  Suzanne Albertson
Cover Design: Erin Seaward-Hiatt
Interior Design: Darren Alessi
Moon Logo: Tim McGrath
Map Editor: Albert Angulo
Cartographers: Albert Angulo and Andrew Dolan
Proofreader: Caroline Trefler
Indexer: Greg Jewett

ISBN-13: 978-1-64049-214-1
Printing History
1st Edition — March 2020
5 4 3 2 1

Front cover photo: © Tobin Akehurst | Shutterstock

Printed in China by RR Donnelley